Want your practice SAT essay
scored and critiqued?

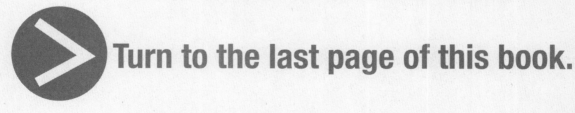 Turn to the last page of this book.

PETERSON'S

ULTIMATE

New SAT

TOOL KIT

Drew Johnson

THOMSON

PETERSON'S

Australia • Canada • Mexico • Singapore • Spain • United Kingdom • United States

THOMSON

PETERSON'S

About Thomson Peterson's

Thomson Peterson's (www.petersons.com) is a leading provider of education information and advice, with books and online resources focusing on education search, test preparation, and financial aid. Its Web site offers searchable databases and interactive tools for contacting educational institutions, online practice tests and instruction, and planning tools for securing financial aid. Thomson Peterson's serves 110 million education consumers annually.

For more information, contact Thomson Peterson's, 2000 Lenox Drive, Lawrenceville, NJ 08648; 800-338-3282; or find us on the World Wide Web at www.petersons.com/about.

Acknowledgments:
Head Writer: Drew D. Johnson; Contributing Writers: Maria Hong, Cameron Scott, Teresa Diaz, and Keith Cox.

Editor: Wallie Walker-Hammond; Production Editor: Alysha Bullock; Manufacturing Manager: Judy Coleman; Composition Manager: Gary Rozmierski; CD Producer: Carol Aickley; CD Quality Assurance: Jeff Pagano and Viral Modi.

ISBN 0-7689-1431-0

Printed in the United States of America

10 9 8 7 6 5 4 3 2 1   07 06 05

First Edition

Contents

About This Tool Kit

Your Tools

Peterson's Ultimate New SAT Tool Kit provides the complete package you need to score your personal best on the SAT and get into your top-choice college. Unlike any book previously published, this tool kit contains many features that used to be available *only* to those who purchased expensive test-prep classes.

e-Tutoring

Use the CD to go on line to register for one-on-one math help from a live expert whenever you need it. Tutoring is offered using an on-line whiteboard shared by you and the tutor, which allows you to communicate with one another in real time. However, if you prefer, you can submit your math question in writing instead and receive a written answer within 24 hours.

The free tutoring offered with this product is limited to 30 minutes, although you may purchase more time if you need it. A written response to a submitted question counts as 20 minutes. The tutoring service is available for six months from the date you register on line.

Note: The e-tutoring service offered to purchasers of this 2005 edition will expire on January 1, 2006.

This service is available 24 hours a day, seven days a week for most of the year. During the summer the service is available from 9 a.m. to 1 a.m. Eastern Standard Time. Due to low demand, the service is not available during several holiday periods, including Thanksgiving, Christmas, Easter, Labor Day, and Memorial Day.

Remember, to register for this service, you will need the CD that accompanies this book. You will also need to refer to this book to provide the access code when prompted.

Essay Scoring

The CD that accompanies this book allows you to write 1 practice test essay on line and receive a score on it, which approximates your performance on the essay in the actual SAT. In addition to a score, you will also receive constructive feedback on your essay, including tips to improve your score.

With this tool kit, you get scoring for 1 practice test essay. If you wish, for a fee, you may obtain scoring information and feedback for additional practice essays you write on line.

To register for the essay-scoring service you need the CD that accompanies this book. In addition, you will need to refer to this book to provide the access code when prompted.

Note: The scoring of the 1 essay is offered *free* to purchasers of this edition and this offer will expire on December 31, 2005.

The CD

There are 2 full-length practice tests for the SAT on the CD-ROM that accompanies this book. These tests, along with the 3 full-length practice tests in this book, provide a total of 5 simulated tests you can incorporate into your test-prep plan. Since the actual SAT is a paper-and-pencil test, be sure to go through at least one of the tests printed in this book. (The CD version will automatically time your test and compute your score.)

The Flash Cards

Vocabulary flash cards are bound into the back of this book. Separate these at the perforations to create a deck of 216 SAT vocabulary flashcards to help you expand your vocabulary. While no questions on the SAT will specifically ask you to provide definitions of any words, building a better vocabulary will improve your performance on the SAT, especially the Critical Reading and the Writing sections.

Introduction

About This Book

Most colleges require applicants to take the SAT, the standardized test that's been around for decades. If you haven't already taken an SAT, you may have taken the PSAT, which is like the SAT's cousin. Both tests are primarily timed multiple-choice tests that cover math and English skills. Your SAT score is an ingredient colleges add to the mysterious soup known as the admissions process. In this respect the SAT is like salt, since almost every soup uses salt to some degree or another.

Sometimes your SAT score is a big factor in your selection, and sometimes it isn't. There's no way to tell one way or the other, but all you really need to know is that a good SAT score helps your chances of getting into a college. You might think it's unfair that a single standardized test has such an impact on your chances of getting accepted, and you're not alone. Other people have questioned why a single exam given one morning could matter as much as twelve years of schoolwork and grades. The debate about the merits of the SAT has gone on for decades, but one thing hasn't changed. The SAT is the only standard measure that colleges can use to compare one potential student to another. Every high school is different, so an A in algebra from Lawrence High School might mean something different than an A in algebra from Pennington Prep. Even the algebra classes themselves might cover different topics, so it's impossible to say which A student is better at algebra. But the SAT is a standardized test, which is supposed to mean that a math score of 590 equals a score of 590 equals a score of 590 no matter where you come from or when you took the test.

This is the practical reason that colleges like the SAT. It makes wading through a mountain of applications much easier. For instance, some public schools will let students enroll if their SAT scores are over a certain number. Sometimes the SAT score is combined with GPA to help decide automatic enrollment. At very competitive schools, having a high score gets you into the pile of applications that is examined first. You still might not get in to that school, but a high score gives you a better chance than a lower score would. SAT scores help admissions people slice the mountain of applications into smaller piles, and this makes their tough job a little easier.

Note

What Does SAT Stand For?

The SAT is such a well-known test that most people refer to it by its initials. There's a reason for this. For most of its life the letters S.A.T. stood for Scholastic Aptitude Test, and people referred to the test by name or initials. Since 1993, however, the College Board—the organization that administers and controls the test—has taken to referring to the test only as "the SAT." The reason for the change lies in the middle letter "A." It used to stand for *aptitude*, but the College Board doesn't want the SAT to be thought of as an aptitude test anymore. (Aptitude tests are supposed to test intelligence or a person's ability to learn.) The College Board doesn't want to change the name of its most famous product, either, so the SAT is still the SAT.

This Isn't Your Parents' SAT— It's Not Even Your Older Brother's SAT

A new version of the SAT debuts in 2005. All the known details of the new SAT are covered starting in the next chapter, but here are the main changes:

1. A new section, Writing, will be introduced. Writing will be given its own 200–800 score, so there are now three sections in which students will get a 200–800 score. (Mathematics and Critical Reading are the other two sections.)

2. There is an essay, which will be graded by professional readers. Since readers will be needed, the cost of the SAT is increasing by roughly ten dollars, give or take a buck. The essay will count as 30 percent of your Writing score.

3. Analogy questions will no longer be used on the new SAT. If you never learned how to do analogies, you don't have to start now.

A new version of any test puts all test-takers at a disadvantage. Previous versions of a test can often give you a good idea of what to expect. You don't have that option with the new SAT. Even so, there's no need to freak out. Just because the new SAT is *different* doesn't mean that it's *harder* or that it's been completely created from scratch. Let's use the Writing section as an example. Even though this section is new to the SAT, the question

2

types are not unique by any means. The same type of multiple-choice grammar questions that will appear on the new SAT can be found in many other standardized tests. Similar questions appear on the SAT II: Writing test, the Stanford Series of standardized tests, as well as some state exams like Texas's TAKS. Many state exams also require an essay, so for many of you the idea of a graded essay won't seem like it came from the moon.

> **Note**
>
> Basic elimination strategies can be found in Chapter 2, while section-specific strategies (Math, Critical Reading, and Writing) can be found beginning in Chapter 4.

The new SAT differs from the old one, but in the end it's just another version of a standardized test. As with all standardized tests, the key to success is to know what to expect on the exam so that you can prepare for it ahead of time. The book you have in your hands, *Peterson's Ultimate New SAT Tool Kit*, can help you do just that. Included in this book are general test strategies, specific question strategies, and a great deal of the factual knowledge you will need to get a good score. There are also three sample tests with explanations, as well as an early diagnostic that will give you an idea of how you might do if you were to take the new SAT without preparing. We can give you the vital information, skills, and strategies necessary to blow the SAT out of the water, "new" test or not.

The Peterson's Approach to the New SAT

Some students only want a decent score on the SAT, while others are shooting for a great score. This book takes these different goals into account. Throughout each of the main three subject-review chapters, there are "Take It to the Next Level" sections that cover harder material. People bucking for a 700+ on all sections will want to pay attention to these tougher problems. Others might want to focus on the basic knowledge and not worry about hard topics that may or may not even appear on the new SAT. The book gives you the flexibility to make this decision for yourself.

This book is divided into three main parts. The first part gives you the details of the new SAT, the basic strategies needed to master it, and a diagnostic test to give you an idea of what you need to work on. Chapters 1 and 2 cover general test-taking strategies and give you a Big Picture idea of the new SAT. You'll learn what changes were made and why, and get information that will help you approach the test with the right mental framework.

After learning about the new SAT, you will take a diagnostic test. This exam is based on the new SAT, and should give you a rough idea of how you would fare on the actual exam. You can take the results of your diagnostic and use them to tailor your approach to the middle chapters of this book.

Chapters 4 through 7—the middle part of the book—cover the Reading, Writing, and Mathematics portions of the test, respectively. These chapters provide you with the basic facts every test-taker should have. More important, they give you a clear picture of the techniques needed to handle each question type effectively.

Finally, the last part of the book is devoted to three full-length practice tests (with explanations). We suggest you hold off on taking these practice exams until you cover all of the material in the book. The tests will allow you the chance to try out the techniques and strategies discussed in Chapters 1–2. By the time you are finished with all three practice tests, you will have a very good idea of what taking the new SAT will be like for you. You will also know what techniques and strategies you'll need in each section.

Combining factual knowledge with a sound strategic approach is the best way to score well on any standardized test, not just the new SAT. This book will provide you with the facts and strategies you need to succeed. The first step is to learn about the new SAT, covered in the next chapter.

About the Sidebars in This Book

Throughout this book you'll encounter four different iconic symbols. (Flip through this book, and you'll see oodles of each one.) Here's what these symbols are and what they mean:

Alert!
This sidebar warns you about a common blunder or testing trap, trick, or ploy that might trip you up during the test if you're not careful.

Note
This sidebar signals information that, although isn't a "need-to-know" fact, you might find interesting and that rounds out your knowledge of the topic at hand.

4

Tip

This sidebar signals a tip, strategy, or fine point related to the topic or example at hand.

X-Ref

This sidebar signals a reference to a concept or other information located elsewhere in the book.

Understanding the SAT

Chapter
1

Straight from Jersey, It's the New SAT!

Whenever SAT scores are released, the following scene happens somewhere in America: A student with average grades gets a high score, while a straight-A student does not do as well as she wanted. Usually the first student is described as a "good test-taker," while the straight-A student either had a "bad test day" or "didn't test well." What are the differences between these two test-takers?

Sometimes the only thing that separates a good test-taker from a poor one is a feeling of confidence. Good test-takers feel confident about their chances, even if they have no reason to feel that way. Poor test-takers are often nervous and anxious. There's a lot of pressure surrounding the SAT, and feeling that pressure during the test can cause you to rush problems and make careless mistakes.

So how do you gain confidence and reduce anxiety? For starters, you should learn everything you can about the format of the new SAT. The more you know what to expect, the less mysterious the test will be. Once you learn all about the test, you'll realize that the SAT is not really that different from other standardized tests you have taken.

Format of the New SAT

Total Time: about 3 hours and 45 minutes

Scoring: There will be three scores from 200–800 in the areas of Mathematics, Critical Reading, and Writing. The Writing score will factor in your essay score, which is graded on a scale of 0 (low) to 6 (high).

Sections

Mathematics has three sections—two 25-minute sections and one 20-minute section. Typically, the 25-minute sections contain five-choice multiple-choice questions, while the 20-minute section requires student-produced responses. The questions in the Mathematics sections are short-answer and fill-in-the-blank type problems. Calculators are allowed, as long as they are not the super-brainy calculators that can surf the 'Net and do your laundry for you. Four-function, graphing, and scientific calculators are the ones to use.

Critical Reading also has three sections. Two sections are 25 minutes long, and the other one is 20 minutes. All sections consist of five-choice multiple-choice questions. Analogies have been eliminated from the new test, but Sentence Completion problems will still make an appearance. Reading Comprehension passages on the SAT are still long (500–800 words), but the new SAT will have shorter passages as well. These "paragraph-length" passages will be around 100 words. Whatever the length, it's still about reading a passage and then answering questions about it.

The **Writing** portion of the SAT is the big new wrinkle. The total time for this section is 50 minutes, probably divided into two 25-minute sections. One section uses multiple-choice questions to test your grammar skills. There are three different types of multiple-choice grammar questions, and you will learn more about each type starting on page 14. The other section contains an essay prompt. This prompt will ask a very broad question like, "What is the importance of education?" in order to give you a lot of leeway to decide what to write. Your essay score is factored into your overall 200–800 score in a way that has not yet been revealed by ETS.

> **Note**
>
> These are the facts about the new SAT at the time this book was printed. Any new updates about the test format can be found at Peterson's Web site at: www.petersons.com/testprep. This site will keep track of any changes that might give you more information about the new format.

Understanding the basic format of the test should reduce some anxiety. Many kids show up to take the SAT knowing only that it's a timed test that can mess up their chances of getting into college. As you might expect, these kids are pretty nervous about the exam and likely to make careless errors once it starts. You can avoid this pitfall by memorizing the test format you just read. Sure, the SAT is still important, but at least you know what to expect in each section and for the whole test in general.

The Mysterious Section 9

The new SAT should take:

> 70 minutes Math + 70 minutes Critical Reading + 60 minutes Writing = 200 minutes.

This works out to three hours, 20 minutes. But earlier, we stated that the total testing time is about three hours, 45 minutes. There's a difference of 35 minutes that's unexplained. Before you dash off to the computer and check out some Web conspiracy sites, you should know that the eight SAT sections described in the chart are the eight sections that *will count towards your score*. There will be a Section 9, though, containing only "sample or experimental" questions.

In one sense, this "sample" section helps ensure some fairness in future SATs. In another sense, it is a waste of time that uses you as a guinea pig. It all depends on your point of view. Educational Testing Service—the company that writes the SAT questions—uses the sample section to "test" questions for future SATs. The results help ETS to identify and discard questions that are bad and determine which questions are easy, medium, or hard. So the sample section does help ensure equanimity between tests from year to year, decreasing the chance that one SAT will be much harder than another. That levels the playing field from one SAT to the next. And, that's a good thing. The sample section also means that you will have to answer a bunch of questions that will have no impact on your score. There's no way to tell which section is the sample section, so you have to approach them all as if they count. For example, if you have four math sections, then you know that one of them is the sample section, since only three count toward your score. But which one? You could guess, but it would be a foolish maneuver on your part. You need to tackle **every** section as if the questions are real. In the back of your mind, though, you know that one of the sections will not count toward your score. Having to expend mental energy on problems that do not count is a bad thing, for you at least.

Knowing that there is a sample section won't translate directly into a higher score, but it does help you understand the SAT testing process better. Place this in your rapidly growing "Knowledge is Power" file on the SAT along with everything else. Whenever you start to feel anxious about the test, review the facts in this file until you calm down and realize that the new SAT is just another test.

> **Note**
>
> The sample section could be in Math, Critical Reading, or Writing. Sometimes different standardized tests will have different sample sections, so the person next to you might get a sample Math section while you're stuck with a sample Writing section. This allows ETS to test a greater number of sample questions. Both of you get the same eight sections that count, of course.

At this point, you should have a good idea about *how* the SAT has changed. It will also help your cause if you understand *why* the SAT has changed. There are a host of reasons why the SAT changed formats, and some of them have a direct impact on how the new SAT will look.

Some Reasons the SAT Changed

The SAT Has Always Changed

Like fashion, the field of education has trends and fads. Some educational ideas get hot while others get pushed to the back of the closet next to the parachute pants. Classrooms today are very different from the high school classrooms of America in the 1920s, when the SAT first was introduced. If the SAT kept the exact same form every year, it would run the risk of becoming outdated and irrelevant in about a decade. So the test is constantly being tweaked or modified to remain topical. The next big change might be to a computerized SAT, since this is already being done with other standardized tests.

The New SAT Is More about Mastery of Subject Skills than Aptitude

The changes to the SAT might allow it to become more than just a college admissions test. Theoretically, some time in the future the new SAT could be used to see how well students have mastered a basic curriculum of math and English.

As it now stands, many states require high school students to take a state standardized test in order to graduate. These exams—such as the MCAS in Massachusetts, TAKS in Texas, and FCAT in Florida—are designed to see how well students have mastered their state's learning objectives. The new SAT is going to be like these tests, since it will try to accurately gauge how well students meet some basic learning standards.

So the new SAT is poised to be more of an achievement test than an aptitude test. To illustrate this key difference, imagine a high school biology textbook. A biology *aptitude* test would ask questions to see how well a

PETERSON'S
getting you there

student *could* learn biology. In theory, Jill Student would not have to know biology beforehand. The question would be designed to see how well she could learn biology. The aptitude test is like an intelligence test. In contrast, a biology *achievement* test would test the material in the textbook. Students who had read the material would likely do well on this test, while students who did not know biology would probably score poorly.

> **Note**
>
> **aptitude**—1. an inherent ability to learn; a talent. 2. quickness in learning or understanding.

All of this doesn't mean that the new SAT is going to be a radical departure from the previous version. At the end of the day, the new and old SATs are both standardized tests of basic math and English. Fundamentally, the two tests will be similar, and there's a good reason for this. A balance between the old and new versions is necessary so that older SAT scores can still be compared to the new scores.

The new SAT is going to be more of an achievement test, and it's true that it will have some different questions and sections, but it's still primarily a test of high school math and English. That won't change, regardless of the introduction of "paragraph-length" reading passages.

The proposed shift from aptitude to achievement does a good job of explaining why the test has changed the way it has. A writing portion can now be added because grammar is an important subject you should have learned. You can't have a grammar aptitude test, since grammar is not intuitive. But you can have a grammar achievement test that tracks how well students know their grammar rules.

Analogy questions were a standard aptitude question, so they're gone. Sentence Completion problems are a form of vocabulary question, so they remain to test your achievement level in vocabulary. New SAT reading passages might contain questions that ask you about *metaphors* or *similes*. These are basic literary terms that most high school English students are required to know. The same holds true for the Math section. Instead of questions designed to see if you could master algebra, you'll be given straight algebra problems like:

If, $x^{\frac{1}{3}} = \sqrt{144}$, what is the value of x?

(A) 4
(B) 12
(C) 36
(D) 144
(E) 1728

There's not a lot of aptitude here. What's needed is a firm knowledge of how to manipulate variables, radicals, and exponents. These skills are *achieved* in a high school algebra class.

The transformation from an aptitude test to an achievement test obviously affects the way you should prepare for the new SAT. This book provides you with three entire practice tests. The CD that accompanies it will provide you with two additional practice tests.

You should have a pretty good idea of what the new SAT is about by now. Since the framework for understanding the new SAT is in place, the next step is to learn some general strategies to help you on the test.

Chapter 2

Standard Test-Taking Tools for Standardized Tests

Think of the general test-taking strategies in this chapter as the hammer, screwdriver, and pliers of test preparation. They are the basic tools that every good test-taker should carry in his or her test-prep utility belt. More specific tools are needed for certain jobs, but you always need the essential items at some point. Like a good carpenter, a good test-taker comes up with clever ways to use these tools in order to complete a task well.

Pacing

There are three major ways in which the new SAT can cause anxiety:

1. The mysterious, unknown factor of the exam.

2. The fact that the test effects your college admissions hopes.

3. The timed nature of the test, which means that as you answer each problem TIME IS RUNNING OUT!

Let's look at the points above. Hopefully, the last chapter has addressed number 1 and helped reduce your anxiety about the test. There's nothing you can do about number 2, so there's no point in worrying about it. That leaves number 3. This problem can be solved by **pacing**.

> **Note**
>
> There are circumstances under which extended test-taking time might be granted. These usually have to do with special conditions regarding the test-taker. In order to be eligible to take a test with extended time periods, a number of conditions must be met. If you feel you might qualify for one of these exams, visit the College Board Web site at:
>
> http://www.collegeboard.com/disable/students/html/indx000.html.

Pacing is the deceptively simple idea that you should give yourself an adequate amount of time to attempt every question. It sounds easy, but in practice good pacing is harder to accomplish than you might think. The problem is that most people are stuck with the idea that they must answer every question. To achieve this, they rush through the early questions in order to have more time to answer the harder questions at the end.

There are many pitfalls with this plan. First, rushing through the easy and medium problems often leads to careless errors. You don't get extra credit for the harder questions, so if you miss the first question and get the last question right, you've done yourself little good. You would get the same score as someone who got the first (easy) question right and missed the really tough problem at the end. Second, the hard problems are hard for a reason. You could stare at some of them for three hours and still not come up with the right answer. This is especially true with some achievement tests. If the question is testing you on negative exponents, and you don't know how to handle negative exponents, then it's unlikely you'll solve this problem in the regular manner.

You might be wondering what constitutes an easy, medium, or hard test question. A lot of this depends on you, since everyone has strengths and weaknesses. If you find a question tough, then it's a tough question. Previous SATs have had questions that progress in order from easiest to hardest. The first third are easy, the middle third are medium, and the final third are the toughest problems. This may still be the case on the new SAT, but it doesn't apply neatly to every section. The Math sections are the best fit, and you can expect a nice progression from easy to hard. The multiple-choice Writing section might be different, since there are three distinct question types. Each group of similar questions might go from easy to hard, although at this point there's no definitive word from ETS or the College Board about this. The situation is a little different in the Critical Reading section as well. The questions don't vary in difficulty, but the passages do. There will be some passages that are tougher or longer than others. For the Critical Reading sections, it's a good idea to flip through a section at the beginning and glance at each of the passages. You might want to start with the passage that's closest to your interests. You can also start with the passage that has the most questions attached to it. Whatever you do, don't believe that you must start with Question 1 and answer every question in order. The bottom line is: Whether or not a question is tough often boils down to your personal opinion. You should take charge and answer the questions in a way that works best for you.

A standard pacing technique is the "two-pass" method where you go through a section twice. On the first pass, the goal is to answer all the questions that do not pose too much difficulty. On the first pass, you want to spend at least 20 seconds on every question, since you don't want to cut corners and answer something too quickly. However, you don't want to spend too long on any problem, either, since there might be simpler problems after it. Therefore, spend a minute on a problem, and if you can't wrangle an answer in that time, mark it for later and move on. You want to look for easier problems before spending more time on difficult ones.

> **Tip**
>
> As you might expect, pacing is impossible if you can't tell the time. The best plan is to use a small, non-beepy digital clock, since there's no guarantee that there will be a clock in plain view when you take the real exam. Make sure, though, that you check the list of approved timers from The College Board.

The second pass is where you go back and tackle the harder problems that were giving you grief. You can take extra time on the second pass. Again, though, there's no point in spending ten minutes on a single question. If you stare at a problem for two minutes and still cannot get anywhere, take a qualified guess and move on. Sometimes the extra time on the second pass will help you solve the problem, but sometimes it won't.

Ideally, you will finish your second pass with about three minutes remaining. This will give you time to go over the section and check your answers. Use the opportunity to make sure you didn't fill in the wrong oval somewhere or make some other simple mistake.

That explains pacing. Many of you probably do it a bit naturally. On every practice section you take in this book, work on refining your pacing approach. Use the two-pass system and see how many easy questions you answer after you leap over that first hard problem. Students who are good pacers give themselves the best chance to answer the greatest number of questions correctly.

Now, suppose you come to a problem on the second pass and still can't figure it out. You don't want to spend any more time on it, but you don't want to leave it blank either. What should you do?

Process of Elimination

Using the process of elimination (POE) is probably not a new concept to you. The idea is that you can eliminate some answer choices that you know are wrong and then take a guess from the remaining choices. You might not guess correctly on every problem, but you do increase your chances on scoring higher over the course of the whole test.

> **Tip**
>
> There is a guessing penalty for incorrect answers. This often discourages students from being aggressive with their guessing. The guessing penalty does negate points if you are simply taking a one-in-five stab at a question. But if you can eliminate even a single answer choice and then guess, the law of averages should translate into more points over the course of the whole test. So if you can eliminate even a single answer choice, you should take a guess on that problem.

Even though people *understand* POE, that doesn't mean they actually *use* it on the test. Once the pressure gets cranked up, POE is one of the first things to be jettisoned. Part of the problem lies in the "one question-one solution" idea that is fixed in people's minds. Before jumping into an SAT example of POE, let's first talk about multiple-choice tests and the mistake behind the "one question-one solution" concept.

Suppose your history teacher stood in front of the class and asked, "Who won the naval Battle of Tsushima in 1905? Write your answer down on a sheet of paper." There's only one answer to this question, and you must search through your brain to come up with it. Either you have the right fact in your head, or you don't. This is a typical one question-one solution problem, and it's what you often experience in school.

Yet six out of eight sections of the SAT consist of multiple-choice problems. With a multiple-choice test, *the correct answer is given to you for every question*. It's already there, every time. The only problem is that it is surrounded by four incorrect answer choices. Still, since all the answers are there in front of you, you have ways of getting the correct answer other than simply pulling the right fact from your head.

Who won the naval Battle of Tsushima in 1905?
- (A) The United States
- (B) Japan
- (C) Russia
- (D) Mongolia
- (E) China

PETERSON'S
getting you there

It would be great if you could pull the right fact out of your head, but it is not the end of the world if you can't. Many students mistakenly get discouraged at this point, believing that there is only one way to answer it. If you get nothing else from this section, you should walk away with the knowledge that there is always more than one way to tackle an SAT problem.

If you can't pull the correct fact out of your head, try some POE. The United States wasn't at war in 1905, so it's unlikely that (A) is the answer. You might not know much about the history of the other four countries, but you probably know some U.S. history, and a naval battle during a time when our nation was at peace would stick out a bit. Choice (A) can be crossed out. Take a guess at this point, or look over the other choices and search for faults.

If you know geography, you'll realize that Mongolia is a landlocked nation. It's doubtful a landlocked country would have a navy, isn't it? Choice (D) can be crossed out. It's down to three choices. At this point, you can go a bit further and say that the word "Tsushima" does not sound very Russian, so you can eliminate (C). That leaves two remaining choices, (B) and (E), both of which are pretty good. Take a qualified guess and move on.

Say you had it down to two choices and picked (B). The person next to you was named Bill, so he picked (B) because it's the first letter of his name. The girl next to Bill actually knew that the Japanese defeated the Russians at the Battle of Tsushima, so she picked (B) also. All three of you got the right answer, but you took different paths to get there. However, the path you take doesn't matter on a multiple-choice test. All that matters is marking in the correct oval, and POE can help you do that.

Here's an SAT math question from earlier. The number 24 has been placed in front of it, but otherwise the question is the same. The question number is important, since it shows that this is one of the later, and, theoretically, more difficult questions in a section. On a tougher question, finding the correct answer will NOT be as easy as simply looking at the numbers in the question and picking an answer choice that has the same number.

24. If $x^{\frac{1}{3}} = \sqrt{144}$, what is the value of x?

   (A) 4
   (B) 12
   (C) 36
   (D) 144
   (E) 1728

Let's look at the answer choices. Choice (D) is out, since it just takes the number 144 from the question itself and places it in the answer choice. Also, if you multiply $\frac{1}{3} \times 144$ you get 36, choice (C). But the whole problem is filled with exponents and square roots, so the answer will not be found by simply multiplying the two numbers you do have together. Choice (C) can be eliminated.

Many of you might stop and take a guess right here, which would be fine. Others might pull out their calculators and figure out what the square root of 144 ($\sqrt{144}$) is. It works out to $\sqrt{144} = 12$, which is answer (B). You could pick (B) if you're willing to forget that freaky $\frac{1}{3}$ exponent above the variable x. Keep in mind that mathematicians aren't allowed to forget things they don't like, which means that (B) is probably not the right answer either. Take a guess from the two remaining choices. The answer is (E).

This is just one way you can use POE on a math problem. There are other POE techniques for the Math, Reading, and Grammar sections, and they'll be discussed throughout the book. For now, just be sure to move away from the one-problem one-solution mindset. Keeping this rigid idea around does no good. Instead, if you find yourself unsure of how to proceed on a question, snap down to the answer choices. Your goal is to separate the correct answer from the four impostors, so if you can eliminate any choices, you are on the right path.

Using POE in the Reading section is often about looking for the bland while eliminating the spicy. In general, correct answers are:

- Vaguely positive and upbeat

- Vaguely worded

- A nice paraphrase of what was written in the passage

The SAT is taken by bazillions of students each year, and the College Board can't afford to be controversial or edgy in any way. So the reading passages are on safe, noncontroversial topics, and the answers are similarly bland and noncontroversial. With this in mind, in many instances you can look over the answer choices and eliminate any that are too negative or strongly worded.

> The experiment described in the third paragraph helps the author prove that
>
> (A) the scientists are unwilling to accept new ideas.
> (B) mainstream opinion had little effect on people's feelings
> (C) educators were not interested in the subject.
> (D) the old popular belief actually had some basis in fact.
> (E) the new theory was wholly original.

It doesn't matter that you have no idea what the "experiment" is. All you need to do is peruse the answer choices and get rid of the answers that are negative, radical, or controversial. Take choice (A). This statement is not very pro-education, is it? It claims that scientists, people devoted to learning new truths, are unwilling to accept new ideas. This radical, anti-education stance is not going to be the right answer on a national standardized test like the SAT. You can cross it out. Choice (C) can be crossed out for the same anti-educational stance.

Choices (E) and (D) provide a good contrast, and they show the difference between a likely answer and an unlikely one. Choice (E) uses strong wording, claiming the theory was "wholly original." That means if only one tiny, tiny part of the theory was NOT original, then answer choice (E) would be incorrect. Since it would be hard to prove that every single facet of the theory was wholly original, choice (E) can be eliminated for being too extreme. In contrast, choice (D) uses the phrase "some basis in fact." It doesn't say it was totally, completely based in fact. Saying this would make it hard to prove. However, saying only that it has *some* basis in fact makes it much easier to prove. It means that if you can find a single thing that has basis in fact, you have *some* basis in fact. This means choice (D) is a nice, vaguely worded answer that doesn't say anything too radical or controversial. If you had to choose between (B) and (D), choice (D) would be your best guess.

Using POE on the Math and Reading portions of the SAT is a straightforward process. You will find and can eliminate extreme answer choices on the SAT Reading, and answers that consist of numbers exactly like those in the question in the SAT Math section. Using POE in the Writing section is not quite so helpful for two main reasons. One is that half of the Writing section is an essay, and there's no way to use the process of elimination on an essay. The second problem deals with the fact that the Writing portion of the test is very new. This makes it impossible to spot any common incorrect choices that appear time and time again.

Yet although POE is not as helpful on the Writing section, it still can be used. Many incorrect choices in the multiple-choice portion of the SAT Writing section are based on the idea that "grammar is hard, so the hard-looking answer must be correct." Very few Americans—and this includes *some* English teachers—truly believe that they are good at taming the seven-headed monster known as English Grammar. These individuals might fall for the very, very complicated answer simply because they believe grammar is difficult and complicated. However, extremely complicated answers are often incorrect and should be eliminated using POE. Remember, most of us are better at grammar than we think, and we use the right word even when we can't explain exactly why that word is right. So if you don't know the exact answer to a grammar problem you should always trust your ear, and it will guide to the right answer more often than not.

> We were hoping to catch the opening act of the concert, but car troubles cause us to be 30 minutes late to the show.
>
> (A) cause us to be
> (B) are causing us to have been
> (C) caused us to be
> (D) will be causing us to be
> (E) are having to cause us to be

Note

This is one of the new SAT question types known officially as "improving sentences." You are given a sentence with an underlined portion that may or may not contain a grammatical error. If you think there's no error, you pick choice (A), which is an exact copy of the original underlined phrase. If you think there is an error, your goal is to choose the answer that corrects the grammatical mistake.

This sentence probably doesn't sound right to you, so trust your ear and eliminate choice (A). Choices (B), (D), and (E) are all filled with many small words and they sound impressive, or at least complicated. But none of them are the right answer. The tense of the verb *cause* is incorrect, since cause is present tense and the troubles happened in the past. All you need to fix the sentence is the past tense, *caused*, which is choice (C). The other choices create complicated verb tenses by using *have*, *having*, *will*, and *-ing*, but grammar isn't always that complicated and wordy.

Therefore, if you find yourself struggling on a tough grammar problem, cross out one or two of the most complicated answer choices, and then take your best guess. With POE, you won't always get the right answer, but over the course of the whole SAT you will increase your chances of scoring higher.

Now that we've reviewed some of the most basic test-taking strategies and considered how they apply to the three main sections of the new SAT, you're ready to take the diagnostic test in Chapter 3.

Part
II

Diagnosing Strengths and Weaknesses

Chapter 3

The Diagnostic—
Test Driving the New SAT

At this point, you should have a good general idea about what the new SAT is like. You should know the basic format of the test and understand the idea behind pacing and process of elimination.

Before diving into the subject-review sections, in chapters 4–7, it's a good idea to take a sample SAT at this point. There are four reasons for this:

1. You'll get a rough idea of how you might do if you were to take the real new SAT without studying anything.

2. You can determine your SAT strengths and weaknesses. There will be some sections you ace, and others you have a lot of trouble with. This knowledge can be used to fine-tune your study plans.

3. No matter how you do on the diagnostic, *it doesn't count.*

4. Really, it doesn't count.

Points 3 and 4 are there for a reason. Some people take a practice test, don't do as well as they had hoped, and then freak out. It's just a practice test, nothing more. The diagnostic is like a photographic snapshot, giving you an idea about your relative SAT strengths and weaknesses at this one moment in time. You can then use this information to help guide your studying. Simply put, you want to determine your weak points, and then focus on shoring up your knowledge in these areas. Improving your weaker points will translate to a higher score on the real test.

Where Did We Get This New SAT?

We made this practice test up, but that doesn't mean we just took a wild guess. The College Board has released some morsels of information about the new SAT, and every morsel was used to create a test that closely resembles the real SAT in as many ways as possible. Information about the relevant SAT II tests was also included in the creation of this diagnostic, along with decades of experience in the test-preparation field. The result is a diagnostic exam that will give you a very good—but not perfect—idea of what it will be like to take the new SAT.

Note

Quiet on the Set

You should try to take this diagnostic under actual SAT conditions. It would be nice to get up during a section and chat with your friends on the phone, but you don't get to do that on the real test. Ideally, you will block out three hours of time on a weekend morning in a place where you won't be bothered or interrupted. Then you can take the exam exactly as you will take the real SAT. This sounds like torture, but you will be amazed at how much this can help prepare you for the real test. Most students aren't used to getting up early on a Saturday morning and taking a long test, so getting some practice at doing this really does a great deal of good.

However, while taking the whole test on a Saturday is ideal, many people have such busy lives that this is impossible. You might not be able to take the whole SAT in one shot, but you should still try to take each section under timed conditions. This will give you an accurate idea of the time you have to answer the questions in each section. Timing yourself on the diagnostic gives you a chance to work on your pacing, so remember to use the two-pass system for every section.

When you finish the entire diagnostic, turn to page 72 and check your answers. Use the results to formulate a study plan that best suits you. Here are some of the kinds of questions you can ask about each particular section.

PETERSON'S
getting you there

Questions to Ask Yourself about
Your Critical Reading Diagnostic Score

1. How did I do on the Sentence Completions problems?

   a. Did I do better or worse on the two-blank problems? *If you did worse on the two-blank problems, you might be looking at both blanks at the same time. Looking over the techniques described starting on page 87 will help you correct this approach.*

2. How did I do on the Reading passages questions?

   a. Did I do better or worse on the longer passages? *Suppose you answered many of the paragraph-length questions right, but missed questions on the longer passages. This could mean that you are skimming through the longer passages too quickly and not spending enough time on these problems. To correct this, you would want to spend more time on these passages. This might mean you skip reading one passage and just guess on those questions, but overall it will help you answer more problems correctly.*

   b. Which passage did I enjoy reading the most? How well did I answer those questions? *Most people pay more attention to subjects they like, so they end up answering questions about it correctly. If this is the case with you, make it a point to go through every subsequent Reading section and start with the passages you like the most. Of course, there might not be any passages that you like, but there should be some subjects that you hate less than others.*

3. How many questions did I answer on the first pass? How many of these did I get correct? *If you missed a lot of questions you thought you answered correctly, your problem is one of speed. You are probably going too fast and picking wrong answers that look great but are actually traps meant to snare people in a rush. Slow down, take the time to do the work needed (like looking back in the passage for the right answer), and don't worry so much about speed.*

4. How much time did I have for the second pass? Did I have enough time to review the section?

5. How often did I use POE when forced to make an educated guess? *If the answer is "never," you should go back and look at the problems you missed. Think about the answer choices and decide if there were any you could have eliminated for being too extreme.*

6. Was I better at Sentence Completions or the Reading questions? *You can look at being "better" as either having more correct answers or a greater percentage of correct answers. There might not be a big difference between the two question types. If there is a big difference, spend some extra time on the question type you had trouble with.*

You should ask similar questions for the other two sections. For Math, look at where your mistakes occurred. Were your mistakes in the easy, medium, or hard section? If you have more than two wrong answers in the easy section, you need to look over those problems. It is likely that you are going too fast or not doing enough work on these problems. Remember that the best way to improve your math score is to eliminate mistakes on the easy and medium problems, not get more hard questions correct. Your score will increase if you make no errors on the easy problems, get most of the medium problems correct, and then attack the hard questions with some tough work and a sprinkling of educated guesses.

> **Note**
>
> For Math, you can also look to see if there is any particular subject—like geometry or algebra—that you are having trouble with. Sometimes this is not easy to determine, since there are few SAT questions that draw on concepts from only one math area. Solving most questions requires knowledge of several subjects. Even so, over three Math sections you should be able to look at the problems you missed and spot a pattern if there is one.

The Writing section is the hardest one to diagnose. You can always take your essay and ask someone to review it for you. This person could be a teacher, a fellow student, or a parent. Just ask nicely and understand that any criticism you receive will help you to write a better essay for the real SAT. The multiple-choice Writing section is only approximately 25 questions, so it won't be as easy to determine if there's a pattern to your mistakes. Look over this section in two ways. First, the section has three different question types, so look to see how well you did with each question type. Is there a question type you are strongest at, or one that you have the most trouble with? Modify your study plans accordingly. Second, look over your incorrect answers and see if there's a connection. For example, do all your mistakes concern pronouns, or do you have trouble with verbs? Again, this information can help you modify your study plans to shore up any weak areas.

When you're ready to take the test:

1. Grab some scratch paper and some Number 2 pencils.
2. Unplug/turn off the phone.
3. Get out your timer.
4. Start the Diagnostic.

Answer Sheets

SECTION 1

1 Ⓐ Ⓑ Ⓒ Ⓓ Ⓔ	6 Ⓐ Ⓑ Ⓒ Ⓓ Ⓔ	11 Ⓐ Ⓑ Ⓒ Ⓓ Ⓔ	16 Ⓐ Ⓑ Ⓒ Ⓓ Ⓔ
2 Ⓐ Ⓑ Ⓒ Ⓓ Ⓔ	7 Ⓐ Ⓑ Ⓒ Ⓓ Ⓔ	12 Ⓐ Ⓑ Ⓒ Ⓓ Ⓔ	17 Ⓐ Ⓑ Ⓒ Ⓓ Ⓔ
3 Ⓐ Ⓑ Ⓒ Ⓓ Ⓔ	8 Ⓐ Ⓑ Ⓒ Ⓓ Ⓔ	13 Ⓐ Ⓑ Ⓒ Ⓓ Ⓔ	18 Ⓐ Ⓑ Ⓒ Ⓓ Ⓔ
4 Ⓐ Ⓑ Ⓒ Ⓓ Ⓔ	9 Ⓐ Ⓑ Ⓒ Ⓓ Ⓔ	14 Ⓐ Ⓑ Ⓒ Ⓓ Ⓔ	19 Ⓐ Ⓑ Ⓒ Ⓓ Ⓔ
5 Ⓐ Ⓑ Ⓒ Ⓓ Ⓔ	10 Ⓐ Ⓑ Ⓒ Ⓓ Ⓔ	15 Ⓐ Ⓑ Ⓒ Ⓓ Ⓔ	20 Ⓐ Ⓑ Ⓒ Ⓓ Ⓔ

SECTION 2

1 Ⓐ Ⓑ Ⓒ Ⓓ Ⓔ	7 Ⓐ Ⓑ Ⓒ Ⓓ Ⓔ	12 Ⓐ Ⓑ Ⓒ Ⓓ Ⓔ	17 Ⓐ Ⓑ Ⓒ Ⓓ Ⓔ
2 Ⓐ Ⓑ Ⓒ Ⓓ Ⓔ	8 Ⓐ Ⓑ Ⓒ Ⓓ Ⓔ	13 Ⓐ Ⓑ Ⓒ Ⓓ Ⓔ	18 Ⓐ Ⓑ Ⓒ Ⓓ Ⓔ
3 Ⓐ Ⓑ Ⓒ Ⓓ Ⓔ	9 Ⓐ Ⓑ Ⓒ Ⓓ Ⓔ	14 Ⓐ Ⓑ Ⓒ Ⓓ Ⓔ	19 Ⓐ Ⓑ Ⓒ Ⓓ Ⓔ
4 Ⓐ Ⓑ Ⓒ Ⓓ Ⓔ	10 Ⓐ Ⓑ Ⓒ Ⓓ Ⓔ	15 Ⓐ Ⓑ Ⓒ Ⓓ Ⓔ	20 Ⓐ Ⓑ Ⓒ Ⓓ Ⓔ
5 Ⓐ Ⓑ Ⓒ Ⓓ Ⓔ	11 Ⓐ Ⓑ Ⓒ Ⓓ Ⓔ	16 Ⓐ Ⓑ Ⓒ Ⓓ Ⓔ	21 Ⓐ Ⓑ Ⓒ Ⓓ Ⓔ
6 Ⓐ Ⓑ Ⓒ Ⓓ Ⓔ			

SECTION 3

1 Ⓐ Ⓑ Ⓒ Ⓓ Ⓔ	9 Ⓐ Ⓑ Ⓒ Ⓓ Ⓔ	17 Ⓐ Ⓑ Ⓒ Ⓓ Ⓔ	24 Ⓐ Ⓑ Ⓒ Ⓓ Ⓔ
2 Ⓐ Ⓑ Ⓒ Ⓓ Ⓔ	10 Ⓐ Ⓑ Ⓒ Ⓓ Ⓔ	18 Ⓐ Ⓑ Ⓒ Ⓓ Ⓔ	25 Ⓐ Ⓑ Ⓒ Ⓓ Ⓔ
3 Ⓐ Ⓑ Ⓒ Ⓓ Ⓔ	11 Ⓐ Ⓑ Ⓒ Ⓓ Ⓔ	19 Ⓐ Ⓑ Ⓒ Ⓓ Ⓔ	26 Ⓐ Ⓑ Ⓒ Ⓓ Ⓔ
4 Ⓐ Ⓑ Ⓒ Ⓓ Ⓔ	12 Ⓐ Ⓑ Ⓒ Ⓓ Ⓔ	20 Ⓐ Ⓑ Ⓒ Ⓓ Ⓔ	27 Ⓐ Ⓑ Ⓒ Ⓓ Ⓔ
5 Ⓐ Ⓑ Ⓒ Ⓓ Ⓔ	13 Ⓐ Ⓑ Ⓒ Ⓓ Ⓔ	21 Ⓐ Ⓑ Ⓒ Ⓓ Ⓔ	28 Ⓐ Ⓑ Ⓒ Ⓓ Ⓔ
6 Ⓐ Ⓑ Ⓒ Ⓓ Ⓔ	14 Ⓐ Ⓑ Ⓒ Ⓓ Ⓔ	22 Ⓐ Ⓑ Ⓒ Ⓓ Ⓔ	29 Ⓐ Ⓑ Ⓒ Ⓓ Ⓔ
7 Ⓐ Ⓑ Ⓒ Ⓓ Ⓔ	15 Ⓐ Ⓑ Ⓒ Ⓓ Ⓔ	23 Ⓐ Ⓑ Ⓒ Ⓓ Ⓔ	30 Ⓐ Ⓑ Ⓒ Ⓓ Ⓔ
8 Ⓐ Ⓑ Ⓒ Ⓓ Ⓔ	16 Ⓐ Ⓑ Ⓒ Ⓓ Ⓔ		

SECTION 4

1 Ⓐ Ⓑ Ⓒ Ⓓ Ⓔ	8 Ⓐ Ⓑ Ⓒ Ⓓ Ⓔ	15 Ⓐ Ⓑ Ⓒ Ⓓ Ⓔ	22 Ⓐ Ⓑ Ⓒ Ⓓ Ⓔ
2 Ⓐ Ⓑ Ⓒ Ⓓ Ⓔ	9 Ⓐ Ⓑ Ⓒ Ⓓ Ⓔ	16 Ⓐ Ⓑ Ⓒ Ⓓ Ⓔ	23 Ⓐ Ⓑ Ⓒ Ⓓ Ⓔ
3 Ⓐ Ⓑ Ⓒ Ⓓ Ⓔ	10 Ⓐ Ⓑ Ⓒ Ⓓ Ⓔ	17 Ⓐ Ⓑ Ⓒ Ⓓ Ⓔ	24 Ⓐ Ⓑ Ⓒ Ⓓ Ⓔ
4 Ⓐ Ⓑ Ⓒ Ⓓ Ⓔ	11 Ⓐ Ⓑ Ⓒ Ⓓ Ⓔ	18 Ⓐ Ⓑ Ⓒ Ⓓ Ⓔ	25 Ⓐ Ⓑ Ⓒ Ⓓ Ⓔ
5 Ⓐ Ⓑ Ⓒ Ⓓ Ⓔ	12 Ⓐ Ⓑ Ⓒ Ⓓ Ⓔ	19 Ⓐ Ⓑ Ⓒ Ⓓ Ⓔ	26 Ⓐ Ⓑ Ⓒ Ⓓ Ⓔ
6 Ⓐ Ⓑ Ⓒ Ⓓ Ⓔ	13 Ⓐ Ⓑ Ⓒ Ⓓ Ⓔ	20 Ⓐ Ⓑ Ⓒ Ⓓ Ⓔ	27 Ⓐ Ⓑ Ⓒ Ⓓ Ⓔ
7 Ⓐ Ⓑ Ⓒ Ⓓ Ⓔ	14 Ⓐ Ⓑ Ⓒ Ⓓ Ⓔ	21 Ⓐ Ⓑ Ⓒ Ⓓ Ⓔ	

SECTION 5

1 Ⓐ Ⓑ Ⓒ Ⓓ Ⓔ	7 Ⓐ Ⓑ Ⓒ Ⓓ Ⓔ	12 Ⓐ Ⓑ Ⓒ Ⓓ Ⓔ	17 Ⓐ Ⓑ Ⓒ Ⓓ Ⓔ
2 Ⓐ Ⓑ Ⓒ Ⓓ Ⓔ	8 Ⓐ Ⓑ Ⓒ Ⓓ Ⓔ	13 Ⓐ Ⓑ Ⓒ Ⓓ Ⓔ	18 Ⓐ Ⓑ Ⓒ Ⓓ Ⓔ
3 Ⓐ Ⓑ Ⓒ Ⓓ Ⓔ	9 Ⓐ Ⓑ Ⓒ Ⓓ Ⓔ	14 Ⓐ Ⓑ Ⓒ Ⓓ Ⓔ	19 Ⓐ Ⓑ Ⓒ Ⓓ Ⓔ
4 Ⓐ Ⓑ Ⓒ Ⓓ Ⓔ	10 Ⓐ Ⓑ Ⓒ Ⓓ Ⓔ	15 Ⓐ Ⓑ Ⓒ Ⓓ Ⓔ	20 Ⓐ Ⓑ Ⓒ Ⓓ Ⓔ
5 Ⓐ Ⓑ Ⓒ Ⓓ Ⓔ	11 Ⓐ Ⓑ Ⓒ Ⓓ Ⓔ	16 Ⓐ Ⓑ Ⓒ Ⓓ Ⓔ	21 Ⓐ Ⓑ Ⓒ Ⓓ Ⓔ
6 Ⓐ Ⓑ Ⓒ Ⓓ Ⓔ			

Answer Sheets

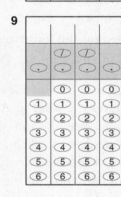
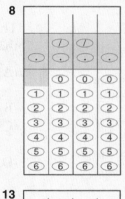
29

PETERSON'S
getting you there

Diagnostic

Test

Section 1

20 Questions ■ **Time—25 Minutes**

Directions: Read each of the passages carefully, then answer the questions that come after them. The answer to each question may be stated overtly or only implied. You will not have to use outside knowledge to answer the questions—all the material you will need will be in the passage itself. In some cases, you will be asked to read two related passages and answer questions about their relationship to one another. Mark the letter of your choice on your answer sheet.

Questions 1–2 are based on the following passage.

The *Iliad*, one of the great works of the ancient Greek poet Homer, relates the story of Achilles. As Homer tells it, Achilles was the son of Peleus, king of the Myrmidons of Phthia in Thessaly. His paternal grandfather Aeacus was, according to the legend recounted in the *Iliad*, the son of Zeus himself. The story of the childhood of Achilles in Homer differs from that given by later writers. According to Homer, Achilles was brought up by his mother in Phthia with his cousin and intimate friend Patroclus. Achilles learned the arts of war and eloquence from Phoenix, while Chiron (a Centaur) taught him music and medicine.

1. The passage makes clear that writers other than Homer describe Achilles's

   (A) childhood as different than Homer's description.
   (B) closest friend as not being Patroclus.
   (C) succession to the Myrmidonian throne as going unchallenged.
   (D) primary instructors as his mother and father and not Phoenix and Chiron.
   (E) childhood in more detail than does Homer.

2. According to the passage, Peleus's father was

   (A) Phthia
   (B) Patroclus
   (C) Aeacus
   (D) Chiron
   (E) Zeus

30

"The Address" is an English parliamentary term for the reply to the speech of the sovereign at the opening of a new parliament or session. There are certain formalities that distinguish this stage of parliamentary proceedings. The speech of the sovereign, or the "king's speech," itself is divided into three sections. The first, addressed to "My Lords," touches on foreign affairs. The second, to the "Gentlemen of the House of Commons," discusses financial issues related to the Treasury. The third, to "My Lords and Gentlemen," outlines the proposed legislation for the session.

3. According to the passage, "The Address" is the

(A) sovereign speaking to the Parliament
(B) House of Lords addressing the House of Commons
(C) Parliament replying to a speech of the sovereign
(D) Parliament addressing the English public
(E) House of Commons replying to the inquiries of the House of Lords

4. Which of the following might be included in the third section of the "king's speech?"

(A) trade relations with France
(B) foreign debt
(C) the appointment of a new head of the Treasury
(D) business growth in urban settings
(E) a newly proposed bill to readjust education spending

Questions 5–10 are based on the following passage.

In this passage the author, a historian, argues that the construction of Egypt's pyramids is readily explainable.

Line Even though thousands of years have passed since their construction, the pyramids of Egypt's Nile basin still evoke awe and wonder at their magnitude and (5) majesty. The pyramids prove that the Egyptians of that early day had attained a knowledge of practical mechanics which, even from the twentieth-century point of view, is not to be spoken of (10) lightly. It is amazing to think that until the introduction of skyscrapers in the twentieth century, these ancient pyramids ranked as some of the tallest manmade structures ever built.

(15) It has sometimes been suggested that these mighty pyramids, built as they are of great blocks of stone, speak to an almost miraculous knowledge on the part of their builders. Theories about extrater- (20) restrial help have been put forth to explain the Egyptians' accomplishment. These theories make for good storytell- ing, but have absolutely no basis in truth. A saner assessment of the conditions can (25) be found in the writings of Diodorus. A Sicilian, Diodorus lived centuries after the Great Pyramids were constructed, so he does not provide an eyewitness account. Even so, his explanation strikes (30) many as being very plausible.

In his famous *World's History* written nearly two thousand years ago, Diodorus explains the building of the pyramids by suggesting that great (35) quantities of earth were piled against the side of the rising structure to form an inclined plane. The massive blocks of

GO ON TO THE NEXT PAGE

stone used to build the pyramids were then dragged up this slanted surface.
(40) Diodorus gives us certain figures, based, doubtless, on reports made to him by Egyptian priests, who in turn drew upon the traditions of their country, perhaps even upon written records no longer
(45) preserved. He says that as much as 120,000 people were employed in the construction of the largest pyramids, and that, notwithstanding the size of this host of workers, such tasks still required
(50) twenty or more years to complete.

Of course, we must not place too much dependence upon such figures as these. Ancient historians were not as fastidious as contemporary historians in
(55) recording numbers and figures. But this does not mean Diodorus is not an important source of information on the construction of the pyramids. We need not doubt that he is generally accurate in
(60) his outlines of the methods used to construct the pyramids. Imagine a host of workers numbering in the tens of thousands. Their combined weight and strength could be applied to the task and
(65) supplemented with the aid of ropes, pulleys, rollers, and levers. With the help of the inclined plane, these workers could undoubtedly move, elevate, and place in position the largest blocks that were used
(70) to construct the pyramids. Using simple human muscle aided by basic tools, these workers could even raise the most gigantic obelisks, without the aid of any other kind of mechanism or occult
(75) power. These same human hands could, as Diodorus suggests, remove all trace of the debris of construction and leave the pyramids and obelisks standing in weird isolation, as if sprung into being through
(80) a miracle.

5. It is clear from the passage that the author views the Egyptian pyramids as

(A) a great feat of engineering.
(B) easily reproducible with current technologies.
(C) the supreme expression of the Egyptian exaltation of their pharaohs.
(D) a mechanical failure since they are losing their original shape.
(E) a marked advance in the use of sand materials in ancient construction.

6. The author uses Diodorus's writings primarily to

(A) argue that the Egyptian priests were instrumental in the construction of the pyramids.
(B) help date the building of the pyramids.
(C) illustrate the imprecision of ancient historians.
(D) argue that the building of the pyramids is explainable in terms of the technologies available to the ancient Egyptians.
(E) argue that the obelisks were the most difficult of the ancient structures to build.

7. The word "saner" line 24, without changing the meaning of the sentence, could be replaced with

(A) more stable
(B) more articulate
(C) more reasonable
(D) hardier
(E) more elusive

32

8. The author's attitude towards the hypothesis that the construction of the pyramids is unexplainable is one of

(A) tentative acceptance
(B) firm denial
(C) mild skepticism
(D) stated indecision
(E) exclusive allegiance

9. All of the following are problems regarding the credibility of Diodorus that the author of the passage addresses EXCEPT

(A) Diodorus's work took over twenty years to complete.
(B) Diodorus's work was written centuries after the pyramids were constructed.
(C) Diodorus does not provide mathematical detail.
(D) Diodorus's history was based on the writing of priests', which was based on oral history.
(E) Some of Diodorus's descriptions are exaggerated.

10. Based on the author's beliefs about the construction of the Egyptian pyramids the author would most likely view the building of other pyramids by ancient civilizations as

(A) explainable by undiscovered technologies.
(B) unexplainable since we do not have direct evidence of their building techniques.
(C) mysterious since we know of no communication between the Egyptians and these other ancient civilizations.
(D) explainable by use of the technologies we know they possessed.
(E) explainable by reference to the governmental systems of these civilizations.

Questions 11–20 are based on the following passage.

The following excerpts have been adapted from an autobiography of Theodore Roosevelt, an American president from the early twentieth century.

Line Sometime around 1644, Klaes Martensen van Roosevelt came from Holland to New Amsterdam, now New York City. For the next seven generations, every one
(5) of us was born on Manhattan Island. On October 27, 1858, I was born at No. 28 East Twentieth Street, New York City.

My father, Theodore Roosevelt, was the best man I ever knew. He combined
(10) strength and courage with gentleness and great unselfishness. He would not tolerate in his children selfishness, idleness, cowardice, or untruthfulness. As we grew older he also made us under-
(15) stand that the same standard of clean living was demanded for boys as for girls. With great love and patience, he combined insistence on discipline. He never physically punished me but once, yet he
(20) was the only man of whom I was ever really afraid.

My father worked hard at his business, and he died when he was forty-six. He was interested in every
(25) social reform movement, and he did an immense amount of charitable work himself. He was a big, powerful man, with his heart filled with gentleness for those who needed help or protection, and
(30) with the possibility of much wrath against a bully or an oppressor.

My father was particularly interested in a lodging house for underprivileged boys and in getting the children off the
(35) city streets and out on farms in the West. At very early ages we children were taken

33

with him to help at the lodging house. When I was President, the Governor of Alaska under me was one of these boys (40) who had been sent from New York out West by my father.

While still a small boy I began to take an interest in natural history. At once, I began to write a natural history. It was (45) written down in a blank book wholly unscientifically and in simplified spelling. After that, my two cousins and I promptly started what we ambitiously called the "Roosevelt Museum of (50) Natural History." The collections were at first kept in my room, and later moved up to a bookcase in the back hall. My father and mother encouraged me warmly in this, as they always did in (55) anything that could give me wholesome pleasure or help to develop me.

Quite unknown to myself, I was, while a boy, under a hopeless disadvantage in studying nature. I was very (60) near-sighted. I realized it when one day my friends read aloud an advertisement in huge letters on a distant billboard. Not only was I unable to read the sign, but I could not even see the letters. I spoke of (65) this to my father, and soon afterwards got my first pair of spectacles, which opened an entirely new world to me. I had been a clumsy and awkward little boy, and a good deal of it had been due (70) to the fact that I could not see. The recollection of this experience gives me a keen sympathy for those who are trying in our public schools and elsewhere to remove the physical causes of deficiency (75) in children, who are often unjustly blamed for being obstinate or unambitious.

By the time I left college and entered the big world, I owed more than I can (80) express to the training I had received, especially in my own home. But I still had much to learn if I were to become really fitted to do my part in the work that lay ahead for my generation of (85) Americans. I had, consciously or unconsciously, been taught that socially and industrially pretty much the whole duty of the man lay in thus making the best of himself—that he should be honest in his (90) dealings with others and charitable to the unfortunate, but that it was no part of his business to join with others in trying to make things better for the many by curbing the excessive development of (95) individualism in a few. Now I do not mean that this training was by any means all bad. But such teaching, if not corrected by other teaching, means acquiescence in a riot of lawless business (100) individualism which would be as destructive to real civilization as the lawless military individualism of the Dark Ages.

11. From the sentence beginning "He was a big . . ." (lines 27–28), it can be inferred that Theodore Roosevelt's father

(A) got a thrill from his power
(B) was physically large, but sweet-tempered
(C) had a great deal of money
(D) was provoked by weakness
(E) could be frightening when he had good reason to be

34

12. Which of the following best describes Roosevelt's tone in the passage?

    (A) genuine
    (B) somber
    (C) adamant
    (D) reactionary
    (E) self-important

13. The word "ambitiously" in line 48, paragraph 5 primarily serves to convey

    (A) the strength of Roosevelt's desire to become an important man
    (B) the young age at which Roosevelt planned to found a museum
    (C) Roosevelt's admiration for his father's successes
    (D) the insignificance of Roosevelt's collection
    (E) Roosevelt's love of adult vocabulary

14. The purpose of paragraph 5 is to show that Roosevelt's interest in natural history

    (A) was an outgrowth of his love of reading
    (B) was unschooled and naïve
    (C) was a precursor to his passion for politics
    (D) was rigorous from the outset
    (E) was an expression of genius

15. Roosevelt includes the detail about the governor of Alaska in order to emphasize

    (A) how successful his father's program was
    (B) how connected his father was politically
    (C) how far west they sent the boys
    (D) how humble the governor's background was
    (E) how generous Roosevelt was as president

16. It can be inferred from the passage that which of the following was a lesson Roosevelt learned from his father?

    (A) It is especially important for men to have strong morals.
    (B) Society must have safeguards to protect the poor.
    (C) Individuals have a moral duty to strive to their highest possible level of achievement.
    (D) Children who struggle in school deserve patience and compassion.
    (E) Intellectual pursuit is more important than sport.

17. Roosevelt's ultimate purpose in the passage is to

    (A) provide an explanation for having ideas that might otherwise seem contradictory
    (B) demonstrate that he is an average American
    (C) celebrate his father
    (D) justify his establishment of a school for underprivileged boys
    (E) explain his shift from natural sciences to politics

18. In line 94, paragraph 7, "curbing" most nearly means

    (A) supplanting
    (B) sidetracking
    (C) curtailing
    (D) spurring
    (E) condemning

19. The main idea of paragraph 7 can best be expressed as

    (A) Roosevelt would later reject the idea that all business dealings must be honest.

    (B) Roosevelt had concluded that individual enterprise was ruthless.

    (C) Roosevelt would later conclude that individual success was not as important as his father thought.

    (D) Roosevelt would later decide that government has to limit individual profit to protect the poor.

    (E) Roosevelt had established all of his important views by the time he finished college.

20. The author includes the phrase "consciously or unconsciously" (lines 85–86, paragraph 7) to emphasize that

    (A) he was still too young to have a concrete understanding of these opinions

    (B) his teachers had been very insistent on the value of the individual

    (C) his desire to be successful was an unconscious attempt to please his father

    (D) he had been taught in a variety of ways

    (E) his mentors were not heartless

STOP Do not proceed to the next section until time is up.

Section 2

21 Questions ■ Time—25 Minutes

Directions: Solve the following problems using any available space on the page for scratchwork. Mark the letter of your choice on the answer sheet that best corresponds to the correct answer.

Notes:

1. You may use a calculator. All of the numbers used are real numbers.

2. You may use the figures that accompany the problems to help you find the solution. Unless the instructions say that a figure is not drawn to scale, assume that it has been drawn accurately. Each figure lies in a plane unless the instructions say otherwise.

Reference Information

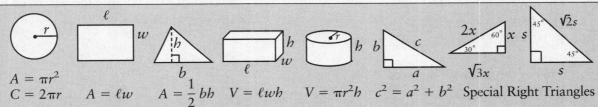

$A = \pi r^2$
$C = 2\pi r$ $A = \ell w$ $A = \dfrac{1}{2} bh$ $V = \ell wh$ $V = \pi r^2 h$ $c^2 = a^2 + b^2$ Special Right Triangles

The number of degrees of arc in a circle is 360.
The measure in degrees of a straight angle is 180.
The sum of the measures in degrees of the angles of a triangle is 180.

---

1. If $3(x + y + z) - y = 3z + 2y + 12$ then $x =$

(A) 2
(B) 3
(C) 4
(D) 5
(E) 6

2. If a bolt machine makes three bolts every 5 seconds, how many bolts will the machine make in ten minutes?

(A) 100
(B) 160
(C) 240
(D) 360
(E) 600

GO ON TO THE NEXT PAGE

3.

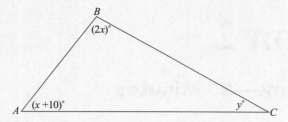

If the measure of ∠*A* is 50°, what is the value of *y*?

(A) 40
(B) 50
(C) 80
(D) 85
(E) 100

4. Which of the following numbers is a multiple of 3 and 9?

(A) 127
(B) 231
(C) 267
(D) 684
(E) 775

5. What is the distance between *P* (3, 2) and *Q* (0, 1)?

(A) 2
(B) 3
(C) $\sqrt{10}$
(D) $\sqrt{11}$
(E) 4

6. If $f(x) = 3 - x^2$ then which of the following values are outside the range of $f(x)$?

(A) −4
(B) −2
(C) 0
(D) 2
(E) 4

7. What is the area of a right triangle with one side of length 6 and a hypotenuse of length 10?

(A) 20
(B) 24
(C) 30
(D) 36
(E) 48

8.

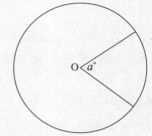

Circle O in the above figure has a diameter of 6. If the central angle formed measures 60°, what is the length of the intercepted arc?

A. $\dfrac{\pi}{2}$

B. π

C. $\dfrac{3\pi}{2}$

D. 2π

E. 3π

9. A stock's price went up 25 percent in the first half of a year and then went down 20 percent in the second half of the year. For the entire year, the price

(A) decreased by 10 percent.
(B) decreased by 5 percent.
(C) did not change.
(D) increased by 5 percent.
(E) increased by 10 percent.

10. In a certain school there are x halls each with y classrooms. Each classroom has z desks. Which of the following correctly expresses the number of desks in the school?

 (A) $x + yz$
 (B) $y(x + z)$
 (C) xyz
 (D) $x(y + z)$
 (E) $x + y$

11. The perimeter of a square is 20. What is the shortest distance between opposite corners?

 (A) 5
 (B) $5\sqrt{2}$
 (C) 8
 (D) $5\sqrt{3}$
 (E) 10

12.

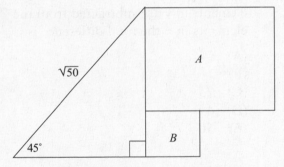

 If in the figure above A and B are squares, and the area of A is sixteen. What is the area of B?

 (A) 0.25
 (B) 1
 (C) 2.25
 (D) 4
 (E) 9

13.

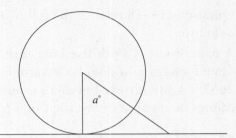

 In the figure above the line is tangent to the circle. If m∠a is 45° degrees, and the radius of the circle is $\sqrt{5}$, what is the length of the hypotenuse of the triangle?

 (A) $\sqrt{2}$
 (B) $\sqrt{3}$
 (C) 3
 (D) $\sqrt{10}$
 (E) 5

14.

 In the figure above if AC is $3x + 7$, what is CD?

 (A) 7
 (B) 6
 (C) 3
 (D) $x + 3$
 (E) $x + 6$

15. There are three routes from Stuben to Tejanos. There are three routes from Tejanos to Verona. There are four routes from Verona to Galson. If a driver is to go from Stuben to Galson, only passing through Tejanos and Verona once, how many different possible routes are there?

 (A) 10
 (B) 12
 (C) 16
 (D) 24
 (E) 36

39

Questions 16–18 refer to the following definition.

A palindrome is a positive integer that reads the same forward as it does backward. For instance, 2662 is a palindrome but 2626 is not. Also, zero cannot be the first or last digit of a palindrome.

16. Which of the following is a palindrome?

(A) 360
(B) 306
(C) 3636
(D) −6336
(E) 3663

17. If 9A6B9 is a palindrome, and 3A43 is a palindrome, what is the value of B?

(A) 3
(B) 4
(C) 6
(D) 9
(E) It cannot be determined.

18. What is the difference between the next greatest and next smallest palindrome in relation to 4554?

(A) 20
(B) 22
(C) 200
(D) 220
(E) 322

19. If 3, 6, 12 . . . is a geometric sequence, what is the 13th term in this sequence?

(A) 156
(B) 892
(C) 3,024
(D) 12,288
(E) 24,576

20. If p, q, and n are distinct digits, how many different 4-digit numbers that only include p, q, and n, but always uses all three, could they possibly form?

(A) 8
(B) 30
(C) 36
(D) 54
(E) 104

21. If x is the set of positive even integers 0 to 100 inclusive, and y is the set of positive odd integers 0 to 100 inclusive, and the elements in y are subtracted from the elements in x the total difference is

(A) 0
(B) 1
(C) 25
(D) 49
(E) 50

S T O P Do not proceed to the next section until time is up.

Section 3

Identifying Sentence Errors

Directions: Mark the letter of your choice on the answer sheet that best corresponds to the correct answer.

Notes:

1. The following questions test your knowledge of the rules of English grammar, as well as word usage, word choice, and idioms.

2. Some sentences are correct, but others contain a single error. No sentence contains more than one error.

3. Any errors that occur will be found in the underlined portion of the sentence. Choose the letter underneath the error to indicate the part of the sentence that must be changed.

4. If there is no error, pick answer choice (E).

5. There will be no change in any parts of the sentence that are not underlined.

1. Mrs. Thompson did not go with Smythe
                     A
   and I on the trip because her plane arrived
   B   C
   late, and she missed her connecting flight.
                        D
   No error.
   E

2. It is likely that the first day of the race,

   originally set for September 20, would be
   A   B   C
   postponed on account of bad weather.
              D
   No error.
   E

3. Modern art, though often used as a
                           A
   catch-all term for all contemporary art, is
                                           B
   generally defined as having a definite
   C
   beginning in the early decades of the
                           D
   twentieth century. No error.
                       E

4. Thomas had, in the past, stated that Alicia
            A   B
   was a more natural speaker than him.
          C   D
   No error.
   E

GO ON TO THE NEXT PAGE

5. In 1953 Watson and Crick <u>unlocked</u> the
   A
   structure of the DNA molecule and

   <u>set into motion</u> the modern study of
   B
   genetics, <u>which</u> <u>was</u> currently one of the
   C   D
   most vibrant fields of scientific research.

   <u>No error.</u>
   E

6. Enrique Fermi, one of the great <u>physicists</u>
   A
   of the last century, <u>was</u> a good friend of
   B
   Albert Einstein; <u>they</u> met after one of <u>his</u>
   C   D
   lectures at Princeton. <u>No error.</u>
   E

7. The group, <u>including</u> the speakers, <u>were</u>
   A   B
   ready for the second half of the conference

   which <u>was going to be held</u>
   C
   <u>in the main amphitheater.</u> <u>No error.</u>
   D   E

8. Recent, studies <u>on the topic</u> of biodiversity
   A   B
   in aquamarine settings <u>have raised</u>
   C
   concerns related to the <u>rising</u> levels of
   D
   oxygen in the Pacific Ocean. <u>No error.</u>
   E

9. The report <u>unambiguously</u> <u>stated</u> that
   A   B
   <u>in respect of</u> the new regulations, the
   C
   company <u>would</u> not be in compliance.
   D
   <u>No error.</u>
   E

10. <u>Many of the employees</u> <u>thought</u> that filing
    A   B
    the paperwork <u>was</u> more time consuming
    C
    <u>than the computer entries.</u> <u>No error.</u>
    D   E

Improving Sentences

Directions:

1. The following questions test your knowledge of English grammar, word usage, word choice, sentence construction, and punctuation.

2. Every sentence contains a portion that is underlined.

3. Any errors that occur will be found in the underlined portion of the sentence. If you believe there is an error, choose the answer choice that corrects the original mistake. Answer choices (B), (C), (D), and (E) contain alternative phrasings of the underlined portion. If the sentence contains an error, one of these alternate phrasings will correct it.

4. Choice (A) repeats the original underlined portion. If you believe the underlined portion does not contain any errors, select answer choice (A).

5. There will be no change in any parts of the sentence that are not underlined.

11. With all the receipts in hand, it was not unclear how many people had bought tickets.

    (A) was not unclear
    (B) was clearly
    (C) was clear
    (D) was not unclearly
    (E) wasn't unclear

12. The Cours Mirabeau, a wide thoroughfare planted with double rows of plane-trees and bordered by fine houses, divides the town into two portions.

    (A) planted with double rows of plane-trees
    (B) which has been planted with double rows of plane-trees
    (C) that was planted in the past with double rows of plane-trees
    (D) with double-rows of plane-trees which were planted in the past
    (E) in the past was planted with a double row of plane-trees

13. Philosophy, as an academic discipline, had its inception over twenty-four centuries ago in ancient Greece with Plato's Academy.

    (A) as an academic discipline
    (B) a discipline which is academic
    (C) as a discipline academically
    (D) as a discipline for the academic
    (E) as a discipline which is practiced academically

14. As the team of geologists began their descent into the canyon, it became really most clear to them that previous dating schemes of the canyon formation were inaccurate.

    (A) it became really clear
    (B) it became really clearer
    (C) it had become really clear
    (D) it had become clearer
    (E) it became clear

15. The medical establishment under pressure from government regulators stopped the relaxation of standards for earning a medical license.

    (A) establishment under pressure from government regulators stopped the relaxation

    (B) establishment, under pressure from government regulators, it stopped the relaxation

    (C) establishment—under pressure from government regulators—stopped, the relaxation

    (D) establishment, under pressure from government regulators; stopped the relaxation

    (E) establishment, under pressure from government regulators, stopped the relaxation

16. Large numbers of geese migrate along the southern route to the milder climates of Mexico grouping together to form super flocks.

    (A) geese migrate along the southern route to the milder climates of Mexico grouping together

    (B) goose migrating along the southern route to the milder climates of Mexico and grouping together

    (C) geese migrate along the southern route to the milder climates of Mexico and group together

    (D) geese migrate along the southern route to the mildest climates of Mexico, grouping together

    (E) geese, migrating along the southern route to the milder climates of Mexico, and then grouping together

17. Franklin Delano Roosevelt was an important figure in twentieth century America, he was president during the Great Depression and the Second World War.

    (A) Franklin Delano Roosevelt was an important figure in twentieth century America, he was president during the Great Depression and the Second World War.

    (B) Franklin Delano Roosevelt was an important figure in twentieth century America, and he was president during the Great Depression, and also the Second World War.

    (C) Franklin Delano Roosevelt was an important figure in twentieth century America. He was president during the Great Depression and the Second World War.

    (D) Franklin Delano Roosevelt was an important figure in twentieth century America: president during the Great Depression and the Second World War.

    (E) Franklin Delano Roosevelt was an important figure in twentieth century America; was president during the Great Depression and the Second World War.

18. It is vital for success in college both to employ good study skills and being a good listener in class lectures.

    (A) being a good listener
    (B) listening well
    (C) to listen good
    (D) to listen well
    (E) being a goodly listener

19. To this day, the Yamato clan can trace <u>its imperial lineage</u> to the pre-history of ancient Japan.

(A) its imperial lineage
(B) it's imperial lineage
(C) their line of imperialism
(D) they're imperial lineage
(E) their imperial lineage of the Yamato clan

20. Unlike many of his colleagues, Thompson <u>did not think that the Houghton space Project was going</u> to be a scientifically fruitful endeavor.

(A) did not think that the Houghton space Project was going
(B) did not think the Houghton Space Project was going
(C) did not think the Houghton space project would be going
(D) did not think that the Houghton Space Project would be
(E) did not think that the Houghton Space Project will be

Improving Paragraphs

Directions:

1. The following questions test your knowledge of paragraph and sentence construction.

2. The following passage is a rough draft of an essay. This rough draft contains various errors.

3. Read the rough draft and then answer the questions that follow. Some questions will focus on specific sentences and ask if there are any problems with that sentence's word choice, word usage, or overall structure. Other questions will ask about the paragraph itself. These questions will focus on paragraph organization and development.

4. Select the answer that best reflects the rules of English grammar and proper essay and paragraph writing.

Questions 21–25 refer to the following passage.

The following is the first few paragraphs of an early draft of an essay on Yusuf Komunyakaa, an African-American poet.

Line   On April 29 1947, Yusef Komunyakaa was born in Bogalusa, Louisiana. He is the eldest of five children. Komunyakaa employs his childhood experiences in his
(5)   works: his familial relationships and his maturation in a rural Southern community provide fundamental themes for several of his volumes.

Military service during when he was
(10)   a young man also proved to be a formative thing to the budding poet. After graduating from Bogalusa's Central High School in 1965, Komunyakaa enlisted in the United States Army to
(15)   begin a tour of duty in Vietnam. While there, he started writing, sometime between 1969 and 1970. As a correspon-

45

GO ON TO THE NEXT PAGE

(20)
dent for and later editor of the military newspaper, *The Southern Cross*, Komunyakaa mastered a journalistic style which he would later use in poetic efforts to assess objectively his time spent engaged in warfare. He was awarded the Bronze Star for his work with the paper.

(25)
Komunyakaa enrolled at the University of Colorado and received a B.A. in 1975. While at Colorado, he discovered his undiscovered abilities as a poet in a creative writing workshop. The work-

(30)
shop, notes the author, was the first chance he had to write for himself. Even though he had long been an avid reader of poetry and a lover of literature, his attempts to write creatively—mainly

(35)
short stories—had been unsuccessful. He had tried numerous times to write short stories but he had never felt that he had succeeded in this task.

21. What is the best way to revise the first sentence of the first paragraph?

   (A) Omit the comma after "1947"
   (B) Omit the comma after "Bogalusa"
   (C) Change the comma after "1947" to a semicolon
   (D) Insert a comma after "29"
   (E) Change the capitalization of the word "April" to "april"

22. Which of the following sentences would be the best revision of the first sentence in the second paragraph?

   (A) Military service during young adulthood also proves formative for the budding poet.
   (B) Military service when as a young adult proved to be really formative for the budding poet.
   (C) Although a young adult, military service proved to be really formative for the budding poet.
   (D) Military service during his youthfulness was really important to his formation as a budding poet.
   (E) Military service as a young adult also proved formative to the budding poet.

23. Which of the following is the best transitional phrase to place in the beginning of the third paragraph?

   (A) After leaving the army in the early 1970s,
   (B) Since he left the army in the early 1970s,
   (C) While leaving the army in the early 1970s,
   (D) Because he left the army in the early 1970s,
   (E) On account of his leaving the army in the early 1970s,

24. Which of the following is the best choice to replace the word "undiscovered" in the second sentence of the third paragraph?

   (A) basic
   (B) nascent
   (C) complex
   (D) unusual
   (E) waxing

46

25. The essay would be stronger if the last sentence were

(A) omitted entirely.
(B) split into two smaller sentences.
(C) moved so that it became the second sentence of the paragraph.
(D) revised to, "He had tried numerous times to write short stories but never felt that he succeeded in this task."
(E) revised to, "He had tried numerous times to write short stories but had never felt successful at it."

Questions 26–30 refer to the following passage.

The following is a short piece on Amarapura, a historic Burmese city.

Line   Once in the past the capital of the Burmese kingdom, Amarapura is now a suburb of Mandalay, Burma. The town was founded in 1783 to form a new
(5)   capital about six miles to the northeast of Ava. It increased rapidly in size and population, and in 1810 was estimated to contain 170,000 inhabitants; but in that year the town was destroyed by fire,
(10)   and this disaster, together with the removal of the royal court to Ava in 1823, caused a decline in the prosperity of the city. In 1827 its population was estimated at only 30,000. It suffered
(15)   severe calamity from an earthquake, which in 1839 destroyed the greater part of the city. It was finally abandoned in 1860, when king Mindon occupied Mandalay, roughly five miles farther
(20)   north.
       Amarapura was also laid out on much the same plan as Ava. The ruins of the city wall, now overgrown with jungle, show it to have been a square
(25)   with a side of about three-quarters of a

mile in length. At each corner stood a solid brick pagoda about 100 feet high. The most remarkable edifice was a celebrated temple, adorned with 250
(30)   lofty pillars of gilt wood. The remains of the former palace of the Burmese monarchs still survive in the center of the town. During the time of its prosperity Amarapura was defended by a rampart
(35)   and a large square citadel, with a broad moat, the walls being 7000 feet long and 20 feet high; with a bastion at each corner. The Burmese now refer to Amarapura as Myohaung, "the old city."
(40)   It has a station on the Rangoon-Mandalay railway, and is the junction for the line to Maymyo and the Kunlong ferry.

26. The opening words of the passage "Once in the past" would best be replaced by

(A) A long time ago
(B) Formerly
(C) Once upon a time
(D) In the past
(E) Millenia ago

27. The third sentence in the first paragraph might be revisable because it

(A) has subject-verb disagreement
(B) does not flow with the previous sentence
(C) is very long
(D) contains too many numbers and figures
(E) contains vague pronoun references

47

PETERSON'S
getting you there

28. The entire rough draft suffers from the fact that

(A) the town of Ava is repeatedly mentioned, but its overall importance or relationship to Amarapura is never explained.

(B) no explanation is given for why Amarapura waned in importance.

(C) the city of Mandalay is never described in sufficient detail

(D) the rituals of the ancient Burmese royal court are not delineated

(E) No mention is given to Amarapura's current state.

29. The word "edifice" in line 28 could most reasonably be replaced with

(A) structure
(B) place
(C) location
(D) construction site
(E) architect

30. Which of the following is the best way to revise the sentence in the second paragraph shown below?

During the time of its prosperity Amarapura was defended by a rampart and a large square citadel, with a broad moat, the walls being 7000 feet long and 20 feet high; with a bastion at each corner.

(A) Amarapura defended itself with a rampart and a large square citadel with a broad moat. The walls were 7000 feet long and 20 feet high with a bastion at each corner.

(B) Amarapura was defended by a rampart and a large square citadel with a broad moat. The citadel walls were 7000 feet long and 20 feet high and had a bastion at each corner.

(C) Amarapura was defended by a rampart and a large square citadel, with a broad moat, the walls being 7000 feet long and 20 feet high, with a bastion at each corner.

(D) Amarapura was defended by a rampart, a large square citadel, a broad moat, walls measuring 7000 feet long and 20 feet high with a bastion at each corner.

(E) Amarapura was defended by a rampart and a large square citadel with a broad moat. Amarapura, with walls being 7000 feet long and 20 feet high, had a bastion at each corner.

STOP Do not proceed to the next section until time is up.

48

Section 4

27 Questions ■ Time—25 Minutes

Directions: Each sentence below has either one or two blanks in it and is followed by five choices, labeled (A) through (E). These choices represent words or phrases that have been left out. Choose the word or phrase that, if inserted into the sentence, would best fit the meaning of the sentence as a whole.

Example:

Canine massage is a veterinary technique for calming dogs that are extremely _____.

(A) inept
(B) disciplined
(C) controlled
(D) stressed
(E) restrained

Ⓐ Ⓑ Ⓒ ● Ⓔ

1. Though thought _____, recently a small number of living *lingis terracotis* organisms were discovered.

   (A) defunct
   (B) exiled
   (C) deserted
   (D) extinct
   (E) overpopulated

2. The most _____ factor in the computer revolution was size: the greatly diminished size of more modern computers has made them far more _____.

   (A) irrelevant..common
   (B) complex..unpredictable
   (C) salient..indispensable
   (D) concrete..valuable
   (E) essential..practical

GO ON TO THE NEXT PAGE

3. Though many traditional forms of medicine have been practiced for centuries, members of the modern medical establishment still often view these treatments as _____, since many have not been tested scientifically.

   (A) dubious
   (B) dogmatic
   (C) ineffective
   (D) surreptitious
   (E) disingenuous

4. The Barbary Pirates _____ the Strait of Gibraltar for centuries, attacking passing ships and impeding trade.

   (A) menaced
   (B) cultivated
   (C) arraigned
   (D) appropriated
   (E) disclaimed

5. The specks of paint were small, nearly _____ in fact, but they still were _____ by the inspector.

   (A) minuscule..ignored
   (B) microcosmic..upbraided
   (C) infinitesimal..detected
   (D) inestimable..noticed
   (E) ignominious..rejected

6. The _____ play was _____ even to its author, who later disavowed it.

   (A) bland..anathema
   (B) vulgar..offensive
   (C) heinous..maladroit
   (D) crafty..fearsome
   (E) inarticulate..comprehensible

7. Thomas was _____ the business deal since he had been swindled in a similar situation in the past.

   (A) enthusiastic about
   (B) terrified of
   (C) prideful of
   (D) leery of
   (E) nonchalant about

8. Maintaining the integrity of the soil specimens was _____, and ultimately the scientists were _____ in their attempts to keep the soil free of foreign particles.

   (A) straightforward..triumphant
   (B) challenging..unsuccessful
   (C) laborious..inundated
   (D) vexing..victorious
   (E) problematic..reticent

9. Though considered a traditionalist by many of her critics, the artist saw her work as _____ new techniques and forms.

   (A) undermining
   (B) enforcing
   (C) precluding
   (D) rejecting
   (E) employing

10. Although normally _____, the teacher became _____ when the students expressed frustration with the assignment.

    (A) impassive..defensive
    (B) serene..irritable
    (C) conscientious..irreverent
    (D) impatient..understanding
    (E) volatile..heated

11. The _____ between the politicians originated with a deeply _____ piece of legislation.

(A) rapprochement..ideological
(B) tension..meaningful
(C) rift..controversial
(D) argument..visceral
(E) tedium..complex

12. Though the author's prose was natural and fluid, her speech at the press club was halting and _____.

(A) condescending
(B) florid
(C) stilted
(D) Intricate
(E) elegant

13. Caught in indecision, the customer _____ between purchasing the laptop or the desktop.

(A) struggled
(B) determined
(C) vied
(D) vacillated
(E) protracted

14. The candidate's platform _____ greater fiscal responsibility and improvements in education, but few in the electorate believed the candidate would _____ these goals.

(A) promised..critique
(B) eschewed..uphold
(C) advocated..prioritize
(D) rejected..abhor
(E) proclaimed..satirize

15. Clark Gable, the legendary movie actor, was famous for his _____ and social savvy, two characteristics with which he _____ many adoring fans.

(A) obtuseness..ingratiated
(B) sanctimony..cultivated
(C) earnestness..accosted
(D) acumen..disgusted
(E) panache..charmed

Questions 16–27 refer to the following passage.
This is an excerpt from Mark Twain's speech entitled "Compliments and Degrees," a speech in which he discusses receiving compliments. Widely considered one of America's greatest novelists, Twain also won great acclaim as a humorist in his own day.

Line   It is very difficult to take compliments. I do not care whether you deserve the compliments or not, it is just as difficult to take them. The other night I was at the
(5)   Engineers' Club, and enjoyed the sufferings of Mr. Carnegie. They were complimenting him there; there it was all compliments, and none of them deserved. They say that you cannot live by bread
(10)   alone, but I can live on compliments.
     I do not make any pretence that I dislike compliments. The stronger the better, and I can manage to digest them. I think I have lost so much by not making
(15)   a collection of compliments, to put them away and take them out again once in a while. When in England I said that I would start to collect compliments, and I began there and I have brought some of
(20)   them along.
     The first one of these lies—I wrote them down and preserved them— I think they are mighty good and extremely just. It is one of Hamilton Mabie's compli-
(25)   ments. He said that La Salle was the first

51

PETERSON'S
getting you there

one to make a voyage of the Mississippi, but Mark Twain was the first to chart, light, and navigate it for the whole world. If that had been published at the
(30) time that I issued that book *Life on the Mississippi*, it would have been money in my pocket. I tell you, it is a talent by itself to pay compliments gracefully and have them ring true. It's an art by itself.

(35)   W. D. Howells spoke of me as first of Hartford, and ultimately of the solar system, not to say of the universe. If it can be proved that my fame reaches to Neptune and Saturn, that will satisfy
(40) even me. You know how modest and retiring Howells seems to be, but deep down he is as vain as I am. Mr. Howells had been granted a degree at Oxford, whose gown was red. He had been
(45) invited to an exercise at Columbia, and upon inquiry had been told that it was usual to wear the black gown. Later he had found that three other men wore bright gowns, and he had lamented that
(50) he had been one of the black mass, and not a red torch.

    Now here is a gold-miner's compliment. It is forty-two years old. It was my introduction to an audience to which I
(55) lectured in a log schoolhouse. There were no ladies there. I wasn't famous then. They didn't know me. Only the miners were there, with their breeches tucked into their boot-tops and with clay all
(60) over them. They wanted someone to introduce me, and they selected a miner, who protested, saying: "I don't know anything about this man. Anyhow, I only know two things about him. One is, he
(65) has never been in jail, and the other is, I don't know why."

    There's one thing I want to say about that English trip. One thing that I regret

was that some newspapers said I talked
(70) with the Queen of England with my hat on. I don't do that with any woman. I did not put it on until she asked me to. Then she told me to put it on, and it's a command there. I thought I had carried
(75) my American democracy far enough. So I put it on. I have no use for a hat, and never did have.

    The happiest experience I had in England was at a dinner given in the
(80) building of the Punch publication, a humorous paper which is appreciated by all Englishmen. It was the greatest privilege ever allowed a foreigner. I entered the diningroom of the building,
(85) where those men get together who have been running the paper for over fifty years. We were about to begin dinner when the toastmaster said: "Just a minute; there ought to be a little cer-
(90) emony." Then there was that meditating silence for a while, and out of a closet there came a beautiful little girl dressed in pink, holding in her hand a copy of the previous week's paper, which had in
(95) it my cartoon. It broke me all up. I could not even say "Thank you." That was the prettiest incident of the dinner, the delight of all that wonderful table. When she was about to go, I said, "My child,
(100) you are not going to leave me; I have hardly got acquainted with you." She replied, "You know I've got to go; they never let me come in here before, and they never will again." That is one of the
(105) beautiful incidents that I cherish.

52

16. The word "sufferings" in line 6 refers to

(A) the physical illness which ailed Mr. Carnegie.

(B) the difficulty of listening to others complimented deservedly.

(C) the difficulty of receiving compliments well.

(D) the hardships he had overcome, for which the engineers complimented him.

(E) the difficulty of devising false compliments.

17. The passage as a whole indicates that Twain thinks compliments are

(A) always profoundly flattering.

(B) an important social function.

(C) difficult to receive well but easy to give well.

(D) easily recorded but remembered only with difficulty.

(E) often grossly exaggerated.

18. When Twain says of compliments, "The stronger the better, and I can manage to digest them," he means to

(A) sardonically depict loving compliments as a noble act.

(B) adamantly maintain that one can live off compliments only with difficulty.

(C) earnestly encourage the audience to come up with great compliments for him.

(D) mournfully compare his present successes with his past struggles.

(E) indignantly insist that he is better at receiving compliments than Mr. Carnegie.

19. In lines 32–34, the author implies that

(A) Mr. Mabie made both an eloquent and well-timed compliment.

(B) a truly fine compliment can have monetary value.

(C) he would pay money to be able to make such a fine compliment himself.

(D) if Mr. Mabie had praised the book sooner, more copies would have been sold.

(E) it is distasteful to think of compliments in economic terms.

20. Twain's response to W. D. Howells's compliment in paragraph 4 suggests that

(A) Twain thinks the compliment is excessive.

(B) Twain believes every compliment should be met with another.

(C) Twain thirsts for greater and greater compliments.

(D) Twain prides himself on the universality of his themes.

(E) Twain has little regard for people who pay him compliments.

21. The phrase "red torch" lines 51 is used to emphasize

(A) the importance of the role Mr. Howells played in the ceremony.

(B) the flamboyance of Mr. Howells's wish.

(C) the garish hue of the gown.

(D) the colorfulness of the ceremony.

(E) the drabness of the other gowns.

22. In line 41 of paragraph 4, "retiring" most closely means

(A) elderly

(B) humble

(C) aloof

(D) lethargic

(E) arrogant

23. Twain relays the anecdote of the miner's introduction lines 62–66 to

(A) show how a spontaneous compliment can be the best kind.

(B) illustrate what a backhanded compliment is.

(C) provide a humorous example of how he was received before he became famous.

(D) provide a contrast with how the Queen of England welcomed him.

(E) show the nobility of the miner's intentions.

24. The underlying sentiment in Twain's remark that "I thought I had carried my American democracy far enough" (lines 74–75) is best described as

(A) mild affront at having been ordered by the Queen.

(B) self-satisfaction at having proved a point to the Queen.

(C) bashful humility in the Queen's presence.

(D) bold patriotism in a foreign setting.

(E) indifference to what the Queen wanted.

25. The author includes the little girl's remark in the last paragraph in order to

(A) show how young the girl really was.

(B) criticize the hosts for not allowing her to stay.

(C) reveal that he can pay pleasant compliments in conversation.

(D) demonstrate that children also enjoy his work.

(E) emphasize what a special occasion it was.

26. In lines 95–96, the author conveys that he

(A) couldn't help laughing at the hosts' surprise.

(B) was taken completely off guard.

(C) was too moved by the gesture to speak.

(D) was flattered, but forgot to say thank you.

(E) was flustered that his presentation had been interrupted.

27. This speech would best be compared to a speech in which a

(A) politician spoke on her platform.

(B) comedian performed his routine.

(C) journalist offered personal reflections on her career.

(D) novelist spoke on the issues his latest novel addressed.

(E) writer reflected on the reception of her writing.

STOP Do not proceed to the next section until time is up.

Section 5

21 Questions ■ Time—25 Minutes

Directions: Solve the following problems using any available space on the page for scratchwork. Mark the letter of your choice on the answer sheet that best corresponds to the correct answer.

Notes:

1. You may use a calculator. All of the numbers used are real numbers.

2. You may use the figures that accompany the problems to help you find the solution. Unless the instructions say that a figure is not drawn to scale, assume that it has been drawn accurately. Each figure lies in a plane unless the instructions say otherwise.

Reference Information

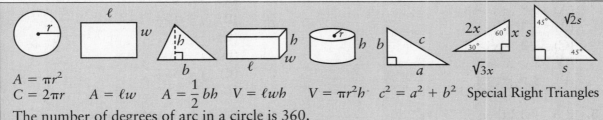

$A = \pi r^2$
$C = 2\pi r$ $\quad A = \ell w \quad A = \frac{1}{2}bh \quad V = \ell wh \quad V = \pi r^2 h \quad c^2 = a^2 + b^2$ Special Right Triangles

The number of degrees of arc in a circle is 360.
The measure in degrees of a straight angle is 180.
The sum of the measures in degrees of the angles of a triangle is 180.

1. If $5\sqrt{x} + 14 = 20$ then x equals

   A. $\frac{6}{5}$

   B. $1\frac{11}{25}$

   C. $\frac{48}{5}$

   D. 25

   E. 900

2. A class has x students. Four students join the class and the class size increases 20%. What was the original class size?

   (A) 16
   (B) 18
   (C) 20
   (D) 22
   (E) 24

55

GO ON TO THE NEXT PAGE

3.

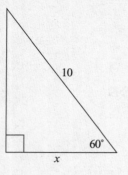

What is the value of x?

(A) 2
(B) 3
(C) 5
(D) $5\sqrt{2}$
(E) $5\sqrt{3}$

4. If $|x - 5| > 3$ then which of the following is true?

(A) $-8 > x > 8$
(B) $-3 > x > 2$
(C) $-2 > x > 5$
(D) $2 > x > 8$
(E) $5 > x > 8$

5. If $3^x = 12$ then $3^{2 + x} =$

(A) 6
(B) 12
(C) 36
(D) 108
(E) 144

6. A bag of marbles contains 6 red marbles, 8 green marbles, and 10 black marbles. What is the probability of picking out a red marble on one random try?

A. $\dfrac{1}{5}$

B. $\dfrac{1}{4}$

C. $\dfrac{1}{3}$

D. $\dfrac{2}{5}$

E. $\dfrac{5}{12}$

7. If j is an integer divisible by 2, 3, 6, 9, and 12 what is the next integer divisible by these numbers?

(A) $j + 9$
(B) $j + 12$
(C) $j + 24$
(D) $j + 30$
(E) $j + 36$

8. For how many integer values of x will $\dfrac{5}{x}$ be less than $\dfrac{1}{3}$ but greater than $\dfrac{1}{5}$?

(A) 9
(B) 7
(C) 6
(D) 4
(E) an infinite number

9.

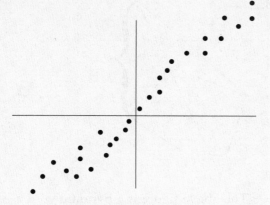

If a best fit line were fitted to the scatter-plot above, its slope would be

(A)   negative
(B)   nearly 0
(C)   0.05
(D)   0.50
(E)   about 1

10.   What is the midpoint between P (4, 2) and Q (0, 8)?

(A)   (0, 5)
(B)   (2, 5)
(C)   (2, 6)
(D)   (3, 4)
(E)   (3, 5)

11.   If y is a multiple of x by a factor of k, where k is a positive integer, and $x < y$ then

A. $\dfrac{y}{x} = k$

B. $\dfrac{3x}{y} = 3k$

C. $2(x - y) = 2k$

D. $(x - y)(y - x) = k$

E. $\dfrac{(x - y)}{(y - x)} = k$

12.   If $2^{-x} = (8)^{-1}$ then $x =$

(A) -4
(B) -3
(C)   2
(D)   3
(E)   4

13.   Jorge has 6 square tiles that are nine inches square each. If Jorge cuts each tile into the largest circle possible, what will the area of the left over tiles be in square inches?

(A) $54 - 7\pi$
(B) $6(9 - \pi)$
(C) $9(6 - \pi)$
(D) $54 - 13.5\pi$
(E) $12(9 - \pi)$

14.   In a coordinate plane, if distinct points A $(2, p)$ and B $(p, 2)$ lie on a line with a slope of negative one, which of the following could be values of p?

(A)   1, 2
(B)   1, 3
(C)   2, 2
(D)   2, 4
(E)   2, 5

GO ON TO THE NEXT PAGE

15. Which of the following numbers is a relative prime of 27?

    (A) 24
    (B) 35
    (C) 45
    (D) 54
    (E) 60

16. A rectangular solid has a height and width of 4. If the solid can be cut in half, across its length, such that two cubes result, what is the volume of the original solid?

    (A) 64
    (B) 78
    (C) 92
    (D) 110
    (E) 128

17. If $\dfrac{6x^2 + 16x + 10}{x^3 - 4x^2} = 0$ then $x =$

    A. $-1, -\dfrac{5}{3}$

    B. $-2, 2$

    C. $3, \dfrac{4}{5}$

    D. $1, 3$

    E. $2, 6$

18.

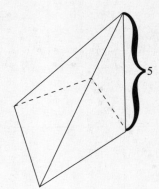

The above figure is a pyramid with a square base. If the height of the pyramid is 4, then what is the area of the base of the pyramid?

    (A) $3\sqrt{2}$
    (B) 9
    (C) 18
    (D) 25
    (E) 36

19.

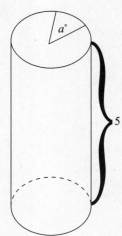

If the area of the sector is 6π, and the measure of angle a is 60°, what is the volume of the cylinder?

    (A) 120π
    (B) 140π
    (C) 160π
    (D) 180π
    (E) 200π

20. A circular dart board is divided into 20 equal sectors. One dart is thrown randomly at the board and lands in one of the sectors. What is the probability that a second dart, also thrown randomly, will land in the same sector?

A. $\dfrac{1}{400}$

B. $\dfrac{1}{380}$

C. $\dfrac{1}{20}$

D. $\dfrac{1}{19}$

E. $\dfrac{1}{10}$

21.

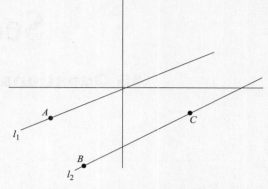

In the figure above, $l_1 \| l_2$, A is at $(-3, -2)$, B is at $(-2, -3)$, and C is at $(2, -1)$. What is the y-intercept of $l O_1$?

(A) -3
(B) -2
(C) -0.5
(D) 1
(E) 4

S T O P Do not proceed to the next section until time is up.

Section 6

16 Questions ■ Time—20 Minutes

The question of whether the ancient Greeks borrowed their algebra from the ancient Hindus or vice versa has been the subject of much discussion. There is no doubt that there was constant traffic between Greece and India beginning over three millennia ago, and it is very likely that an exchange of produce would be accompanied by a transference of ideas. In certain respects it appears that Hindu solutions to some basic algebraic equations were influenced by the Greeks. This is thought to be the case because Greek notation is employed in a few ancient texts of Hindu mathematics. Even so, it is certain that the Hindu algebraists were far in advance of the Greek algebraists. Hindu algebraists solved complex problems involving negative numbers, a feat not attained by the ancient Greeks.

1. The passage argues that

   (A) the Greek algebraists were more advanced than the Hindus.
   (B) Hindu and Greek algebraists were equally influenced by one another.
   (C) Hindu algebraists definitely influenced the Greeks more than vice versa.
   (D) Greek algebraists definitely influenced the Hindus more than vice versa.
   (E) the Hindu algebraists were influenced by the Greeks, but attained greater successes.

The United States Department of Agriculture dates its rank as an executive department from 1889. It was first established as a department in 1862, ranking as a bureau, with a commissioner in charge. In addition to the commissioner, there was a statistician, a chemist, an entomologist, and a superintendent of experimental farming. The bureau's scope was initially somewhat limited, but its work was gradually enlarged by the appointment of a botanist in 1868, the creation of a forestry department in 1877, and the establishment of agricultural experiment stations throughout the country in 1887. In 1889 the department became an executive department, the principal official being designated Secretary of Agriculture, with a seat in the president's cabinet.

2. The passage describes the United States Department of Agriculture as

(A) becoming more bureaucratic through the late nineteenth century.
(B) becoming more specialized in experimental farming through the late nineteenth century.
(C) growing in political clout through the early twentieth century.
(D) growing in size through the late nineteenth century.
(E) narrowing its scope of operations in the late nineteenth century.

3. It can be inferred from the passage that the U. S. Department of Agriculture becoming an executive department

(A) was beneficial for the farmers of the American Midwest.
(B) earned the department a seat on the president's cabinet.
(C) meant the department could hire a chemist and an entomologist.
(D) was a decision made by the future Secretary of Agriculture himself.
(E) made the Department of Agriculture a part of a different branch of government.

The Alder genus of plants comprises a few species of shrubs and trees, most of which do not reach a large size. They are geographically distributed throughout the north temperate zone of South America, which stretches along the Andes southward to Chile. One of the rare exceptions to the small size of the Alder genus is the Tuvian tree. Under favorable circumstances Tuvian trees will grow to a height of 40 or 50 feet, dwarfing the other members of its genus. Other than size, the Tuvian tree possesses the major characteristics of the Alder genus: the large wedge-shaped leaf, the saplike secretions at the base of the plant, and the production of large seeds.

4. Which of the following questions is *not* explicitly answered in the passage?

(A) What are the characteristics of leaves of plants in the Alder genus?
(B) Do plants other than the Tuvian tree in the Alder genus produce sap?
(C) How large are other plants in the Alder genus?
(D) Where do plants other than the Tuvian tree in the Alder genus grow?
(E) How large is a Tuvian tree?

Questions 5–16 refer to the following passage.

The following two passages discuss neuroscience, the study of the brain. Specifically, they address the notion of progress in the field of neuroscience.

Passage 1

Line   When NASA put a man on the moon
some four decades ago, a new frontier of
human endeavor began: the exploration
of outer space. In the last decade,
(5)   humanity again has entered into a new
frontier: the exploration of inner space.
This new frontier is the brain, and its
heroes are not astronauts but neuroscientists. Just as outer space holds vast
(10)   expanses to be explored, so also the
human brain holds great promise for
human exploration and discovery in its
vast uncharted domains. The great strides
made in neuroscience in the last decade
(15)   and the promise of future discoveries
make neuroscience arguably the most
important scientific field of our time.

One example of the promise of
neuroscience is the progress already made
(20)   with neurogenesis, the growth of new
neurons. Neurons are the basic cellular
building blocks of the brain. It had long
been dogma in neuroscience that adult
brains could not grow new neurons, but
(25)   recent research has shown that the
human brain has an incredible ability to
generate all kinds of new brain cells,
including neurons. Our increasing
understanding of the processes of
(30)   neurogenesis augurs an astounding
potential for medical application.
Researchers are already setting their
sights on the myriad neural diseases, such
as Alzheimer's and Parkinson's Disease.
(35)   The advancement of neuroscience
does not just anticipate the elimination of
neural diseases, but also holds the
possibility of enhancing the abilities of
healthy brains. New neural drug regimes
(40)   could increase memory or even heighten
our powers of perception, such as sight.
These exciting possibilities remain, for
the present, shrouded in mystery like
the brain itself, but the exploration of
(45)   the inner space of our brain has begun
in earnest.

Passage 2

Line   The 1990s were the "Decade of the
Brain." In that illustrious decade of brain
investigations, we were told of the great
promise of neuroscience. The end of
(5)   brain ailments from Alzheimer's disease
to depression, it was heralded, was just
around the corner. But the "Decade of
the Brain" has ended, and brain diseases
have not.

(10)   Depression is a good case study in the
progress of neuroscience. The history of
depression extends at least as far back as
Hippocrates, the founder of medicine in
ancient Greece. He prescribed herbal oral
(15)   remedies for depression and theorized
that depression was the result of imbalanced brain "biles." The herbal treatments were thought to help balance the
brain biles. His theory might sound crude
(20)   to modern ears, but we should not be so
quick to suppose that our understanding
and treatment regimes are much in
advance of Hippocrates. Like him, we
prescribe oral remedies for depression,
(25)   and like him, we have only a vague sense
of how these chemicals alter the balance
of chemicals in the brain. We have even
less idea of how or why these remedies
work when they do. There are various
(30)   explanations for why oral treatments—
from the earlier tricyclics to the iconic

1990s medication, Prozac—are beneficial to the depressed patient, but none of the explanations are ultimately satisfactory.
(35) For the most part, neither doctors nor pharmaceutical researchers have a fundamental grasp of how these medications work.

Before we scientists can declare
(40) neuroscience the harbinger of the end of mental illness and brain disease, we need to have a better grasp of the whys and wherefores of our discoveries.

5. NASA is mentioned in the first paragraph of Passage 1 to illustrate

- **(A)** the spatial dimensions of the brain.
- **(B)** the relation of brain research to astronomical research.
- **(C)** the importance of neuroscience, according to NASA.
- **(D)** the importance of pursuing more than one kind of scientific inquiry at once.
- **(E)** the comparable importance of neuroscience in the present to space exploration in the past.

6. The author of Passage 1 believes that neuroscience is "arguably the most important scientific field of our time" because it

- **(A)** has important political implications.
- **(B)** seeks to explain something we know virtually nothing about.
- **(C)** has the potential to improve the quality of human life.
- **(D)** can tell us more about the origin and meaning of life.
- **(E)** is the only science primarily devoted to understanding how humans work.

7. In Passage 1, the author's attitude toward enhancing normal brains is

- **(A)** markedly less enthusiastic than his or her response to possible cures for diseases.
- **(B)** indicative of his or her unconditional embrace of scientific advances.
- **(C)** clinical and objective.
- **(D)** defensive about the moral value of such advances.
- **(E)** skeptical, in contrast to his or her general optimism about scientific advances.

8. Neurogenesis is important to the argument of Passage 1 primarily because it

- **(A)** provides concrete evidence to support the author's claim that neuroscience has made important advances.
- **(B)** disproves the suggestion in the first paragraph that the brain is "uncharted territory."
- **(C)** provides a contrast to the view that neuroscience will enhance our perceptions.
- **(D)** demonstrates that neuroscience was relatively undeveloped before the 1990s.
- **(E)** poetically extends the metaphor of the brain as the new frontier.

9. The word "dogma" in line 23 of Passage 1 most closely means

- **(A)** strongly held belief.
- **(B)** question of faith rather than intellect.
- **(C)** anathema.
- **(D)** loosely held tenet.
- **(E)** tangential consideration.

63

10. For Passage 2, which of the following best describe the author's attitude toward neuroscience?

(A) hopeful expectation
(B) moral opposition
(C) begrudging acceptance
(D) moderate anticipation
(E) forceful rejection

11. The author of Passage 2 suggests that real progress toward curing mental illness and brain disease should be characterized by a

(A) firmer notion of what causes various illnesses.
(B) decreased reliance on oral medications for brain-related conditions.
(C) deeper consideration of the side effects of medical treatments.
(D) more methodical understanding of how current treatments work.
(E) greater sense of creativity in approaching problems.

12. The author compares Hippocrates's approach to depression with modern approaches primarily suggest that

(A) oral remedies for depression are unlikely to work.
(B) doctors suffer from depression as much as their patients.
(C) neuroscience has made no progress since Hippocrates's time.
(D) modern doctors' claim to balance chemicals they don't understand is unconvincing.
(E) today's methods are far more technologically sophisticated than Hippocrates's.

13. The author probably calls Prozac an "iconic 1990s medication" primarily to convey that

(A) the importance of Prozac, like the other 1990s antidepressants, was more about hype than effectiveness.
(B) Prozac is indicative of the developments of the 1990s.
(C) the author is disinterested in discussing the specifics of the different oral medications.
(D) Prozac represented a drastic shift in approach from the earlier medications.
(E) Prozac is particularly overrated as a treatment for depression.

14. The authors of Passages 1 and 2 would be most likely to agree that

(A) the last decade saw breakthrough developments in neuroscience.
(B) neuroscientists will soon find a cure for Alzheimer's disease.
(C) Alzheimer's disease is a more important disease than depression.
(D) the discovery of neurogenesis will have practical applications.
(E) neuroscientists are the appropriate people to search for a cure for Alzheimer's disease.

64

15. Which of the following questions is not answered by either passage?

(A) How does the discovery of neurogenesis promise treatment for brain diseases?

(B) Which developments made the 1990s an important decade for neuroscience?

(C) What recent advances have been made to treat Alzheimer's disease?

(D) What aspect of brain functioning do antidepressants affect?

(E) How is the development of neuroscience likely to affect healthy people?

16. The author of the second passage would probably describe the author of the first passage as

(A) too simplistic in his or her assumption that theoretical discoveries and practical applications go hand in hand.

(B) overly critical about the state of neuroscience prior to the 1990s.

(C) unaware of the complete lack of new neuroscience research.

(D) not attentive enough to the practical developments neuroscience research has already made possible.

(E) too focused on the importance of Alzheimer's and Parkinson's Diseases.

STOP Do not proceed to the next section until time is up.

Section 7

13 Questions ■ Time—20 Minutes

Directions for Student Produced Responses

Notes:

1. All numbers used are real numbers.

2. All angle measurements can be assumed to be positive unless otherwise noted.

3. All figures lie in the same plane unless otherwise noted.

4. Drawings that accompany questions are intended to provide information useful in answering the question. The figures are drawn closely to scale unless otherwise noted.

Enter your responses to questions 1–13 in the special grids provided on your answer sheet. Input your answers as indicated in the directions below.

Answer: $\frac{4}{9}$ or 4/9

Answer: 1.4
Either position is correct.

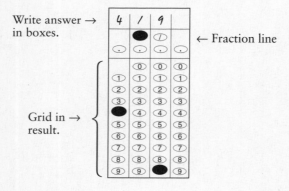

Note: You may begin your answer in any column, space permitting. Leave blank any columns not needed.

- Writing your answer in the boxes at the top of the columns will help you accurately grid your answer, but it is not required. **You will only receive credit for an answer if the ovals are filled in properly.**

- Only fill in one oval in each column.

- If a problem has several correct answers, just grid in one of them.

- There are no negative answers.

- **Never grid in mixed numbers.** The answer $3\frac{1}{5}$ must be gridded as 16/5 or 3.2. If

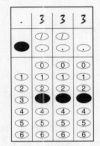

is gridded, it will be read as $\frac{31}{5}$, not $3\frac{1}{5}$.

Decimal Accuracy

Decimal answers must be gridded as accurately as possible. The answer 0.3333 . . . must be gridded as .333.

Less accurate values, such as .33 are not acceptable.

Acceptable ways to grid $\frac{1}{3}$ = .3333 . . .

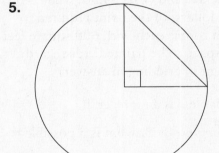

---

1. A fair six-sided die has a number on each side one through six. If the die is cast, what is the probability of rolling a prime number?

2. Five lines intersect at one point forming ten congruent angles. What is the sum of the measures of two of those angles?

3. If $(3x^2 + 6x + 4)(2x + 4) = ax^3 + bx^2 + cx + d$, what is the value of b for all values of x?

4. If $f(x) = x + 2^x$ then $f(3)$ equals

5.

If the radius of the above circle is $\sqrt{8}$, what is the hypotenuse of the triangle?

6. Car sales in County X jumped 10% from May to June. If in June 220 cars were sold, how many were sold in May?

67

PETERSON'S
getting you there

7.

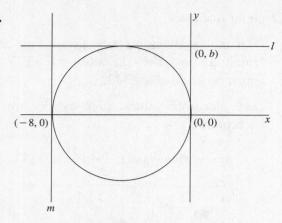

In the figure above, lines l and m are perpendicular and are tangent to the circle. What is the value of b?

8. If n is an integer whose cube root is an integer, and $7n > n^2$, what is n?

9. If a gallon of paint covers 400 square feet of wall space and costs $4.50, what is the cost, in dollars, of the paint required to paint ten rooms each with 600 square feet of wall space to be painted? (disregard dollar sign in gridding in answer)

10. The variable a is an integer. If
$$-a < \frac{2a}{5} - 6 < -3,$$ what is a possible value of a?

11. The average (arithmetic mean) of four distinct positive integers is 45. What is the greatest possible value of one of those four integers?

12. If $b^{\frac{3}{4}}b^{\frac{3}{4}}b^{\frac{3}{2}} = 8$ then what does b equal?

13.

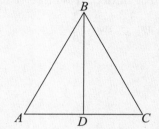

In the figure above ΔABD is congruent to ΔCBD, and m$\angle B = 60$. If $AD = 3$, what is the perimeter of ΔABC?

S T O P   Do not proceed to the next section until time is up.

Section 8
Essay

Time—25 Minutes

Directions: Think carefully about the statement below and the assignment that follows it.

Consider the following statement.

Because of technological advances, the world is becoming _____.

Assignment: Write an essay in which you complete the preceding statement. Explain the reasons behind how you completed the statement. Develop your point of view on this statement and be sure to support your stance with sufficient details.

STOP When you are finished with your essay put your pencil down until the time allotted is over.

Answer Key

Section 1 Critical Reading		Section 2 Math		Section 3 Writing		Section 4 Critical Reading	
1. A	11. E	1. C	12. B	1. B	16. C	1. D	15. E
2. C	12. A	2. D	13. D	2. C	17. C	2. E	16. C
3. C	13. D	3. B	14. A	3. E	18. D	3. A	17. E
4. E	14. B	4. D	15. E	4. D	19. A	4. A	18. A
5. A	15. A	5. C	16. E	5. D	20. B	5. C	19. D
6. D	16. C	6. E	17. B	6. D	21. D	6. B	20. A
7. C	17. A	7. B	18. D	7. B	22. E	7. D	21. B
8. B	18. C	8. B	19. D	8. A	23. A	8. B	22. B
9. A	19. D	9. C	20. C	9. C	24. B	9. E	23. C
10. A	20. E	10. C	21. E	10. D	25. A	10. B	24. A
		11. B		11. C	26. B	11. C	25. E
				12. A	27. C	12. C	26. C
				13. A	28. A	13. D	27. B
				14. E	29. A	14. C	
				15. E	30. B		

Section 5 Math		Section 6 Critical Writing		Section 7 Math	
1. B	12. D	1. E	9. A	1. 0.5 or 1/2	8. 1
2. C	13. D	2. D	10. C	2. 72	9. 67.5
3. C	14. B	3. B	11. D	3. 24	10. 5, 6, or 7
4. D	15. B	4. C	12. D	4. 11	11. 174
5. D	16. E	5. E	13. B	5. 4	12. 2
6. B	17. A	6. C	14. E	6. 200	13. 18
7. E	18. C	7. B	15. D	7. 4	
8. A	19. D	8. A	16. A		
9. E	20. C				
10. B	21. C				
11. A					

Section 8
Essay

As you might expect, answers will vary. If possible, politely ask a teacher, fellow student, or some other person knowledgeable about formal essay writing to review your essay and provide feedback on ways in which your essay is commendable and on areas where it could be improved.

Or, you can go to www.petersons.com/satessayedge for scoring and review of your essay.

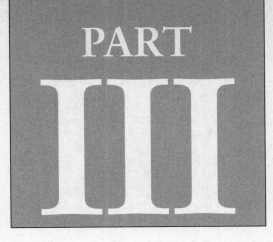

PART III

Reviewing the Sections

PART III

Chapter 4

Critical Reading Section—A Game of Words You CAN Win

The Critical Reading section on the new SAT was known as the Verbal section on the old tests. Although the name has changed, most of the section remains the same. It is still composed of reading passages (500–800 words) followed by questions. Sentence completion problems are still around but analogy questions are no longer part of the SAT. To replace the analogy questions, the College Board added spunky paragraph-length critical reading passages (approximately 100 words) with corresponding questions. Think of these passages as Chihuahuas and the 500–800 words passages as Great Danes. They're the same animal—just different sizes.

To review, the new Critical Reading (CR) section is made up of the following three sub-sections:

- Sentence Completions

- Paragraph-length Critical Reading: Short reading passages (100 words approximately) and corresponding questions

- Reading Comprehension: Long reading passages (500–800 words) and corresponding questions

In this chapter, we'll take a close look at each of the question types you'll see in the Critical Reading section and offer strategies to use when faced with the real thing at test time. Please note, this chapter focuses on reading comprehension questions as they appear on the new SAT, but it is doubtful that this will be the last time you ever face a reading comprehension question. In fact, following the reading guidelines here might just make you a better reader on the whole, which is something that will help you throughout the rest of your life. For now, though, the focus remains on the SAT.

A Leg Up on Reading Comprehension

Preparing for the Critical Reading section is similar to preparing for a marathon—work early, slowly, and consistently to achieve the best results. How soon you start studying depends on how many other activities you have going on in your life. The goal is to work through this book on a consistent basis so, if you are a member of four different charities and three sports teams, you might want to open this book six months ahead of when you plan to take the test. The same is true if you have a job that requires you to work a lot. On the other hand, if you are able to clear your schedule and focus solely on the new SAT, two months is probably a good amount of time. It will allow you to cover all the information at a nice pace and then take the SAT while your preparation is still fresh in your mind.

> Figuring out how much time you need to prepare effectively might require you to make a schedule. Many people are schedule-phobic, but it is very helpful if you can devote a specific number of hours each week to studying, and then stick to that schedule—"plan."

Don't fret if you're just cracking open this book two weeks before you face the test for real. There are some simple and potentially entertaining activities you can do to help boost your reading fluency. These are most helpful when mixed in with the drill-and-practice methods most people focus on when thinking about test preparation. The drill stuff is necessary, but it can be mentally tiresome. In contrast, the activities below are not so dully "test-preppy," so they present a nice change of pace if you find yourself tired of working multiple-choice questions.

Activities to Increase Your Reading Comprehension

1. Read books, Web sites, CD covers, the backs of cereal boxes . . .

Without a doubt, anything you read makes you a better reader, even if you read gossip rags and monster truck magazines. Read whatever you want, but if you want to gain an advantage over your "test-mates," reach for something other than the latest issue of *Bubblegum Pop Weekly*. Why? The more experience you have reading about stuff like science, social issues, humanities, and current events, the more comfortable you'll be with the kind of subjects you'll encounter on the exam.

The newspaper is a great, all-in-one resource for pumping up your reading prowess. It's like one-stop shopping for readers, providing texts in different

PETERSON'S
getting you there

formats, covering different topics, perspectives, and purposes. If you read an article from each newspaper section on a daily or weekly basis, you'll expose yourself to new information and practice reading different types of texts similar to those in the CR section. For example, a cover story might be informational, an editorial will express an opinion, an article from the business section may reveal a cause-effect relationship, and a movie review will analyze a film with a critical eye. All of these types of articles are reflected in the reading passages you'll see on the test. Seeing them often in different contexts will increase your comfort level and skill for the real thing later.

Regardless of what you read, make it a habit. You may need to shift your schedule and cut out some of your preferred pastimes, like watching television or shopping with friends, but hey, this is not just any test. If you cut out television a few weeks before the test, you can also console yourself with the fact that there are always reruns.

Tip

Another way to work reading into your daily schedule is to do it online. Choose a local or national newspaper and make a point to read one or two articles from it everyday before checking e-mail or surfing the Internet.

2. Get Classic!

While you read whatever you can get your hands on, don't leave out good ol' literature. Even if you think you read enough novels in your language arts class, it never hurts to read a book or two on your own. The new SAT will include literary fiction passages for the first time ever. Of course, there are hundreds of books the College Board will choose from, but alternating your reading workout between simple periodical fare and more substantial novels touches on all of your "reading muscles" with equal weight.

3. Hey Stripling, Augment Your Lexicon

When it comes to preparing for the CR section, reading comprehension and vocabulary development go hand in hand. A natural part of improving your own reading comprehension is also increasing (*augment*ing) your working vocabulary. A working vocabulary is exactly that—it works for you, not against you. To get your *lexicon* (stock of words that you know) into shape for the SAT, incorporate one or more of these verbal activities into your test-preparation routine.

76

Keeping Track of New Words

To really know a word, experts say you must encounter it and use it in more than one instance. You have to see it, hear it, and use it all in context. Pause to look up any unknown words you come across while you read. If you read online, it's easy to open an online dictionary and type in the word. You could also jot it down to look up later.

However, if you don't want to interrupt your reading flow, try to come up with a definition of the word on your own by looking at the context and comparing your definition to the real thing at a later time. You can use this process to answer sentence completion and reading comprehension questions.

Learn Words Directly through Word Study

There are lots of great SAT vocabulary books available if you want to take the direct approach to vocabulary study. Some titles include *Get Wise! Mastering Vocabulary Skills* and *Ultimate Word Success*, which just happen to be published by the same company that publishes this book. There is also the Ultimate Word List (Chapter 5), which does its best to include words that tend to appear frequently on standardized tests.

But, how do you do it? How do you move a new word from your mental desktop to your long-term hard drive? Well, you have to activate your memory by connecting the new with the old. In this case, mentally connect the new word with stuff you already know or have experienced. A simple way to accomplish this is by making up sentences using the new vocabulary words. These sentences should apply to you in some way. For example, suppose you've just encountered the word *lugubrious*, and you have a cousin named Willy who's always sad and depressed. You could write the sentence:

My cousin is so *lugubrious* we should call him, "Weeping Willy."

The word *lugubrious* and its meaning are now attached to something that already existed in your mind.

Study the Roots, Suffixes, and Prefixes

Some vocabulary study books emphasize the study of word parts, such as roots, bases, prefixes and suffixes. Studying word parts is a great way to maximize your time and effort on vocabulary development. Knowledge of the root words of Latin, Greek, and French will help you recognize those word parts in other SAT words and will increase your vocabulary simply by

association. If you know a root word and recognize it in a SAT word, but aren't sure of the exact meaning, you should be able to more easily infer the meaning than if you had no prior knowledge of the root. For example, if you come across the word *malevolent* and recognized the Latin root *male,* which means "badly," you can safely guess that malevolent has a negative meaning.

Word Play

Another way to boost your vocabulary is to do some crossword puzzles. You'll learn to see words in new contexts and exercise your synonym replication skills which are handy and necessary for taking the CR section. Check out the numerous free online sites that offer word games, vocabulary-building activities and crossword puzzles for other ways to play with words and build your lexicon.

> **Note**
>
> You'll begin to increase your vocabulary just by reading, even if you're too lazy to stop and think about words you don't know. The more you read, the greater the chance of encountering unknown words. Even if you've only seen the word once, it's better than never, and your recall of the initial encounter of the word might be enough prior knowledge to help you answer a question correctly when you see the word again on the test.

Sentence Completion: More than Meets the _____

One of the best tricks to help you be comfortable and save time on the SAT is to familiarize yourself with the directions for the Sentence Completion (SC) section before you take the test. The directions will look something like this:

> **Directions:** Each of the following questions consists of an incomplete sentence followed by five words or pairs of words. Choose that word or pair of words which, when substituted for the blank space or spaces, best completes the meaning of the sentence as a whole.

Sentence completions are no great mystery. They're just a sentence with one or two missing words followed by five answer choices. In previous years, the questions in this section were organized from easiest to most difficult and they appeared in groups of approximately 10 questions. The odds are

78

good that the questions in this section will still be ranked from easiest to difficult on the new exam and that they will also appear in a group. The probability that the new SAT will have sentence completion questions sprinkled throughout a section exits, but it is slight. Remember that the new test is not, in all sections, a radical departure from the old. It's just a slight tweaking.

Sentence completion questions focus on two things:

1. Do you know the meaning of words in the sentence and answer choices?

2. Do you understand the basic logic of the sentence?

> **Tip**
>
> Pacing is important on the SAT. Try spending about 1 minute on every practice SC question on the first pass. If you have a good idea of the sentence's meaning and recognize all the words in the answer choices, you may find you need only 30 seconds to answer. If 1 minute goes by and you're still looking for the word, skip over that question and come back to it later.

If you can identify the structure and meaning of each sentence, you'll find the best words to complete it. Vocabulary is an important part of this section. You may understand all of the words in the sentence but have trouble with the hard words in the answer choices. On the other hand, you may know the meaning of all of the answer choices, but not understand the sentence. Combining points 1 and 2 above will provide you with the best chance for success.

"Sentence logic" describes the way the sentence is organized—its building blocks—and the main idea of the sentence. Understanding the sentence's logic means you're looking at both the structure and the meaning. With SC questions, the word that does *not* appear is often critical to the meaning of the sentence. The words that do appear offer clues to the missing word, and you must follow these clues to determine the missing word. The missing word's location in the overall structure of the sentence also provides a clue to the meaning of the missing word. Where a word appears in relation to other words in a sentence is known as *context*. Context plays a huge part in figuring out what word goes where.

SC questions with two blanks compound the task by requiring you to also determine the relationship between the two words that should be there, but aren't. Before learning more about these double-blank delights, let's first look at the basic steps you can use to answer an SC question.

PETERSON'S
getting you there

Basic Steps for Answering a Sentence Completion Question

1. Read For the "Gist" of the Sentence

Every sentence has a purpose. For example, some sentences state an opinion or viewpoint, others inform, and still others compare and contrast (to name just a few types). You must understand the main point, or gist, of a sentence completion sentence.

In any SC question, use the sentence structure to help spot the type of word you're looking for. Read the sentence to get a basic understanding of what it is about. When reading, make note of:

- Clue words that tip you off to the structure of the sentence and the words that will best fit in the blanks.

- Punctuation that helps with emphasis and word choice

2. Make Up A Word that Would Fit In Each Blank

Look at the stem sentence and think of the type of word that would best complete it WITHOUT looking at the choices. Make a prediction based on what you infer from the stem sentence. You don't have to use a fancy word to make your prediction, since the goal is to capture the right meaning, not the exact word.

Read through the sentence again with your own word(s) inserted to get a basic idea of what the sentence needs to make it logically plausible and grammatically correct.

3. Compare Your Word with the Answer Choices

Look at all five answer choices and pick one that most closely matches the word you inserted on your own. Eliminate choices that contrast with your prediction. Sometimes the right answer will simply be a difficult synonym of the word you imagined. For example, suppose you read a sentence, judged the clues, and decided that the missing word meant "sad" or something along the lines of "really depressing." You then look at the answer choices and spot the word *lugubrious*, which you know from earlier in this chapter, is a tough vocabulary word that means "extremely sad or depressing." There's your answer! It doesn't matter that you didn't come up with the word *lugubrious* to start with. What's important is that you had the right idea, and you used that correct meaning to find the correct answer.

Put Things into Perspective—or Context, Rather

Use clues within a sentence to determine the context of that sentence. If you miss these subtle clues, then more than one answer choice may seem to work. This is no unlucky coincidence. The sentences and choices are deliberately close in meaning in order to make sure you read carefully and closely.

Every question will have its own context-specific clue words that you can use to find the right answer. Some sentences may also be written in a way that allow you to maximize the context of the sentence in order to determine (or at least begin to determine) the meanings of words that should go in the blanks.

The most frequently used context clues for SC questions will come in the form of:

1. Contrast/antonym clues
2. Definition/explanation clues
3. General/inference clues.

Let's take a closer look at these common SC clues.

Alert!

All practice questions in this SC section will have a number in front of them ranging from [1] to [10]. This is done to simulate an actual SAT Sentence Completion section with ten questions ranging from easiest to hardest. The question here is number 5, meaning that should be of about medium difficulty. Looking at the answer choices, you can see that some of these words are tough, but that's pretty normal for a one-blank-only medium question.

Contrast/Antonym Clues

Contrast/antonym clues indicate a change or contrast between one thing and the other. Here's an example:

[5] Unlike his earlier paintings, which attracted lukewarm response and were considered _____, his mid-career retrospective has received praise for its energetic originality and complexity.

In this SC question, your first clue is the first word of the sentence, "unlike." As you read on, you see that the sentence is basically contrasting an artist's earlier work to his later work. Since the artist's later work was considered *energetic, original,* and *complex,* your job is to think of the opposite of those words to fill in the blank. Some contrasting words might be *boring, bland, unoriginal,* and *simplistic.*

With one of these possible words in mind, you can zero in on the best answer choice can be done by eliminating words that don't match your own idea.

[5] Unlike his earlier paintings, which attracted lukewarm response and were considered _____, his mid-career retrospective has received praise for its energetic originality and complexity.

   (A) insipid
   (B) laconic
   (C) novel
   (D) prudish
   (E) profuse

The words *boring, bland,* or *simplistic* would seem to fit in the blank, but are not among the answer choices. So, which of these words is close in meaning to *boring, bland* or *simplistic*? Answer choice (C) is a positive word that means "original" or "new," so it is the opposite of what you're looking for. It's there to catch students who didn't get the fact that the word *unlike* created a contrast between the artist's new work and his old. Choice (A), *insipid,* has similar meaning to *boring* and *unoriginal.* It's your answer, and you can feel good about picking it because you anticipated it—or something like it—would be in the answer choices.

Definition/Explanation Clues

Sometimes you'll see an SC question that actually defines or explains the word you're looking for. These often come with helpful punctuation in the form of colons or semicolons which break the flow of the sentence and indicate elaboration of some kind, usually on the missing word. The structure is loosely based on a common dictionary format, which presents the word followed by a colon and its explanation.

[8] Mrs. Crumb has long been considered a _____; she always insists that her students follow her classroom procedures without exception.

   (A) hypocrite
   (B) dilettante
   (C) martinet
   (D) martyr
   (E) sycophant

82

In this question, you can see how the semicolon breaks the sentence between the missing word and its explanation. Looking at this context, the missing word should be something that indicates strictness and unwavering attitude, based on the description of Mrs. Crumb as a pretty inflexible person. Equipped with this description, you can bet that the answer won't be *martyr,* which means, "someone who makes sacrifices to further a cause," since that doesn't make any sense whatsoever given the sentence's setting. You can eliminate choice (D) right off the bat.

Hard SC problems can have some tough words in the answer choices, and this can be a bit frustrating. You might approach a sentence, decipher the clues well enough to divine the sentence's meaning, and then come up with a good word. But then you look down at the answer choices and find five words you've never seen before. This illustrates how your knowledge of vocabulary plays an important part in your overall reading score. Before you snap your Number 2 pencil in fury, know that there are still techniques you can use to answer an SC question even if you don't know what some of the answer choice words are. These techniques will be covered later in this chapter. Until then, keep learning vocabulary!

It turns out Mrs. Crumb is a *martinet,* someone very strict about rules.

Inference/General Context Clues

Another aspect of answering sentence completions involves your ability to make inferences. Making inferences can be tricky, because the process involves combining evidence you see in the sentence in combination with your own experiences and knowledge. Words or phrases will not be immediately clarified in these SC questions, because it's your job to infer their meanings and relationships to each other and the sentence as a whole. You'll have to draw on your prior knowledge of the sentence's key words and how you've seen them used in the past.

In these instances, you have to rely on your own powers of inference—the ability to piece together meaning from contextual clues in the sentence and what you already know or can deduce. The process is complicated by the types of words missing. These absent words are often forms of verbs or adjectives, which can be used in a variety of contexts and aren't bound to a particular subject or topic. Careful reading is key here, and you must also be aggressive and take a guess or two about the missing word. You might guess wrong at first, but taking charge of the question will lead you to the right answer more often than not.

PETERSON'S
getting you there

[4] Due to destructive fishing practices, such as bycatch, certain seafood populations are in _____ decline.

- **(A)** steep
- **(B)** temperate
- **(C)** voluminous
- **(D)** erratic
- **(E)** halting

With this SC question, you can see how inferring meaning comes from the clues plus your own prior knowledge. The first word clues are *Due to*, which tells you that one thing caused another—due to *this*, *that* is the result. The next clue is the phrase *destructive practices*. This is the actual cause of something, and it wasn't positive, since the word *destructive* means something negative. Having prior knowledge of the fishing term *bycatch* could help you here, but you don't need to know what it means. You can infer that it's not a good method, simply from the way it's used as an example of destructive fishing. The last clue comes at the end—*decline*. Usually a decline indicates something negative, too. So based on your knowledge of these words, and the cause/effect pattern of this sentence, the word you're looking for should be something negative. It might be a word like *dangerous, scary,* or *depressing*, or it might be an adjective that reinforces the word decline. Answer choice (A), *steep*, reinforces the severity of the decline, and it's the best answer of the lot.

Clue in to Clue Words

Sentence completion questions will often contain some type of signal or key word. These words sometimes reinforce the way a sentence is going, like the word *and* in the following sentence:

Everyone on the tour was thrilled by the grand and _____ palace.

For such a small sentence, it's got a ton of clues. You know that it's a *grand palace*, and that everyone was *thrilled*. The word after *and* is going to keep up the positive, gushy-gushy nature of this sentence. Think of something like *magnificent* or *exquisite*. They mean roughly the same thing, but *exquisite* is the less common word.

Words like *and* make things easier since they continue the flow of the sentence. You won't get too many of these on the softball SC questions on the SAT, but when you do, hit them out of the park. Words that change the direction of a sentence occur more often than words that continue the flow. This makes sense, since it's a simple way to make a sentence tougher to decipher. The word *Unlike* in the previous example on page 82 is one word that changes the flow. You saw how the artist started out as *insipid*, but then ended up being *energetically original*.

The following words are all clue words that either continue or change the flow of a sentence. Review the words and determine for yourself if each word is likely to change the flow or continue the flow.

but	until	while
however	so	unlike
and	for	before
although	because	never
despite	still	even though
unfortunately	but	therefore
regardless	not	as a result
actually	by contrast	due to
after		

Look for these words whenever you read and you will see them in action, changing the context of a sentence faster than a speeding bullet. Once you start looking for them, you'll find them everywhere, including the pages of this book. (I confess that I am a big fan of *however*.) If you spend time learning how they work on non-SAT sentences, it will help you whenever you encounter them on an SAT sentence completion question.

By now, you should have a fairly good idea of how to approach a SC problem. Here's a sample question and step-by-step discussion of proper strategy in case you are a little fuzzy about anything.

[4] Although no bigger than a bottle cap, the coqui frog emits a _____ screech as loud as a vacuum cleaner.

(A) keen
(B) malodorous
(C) strident
(D) subtle
(E) reticent

Step 1: Decode the Sentence for Meaning

Don't worry about whether you've ever heard of a *coqui frog* before. All you need to know about this little fellow is the kind of noise it makes. If you wanted to restate the sentence in your own words, you could say something like, "The sentence deals with a little frog that makes a noise that sounds like a household appliance."

Now, focus on any clue words. The clue word *although* signals a contrast between the appearance of the frog and what it can do. Even though the frog is super small, it can be as loud as a *vacuum cleaner*. Vacuum cleaners are typically pretty loud. Adding the fact that this tiny creature's call is being compared to a vacuum cleaner's noise means it can't be pleasant. How many vacuum cleaners purr like a kitten? Other contextual clue words are *screech as loud as*. A *screech* is an unpleasant sound. Taking all these clues into account, what you're looking for is a word that shows how loud, and annoying, this frog can be.

Step 2: Supply Your Own Word

If you were to supply your own word for the blank, what would it be? Say the sentence aloud in your mind, including "blank" for the blank space. Doing this can help activate your brain into substituting appropriate words to complete the sentence. The question is asking for an adjective that describes the quality of the sound the coqui frog makes. You're looking for a word that deals with sound, and an unpleasant sound at that.

Some possibilities:

> Although no bigger than a bottle cap, the coqui frog emits a harsh, annoying, noisy, irritating screech as loud as a vacuum cleaner.

Step 3: Compare Your Word(s) to the Answer Choices

Look at the choices to see which word(s) works. Which of these choices best match your imagined word?

Choice (A) wouldn't work, since *keen* can mean "sharp" or "sensitive." Neither definition is what you are looking for.

Choice (B) is out, because the frog isn't stinky, just noisy, and *malodorous* basically means "bad smelling."

Choice (C), *strident*, could work, and if you were unsure about its meaning, you'd have to go on to the other choices before making a final selection.

Choices (D) and (E) don't work either, because they just plain don't make sense. Something *subtle* is something that's hard to notice, and the frog doesn't seem *reticent,* or "unwilling," to belt out sound, especially if it's compared to a vacuum cleaner.

So, it's back to choice (C), *strident*. Because everything else has been eliminated for good reason, that's your answer. In this case, you didn't find the right answer so much as cross out all the wrong answers and pick the only answer remaining. That's good, since it shows how using good technique can help you get a right answer even if you don't know what a word means.

Blankity-Blank: Sentence Completions with Two Words Missing

A sentence completion with two blanks is both a blessing and a curse. It's a blessing since both words have to work in the sentence, which can make eliminating some answer choices easy. It's a curse since you have to figure out the relationship between the two words in the pair before determining which answer choices will most logically complete the sentence.

With these SC questions, it's all about relationship. How do the missing words relate to each other? Do they compare and contrast? Do they establish a cause and effect? Are they synonyms or antonyms?

With two-blank sentences, there are two things to remember:

1. Figure out the relationship between the pair of words.

2. Both words in the answer choices have to work in the blanks.

Although there are two blanks, these are still SC problems. This means you should follow the same basic steps you did with a one-blank problem. Use clues in the sentence and try to figure out which words best fit in the blanks. Sometimes you'll find clues in the pair of missing words in the answer choices rather than in the sentence. To describe this, think of this sentence about the weather.

> The weather this afternoon was _____ and _____.

There are no clues in the sentence to tell you how the weather is. However, you do know the relationship between the two missing words. They're related, linked together by the continue-the-flow word *and*. If your choices were:

> hot..cold   wet..muggy   dry..humid

The answer would have to be the words *wet* and *muggy*. The other two choices contain words that are opposite in meaning, and you know from the word *and* that the two words have to be similar in meaning.

[9] Despite Nikolai Tesla's contemporary status as a _____ scientist, people in the 1800s initially considered his ideas about wireless communication highly _____.

- **(A)** admirable..plausible
- **(B)** frivolous..spurious
- **(C)** laudable..farcical
- **(D)** loathed..licentious
- **(E)** talented..prescient

First read for the gist of the sentence. Basically, the sentence deals with a change in people's perception and attitude toward Tesla over time. The clue words that indicate this transition are *despite, contemporary*, and *people in the 1800s initially*. *Despite* signals a contrast between the way people think of him now (*contemporary*), and the way *people in the 1800s initially* thought of him in his own day. More specifically, people's attitudes toward Tesla have changed as a result of technological advances in the wireless communications industry. In the 1800s, scientists were still working on getting electricity up and running, and wires were a big part of making this happen. So wireless communication back then may have seemed as wacky a concept as sending a man to the moon, which we know is not such an impossible feat, either.

If you were to predict what words that might fill in the blanks, what would they be? To do this, use your understanding of the sentence's logic and meaning. The relationship between the two blanks is one of contrast. Both words will be adjectives describing that contrast, so the words will have opposite meanings. Since Tesla's status has changed for the better, the first word should be one indicating a positive attitude about his reputation. The second blank is negative in connotation, since Tesla's own contemporaries were skeptical about anything so ahead of its time.

Looking at the relationship between these missing words, generate your own words to fill in the blanks:

> Despite Nikolai Tesla's contemporary status as a <u>great, smart, innovative, clever, respected</u> scientist, people in the 1800s initially considered his ideas about wireless communication highly *wacky, off-base, unbelievable, impossible*.

The best way to attack a two-blank SC problem is to go **one blank at a time**. Remember, both words need to work in their respective blanks equally well. If you work one blank at a time, you can use POE to help you eliminate choices that are half-great, half-bad. All too often, students working a two-blank SC problem pick an answer that has one word that works great

88

even though the second word is not a good fit. They do this because they don't look at each blank individually. If you do, you will end up with an answer that has two words that work in the sentence, even if they're not the most spectacular pair.

> **Note**
>
> Think of these as a pair of shoes—both should fit equally well in order to balance out the sentence's logic.

For this sample question, start with the first blank. (The order is not really important, and you can start with the second word if you want that to be your "thing.") You want a positive adjective to describe Tesla's reputation, so you are looking for a word along the lines of *great, smart, innovative, clever, respected.*

- **(A)** admirable..plausible
- **(B)** ~~frivolous~~..spurious
- **(C)** laudable..farcical
- **(D)** ~~loathed~~..licentious
- **(E)** talented..prescient

Choices (B) and (D) are definitely out. *Frivolous* doesn't make any sense; his ideas in his heyday may have seemed frivolous, but not now. Also, Tesla isn't *loathed* today, he's actually respected.

By using POE and working one blank at a time, you give yourself an advantage on every two-blank question. If you had no idea what was in the second blank of this problem, you would still have a one-in-three chance of getting it correct now that (B) and (D) are crossed out. If you don't know any of the vocabulary words in the remaining three answer choices, you could still take a guess. Odds of one-in-three might not sound great, but on a hard problem they're pretty good.

Guessing aside, choices (A), (C), and (E) require some closer inspection. The first words of these pairs could all work, since they positively describe Tesla's status. Move on to the second word in each pair and compare them to your predictions for the second blank. Which word most closely matches *wacky, off-base, unbelievable,* or *impossible*? *Plausible* is the opposite of *impossible*, so choice (A) can be eliminated. Your next choice is *farcical*, which means "ridiculous," based on the word *farce*. So choice (C) might work, since you want a word that is close in meaning to *wacky* or *unbelievable*. Before choosing (C), you have to look at choice (E). *Prescient* means "to have foresight." Someone who is *prescient* is someone who is ahead of his time. Tesla was ahead of his time if he was able to come up with wireless communication, but according to the sentence, people thought those ideas were ridiculous. So, (E) wouldn't work. The best answer is choice (C).

Note

If you didn't know the meaning of *plausible*, you may have inferred what it means since that word has been used twice already in this chapter.

As the example shows, two-blank SC problems often contain a high number of difficult vocabulary words. That's why working one blank at a time and using POE is such an important strategy for these problems. If you do this, you should be able to eliminate some answer choices and then take a good guess.

The Positives and Negatives of SC

Thinking in terms of positive and negative can help narrow down answer choices when you've maxed out other techniques. The positive and negative meanings of words are based in their denotative and connotative meanings. For instance, the word *thrifty* conjures up specific ideas and associations in comparison with those for the word *stingy*. If you were to give a positive or negative sign to these words, chances are *thrifty* would be positive, and *stingy* would be negative, although they are very close in meaning. If you can determine whether the missing word is supposed to be positive or negative, you can use the "connotative vibe" of that word to generate your own possible synonyms while eliminating those from the answer choices that don't make sense.

Tip

Connotation and Denotation

Every word has at least one denotative and connotative meaning. The easiest way to remember which is which is to connect *denotative* to a word's dictionary definition, and *connotative* to the "gut reaction" response you have to the word. Connotative meanings are more emotional and suggestive, whereas a word's denotative meaning is literal. Because of the subjective nature of connotations, they can be positive or negative. Denotations tend to be more neutral.

Use the fact that *denote* and *dictionary* both start with the letter "d" to link those two concepts together in your head.

To use the plus/minus method, you should have already gone through the basic steps for answering a SC question, including coming up with your own answer. Read the sentence again to see whether the blank or blanks should be filled by a positive or negative word. You can even write a minus sign (−) or a plus sign (+) in the blanks to represent the type of word that should go there. Now, look at the answer choices and eliminate those that don't match the positive/negative connotations of your projected answer.

Be careful, however, of answer choices that may seem positive or negative, but also have completely different meanings. If you're looking for a word that is positive, and there are three answer choices with positive connotations, you can't safely bet that your choice will be correct. You have to try some of the other sleuthing methods offered here in this chapter, such as looking at the roots/word parts while making connections between words you know and similarities you see in the answer choices.

To be honest, using positive/negative will never be considered the world's greatest technique. However, it is yet another tool you have at your disposal, and can help you get closer to the right answer on certain SC problems.

Reading Comprehension: So Many Words, So Little Time

Most of your time on the Critical Reading section will be spent working on the longer reading passages. These passages take the most time to read, and they have the most questions attached to them. It makes sense to learn about these lengthier passages first, and then move on to the morsel-sized (100-word) reading passages.

The Long Reading Comprehension Passages

The Reading Comprehension section of the SAT is typical of most standardized tests. There's a passage composed of several paragraphs followed by several multiple-choice questions. You may have one very long passage, two shorter separate passages, or two paired passages. All of these variations will then have five to thirteen questions after them. The passages themselves will range from 500 to 800 words.

PETERSON'S
getting you there

This long reading comprehension passages make up a section that is appropriately named *Critical Reading* (CR), since you will be tested on how carefully and keenly you read in a short period of time. Not only must you understand what's happening in the passage, you also need to:

- Figure out the meanings of words in context.

- Isolate and connect details.

- Determine the author's perspective.

- Understand the point of view.

- Determine the main idea.

Those are the main items, but there are others, too. You'll also be asked to infer meaning based on stated details, which is one of the more complex tasks of reading.

In a nutshell, the CR section tests your reading fluency. It wants to see how well you can read for the details, meaning, and message of a text. The reading passages are designed to measure your ability to identify genre, relationships among parts of a text, cause and effect, rhetorical devices, and comparative arguments. They will be crafted to more closely reflect the types of reading and critical analysis you're already doing as part of your high school coursework.

Note

The passages themselves will come from a range of fields:

- Natural Sciences
- Humanities
- Social Sciences
- Literary Fiction—*this is new!*

The questions after each passage are NOT arranged by difficulty. That means that the first question may be the most challenging to answer, rather than the last one. Instead, the questions are arranged in rough chronological order as they relate to the passage. For example, a question that relates to the first sentence in paragraph 1 will appear first in the set of questions that follows that passage. Most questions will also include a reference to a specific paragraph or line number that corresponds to the passage.

The directions for this section are quite simple and to the point. They will look something like this:

Directions: Answer the questions below based on the information in the accompanying passage.

Getting Into the Act of Active Reading

It would be hard to describe the content of reading passages as "exciting" or "riveting." It could be done, but probably only on a dare. You might find a passage about some historical figure or current trend that you're really into, but it's doubtful. Instead, expect to encounter dry writing about bland topics. Such bland safe writing can be a chore to read, since it can cause your mind to wander in search of better things to think about. Worse, you might groan and jump to the questions, randomly choosing answers to put yourself out of your misery.

The way to avoid this trap is to practice active reading, or reading with a purpose. The most obvious purpose is to read to answer the questions. To do this, you first want to actively search for the overall idea of the passage. Often the main idea is connected to the author's purpose or perspective. Each paragraph, linked together, forms the whole picture of the passage, and the individual paragraphs hold the details that support that main idea. As you read, try to decipher the author's main purpose for writing the text, and what the overall idea might be.

Every passage will have a brief italicized introduction before it. Don't skip this! It can offer clues about the author's purpose and possibly the main idea of the passage. Besides clues, it will often flat out tell you the type of passage it is—an excerpt from a novel, a speech, a journal article, a descriptive essay.

Here's an example passage introduction:

The following passage analyzes one of Eudora Welty's short stories.

You don't need to know who Eudora Welty is, but note the word *analyzes,* which is a word you do know. The purpose of this passage is to analyze the story. This means the author will be critical. Knowing this, ask yourself, "What kind of argument does the author make about this story?" This point, or purpose, is basically the main idea of the passage. You want to figure out the author's thesis, then look and see what details support this controlling idea—what evidence is there in the passage to back it up. There will only be one central idea in each passage, with lots of supporting details. Reading actively will help you trace the development of an argument over several paragraphs.

> **Tip**
>
> There is a great deal of overlap between actively reading a CR passage and creating your essay for the Writing section of the SAT. For the reading passages, you are analyzing existing writing to understand how the main idea and supporting details fit together. When you get to the essay section in Chapter 6, the process will be reversed. You will be creating the main idea and supporting details, and the SAT essay readers will be analyzing your essay the same way you judged the reading passages.

Using your pencil is another quality of active reading. Make notations or underline key points as you read. Each paragraph should have its own main idea, usually conveyed in a topic sentence at the beginning of the paragraph. Underline these if you see them. This isn't a failsafe method, though, because some paragraphs make their point at the end or combine several sentences to get the idea across to the reader. What you can do is come up with a "main idea" word, phrase, or sentence for each paragraph and jot it down in the margin. You can use those notes later when delving back into the passage to answer specific questions.

Fact vs. Fiction: Types of CR Passages

In the past, the SAT's reading passages were strictly expository nonfiction, which means they were very information-based and fact heavy. The new SAT will include passages of literary fiction, which is quite different from expository writing. Armed with this knowledge, you won't be thrown by an excerpt from Hemingway, followed by an articles about erosion and the Grand Canyon—a juxtaposition (good vocabulary word!) that could happen on the new test.

Expository Writing

Expository writing is used to explain, describe, give information or inform. The basic intent is to expose the reader to new ideas, often with the intent to persuade or argue. It may include facts, statistics, research findings, or quotations as evidence to support a view. These passages may also include more specialized vocabulary. However, any unfamiliar technical words will be defined in the margins of each passage.

94

Textual Pattern	Description	Signal Words	While Reading . . .
Description	Author describes a topic through examples, listing features or characteristics	*for example, characteristics are*	Think about how the description supports the main idea
Sequence/ Chronology	Author lists facts, events, concepts in chronological or numerical order	*on* (date), *not long after, now, as, before, after, when, first, second, then, finally, during, until*	Note how the sequence connects to the author's purpose
Comparison-Contrast	Author discusses similarities or differences about one or more issues, or aspects of a topic. NOTE: Paired passages may show contrasting views on a topic.	*despite, only...but also, meanwhile, although, however, but, as well as, on the other hand, not either...or, while, yet, unless, nevertheless, otherwise, similarly, compared to*	Look for opposites/ contrasting sides of the topics discussed
Cause-Effect	Author lists	*cause, effect, because, since, therefore, consequently, as a result, this led to, so, so that, nevertheless, accordingly, if . . . then, thus*	Note the "chain reaction" effect of the causes and effects.
Problem-Solution	Author traces a problem and its resulting solution	*because, cause, since, therefore, consequently, as a result, this led to, so, so that, nevertheless, accordingly, if-....then, thus*	Identify the problems first and see what solutions are offered.

PETERSON'S
getting you there

Expository writing from three of the four fields—natural sciences, social sciences, and the humanities—will usually fall into one of these formats, or textual patterns, described in the chart on page 95. These patterns will apply to the passages you'll see from three of the four fields: natural sciences, social sciences, and the humanities.

Literary Fiction

A literary fiction passage is like a story. There is a beginning, middle, and an end, usually in that order unless the author gets all "artsy" and start things at the end. The passages could be from a short story or from a novel. Even though they will be narrative in nature, the passages may be very descriptive or introspective rather than action-based. Most likely the selected passage will come from somewhere deep within the source novel or story, with just a simple italicized blurb before it. The questions will ask you to reflect on and evaluate some aspect of that passage, such as on a character's decisions or motivations, just as you would the author's purpose in an expository passage.

Basic Strategy for Tackling all the Long Critical Reading Passages

You can approach any text in the same way.

1. **Read the Italicized Introduction**
    This can often clue you in to the author's purpose and attitude toward the subject. Note any words that suggest the type of passage, the kind of argument the author might make, and the passage's overall main idea.

2. **Read the Questions Next**
    People debate back and forth about whether you should read the passage first or the questions first. In a perfect world, you would read the passage at your leisure and respond at length to any question asked. Since a timed test is not a perfect world, you have to cut corners wherever you can. Read the questions before diving into the passage. You can underline key words in the question stems and keep them in mind as you read. The questions will direct you to the part of the passage that you'll need to help answer them, usually in the form of line or paragraph references.

    If you come across something in a paragraph that connects to a question, mark it in the passage. Often, a question connects to a detail or issue in the passage that will change or develop through a series of paragraphs. If a reference line number is not given, then you can use your notes to go back to the passage and double-check what the best possible answer may be.

3. **Skim the Passage, (Keeping Questions In Mind).**

   Skimming the passage means reading with big but fast eyes—reading as quickly as you can while still understanding the material. You should have the questions in mind, and keep a lookout for details that relate to those questions. At the same time, you're also reading to get the gist of the passage as a whole. Don't mull over every little detail, since that will just slow you down, and might not be relevant to any of the questions. Think of it as mentally jogging. You're not sprinting, but not lazily strolling, either.

4. **Answer the Questions As You Skim the Passage**

   Skip harder questions and come back to them after answering the easier ones. If you come across a question that deals with the general tone or summary of the passage, you may need to answer the other questions first, simply because the answers to the other questions can help give you a good idea as to the overall picture of the text and a better chance at answering the question correctly.

   Once you answer all the questions, stop reading. The goal is to answer questions, not read the passage. Move on to the next passage and repeat the four steps just described.

2gether 4ever: The Paired Passages

Most reading passages you encounter will be stand-alone essays, but occasionally two passages will appear together. These are commonly known as the paired reading passages. Paired passages give you two different views on a related topic or theme. These views may be related, they may contrast, or they may connect or support one another. Some questions will pertain to a specific passage, and others will relate to both passages together.

> **Note**
>
> Imagine two passages praising peanut butter and jelly sandwiches. The first passage talks about the history of peanut butter, while the second passage focuses on how grape jelly is made. Both passages talk about pb&j sandwiches, but they have different views about the same topic.

Definitely answer all the questions on the first passage first and then answer all the questions about the second passage. Then move on to the questions that refer to both passages. Be mindful that since these questions are arranged chronologically, those on both passages may not necessarily be the hardest, but answering them last gives you the added advantage of having

PETERSON'S
getting you there

thought about the passages more by responding to them individually with their own questions.

Paired passages may look strange, but you should handle them as you would any other stand-alone RC passages. The only real difference is the dual-passage questions. Before tackling these problems it helps to ask yourself, "How are the two passages related to each other?" "Do they contrast viewpoints, or do they agree?" Understanding the similarities and differences between the two passages will help you answer the question about both passages.

If the dual passage questions seem tough to you, simply save the paired passages until the end and answer all the other questions in the section first. You can then answer all the one passage questions first. If you don't have a great deal of time to spend on the dual passage questions, look them over and see if you can take an educated guess. These problems typically require some work to answer, and there are better ways to earn points than spending large amounts of time answering them. Another way to state this is to say, "Don't rush through easier problems in order to have more time to work on difficult, involved questions. Every question counts the same."

Critical Reading Question Types: Seeing the Forest for the Trees

According to the College Board, there are three categories of questions following the critical reading passages:

Question	Description
Vocabulary in Context	covers vocabulary used in a specific context in the passage.
Literal Comprehension	deals with supporting details and ideas, marked by the use of line or paragraph references.
Extended Reasoning	requires you to synthesize and analyze information. These questions include identifying cause and effect, making inferences, recognizing implications, evaluating the author's assumptions and purpose, and following the logic of an argument. Most of the questions in this section will be in this category.

There are variations of these question types that we'll break down further. After learning about each of them, you'll get a chance to see them in action in connection with the sample passage on page 106.

Vocabulary-in-Context Questions

Vocabulary-in-context questions are very direct. They ask you about the meaning of a vocabulary word within a specific context in the passage. They include a line reference and five choices. The words usually have more than one meaning, which can make the questions tricky. What's important to remember is that the most obvious definition of the word is not necessarily the best choice. The key is context, and the test-makers will intentionally choose a word with shades of meaning that are dependent on the context of the sentence.

Vocab-in-Context questions will look something like:

> The word *trifling* in line 5 could best be replaced by

> In line 53, the word *inculcated* means

When faced with a vocabulary question, you can apply techniques similar to the ones used to answer a sentence completion question:

- Reread the line containing the word or phrase, along with the lines above and below it, especially if the line is the first sentence in a new paragraph. Another good way to state this is to read the sentence before the word occurs, the sentence the word occurs in, and then the sentence after the word occurs. This should give you sufficient context to understand the meaning of the word.

- Think of your own word or phrase to replace the one in question. With your substitution in mind, read through the answer choices and choose the one that best matches your own word choice.

The fact that you use the same strategy on RC vocab questions and SC problems illustrates an important point. Most strategies are recyclable. The more comfortable you get using them, the more opportunities you find to use them. The process feeds on itself, and this is why it's important for you to try strategies and techniques on all the sample questions you encounter in this book. The better acquainted you become with the strategies, the easier it will be for you to use them on the real SAT.

Phrase/Expression Questions

Chances are good that you'll see at least one of these questions. A common phrase or expression is framed in quotation marks or italicized, and you're asked to either interpret its meaning or decide how or why it is used by the author. In some cases, these questions are similar to vocabulary-in-context questions, because they ask you to paraphrase the highlighted phrase. In other situations, you have to first interpret its meaning, and then figure out what the author meant—the intention behind the expression, so to speak.

Phrase/Expressions questions will look like:

> In context, *nail-biting experience* (line 23) suggests that

> The phrase *back on his feet* (line 49) most nearly means

To solve these questions, apply the same techniques you used to solve the vocabulary-in-context questions. (Recycling at work again!) The phrase can be translated into more common words with more obvious connotative meanings.

Literal Comprehension Questions

Literal comprehension questions can be the most straightforward and easiest of the types of questions you'll see in this section. Some questions will focus on textual details. Others will involve the technical aspects of the passage, such as its organization, the author's techniques, and details that support the main idea. Some of the answers to these are literally located within the passage, and other answers are paraphrases of actual lines. Answering other comprehension questions might involve rereading and understanding the passage, but skimming can be your best tactic with literal comprehension questions.

Literal comprehension questions can look like:

> In line 5, the animal described is a

> All of these factors support the author's point of view except—

> The author's point about the role of the media is made mainly through . . .

> The last three sentences in the passage provide—

To answer these questions, use your notations and any key words in the question that direct you to a specific part of the passage. The answers can help with this, too. Use them to fact check against what was actually stated in the passage. If only part of the answer applies, then it isn't a good choice.

Literary Terms Questions

On the new SAT, there will be some questions containing literary terminology. These should be terms you've seen before in your English or literature classes, such as *simile*, *personification*, and *metaphor*. The more obscure or unusual terms won't be included. Brushing up on the most popular literary terms is a good idea for two reasons—familiarity will make it easier to deal with these types of questions and can save you time. Use the following chart as a reference for literary terms, their definitions, and examples of each.

Literary Term	Definition	Example
Simile	Comparison of two different things or ideas through the use of the words *like* or *as*	Love is like a blooming rose.
Metaphor	Comparison without the use of *like* or *as*	Love is a rose.
Personification	A type of metaphor. It gives inanimate objects or abstract ideas human characteristics	The rose spoke of love.
Hyperbole	Extreme, outrageous exaggeration used for effect	She wore so much makeup she had to use a chisel to get it off.
Irony	Statement that says one thing but means the opposite	The roses lasted much longer than their love.
Symbol	An object that stands for something else	The rose represents love.
Tone	The attitude created by the author, indicated through word choice	The author's tone can range from optimistic and joyful to pessimistic and depressing.
Oxymoron	Type of paradox that combines a pair of contrary terms into a single expression	Sweet sorrow, beautiful disaster.

Literary Term	Definition	Example
Mood	The atmosphere or tone of a literary work	The mood is connected to emotions—how the reader feels when reading the passage.
Allegory	Any writing that has a double meaning—the first literal meaning, and a second more symbolic/ conceptual meaning	In Dante's *Divine Comedy,* the character Beatrice represents both the actual woman Dante knew and his concept of divine revelation.
Allusion	Reference to a mythological, literary, historical, or Biblical person, place, or thing	Standardized tests can be a person's Achilles heel.
Parody	A work that mimics the manner and characteristics of a particular literary work in order to make fun of those same features.	*Don Quixote* is Cervantes's parody of a medieval romance.
Paradox	Contradictory statement that seems absurd but reveals a truth	Youth is wasted on the young.

Brushing up on these terms is the best way to arm yourself for literary terms questions. Simile, metaphor, and personification are easier to recognize than some of the others simply because they are so pervasive in speaking and writing inside and outside of a literature class. If you can't readily come up with an example for a particular term in the chart, make learning the term a priority and learn it well so it doesn't become your Achilles' heel. (Ah ha! Allusion!)

Extended Reasoning Questions

A lot of extended-reasoning questions will have the word "author" in them. They can be about a variety of things—the author's purpose, opinion, tone, you name it. What they're really asking is for you to make inferences in order to answer the question.

You have to draw a conclusion or make an assumption based on what is implied in the passage. In other words, you have to infer meaning by reading between the lines. Answering these questions is very much like answering SC problems, since once again you have to find clues that will lead you to the correct answer. The clues for an extended-response question are found in the passage sentences. You have to analyze the connotative and denotative meanings of words, incorporating the other bits and pieces of information you gleaned while reading, and consider the author's purpose and attitude.

One trick when answering these questions is to disregard answer choices that repeat something that was mentioned explicitly in the passage. You're looking for what is not said, rather than what is. Since the range of these questions is larger in scope than in the other two question categories, the major question stems you're likely to see are discussed here so you can zone in on those that are more challenging or sneaky, depending on your level of preparedness and familiarity.

Following are some variations of extended-reasoning questions:

1. Tone/Attitude Questions

Tone questions will ask you to figure out the author's attitude toward a subject, a character, or the reader. These questions could also involve a character's attitude, since literary fiction passages will undoubtedly involve characters and their motivations or feelings.

Usually when you interpret tone, it involves words said aloud in tandem with the word choice. In these situations, you're interpreting the tone of someone's voice along with what is said. Unfortunately, in written work you can't actually hear the author read aloud the passage to figure out how he feels about it, so all you can do is look carefully at the words the author uses.

> **Note**
>
> For an example of how voice affects tone, consider a science teacher saying, "You did what?" Think about how this phrase would sound after you told your teacher that you just melted down the lab because you were napping. Now think about how those same words would sound after you told your science teacher you just figured out a way to travel faster than light. The first statement would have an angry tone, while the second utterance would have a bewildered, incredulous tone.

PETERSON'S

getting you there

Example of tone/attitude questions:

The author's description of the tenement conditions in lines 47–53 is . . .

The character's attitude toward the changes in her hometown since the hurricane can best be described as one of . . .

Which best describes the author's view of the rights of teenagers?

Being prepared for tone/attitude questions is easier if you think about the author's attitude as you skim, and try to categorize it as positive, negative, or neutral. The attitude can be linked to the purpose. If the purpose is very informational, then the author's attitude may be neutral, especially if you can't figure out how he feels one way or the other about the topic at hand. There are no hard-and-fast correlations between purpose and attitude, but knowing that one influences the other, can help you identify clues such as word choice and supportive details to determine whether the author's tone is critical versus comical, for instance.

Although there's no trick to answering these questions, the right answer is usually not the most radical or extreme of the choices. Regardless of how emphatic an author may seem about the topic at hand, the correct answer will never be extreme or worded so strongly as to make the author sound too wacky or irrational. If the question refers to a specific sentence or paragraph, concentrate on the connotative meanings of the words in the sentence. If the question addresses a larger portion of the passage or the passage as a whole, keep in mind what the author said that gave you an impression of how he/she feels about his/her topic. Especially note if the tone changes throughout the passage, since that's prime material for a juicy question. Probably the best tactic for solving these problems is to read the question and come up with your own answers, just as you would for the questions about main idea and author's purpose.

2. Author's Purpose or Intent Questions

You might think that you have to be a mind reader to figure out what the author really means or suggests by saying something. Actually, you just have to be a careful reader. Author's purpose questions involve asking you to figure out why the author made the decisions he or she made in writing something in the passage.

Questions of this type might resemble:

In the third paragraph, the author mentions faded roses in order to emphasize which point about the main character?

The information in lines 27–31 suggests that the author is very concerned about

In the second example, the key word is *suggests*. From this, you can immediately tell that you're not looking for a specific fact or statement in the passage. Instead, you're supposed to make an inference about the author's intention—the message behind the words.

With any variation of this type of question, the answers that seem the most extreme are likely to be wrong. Think about what the author is advocating overall in the passage, and use that to guide your process of elimination with the answer choices. Often the italicized introductions to the passages provide more information than you might think about the author's perspective, and thus what he or she implies by certain statements throughout the passage.

3. Main Idea or Focus Questions

If you've been actively reading, then main idea or focus questions are often ripe for the plucking. They'll ask you to state the main idea that you've been searching for while skimming through the passage. These questions may deal with the main idea of the whole passage, or ask specifically about the main purpose of a single paragraph.

Main Idea/Focus questions start out like:

The primary focus of this passage is on

The primary purpose of this passage is

Both passages focus primarily on . . .

The passage as a whole is most concerned with

If you like, you can skip these questions and answer the others first, since those can help you come to a conclusion about the main idea or theme by examining the passage's details. On the other hand, if you feel you've done a good job at determining the main idea of the passage, then go and look at the answer choices. If your main idea is stated in some form in the answer choices, pick that answer and move on.

 Tip
If a question asks for the main idea of a specific paragraph, look back at the first and last sentences, since those may provide a clearer picture of how an idea was introduced and then concluded in that particular paragraph.

PETERSON'S
getting you there

Watch out for answer choices that are partially correct. These choices mention smaller ideas or issues from the passage, but are too narrow if you really step back mentally and think about everything the passage is about. There will be distractor-like choices which may include an aspect of the passage's main idea, but just miss the mark a little. So, again, reading actively while you skim can help keep these diversionary choices out of your line of vision when concentrating on the big picture of a passage.

Applying the Four-Step Process to Critical Reading Passages

Now it's time to put your skills and strategies to work all at once. Read through this passage and then answer the questions that follow. After you take a shot at answering each question, read through the explanations for them, pinpointing any question types that you need more practice on.

Directions: Answer the questions below based on the information in the accompanying passage.

The following passage is excerpted from a popular journal of humanities.

Line Initially considered an indulgence for the affluent, the growing trend in spa vacations in tandem with the burgeoning number of day spas sprouting up throughout metropolitan areas will soon make them as ubiquitous as other traditional retreats. Yet, this

(5) trend in relaxation and rejuvenation has its roots in an ancient and well-perfected form of bathing. The founders of this growth industry were none other than the Romans, who merged together their mastery of intricate engineering, their love of cleanliness, and their desire to dominate and convert conquered subjects to

(10) their favored lifestyle through the establishment of bathing as a necessary pastime.

The art of bathing has been practiced for centuries, dating back to early Egypt; historians assert that Egyptian palaces contained bathing rooms, although scant physical remains exist

(15) today. Bathing also played an important role in the lives of the Greeks, supported with archaeological evidence of bathing rooms located in the palace of Knossos, circa 1700 B.C. Yet, it was during the heyday of the Roman Empire that bathing was elevated to a level of sophistication and complexity yet to be

(20) replicated in even the most elite and fancy resorts.

106

The intricate and systematic ritual of Roman bathing is most revealing via the architectural structure of the baths, or *thermae*, themselves. Beyond each *thermae's* entrance was usually an open courtyard, called a *palaestra*, which could be considered the

(25) forerunner to a modern gymnasium. In this courtyard, visitors would exercise to elevate body temperatures and perspire, which was seen as a prerequisite to entering the baths. While men engaged in more vigorous forms of exertion, such as lifting weights or wrestling, women usually swam or tried their hand at

(30) a more feminine pursuit called *Trochus*, a game involving rolling a metal hoop with a hooked stick. Post exercise, the *apodyterium* allowed bathers space to change and prepare for bathing, the equivalent to today's locker rooms.

The most noteworthy feature of the baths involved a series of

(35) rooms with controlled air and water temperatures. The first in the sequence, the *tepidarium,* or warm room, was a place for further bathing preparation; a slave would use a metal instrument called a *strigil* to scrape dirt, sweat, and oil from the body. Depilation was also available for those more hirsute bathers,

(40) reflecting the fashionable obsession with hairless bodies. After having one or more of these "spa treatments," bathers would submerge themselves in tepid, lukewarm water.

The hottest room in the bath's labyrinth contained a large pool approximately three feet in depth. The *calidarium* served to

(45) create a very steamy atmosphere to open the pores and release toxins from the body. The air and water remained a constant high temperature well above 100 degrees Fahrenheit, heated by the ingenious under floor heating system called the *hypocaust*. Scholars still marvel today at the effectiveness of this brilliantly

(50) efficient furnace system below ground that transported water to the appropriate pool while drawing hot air underneath the flooring and through its hollow-brick walls.

The actual order of bathing activities has been a contentious topic among scholars, since no actual documents remain that

(55) outline the order in which each room was used in the baths. Other steam rooms, such as the *sudatorium* or *laconicum,* may have diverted bathers on their path to the final destination, the *frigidarium.* In this cold room, bathers would commence their cleansing practices by immersing themselves in cold water,

(60) closing their pores and leaving refreshed.

The function of Roman baths served much more than to
cleanse the body. Baths were often the nexus of social interaction,
acting as a community center, fitness and health facility, and a
source of public entertainment. The bathing complex often
(65)   included a performance area where local entertainment from
juggling to philosophical oratory was offered as icing on the cake
to the overall experience. Food and drink were available to
purchase, and often whole families would come to socialize and
recreate while attending to their personal hygiene.
(70)   The societal significance of these baths is also mirrored in
their opulent decoration and extensive statuary, many of which
were plundered over time for use in later structures and monu-
ments. The elaborate mosaics and frescoes that adorned the
floors and walls of many bathing rooms stand as further cultural
(75)   and architectural evidence of how the baths were revered for
their form and function in ancient Roman society.

1. The word *merged* in line 7 most nearly means

    (A) enhanced.
    (B) combined.
    (C) separated.
    (D) connected.
    (E) compressed.

2. In paragraph 2, the author's inclusion of the history of bathing
    primarily serves to

    (A) discuss the evolution of an ancient practice.
    (B) explain why bathing is an important ritual.
    (C) establish a basis/context for the rest of the passage.
    (D) compare ancient practices to modern methods.
    (E) emphasize other cultures that practiced the ritual.

3. According to paragraph 3, after entering each *thermae*, bathers
    would

    (A) change into their bathing clothes.
    (B) exercise in the open courtyard.
    (C) play games such as *Trochus*.
    (D) scrape their bodies with a *strigil*.
    (E) elevate their body temperatures.

4. In paragraph 5, the author's description of the underground furnace system is

    (A) didactic.
    (B) enthusiastic.
    (C) pretentious.
    (D) admiring.
    (E) colloquial.

5. The information in lines 56–60 primarily serves to

    (A) illustrate the debate about the bathing sequence.
    (B) show the complexity of bathing structures.
    (C) offer other alternatives to the bathing sequence.
    (D) refute the bathing sequence outlined by scholars.
    (E) explain the importance of the final bathing room.

6. In context, the phrase *icing on the cake* (line 66) means

    (A) extra food.
    (B) required activity.
    (C) free dessert.
    (D) amusing bonus.
    (E) open performances.

7. The information in the last paragraph provides

    (A) a summary of the points made earlier.
    (B) an additional aspect of the main topic.
    (C) a reason for the significance of the topic.
    (D) an explanation of the topic's importance.
    (E) a context for why baths were used.

8. The primary focus of this passage is on

    (A) the similarities between modern-day spas and ancient baths.
    (B) the evolution of bathing over time.
    (C) the significance of bathing to the Romans.
    (D) the ancient ritualized process of Roman bathing.
    (E) the architectural and cultural significance of Roman bathing.

PETERSON'S
getting you there

Explanation of Questions and Answers

Question 1: Vocabulary-in-Context

The correct answer is B. This is a perfect example of a vocabulary-in-context question. To find a synonym for *merged* that fits the context, go back to the actual sentence in the paragraph. You can see how *merged* is used to show how baths joined together three different elements considered important to the Romans—engineering, cleanliness, and converting/controlling their subjects. So B is the best replacement word. The Romans combined those concepts, rather than keeping them separate, yet close together.

Choices (A) and (E) don't make sense in this context, because they didn't improve upon these things or compact them together. Choice (C) is the antonym of the word's meaning, so that can also be eliminated. Choices (B) and (D) are similar, yet (D) has connotations of three separate things placed side by side, rather than being blended together.

Question 2: Author's Purpose/Intent; Literal Comprehension

The correct answer is C. This question asks you to determine the purpose of the historical background about bathing in relation to the passage as a whole. To see how this connects to the whole passage, you have to think about what the majority of the passage discusses. The passage is not just about the history of bathing. It's mostly about the layout and use of the baths by the Romans. The background information about Egyptians and Greeks helps establish a context for why the passage details Roman baths instead of their predecessors' versions. So, choice (C) is the best answer.

Choice (A) is true in general about the content of paragraph 2, but it's not the *purpose of* that paragraph. The paragraph states that bathing was important, but it doesn't mention why, so choice (B) is wrong, too. Choice (D) is irrelevant, since the paragraph doesn't make comparisons between the past and the present, even though the last sentence makes reference to contemporary spa resorts. Choice (E) is partially correct, since the paragraph mentions other cultures that also believed bathing was important. However, the purpose of this information goes back to supporting the rest of the passage, which is about the development and importance of Roman baths.

Question 3: Literal Comprehension

The correct answer is B. This question involves asking you to sequence events in the order mentioned in the passage. After thinking of the answer on your own, compare your answer to what happens next in the paragraph. From lines 25–27, you can see that after entering the *thermae*, "visitors would exercise to elevate body temperatures" before changing for the baths. The correct answer is choice (B). Choices (A), (D), and (E) occur after the initial exercise, and choice (C) is specific only to women, according to the passage.

Question 4: Author's Tone/Attitude

The correct answer is D. This question asks you to determine the author's tone for a specific paragraph. To answer this, you have to look back at the words the author uses to describe the furnace. In lines 48–50, the adjectives "ingenious" and brilliantly efficient" are used to describe the furnace system, which sounds like the author thinks as highly of this system as the scholars who "marvel" at it even today. The author's attitude seems very complimentary and flattering. Scanning the answer choices, the best match is choice (D)

Choices (A) and (E) don't match, since the author is not trying to moralize nor does he use very informal language. Even if the author seems a little formal or pretentious in other paragraphs, you're concentrating only on one part of the passage—the description of the hypocaust, so choice (C) is incorrect. Although the author is very positive about the furnace system, choice (B) is not as close to the author's tone as is choice (D), since *enthusiastic* has connotations related more to excitement than to admiration and respect, which is the effect created by the adjectives used in lines 48–50.

Question 5: Literal Comprehension

The correct answer is A. This question asks you to look at how one sentence supports or explains another. The first sentence in the paragraph states that scholars aren't exactly sure in what order the ancient Romans used the bathing rooms. The line referred to in the question is the next sentence in the paragraph. That sentence mentions other rooms that were a part of the sequence, but the words "may have diverted" suggest that the author is not sure about when bathers used these rooms or not. So, the ideas in this sentence support the first, offering examples of what is mentioned in the previous sentence. The correct answer is (A).

In terms of the other choices, B and E are not supported in that specific paragraph. The complexity of the bathhouses comes from the passage as a whole, and only the purpose of the final bathing room is discussed. Choice (C) is partially accurate, since lines 56-60 point out other bathing rooms, but don't offer up a different bathing sequence that may have been used. Choice (D) is the opposite of what you want, since you're looking for an answer that supports, not negates, the ideas already mentioned in the paragraph's previous sentence.

Question 6: Phrase/Expression

The correct answer is D. This question is a variation of a vocabulary-in-context question. To answer this one, look back at the sentence. Read the

PETERSON'S
getting you there

sentence with that phrase missing, and substitute your own answer. You should've come up with something like "interesting benefit." Looking at the answer choices, the closest in meaning to the phrase used in context is choice (D) Choices (A) and (C) don't make sense, since the only reference to food is in the next sentence. The juggling and other entertainment discussed is not mandatory to watch, so choice (B) is wrong. Choice (E) is redundant, and therefore doesn't make sense if substituted for the phrase in question.

Question 7: Literal Comprehension

The correct answer is B. The last paragraph raises the social importance of the baths by mentioning the tile work and other art Romans used as decoration in the baths. This is the first time it is discussed in the passage, so the best answer is choice (B). The paragraph doesn't summarize any of the other points made, so choice (A) can be eliminated. Choices (C), (D), and (E) don't make sense if you think about what they are really saying.

Question 8: Main Idea/Focus

The correct answer is D. To answer this question, you have to think about what the majority of the passage is about. What does the author focus on most? The best answer is choice (D).

Bathing is definitely significant to the Romans, but the passage concentrates more on the layout and use of the bathhouses, and only toward the end refers to the cultural and social importance of the baths, so you can eliminate choice (C). Choice (A) is wrong, since modern-day spas are only mentioned in the first paragraph. The evolution of bathing is referred to early in the passage, but is not revisited, so choice (B) can also be eliminated. Choice (E) only includes part of what the passage is about, so that's not a good choice.

> **Note**
>
> If you look at the passage and simply count up the number of paragraphs devoted to each answer choice, you'll see how the middle 4–5 paragraphs discuss the ritualized process of Roman bathing. Other choices, like (C) and (E), appear in single paragraphs, but they are not the larger focus of the passage.

If you had no problems answering any of these questions, you should feel good about your chances on the long SAT reading passages. You're obviously doing things like actively reading and going back to find the answer in the passage correctly. If you missed some questions, use this opportunity to learn from your mistakes. Look over the questions you missed and determine where you made the error. Did you forget to go back to the passage to find the answer? Did you have a clear picture of the main idea when you finished skimming it?

Learning new techniques can take some time, and everyone is going to miss a question or two during the learning process. Take the time to practice these techniques, since they will give you your best shot at a good score on the real SAT, the only test that matters.

Paragraph-Length Critical Reading: Pint-sized but Feisty Passages

The College Board didn't leave you empty-handed when they eliminated the analogies. Instead, the test now contains "snack-sized" versions of the longer critical reading passages. These paragraph-length passages are approximately 100 words long, followed by two to four multiple-choice questions in the same format and style as those for the longer reading passages.

Although these compact passages are indeed shorter, they aren't completely harmless. Because they are so short, your "critical eye" as a reader will have to be all the more aware of the stated and inferred meanings of the content. The College Board refers to these questions as "discrete reading," which translates as, "reading isolated paragraphs closely and carefully."

One thing to remember is that unlike the sentence completions, you don't have to rely on experiences or knowledge outside of what is stated in the passages. All you need to know to answer the questions will be within the passages themselves. However, you will have to make inferences, since the directions clearly state that you should answer the questions on the basis of "what is stated or implied" in the passage.

> **Note**
>
> Internalize the directions for the short reading passage section to save time. The directions will look similar to this:
>
> **Directions:** The passage below is followed by questions based on its content. Answer the questions on the basis of what is stated or implied in the passage.

Types of Questions

Questions here will be similar to those for longer CR questions. They'll cut to the chase, specifically asking about the significance of a particular phrase, the contextual use of a word, the reason behind an author's word choice, as well as the author's purpose or attitude. For these questions, you'll

PETERSON'S
getting you there

definitely make inferences to help pinpoint the answer. Since the passages are short, the College Board wants to see how well you can make smart assumptions rather than recall information.

Some potential question stems are:

- The author most likely mentions the faded wallpaper in order to...

- According to the passage, it can be most reasonably inferred that . . .

- According to the passage, Welty aimed to convey through her writing . . .

- The reference to the "aging population" (line 3) primarily serves to emphasize . . .

Dealing with the Passages

To answer these questions, apply the same process as that used for the longer reading passages, EXCEPT for skimming. Skimming will be your downfall with these questions. Since you have so little to work with in terms of words, every word will count. Don't memorize the paragraph, but definitely read it both line by line and for its overarching idea.

Keep in mind the following things when reading these short passages:

- Follow the author's reasoning carefully. Notice the style, the author's attitude, and the tone.

- When answering the questions, do so based on what is either stated or implied in the passage. Just because an answer choice is true on its own doesn't make it a correct answer. Example: "Life is not easy." We'd all agree that this is a true statement, right? Well, it may be easier for some, but we won't get into that. Even though you may feel that this is a true statement, if it is not stated or implied in the passage, then it is not the right answer.

Try these.

Passage 1

Line   American artist James McNeill Whistler may be best known for his 1871 painting of his mother seated in a rocking chair, but very few know of his talents beyond the canvas—that of an exhibition designer. His monochromatic, spare approach initially

(5)   threw stuffy Victorian gallery-goers, who were accustomed to darkly draperied rooms cluttered with wall-to-wall artwork, into a tizzy. Dictating the décor of his exhibitions down to the wall

color and flower vases may seem beyond the norm for an artist, but his nutty micromanaging tendencies actually caused a
(10) constructive ripple effect on exhibition design, which evolved into standard practice for museums and galleries today.

1. The use of the phrase "threw . . . into a tizzy" (lines 5–7) primarily serves to

   (A) show a contrast between their expectations and the actual experience.
   (B) suggest that Victorians didn't like change.
   (C) introduce a controversial form of gallery exhibition.
   (D) question a contemporary method of art display.
   (E) challenge the way exhibitions were displayed then.

2. The author's tone throughout the passage is

   (A) critical.
   (B) playful.
   (C) mocking.
   (D) sentimental.
   (E) detached

1. **The correct answer is A.** The Victorian reaction to Whistler's form of exhibitions was in stark contrast to what they had previously experienced and therefore expected when going to see art. That's Choice (A). Choice B is incorrect, because it makes too big of an assumption about Victorian attitudes. Choices C, D and E are incorrect because they don't make logical sense. The last three choices all have words in them that relate to the overall passage, but these words are not used in the proper "context." That word gets around, doesn't it?

2. **The correct answer is B.** The overall attitude the author conveys is positive and humorous in tone, through the use of words such as "tizzy" and "nutty." The author is not critical but complimentary of Whistler, so choice A is wrong. The author seems involved in the subject, so choice E is out. Choices C and D are not supported by the words the author uses to describe Whistler's impact, so those are also incorrect.

As you can see, it's really just like the long reading passages, only (1) the passages are shorter, and (2) the questions focus on inferences.

Passage 2

Line   "For all serious daring starts from within," Eudora Welty stated
in her autobiography's conclusion. A self-proclaimed "sheltered"
writer, her stories dared to capture a vividly evocative view of
human life via her zealous imagination. Her form of storytelling,
(5)   steeped in description paired with the bittersweet truth of human
nature and experience, continuously caused critics and admirers
alike to query Welty's muse, especially considering her simple,
quiet life in Mississippi. Yet this understated woman ventured
often into settings rich with life's beauty and pain while docu-
(10)   menting the Great Depression in photographs for the WPA
during the 1930s.

3. According to the passage, Welty aimed to convey through her writing

   (A) an appreciation of human nature.
   (B) an inventive yet accurate portrait of life.
   (C) a readily accessible story.
   (D) life's hardships during the 1930s.
   (E) strategies for vivid description.

4. The author mentions Welty's job as a WPA photographer to suggest that

   (A) her work influenced her craft.
   (B) photography was her first passion.
   (C) storytelling is based in the visual realm.
   (D) documenting life is a dual process.
   (E) her daring nature grew from photography.

3. **The correct answer is B.** The passage states that Welty strove to combine her imagination with the reality of people's lives. Choice A only contains one aspect of what Welty strove for in her writing. C and E are incorrect because the passage doesn't indicate either of these assumptions. D is incorrect because it is too narrow and specific. Although Welty may have drawn upon her experiences as a photographer in the 1930s when writing, there's nothing in the passage that says her writing reflected only one time period.

4. **The correct answer is A.** The author asks the reader to make the connection between how Welty's writing was influenced by her work experience without coming out and saying so. Choice B is not supported in the passage, so it is incorrect. Although choices C, D and E may seem true, they have no relevance to the question, and should be eliminated as wrong answers.

Take It to the Next Level

What Makes for a Tough Sentence Completion Question?

Most of the 19 sentence completions you'll encounter on the SAT will be no-brainers for you. One feature that makes for a no-brainer question is easy vocabulary. Another feature that makes for a "gimmee" question is a short, simple sentence—an easily understood statement that doesn't take too many twists or turns as it goes. Here's an example of the kinds of straightforward, easy-to-understand sentences and answer choices that you'll find in comparatively easy sentence completion questions:

1. Many stage actors are intimidated by the _____ of drama critics, whose reviews can determine the fate of a play in a single night.

    (A) tastes
    (B) power
    (C) expertise
    (D) criticism
    (E) reviews

The correct answer is (B). Of the five word choices, the one that it makes most sense to be *intimidated by* is *power*. And this word makes perfect sense in the context of the sentence: The ability to determine the fate of a play in a single night is a good description of a certain type of *power*. Just for the record, here's why none of the four wrong-answer choices can compete with (B):

    (A) It makes no sense to be intimidated by *tastes,* so you can easily eliminate (A) without even considering the second part of the sentence.

(C) Although it might make sense to be intimidated by someone's "expertise" (knowledge or skill gained from experience), this kind of intimidation doesn't make as much sense as choice (B), when you consider the second part of the sentence as well.

(D) It makes no sense to be intimidated by "criticism of drama critics," a phrase that suggests that it is the drama critics who are being criticized.

(E) This choice provides a completion that results in the redundant, and very awkward, use of the word "reviews."

> **Note**
>
> No knowledge of rocket science is needed to handle questions like this one! And, believe it or not, you'll find some SAT sentence completions to be even easier! Don't worry, we won't waste any more time in this lesson on no-brainers. From here on, we'll handle only the tougher questions.

To crank up the difficulty level of the drama-critic question you just looked at, the test-makers might:

- Use more advanced vocabulary (in the sentence as well as the answer choices)

- Provide "runner-up" answer choices that require closer judgment calls

- Add a second blank

Here's a souped-up variation on the drama-critic question, made tougher in all three ways:

2. Friends of the theater have long decried the _____ of big-city drama critics, whose reviews can determine the _____ of a play in a single night.

   (A) tactlessness..popularity
   (B) callous indifference..outcome
   (C) incisive judgment..attendance
   (D) disingenuousness..success
   (E) unfettered sway..fate

The correct answer is (E). To handle this more difficult version of the question, it helps to know that the word *decry* means "to discredit or criticize." It wouldn't make much sense for "friends of the theater" to discredit or criticize a drama critic's "incisive judgement." (The word *incisive* in this context means "keen or sharp.") So, you can at least eliminate choice (C), without even considering the second blank. But the remaining four choices for completing the first blank all make sense as characteristics of big-city drama critics as seen by friends of the theater. (Of course, it helps to know that *disingenuousness* means "insincerity" and that *unfettered sway* means "unconstrained influence or power.") So, you'll need to consider the second blank.

Choice (B) doesn't make sense for the second blank. It's the playwright, not the critic, that determines the *outcome* of a play. Therefore, you can narrow your choices to (A), (D), and (E), all of which make sense for completing the second blank. (A drama critic's review can determine a play's *popularity*, *success*, or *fate*.) But of the three choices, (E) makes the most sense when you consider the completed sentence. Regardless of which word (*popularity*, *success*, or *fate*) you use to complete the second blank, the second part of the sentence provides a better description of *unfettered sway* than either *tactlessness* or *disingenuousness*. In other words, with (E) the sentence as a whole is more consistent and cohesive.

If you were paying attention to the analysis of the preceding question, you noticed some pretty subtle distinctions between the best answer choice and the others. That's exactly how many of the toughest sentence completion questions earn their stripes. By tuning-in to these subtleties, you'll be ready for the toughest completions the test-makers can dish out.

> **Note**
>
> Test-makers have another way to boost the difficulty level of sentence completions: they construct longer, more complex sentences that contain "signpost" words. These words connect the sentence's parts together to form a cohesive whole that makes sense with the right completion. We'll examine the test-makers' four favorite types of connections, and their signposts, later in this lesson.

Take It to the Next Level

PETERSON'S
getting you there

Strategies for Sentence Completion Questions

Here you'll learn some strategies that you can use for handling sentence completion questions. But first, attempt each of the following "tougher than average" sample questions. Then, carefully read the explanations, which reveal some of these strategies.

3. Sleep researchers now view sleep as involving degrees of detachment from the surrounding world, a _____ whose rhythm is as unique and as consistent as a signature.

   (A) realm
   (B) progression
   (C) science
   (D) restfulness
   (E) condition

The correct answer is (B). The sentence as a whole seems to suggest that sleep is a dynamic process involving a series of different stages defined by degree of detachment. Notice that the purpose of the second clause is to describe, or restate, what sleep is. This observation is key in getting to the correct answer. The missing word refers to "sleep," so perhaps a word such as *state* or *condition* might occur to you as a logical completion. Choices (C) and (D) make no sense as characterizations of sleep, so eliminate them. Notice also that "rhythm" is mentioned as a feature or trait of the missing word ("_____ whose rhythm . . ."). To describe a "realm" as having a rhythm makes no sense, so eliminate (A). You've narrowed the choices down to (B) and (E). Read the sentence with each word in turn. Ask yourself which word is more appropriate and effective in conveying the thrust of the sentence—that sleep is a dynamic process involving a series of different stages. The word *progression* clearly drives home this notion more pointedly and effectively than the word *condition*.

4. African-American legislators today not only _____ their constituencies but also serve as proxies in the democratic process for all African Americans; yet the records of some of them _____ their struggle to extend certain ideals to encompass all citizens.

   (A) serve..describe
   (B) abandon..affirm
   (C) promote..criticize
   (D) represent..belie
   (E) influence..discredit

The correct answer is (D). Notice that the sentence changes direction midway through. This change is signaled by the key word *yet*, which provides a clue that the second part of the sentence sets up a contrast or contradiction to the first part. The words "not only . . . but also" are important clues that the first blank must complement the phrase "serve as proxies . . . ." (*Proxy* means "substitute.") A negatively charged word such as *harm*, *ignore*, or *disagree with* would make no sense in the first blank; however, a word such as *serve*, *represent*, or *aid* would fit nicely. The meaning of the second clause should reflect a contrast to that of the first one. Therefore, a word such as *ignore*, *de-emphasize*, or *trivialize* would make sense here. Here's a good paraphrase of the sentence that shows the idea that it is probably trying to convey:

In doing their jobs, these legislators have helped (*aided*) all African Americans, yet the records of some of them don't reflect (they *ignore*) the efforts of these legislators as a group. Now analyze each answer choice to see how effectively it conveys these ideas:

(A) *Served* fits nicely, but *describe* fails to establish the necessary contrast between the two parts of the sentence. Eliminate (A).

(B) *Abandoned* doesn't fit, because it doesn't complement "served as proxies. . . ." You can eliminate (B) even without considering the second word (*affirm*).

(C) *Promoted* and *criticize* each seem to make sense in context, and together they set up a sense of contrast between the two clauses. So (C) is in the running. However, it is the *goals* or *interests* of a constituency, not the constituency itself that an elected representative promotes. So *promoted* sets up an improper idiomatic expression. What's more, for the word *criticize* to establish a clear contrast, the first clause should at least suggest the opposing notion of *approval*, but it doesn't. Even though the "flavor" of *criticize* is in the right direction, it is not a perfect fit in the context of the sentence as a whole.

(D) *Represented* fits nicely. If you don't know what *belie* means, perhaps you can guess based on its root *lie* (falsehood), which provides the sort of contrast between the two clauses you're looking for. To *belie* is to misrepresent or contradict. For example, a smile belies sadness. Similarly, a biography can belie the struggle described in the sentence, perhaps by mis-describing it as an easier effort than it has in fact been. (D) appears to be a logical answer choice.

Take It to the Next Level

(E) *Influenced* establishes a different meaning for the first clause than the one you're inferring. But *influenced* does make some sense in the first clause. *Discredit* makes sense as well and sets off the necessary contrast between the two clauses. However, this version of the sentence inappropriately *discredits* a *struggle*, while it makes better sense to discredit the *strugglers*. You can eliminate (E) based on this defect alone. What's more, although the word *influence* makes sense in context, it doesn't establish the close parallel in ideas that the correlative phrases "not only . . . but also . . . "call for. (D) is better in this respect.

Strategies

If you read the explanations for the preceding two questions, you already picked up some valuable ideas for gaining a tactical advantage on SAT sentence completion questions. Here, you'll review those ideas, and pick up some additional ones. These strategies will help you gain insights into sentence completions so that you can handle them efficiently, while avoiding the kinds of blunders that average test-takers might make.

1. **First try to understand the sentence, paying particular attention to "signpost" words and phrases that connect parts of the sentence together.**

   Initially, read the sentence in its entirety, without worrying about how to fill in the blanks yet. Try to get a feel for the topic and the "thrust" of the sentence. Ask yourself about the point the sentence is trying to make. Pay particular attention to key, or "signpost," words that indicate any of the following:

   - A contrast (pointing out a difference, contradiction, or distinction)

   - A similarity (pointing out how two things are analogous or otherwise the same)

   - A restatement (paraphrasing, describing, or clarifying) An effect (pointing out a conclusion, consequence, or result of a cause or influence)

"Signpost" words can tell you where the sentence is going. Is it continuing along one line of thought? If so, you're looking for a word that supports that thought. Is it changing direction in midstream? If so, you're looking for a word that sets up a contrast between the thoughts in the sentence.

Words that signal blanks that go with the flow:	Words that signal blanks that shift gears:
and	but
also	yet
consequently	although
as a result	on the other hand
thus	in contrast
hence	however
so	nevertheless
for example	

Question 3

The sentence as a whole seems to suggest that sleep is a dynamic process involving a series of different stages defined by degree of detachment. Notice that the purpose of the second clause is to describe what sleep is. This observation is key in getting to the correct answer.

Question 4

In reading this sentence, you should have noticed that it changes direction midway through. This change is signaled by the keyword *yet*, which provides a clue that the second part of the sentence sets up a contrast or contradiction to the first part. You can bet that this structural clue will be crucial in determining the best answer.

2. As a starting point, complete the sentence with your own words before looking at the answer choices.

Filling in the blank(s) with your own words first will help get your mental wheels turning and get you into the question. If you use this approach, you'll have a much easier time spotting "sucker bait" answer choices (and you'll see plenty of them in sentence completions). If the question includes two blanks, be sure that your two "home-grown" words make sense considered together.

Take It to the Next Level

PETERSON'S
getting you there

Question 4

The words "not only . . . but also" provided clues that the first blank must complement the phrase "served as proxies . . . ." The word *aided* fit nicely. Since the sentence's second clause should set up a contrast to the first one, a word such as *ignore* made sense. With these two words, you've made overall sense of the sentence, and you can eliminate conflicting answer choices.

3. Don't waste time trying to make sense of answer choices that don't fit.

For any sentence completion question, you're bound to find at least one or two choices that make little or no sense in the context of the sentence. Clear those away first, so that you can focus your attention on the viable candidates. If the sentence contains two blanks, you can eliminate any answer choice in which one of the words considered alone makes no sense.

Question 3

The correct answer must make sense as a characterization of sleep. Choices (C) and (D) obviously make no sense, so you can easily eliminate them. Since it makes no sense to describe a "realm" as having a rhythm, you can also eliminate choice (A).

Question 4

You can eliminate choice (B) because *abandon* doesn't make sense in the first clause. You don't even need to analyze the second word (*affirm*).

4. Don't stop short of considering each and every answer choice.

Okay, you've thought up your own answer first, and one of the five choices looks perfect. Should you select it and move on, without considering the others? No! Remember: The qualitative difference between the best and second best answer can be subtle.

> **Alert!**
>
> Keep in mind that filling in the blanks with your own words is only a starting point. Don't expect to find your answer verbatim among the choices because most SAT sentence completions are not that easy. For example, in question 3, if you were filling in the blank yourself (without the aid of the answer choices), what word would you use? The missing word refers to "sleep," so perhaps a word such as *state* or *condition* might occur to you as a logical completion. While choice (E) provides the word "condition," another choice turned out to be better.

124

Question 3

If choices (B) and (E) were switched, you might have been tempted to select (B) without considering other choices. But you'd have been wrong!

Question 4

Choice (C) seemed to fit okay, but if you selected it and moved on without considering later choices, you'd have missed the best answer, choice (D).

5. Don't choose an answer to a dual-blank question just because one of the words is a perfect fit.

As often as not, one word that fits perfectly is paired with another word that doesn't fit well at all. When it comes to dual-blank questions, this is the test-makers' favorite trap. Don't fall for it!

Question 4

The word *serve* in choice (A) is a perfect fit for the first blank; yet, (A) is not the correct answer choice.

6. Don't choose an answer just because it contains a tough word.

Expect to encounter some tough vocabulary words in later sentence completion questions. But don't choose an answer just because it includes a difficult word. By the same token, don't rule it out for this reason. That's not how the test-makers design sentence completions. Instead, try to take your best guess as to what the word might mean (perhaps it looks a bit like a familiar word). A reasoned guess is better than an unreasoned one, right?

Question 4

The word *belie* happened to be part of the best answer; but that's just the way this question turned out. Don't generalize from this single example!

7. Choose between the best choices by checking for idiom, usage, and awkwardness.

Don't forget that the test-makers are covering not just overall sentence sense but also word usage (whether a word is used properly) and idiom (how ideas are expressed as phrases). If you're having trouble deciding between choices, check for these two problems, and eliminate any answer choice that makes any part of the sentence confusing or awkward.

Question 4

Both (C) and (E) contain subtle usage and idiom problems that distinguish them from the best answer choice (D).

PETERSON'S
getting you there

The Test-Makers' Favorite Sentence Connections

Earlier in this lesson, we looked at how advanced vocabulary and subtle distinctions between best and second-best answer choices can make for tougher sentence completion questions. Yet another feature that makes for a tougher question is a sentence with a complex logical structure. In this kind of sentence, signpost words are included to connect the sentence's parts together to form a complete idea that makes sense (assuming the right words are used to fill in the blanks.) For the remainder of this lesson, we'll focus on the test-makers' four favorite types of connections and the "signpost" words used for each type.

The test-makers are rather predictable when it comes to how they construct complex sentences that contain "signpost" words. Once you see enough of these sentences, you'll begin to recognize certain patterns in how parts of the sentences connect together logically. Here are the types of connections that you're most likely to encounter, and should learn to recognize:

- Contrast
- Similarity
- Restatement
- Cause and effect

Note

Not every tough sentence completion question will illustrate one of these four connections; but most will.

Contrast

In a sentence fitting this pattern, one part of a sentence contains an idea that contrasts with, or is opposed to, an idea in another part of the sentence. Here's an example:

5. Whereas Wordsworth wrote his best poetry during _____, Yeats wrote some of his finest poems when he was over 70-years old.

- **(A)** illness
- **(B)** war
- **(C)** youth
- **(D)** marriage
- **(E)** convalescence

126

The correct answer is (C). What is there about the sentence that tells you to look for a contrast? It's the word "Whereas," isn't it? Without this word, you couldn't make the Contrast connection. If you doubt this, think about how you'd fill in the blank without the word, as in this variation:

Wordsworth wrote his best poetry during _____, *and* Yeats wrote some of his finest poems when he was over 70-years old.

The single word "Whereas" makes all the difference. It tells you that a contrast is coming. In other words, the first part of the sentence tells you something about Wordsworth that *should contrast* with what the second part of the sentence tells you about Yeats. Since the second part says that Yeats wrote his best poetry when he was old ("over 70-years old"), Wordsworth must have written his best poetry when he was young. The only answer choice that provides this contrast is (C).

Here are some other "signpost" words used to signal a Contrast connection:

although	*however*	*on the other hand*
but	*nevertheless*	*unlike*
by contrast	*nonetheless*	*yet*
despite		

Note

For the sentence involving Wordsworth and Yeats, you could use almost any word from the preceding list instead of "whereas" to set up the same contrast. Some you'd use to introduce the first part of the sentence; others you'd use to introduce the second part of the sentence. Try each one to see if it fits (and, if so, where).

Similarity

In a sentence fitting this pattern, one part describes something that is similar to something described in another part of the sentence. Here's an example:

6. Just as musicians in the 1970s were amazed by the powers of the electronic synthesizer, musicians during the time of Bach _____ the organ, the technical wonder of its day.

   (A) were reluctant to play
   (B) marveled at
   (C) were intimidated by
   (D) were anxious to master
   (E) misunderstood

Take It to the Next Level

PETERSON'S
getting you there

The correct answer is (B). In this sentence, the words "Just as" tell you that the two parts of the sentence are describing similar situations. In other words, musicians during Bach's time reacted to the organ in the same way that musicians in the 1970s reacted to the synthesizer. Since the sentence indicates that musicians of the 1970s "were amazed by" the synthesizer, the words for the blank should express something similar about the reaction to the organ. Only choice (B), "marveled at," provides the similarity, so it's the best answer choice.

Here are some other words and phrases that act as Similarity "signposts":

as	*like*	*similarly*
in the same way	*likewise*	

Try redrafting the sentence about synthesizers using each of these signposts instead of the words "just as." You'll notice that some words work only to begin the first clause, whereas others work only to begin the second clause.

Restatement

In a sentence fitting this pattern, one part paraphrases, defines or clarifies what is said in another part of the sentence. Here's an example:

7. Public attitudes toward business _____ are somewhat _____; most people resent intrusive government rules, yet they expect government to prevent businesses from defrauding, endangering, or exploiting the public.

   (A) ethics..divided
   (B) investment..confused
   (C) practices..emotional
   (D) regulation..ambiguous
   (E) leaders..skeptical

The correct answer is (D). As you read the sentence as a whole, you get the distinct idea that the second part is intended to elucidate (clarify or explain) the first part. What provides the clue for this connection? In this sentence, there are two keys: the semicolon and the syntax. The first part is much briefer than the second, and there are no connecting words that signal anything but restatement.

> **Note**
>
> Think of the brief phrase as a dictionary entry, and the longer phrase as its definition. A dictionary might separate the entry from its definition with a colon; here a semicolon serves a similar purpose.

In this sentence, the second part (following the semicolon) describes in some detail the public's attitude about government rules for business. As you can see, the attitude described is self-contradictory in that the same person typically has conflicting expectations when it comes to government rules for business. (Notice the keyword "yet," which signals the contradiction.) Try starting with the second blank. You're looking for a word that accurately captures the public attitude. Choices (A), (B) and (D) work best; "divided," "confused," and "ambiguous" all convey the general idea that the public wants two things that don't go together very well. For the first blank, you want a word that describes what the second part of the sentence also describes. Choice (D) appears to be the best fit; the sentence as a whole has to do with "business regulation," that is, the rules laid down by government for business. Two other choices, (A) and (C), work okay for the first blank. But "ethics" is a bit too specific, while "practices" is a bit too vague. (You already eliminated choice (C) based on the second missing word.) So, the best answer choice is (D).

As you just saw, the semicolon without a connector word might provide a wordless warning that a Restatement might be taking place. Also, look for these keywords and phrases, which often mark Restatement connections:

in fact in other words	in short namely	that is

Note

Three of these markers could easily be inserted into the sentence about business regulation to strengthen the signal that a Restatement is taking place. Try redrafting the sentence with the addition of each marker in turn, and you'll find out which three work.

Take It to the Next Level

Cause and Effect

In a sentence fitting this pattern, one part describes something that causes, produces, or influences what's described in another part. Here's an example:

8. When waging election campaigns against challengers, most incumbent politicians have significant _____ as a result of the power and recognition that are typically part and parcel of holding public office.

    (A) propensities
    (B) expenses
    (C) contributions
    (D) budgets
    (E) advantages

The correct answer is (E). In this sentence, the operative phrase is "as a result." What precedes this phrase describes the effect, or result, of the "power and recognition" that goes with holding an official position in the government. Or, put another way, the power and recognition of public office causes or influences what the earlier part of the sentence intends to describe. Logically, what effects would be caused by the power and recognition of public office? One natural effect would be to make it easier to run for reelection, if only because the current office holder is already well known. So, "advantages" is an apt expression of this natural effect. The most tempting wrong answer choices are probably (C) and (D). However, significant "contributions" or "budgets" wouldn't necessarily be logical, or natural, effects of having power and recognition, would they? A candidate with a lot of power and recognition could perhaps spend as much, or as little, as he would like. What's more, the phrase "have . . . contributions" is an awkward idiom. (A more effective and clearer phrase is "receive contributions.") So, on this count as well, choice (C) cannot be the best one.

> **Note**
>
> To understand the preceding sentence, it helps to know that an "incumbent politician" is one who is already in office. Even if you don't know what "incumbent" means, you can still make an educated guess based on the sentence as a whole. "Incumbent politicians" are depicted here as running against "challengers," and a "challenger" is typically a person who goes up against a current title holder. So, it would be a good guess that an incumbent candidate is the current office holder.

In the preceding example, the words "as a result" marked the Cause-and-Effect connection. Here are some other "signposts" that mark this kind of connection:

because	leads to	since
hence	produces	therefore
consequently	results in	thus
due to		

You can redraft the sentence about incumbent candidates using any of these "signposts" instead of "as a result." You'll find that you can plug in some as substitutes for "as a result," but others require that you restructure the sentence.

Reading Passages

As SAT reading passages go, this next one is not especially difficult to understand. What you'll be focusing on here are not tough passages, but rather tough questions.

Francis Bacon was a sixteenth-century philosopher of science. The passage below explores the link between his thinking and that of the modern-day scientific establishment.

Line   Francis Bacon contributed to the scientific enterprise a prophetic
        understanding of how science would one day be put to use in the
        service of technology, and how such a symbiosis between the two
        would radically impact both man and his surroundings. As
(5)   inseparable as they are today, it is hard to imagine science and
        technology as inhabiting separate domains. But in Bacon's world
        of the sixteenth century, science was not generally viewed as a
        practical instrument for improving the physical conditions of life.
        Anticipating Jules Verne and H.G. Wells* by three hundred years,
(10)   Bacon foresaw not only the extent to which science would
        contribute to the enlargement of technology, but also how
        technology would come to be seen as the ultimate justification
        of science.
            There is little doubt that others before Bacon understood that
(15)   discovering the mysteries of air, water, fire, and earth could lead
        to useful applications. But Bacon's systematic elaboration of the

---

* Nineteenth-century science fiction writers.

PETERSON'S

getting you there

promise of joining science with technology was a major leap forward in closing the gap between the two endeavors. He, more than any before him, stressed the need for collective organiza-

(20) tions for scientific inquiry and application—the forerunners of our vast government, academic, and corporate-sponsored research and development departments. Bacon did not ignore the necessity for creative and dedicated individuals to spur science onwards. Rather, he declared that such individuals would need

(25) the help of state aid, corporate organization, official conferences and publications, and regulated social and pecuniary incentives in order for their experiments and insights to have the widest possible application.

The danger that Bacon did not foresee was that corporate

(30) influences could restrict the opportunities of the individual scientist, and that a time could come when no scientific work would be possible without corporate support. The most important ramification of these new conditions is that the judgment and moral grounding possible of individual scientists must now

(35) compete with the concerns of industrial collectives. Entangled within the scientific/technological system, the modern scientist has jeopardized the qualities once exalted as the very hallmarks of science: the detachment from worldly gains and the disinterested pursuit of truth. Influenced by political and economic

(40) pressures, scientists have less and less power to enact any controls over the scientific establishment that pursues the Baconian ideals of riches and power over another of his stated uses for science, "the relief of man's estate." Scientists are losing the power to say "No."

(45) No one questions the immense benefits already conferred by science's efficient methodology. However, since individual scientists must now choose between improving standards of living and obtaining financial support for their research, there is cause for concern. In light of current circumstances, we must ask

(50) certain questions about science that Bacon, from a sixteenth-century perspective, could not possibly have put to himself.

Assumption Questions

Assumption questions ask you to fill in gaps in the author's argument or in a position put forth by some other character in the passage. An assumption is an unstated yet necessary part of an argument. These questions can be difficult because, in order to recognize the assumption required to hold the argument together, you must understand both the conclusion that's drawn and the evidence offered in support of it.

An SAT assumption question usually contains some form of the word *assumption* or *assume*. Here are a few typical examples:

"The author's discussion about . . . assumes that"

"The author's argument is based on the assumption that"

> **Note**
>
> An assumption in a passage will not necessarily be the author's. It might instead be an assumption made by a character or other person discussed in the passage.

When you see an assumption question, you should follow these three steps:

1. Focus on the point established (the conclusion) and the evidence used to support it.

2. Look for a link between the evidence and the conclusion that is necessary to the logic yet not explicitly stated in the passage.

3. Eliminate choices that are outside the scope of the argument. In order for something to be necessary to an argument, it must first be relevant.

Now apply these steps to a question that relates to the passage about Francis Bacon. Use the line reference to find the phrase in question, and read the entire sentence carefully. As you read it, try to figure out what the author is NOT saying that nevertheless must be true for the argument in that sentence to make sense. That unstated premise is the assumption.

Take It to the Next Level

PETERSON'S
getting you there

1. In stating the case for his "cause for concern" (line 29), the author assumes that

   (A) individual scientists have sacrificed all power of choice with regard to the direction of their research.
   (B) it is not in the financial interest of the scientific establishment to improve standards of living.
   (C) science's efficient methodology has led to the solution of most of society's problems.
   (D) no scientists will choose to devote their time to improving standards of living.
   (E) non-scientists are incapable improving their own standard of living.

The correct answer is (B). The author is concerned that scientists will have to choose between improving standards of living and getting money from the scientific establishment for their research. But if scientists receive money from the establishment for projects that will improve the standards of living, then this concern is not so well founded. In making his argument, the author must *assume* that the scientific establishment does not have an interest in improving standards of living. If it *did*, then the author's concern would make less sense. Let's examine the other four choices to see why none can compete with choice (B):

Choice (A): The author need not assume that scientists have sacrificed all control over their work. In fact, the argument in question indicates that scientists still have a choice regarding what they do. The author is concerned because it is a choice that may not bode well for society, but his concern does not rely on the notion in choice (A).

Choice (C): The reference to "science's efficient methodology" comes from the previous sentence and is just there to acknowledge science's achievements before the author states his concern. This concern does not rely on the notion that science has solved most of society's problems, so choice (C) is not the assumption we're looking for here.

Choice (D): The argument in question indicates that scientists still have a choice regarding what they do. The author's concern does not rely on the idea that not one single scientist will choose to improve standards of living. A handful may, and the author would still be concerned because the nature of the choice that has arisen in the modern scientific community does not bode well for society overall. So, choice (D) is not the necessary assumption we seek.

Choice (E): This choice is not the assumption you're looking for because non-scientists are outside the scope. The passage, and the specific concern that's the focus of this question, concerns only the situation of scientists.

Additional Information Questions

Additional Information questions ask you to recognize an additional fact that would make an argument within the passage either more or less convincing—that is, stronger or weaker. These two question types are tougher than average because they require you to challenge the text and to think for yourself as an active reader rather than passively assimilate what's on the page.

An SAT *strengthen* question typically contains a word such as *support* or *strengthen*, as in these two question stems:

Which of the following, if true, would provide the most direct support for the author's assertion that _____ ?

a specific claim made by the author

Which of the following statements, if true, would best strengthen the contention that _____?

a specific point mentioned in the passage

To identify a *Weaken* question on the SAT, look for a word such as *weaken*, *undermine*, *contradict*, or *refute*, as in these two question stems:

Which of the following statements, if true, would contradict most directly the author's claim that _____ ?

a specific claim made by the author

Which of the following, if true, would most seriously weaken the author's argument that _____ ?

a specific conclusion made by the author

To handle a strengthen or weaken question, follow these steps:

1. Make sure you're clear on the argument. You won't have much luck strengthening or weakening an argument that you don't understand.

2. Look for assumptions in the argument. Often, the key to strengthening or weakening an argument lies in building up or breaking down an author's central assumption.

Take It to the Next Level

135

3. Beware of choices that are true but that don't have the desired effect. A choice may perfectly reflect what's in the passage, but if it doesn't strengthen or weaken the argument (whichever you're asked to do), then it cannot be correct. Don't select a choice simply because it seems "true"; that may not be good enough.

Apply these steps to the following weaken question about the Francis Bacon passage. To handle the question, find the relevant text and reread what the author says about what Bacon didn't foresee—that is, what Bacon missed in his analysis. Keep in mind that you're being asked to weaken the *author's* point, not any arguments that Bacon himself makes. Therefore, get into the mindset of challenging the author as you go back to read this part of the passage.

2. The author's assertion regarding what "Bacon did not foresee" (line 18) would be most seriously weakened if it were determined that Bacon

   (A) outlined the mechanisms of corporate support necessary to adequately fund scientific research.
   (B) stated in his writings that the economic and political requirements for a stable society were intertwined with the efficient functioning of the scientific establishment.
   (C) suggested that passionate and creative people were indispensable to the advancement of the scientific enterprise.
   (D) was generally perceptive regarding most scientific topics.
   (E) warned of the dangers to scientific inquiry that would result if collective organization became an integral part of scientific research.

The correct answer is (E). Paraphrasing the text, the author says that Bacon didn't realize that corporate/institutional support would become so essential to science that no science would be possible without it. If, however, we find that Bacon *did* in fact warn of the dangers to science of such corporate control ("collective organization"), then the author's argument here would carry much less weight. Choice (E) is the best "weakener" of the bunch. Let's examine the other four choices to see why none can compete with choice (D):

Choice (A): The author credits Bacon with the idea that corporate support would be necessary for science to flourish. If it were determined that somewhere Bacon spells out just what that support would consist of, that would still do nothing to damage the author's claim that Bacon missed the point that such corporate control of science could have negative consequences.

Choice (B): It wouldn't be surprising to find the claim stated in choice (B) in Bacon's writings, considering what we know about his ideas from the passage. However, this wouldn't in any way damage the author's claim that Bacon missed the point that corporate control of science could have negative consequences.

Choice (C): The author states that "Bacon did not ignore the necessity for creative and dedicated individuals to spur science onwards," so it wouldn't be surprising to find the suggestion described in choice (C) in Bacon's writings. However, this wouldn't in any way damage the author's claim that Bacon missed the point that corporate control of science could have negative consequences.

Choice (D): Based on the passage, Bacon seems to be a fairly perceptive fellow, so we wouldn't be surprised to find he was totally up on his science. However, as with all the other wrong choices here, this in no way hurts the author's argument that Bacon missed the point that corporate control of science could have negative consequences. That's the claim we're trying to weaken, and choice (D) doesn't do it.

Application Questions

Application questions ask you to relate ideas and situations described in the passage to outside scenarios. In other words, they test whether you can understand how examples represented in the passage might be applied in a different context. Application questions are inherently difficult because the choices involve situations foreign to the topic of the passage, and a leap is required on your part to connect the correct choice to the relevant idea or example in the passage. Here is what application questions typically look like:

"As described in the passage, _____ is most
something the author describes
nearly analogous to which of the following?"

Which of the following best exemplifies _____
something mentioned in the
_____?
passage

Which of the following would the author consider to be most similar to _____?
something mentioned in the passage

Take It to the Next Level

PETERSON'S
getting you there

When you see an application question, you should follow these three steps:

1. Go back to the example or idea in question and reread it to make sure you have a firm grasp of it.

2. Put the example or idea into general terms. This helps because it is the general logic of the example that will somehow relate to the correct answer choice.

3. Test the choices to see whether each one matches the example or idea in question. Beware of choices that distort the meaning of the example.

Now, try to answer an application question about the Francis Bacon passage. Remember that the key to an application question is to generalize a situation and recognize it in another context. Think about the plight of the modern scientist and try to put it into general terms. Then, check the choices to see which one corresponds best to such a scenario.

3. The situation of the modern scientist as described in the passage is most nearly analogous to that of

   (A) a painter who participates in an artistic community in order to gain exposure for his works.
   (B) a doctor who is required to attend a yearly conference in order to keep up with developments in her field.
   (C) a musician who needs to alter her vision for a recording project in order to maintain the support of her record company.
   (D) an executive who is fired for disobeying company policy.
   (E) a union member who organizes a strike to protest against poor working conditions.

The correct answer is (C). According to the author, the modern scientist depends on support from a large organization that forces him to conduct his work according to the demands of the organization. Similarly, the musician in choice (C) depends on a record company that forces her to change what she wants to create in order to please the company. Choice (C) offers the best analogy to the author's description of the modern scientist's plight. Let's examine the other four choices to see why none can compete with choice (C):

Choice (A): According to the author, the modern scientist depends for support on a large organization that forces him to conduct his work according to the demands of the organization. This results in a problem for the scientist, whereas the painter in choice (A) benefits from his attachment to the artistic community.

Choice (B): According to the author, the modern scientist depends for support on a large organization that forces him to conduct his work according to the demands of the organization. A doctor required to attend a conference is not in the same situation, since nothing implies that the doctor must alter, against her will, the way she goes about practicing medicine.

Choice (D): According to the author, the modern scientist depends for support on a large organization that forces him to conduct his work according to the demands of that organization. A fired executive need not fit into the same general category. Maybe he deserved to be fired, maybe not, but either way a company has a right to determine how its employees should behave. However, the scientist, according to the author, was once independent and needs to be independent for society to benefit. The predicament of the scientist that the author laments is therefore not similar to the situation of a fired executive.

Choice (E): According to the author, the modern scientist depends for support on a large organization that forces him to conduct his work according to the demands of the organization. That's the situation we need to mirror. A union worker organizing a protest doesn't match the scenario in the question stem. We never hear about scientists fighting back—the author simply voices his concern regarding their ability to work independent of corporate influence.

Method Questions

Method questions ask you to recognize what the author is doing in the passage, or, how the author goes about making her points. Some method questions ask for the author's overall approach in the passage, while others ask about how a specific point is made or about the structure of a particular paragraph. Method questions can be difficult because the answer choices are usually stated very generally, and it's up to you to connect the general wording of the choices with what's going on in the passage.

A Method question can come in many different forms. Here are just a few examples of what the question stem might look like:

Which of the following best describes the approach of the passage?

In the last paragraph, the author proceeds by . . .

How does the fourth paragraph function in relation to the third paragraph?

Which of the following most accurately describes the organization of the second paragraph?

Which of the following techniques is used in the last sentence of paragraph 3?

When you see a method question, you should follow these steps:

1. Let the question guide you to the appropriate area of the passage and reread that section carefully.

2. Focus on what the author is doing—don't get bogged down in details. Method questions concern how the author makes his/her points, not what those points are. The latter is the subject of Detail and Inference questions.

3. Test the choices rigorously. Every word in the correct choice must be consistent with what's going on in the passage. Wrong choices will contain elements that go against the author's approach, or that are simply not represented in the passage.

Now apply these steps to a Method question about the Francis Bacon passage. The final paragraph is short enough to skim quickly before checking out the choices. But read it with a very specific goal in mind—to see what the author is doing in these few lines. Don't get bogged down in details—they really won't help you here. Test the choices, making sure every word of the choice you select matches what's going on in this part of the passage.

4. Which of the following most accurately describes the organization of the last paragraph of the passage?

   (A) An assertion is made and is backed up by evidence.
   (B) A viewpoint is expressed and an opposing viewpoint is stated and countered.
   (C) An admission is offered and is followed by a warning and recommendation.
   (D) Contradictory claims are presented and then reconciled.
   (E) A problem is outlined and a solution is proposed and defended.

The correct answer is C. The notion that no one questions the benefits of science does qualify as an admission in the context of the paragraph; that is, the author admits that science has given humankind enormous benefits, but then goes on to voice his concern regarding the current state of the scientific enterprise. Note how the contrast signal word "however" screams at us that some kind of change must come after the author admits that science has conferred immense benefits, and indeed, what comes next is, as choice (C) puts it, a warning: there is cause for concern. The recommendation that rounds out choice (C) appears in the final sentence, highlighted by the words "we must ask certain questions . . ." Every element in choice (C) is present and accounted for, so choice (C) correctly describes the organization of the paragraph. Let's examine the other four choices to see why none can compete with choice (C):

Choice (A): This choice says that the paragraph begins with an assertion, and we can surely accept that: the assertion that no one questions the benefits of science. Is this then backed up by evidence? No. The contrast signal word "however" alerts us that some kind of change is coming, not evidence for the statement in the first sentence. And indeed, the rest does go off in a different direction.

Choice (B): This choice doesn't reflect what's going on here. It says that the final paragraph begins with a viewpoint, and we can surely accept that: the view that no one questions the benefits of science. But does an opposing viewpoint follow—that is, an argument against the benefits of science? No, the author doesn't go there. He is concerned about the way science is now conducted. He doesn't mention or counter the position that tries to downplay what science has already accomplished.

Choice (C): The contrast signal word "however" offers a promising start for the organization described in choice (C): it flags some kind of upcoming change, so it would certainly sound reasonable for an opposing viewpoint to enter the story here. But it doesn't—the author goes in a different direction from what is described at the end of this choice.

Choice (D): This choice is incorrect because there are no contradictory claims here. The author admits that science has given humankind enormous benefits, but then goes on to voice his concern regarding the current state of the scientific enterprise. These things aren't contradictory, and nothing in the paragraph contradicts either of these things, so choice (D) can't be correct.

Take It to the Next Level

PETERSON'S
getting you there

Choice (E): It's fair to say that a problem is outlined—the problem that securing financial support for scientific work might get in the way of scientists improving standards of living. But does the author propose a solution? No. He recommends that serious questions be asked about the problem, but offers no solution of his own. Even if you viewed his recommendation as a solution, you'd still have to bog down on the "defended" part of choice (E). The passage ends before any kind of defense of his recommendation is offered.

Six Next Level Techniques for Effective Reading

You're a voracious reader who's already developed the kinds of effective reading habits that will serve you well in SAT critical reading. So, there's certainly no need here for an *ad nauseum* discourse on how to read effectively. But it can't hurt to review the basic reading techniques that apply most directly to the SAT.

Alert!

Don't expect to just walk into the SAT testing room and apply the techniques you'll learn about here without practicing them first. You'll need to try them out first, during your SAT practice testing, until you become comfortable with them.

Most test-takers approach critical reading passages *passively*. They give equal time and attention to every sentence in a passage, reading the passage from beginning to end without interruption and with very little thought as to what particular information is most important in order to respond to the specific questions. This strategy is actually better characterized as a *non*-strategy. What's the result? The test-taker might remember some scattered facts and ideas, which will help him/her respond correctly to some easier questions.

But the passive mind-set won't take the test-taker very far when it comes to tougher questions. As you're no doubt aware by now, tougher critical reading questions are tougher because they measure your ability to *understand* the ideas in the passage rather than to simply *recall* information. In order to understand a passage, you must be able to (1) identify the thesis (or main idea) and the author's primary purpose and (2) follow the author's line of reasoning from paragraph to paragraph. Both tasks require an *active* frame of mind in which you constantly interact with the text as you read.

142

1. Mark up the passage. (That's what your pencil is for!)

Selective annotating (e.g., circling and underlining key words and phrases) serves three important purposes:

1. It helps you to maintain an active frame of mind since you are shopping for ideas and information that are sufficiently important to earmark.

2. It provides a pre-written outline. After you read (and annotate) the entire passage, reviewing the annotated words and phrases can be an effective way to recap the passage for yourself.

3. If you need to refer to the passage as you answer the questions, effective annotating will help you quickly locate the information you need.

What sort of information should you annotate? If you under-annotate, you will not be able to effectively recap the passage by reviewing your annotations. On the other hand, if you over-annotate, your annotations lose their meaning, and you might as well not have annotated at all. Here are some suggestions for finding just the right balance:

- Mark areas of discussion that you may need to locate again to answer one or more of the questions.

- Instead of underlining complete sentences, select keywords or phrases that "trigger" for you the idea or point that is made in this sentence or this part of the paragraph.

- Mark structural connectors—keywords that connect the logical building blocks of the passage.

- In chronological passages, mark historical benchmarks and divisions—centuries, years, decades, or historical periods—that help to form the structure of the author's discussion.

- Use arrows to physically connect words that signify ideas that are connected; for example:

  - To clarify cause and effect in the natural sciences or in the context of historical events

  - To indicate who was influenced by whom in literature, music, psychology, etc.

  - To connect names (philosophers, scientists, authors, etc.) with dates, events, other names, theories, or schools of thought, works, etc.

143

- To indicate the chronological order in which historical events occurred

- Create your own visual cues to earmark possible thesis statements, major supporting points, and points of author disagreement.

2. Make margin notes and (for some passages) outlines.

In the left-hand margin, make shorthand notes to summarize paragraphs, earmark areas of discussion, and otherwise provide signals for yourself so that you can locate details more quickly and recap the passage more effectively. Keep your notes as brief as possible; two or three words should provide a sufficient cue.

Don't bother constructing a formal outline of the passage. This takes more time than it's worth. Instead, rely on your margin notes and annotations to indicate the flow of the discussion. For certain high-density passages, however, some organized notes—a "mini-outline"—may be necessary to organize information. Shorthand notes at the bottom of the page may help to keep particular details straight in your mind. The following scenarios typically call for the mini-outline:

- If the passage categorizes or classifies various phenomena, notes may help clarify which phenomena belong in which categories.

- If the passage mentions numerous individual names (e.g., of authors, artists, political figures, etc.), use notes to link them according to influence, agreement or disagreement, and so forth.

3. Pay attention to the overall structure of the passage.

Different types of reading passages are organized in different ways. For example:

- A passage that traces historical causes or consequences will probably be organized chronologically.

- A passage that critiques a theory will probably describe the theory first, and then explain its problems, one at a time.

- A passage that draws a comparison (pointing out similarities and differences) between two things might first list similarities, then differences.

144

- A passage that describes a classification system will probably begin by defining the main class, then branch out to each sub-class level.

Understanding how the passage is organized—in other words, recognizing its structure—will help you to articulate the passage's main idea and primary purpose, to understand the author's purpose in mentioning various details, and to distinguish between main points and minor details—all of which will help you answer the questions.

4. Look for structural clues or "triggers."

Triggers are key words and phrases that provide clues about the structure and organization of the passage and the direction in which the discussion is flowing. The lists below contain many common trigger words and phrases. Underline or circle trigger words as you read the passage. Review your annotations to help you recap the passage and see its structure and organization.

- These words precede an item in a list (e.g., examples, classes, reasons, or characteristics):

  first, second (etc.)

  in addition, also, another

- These words signal that the author is contrasting two phenomena:

  alternatively, by contrast, however, on the other hand, rather than, while, yet

- These words signal a logical conclusion based upon preceding material:

  consequently, in conclusion, then, thus, therefore, as a result, accordingly

- These words signal that the author is comparing (identifying similarities between) two phenomena:

  similarly, in the same way, analogous, parallel, likewise, just as, also, as

- These words signal evidence (factual information) used to support the author's argument:

  because, since, in light of

- These words signal an example of a phenomenon:

  for instance, e.g., such as, . . . is an illustration of

Take It to the Next Level

PETERSON'S
getting you there

5. Don't get bogged down in details as you read.

SAT reading passages are packed with details: lists, statistics and other numbers, dates, titles, and so forth. If you try to absorb all of the details as you read, you'll not only lose sight of the main points but also lose reading speed. Don't get bogged down in the details; gloss over them. In the left-hand margin, note where particular examples, lists, and other details are located. Then, if a particular question involving those details is included, you can quickly and easily locate them and read them more carefully.

6. Sum up the passage after you read it.

After reading the entire passage, take a few seconds to recap it. What was the author's main point and what were the major supporting points? Remind yourself about the flow of the discussion without thinking about all the details. Chances are, you'll be able to answer at least one or two of the questions based just on your recap.

In Conclusion

Many passages have a conclusion, so it's only right that our chapter about passages has one, too. Most of the techniques discussed here are things that you already do in some form already. This chapter has shown how strategies such as "using context" and "finding the main idea" apply to the reading section of the SAT. When you work the sample passages in this book, focus on using the techniques. Cover the answer choices of a sentence completion problem while you come up with your own word. Jot down quick summaries of a passage while you're reading it. The techniques are highly effective, and all you need to do is practice them to the point where they become second nature. When you get to that level of comfort, you will see how beneficial they are in answering easy, medium, and hard problems.

Chapter 5

The Ultimate Word List

Use the Words You Learn

Vocabulary *as such* is not tested on the SAT. But there are plenty of *indirect* and *hidden* vocabulary questions on the SAT:

1. **Reading comprehension passages** include vocabulary-in-context questions. These focus on particular words in the passage and ask you to determine their meaning in the passage. Sometimes the words chosen are obviously hard words (*latent, replete,* and *eminent,* to name three real examples). More often they are seemingly easy words that are tricky because they have many possible meanings (*camp, idea,* and *hard,* for example). In both cases, the broader, more varied, and more accurate your vocabulary knowledge, the better your chances of answering these questions quickly and correctly.

2. The better your vocabulary knowledge, the easier you'll find it to understand both **critical reading passages** and **sentence completion items** (which are, in effect, mini-reading passages, each one sentence long). Even an occasional math item is made a little more complicated by the use of a challenging vocabulary word.

So vocabulary knowledge makes a clear and significant difference in your performance on the SAT. Fortunately, the kinds of words that regularly appear fall into definite patterns.

The SAT is written and edited by bookish people for the benefit of the other bookish people who run colleges and universities. They're designed to test your ability to handle the kinds of bookish tasks college students usually have to master: reading textbooks, finding information in reference books, deciphering scholarly journals, studying research abstracts, and writing impressive-sounding term papers.

So the hard words on the tests are hard words of a particular sort: bookish hard words that deal, broadly speaking, with the manipulation and communication of *ideas*—words like *ambiguous, amplify, arbitrary,* and *arcane*. The better you master this sort of vocabulary, the better you'll do on your exam.

Happily, you don't need to find these words on your own. We've done the spadework for you. We've been able to come up with a list of the words most commonly used in reading passages and sentence completions, including both the question stems and the answer choices. This list has become the *Ultimate Word List*. It includes about 500 primary words that are most likely to appear in one form or another on the SAT. It also includes hundreds of related words—words that are either variants of the primary words (*ambiguity* as a variant of *ambiguous*, for example) or that share a common word root (like *ample, amplify,* and *amplitude*). Many of these words have already been covered in this book; some even appear in the flashcards at the back. By placing them all in a single location, however, we hope to give you one more *tool* to enhance your vocabulary study.

A

abbreviate (verb)   to make briefer, to shorten. *Because time was running out, the speaker had to abbreviate his remarks.* **abbreviation** (noun).

abrasive (adjective)   irritating, grinding, rough. *The manager's rude, abrasive way of criticizing the workers was bad for morale.* **abrasion** (noun).

abridge (verb)   to shorten, to reduce. *The Bill of Rights is designed to prevent Congress from abridging the rights of Americans.* **abridgment** (noun).

absolve (verb)   to free from guilt, to exonerate. *The criminal jury absolved O. J. Simpson of the murder of his ex-wife and her friend.* **absolution** (noun).

abstain (verb)   to refrain, to hold back. *After his heart attack, he was warned by the doctor to abstain from smoking, drinking, and overeating.* **abstinence** (noun), **abstemious** (adjective).

accentuate (verb)   to emphasize, to stress. *The overcast skies and chill winds accentuated our gloomy mood.* **accentuation** (noun).

acrimonious (adjective)   biting, harsh, caustic. *The election campaign became acrimonious, as the candidates traded insults and accusations.* **acrimony** (noun).

adaptable (adjective)   able to be changed to be suitable for a new purpose. *Some scientists say that the mammals outlived the dinosaurs because they were more adaptable to a changing climate.* **adapt** (verb), **adaptation** (noun).

adulation (noun)   extreme admiration. *Few young actors have received greater adulation than did Marlon Brando after his performance in* A Streetcar Named Desire. **adulate** (verb), **adulatory** (adjective).

adversary (noun)   an enemy or opponent. *When the former Soviet Union became an American ally, the United States lost its last major adversary.*

adversity (noun)   misfortune. *It's easy to be patient and generous when things are going well; a person's true character is revealed under adversity.* **adverse** (adjective).

aesthetic (adjective)   relating to art or beauty. *Mapplethorpe's photos may be attacked on moral grounds, but no one questions their aesthetic value—they are beautiful.* **aestheticism** (noun).

affected (adjective)   false, artificial. *At one time, Japanese women were taught to speak in an affected high-pitched voice, which was thought girlishly attractive.* **affect** (verb), **affectation** (noun).

aggressive (adjective)   forceful, energetic, and attacking. *A football player needs a more aggressive style of play than a soccer player.* **aggression** (noun).

alacrity (noun)   promptness, speed. *Thrilled with the job offer, he accepted with alacrity—"Before they can change their minds!" he thought.*

allege (verb)   to state without proof. *Some have alleged that Foster was murdered, but all the evidence points to suicide.* **allegation** (noun).

alleviate (verb)   to make lighter or more bearable. *Although no cure for AIDS has been found, doctors are able to alleviate the suffering of those with the disease.* **alleviation** (noun).

ambiguous (adjective)   having two or more possible meanings. *The phrase, "Let's table that discussion" is ambiguous; some think it means, "Let's discuss it now," while others think it means, "Let's save it for later."* **ambiguity** (noun).

ambivalent (adjective)   having two or more contradictory feelings or attitudes; uncertain. *She was ambivalent toward her impending marriage; at times she was eager to go ahead, while at other times she wanted to call it off.* **ambivalence** (noun).

amiable (adjective)   likable, agreeable, friendly. *He was an amiable lab partner, always smiling, on time, and ready to work.* **amiability** (verb).

amicable (adjective)   friendly, peaceable. *Although they agreed to divorce, their settlement was amicable and they remained friends afterward.*

amplify (verb)   to enlarge, expand, or increase. *Uncertain as to whether they understood, the students asked the teacher to amplify his explanation.* **amplification** (noun).

anachronistic (adjective)   out of the proper time. *The reference, in Shakespeare's* Julius Caesar, *to "the clock striking twelve" is anachronistic, since there were no striking timepieces in ancient Rome.* **anachronism** (noun).

anarchy (noun)   absence of law or order. *For several months after the Nazi government was destroyed, there was no effective government in parts of Germany, and anarchy ruled.* **anarchic** (adjective).

anomaly (noun)   something different or irregular. *The tiny planet Pluto, orbiting next to the giants Jupiter, Saturn, and Neptune, has long appeared to be an anomaly.* **anomalous** (adjective).

antagonism (noun)   hostility, conflict, opposition. *As more and more reporters investigated the Watergate scandal, antagonism between Nixon and the press increased.* **antagonistic** (adjective), **antagonize** (verb).

antiseptic (adjective)   fighting infection; extremely clean. *A wound should be washed with an antiseptic solution. The all-white offices were bare and almost antiseptic in their starkness.*

apathy (noun)   lack of interest, concern, or emotion. *American voters are showing increasing apathy over politics; fewer than half voted in the last election.* **apathetic** (adjective).

arable (adjective)   able to be cultivated for growing crops. *Rocky New England has relatively little arable farmland.*

arbiter (noun)   someone able to settle dispute; a judge or referee. *The public is the ultimate arbiter of commercial value; it decides what sells and what doesn't.*

arbitrary (adjective)   based on random or merely personal preference. *Both computers cost the same and had the same features, so in the end I made an arbitrary decision about which one to buy.*

arcane (adjective)   little-known, mysterious, obscure. *Eliot's* Waste Land *is filled with arcane lore, including quotations in Latin, Greek, French, German, and Sanskrit.* **arcana** (noun, plural).

ardor (noun)   a strong feeling of passion, energy, or zeal. *The young revolutionary proclaimed his convictions with an ardor that excited the crowd.* **ardent** (adjective).

arid (adjective)   very dry; boring and meaningless. *The arid climate of Arizona makes farming difficult. Some find the law a fascinating topic, but for me it is an arid discipline.* **aridity** (noun).

ascetic (adjective)   practicing strict self-discipline for moral or spiritual reasons. *The so-called Desert Fathers were hermits who lived an ascetic life of fasting, study, and prayer.* **asceticism** (verb).

assiduous (verb)   working with care, attention, and diligence. *Although Karen is not a naturally gifted math student, by assiduous study she managed to earn an A in trigonometry.* **assiduity** (noun).

astute (adjective) observant, intelligent, and shrewd. *Safire's years of experience in Washington and his personal acquaintance with many political insiders make him an astute commentator on politics.*

atypical (adjective) not typical; unusual. *In* The Razor's Edge, *Bill Murray, best known as a comic actor, gave an atypical dramatic performance.*

audacious (adjective) bold, daring, adventurous. *Her plan to cross the Atlantic single-handed in a 12-foot sailboat was audacious, if not reckless.* **audacity** (noun).

audible (adjective) able to be heard. *Although she whispered, her voice was picked up by the microphone, and her words were audible throughout the theater.* **audibility** (noun).

auspicious (adjective) promising good fortune; propitious. *The news that a team of British climbers had reached the summit of Everest seemed an auspicious sign for the reign of newly crowned Queen Elizabeth II.*

authoritarian (adjective) favoring or demanding blind obedience to leaders. *Despite Americans' belief in democracy, the American government has supported authoritarian regimes in other countries.* **authoritarianism** (noun)

B

belated (adjective) delayed past the proper time. *She called her mother on January 5th to offer her a belated "Happy New Year."*

belie (verb) to present a false or contradictory appearance. *Lena Horne's youthful appearance belies her long, distinguished career in show business.*

benevolent (adjective) wishing or doing good. *In old age, Carnegie used his wealth for benevolent purposes, donating large sums to found libraries and schools.* **benevolence** (noun).

berate (verb) to scold or criticize harshly. *The judge angrily berated the two lawyers for their unprofessional behavior.*

bereft (adjective) lacking or deprived of something. *Bereft of parental love, orphans sometimes grow up to be insecure.*

152

bombastic (adjective)   inflated or pompous in style. *Old-fashioned bombastic political speeches don't work on television, which demands a more intimate style of communication.* **bombast** (noun).

bourgeois (adjective)   middle-class or reflecting middle-class values. *The Dadaists of the 1920s produced art deliberately designed to offend bourgeois art collectors, with their taste for respectable, refined, uncontroversial pictures.* **bourgeois** (noun).

buttress (noun)   something that supports or strengthens. *The endorsement of the American Medical Association is a powerful buttress for the claims made about this new medicine.* **buttress** (verb).

C

camaraderie (noun)   a spirit of friendship. *Spending long days and nights together on the road, the members of a traveling theater group develop a strong sense of camaraderie.*

candor (noun)   openness, honesty, frankness. *In his memoir about the Vietnam War, former defense secretary McNamara describes his mistakes with remarkable candor.* **candid** (adjective).

capricious (adjective)   unpredictable, whimsical. *The pop star Madonna has changed her image so many times that each new transformation now appears capricious rather than purposeful.* **caprice** (noun).

carnivorous (adjective)   meat-eating. *The long, dagger-like teeth of the Tyrannosaurus make it obvious that this was a carnivorous dinosaur.* **carnivore** (noun).

carping (adjective)   unfairly or excessively critical; querulous. *New York is famous for its demanding critics, but none is harder to please than the carping John Simon, said to have single-handedly destroyed many acting careers.* **carp** (verb).

catalytic (adjective)   bringing about, causing, or producing some result. *The conditions for revolution existed in America by 1765; the disputes about taxation that arose later were the catalytic events that sparked the rebellion.* **catalyze** (verb).

caustic (adjective)   burning, corrosive. *No one was safe when the satirist H. L. Mencken unleashed his caustic wit.*

censure (noun)   blame, condemnation. *The news that Senator Packwood had harassed several women brought censure from many feminists.* **censure** (verb).

chaos (noun)   disorder, confusion, chance. *The first few moments after the explosion were pure chaos: no one was sure what had happened, and the area was filled with people running and yelling.* **chaotic** (adjective).

circuitous (adjective)   winding or indirect. *We drove to the cottage by a circuitous route so we could see as much of the surrounding countryside as possible.*

circumlocution (noun)   speaking in a roundabout way; wordiness. *Legal documents often contain circumlocutions which make them difficult to understand.*

circumscribe (verb)   to define by a limit or boundary. *Originally, the role of the executive branch of government was clearly circumscribed, but that role has greatly expanded over time.* **circumscription** (noun).

circumvent (verb)   to get around. *When Jerry was caught speeding, he tried to circumvent the law by offering the police officer a bribe.*

clandestine (adjective)   secret, surreptitious. *As a member of the underground, Balas took part in clandestine meetings to discuss ways of sabotaging the Nazi forces.*

cloying (adjective)   overly sweet or sentimental. *The deathbed scenes in the novels of Dickens are famously cloying: as Oscar Wilde said, "One would need a heart of stone to read the death of Little Nell without laughing."*

cogent (adjective)   forceful and convincing. *The committee members were won over to the project by the cogent arguments of the chairman.* **cogency** (noun).

cognizant (adjective)   aware, mindful. *Cognizant of the fact that it was getting late, the master of ceremonies cut short the last speech.* **cognizance** (noun).

cohesive (adjective)   sticking together, unified. *An effective military unit must be a cohesive team, all its members working together for a common goal.* **cohere** (verb), **cohesion** (noun).

collaborate (verb)   to work together. *To create a truly successful movie, the director, writers, actors, and many others must collaborate closely.* **collaboration** (noun), **collaborative** (adjective).

colloquial (adjective)   informal in language; conversational. *Some expressions from Shakespeare, such as the use of thou and thee, sound formal today but were colloquial English in Shakespeare's time.*

competent (adjective)   having the skill and knowledge needed for a particular task; capable. *Any competent lawyer can draw up a will.* **competence** (noun).

complacent (adjective)   smug, self-satisfied. *During the 1970s, American auto makers became complacent, believing that they would continue to be successful with little effort.* **complacency** (noun).

composure (noun)   calm, self-assurance. *The president managed to keep his composure during his speech even when the Teleprompter broke down, leaving him without a script.* **composed** (adjective).

conciliatory (adjective)   seeking agreement, compromise, or reconciliation. *As a conciliatory gesture, the union leaders agreed to postpone a strike and to continue negotiations with management.* **conciliate** (verb), **conciliation** (noun).

concise (adjective)   expressed briefly and simply; succinct. *Less than a page long, the Bill of Rights is a concise statement of the freedoms enjoyed by all Americans.* **concision** (noun).

condescending (adjective)   having an attitude of superiority toward another; patronizing. *"What a cute little car!" she remarked in a condescending style. "I suppose it's the nicest one someone like you could afford!"* **condescension** (noun).

condolence (noun)   pity for someone else's sorrow or loss; sympathy. *After the sudden death of Princess Diana, thousands of messages of condolence were sent to her family.* **condole** (verb).

confidant (noun)   someone entrusted with another's secrets. *No one knew about Janee's engagement except Sarah, her confidant.* **confide** (verb), **confidential** (adjective).

conformity (noun)   agreement with or adherence to custom or rule. *In my high school, conformity was the rule: everyone dressed the same, talked the same, and listened to the same music.* **conform** (verb), **conformist** (adjective).

consensus (noun)   general agreement among a group. *Among Quakers, voting traditionally is not used; instead, discussion continues until the entire group forms a consensus.*

consolation (noun)   relief or comfort in sorrow or suffering. *Although we miss our dog very much, it is a consolation to know that she died quickly, without suffering.* **console** (verb).

consternation (noun)   shock, amazement, dismay. *When a voice in the back of the church shouted out, "I know why they should not be married!" the entire gathering was thrown into consternation.*

consummate (verb)   to complete, finish, or perfect. *The deal was consummated with a handshake and the payment of the agreed-upon fee.* **consummate** (adjective), **consummation** (noun).

contaminate (verb)   to make impure. *Chemicals dumped in a nearby forest had seeped into the soil and contaminated the local water supply.* **contamination** (noun).

contemporary (adjective)   modern, current; from the same time. *I prefer old-fashioned furniture rather than contemporary styles. The composer Vivaldi was roughly contemporary with Bach.* **contemporary** (noun).

contrite (adjective)   sorry for past misdeeds. *The public is often willing to forgive celebrities who are involved in some scandal, as long as they appear contrite.* **contrition** (noun).

conundrum (noun)   a riddle, puzzle, or problem. *The question of why an all-powerful, all-loving God allows evil to exist is a conundrum many philosophers have pondered.*

convergence (noun)   the act of coming together in unity or similarity. *A remarkable example of evolutionary convergence can be seen in the shark and the dolphin, two sea creatures that developed from different origins to become very similar in form.* **converge** (verb).

convoluted (adjective)   twisting, complicated, intricate. *Tax law has become so convoluted that it's easy for people to accidentally violate it.* **convolute** (verb), **convolution** (noun).

corroborating (adjective)   supporting with evidence; confirming. *A passerby who had witnessed the crime gave corroborating testimony about the presence of the accused person.* **corroborate** (verb), **corroboration** (noun).

corrosive (adjective)   eating away, gnawing, or destroying. *Years of poverty and hard work had a corrosive effect on her beauty.* **corrode** (verb), **corrosion** (noun).

credulity (noun)   willingness to believe, even with little evidence. *Con artists fool people by taking advantage of their credulity.* **credulous** (adjective).

criterion (noun)   a standard of measurement or judgment. (The plural is criteria.) *In choosing a design for the new taxicabs, reliability will be our main criterion.*

critique (noun)   a critical evaluation. *The editor gave a detailed critique of the manuscript, explaining its strengths and its weaknesses.* **critique** (verb).

culpable (adjective)   deserving blame, guilty. *Although he committed the crime, because he was mentally ill he should not be considered culpable for his actions.* **culpability** (noun).

cumulative (adjective)   made up of successive additions. *Smallpox was eliminated only through the cumulative efforts of several generations of doctors and scientists.* **accumulation** (noun), **accumulate** (verb).

curtail (verb)   to shorten. *Because of the military emergency, all soldiers on leave were ordered to curtail their absences and return to duty.*

D

debased (adjective)   lowered in quality, character, or esteem. *The quality of TV journalism has been debased by the many new tabloid-style talk shows.* **debase** (verb).

debunk (verb)   to expose as false or worthless. *Magician James Randi loves to debunk psychics, mediums, clairvoyants, and others who claim supernatural powers.*

decorous (adjective)   having good taste; proper, appropriate. *The once reserved and decorous style of the British monarchy began to change when the chic, flamboyant young Diana Spencer joined the family.* **decorum** (noun).

decry (verb)   to criticize or condemn. *Cigarette ads aimed at youngsters have led many to decry the marketing tactics of the tobacco industry.*

deduction (noun)   a logical conclusion, especially a specific conclusion based on general principles. *Based on what is known about the effects of greenhouse gases on atmospheric temperature, scientists have made several deductions about the likelihood of global warming.* **deduce** (verb).

delegate (verb)   to give authority or responsibility. *The president delegated the vice president to represent the administration at the peace talks.* **delegate** (noun).

deleterious (adjective)   harmful. *About thirty years ago, scientists proved that working with asbestos could be deleterious to one's health, producing cancer and other diseases.*

delineate (verb)   to outline or describe. *Naturalists had long suspected the fact of evolution, but Darwin was the first to delineate a process—natural selection—through which evolution could occur.*

demagogue (noun)   a leader who plays dishonestly on the prejudices and emotions of his followers. *Senator Joseph McCarthy was a demagogue who used the paranoia of the anti-Communist 1950s as a way of seizing fame and power in Washington.* **demagoguery** (noun).

demure (adjective)   modest or shy. *The demure heroines of Victorian fiction have given way to today's stronger, more opinionated, and more independent female characters.*

denigrate (verb)   to criticize or belittle. *The firm's new president tried to explain his plans for improving the company without seeming to denigrate the work of his predecessor.* **denigration** (noun).

depose (verb)   to remove from office, especially from a throne. *Iran was formerly ruled by a monarch called the Shah, who was deposed in 1976.*

derelict (adjective)   neglecting one's duty. *The train crash was blamed on a switchman who was derelict, having fallen asleep while on duty.* **dereliction** (noun).

derivative (adjective)   taken from a particular source. *When a person first writes poetry, her poems are apt to be derivative of whatever poetry she most enjoys reading.* **derivation** (noun), **derive** (verb).

desolate (adjective)   empty, lifeless, and deserted; hopeless, gloomy. *Robinson Crusoe was shipwrecked and had to learn to survive alone on a desolate island. The murder of her husband left Mary Lincoln desolate.* **desolation** (noun).

destitute (adjective)   very poor. *Years of rule by a dictator who stole the wealth of the country had left the people of the Philippines destitute.* **destitution** (noun).

deter (verb) to discourage from acting. *The best way to deter crime is to insure that criminals will receive swift and certain punishment.* **deterrence** (noun), **deterrent** (adjective).

detractor (noun) someone who belittles or disparages. *Neil Diamond has many detractors who consider his music boring, inane, and sentimental.* **detract** (verb).

deviate (verb) to depart from a standard or norm. *Having agreed upon a spending budget for the company, we mustn't deviate from it; if we do, we may run out of money soon.* **deviation** (noun).

devious (adjective) tricky, deceptive. *Milken's devious financial tactics were designed to enrich his firm while confusing or misleading government regulators.*

didactic (adjective) intended to teach, instructive. *The children's TV show* Sesame Street *is designed to be both entertaining and didactic.*

diffident (adjective) hesitant, reserved, shy. *Someone with a diffident personality should pursue a career that involves little public contact.* **diffidence** (noun).

diffuse (verb) to spread out, to scatter. *The red dye quickly became diffused through the water, turning it a very pale pink.* **diffusion** (noun).

digress (verb) to wander from the main path or the main topic. *My high school biology teacher loved to digress from science into personal anecdotes about his college adventures.* **digression** (noun), **digressive** (adjective).

dilatory (adjective) delaying, procrastinating. *The lawyer used various dilatory tactics, hoping that his opponent would get tired of waiting for a trial and drop the case.*

diligent (adjective) working hard and steadily. *Through diligent efforts, the townspeople were able to clear away the debris from the flood in a matter of days.* **diligence** (noun).

diminutive (adjective) unusually small, tiny. *Children are fond of Shetland ponies because their diminutive size makes them easy to ride.* **diminution** (noun).

discern (verb) to detect, notice, or observe. *I could discern the shape of a whale off the starboard bow, but it was too far away to determine its size or species.* **discernment** (noun).

159

disclose (verb) to make known; to reveal. *Election laws require candidates to disclose the names of those who contribute money to their campaigns.* **disclosure** (noun).

discomfit (verb) to frustrate, thwart, or embarrass. *Discomfited by the interviewer's unexpected question, Peter could only stammer in reply.* **discomfiture** (noun).

disconcert (verb) to confuse or embarrass. *When the hallway bells began to ring halfway through her lecture, the speaker was disconcerted and didn't know what to do.*

discredit (verb) to cause disbelief in the accuracy of some statement or the reliability of a person. *Although many people still believe in UFOs, among scientists the reports of "alien encounters" have been thoroughly discredited.*

discreet (adjective) showing good judgment in speech and behavior. *Be discreet when discussing confidential business matters—don't talk among strangers on the elevator, for example.* **discretion** (noun).

discrepancy (noun) a difference or variance between two or more things. *The discrepancies between the two witnesses' stories show that one of them must be lying.* **discrepant** (adjective).

disdain (noun) contempt, scorn. *Millionaire Leona Helmsley was disliked by many people because she treated "little people" with such disdain.* **disdain** (verb), **disdainful** (adjective).

disingenuous (adjective) pretending to be candid, simple, and frank. *When Texas billionaire H. Ross Perot ran for president, many considered his "jest plain folks" style disingenuous.*

disparage (verb) to speak disrespectfully about, to belittle. *Many political ads today both praise their own candidate and disparage his or her opponent.* **disparagement** (noun), **disparaging** (adjective).

disparity (noun) difference in quality or kind. *There is often a disparity between the kind of high-quality television people say they want and the low-brow programs they actually watch.* **disparate** (adjective).

disregard (verb) to ignore, to neglect. *If you don't write a will, when you die, your survivors may disregard your wishes about how your property should be handled.* **disregard** (noun).

disruptive (adjective)   causing disorder, interrupting. *When the senator spoke at our college, angry demonstrators picketed, heckled, and engaged in other disruptive activities.* **disrupt** (verb), **disruption** (noun).

dissemble (verb)   to pretend, to simulate. *When the police questioned her about the crime, she dissembled innocence.*

dissipate (verb)   to spread out or scatter. *The windows and doors were opened, allowing the smoke that had filled the room to dissipate.* **dissipation** (noun).

dissonance (noun)   lack of music harmony; lack of agreement between ideas. *Most modern music is characterized by dissonance, which many listeners find hard to enjoy. There is a noticeable dissonance between two common beliefs of most conservatives: their faith in unfettered free markets and their preference for traditional social values.* **dissonant** (adjective).

diverge (verb)   to move in different directions. *Frost's poem* The Road Less Traveled *tells of the choice he made when "Two roads diverged in a yellow wood."* **divergence** (noun), **divergent** (adjective).

diversion (noun)   a distraction or pastime. *During the two hours he spent in the doctor's waiting room, his hand-held computer game was a welcome diversion.* **divert** (verb).

divination (noun)   the art of predicting the future. *In ancient Greece, people wanting to know their fate would visit the priests at Delphi, supposedly skilled at divination.* **divine** (verb).

divisive (adjective)   causing disagreement or disunity. *Throughout history, race has been the most divisive issue in American society.*

divulge (verb)   to reveal. *The people who count the votes for the Oscar awards are under strict orders not to divulge the names of the winners.*

dogmatic (adjective)   holding firmly to a particular set of beliefs with little or no basis. *Believers in Marxist doctrine tend to be dogmatic, ignoring evidence that contradicts their beliefs.* **dogmatism** (noun).

dominant (adjective)   greatest in importance or power. *Turner's* Frontier Thesis *suggests that the existence of the frontier had a dominant influence on American culture.* **dominate** (verb), **domination** (noun).

dubious (adjective)   doubtful, uncertain. *Despite the chairman's attempts to convince the committee members that his plan would succeed, most of them remained dubious.* **dubiety** (noun).

durable (adjective)   long lasting. *Denim is a popular material for work clothes because it is strong and durable.*

duress (noun)   compulsion or restraint. *Fearing that the police might beat him, he confessed to the crime, not willingly but under duress.*

E

eclectic (adjective)   drawn from many sources; varied, heterogeneous. *The Mellon family art collection is an eclectic one, including works ranging from ancient Greek sculptures to modern paintings.* **eclecticism** (noun).

efficacious (adjective)   able to produce a desired effect. *Though thousands of people today are taking herbal supplements to treat depression, researchers have not yet proved them efficacious.* **efficacy** (noun).

effrontery (noun)   shameless boldness. *The sports world was shocked when a pro basketball player had the effrontery to choke his head coach during a practice session.*

effusive (adjective)   pouring forth one's emotions very freely. *Having won the Oscar for Best Actress, Sally Field gave an effusive acceptance speech in which she marveled, "You like me! You really like me!"* **effusion** (noun).

egoism (noun)   excessive concern with oneself; conceit. *Robert's egoism was so great that all he could talk about was the importance—and the brilliance—of his own opinions.* **egoistic** (adjective).

egregious (adjective)   obvious, conspicuous, flagrant. *It's hard to imagine how the editor could allow such an egregious error to appear.*

elated (adjective)   excited and happy; exultant. *When the Green Bay Packers' last, desperate pass was dropped, the elated fans of the Denver Broncos began to celebrate.* **elate** (verb), **elation** (noun).

elliptical (adjective)   very terse or concise in writing or speech; difficult to understand. *Rather than speak plainly, she hinted at her meaning through a series of nods, gestures, and elliptical half sentences.*

elusive (adjective)   hard to capture, grasp, or understand. *Though everyone thinks they know what "justice" is, when you try to define the concept precisely, it proves to be quite elusive.*

embezzle (verb) to steal money or property that has been entrusted to your care. *The church treasurer was found to have embezzled thousands of dollars by writing phony checks on the church bank account.* **embezzlement** (noun).

emend (verb) to correct. *Before the letter is mailed, please emend the two spelling errors.* **emendation** (noun).

emigrate (verb) to leave one place or country to settle elsewhere. *Millions of Irish emigrated to the New World in the wake of the great Irish famines of the 1840s.* **emigrant** (noun), **emigration** (noun).

eminent (adjective) noteworthy, famous. *Vaclav Havel was an eminent author before being elected president of the Czech Republic.* **eminence** (noun).

emissary (noun) someone who represents another. *In an effort to avoid a military showdown, Carter was sent as an emissary to Korea to negotiate a settlement.*

emollient (noun) something that softens or soothes. *She used a hand cream as an emollient on her dry, work-roughened hands.* **emollient** (adjective).

empathy (noun) imaginative sharing of the feelings, thoughts, or experiences of another. *It's easy for a parent to have empathy for the sorrow of another parent whose child has died.* **empathetic** (adjective).

empirical (adjective) based on experience or personal observation. *Although many people believe in ESP, scientists have found no empirical evidence of its existence.* **empiricism** (noun).

emulate (verb) to imitate or copy. *The British band Oasis admitted their desire to emulate their idols, the Beatles.* **emulation** (noun).

encroach (verb) to go beyond acceptable limits; to trespass. *By quietly seizing more and more authority, Robert Moses continually encroached on the powers of other government leaders.* **encroachment** (noun).

enervate (verb) to reduce the energy or strength of someone or something. *The stress of the operation left her feeling enervated for about two weeks.*

engender (verb) to produce, to cause. *Countless disagreements over the proper use of national forests have engendered feelings of hostility between ranchers and environmentalists.*

enhance (verb)   to improve in value or quality. *New kitchen appliances will enhance your house and increase the amount of money you'll make when you sell it.* **enhancement** (noun).

enmity (noun)   hatred, hostility, ill will. *Long-standing enmity, like that between the Protestants and Catholics in Northern Ireland, is difficult to overcome.*

enthrall (verb)   to enchant or charm. *When the Swedish singer Jenny Lind toured America in the nineteenth century, audiences were enthralled by her beauty and talent.*

ephemeral (adjective)   quickly disappearing; transient. *Stardom in pop music is ephemeral; most of the top acts of ten years ago are forgotten today.*

equanimity (noun)   calmness of mind, especially under stress. *Roosevelt had the gift of facing the great crises of his presidency—the Depression and the Second World War—with equanimity and even humor.*

eradicate (verb)   to destroy completely. *American society has failed to eradicate racism, although some of its worst effects have been reduced.*

espouse (verb)   to take up as a cause; to adopt. *No politician in American today will openly espouse racism, although some behave and speak in racially prejudiced ways.*

euphoric (adjective)   a feeling of extreme happiness and well-being; elation. *One often feels euphoric during the earliest days of a new love affair.* **euphoria** (noun).

evanescent (adjective)   vanishing like a vapor; fragile and transient. *As she walked by, the evanescent fragrance of her perfume reached me for just an instant.*

exacerbate (verb)   to make worse or more severe. *The roads in our town already have too much traffic; building a new shopping mall will exacerbate the problem.*

exasperate (verb)   to irritate or annoy. *Because she was trying to study, Sharon was exasperated by the yelling of her neighbors' children.*

exculpate (verb)   to free from blame or guilt. *When someone else confessed to the crime, the previous suspect was exculpated.* **exculpation** (noun), **exculpatory** (adjective).

exemplary (adjective)   worthy to serve as a model. *The Baldrige Award is given to a company with exemplary standards of excellence in products and service.* **exemplar** (noun), **exemplify** (verb).

exonerate (verb)   to free from blame. *Although Jewell was suspected at first of being involved in the bombing, later evidence exonerated him.* **exoneration** (noun), **exonerative** (adjective).

expansive (adjective)   broad and large; speaking openly and freely. *The LBJ Ranch is located on an expansive tract of land in Texas. Over dinner, she became expansive in describing her dreams for the future.*

expedite (verb)   to carry out promptly. *As the flood waters rose, the governor ordered state agencies to expedite their rescue efforts.*

expertise (noun)   skill, mastery. *The software company was eager to hire new graduates with programming expertise.*

expiate (verb)   to atone for. *The president's apology to the survivors of the notorious Tuskegee experiments was his attempt to expiate the nation's guilt over their mistreatment.* **expiation** (noun).

expropriate (verb)   to seize ownership of. *When the Communists came to power in China, they expropriated most businesses and turned them over to government-appointed managers.* **expropriation** (noun).

extant (adjective)   currently in existence. *Of the seven ancient* Wonders of the World, *only the pyramids of Egypt are still extant.*

extenuate (verb)   to make less serious. *Karen's guilt is extenuated by the fact that she was only twelve when she committed the theft.* **extenuating** (adjective), **extenuation** (noun).

extol (verb)   to greatly praise. *At the party convention, speaker after speaker rose to extol their candidate for the presidency.*

extricate (verb)   to free from a difficult or complicated situation. *Much of the humor in the TV show* I Love Lucy *comes in watching Lucy try to extricate herself from the problems she creates by fibbing or trickery.* **extricable** (adjective).

extrinsic (adjective)   not an innate part or aspect of something; external. *The high price of old baseball cards is due to extrinsic factors, such as the nostalgia felt by baseball fans for the stars of their youth, rather than the inherent beauty or value of the cards themselves.*

exuberant (adjective)   wildly joyous and enthusiastic. *As the final seconds of the game ticked away, the fans of the winning team began an exuberant celebration.* **exuberance** (noun).

F

facile (adjective)   easy; shallow or superficial. *The one-minute political commercial favors a candidate with facile opinions rather than serious, thoughtful solutions.* **facilitate** (verb), **facility** (noun).

fallacy (noun)   an error in fact or logic. *It's a fallacy to think that "natural" means "healthful"; after all, the deadly poison arsenic is completely natural.* **fallacious** (adjective).

felicitous (adjective)   pleasing, fortunate, apt. *The sudden blossoming of the dogwood trees on the morning of Matt's wedding seemed a felicitous sign of good luck.* **felicity** (noun).

feral (adjective)   wild. *The garbage dump was inhabited by a pack of feral dogs, that had escaped from their owners and become completely wild.*

fervent (adjective)   full of intense feeling; ardent, zealous. *In the days just after his religious conversion, his piety was at its most fervent.* **fervid** (adjective), **fervor** (noun).

flagrant (adjective)   obviously wrong; offensive. *Nixon was forced to resign the presidency after a series of flagrant crimes against the U.S. Constitution.* **flagrancy** (noun).

flamboyant (adjective)   very colorful, showy, or elaborate. *At Mardi Gras, partygoers compete to show off the most wild and flamboyant outfits.*

florid (adjective)   flowery, fancy; reddish. *The grand ballroom was decorated in a florid style. Years of heavy drinking had given him a florid complexion.*

foppish (adjective)   describing a man who is foolishly vain about his dress or appearance. *The foppish character of the 1890s wore bright-colored spats and a top hat; in the 1980s, he wore fancy suspenders and a shirt with a contrasting collar.* **fop** (noun).

formidable (adjective)   awesome, impressive, or frightening. *According to his plaque in the Baseball Hall of Fame, pitcher Tom Seaver turned the New York Mets "from lovable losers into formidable foes."*

fortuitous (adjective)   lucky, fortunate. *Although the mayor claimed credit for the falling crime rate, it was really caused by several fortuitous trends.*

fractious (adjective)   troublesome, unruly. *Members of the British Parliament are often fractious, shouting insults and sarcastic questions during debates.*

fragility (noun)   the quality of being easy to break; delicacy, weakness. *Because of their fragility, few stained glass windows from the early Middle Ages have survived.* **fragile** (adjective).

fraternize (verb)   to associate with on friendly terms. *Although baseball players aren't supposed to fraternize with their opponents, players from opposing teams often chat before games.* **fraternization** (noun).

frenetic (adjective)   chaotic, frantic. *The floor of the stock exchange, filled with traders shouting and gesturing, is a scene of frenetic activity.*

frivolity (noun)   lack of seriousness; levity. *The frivolity of the Mardi Gras carnival is in contrast to the seriousness of the religious season of Lent that follows.* **frivolous** (adjective).

frugal (adjective)   spending little. *With our last few dollars, we bought a frugal dinner: a loaf of bread and a piece of cheese.* **frugality** (noun).

fugitive (noun)   someone trying to escape. *When two prisoners broke out of the local jail, police were warned to keep an eye out for the fugitives.* **fugitive** (adjective).

G

gargantuan (adjective)   huge, colossal. *The building of the Great Wall of China was one of the most gargantuan projects ever undertaken.*

genial (adjective)   friendly, gracious. *A good host welcomes all visitors in a warm and genial fashion.*

grandiose (adjective)   overly large, pretentious, or showy. *Among Hitler's grandiose plans for Berlin was a gigantic building with a dome several times larger than any ever built.* **grandiosity** (noun).

gratuitous (adjective)   given freely or without cause. *Since her opinion was not requested, her harsh criticism of his singing seemed a gratuitous insult.*

gregarious (adjective)   enjoying the company of others; sociable. *Marty is naturally gregarious, a popular member of several clubs and a sought-after lunch companion.*

guileless (adjective) without cunning; innocent. *Deborah's guileless personality and complete honesty make it hard for her to survive in the harsh world of politics.*

gullible (adjective) easily fooled. *When the sweepstakes entry form arrived bearing the message, "You may be a winner!" my gullible neighbor tried to claim a prize.* **gullibility** (noun).

H

hackneyed (adjective) without originality, trite. *When someone invented the phrase, "No pain, no gain," it was clever, but now it is so commonly heard that it seems hackneyed.*

haughty (adjective) overly proud. *The fashion model strode down the runway, her hips thrust forward and a haughty expression, like a sneer, on her face.* **haughtiness** (noun).

hedonist (noun) someone who lives mainly to pursue pleasure. *Having inherited great wealth, he chose to live the life of a hedonist, traveling the world in luxury.* **hedonism** (noun), **hedonistic** (adjective).

heinous (adjective) very evil, hateful. *The massacre by Pol Pot of more than a million Cambodians is one of the twentieth century's most heinous crimes.*

hierarchy (noun) a ranking of people, things, or ideas from highest to lowest. *A cabinet secretary ranks just below the president and vice president in the hierarchy of the executive branch.* **hierarchical** (adjective).

hypocrisy (noun) a false pretense of virtue. *When the sexual misconduct of the television preacher was exposed, his followers were shocked at his hypocrisy.* **hypocritical** (adjective).

I

iconoclast (noun) someone who attacks traditional beliefs or institutions. *Comedian Dennis Miller enjoys his reputation as an iconoclast, though people in power often resent his satirical jabs.* **iconoclasm** (noun), **iconoclastic** (adjective).

idiosyncratic (adjective) peculiar to an individual; eccentric. *Cyndi Lauper sings pop music in an idiosyncratic style, mingling high-pitched whoops and squeals with throaty gurgles.* **idiosyncrasy** (noun).

idolatry (noun) the worship of a person, thing, or institution as a god. *In Communist China, Chairman Mao was the subject of idolatry; his picture was displayed everywhere, and millions of Chinese memorized his sayings.* **idolatrous** (adjective).

impartial (adjective) fair, equal, unbiased. *If a judge is not impartial, then all of her rulings are questionable.* **impartiality** (noun).

impeccable (adjective) flawless. *The crooks printed impeccable copies of the Super Bowl tickets, making it impossible to distinguish them from the real ones.*

impetuous (adjective) acting hastily or impulsively. *Ben's resignation was an impetuous act; he did it without thinking, and he soon regretted it.* **impetuosity** (noun).

impinge (verb) to encroach upon, touch, or affect. *You have a right to do whatever you want, so long as your actions don't impinge on the rights of others.*

implicit (adjective) understood without being openly expressed; implied. *Although most clubs had no rules excluding students, many had an implicit understanding that no students would be allowed to join.*

impute (verb) to credit or give responsibility to; to attribute. *Although Sarah's comments embarrassed me, I don't impute any ill will to her; I think she didn't realize what she was saying.* **imputation** (noun).

inarticulate (adjective) unable to speak or express oneself clearly and understandably. *A skilled athlete may be an inarticulate public speaker, as demonstrated by many post-game interviews.*

incisive (adjective) expressed clearly and directly. *Franklin settled the debate with a few incisive remarks that summed up the issue perfectly.*

incompatible (adjective) unable to exist together; conflicting. *Many people hold seemingly incompatible beliefs: for example, supporting the death penalty while believing in the sacredness of human life.* **incompatibility** (noun).

inconsequential (adjective) of little importance. *When the stereo was delivered, it was a different shade of gray than I expected, but the difference was inconsequential.*

incontrovertible (adjective)   impossible to question. *The fact that Sheila's fingerprints were the only ones on the murder weapon made her guilt seem incontrovertible.*

incorrigible (adjective)   impossible to manage or reform. *Lou is an incorrigible trickster, constantly playing practical jokes no matter how much his friends complain.*

incremental (adjective)   increasing gradually by small amounts. *Although the initial cost of the Medicare program was small, the incremental expenses have grown to be very large.* **increment** (noun).

incriminate (adjective)   to give evidence of guilt. *The fifth amendment to the Constitution says that no one is required to reveal information that would incriminate him in a crime.* **incriminating** (adjective).

incumbent (noun)   someone who occupies an office or position. *It is often difficult for a challenger to win a seat in Congress from the incumbent.* **incumbency** (noun), **incumbent** (adjective).

indeterminate (adjective)   not definitely known. *The college plans to enroll an indeterminate number of students; the size of the class will depend on the number of applicants and how many accept offers of admission.* **determine** (verb).

indifferent (adjective)   unconcerned, apathetic. *The mayor's small proposed budget for education suggests that he is indifferent to the needs of our schools.* **indifference** (noun).

indistinct (adjective)   unclear, uncertain. *We could see boats on the water, but in the thick morning fog their shapes were indistinct.*

indomitable (adjective)   unable to be conquered or controlled. *The world admired the indomitable spirit of Nelson Mandela; he remained courageous despite years of imprisonment.*

induce (verb)   to cause. *The doctor prescribed a medicine that was supposed to induce a lowering of the blood pressure.* **induction** (noun).

ineffable (adjective)   difficult to describe or express. *He gazed in silence at the sunrise over the Taj Mahal, his eyes reflecting an ineffable sense of wonder.*

inevitable (adjective)   unable to be avoided. *Once the Japanese attacked Pearl Harbor, American involvement in World War II was inevitable.* **inevitability** (noun).

inexorable (adjective)   unable to be deterred; relentless. *It's difficult to imagine how the mythic character of Oedipus could have avoided his evil destiny; his fate appears inexorable.*

ingenious (adjective)   showing cleverness and originality. *The Post-it note is an ingenious solution to a common problem—how to mark papers without spoiling them.* **ingenuity** (noun).

inherent (adjective)   naturally part of something. *Compromise is inherent in democracy, since everyone cannot get his way.* **inhere** (verb), **inherence** (noun).

innate (adjective)   inborn, native. *Not everyone who takes piano lessons becomes a fine musician, which shows that music requires innate talent as well as training.*

innocuous (adjective)   harmless, inoffensive. *I was surprised that Andrea took offense at such an innocuous joke.*

inoculate (verb)   to prevent a disease by infusing with a disease-causing organism. *Pasteur found he could prevent rabies by inoculating patients with the virus that causes the disease.* **inoculation** (noun).

insipid (adjective)   flavorless, uninteresting. *Most TV shows are so insipid that you can watch them while reading without missing a thing.* **insipidity** (noun).

insolence (noun)   an attitude or behavior that is bold and disrespectful. *Some feel that news reporters who shout questions at the president are behaving with insolence.* **insolent** (adjective).

insular (adjective)   narrow or isolated in attitude or viewpoint. *Americans are famous for their insular attitudes; they seem to think that nothing important has ever happened outside of their country.* **insularity** (noun).

insurgency (noun)   uprising, rebellion. *The angry townspeople had begun an insurgency bordering on downright revolution; they were collecting arms, holding secret meetings, and refusing to pay certain taxes.* **insurgent** (adjective).

integrity (noun)   honesty, uprightness; soundness, completeness. *"Honest Abe" Lincoln is considered a model of political integrity. Inspectors examined the building's support beams and foundation and found no reason to doubt its structural integrity.*

interlocutor (noun)   someone taking part in a dialogue or conversation. *Annoyed by the constant questions from someone in the crowd, the speaker challenged his interlocutor to offer a better plan.* **interlocutory** (adjective).

interlude (noun)   an interrupting period or performance. *The two most dramatic scenes in King Lear are separated, strangely, by a comic interlude starring the king's jester.*

interminable (adjective)   endless or seemingly endless. *Addressing the United Nations, Castro announced, "We will be brief"—then delivered an interminable 4-hour speech.*

intransigent (adjective)   unwilling to compromise. *Despite the mediator's attempts to suggest a fair solution, the two parties were intransigent, forcing a showdown.* **intransigence** (noun).

intrepid (adjective)   fearless and resolute. *Only an intrepid adventurer is willing to undertake the long and dangerous trip by sled to the South Pole.* **intrepidity** (noun).

intrusive (adjective)   forcing a way in without being welcome. *The legal requirement of a search warrant is supposed to protect Americans from intrusive searches by the police.* **intrude** (verb), **intrusion** (noun).

intuitive (adjective)   known directly, without apparent thought or effort. *An experienced chess player sometimes has an intuitive sense of the best move to make, even if she can't explain it.* **intuit** (verb), **intuition** (noun).

inundate (verb)   to flood; to overwhelm. *As soon as playoff tickets went on sale, eager fans inundated the box office with orders.*

invariable (adjective)   unchanging, constant. *When writing a book, it was her invariable habit to rise at 6 and work at her desk from 7 to 12.* **invariability** (noun).

inversion (noun)   a turning backwards, inside-out, or upside-down; a reversal. *Latin poetry often features inversion of word order; for example, the first line of Virgil's Aeneid: "Arms and the man I sing."* **invert** (verb), **inverted** (adjective).

inveterate (adjective)   persistent, habitual. *It's very difficult for an inveterate gambler to give up the pastime.* **inveteracy** (noun).

invigorate (verb)   to give energy to, to stimulate. *As her car climbed the mountain road, Lucinda felt invigorated by the clear air and the cool breezes.*

172

invincible (adjective)   impossible to conquer or overcome. *For three years at the height of his career, boxer Mike Tyson seemed invincible.*

inviolable (adjective)   impossible to attack or trespass upon. *In the president's remote hideaway at Camp David, guarded by the Secret Service, his privacy is, for once, inviolable.*

irrational (adjective)   unreasonable. *Charles knew that his fear of insects was irrational, but he was unable to overcome it.* **irrationality** (noun).

irresolute (adjective)   uncertain how to act, indecisive. *When McGovern first said he supported his vice presidential candidate "one thousand percent," then dropped him from the ticket, it made McGovern appear irresolute.* **irresolution** (noun).

J

jeopardize (verb)   to put in danger. *Terrorist attacks jeopardize the fragile peace in the Middle East.* **jeopardy** (noun).

juxtapose (verb)   to put side by side. *It was strange to see the old-time actor Charlton Heston and rock icon Bob Dylan juxtaposed at the awards ceremony.* **juxtaposition** (noun).

L

languid (adjective)   without energy; slow, sluggish, listless. *The hot, humid weather of late August can make anyone feel languid.* **languish** (verb), **languor** (noun).

latent (adjective)   not currently obvious or active; hidden. *Although he had committed only a single act of violence, the psychiatrist who examined him said he had probably always had a latent tendency toward violence.* **latency** (noun).

laudatory (adjective)   giving praise. *The ads for the movie are filled with laudatory comments from critics.*

lenient (adjective)   mild, soothing, or forgiving. *The judge was known for his lenient disposition; he rarely imposed long jail sentences on criminals.* **leniency** (noun).

lethargic (adjective)   lacking energy; sluggish. *Visitors to the zoo are surprised that the lions appear so lethargic, but, in the wild, lions sleep up to 18 hours a day.* **lethargy** (noun).

liability (noun)   an obligation or debt; a weakness or drawback. *The insurance company had a liability of millions of dollars after the town was destroyed by a tornado. Slowness afoot is a serious liability in an aspiring basketball player.* **liable** (adjective).

lithe (adjective)   flexible and graceful. *The ballet dancer was almost as lithe as a cat.*

longevity (noun)   length of life; durability. *The reduction in early deaths from infectious diseases is responsible for most of the increase in human longevity over the past two centuries.*

lucid (adjective)   clear and understandable. *Hawking's* A Short History of the Universe *is a lucid explanation of modern scientific theories about the origin of the universe.* **lucidity** (noun).

lurid (adjective)   shocking, gruesome. *While the serial killer was on the loose, the newspapers were filled with lurid stories about his crimes.*

M

malediction (noun)   curse. *In the fairy tale "Sleeping Beauty," the princess is trapped in a death-like sleep because of the malediction uttered by an angry witch.*

malevolence (noun)   hatred, ill will. *Critics say that Iago, the villain in Shakespeare's* Othello, *seems to exhibit malevolence with no real cause.* **malevolent** (adjective).

malinger (verb)   to pretend incapacity or illness to avoid a duty or work. *During the labor dispute, hundreds of employees malingered, forcing the company to slow production and costing it millions in profits.*

malleable (adjective)   able to be changed, shaped, or formed by outside pressures. *Gold is a very useful metal because it is so malleable. A child's personality is malleable and deeply influenced by the things her parents say and do.* **malleability** (noun).

mandate (noun)   order, command. *The new policy on gays in the military went into effect as soon as the president issued his mandate about it.* **mandate** (verb), **mandatory** (adjective).

174

maturation (noun)   the process of becoming fully grown or developed. *Free markets in the former Communist nations are likely to operate smoothly only after a long period of maturation.* **mature** (adjective and verb), **maturity** (noun).

mediate (verb)   to act to reconcile differences between two parties. *During the baseball strike, both the players and the club owners were willing to have the president mediate the dispute.* **mediation** (noun).

mediocrity (noun)   the state of being middling or poor in quality. *The New York Mets, finished in ninth place in 1968, won the world's championship in 1969, going from horrible to great in a single year and skipping mediocrity.* **mediocre** (adjective).

mercurial (adjective)   changing quickly and unpredictably. *The mercurial personality of Robin Williams, with his many voices and styles, made him perfect for the role of the ever-changing genie in* Aladdin.

meticulous (adjective)   very careful with details. *Repairing watches calls for a craftsperson who is patient and meticulous.*

mimicry (noun)   imitation, aping. *The continued popularity of Elvis Presley has given rise to a class of entertainers who make a living through mimicry of "The King."* **mimic** (noun and verb).

misconception (noun)   a mistaken idea. *Columbus sailed west with the misconception that he would reach the shores of Asia.* **misconceive** (verb).

mitigate (verb)   to make less severe; to relieve. *Wallace certainly committed the assault, but the verbal abuse he'd received helps to explain his behavior and somewhat mitigates his guilt.* **mitigation** (noun).

modicum (noun)   a small amount. *The plan for your new business is well designed; with a modicum of luck, you should be successful.*

mollify (verb)   to soothe or calm; to appease. *Carla tried to mollify the angry customer by promising him a full refund.*

morose (adjective)   gloomy, sullen. *After Chuck's girlfriend dumped him, he lay around the house for a couple of days, feeling morose.*

mundane (adjective)   everyday, ordinary, commonplace. *Moviegoers in the 1930s liked the glamorous films of Fred Astaire because they provided an escape from the mundane problems of life during the Great Depression.*

munificent (adjective)   very generous; lavish. *Ted Turner's billion-dollar donation to the United Nations is probably the most munificent act of charity in history.* **munificence** (noun).

mutable (adjective)   likely to change. *A politician's reputation can be highly mutable, as seen in the case of Harry Truman—mocked during his lifetime, revered afterward.*

N

narcissistic (adjective)   showing excessive love for oneself; egoistic. *Andre's room, decorated with photos of himself and the sports trophies he has won, suggests a narcissistic personality.* **narcissism** (noun).

nocturnal (adjective)   of the night; active at night. *Travelers on the Underground Railroad escaped from slavery to the North by a series of nocturnal flights. The eyes of nocturnal animals must be sensitive in dim light.*

nonchalant (adjective)   appearing to be unconcerned. *Unlike the other players on the football team, who pumped their fists when their names were announced, John ran on the field with a nonchalant wave.* **nonchalance** (noun).

nondescript (adjective)   without distinctive qualities; drab. *The bank robber's clothes were nondescript; none of the witnesses could remember their color or style.*

notorious (adjective)   famous, especially for evil actions or qualities. *Warner Brothers produced a series of movies about notorious gangsters such as John Dillinger and Al Capone.* **notoriety** (noun).

novice (noun)   beginner, tyro. *Lifting your head before you finish your swing is a typical mistake committed by the novice at golf.*

nuance (noun)   a subtle difference or quality. *At first glance, Monet's paintings of water lilies all look much alike, but the more you study them, the more you appreciate the nuances of color and shading that distinguish them.*

nurture (verb)   to nourish or help to grow. *The money given by the National Endowment for the Arts helps nurture local arts organizations throughout the country.* **nurture** (noun).

o

obdurate (adjective) unwilling to change; stubborn, inflexible. *Despite the many pleas he received, the governor was obdurate in his refusal to grant clemency to the convicted murderer.*

objective (adjective) dealing with observable facts rather than opinions or interpretations. *When a legal case involves a shocking crime, it may be hard for a judge to remain objective in his rulings.*

oblivious (adjective) unaware, unconscious. *Karen practiced her oboe with complete concentration, oblivious to the noise and activity around her.* **oblivion** (noun), **obliviousness** (noun).

obscure (adjective) little known; hard to understand. *Mendel was an obscure monk until decades after his death, when his scientific work was finally discovered. Most people find the writings of James Joyce obscure; hence the popularity of books that explain his books.* **obscure** (verb), **obscurity** (noun).

obsessive (adjective) haunted or preoccupied by an idea or feeling. *His concern with cleanliness became so obsessive that he washed his hands twenty times every day.* **obsess** (verb), **obsession** (noun).

obsolete (adjective) no longer current; old-fashioned. *W. H. Auden said that his ideal landscape would include water wheels, wooden grain mills, and other forms of obsolete machinery.* **obsolescence** (noun).

obstinate (adjective) stubborn, unyielding. *Despite years of effort, the problem of drug abuse remains obstinate.* **obstinacy** (noun).

obtrusive (adjective) overly prominent. *Philip should sing more softly; his bass is so obtrusive that the other singers can barely be heard.* **obtrude** (verb), **obtrusion** (noun).

ominous (adjective) foretelling evil. *Ominous black clouds gathered on the horizon, for a violent storm was fast approaching.* **omen** (noun).

onerous (adjective) heavy, burdensome. *The hero Hercules was ordered to clean the Augean Stables, one of several onerous tasks known as "the labors of Hercules."* **onus** (noun).

opportunistic (adjective) eagerly seizing chances as they arise. *When Princess Diana died suddenly, opportunistic publishers quickly released books about her life and death.* **opportunism** (noun).

opulent (adjective)   rich, lavish. *The mansion of newspaper tycoon Hearst is famous for its opulent decor.* **opulence** (noun).

ornate (adjective)   highly decorated, elaborate. *Baroque architecture is often highly ornate, featuring surfaces covered with carving, sinuous curves, and painted scenes.*

ostentatious (adjective)   overly showy, pretentious. *To show off his wealth, the millionaire threw an ostentatious party featuring a full orchestra, a famous singer, and tens of thousands of dollars worth of food.*

ostracize (verb)   to exclude from a group. *In Biblical times, those who suffered from the disease of leprosy were ostracized and forced to live alone.* **ostracism** (noun).

P

pallid (adjective)   pale; dull. *Working all day in the coal mine had given him a pallid complexion. The new musical offers only pallid entertainment: the music is lifeless, the acting dull, the story absurd.*

parched (adjective)   very dry; thirsty. *After two months without rain, the crops were shriveled and parched by the sun.* **parch** (verb).

pariah (noun)   outcast. *Accused of robbery, he became a pariah; his neighbors stopped talking to him, and people he'd considered friends no longer called.*

partisan (adjective)   reflecting strong allegiance to a particular party or cause. *The vote on the president's budget was strictly partisan: every member of the president's party voted yes, and all others voted no.* **partisan** (noun).

pathology (noun)   disease or the study of disease; extreme abnormality. *Some people believe that high rates of crime are symptoms of an underlying social pathology.* **pathological** (adjective).

pellucid (adjective)   very clear; transparent; easy to understand. *The water in the mountain stream was cold and pellucid. Thanks to the professor's pellucid explanation, I finally understand relativity theory.*

penitent (adjective)   feeling sorry for past crimes or sins. *Having grown penitent, he wrote a long letter of apology, asking forgiveness.*

penurious (adjective)   extremely frugal; stingy. *Haunted by memories of poverty, he lived in penurious fashion, driving a twelve-year-old car and wearing only the cheapest clothes.* **penury** (noun).

perceptive (adjective)   quick to notice, observant. *With his perceptive intelligence, Holmes was the first to notice the importance of this clue.* **perceptible** (adjective), **perception** (noun).

perfidious (adjective)   disloyal, treacherous. *Although he was one of the most talented generals of the American Revolution, Benedict Arnold is remembered today as a perfidious betrayer of his country.* **perfidy** (noun).

perfunctory (adjective)   unenthusiastic, routine, or mechanical. *When the play opened, the actors sparkled, but by the thousandth night their performance had become perfunctory.*

permeate (verb)   to spread through or penetrate. *Little by little, the smell of gas from the broken pipe permeated the house.*

persevere (adjective)   to continue despite difficulties. *Although several of her teammates dropped out of the marathon, Laura persevered.* **perseverance** (noun).

perspicacity (noun)   keenness of observation or understanding. *Journalist Murray Kempton was famous for the perspicacity of his comments on social and political issues.* **perspicacious** (adjective).

peruse (verb)   to examine or study. *Mary-Jo perused the contract carefully before she signed it.* **perusal** (noun).

pervasive (adjective)   spreading throughout. *As news of the disaster reached the town, a pervasive sense of gloom could be felt.* **pervade** (verb).

phlegmatic (adjective)   sluggish and unemotional in temperament. *It was surprising to see Tom, who is normally so phlegmatic, acting excited.*

placate (verb)   to soothe or appease. *The waiter tried to placate the angry customer with the offer of a free dessert.* **placatory** (adjective).

plastic (adjective)   able to be molded or reshaped. *Because it is highly plastic, clay is an easy material for beginning sculptors to use.*

plausible (adjective)   apparently believable. *The idea that a widespread conspiracy to kill President Kennedy has been kept secret for over thirty years hardly seems plausible.* **plausibility** (noun).

polarize (adjective)   to separate into opposing groups or forces. *For years, the abortion debate polarized the American people, with many people voicing extreme views and few trying to find a middle ground.* **polarization** (noun).

portend (verb)   to indicate a future event; to forebode. *According to folklore, a red sky at dawn portends a day of stormy weather.*

potentate (noun)   a powerful ruler. *Before the Russian Revolution, the Tsar was one of the last hereditary potentates of Europe.*

pragmatism (noun)   a belief in approaching problems through practical rather than theoretical means. *Roosevelt's approach toward the Great Depression was based on pragmatism: "Try something," he said; "If it doesn't work, try something else."* **pragmatic** (adjective).

preamble (noun)   an introductory statement. *The preamble to the Constitution begins with the famous words, "We the people of the United States of America . . ."*

precocious (adjective)   mature at an unusually early age. *Picasso was so precocious as an artist that, at nine, he is said to have painted far better pictures than his teacher.* **precocity** (noun).

predatory (adjective)   living by killing and eating other animals; exploiting others for personal gain. *The tiger is the largest predatory animal native to Asia. Microsoft has been accused of predatory business practices that prevent other software companies from competing with them.* **predation** (noun), **predator** (noun).

predilection (noun)   a liking or preference. *To relax from his presidential duties, Kennedy had a predilection for spy novels featuring James Bond.*

predominant (adjective)   greatest in numbers or influence. *Although hundreds of religions are practiced in India, the predominant faith is Hinduism.* **predominance** (noun), **predominate** (verb).

prepossessing (adjective)   attractive. *Smart, lovely, and talented, she has all the prepossessing qualities that mark a potential movie star.*

presumptuous (adjective)   going beyond the limits of courtesy or appropriateness. *The senator winced when the presumptuous young staffer addressed him as "Chuck."* **presume** (verb), **presumption** (noun).

pretentious (adjective)   claiming excessive value or importance. *For a shoe salesman to call himself a "Personal Foot Apparel Consultant" seems awfully pretentious.* **pretension** (noun).

180

procrastinate (verb)   to put off, to delay. *If you habitually procrastinate, try this technique: never touch a piece of paper without either filing it, responding to it, or throwing it out.* **procrastination** (noun).

profane (adjective)   impure, unholy. *It seems inappropriate to have such profane activities as roller blading and disco dancing in a church.* **profane** (verb), **profanity** (noun).

proficient (adjective)   skillful, adept. *A proficient artist, Louise quickly and accurately sketched the scene.* **proficiency** (noun).

proliferate (verb)   to increase or multiply. *Over the past 15 years, high-tech companies have proliferated in northern California, Massachusetts, and other regions.* **proliferation** (noun).

prolific (adjective)   producing many offspring or creations. *With more than three hundred books to his credit, Isaac Asimov was one of the most prolific writers of all time.*

prominence (noun)   the quality of standing out; fame. *Kennedy's victory in the West Virginia primary gave him a position of prominence among the Democratic candidates for president.* **prominent** (adjective).

promulgate (verb)   to make public, to declare. *Lincoln signed the proclamation that freed the slaves in 1862, but he waited several months to promulgate it.*

propagate (verb)   to cause to grow; to foster. *John Smithson's will left his fortune for the founding of an institution to propagate knowledge, without saying whether that meant a university, a library, or a museum.* **propagation** (noun).

propriety (noun)   appropriateness. *Some people had doubts about the propriety of Clinton's discussing his underwear on MTV.*

prosaic (adjective)   everyday, ordinary, dull. *"Paul's Case" tells the story of a boy who longs to escape from the prosaic life of a clerk into a world of wealth, glamour, and beauty.*

protagonist (noun)   the main character in a story or play; the main supporter of an idea. *Leopold Bloom is the protagonist of James Joyce's great novel*, Ulysses.

provocative (adjective)   likely to stimulate emotions, ideas, or controversy. *The demonstrators began chanting obscenities, a provocative act that they hoped would cause the police to lose control.* **provoke** (verb), **provocation** (noun).

proximity (noun) closeness, nearness. *Neighborhood residents were angry over the proximity of the sewage plant to the local school.* **proximate** (adjective).

prudent (adjective) wise, cautious, and practical. *A prudent investor will avoid putting all of her money into any single investment.* **prudence** (noun), **prudential** (adjective).

pugnacious (adjective) combative, bellicose, truculent; ready to fight. *Ty Cobb, the pugnacious outfielder for the Detroit Tigers, got into more than his fair share of brawls, both on and off the field.* **pugnacity** (noun).

punctilious (adjective) very concerned about proper forms of behavior and manners. *A punctilious dresser like James would rather skip the party altogether than wear the wrong color tie.* **punctilio** (noun).

pundit (noun) someone who offers opinions in an authoritative style. *The Sunday afternoon talk shows are filled with pundits, each with his or her own theory about the week's political news.*

punitive (adjective) inflicting punishment. *The jury awarded the plaintiff one million dollars in punitive damages, hoping to teach the defendant a lesson.*

purify (verb) to make pure, clean, or perfect. *The new plant is supposed to purify the drinking water provided to everyone in the nearby towns.* **purification** (noun).

Q

quell (verb) to quiet, to suppress. *It took a huge number of police to quell the rioting.*

querulous (adjective) complaining, whining. *The nursing home attendant needed a lot of patience to care for the three querulous, unpleasant residents on his floor.*

R

rancorous (adjective) expressing bitter hostility. *Many Americans are disgusted by recent political campaigns, which seem more rancorous than ever before.* **rancor** (noun).

182

rationale (noun)   an underlying reason or explanation. *At first, it seemed strange that several camera companies would freely share their newest technology; but their rationale was that offering one new style of film would benefit them all.*

raze (verb)   to completely destroy; demolish. *The old Coliseum building will soon be razed to make room for a new hotel.*

reciprocate (verb)   to make a return for something. *If you'll baby-sit for my kids tonight, I'll reciprocate by taking care of yours tomorrow.* **reciprocity** (noun).

reclusive (adjective)   withdrawn from society. *During the last years of her life, actress Greta Garbo led a reclusive existence, rarely appearing in public.* **recluse** (noun).

reconcile (verb)   to make consistent or harmonious. *Roosevelt's greatness as a leader can be seen in his ability to reconcile the demands and values of the varied groups that supported him.* **reconciliation** (noun).

recriminate (verb)   to accuse, often in response to an accusation. *Divorce proceedings sometimes become bitter, as the two parties recriminate each other over the causes of the breakup.* **recrimination** (noun), **recriminatory** (adjective).

recuperate (verb)   to regain health after an illness. *Although she left the hospital two days after her operation, it took her a few weeks to fully recuperate.* **recuperation** (noun), **recuperative** (adjective).

redoubtable (adjective)   inspiring respect, awe, or fear. *Johnson's knowledge, experience, and personal clout made him a redoubtable political opponent.*

refurbish (verb)   to fix up; renovate. *It took three days' work by a team of carpenters, painters, and decorators to completely refurbish the apartment.*

refute (adjective)   to prove false. *The company invited reporters to visit their plant in an effort to refute the charges of unsafe working conditions.* **refutation** (noun).

relevance (noun)   connection to the matter at hand; pertinence. *Testimony in a criminal trial may be admitted only if it has clear relevance to the question of guilt or innocence.* **relevant** (adjective).

remedial (adjective)   serving to remedy, cure, or correct some condition. *Affirmative action can be justified as a remedial step to help minority members overcome the effects of past discrimination.* **remediation** (noun), **remedy** (verb).

remorse (noun)   a painful sense of guilt over wrongdoing. *In Poe's story "The Tell-Tale Heart," a murderer is driven insane by remorse over his crime.* **remorseful** (adjective).

remuneration (noun)   pay. *In a civil lawsuit, the attorney often receives part of the financial settlement as his or her remuneration.* **remunerate** (verb), **remunerative** (adjective).

renovate (verb)   to renew by repairing or rebuilding. *The television program "This Old House" shows how skilled craftspeople renovate houses.* **renovation** (noun).

renunciation (noun)   the act of rejecting or refusing something. *King Edward VII's renunciation of the British throne was caused by his desire to marry an American divorcee, something he couldn't do as king.* **renounce** (verb).

replete (adjective)   filled abundantly. *Graham's book is replete with wonderful stories about the famous people she has known.*

reprehensible (adjective)   deserving criticism or censure. *Although Pete Rose's misdeeds were reprehensible, not all fans agree that he deserves to be excluded from the Baseball Hall of Fame.* **reprehend** (verb), **reprehension** (noun).

repudiate (verb)   to reject, to renounce. *After it became known that Duke had been a leader of the Ku Klux Klan, most Republican leaders repudiated him.* **repudiation** (noun).

reputable (adjective)   having a good reputation; respected. *Find a reputable auto mechanic by asking your friends for recommendations based on their own experiences.* **reputation** (noun), **repute** (noun).

resilient (adjective)   able to recover from difficulty. *A pro athlete must be resilient, able to lose a game one day and come back the next with confidence and enthusiasm.* **resilience** (adjective).

resplendent (adjective)   glowing, shining. *In late December, midtown New York is resplendent with holiday lights and decorations.* **resplendence** (noun).

responsive (adjective) reacting quickly and appropriately. *The new director of the Internal Revenue Service has promised to make the agency more responsive to public complaints.* **respond** (verb), **response** (noun).

restitution (noun) return of something to its original owner; repayment. *Some Native American leaders are demanding that the U.S. government make restitution for the lands taken from them by white settlers.*

revere (verb) to admire deeply, to honor. *Millions of people around the world revered Mother Teresa for her saintly generosity.* **reverence** (noun), **reverent** (adjective).

rhapsodize (verb) to praise in a wildly emotional way. *That critic is such a huge fan of Toni Morrison that she will surely rhapsodize over the writer's next novel.* **rhapsodic** (adjective).

s

sagacious (adjective) discerning, wise. *Only a leader as sagacious as Nelson Mandela could have united South Africa so successfully and peacefully.* **sagacity** (noun).

salvage (verb) to save from wreck or ruin. *After the earthquake destroyed her home, she was able to salvage only a few of her belongings.* **salvage** (noun), **salvageable** (adjective).

sanctimonious (adjective) showing false or excessive piety. *The sanctimonious prayers of the TV preacher were interspersed with requests that the viewers send him money.* **sanctimony** (noun).

scapegoat (noun) someone who bears the blame for others' acts; someone hated for no apparent reason. *Although Buckner's error was only one reason the Red Sox lost, many fans made him the scapegoat, booing him mercilessly.*

scrupulous (adjective) acting with extreme care; painstaking. *Disney theme parks are famous for their scrupulous attention to small details.* **scruple** (noun).

scrutinize (verb) to study closely. *The lawyer scrutinized the contract, searching for any sentence that could pose a risk for her client.* **scrutiny** (noun).

secrete (verb) to emit; to hide. *Glands in the mouth secrete saliva, a liquid that helps in digestion. The jewel thieves secreted the necklace in a tin box buried underground.*

sedentary (adjective)   requiring much sitting. *When Officer Samson was given a desk job, she had trouble getting used to sedentary work after years on the street.*

sequential (adjective)   arranged in an order or series. *The courses for the chemistry major are sequential; you must take them in the order, since each course builds on the previous ones.* **sequence** (noun).

serendipity (noun)   the ability to make lucky accidental discoveries. *Great inventions sometimes come about through deliberate research and hard work, sometimes through pure serendipity.* **serendipitous** (adjective).

servile (adjective)   like a slave or servant; submissive. *The tycoon demanded that his underlings behave in a servile manner, agreeing quickly with everything he said.* **servility** (noun).

simulated (adjective)   imitating something else; artificial. *High-quality simulated gems must be examined under a magnifying glass to be distinguished from real ones.* **simulate** (verb), **simulation** (noun).

solace (verb)   to comfort or console. *There was little the rabbi could say to solace the husband after his wife's death.* **solace** (noun).

spontaneous (adjective)   happening without plan or outside cause. *When the news of Kennedy's assassination broke, people everywhere gathered in a spontaneous effort to share their shock and grief.* **spontaneity** (noun).

spurious (adjective)   false, fake. *The so-called Piltdown Man, supposed to be the fossil of a primitive human, turned out to be spurious, although who created the hoax is still uncertain.*

squander (verb)   to use up carelessly, to waste. *Those who had made donations to the charity were outraged to learn that its director had squandered millions on fancy dinners and first-class travel.*

stagnate (verb)   to become stale through lack of movement or change. *Having had no contact with the outside world for generations, Japan's culture gradually stagnated.* **stagnant** (adjective), **stagnation** (noun).

staid (adjective)   sedate, serious, and grave. *This college is no "party school"; the students all work hard, and the campus has a reputation for being staid.*

stimulus (noun)   something that excites a response or provokes an action. *The arrival of merchants and missionaries from the West provided a stimulus for change in Japanese society.* **stimulate** (verb).

stoic (adjective)   showing little feeling, even in response to pain or sorrow. *A soldier must respond to the death of his comrades in stoic fashion, since the fighting will not stop for his grief.* **stoicism** (noun).

strenuous (adjective)   requiring energy and strength. *Hiking in the foothills of the Rockies is fairly easy, but climbing the higher peaks can be strenuous.*

submissive (adjective)   accepting the will of others; humble, compliant. *At the end of Ibsen's play* A Doll's House, *Nora leaves her husband and abandons the role of submissive housewife.*

substantiated (adjective)   verified or supported by evidence. *The charge that Nixon had helped to cover up crimes was substantiated by his comments about it on a series of audio tapes.* **substantiate** (verb), **substantiation** (noun).

sully (verb)   to soil, stain, or defile. *Nixon's misdeeds as president did much to sully the reputation of the American government.*

superficial (adjective)   on the surface only; without depth or substance. *Her wound was superficial and required only a light bandage. His superficial attractiveness hides the fact that his personality is lifeless and his mind is dull.* **superficiality** (noun).

superfluous (adjective)   more than is needed, excessive. *Once you've won the debate, don't keep talking; superfluous arguments will only bore and annoy the audience.*

suppress (verb)   to put down or restrain. *As soon as the unrest began, thousands of helmeted police were sent into the streets to suppress the riots.* **suppression** (noun).

surfeit (noun)   an excess. *Most American families have a surfeit of food and drink on Thanksgiving Day.* **surfeit** (verb).

surreptitious (adjective)   done in secret. *Because Iraq has avoided weapons inspections, many believe it has a surreptitious weapons development program.*

surrogate (noun)   a substitute. *When the congressman died in office, his wife was named to serve the rest of his term as a surrogate.* **surrogate** (adjective).

sustain (verb)   to keep up, to continue; to support. *Because of fatigue, he was unable to sustain the effort needed to finish the marathon.*

PETERSON'S
getting you there

T

tactile (adjective)   relating to the sense of touch. *The thick brush strokes and gobs of color give the paintings of Van Gogh a strongly tactile quality.* **tactility** (noun).

talisman (noun)   an object supposed to have magical effects or qualities. *Superstitious people sometimes carry a rabbit's foot, a lucky coin, or some other talisman.*

tangential (adjective)   touching lightly; only slightly connected or related. *Having enrolled in a class on African-American history, the students found the teacher's stories about his travels in South America only of tangential interest.* **tangent** (noun).

tedium (noun)   boredom. *For most people, watching the Weather Channel for 24 hours would be sheer tedium.* **tedious** (adjective).

temerity (noun)   boldness, rashness, excessive daring. *Only someone who didn't understand the danger would have the temerity to try to climb Everest without a guide.* **temerarious** (adjective).

temperance (noun)   moderation or restraint in feelings and behavior. *Most professional athletes practice temperance in their personal habits; too much eating or drinking, they know, can harm their performance.* **temperate** (adjective).

tenacious (adjective)   clinging, sticky, or persistent. *Tenacious in pursuit of her goal, she applied for the grant unsuccessfully four times before it was finally approved.* **tenacity** (noun).

tentative (adjective)   subject to change; uncertain. *A firm schedule has not been established, but the Super Bowl in 2005 has been given the tentative date of February 6.*

terminate (verb)   to end, to close. *The Olympic Games terminate with a grand ceremony attended by athletes from every participating country.* **terminal** (noun), **termination** (noun).

terrestrial (adjective)   of the Earth. *The movie* Close Encounters of the Third Kind *tells the story of the first contact between beings from outer space and terrestrial humans.*

therapeutic (adjective)   curing or helping to cure. *Hot-water spas were popular in the nineteenth century among the sickly, who believed that soaking in the water had therapeutic effects.* **therapy** (noun).

188

timorous (adjective)   fearful, timid. *The cowardly lion approached the throne of the wizard with a timorous look on his face.*

toady (noun)   someone who flatters a superior in hopes of gaining favor; a sycophant. *"I can't stand a toady!" declared the movie mogul. "Give me someone who'll tell me the truth—even if it costs him his job!"* **toady** (verb).

tolerant (adjective)   accepting, enduring. *San Franciscans have a tolerant attitude about lifestyles: "Live and let live" seems to be their motto.* **tolerate** (verb), **toleration** (noun).

toxin (noun)   poison. *DDT is a powerful toxin once used to kill insects but now banned in the U.S. because of the risk it poses to human life.* **toxic** (adjective).

tranquillity (noun)   freedom from disturbance or turmoil; calm. *She moved from New York City to rural Vermont seeking the tranquillity of country life.* **tranquil** (adjective).

transgress (verb)   to go past limits; to violate. *If Iraq has developed biological weapons, then it has transgressed the United Nation's rules against weapons of mass destruction.* **transgression** (noun).

transient (adjective)   passing quickly. *Long-term visitors to this hotel pay at a different rate than transient guests who stay for just a day or two.* **transience** (noun).

transitory (adjective)   quickly passing. *Public moods tend to be transitory; people may be anxious and angry one month, but relatively content and optimistic the next.* **transition** (noun).

translucent (adjective)   letting some light pass through. *Blocks of translucent glass let daylight into the room while maintaining privacy.*

transmute (verb)   to change in form or substance. *In the Middle Ages, the alchemists tried to discover ways to transmute metals such as iron into gold.* **transmutation** (noun).

treacherous (adjective)   untrustworthy or disloyal; dangerous or unreliable. *Nazi Germany proved to be a treacherous ally, first signing a peace pact with the Soviet Union, then invading. Be careful crossing the rope bridge; parts are badly frayed and treacherous.* **treachery** (noun).

tremulous (adjective)   trembling or shaking; timid or fearful. *Never having spoken in public before, he began his speech in a tremulous, hesitant voice.*

trite (adjective)   boring because of over-familiarity; hackneyed. *Her letters were filled with trite expressions, like "All's well that ends well" and "So far so good."*

truculent (adjective)   aggressive, hostile, belligerent. *Hitler's truculent behavior in demanding more territory for Germany made it clear that war was inevitable.* **truculence** (noun).

truncate (verb)   to cut off. *The manuscript of the play appeared truncated; the last page ended in the middle of a scene, halfway through the first act.*

turbulent (adjective)   agitated or disturbed. *The night before the championship match, Martina was unable to sleep, her mind turbulent with fears and hopes.* **turbulence** (noun).

U

unheralded (adjective)   little known, unexpected. *In a year of big-budget, much-hyped mega-movies, this unheralded foreign film has surprised everyone with its popularity.*

unpalatable (adjective)   distasteful, unpleasant. *Although I agree with the candidate on many issues, I can't vote for her, because I find her position on capital punishment unpalatable.*

unparalleled (adjective)   with no equal; unique. *Tiger Woods's victory in the Masters golf tournament by a full twelve strokes was an unparalleled accomplishment.*

unstinting (adjective)   giving freely and generously. *Eleanor Roosevelt was much admired for her unstinting efforts on behalf of the poor.*

untenable (adjective)   impossible to defend. *The theory that this painting is a genuine Van Gogh became untenable when the artist who actually painted it came forth.*

untimely (adjective)   out of the natural or proper time. *The untimely death of a youthful Princess Diana seemed far more tragic than Mother Teresa's death of old age.*

unyielding (adjective)   firm, resolute, obdurate. *Despite criticism, Cuomo was unyielding in his opposition to capital punishment; he vetoed several death penalty bills as governor.*

usurper (noun)   someone who takes a place or possession without the right to do so. *Kennedy's most devoted followers tended to regard later presidents as usurpers, holding the office they felt he or his brothers should have held.* **usurp** (verb), **usurpation** (noun).

utilitarian (adjective)   purely of practical benefit. *The design of the Model T car was simple and utilitarian, lacking the luxuries found in later models.*

utopia (noun)   an imaginary, perfect society. *Those who founded the Oneida community dreamed that it could be a kind of utopia—a prosperous state with complete freedom and harmony.* **utopian** (adjective).

V

validate (verb)   to officially approve or confirm. *The election of the president is validated when the members of the Electoral College meet to confirm the choice of the voters.* **valid** (adjective), **validity** (noun).

variegated (adjective)   spotted with different colors. *The brilliant, variegated appearance of butterflies makes them popular among collectors.* **variegation** (noun).

venerate (verb)   to admire or honor. *In Communist China, Chairman Mao Zedong was venerated as an almost god-like figure.* **venerable** (adjective), **veneration** (noun).

verdant (adjective)   green with plant life. *Southern England is famous for its verdant countryside filled with gardens and small farms.* **verdancy** (noun).

vestige (noun)   a trace or remainder. *Today's tiny Sherwood Forest is the last vestige of a woodland that once covered most of England.* **vestigial** (adjective).

vex (verb)   to irritate, annoy, or trouble. *Unproven for generations, Fermat's last theorem was one of the most famous, and most vexing, of all mathematical puzzles.* **vexation** (noun).

vicarious (adjective)   experienced through someone else's actions by way of the imagination. *Great literature broadens our minds by giving us vicarious participation in the lives of other people.*

vindicate (verb)   to confirm, justify, or defend. *Lincoln's Gettysburg Address was intended to vindicate the objectives of the Union in the Civil War.*

PETERSON'S
getting you there

virtuoso (noun)   someone very skilled, especially in an art. *Vladimir Horowitz was one of the great piano virtuosos of the twentieth century.* **virtuosity** (noun).

vivacious (adjective)   lively, sprightly. *The role of Maria in* The Sound of Music *is usually played by a charming, vivacious young actress.* **vivacity** (noun).

volatile (adjective)   quickly changing; fleeting, transitory; prone to violence. *Public opinion is notoriously volatile; a politician who is very popular one month may be voted out of office the next.* **volatility** (noun).

W

whimsical (adjective)   based on a capricious, carefree, or sudden impulse or idea; fanciful, playful. *Dave Barry's* Book of Bad Songs *is filled with the kind of goofy jokes that are typical of his whimsical sense of humor.* **whim** (noun).

Z

zealous (adjective)   filled with eagerness, fervor, or passion. *A crowd of the candidate's most zealous supporters greeted her at the airport with banners, signs, and a marching band.* **zeal** (noun), **zealot** (noun), **zealotry** (noun).

Chapter

6

The SAT Writing Section— Where Grammar Rules Rule

Lucky you—you get to be one the first to take the SAT's Writing Test. Congratulations! Although the prospect of having to take yet another section of the test may not be thrilling, you can approach the latest addition to the SAT with confidence and style. This chapter will tell you what to expect on the Writing section and help you prepare for each type of question you'll encounter.

Words, Words, Words: What's in the Writing Section

As mentioned earlier in the book, the Writing section comes in two parts. One part is the essay, which will ask you to take a position on an issue of general interest and write an essay supporting your viewpoint with examples. The second part consists of three different types of multiple-choice questions:

1. Identifying Sentence Errors (ISE)

2. Improving Sentences

3. Improving Paragraphs

The first three types of questions—identifying sentence errors, improving sentences, and improving paragraphs—are multiple-choice questions that test your knowledge of Standard Written English. To answer these questions, you will have to identify grammatical errors and recognize how to improve sentences and paragraphs.

Both the multiple-choice questions and the essay, will assess your command of English grammar, usage, and word choice. If your immediate reaction to the word grammar is to run away and hide, don't panic. You can take comfort in the fact that only certain types of errors appear repeatedly throughout every test and that you won't be expected to know every rule of grammar in the book. Check out the chart below:

The 13 Deadly Rules of Grammar, Usage, and Word Choice

1. Subject-Verb Agreement

2. Verb Tenses

3. Noun Agreement

4. Pronoun Agreement, Case, and Reference

5. Using Modifiers

6. Homonyms/Easily Confused Words

7. Logical Comparison and Parallel Structure

8. Double Negatives

9. Coordination and Subordination

10. Run-on Sentences

11. Sentence Fragments

12. Eliminating Wordiness

13. Using Idioms and Correct Diction

The good news is that these 13 rules are by far the ones most frequently tested, and the even better news is that you will not be required to define any grammatical rules on the test. You will simply be asked to identify when errors occur and which of the given choices best fixes the errors. If this still sounds overwhelming, don't worry—the process will become clearer to you as we examine each type of question on the test. The truth is, you probably already know more than you think about how to answer the Writing section questions.

> **Note**
>
> As with the Math and Critical Reading sections, the Writing section will be scored on a scale of 200–800. Your ultimate score for the Writing section (between 200 and 800) will be based on two subscores: one for the multiple-choice section on a scale of 20–80 and one for the essay section based on a scale of 2–12. We'll further discuss how the essays are scored in the essay section at the end of this chapter.

Later in this chapter, we will take a closer look at each of the question types you'll see in the Writing section and offer strategies for the real thing during test time. For example, certain types of grammatical errors appear more frequently in certain sections of the test, like errors in subject-verb agreement in the Identifying Sentence Errors section. To give you a good grounding in the types of errors that commonly appear in each section of the test, we will discuss each of the 13 Deadly Rules as we discuss strategies you can use to tackle specific types of question. A chart highlighting the rules of grammar, usage, and word choice explained in each section appears at the beginning of every section.

However, before scrutinizing (how's that for an SAT word?) each type of Writing section question, let's quickly review the 13 Deadly Rules. Although this chapter focuses on strategies, familiarizing yourself with the commonly tested rules of grammar, usage, and word choice will vastly improve your scores in the Writing section and will decrease your anxiety about learning grammar period. Remember, words can't hurt you!

A Quick Overview of the Most Commonly Tested Rules

Here's a quick run-down of the 13 Deadly Rules of grammar, usage, and word choice most often found on the Writing test. While 13 rules may sound like a lot, chances are that you already know most of these rules already from you own reading and writing. Most people are much better at grammar than they think they are—you'll probably surprise yourself with your grasp of grammar as you read about the following rules.

1. Subject-Verb Agreement

Subjects and verbs need to agree in number. In other words, singular subjects take singular verbs and plural subjects take plural verbs. In general, your ear will tell you when there is disagreement between subject and verb as in the following sentence:

She *are* being stubborn.

In this sentence, the singular subject *she* requires the singular verb *is* rather than the plural verb form *are*.

Sometimes, it's a little tricky to identify errors in subject-verb agreement, like when the subject and verb are separated by a phrase or when the subject appears to be plural but isn't. These special cases are favorites of the SAT test-makers and will be discussed in detail in the Identifying Sentence Errors section.

2. Verb Tenses

In addition to agreeing with their subjects, verbs need to be in the correct tense. Here's a sentence in which the verb is in the wrong tense:

In response to her rejection of his work, he *written* her a stinging letter.

The writer of the sentence used the part participle form of the verb "to write," *written,* instead of using the simple past tense of the verb, *wrote.* This substitution of the past participle for the simple past tense is another favorite error of the crafty test creators, but it is one in which again, you can trust your ear to pick out the error. You knew that *written* sounded wrong in the example sentence above! Sometimes, the test-makers substitute other tenses for the correct tense, using the present perfect tense instead of the past perfect tense, for example. Another favorite maneuver is to shift verb tenses within a sentence. We'll examine these kinds of errors in the ISE section as well.

Tip

As you can already see, trusting your ear will often be your best strategy for identifying errors. Another guessing strategy you can use throughout the multiple-choice section is to pick the simple past tense of a verb over the past perfect tense, as in the following sentence:

Yesterday, Jo-jo *had picked up* the pinecone with his paws for the first time.

The past perfect tense isn't necessary in the above sentence, and the shorter simple past form *picked up* works fine. In the Writing section, choosing the more concise choice will often yield the right answer.

3. Noun Agreement

Nouns need to agree in number within a sentence. The following sentence contains an error in noun agreement:

Jean and Dean want to be *a dancer.*

The subject of the sentence is plural: *Jean and Dean*. However, the noun that corresponds to the subject is singular: *a dancer*. To make the nouns agree in number, *a dancer* should be changed to *dancers*. In looking for errors in noun agreement, trust your sense of logic and check to see that nouns that should agree in number do agree.

4. Pronoun Agreement, Case, and Reference

A pronoun is a word such as *me, myself,* or *I* that is used in place of a noun or nouns. Pronouns pop up in the Writing section in several ways. You will probably be asked to identify pronouns in the wrong number or pronouns that do not agree with the nouns they refer to in number. A singular noun takes a singular pronoun; a plural noun takes a plural pronoun. See if you can identify the mistake in the following sentence:

Susan enjoyed eating fish and lifted *their* fork with glee.

The pronoun *their* should be changed to the singular *her* to agree with the antecedent (noun the pronoun refers to) *Susan.*

Pronouns also need to be in the correct case, which shows how the pronoun is used. The test-makers like to throw in errors in pronoun case in compound noun phrases, as in the following sentence:

Her and Al brought fifteen different kinds of apples to the gathering.

In the compound subject *her and Al,* the pronoun is incorrect because it should be acting as the subject and thus should be in the subjective case, *she.*

You will also have to be on the lookout for pronoun shifts, in which the pronouns switch in number or person within a sentence, as in:

If one is having trouble concentrating, *they* should try focusing.

You may have noticed that consistency is very important in English grammar and that the switch from the singular pronoun *one* to the plural pronoun *they* is ungrammatical.

You should also be prepared to encounter vague or ambiguous pronouns that do not clearly refer to antecedents, as in:

The sales clerk gave the customer a break after *his* hairpiece fell off.

Whose hairpiece was it—the sales clerk's or the customer's? This sentence needs to be rewritten to indicate clearly which person owns the hairpiece.

Note

As you can see, pronouns are a goldmine for the test creators. If you are having difficulty understanding any of the four major pronoun problems, ask your teacher to help you understand pronoun rules or practice pronoun problems using a grammar book such as *Get Wise! Mastering Grammar Skills,* published by Thomson Peterson's.

5. *Using Modifiers*

Modifiers describe other words. You may be asked to recognize errors in the use of the one-word modifiers known as adjectives and adverbs. Adjectives modify nouns, while adverbs modify verbs, adjectives, and other adverbs. Look at the next sentence:

The actor read his lines *slow.*

The word *slow* is an adjective, but since *read,* the word being modified, is a verb, the modifier should be changed to the adverb *slowly.* In most errors of this nature, your ear will tell you that the adjective requires the addition of the *-ly* ending to become an adverb.

Sometimes, you'll be asked to identify errors in the comparison of modifiers:

Of all the different flavors, Evan likes raspberry *better.*

The word *better* is a comparative adverb showing comparison between only two things, but the sentence requires the superlative adverb *best,* since more than two things are being compared.

The sneakiest way in which modifiers appear on the test is when they are misplaced or dangling. The next sentence shows how misplaced modifiers may appear on your test:

Gesturing wildly, the pencil flew out of Roberto's hand.

The modifying phrase *Gesturing wildly* should be followed by the subject it modifies but is instead followed by *the pencil.* This is wrong because the pencil is not gesturing wildly, and if it is, something's going on that's much worse than a simple grammatical error! The sentence should be revised to make more sense grammatically and logically:

Gesturing wildly, Robert let the pencil fly out of his hand.

You may also encounter dangling modifiers that don't clearly modify any word or group of words in the sentence, as in:

While slurping loudly, the clock struck midnight.

Who was slurping loudly? In this sentence, the missing information needs to be supplied:

While slurping loudly, we heard the clock strike midnight.

Misplaced and dangling modifiers will most likely appear in the Improving Sentences section of the test. Be on the lookout for modifying phrases, which often contain adjectives or adverbs.

198

6. Homonyms/Easily Confused Words

Be prepared to find a couple ISE questions that contain errors such as the following:

> Orion was under the *allusion* that Jennifer was obsessed with him.

An allusion is a reference to something. The sentence requires the word *illusion*, which is a false idea or conception. Be on the lookout for similar pairs of easily confused words such as set/sit, emigrate/immigrate, accept/except, to name a few.

7. Logical Comparison and Parallel Structure

Sometimes, the test-makers present you with a sentence in which two things that cannot be logically compared are compared:

> Bethany grew more tomatoes than her neighbor's garden.

The comparison is illogical, because *Bethany* (a person) is being compared to *her neighbor's garden* (a thing). To make the comparison logical, *her neighbor's garden* should be changed to *her neighbor did*.

Comparisons can also be grammatically faulty. Parallel structure is the use of the same forms or structures to express equal ideas in a sentence. The test-makers may present you with an error such as the following:

> Anuj likes running, swimming, and *to bicycle*.

or

> Carmela spends her free time at home, at the gym, *and the movie theater*.

In both of the above sentences, the third item in the sentence is not in the same form as the previous items. Remember: Consistency is a key element of English grammar. The correct sentences should read, "Anuj likes running, swimming, and *bicycling*" and "Carmela spends her free time at home, at the gym, and *in* the movie theater."

8. Double Negatives

Don't fret no more about silly grammar problems! Did you hear the double negative in the preceding sentence? Using two negatives such as *no, isn't, hardly, without, no one, hardly, barely,* or *scarcely* in one sentence will cancel the meaning of each negative. Be prepared to encounter errors involving double negatives in the ISE section.

9. Coordination and Subordination

Sentences containing two or more clauses need to be connected logically and grammatically. Coordinating conjunctions such as *and, if, but, or,* and *yet* connect independent clauses that each have a subject and verb. Errors in coordination occur when the coordinating conjunction that is used does not connect the ideas in a logical manner, as in:

> Harriet was renowned as a star basketball player, *and* she was best known as an amazing rock climber.

In this sentence, the conjunction *and* should be replaced with the conjunction *yet* which implies contrast.

Subordinate clauses begin with subordinating conjunctions such as *since, because, although, whenever, after, unless,* and *until.* Errors in subordination occur in the Writing section when the test-makers present you with a bunch of words that contain two subordinate or dependent clauses, as in:

> Although Josh packed his toothbrush the night before, since he left his suitcase at home.

Every sentence requires at least one independent clause containing a subject and a verb. In the above sentence, there is no clear subject, since both clauses are subordinate. To make the second clause independent and correct the error, you should eliminate the subordinating conjunction *since.*

10. Run-On Sentences

A run-on sentence consists of two or more complete sentences (or independent clauses) run together as one. Sometimes two or more independent clauses are joined erroneously by a comma, as in:

> Famke has an extensive CD collection, she also possesses a lot of old vinyl records.

Both clauses in the above sentence could stand alone as a sentence. One way to correct the run-on sentence is to replace the comma with a semicolon. Another way is to join the clauses with an appropriate coordinating or subordinating conjunction:

> Famke has an extensive CD collection, *and* she also possesses a lot of old vinyl records.

We'll explore the different ways to correct run-on sentences in the Improving Sentences section.

200

11. Sentence Fragments

Another favorite error in sentence structure is the sentence fragment, in which there are no independent clauses. This problem can occur when all the clauses in a sentence are dependent:

> As we strolled obliviously through the forest.

What's happening in this sentence? You don't know, because there is no clear verb and the clause begins with a subordinating conjunction. To correct the sentence, information either needs to be added or deleted. Check out the following solutions:

> As we strolled obliviously through the forest, a storm flattened our castle.

> We strolled obliviously through the forest.

When you see a sentence fragment, a little voice should tell you to either add something or take something away.

12. Eliminating Wordiness

Look at the wordy sentence below:

> Wei is of the opinion that the surrounding community in which she resides is under threat from various forces.

The ideas in this sentence can be conveyed much more succinctly:

> Wei believes that her community is under threat.

Avoiding wordiness or the use of unnecessary language is a good rule to follow when composing your essay and when choosing among various multiple-choice choices. Often the shortest, most elegant answer is the correction to choose when you are asked to revise and combine sentences in the Improving Paragraphs section.

> **Note**
>
> Just by reading, you'll improve your grasp of grammar, usage, and diction, whether you're aware of the improvement or not. The more you read, the greater the chance of encountering unknown words and the more finely attuned your ear will be to nuances and peculiarities of the English language. Reading works that employ Standard Written English, whether they are novels or newspaper articles, will put you in position to recognize and correct errors with aplomb.

13. Using Idioms and Correct Diction

Idioms refer to the peculiar expressions in a language. These expressions do not necessarily follow grammatical rules. Idiomatic expressions are correct, because people think they are, and they're defined by custom and usage. For example, the phrase, "How do you do?" is an idiomatic expression, which may sound peculiar if you start to think about it too much, but it is accepted in Standard Written English.

The test-makers create questions that test your idiomatic knowledge of prepositions that follow certain verbs. Notice the incorrect use of the preposition *with* in the next sentence:

Bertrand voted *with* the candidate who won the race.

The correct idiomatic phrase is *voted for.*

The test-makers may also test your grasp of idioms by switching gerunds and infinitives in a sentence. A gerund is a verb form ending in *-ing* that acts as a noun, as in *running* or *dodging*. An infinitive is a verb form, usually preceded by *to,* that can be used as a noun, an adjective, or an adverb, as *to go* or *to be*. Notice the confusion of the gerund for the infinitive in the next sentence:

Ava realized that Sam's effort *at learning* Italian was wearing him out.

Idiomatically, the phrase should be: *effort to learn.* With idioms, you'll have to trust your ear to tell you what sounds right.

Diction is another area in which you'll have to prick up your ears to hone in on errors. Diction is word choice, and the test-makers may ask you to identify the incorrect usage of words as in:

Declan took a *circulatory* path around the lake.

The word *circulatory* means "relating to the circulation of blood," and it should be replaced by the more apt *circuitous*, which means "indirect." (You could also replace it with the word *circular*, although this is not as accurate as circuitous.) In your essay and in the multiple-choice questions, take care to use correct word choice.

Rules Are Just Rules: A Few Last Words

Bear in mind that you will not be asked to name any of the 13 Deadly Rules at any point in the Writing section. The test will never ask you to identify a subordinating conjunction or a dangling modifier as such. The preceding

202

discussion of the 13 Deadly Rules should simply help you know what kinds of grammatical errors to look for in the test.

In the next sections, we will look at the structure of the questions and exactly how these grammatical issues come up in the test, but before we move on, here's a final list of suggestions to help you prepare for the Writing section. As with the other sections, preparing early is always a good idea, but even if the test is only weeks (perhaps days!) away, you can use the following activities to boost your grammatical fluency.

Strengthening Your Grasp of Grammar and Sentence Structure

1. **Ask your English teacher to help you clarify points of grammar, usage, or word choice about which you are unsure.**

   Are there particular areas of grammar that confound you? After reviewing the 13 Deadly Rules, you may want to pinpoint the ones that give you the most trouble and ask your teacher to clarify those rules with you. Your teacher can probably direct you to a number of resources that will give you more practice with these types of questions.

2. **Ask your English teacher or another informed adult to show you examples of grammar and sentence structure in your essays that could be improved.**

   Pull out an old essay or two and ask your teacher to circle and explain errors you may have made. Try revising the essay by correcting those errors and then have someone review the essay again.

3. **Practice revising your essays on your own.**

   Keeping in mind the rules of grammar, usage, and word choice, reread an essay you've written. Identify and correct any errors you've made. Revising your essays will give you great practice with grammar and sentence structure, and the more you do it, the more finely tuned your ear will be to hearing mistakes.

Identifying Sentence Errors (ISE): What's Wrong with This Sentence?

The first section of the Writing test consists of Identifying Sentence Errors (ISE) questions. In these multiple-choice questions, you'll be asked to identify underlined errors in sentences. Here's an example of a typical ISE question:

Example

It is likely that the <u>festivities,</u> previously <u>scheduled for</u> March 1,
               A   B

<u>would be</u> postponed due to the <u>expectation of</u> poor weather. <u>No error</u>
    C   D   E

Note

The directions for ISE problems will look something like this:

Directions: Mark the letter of your choice on the answer sheet that best corresponds to the correct answer.

Notes:

1. The following questions test your knowledge of the rules of English grammar, as well as word usage, word choice, and idioms.

2. Some sentences are correct, but others contain a single error. No sentence contains more than one error.

3. Any errors that occur will be found in the underlined portion of the sentence. Choose the letter underneath the error to indicate the part of the sentence that must be changed.

4. If there is no error, pick answer choice (E).

5. There will be no change in any parts of the sentence that are not underlined.

As in the example above, each of the ISE questions will feature a sentence with four words or phrases underlined, with each of the underlined parts labeled (A) through (D). One of the underlined parts may contain an error. If there is an error in an underlined part, you should mark the corresponding oval (A), (B), (C), or (D). If there is no error, you should mark oval (E) for "No error."

Note that the ISE questions ask only that you find the mistakes in each sentence. You do not have to explain what kind of error was made, as the questions never ask you to define grammatical terms. Remember too that the Writing section only tests your knowledge of grammar, usage, and word choice. The test does not test spelling or capitalization, and punctuation is only tested as a secondary matter as it relates to sentence structure. Before looking at the main types of errors that occur in the ISE section, let's look at how to approach these questions.

Pacing for ISE and Beyond

Use the following three facts to give yourself the best chance of succeeding on the multiple-choice Writing section.

1. A good guess is that the total number of questions will be close to or equal to the total number of minutes allotted for the section. So "one minute per question" is a very good rule of thumb.

2. Different amounts of reading is required for each of the question types. ISE questions will go the fastest, while improving paragraphs questions will take the most time since they have some reading associated with them. Never rush through the ISE questions, because as always, careless errors must be avoided. However, you will probably get through these questions faster than the others, which is good, since you can use the extra time when answering the improving sentences and improving paragraphs problems.

3. A two-pass system is still a good idea, and you can use it two different ways. One way is to make two passes within each question type. In other words, you make one pass through all the ISE problems, skipping any you can't answer immediately. Then you do a second pass through the ISE section (guessing when you have to) before heading on to the next batch of problems.

The advantage to finishing the test section by section is that you use the same set of techniques to answer all of the questions in a particular section before moving on-you don't have to switch back and forth between strategies and question types. The drawback is that you may spend time working a tough ISE question when you could have been answering an easy Improving Paragraphs problem. You can avoid this problem if you do a first and second pass through the entire section. This means you have to switch back and forth between strategies and question types, but you do eliminate the possibility of spending too much time on a hard ISE question when you could be answering easier improving sentences or improving paragraphs questions.

There are pros and cons with each choice. You should decide what works best for you, and then follow that plan. Thinking about pacing and making a choice based on your own inclinations is another way you become a better test-taker.

PETERSON'S
getting you there

What's My Error? How to Tackle the ISE Questions

The ISE questions require you to pinpoint which, if any, underlined parts of sentences need to be changed in order to make the sentences correct. The parts of the sentences that are not underlined are correct and can't be changed. As with all the multiple-choice questions in the Writing section, you should trust your ear to tell you where the mistakes lie. You can follow the steps below to tackle the ISE questions:

How to Tackle the ISE Questions

1. Read the sentence, trusting your ear to identify the error.

2. Read each of the underlined parts again, looking for possible errors.

3. Use POE to find the error, eliminating choices that are error-free.

4. Choose choice (E), "No Error," if there are no mistakes.

Try following these steps to identify the error in the following sentence:

The scientists, <u>who</u> <u>convened</u> in front of the statue, <u>was</u> <u>excited about</u>
        A   B   C   D
the discovery. <u>No error</u>
           E

First, read the sentence—does the error jump out at you? If so, you can mark the appropriate circle and move on. If not, reread each of the underlined parts again, listening for the possible error. The word *who* seems OK, so choice (A) does not contain the error. What about choice (B)? *Convened* also seems to be error-free. Choice (C), however, sounds funny—*was* is a singular verb, but its subject *scientists* is plural. Choice (D), *excited about,* seems to be fine. Choice (C) contains the mistake, so you should mark the oval for C as the answer.

When eliminating choices in the ISE section, you can look for specific types of mistakes that occur frequently in the section. In the preceding example, the error is in subject-verb agreement, a common mistake that you're likely to encounter. When examining the other choices in the sentence, you could also check to make sure the verbs agree with their subjects and that they're in the correct tenses. (They are and they are.)

Alert!

Don't hesitate to select choice (E), "No Error," in answering the ISE questions. Choice (E) will be the correct answer about one-fifth of the time—the test-makers are very equitable in their distribution of possible answers. Don't be tricked into seeing errors where there aren't any!

The same kinds of mistakes occur repeatedly in the ISE section and luckily, there are only a few of them. Knowing what kinds of errors to look out for will help you identify the mistakes in the ISE section. The following chart shows the main types of errors to look for.

Common Errors in the ISE Section

Regular Errors	More Advanced Errors

Subject-Verb Agreement
    Inverted Order
    Subject and Verb Separated by a Phrase
    Fake Compounds (when the subject
        appears to be plural but isn't)
	Collective Nouns

Verb Tenses
    Confusion of Past and Past Participle
    Sequence of Tenses	

Noun Agreement in Number	

Pronouns
    Agreement in Number with Antecedents
    Case in Compound Noun Phrases
    Pronoun Shifts
	Ambiguous and Vague
	Pronoun Reference

Using Modifiers Adjectives and Adverbs	Comparison of Modifiers
Logical Comparison	Parallel Structure
Double Negatives	
Homonyms/Easily Confused Words	Using Correct Diction
Idioms Confusion of infinitive and gerund	Non-idiomatic prepositions after verbs

Notice that we've listed the errors as "Regular" and "More Advanced." For those of you who want to just review the basics, you can stick to the regular types of errors to look out for. For those of you aiming to score super-high on the Writing section, you can review it all: the More Advanced category includes some of the trickier grammatical errors the test-makers will throw at you. In the rest of this section, we will look closely at how each of the common errors occurs in the ISE section.

PETERSON'S
getting you there

Please Be Agreeable: Subject-Verb Agreement

Subjects and verbs must agree in number. Singular subjects require singular verbs, and plural subjects require plural verbs. Chances are that in a regular, everyday sentence, you'll readily recognize when there is subject-verb disagreement, as in:

Sandeep *walk* to the store to buy a newspaper.

The word *walk* probably strikes you as incorrect, since the singular subject *Sandeep* requires the singular verb form *walks*.

However, the pesky test-makers create sentences in which errors in subject-verb agreement may not be so obvious. One way the test-makers do this is by inverting the order of the subject and verb. Try to identify the error in the following sentence:

Although many students <u>believe</u> that carrots <u>taste</u> best raw, there <u>is</u>
                  A   B   C
many others who <u>prefer</u> them cooked. <u>No error</u>
             D   E

The error lies in choice (C), since the plural subject *others* requires a plural verb *are* rather than the singular *is*. Notice how the verb follows the subject in the above sentence. Tricky, isn't it? Be on the lookout for errors in subject-verb agreement when the subject follows the verb, and remember that all you have to do is identify the subject and whether it takes a singular or plural verb.

The test creators also like to separate the subject and the verb with a phrase in ISE items. Look for the error in subject-verb agreement in the next sentence:

The soccer player, <u>a favorite</u> of the <u>team's</u> <u>legions</u> of fans, <u>have</u> a strict
                A   B   C   D
workout routine. <u>No error</u>
            E

The error is in choice (D), since the singular subject *player* should take the singular verb *has* rather than the plural *have*. The phrase that comes between the subject and the verb, *a favorite of the team's legions of fans,* has no affect on the number of the verb.

> **Tip**
>
> When verbs are underlined as possible errors, double check to make sure that they agree in number with their subjects. To identify the subject of the verb, ask who is doing the action stated in the verb and remember that the subject may appear far, far away from the verb. Then figure out whether the subject is singular or plural, and make sure that the verb agrees in number with the subject.

You may also see sentences in the ISE section in which the subject appears to be plural but isn't, as in the next sentence:

Either Jeb or Trisha *are* going to the play with me tonight.

In this sentence there are two separate singular subjects: *Jeb* and *Trisha*, and thus the verb should be in the singular form *is*. In sentences that use the constructions *either* _____ *or* _____ and *neither* _____ *nor* _____, the nouns and the verbs are singular.

Fake Compound Subjects

When you see the following constructions, be on the lookout for subjects that look plural but are not:

either _____ or _____

neither _____ nor _____

_____ along with _____

_____ as well as _____

_____ in addition to _____

Together with _____

That Makes Tense: Getting Verb Tenses Right

Another favorite category for the makers of the Writing section test is verb tenses. Frequently, the test-makers will confuse the simple past and past participle forms of a verb, as in the next sentence:

The snow *fallen* all night long.

Fallen is incorrect, because it is the past participle of the verb *to fall*, and the sentence requires the simple past tense form or *fell*. See if you can pick out the error in the next sentence:

We <u>grabbed</u> our jackets and <u>run</u> outside to <u>make</u> snow people.
    A   B   C   D
<u>No error</u>
   E

If you picked choice (C), you were right! *Run* is the part participle of the verb to run, but the sentence requires the simple past tense: *ran*.

The tense of a verb indicates the time of the action or state of being expressed by the verb. Verbs in English have six tenses: present, past, future, present perfect, past perfect, and future perfect. The chart below explains each of the tenses.

Tense	Definition	Example
Present	existing or happening now	Mimi *has* enough money.
Present Perfect	existing or happening sometime before now	Mimi *has worked* all summer, and now she feels rich.
Simple Past	existing or happening in the past	She *saved* nickels in her piggybank.
Past Perfect	existing or happening before a specific time in the past	Before she counted her bills, Mimi *had taken* them out of her purse.
Future	existing or happening in the future	She will decide how much to spend on a new notebook.
Future Perfect	existing or happening before a specific time in the future	Mimi will have considered many choices, and she will make an informed decision.

When you see more than one verb in a sentence, be on the lookout for the use of the wrong tense in one of those verbs. Try to identify the error in the next sentence:

After she shoveled the sidewalk, Tammie had taken a nap. No error
    A   B   C   D   E

Does that sentence make sense to you? Of course it doesn't, and if you picked choice (D) as the culprit, you were dead-on correct. The verb in the first clause, *shoveled,* is in the simple past tense, while the verb in the second clause, *had taken,* is in the past perfect tense, which implies that the action was completed before another action in the past. However, Tammie has obviously taken her nap after shoveling the sidewalk, so the verb should be in the simple past as well: *took*. When dealing with sentences that involve more than one verb, make sure that the time relation between the verbs seems logical.

Let's All Agree: Noun Agreement

The following sentence contains an error in noun agreement. Let's see if you can spot it:

> The rumor <u>spread</u> <u>that</u> Alexandra and Jane <u>want</u> to be <u>an astronaut.</u>
>   A   B   C   D
> <u>No error</u>
>   E

The error lies with choice (D), because two people (Alexandra and Jane) cannot be one astronaut no matter how hard they try. They can, however, become more than one astronaut. The sentence should read:

> The rumor spread that Alexandra and Jane want to be astronauts.

> The original incorrect sentence contains an error in noun agreement, since the nouns do not agree in number. Remember to identify the subject of the sentence and check to see if the other nouns it relates to agree in number with it.

Pronoun Problems

A pronoun is a word used in place of a noun or nouns. Be on the alert when you see a pronoun underlined, since pronouns are tested in a number of ways.

You will likely encounter a sentence in which the pronoun disagrees with the noun it refers to in number. That's right, pronouns need to agree in number with the nouns they refer to. See if you can spot the error in pronoun number in the sentence below:

> Students <u>who</u> read the novel <u>thoroughly</u> <u>will be</u> rewarded for <u>her</u>
>   A   B   C   D
> efforts. <u>No error</u>
>   E

Choice (D) contains the error, since the pronoun *her* is singular while its antecedent (the noun referred to) *Students* is plural. The correct plural pronoun is *their*.

Another way in which the test-makers present pronoun errors is by putting pronouns in the wrong case. Case is the form of a pronoun that shows how

PETERSON'S
getting you there

the word is used, and pronouns may be in the nominative, objective, and possessive cases. In the next sentence, *I* is in the nominative case; *me* is in the objective case; and *my* is in the possessive case:

> *I* forgot to bring *my* sticker collection with *me* to the meeting.

Don't worry—it's not important for you to name exactly which case a pronoun is in on the test! You just have to be able to recognize when a pronoun is in the wrong case. In addition, these errors in pronoun case will occur most often in compound noun phrases, in which the pronoun is linked with a noun or another pronoun, as in:

> *Him* and Jesse's parents traveled for forty days and nights on a tiny ship called *Invincible*.

In the compound noun phrase *Him and Jesse's parents*, the pronoun *Him* is in the wrong case, because the pronoun should be acting as a subject. Who traveled? *He* did. *Him* can't travel, because *him* is in the objective not subjective case. The trick with these questions is to isolate the pronoun and make sure that it is in the right case. To check the pronoun's case, try reading the phrase without the other part of the compound noun phrase. *Him traveled for forty days . . .* just doesn't work.

Note

When you see a pronoun underlined, check to see if it represents an error in one of the following:

- Number—Does it match the number of the noun it refers to?
- Case—Is it in the right case?
- Shift—Are the pronouns consistent in the sentence?
- Reference—Does it refer clearly to something in the sentence?

A third way in which pronoun errors occur is in pronoun shifts. See if you can identify the pronoun shift in the next sentence:

> Whenever one is bored, you should sing a little ditty.

If you identified the pronoun *you* as the incorrect pronoun, you were right on target. The pronouns in the above sentence refer to the same performer, so they need to be consistent, and *you* should be replaced by the pronoun that was originally used *one*. The test-makers like to try to confuse you by creating pronoun shifts with words such as *you, one,* and *they* that are often used interchangeably in everyday speech but should be consistent in Standard Written English.

The Mod Squad: Using Modifiers Correctly

Adjectives modify or describe nouns or pronouns. Adverbs modify verbs, adjectives, or other adverbs and frequently end in *-ly*. When you see an adjective or adverb underlined in the ISE section, check to see that it is the correct modifier. Try to identify the error in the next sentence:

> Edwin's dog Co-Co, who was named for a fashion designer, ran joyful
>   A   B   C
> through the snow. No error
>   D   E

Cut to the chase and look at choice (C), where the error lies. The word *joyful* is an adjective. However, *joyful* modifies the verb *ran* and should therefore be the adverb *joyfully*. Trust your ear to tell you when there's a mistake in one-word modifiers.

Advanced Topic: Comparison of Modifiers

The next sentence contains an error in the comparison of modifiers:

> This is the *better* meal I have ever eaten.

Assuming that the speaker has eaten more than two meals in her lifetime, you can say that she has used the wrong modifier. Since she is comparing more than two things, she needs to use the superlative form of the modifier, which is *best*. Superlative adjectives and adverbs usually end in *–est* and express comparison among more than two items. The comparative form, usually ending in *–er* shows comparison between two things only.

Modifiers that have more than two syllables form their comparative and superlative degrees with *more* and *most*: *more energetic* and *most energetic*.

Be alert to errors in comparison of modifiers, whenever they are underlined. Check to see how many items are being compared, and then make sure that the modifier is correct.

Logical Comparison: Can I Compare Thee? Maybe, Maybe Not

Not all things can be compared with each other logically in a sentence, and the sneaky test-makers may well try to slip an illogical comparison into your test. Read the next sentence:

> Vain and determined, Franklin aspired to be more admired than his *co-host's reputation*.

When checking for logical comparison, first see what's being compared. In this erroneous sentence, *Franklin* is being compared to his *co-host's reputation*. This comparison doesn't make sense, because you just can't

213

compare a person to a reputation. You can, however, compare a person to a person. The sentence should read:

> Vain and determined, Franklin aspired to be more admired than his co-host.

Sounds better, right?

Double Negatives: Two Wrongs Don't Hardly Make a Right

A double negative is the use of two negative words when one is enough. In Standard Written English, you should use only one negative, unless you intend to cancel out the meanings of both negatives (and you won't want to do that on the test). See if you can identify the error in the next sentence:

> We wanted to splash in the puddles, but there weren't none. No error
>   A   B   C   D   E

Choice (D) contains the error, since it contains the second negative word *none*. In the sentence above, *weren't* adequately conveys the negative meaning.

Here is a list of some common negative words:

Common Negative Words		
barely	nobody	nowhere
hardly	not (also look for the	only
neither	contraction *n't*)	scarcely
no	nothing	without

Except What I Accept: Homonyms/Easily Confused Words

In English, there are homonyms and other word pairs that sound alike but have completely different meanings. Be prepared to identify errors in the usage of such words, as in the next sentence:

> *Accept* for never taking out the garbage, Hercules is a great roommate.

The word *accept* means "to take or tolerate something." In this sentence, the word should be *Except*, which means, "the thing that does not apply to stated rule."

Here's a list of some other easily confused words that you may encounter on the test.

Easily Confused Words	
accept/except	lead/led
advice/advise	leave/let
affect/effect	peace/piece
afflict/inflict	principle/principal
allusion/illusion	raise/rise
break/brake	set/sit
compliment/complement	stationary/stationery
emigrate/immigrate	than/then
formally, formerly	there/their/they're
here/hear	to/too/two
lay/lie	your/you're

Advanced Topic: Using Correct Diction

Diction refers to word choice, and clearly, you should choose the right words whenever you write or speak. The tricky test-makers may give you an ISE question in which they try to confuse you by using incorrect diction. These errors are along the lines of easily confused words, but they may be less common, as in the next example:

Barton has *translocated* the book into five languages.

The word *translocated* means to move from one location to another. The sentence calls for the word *translated,* so the sentence contains an error in diction. There's no real way to prepare for these types of errors, except to be on the alert for them whenever you see a strange word underlined.

Idioms: Weird but True

Idioms refer to the peculiar expressions in a language—expressions that do not necessarily follow grammatical rules. Idiomatic expressions are correct, because people think they are, and they're defined by custom and usage.

The ISE section often features a question in which an infinitive or gerund is used unidiomatically. The infinitive is a verb form, usually preceded by *to,* that can be used as a noun, adjective, or an adverb, as in: *to sleep, to eat, to gesticulate.* A gerund is a verb form ending in *–ing* that is used as a noun, as in: *climbing, singing, castigating.*

PETERSON'S
getting you there

Look for the error in the following sentence:

In spite of rising early every morning to run five miles, Sasha did not
     A   B   C
succeed to conquer her opponent. No error
          D   E

Choice (D) contains the error, because the infinitive *to conquer* should be replaced by the gerund *in conquering*. With idioms, there are no grammatical rules to guide you. You simply have to let your ear tell you if something does or doesn't sound right. However, you should be on the lookout for non-idiomatic phrases whenever you see a gerund or an infinitive underlined on the test.

Non-Idiomatic Prepositions After Verbs

The test-makers also create questions that test your idiomatic knowledge of prepositions that follow certain verbs. Notice the incorrect use of the preposition *on* in the next sentence:

After considering the situation for four days, Tefi told Moon-Jie that she had decided to agree *on* his proposal.

You can agree on many things, but in the sentence above the phrase is used unidiomatically, and the preposition *on* should be replaced with *to*. That's the correct idiomatic expression, and with idioms you'll have to trust your ear to tell you when a preposition is being used incorrectly. When you see a preposition underlined, check to make sure that it's being used correctly.

Studying lists of idioms doesn't make a lot of sense—you'll just know them when you see them. Reading works written in standard English will help you attune your ear to idioms and diction.

ISE Review: Use the Steps to Identify the Error

Congratulations! You've now synthesized the main types of errors you're likely to encounter in the ISE section. Before moving on to the Improving Sentences section, let's see if you can use the steps outlined at the beginning of this section to identify the error in the following sentence:

Although no bigger than a thimble, the fiercely insect terrorized the
                      A   B   C
group of bird-watchers. No error
   D   E

216

Step 1: Listen for mistakes. If you hear the mistake right away, mark the oval, and move on. If not, go on to Step 2.

Step 2: Reread each underlined part, listening for the error. Choice (A) *than* appears to be fine. Choice (B), however, sounds funny—a *fiercely insect?* Knowing that you'll be tested on the use of adjectives and adverbs, choice (B) should come under some scrutiny. You might recognize that since the word in choice (B) modifies a noun, it should be an adjective, not an adverb. It should be a *fierce* insect, since dropping the *–ly* changes the word from an adverb to an adjective. Or you might just realize that it sounds wrong and move on to the next question.

Step 3: If none of the choices sounds funny to you, try the process of elimination. Does choice (C) seem correct? The verb *terrorized* seems to be in the correct tense and it agrees with its subject *insect*. You should probably eliminate choice (C) as a possible error. Complete the same steps with the other choices, then make an educated guess. If the answer isn't obvious to you, don't forget that choice (E), "No error," is always a viable choice.

Tip

Educated guessing can and should be used for all the questions in the Writing section, regardless of the question type.

Improving Sentences: Finding the Correct Corrections

The second section of the Writing test consists of improving sentences questions, which are a bit more elaborate than the ISE questions. Like the ISE questions, the improving sentences questions test your knowledge of basic grammar, usage, and word choice. However, for these problems there will be an emphasis on issues concerning sentence structure. Again, you will not be tested on spelling or capitalization, and punctuation will only be tested as it relates to sentence structure.

As with the ISE questions, you won't have to name grammatical terms or identify exactly what the nature of the error is. You will simply need to recognize when a sentence contains an error and identify the best correction among four given choices. You will not be asked to provide the correction itself.

Note

The directions for Improving Sentences will look something like this:

Directions:

1. The following questions test your knowledge of English grammar, word usage, word choice, sentence construction, and punctuation.

2. Every sentence contains a portion that is underlined.

3. Any errors that occur will be found in the underlined portion of the sentence. If you believe there is an error, choose the answer choice that corrects the original mistake. Answer choices (B), (C), (D), and (E) contain alternative phrasings of the underlined portion. If the sentence contains an error, one of these alternate phrasings will correct it.

4. Choice (A) repeats the original underlined portion. If you believe the underlined portion does not contain any errors, select answer choice (A).

5. There will be no change in any parts of the sentence that are not underlined.

Tackling the Improving Sentences Questions

Let's look at a typical improving sentences question:

Although several players were opposed to riding the bus to the field, other players were as equal in their support of the idea.

(A) were as equal in their support of
(B) held equal support of
(C) were equally supportive of
(D) had supported equally
(E) held support equally of

Look at the underlined portion of the sentence. You will be asked whether that underlined part contains an error, and if so, which of the choices best corrects that part of the sentence.

Notice that choice (A) repeats the underlined portion of the sentence. If you think the underlined portion is fine as it is, you should choose choice (A), which indicates "No correction."

If, however, you think the underlined part sounds wrong, consider choices (B) through (E) as the possible correction. The correction should produce a sentence that is grammatically correct, as well as clear and concise. You can follow these simple steps to tackling improving sentences questions:

1. Read the sentence, listening for an error.

2. If the sentence sounds funny, read choices (B) through (E), mentally plugging in the choices into the sentence.

3. Use POE to eliminate obviously wrong answers.

4. Don't hesitate to select choice A if the sentence sounds right.

Let's try using the steps to find the answer to the example above. Reread the sentence. Something should sound a little odd to you. The phrase "were as equal . . ." is awkward, and its form does not mirror the structure of the first part of the sentence "were opposed to." Since the sentence sounds funny, try mentally plugging each choice into the sentence, to see if it works. When we plug in choice (B), the sentence reads:

> Although several players were opposed to riding the bus to the field, other players held equal support of the idea.

That phrasing still sounds odd. When we plug in choice (C), we get:

> Although several players were opposed to riding the bus to the field, other players were equally supportive of the idea.

That sentence sounds good, and in fact, choice (C) provides the correct answer, because it expresses the second part of the sentence in a way that is parallel, or in equal form, to the first part. You can quickly check the other choices to see if they work better than this one. Choice (D) gives us:

> Although several players were opposed to riding the bus to the field, other players had supported equally the idea.

Choice (D) creates a sentence in which the two verbs are in different forms—*were* is a linking verb and *had supported* is in the past perfect tense—so that choice can be eliminated as incorrect. Choice (E) also yields a sentence that sounds awkward:

> Although several players were opposed to riding the bus to the field, other players held support equally of the idea.

Thus, choice (C) is the best answer. You can double check your answer by plugging it into the sentence again to see if it sounds the best. Since choice (C) provides the best correction, you would mark oval C on the test.

In this sentence, two groups are being compared: players who were opposed to riding the bus and players who were supportive of the idea. Choice (C) creates two phrases that have the same grammatical form. This question tests your knowledge of parallel structure—a common error in the Improving Sentences section. Luckily, the section tests only a few grammatical rules, and by becoming familiar with these rules, you'll be able to rule the Improving Sentences section. Here's a chart showing the grammatical problems we'll cover in this section:

Common Errors in Improving Sentences Questions

Regular	More Advanced

Parallel Structure
    With Connective Words
    In a Series	

Coordination and
    Subordination
Using the Correct
    Conjunction
Two Subordinate Clauses
	Subordinate Clauses: Choosing
	    the Most Concise Choice

Sentence Fragments Creating Independent Clauses	

Run-On Sentences
    Using Semicolons
    Creating Subordinate Clauses
	Creating Compound Predicates
	Using Appositive Phrases

Using Modifiers
    Misplaced and Dangling
        Modifiers	

Notice that we've presented "Regular" and "More Advanced" topics. The "More Advanced" issues are included for those of you who want to ace the test. Those of you who are aiming for a good but not outstanding score can focus on mastering the regular topics.

Since you're a sharpie, you probably also noticed that there are fewer topics to cover in this section than there were in the ISE section. Some of the same grammatical concepts that cropped up in the ISE section will occur in the Improving Sentences section, but the Improving Sentences section is really about the correct flow of sentence.

You already have a good grasp of the basics of grammar, usage, and word choice, and you'll probably be surprised at how good you are at pinpointing issues of sentence structure. Remember, you won't have to use or name grammatical terms on the test. However, knowing what issues to look for will help you know when there is an error and eliminate incorrect choices.

Let's look at the issues.

Equal Ideas in Equal Forms: Parallel Structure

The example question provides a typical improving sentences question involving parallel structure. Whenever items are compared, be sure that they are expressed in the same grammatical forms, using the same verb tenses and types of modifiers.

The test-makers particularly like to create errors in parallel structure in sentences that use pairs of connective words. Notice the connective words in the following sentence:

The more Carolyn advocated for the color green, *the more* Meg argued for the use of blue.

The connective words, *the more . . . the more*, require you to use parallel structure with what follows them, since the connective words imply comparison. The above sentence uses parallel structure effectively, since in both parts of the sentence, there is a noun (*Carolyn/Meg*) followed by a past tense verb (*advocated/argued*) followed by a preposition (*for/for*).

Connective Words Requiring Parallel Structure

- Neither/nor
- Either/or
- Both/and
- Whether/or
- The better/the better

221

- Not only/but also
- The more/ the more

Another way in which the test creators like to test parallelism is in lists of items. Lists require that all the items be in the same form, as in:

Charles *painted the house, cleaned the bathroom,* and *swept the front steps.*

Notice that all three items in the list are in the same form, as they all employ verbs in the same tense (simple past).

Now, see if you can answer the next question. (Guess what? There may be a problem involving parallel structure):

After working all day, Aditi likes to relax by listening to music, lighting candles, <u>and read poetry.</u>

- **(A)** and read poetry
- **(B)** and reading poetry
- **(C)** and be read poetry
- **(D)** and finally in reading poetry
- **(E)** as well as read poetry

Trying the steps to answering improving sentences questions, first read the sentence. The underlined part should sound awkward to you. Since you're a smartie, you probably recognized that the underlined part was not parallel to the other two items in the list. Identifying the error as faulty parallelism will enable you to speed through the next step. As you mentally plug in the other choices to see which one works best, you can look for words ending in *–ing*, which will make the last item parallel. (See how knowing just one grammar rule speeds up the process of elimination!) Choices (B) and (D) contain that construction, but choice (D) also contains the extraneous word *finally in*, which keep the third item from being like the others. Choice (B) is the correct answer.

When you see part of a list underlined, look to see if that item is like the others.

Joined at the Middle: Coordination and Subordination

You may recall that sentences containing two or more clauses need to be connected logically and grammatically. Coordinating conjunctions such as *and, if, but, or,* and *yet* connect independent clauses. An independent clause has a subject and verb and can stand alone as a sentence. Errors in coordination occur when the coordinating conjunction that is used does not connect the ideas in a logical manner. See if you can pick the correct answer to the next improving sentences example:

> Samantha liked to think of herself as a tough cookie, yet she bravely ventured forth into the tiger's cage.

(A) cookie, yet she bravely ventured
(B) cookie; yet, she bravely ventured
(C) cookie; however, she bravely ventured
(D) cookie, so she bravely ventured
(E) cookie only while bravely venture

Does the sentence sound correct to you? Samantha thinks of herself as brave, yet she does a brave thing. That does not make sense, so start looking at choices (B) through (E). You may have surmised that the problem lies with the coordinating conjunction. *Yet* does not logically express the relationship between the two clauses in the sentence, so you should look for an choice that contains a conjunction that does.

Choice (B) merely changes the punctuation of the sentence, so you can eliminate that choice right away. Choice (C) seems to be punctuated correctly, but the connector *however* also does not express the correct relationship between the ideas, so you can cross that choice out. Choice (D), on the other hand, does express a logical relationship, since the conjunction *so* is synonymous with *therefore,* and it makes sense that Samantha would venture into a tiger's cage if she considered herself brave. Choice (E) gives us a verb that is in the wrong tense as well as a mystifying connector. Choice (D) is the correct answer.

Common Subordinating Conjunctions

although	if	until
as	in order that	when
as if	once	whenever
as long as	since	where
because	so that	wherever
before	than	whether
even though	unless	while

Quite sensibly, subordinating conjunctions—like those in the preceding chart—introduce subordinate clauses. Subordinate clauses cannot stand alone as a sentence, since every sentence needs a subject and a verb. Be alert

PETERSON'S
getting you there

to faulty subordination in which the only two clauses in a sentence are both subordinate, as in:

While Grace was brushing her teeth, *when* Janek ran outside.

The subordinating conjunctions at the beginning of each clause will be a big tip-off that something is wrong, and you should look for the correction that creates an independent clause.

Sentence Fragments: Looks Like the Real Thing, but Isn't

This sentence fragment.

The preceding group of words may be punctuated like a sentence, but it isn't one, because it lacks a verb. Sentences must express complete thoughts.

Sometimes, you will see a sentence fragment that consists of only a subordinate clause as in:

Whenever Geneva puts on her wig.

There's no identifiable subject or verb in this group of words. The crafty test-makers will sometimes present you with long sentence fragments posing as sentences. Choose the answer to the next question.

<u>The struggles and triumphs of a class of third-graders, which are movingly depicted in the novel by Yi Munyol.</u>

- **(A)** The struggles and triumphs of a class of third-graders, which are movingly depicted in the novel by Yi Munyol.
- **(B)** The novel by Yi Munyol movingly depicts the struggles and triumphs of a class of third-graders.
- **(C)** Yi Munyol, in his moving novel, depicting the struggles and triumphs of a class of third-graders.
- **(D)** The struggles and triumphs of a class of third-graders being movingly depicted in the novel by Yi Munyol.
- **(E)** Yi Munyol, whose novel movingly depicts a class of third-graders' struggles and triumphs.

You probably noticed that the original sentence is a sentence fragment since it is missing a verb. To determine which of the choices provides the correct revision, look for sentences with subjects and verbs that express complete thoughts.

Is It a Fragment?

Use the following questions to determine if an underlined sentence is a fragment:

1. Does the sentence have a subject?
2. Does it have a verb?
3. Does it express a complete thought?

If the answer is "no" to any of these, the sentence is but a mere fragment.

In the question above, only choice (B) provides a complete sentence, so it is the choice to choose. Use your trusty ear to eliminate choices that are also sentence fragments.

On and On and On: Run-On Sentences

Read the next sentence:

In the movie *Super Comma,* the hero saves the city, he is later engulfed by hordes of clamoring fans.

This sentence is a run-on sentence, because it includes two independent clauses that are joined incorrectly. Remember that independent clauses can stand alone as sentences. In the above sentence, the clauses are erroneously joined by only a comma. There are several ways to correct a run-on sentence. The most obvious way is to replace the comma (or the lack of punctuation) with a period, creating two sentences. However, the test-makers will rarely give you that choice on the Writing test.

Instead, they may offer the choice to change the comma to a semicolon. The semicolon (;) is used to join two sentences that are closely related. The following correction is correct:

In the movie *Super Comma,* the hero saves the city; he is later engulfed by hordes of clamoring fans.

Sometimes the test-makers won't give you the semicolon choice either. In those cases, you should look for an choice that makes one of the independent clauses subordinate. Read the next run-on sentence:

Gus was running late again, Sheila started getting impatient.

A good way to revise this run-on sentence would be to make the first clause subordinate:

225

Because Gus was running late again, Sheila started getting impatient.

To review subordinate clauses and subordinating conjunctions, see pages 200 and 222–224.

Now choose the answer to the next improving sentences question:

You're sure to find people eager <u>to ski, there are</u> snowy vistas.

- **(A)**   to ski, there are
- **(B)**   to ski but there are
- **(C)**   to ski and are
- **(D)**   to ski, meanwhile there are
- **(E)**   to ski, wherever there are

Since each clause in the sentence is independent, the sentence is a run-on and choice (A) is out. Choice (B) doesn't make any sense, and it is punctuated incorrectly, as there should be a comma preceding the coordinating conjunction *but*. Eliminate choice (B). Choice (C) offers a sentence in which the verb *are* is in the wrong number. It's also illogical. Choice (D) provides a grammatically correct choice, but it doesn't make sense. That leaves us with choice (E), which correctly supplies a subordinate clause. Choice (E) is the answer.

Ways to Fix a Run-On

The test-makers may offer any of the following ways to fix a run-on sentence:

1.   Using a semicolon to join the clauses.

2.   Making one clause a subordinate clause.

3.   Turning the clauses into one sentence with a compound predicate.

4.   Using an appositive phrase.

Creating Compound Predicates

Yet another way to fix run-on sentences is to create compound predicates. This is a fancy way of saying that the subject has two or more verbs. When the two independent clauses have the same subject, you can compress the sentence into one clause in which the subject does more than one thing. Look at the next run-on sentence:

The letter *O* probably started as a picture of an eye in Egyptian hieroglyphic writing, it was later given a circular form.

Since the two clauses have the same subject, you can change them into a sentence with a compound predicate:

> The letter *O* probably started as a picture of an eye in Egyptian hieroglyphic writing and was later given a circular form.

> Not too hard, right? Look out for compound predicates among the choices when you encounter run-on sentences.

Using Appositive Phrases

Here's yet another way to correct run-ons. The test-makers may give you a run-on sentence in which the correction involves an appositive phrase. An appositive phrase consists of a noun or pronoun and its modifiers. Appositive phrases give you extra information about the person, place, or thing being described. Here's an example:

> Madonna Ciccone, *a singer from Michigan,* will appear in concert at 8 p.m.

The appositive phrase is *a singer from Michigan*. The test-makers may give the choice of changing an independent clause into an appositive phrase to correct a run-on, so be on the look-out for these kinds of phrases.

Mod Squad II: Misplaced and Dangling Modifiers

Remember your friend the modifier? A modifier is a word or phrase that describes another word in the sentence. Modifiers need to be placed correctly in a sentence, so that it is clear which word is being modified. Funny things happen when you place a modifier too far away from what it should modify, as in the next sentence:

> Born two months ago, we happily adopted the adorable puppies.

The modifying phrase, *Born two months ago,* is misplaced, since as the sentence now reads, the modifier appears to describe the people (*we*). Using your powers of rationality, you can identify that the phrase should modify the puppies, and the sentence should be changed to:

> We adopted the adorable puppies born two months ago.

Dangling modifiers may also crop up on the test. Look at the next sentence:

> Jogging in the park, the clouds move ominously overhead.

Who was jogging? We don't know, because the modifier is missing the word it ought to modify. To correct a dangling modifier, you need to add information:

> Jogging in the park, we noticed the clouds move ominously overhead.

When you see an entire sentence underlined, you should be on the alert for an error in modification. Now try answering the next question:

Roland was pleasantly surprised when he found a package on his doorstep opening the door.

- **(A)** Roland was pleasantly surprised when he found a package on his doorstep opening the door.
- **(B)** Opening the door, Roland was pleasantly surprised to find a package on his doorstep.
- **(C)** Roland was pleasantly surprised when he found a package opening the door on his doorstep.
- **(D)** Roland, on his doorstep, was pleasantly surprised to find a package upon opening.
- **(E)** On his doorstep opening the door, Roland was pleasantly surprised to find a package.

The original sentence is incorrect, because it contains a misplaced modifier; the doorstep appears to be opening the door. Choice (B) presents a logical modification. In this choice, Roland is opening the door, and the package is on the doorstep. Choice (C) can be crossed out, since it presents another misplaced modifier—in this case the package is opening the door! Choices (D) and (E) offer sentences that are within the realm of logic, but their word ordering is awkward. Choice (B) is the best choice. Remember to take a guess, after eliminating obviously wrong choices, if you're not sure of the answer.

Summing Up: Improving Sentences

Phew! Congratulations again—you've finished reviewing the major grammar points for the Improving Sentences section. Remember, there are only five key areas of grammar to keep in mind in this section:

- Parallel Structure

- Coordination and Subordination

- Sentence Fragments

- Run-On Sentences

- Misplaced and Dangling Modifiers

And here's the really good news: you're done with learning about grammar and usage! Knowing what you know already will put you in an excellent position to tackle the Writing section. In the next section, we'll look at a couple of finer points of writing such as avoiding wordiness, but mostly we will focus on how to approach the improving paragraphs questions. Since you're already a grammatical wizard, the next section will be a whiz.

Improving Paragraphs: The (Slightly) Bigger Picture

Give yourself a pat on the back. You've already mastered the basic tasks for the Writing test by learning how to find errors in sentences and how to fix them. The third and final type of multiple-choice questions, improving paragraphs, will take you one step further by asking you to consider errors in the context of paragraphs and short essays.

The Improving Paragraphs questions will present you with paragraphs or short essays, followed by a few questions. Those questions will ask you to do one of three things:

- Correct sentences

- Combine sentences

- Consider organization of the sentences

We'll look at how to approach each of these types of questions in detail, but before doing that, let's look at a typical improving paragraphs question.

Directions:

1. The following questions test your knowledge of paragraph and sentence construction.

2. The following passage is a rough draft of an essay. This rough draft contains various errors.

3. Read the rough draft and then answer the questions that follow. Some questions will focus on specific sentences and ask if there are any problems with that sentence's word choice, word usage, or overall structure. Other questions will ask about the paragraph itself. These questions will focus on paragraph organization and development.

4. Select the answer that best reflects the rules of English grammar and proper essay and paragraph writing.

PETERSON'S
getting you there

This question is based on the following paragraph.

> (1) An estuary is a place where rivers meet the ocean. (2) Fresh water from rivers mixes with salt water from oceans. (3) Estuaries are often shaped like funnels, with the rivers running down the middle of the estuaries toward the ocean. (4) Bays are usually shaped like half-circles; however, some are really estuaries. (5) Any place where fresh water mixes with salt water is an estuary.

1. In context, which is the best way to revise the underlined portion of sentence 4 (reproduced below)?

Bays are usually shaped like half-circles; <u>however, some are really estuaries.</u>

(A) however, they are really estuaries
(B) wherever there are really estuaries
(C) and are really estuaries
(D) however, it is really an estuary
(E) however, some bays are really estuaries

This is an example of the first type of improving paragraphs question, which requires you to correct sentences. This type of question should strike you as familiar, as it similar to the improving sentences questions. The only difference is that with the improving paragraphs questions, you need to look at the context of the whole paragraph to figure out how to best revise the sentence.

In the example above, the original sentence contains an error in ambiguous reference, since it isn't clear what exactly the word *some* refers to. Theoretically, *some* could refer to either *bays* or *half-circles*. Logically, you know that the reference is probably to *bays,* and when you read sentence 5 that instinct is affirmed, since sentence 5 tells you that any place where salt water meets fresh water is an estuary. By reading the whole paragraph, you can correctly surmise that the correct answer is choice (E).

X-Ref

Ambiguous or vague pronoun reference errors are common in the Improving Paragraphs section. If you're not sure how to handle these types of errors, see pages 211–212 in the ISE section.

With any of the improving paragraphs questions, you'll have to read the whole paragraph or essay to determine the correct answers. This portion of the Writing test tests your grasp of information and how sentences work together to effectively convey meaning. You'll be looking for sentences that are weak, redundant, or ambiguous. Often, however, you will have to identify the main idea of a paragraph or essay to arrive at the correct answer. We'll explore this strategy in depth when we discuss the organizational types of questions at the end of this section. Before discussing the three types of questions, let's look at how to tackle the improving paragraphs questions in general.

Basic Strategy for Tackling the Improving Paragraphs Questions

Use the following steps to successfully answer the Improving Paragraphs questions:

1. Read the paragraph or essay, noting any words that clue you in to the passage's main idea. Don't be afraid to underline words as you read.

2. Read the question stem or the part of the question that precedes the five multiple-choice choices. The stem may direct you to specific numbered sentences or it may ask you an organizational question. Determining what kind of question you're being asked will help you hone in on the information you need to answer the question correctly.

3. Reread the parts of the paragraph or essay that you need to reread to answer the question. With the correcting and combining sentences questions, you should reread the numbered sentences in question for sure, but you may also need to reread the sentences that surround them to arrive at the right answer. With the organizational questions, you'll probably have to reread the entire paragraph. The passages are short, so skimming them again shouldn't take too long.

4. When considering the choices, look for an answer that addresses the problem you've identified. For example, if you've already determined that the problem lies with an ambiguous pronoun reference, look for the choice that provides a clear reference.

5. If you come across a question that deals with the main idea or organization of the passage, you may need to answer the other questions first. The answers to the other questions can help you

understand the main idea of the passage and may give you a better chance at answering that type of question correctly.

Now let's look at the three types of Improving Paragraphs questions.

1. Fix It Quick: Correcting Sentences

One type of Improving Paragraphs question requires that you choose the best revision to a given sentence. These questions strongly resemble the Improving Sentences questions from the previous section, but with the Improving Paragraphs questions, you'll have to consider the context of the sentence within the whole passage. Look at the next paragraph and question:

> (1) Fish swim in schools to protect themselves from predators. (2) There is safety in numbers, and young and small fish are safer in a group. (3) Swimming with hundreds or thousands of other fish confuses potential predators, since a school of tiny fish can fool predators by appearing to be a much larger creature. (4) An enemy is less likely to attack it than a single fish swimming by itself.

In the context of the paragraph, which revision is most needed in sentence 4?

(A) Insert "As a matter of fact" at the beginning.
(B) Omit the word "less."
(C) Change "it" to "a school."
(D) Change "than" to "then."
(E) Change "itself" to "themselves."

After reading the paragraph, you can identify that the word *it* in sentence 4 refers to a school of fish, since the whole paragraph is about why fish swim in schools. You should also recognize that the pronoun *it* needs to be changed, because it doesn't have a clear reference. Knowing the context and identifying the grammatical error will tell you that choice C is the best revision to the sentence. Pretty straightforward, right?

Choices (B), (D), and (E) actually introduce grammatical errors into the sentence, so they should all be eliminated. Choice (A) doesn't introduce an error, but it does add unnecessary words to the sentence. Remember that you should always pick the choice that yields the most concise correct construction. We'll say more about the importance of being concise in the next section.

232

2. A Good Mix: Combining Sentences

Some improving paragraphs questions will ask you to choose the best way to combine sentences. Take a look at the next paragraph and question.

(1) The Dutch post-Impressionist painter Vincent van Gogh is famous for his intensely colored, highly textured paintings. (2) His landscapes and portraits are marked by swirling brushstrokes and a passionate sensibility. (3) While creating his artworks, van Gogh sometimes suffered from bouts of mental instability. (4) In 1889, he admitted himself to a hospital in Saint-Rémy. (5) He made some of his greatest paintings while he was at the hospital.

Which of the following is the best way to combine sentences 4 and 5?

In 1889, he admitted himself to a hospital in Saint-Rémy. He made some of his greatest paintings while he was at the hospital.

(A) In 1889, he admitted himself to a hospital in Saint-Rémy, and he made some of his greatest paintings while he was at the hospital.

(B) Having admitted himself to a hospital in Saint-Rémy in 1889, he made some of his greatest paintings while there.

(C) He made some of his paintings, his greatest paintings, in 1889, while admitting himself to a hospital in Saint-Rémy.

(D) Because he admitted himself to a hospital in Saint-Rémy he made some of his greatest paintings in 1889.

(E) In 1889, he admitted himself to a hospital in Saint-Rémy where he made some of his greatest paintings.

Upon reading the paragraph, you probably noticed that part of sentence 5 is redundant, as it repeats what is said in sentence 4. You can surmise that there is a way to combine the ideas in one sentence, and you should look for the choice that combines the ideas effectively and concisely.

Choice (E) offers the best way to combine the sentences, because it provides the most concise way to combine the ideas. Choices (C) and (D) should be eliminated, as they create sentences that are somewhat illogical. Choices (A) and (B) offer sentences that are in the realm of possibility, but choice (E) provides a more succinct and logical connection between the ideas.

In the improving paragraphs questions, you want to choose the answer that eliminates wordiness or unnecessary words. Although the shortest answer is not necessarily the correct one all the time, you should look for the choice that expresses ideas most succinctly.

In order to combine sentences effectively, you should also know the basic rules of punctuation. If you need to refresh your memory concerning commas and the like, take a moment to review the chart below.

Punctuation Review

Punctuation Mark	How to Use the Mark	Example
comma **,**	to separate items in a list	Jon is a runner, a lawyer, and a brother.
	to separate two or more adjectives before a noun	Shabba nearly fell asleep watching the tedious, melodramatic play.
	to set off clauses or phrases that are not essential to the main idea of the sentence	Niko, an excellent mathematician, loves to play the violin.
	after introductory phrases	Before leaving the house, Howie checked to see that the lights were out.
	to separate independent clauses (the comma precedes the conjunction)	Brianna interviewed 14 people for the job, yet she didn't find a suitable employee.
semicolon **;**	to join independent clauses	The iris is Ali's favorite flower; he grows rows of them in his yard.
	to connect independent clauses joined by transitional expressions such as *however, for example, indeed, moreover, therefore,* and *in addition*	Elena felt awkward about barging in on the party; however, she managed to make a grand entrance.

Punctuation Mark	How to Use the Mark	Example
colon :	before a list, definition, or explanation	You will need to bring the following items: a plastic cup, a toothbrush, and a flashlight.
hyphen -	at the end of a line	The party was organ-ized by the president.
	with compound words	twenty-one self-made a well-written story
dash —	to indicate an abrupt break in thought or speech	My pet Marcel—he's a pug—is the most popular dog in the neighborhood.
Apostrophe ,	in contractions	you're, it's, don't
	to show possession	the boy's friend the girls' building blocks

Combining sentences questions are not much more involved than the correcting sentences questions. When you encounter these types of questions, keep in mind the same grammatical rules you've learned while preparing for other parts of the test and use your knowledge to eliminate obviously wrong choices.

3. The Proper Place and Order: Organizational Questions

The third type of improving paragraphs question will require you to make decisions about paragraph development and organization. In these questions you may be asked to:

- Identify which choice would best conclude a paragraph

- Identify which choice would best begin a paragraph—i.e., which sentence would make an appropriate topic sentence

- Identify what the author's purpose is: to describe, analyze, explain, etc.

- Identify which choice would best fit into the overall theme or idea of a given paragraph

As you may have surmised, figuring out the main idea of the essay or paragraph in question will often be necessary when answering these types of questions. Knowing the main idea will help you determine what's needed to complete a paragraph. Determining the main idea is a skill you're probably adept at from tackling the critical reading questions, but if you want to refresh your skills take a look at the following box.

How to Hone in on the Main Idea: A Review

If you've been actively reading, then organizational questions shouldn't throw you for a loop. These questions will usually take more time to answer, simply because they encompass more information. If a question asks which choice would make the best first or last line of a specific paragraph, look back at the first and last sentences, since those may provide a clearer picture of what that paragraph is about.

Look out for answer choices that are partially correct—they mention smaller ideas or issues from the passage. There will be distractor-like choices that may include an aspect of the passage's main idea, but just miss the mark a little. So, again, reading actively while you skim can help keep these diversionary choices out of your line of vision when concentrating on the big picture of a passage.

Let's take a look at a typical organizational question:

(1) The national sport of Korea, tae kwon do is a martial art famous for its flying and spinning kicks. (2) Along with karate and kung fu, it is one of the most popular martial arts in the world. (3) Tae kwon do means "the art of hand and foot fighting." (4) The name comes from three Korean words: *tae* means "foot or kick;" *kwon* means "fist or punch;" and *do* means "the art or way of life." (5) The martial art involves dramatic kicks, which are often done while jumping and spinning. (6) Competitors score points by landing kicks to the body or the head, and students of tae kwon do learn sequences of fighting moves. (7) Students also learn courtesy, determination, and self-control, and tae kwon do emphasizes loyalty and respect for family, teachers, and elders.

236

Which sentence would be most appropriate to follow sentence 7?

(A) Martial arts are becoming more and more popular in the U.S.
(B) I began studying tae kwon do when I was in the fourth grade.
(C) In conclusion, everybody should be familiar with at least one type of martial art.
(D) By studying tae kwon do, students learn many skills and values.
(E) In tae kwon do, the color of the belt shows the person's rank.

To answer this question, you should first determine what the paragraph is about. Reading it through once, you can probably assess that the paragraph describes the martial art tae kwon do. After reading the question, you should reread sentence 7, and determine that the question is asking you to choose the sentence that best concludes the paragraph.

Then consider the choices. Choice (A) provides a sentence that is only tangentially related to the main idea. It is about martial arts in general, not tae kwon do specifically. This is an example of a misleading choice, and you should cross it out. Choice (B) relates to the main idea, but it introduces a different voice or narrator than what was presented in the paragraph, as it uses the first-person *I* form. Choice (B) also offers information that is irrelevant to the ideas in the paragraph. Since the shift in voice and information is not appropriate, you should cross out choice (B). Choice (C) presents a conclusion that would be appropriate to a persuasive paragraph; however, this paragraph is descriptive. It's not trying to persuade you to take up martial arts in general. Choice (C) should also be eliminated.

Choice (D) provides a sentence that does aptly conclude the paragraph, as it describes the kinds of things students of tae kwon do learn. Checking Choice (E), you can conclude that it adds information but doesn't provide a good summary of the ideas in the paragraph. Choice (D) is the best answer.

These types of improving paragraphs questions are the most complex multiple-choice questions you will encounter in the Writing section, and you will only be asked to answer a few organizational questions such as this one. Knowing how to identify what the writer is trying to do and what the passage is about will enable you to answer these questions successfully.

Collective Nouns

A collective noun is singular in form but names a group of persons or things, as in the next sentence:

A *crowd* gathered to watch the paint dry.

Some examples of collective nouns are: *group, audience, class, committee, family, team,* and *majority.* When the group is acting as a unit, use a singular verb, as in the sentence above. When the individuals in the group are acting separately, use a plural verb, as in:

The class have finished their assignments.

In this sentence, the individual members of the class are acting independently to finish their assignments. When you see a collective noun underlined, double check to determine whether it is acting as a singular or plural subject.

Ambiguous and Vague Pronoun Reference

A pronoun should always refer clearly to its antecedent. Sometimes, the test-makers will create erroneous sentences in which the pronoun can refer to more than one noun, as in the next sentence:

When the dog chased the squirrel, *it* was happy.

Who was happy, the dog or the squirrel? The pronoun *it* has ambiguous reference, since the pronoun can refer to either antecedent. When you see a pronoun underlined, make sure that the pronoun refers clearly to a noun in the sentence.

The test creators may also throw you a sentence in which the pronoun has no clear antecedent, as in the next sentence:

On the radio show, *they* announced the release of Pedro's new album.

Who does *they* refer to? We'll never know, since *they* does not have an antecedent. When you see sentences such as the one above, check to make sure the pronouns have clear antecedents. There's a good chance you'll find your error there.

Parallel Structure

Sometimes, you'll see sentences in which the comparison is grammatically faulty or unparallel, as in the following sentence:

In the novel, red flowers require twice as much sun as *pink flowers.*

This type of error can be particularly challenging to spot, since the comparison between the two items is logical. The red flowers can be sensibly compared to the pink flowers. However, Standard Written English requires that you use the same form to compare equal ideas, and in the sentence above, the second item is missing a verb and thus does not match the form of the first item. To be correct, the sentence should read:

In the novel, red flowers require twice as much sun as pink flowers do.

These types of errors test your grasp of parallel structure, which dictates that equal ideas are expressed in equal forms.

Choosing the Most Concise Choice When Combining Clauses

Sometimes the test-makers will present you with a sentence in which an independent clause needs to be replaced by a subordinate clause. This sounds a bit trickier than it actually is, for as always you will not actually have to create the solution. You need only choose the correct answer. However, it is a good idea for you to know what to look for, and since that's what this book is all about, consider the following example:

Wallace wrote his second comic book <u>and he was thirty-seven years old then</u>.

(A) and he was thirty-seven years old then
(B) upon reaching the age of thirty-seven years
(C) at age thirty-seven years
(D) when he was thirty-seven
(E) at the time when he was thirty-seven

When you read the sentence, you probably noticed that the coordinating conjunction *and* does not provide the most logical connection between the two clauses. In addition, the sentence is not punctuated correctly. There should be a comma preceding the *and*. So, choice (A) is definitely out.

Choice (B) presents a logical alternative, but the resulting sentence is wordy. The ideas can be expressed more succinctly than that. Choice (C) provides an awkward and grammatically incorrect solution. People simply do not say "at age thirty-seven years" in English. Choice (D), however, is grammatically correct and succinct. Choice (E) is correct but like (B), quite wordy. Given the choices presented, you should choose the one that is most concise and clear. Choose (D).

Concise and Precise—Very Nice: How to Write an Effective Essay

In the essay section of the Writing test, you will be asked to take a position on an issue and support it with examples from your studies and experience. The question will be open-ended, so that you can answer it successfully in many different ways. You will not have to have any prior knowledge about a specific topic to write an effective essay.

The essay portion of the test is designed to assess your ability to express ideas clearly and effectively. You will need to present a clear viewpoint on a topic, backed up by supporting details. The readers will consider your essay's content, organization, and grammar. By preparing for other sections of the test (the multiple-choice questions), you've already developed a good grasp of grammar, usage, and word choice. You also know how to effectively improve paragraphs. With the essay, you can draw on these skills to write your own effective passage.

> **Note**
>
> The essay will be scored using a holistic approach, meaning that readers will consider the essay as a whole and will judge it based on the overall impression it makes. Errors in punctuation and spelling are of minor importance. Even with a few spelling and punctuation errors, you can score high on the essay. Handwriting will also not count against you, although you do need to write legibly so that the readers can read your essay and score it.

Here's an example of the type of essay question you'll encounter:

Directions: Think carefully about the issue presented in the following excerpt and the assignment below.

"A century ago, the average American had little in the way of real selection. From cornflakes to college, the choices available to most people were limited. Today Americans have so many choices that we are often overwhelmed by too much of a good thing."

Gary Belsky, "A Logical Choice"

Assignment: What is your view on the idea that having too many choices to choose from may be a bad thing? Plan and write an essay in which you develop your point of view on this issue. Support your position with reasoning and examples taken from your reading, studies, experience, or observations.

Notice that you are asked to respond to an issue of general interest and that you can draw on your knowledge of a specific subject such as literature or history or your own experience. The readers will be assessing your ability to express yourself, not your expertise in any particular subject. Now let's look at how to successfully write an essay in response to a question like the one above.

How to Improve Your Writing Skills

The more you write, the better you will become at writing. Here are a few hints for improving your writing skills:

1. Practice writing on a daily basis. Try keeping a journal in a notebook or online, and practice writing thoughtful entries on specific topics.

2. Write about what you read in English and other subjects. Keep a "response journal" in which you write your opinions about what you've read. Writing just a paragraph a day will enable you to clarify your thinking about something you've studied.

3. Explore which writing methods work best for you. For example, try outlining your essays before you write them.

What the Scores Mean

Each reader will give your essay a score from 1 to 6. Here's what each of the numbers indicates:

6	Outstanding
5	Good
4	Adequate
3	Limited
2	Flawed
1	Unacceptable

You should aim to write the best essay you can, but a score of 4 or above is good. To receive a score of 5 or 6, you will need to show a superior command of grammar, usage, and word choice, as well as effective development and logical organization of your ideas.

Steps to Writing an Effective Essay

You may be wondering how long the essay should be. Content is, of course, more important than length. You should never write extra sentences just to make your essay appear longer. However, the ideal length of your essay is three to five paragraphs. Each of those paragraphs should consist of at least three sentences, which develop the main ideas of those paragraphs. The first paragraph, as you may have guessed, should state the main idea of your essay, your point of view on the given topic. The middle one to three paragraphs should provide supporting examples to the main idea and develop the idea further. The concluding paragraph should sum up your main points and give the essay a sense of completion.

The test-makers and readers know that you will be writing under time pressure, so they do not expect you to churn out a perfectly polished, ingenious piece of writing on the spot. What they're looking for is the effective expression of a viewpoint backed up by details. The test-makers will give you enough time to plan the essay before you write it—in fact the word *plan* is in the directions. So, let's look at this first step.

Step 1: Plan Your Essay. Before you begin actually writing the essay, take a few minutes to plan what you will write. Writing down notes or an outline will make the task of writing the essay much easier.

The first thing you should do is decide what your point of view is on the given topic. With the question above, you would need to figure out if you agree or disagree with the statement: Can having too many choices be a bad thing?

Next, you will need to choose how to support your argument. Since you'll be able to draw supporting examples from any of your studies or your experience, you should choose the area in which you feel you know the most. For example, if you've just read William Shakespeare's *Hamlet* and the details of the play are fresh in your mind, you will probably want to discuss the play in the essay. However, if you're particularly knowledgeable about how candidates get elected to the Presidency of the United States, you will want to take your examples from this area. Remember, you can also always draw on your personal experiences to support your argument. It doesn't matter what you write about, as long as you can develop an argument using those examples.

In planning your essay, you may want to first brainstorm as many supporting ideas an examples as you can, jotting them down on a piece of scrap paper. Write down your topic statement, and then list every idea about the subject that comes to you. For the question above, your brainstorming notes might look like this:

242

Yes, having too many choices can be a bad thing.

we have more choices now than ever before
    —hundreds of TV channels to choose from
    —unlimited job choices
    —varieties of jeans

waste time deciding among different choices
    —choosing cereal at the store
    —choosing what kinds of jeans to wear
    —even making bigger decisions like buying cars or
      deciding what college to go to

having more choices, doesn"t necessarily mean better choices

prefer quality over quantity

feeling overwhelmed by too many choices—where to shop?
once at the shop, what kind of jeans to get

After brainstorming your ideas, you can decide which ideas and details you want to include in your essay, perhaps circling the ones that stand out to you. Then, think about how to organize those ideas into the paragraphs that will make up your essay. You may want to quickly write an outline such as the one that follows:

1. Yes, too many choices can be bad.
    —we have more choices than ever before
    —but we waste time choosing among too many choices
    —having so many choices can lead to misery

2. Waste time choosing among too many choices
    —example: trying to buy jeans
    —which store to go to?
    —which types of jeans—low-riders, boot-cut, straight
      leg, flare, faded, dark, pre-washed?

3. Having too many choices can lead to misery
    —I ended up buying nothing, after having wasted four
      hours trying to find the perfect pair.
    —having more choices doesn't mean better
    —illusion of having choices creates pressure on the
      decision maker

PETERSON'S
getting you there

When you outline, you should be thinking about how to organize your ideas into at least three paragraphs: the topic paragraph, a supporting paragraph, and a concluding paragraph. Add any details that occur to you to the outline and feel free to move your ideas around using arrows or whatever method works for you. After outlining your ideas, you'll be prepared to write the essay.

Step 2: Write the Essay

With your notes and outline in hand, you should start writing the topic paragraph. This paragraph should state your opinion and give the main reasons why you have that viewpoint. As you write your essay, don't obsess about punctuation and word choice. You should have time to go back and revise your essay: and matters again are less important than the development of your ideas.

For the question above, a topic paragraph might look like this:

> Having too many choices can indeed be a bad thing. Today, we have more choices than ever before. A typical consumer can choose among 10 different kinds of paper towels, dozens of different cars, and hundreds of TV channels. However, having so many choices can ultimately just be a waste of precious time. A larger array of choices doesn't necessarily translate into better choices, and having to choose among many choices can make a person feel pressured to make perfect choices all the time.

With your introductory paragraph, you should include a topic sentence that clearly states your viewpoint, as in the first sentence above. The topic sentence doesn't necessarily have to come first in the paragraph, but it should appear somewhere. The other sentences should support the main idea by giving details or fleshing out the topic sentence.

Tip

You can support a main idea with different kinds of details including:

- Facts and statistics
- Sensory details appealing to the sense of touch, sight, smell, taste, or hearing
- Examples
- Anecdotes or brief stories

244

After writing the introductory paragraph, write one to three body paragraphs that extend or expand upon the ideas set forth in the first paragraph. You may use the supporting sentences from the first paragraph to start these body paragraphs. In the body of the essay, you should draw on your knowledge of a particular area or your experience to support your viewpoint. Here's an example of a good supporting paragraph:

> I recently had the experience of facing too many choices as a consumer. I wanted to buy a new pair of jeans, but when I went to the store to find a pair, I was confronted with dozens of choices covering three walls of the store. There were boot-cut jeans, straight leg, and flared bottom. There were low-riders, high-waisted, and boy-cut pants. The textures of fabric offered still more choices: prewashed, dark blue, light blue, faded, even something called distressed. Faced with so many choices, I randomly picked a few pairs and tried them on, yet none of the pairs I tried on seemed to fit me well. I left the store empty-handed except for an increased sense of frustration. In this case, having more choices did not deliver a satisfactory outcome.

Supporting paragraphs should contain lots of details to support your argument. Each paragraph should also contain a topic sentence summarizing the main idea of the paragraph. In this body paragraph, the topic sentence is the last one. All the details in the paragraph should support the paragraph's main idea, just as each of the body paragraphs should support the main idea of your essay.

After fleshing out your ideas in the body paragraphs, you should sum up your ideas in the concluding paragraph. The concluding paragraph should give your essay a sense of completeness. Here are some ways to conclude an essay:

Ways to Conclude an Essay
1. Restate the main idea in different words.
2. Summarize your major points.
3. End with a final idea or example.
4. End with a comment on the topic, such as a personal observation or a statement that points to larger related issues.
5. Ask the reader to take action or make a statement to persuade them to do something.

Look at the concluding paragraph for the assignment above:

> Having many choices can, in fact, lead to the opposite of satisfaction. When I left the store without any jeans, I felt not only frustrated but incompetent. Surely with so many choices available to me, I should have been able to find the perfect pair of jeans. Having an abundance of choices can make people feel pressured to make perfect choices all the time. However, that simply was not the case in this situation, nor is it the case in many situations. What people need are good choices, not multitudes of mediocre ones that create more misery.

In the concluding paragraph, you should drive your points home by restating what you've argued in a clear and forceful manner. Summarizing your points and taking them one step further is a good way to conclude your essay. After finishing a draft, you should also take the time to review your essay to make it as clear and precise as it can be.

Step 3: Proofreading Your Essay

Take a few minutes to review what you've written. Keeping in mind the rules of grammar that you've learned, look for grammatical mistakes or errors in spelling or punctuation and correct them. You may also want to replace some phrases with more forceful or concise wording. Proofreading is your opportunity to make the essay as effective as it can be, so don't be afraid to (neatly) cross out words and replace them with better ones.

Tip

Pacing on the Essay

Assuming that you have 25 minutes for your essay, you should break down this time in the following manner:

Step 1, Planning —about 5 minutes

Step 2, Writing—roughly 15 minutes

Step 3, Proofreading—about 5 minutes

246

A Few Final Words about Your Essay

You have all the skills you need to write a persuasive essay. Here are a few final things to keep in mind while writing and proofreading your essay:

1. **Be as concise as possible.** Remember that avoiding wordiness is always a good thing in writing—yours or someone else's. When proofreading your essay, look for ways to say what you've said in the shortest, most elegant way possible.

2. **Eliminate sentences or phrases that are redundant.** Don't include extra sentences just to make your essay appear longer. Chances are that that strategy won't fool your readers, and you want to make sure that every sentence adds something to your essay.

3. **Make sure that the voice you use is consistent.** It's fine to use the first-person *I* as in the paragraphs above, but make sure that whatever voice you use is used throughout the essay. In other words, if you start out using *I* or *one*, don't switch to *you* half-way through the essay.

4. **Avoid using slang/use proper diction.** To be on the safe side, avoid using slang or casual word choice. It's possible that you will get a reader who finds the use of slang charming, but chances are that you won't. When you proofread your essay, check to make sure that your word choices are good.

5. **Check for grammatical errors.** Using your knowledge of grammar, usage, and word choice, you can proofread your essay.

> **Note**
>
> Colleges will be able to view and print your essay only if you send those colleges your test scores. Different colleges will use your writing score in different ways. Colleges may consider your score in admissions decisions or for placement in English Composition courses.

Take It to
the Next Level

The Scoring Rubric for the SAT Essay

The SAT essay is scored from 1 to 6 with 6 being the highest score. Two readers will assess your essay and the scores will be combined, so your final score will range somewhere between 2 and 12. If the scores from the two readers differ by more than one point, a third scorer will read the essay. The two closest scores will then be used.

All the scorers read the essays against the same rubric developed by the College Board and the Educational Testing Service, which administers the SAT. This rubric guides the scorers in considering overall impression, development, organization, diction, sentence structure, grammar, usage, and mechanics. The score guidelines are similar to the following:

Essay Scoring 6 (Outstanding)

- *Overall impression:* develops a point of view with clarity and insight; uses excellent critical thinking in presenting the viewpoint; uses appropriate supporting examples, reasoning, and details

- *Organization:* is well organized with a clear focus; coherent; clear and orderly progression of ideas

- *Diction:* uses appropriate, varied, and accurate vocabulary for interest and clarity

- *Sentence structure:* varies sentence structure

- *Grammar, usage, mechanics:* is almost free of grammar, usage, and mechanics errors

Essay Scoring 5 (Effective)

- *Overall impression:* develops viewpoint effectively; uses strong critical thinking in presenting viewpoint; most examples, reasons, and details are appropriate

- *Organization:* is well organized and focused; coherent; progression of ideas present

- *Diction:* demonstrates skill in the use of appropriate language

- *Sentence structure:* varies sentence structure

- *Grammar, usage, mechanics:* is mostly free of grammar, usage, and mechanics errors

Essay Scoring 4 (Competent)

- *Overall impression:* develops viewpoint; shows competent critical thinking; provides adequate support through the use of examples, reasons, and details

- *Organization:* is mostly organized and focused; coherent for the most part; has some clear progression of ideas

- *Diction:* is inconsistent in the use of appropriate vocabulary; is generally adequate

- *Sentence structure:* uses some varied sentence structure

- *Grammar, usage, mechanics:* makes some grammar, usage, and mechanics errors

Essay Scoring 3 (Inadequate)

- *Overall impression:* develops a point of view; shows some use of critical thinking; may be inconsistent in reasoning; may provide insufficient support

- *Organization:* shows limited organization or some lack of focus; some lack of coherence or progression of ideas

- *Diction:* shows some facility in language use; uses weak or inappropriate vocabulary

- *Sentence structure:* uses little sentence variety; may have problems in use of sentence structures

- *Grammar, usage, mechanics:* shows a number of grammar, usage, and mechanics errors

Essay Scoring 2 (Limited)

- *Overall impression:* develops a vague or limited viewpoint; weak critical thinking; uses inappropriate supporting evidence or too few examples to make the points

- *Organization:* poor or unfocused; serious weaknesses in coherence or progression of ideas

- *Diction:* shows little facility with language; limited word choice; inappropriate vocabulary

- *Sentence structure:* has numerous errors in sentence structure

- *Grammar, usage, mechanics:* has numerous errors in grammar, usage, and mechanics; interfere with meaning

Essay Scoring 1 (Fundamentally Flawed)

- *Overall impression:* has no point of view on the issue or offers little or no support for the point of view

- *Organization:* lacks organization or focus; incoherent; no progression of ideas

- *Diction:* has basic errors in the use of vocabulary

- *Sentence structure:* has serious problems with sentence structure

- *Grammar, usage, mechanics:* has numerous errors in grammar, usage, and mechanics interfering with meaning

Note that a score of 0 will be given if an essay is not based on the writing prompt.

Read the rubric several times. As you practice writing essays for the SAT, keep this rubric in mind. When you write each essay, try to focus on one or two qualities of good writing as measured by the rubric. After you have finished writing your essay, come back to the rubric and see how your essay measures up.

Use the following tables to help you. Give yourself anywhere from 1 to 6 points for each quality of good writing. Then divide the total by 5 to get your score.

Practice Test 1	Practice Test 2	Practice Test 3
Overall impression _____	Overall impression _____	Overall impression _____
Organization _____	Organization _____	Organization _____
Diction _____	Diction _____	Diction _____
Sentence structure _____	Sentence structure _____	Sentence structure _____
Grammar, usage, mechanics _____	Grammar, usage, mechanics _____	Grammar, usage, mechanics _____
Total points: _____	Total points: _____	Total points: _____
Divide by 5 final score: _____	Divide by 5 final score: _____	Divide by 5 final score: _____

Practicing Your Essay Skills

Use the following two essays as practice and as a guide to writing an effective essay. First, read the writing prompt and then write an essay to answer it. Simulate the actual test and give yourself 25 minutes to read the question, plan, and write your essay. Then read the two sample responses for each essay and the critique of each.

Essay 1A

Topic: Were the good old days actually all that good? We must remember that people living in the nineteenth century did not have all the modern conveniences that make our lives easier. There were no airplanes or cars, no washing machines, no television, and no computers. Therefore, it is better to live today, in the modern world, than it was to live in the days of horse-drawn carriages.

Assignment: What is your opinion of the idea that it is better to live today than it was to live in the nineteenth century? Plan and write an essay that develops your ideas logically. Support your opinion with specific evidence taken from your personal experience, your observations of others, or your reading.

Answers and Explanations

Sample Essay 1A

I prefer to be living today rather than when my grandparents were born in the last century or before that even. Today young people can really enjoy themselves they have TV and movies and all sorts of entertainment. Not like long ago when all you did all day was work and then at night you were to tired to do anything accept sleep.

Today we have greater opportunities to do things and to get ahead. There is less prejudism against people because of there race or color or religion. You can go to more kinds of colleges like a two year school or a four year school and there are even many programs to help you if you are financially unable to pay the tuition costs and payments.

I don't believe that the good old days were really that good. I'm very happy to be living today in today world. These are the good days.

Analysis of Sample Essay 1A

1. There is a sense of organization. The essay is divided into three paragraphsan introduction, a development, and a conclusion.

2. The author attempts to stick to the topic and provide examples.

3. Although there are technical errors in the third paragraph, the conclusion provides an interesting summary.

4. There are some problems with sentence structure but the writer attempts to vary sentences.

5. There are serious errors with grammar, usage, and punctuation.

Suggestions for Improvement

1. The essay lacks clarity and is wordy. The opening sentence could have been concluded after "born." In the second paragraph, the first sentence is vague; "to do things" and "to get ahead" should be explained and clarified. The third sentence of the second paragraph needs to be tightened: "There are two- and four-year colleges with various programs to assist those in financial need."

2. There are sentence structure problems. The second sentence of the first paragraph is a run-on sentence. A period should follow "themselves." The sentence that follows is a fragment. "Not like long ago" could be changed to add clarity and also to provide a subject for the sentence: "This is different from times past when all people did. . . ."

3. There are several errors in word choice. In the last sentence of the first paragraph, *to tired* should be changed to *too tired*, and *accept* should be *except*. In the second sentence of the second paragraph, *prejudism* should be *prejudice* and *there* should be *their*.

4. There is an error in the use of the possessive form. In the second sentence of the third paragraph, *today world* should be *today's world*.

5. The ideas could have been better developed had the writer used one paragraph for each idea that he or she introduced in paragraph 2.

Sample Essay 1B

Someone once said that for everything you gain you have to give up something. I agree. We gained the subway, but we have to put up with being crowded like sardines and herded like cattle, being pushed and shoved. We gained large buildings and big cities, but we lost our privacy and we are forced to live in little cubby holes. We gained airplanes and automobiles and with it comes all the dirty air and pollution.

People in the nineteenth century worked hard and didn't have time to relax but maybe they got real pleasure from their work. At least they ate the food that they grew and weren't concerned about all the chemicals and sprays and sickness that came from the fruit and vegetables. Maybe they developed a real feeling of accomplishment too.

They didn't have TV or radios but they had good neighbors and they would enjoy visiting with friends and family. We gained television but we lost the ability to have a good conversation and to enjoy the company of other people.

Every century has its good points and its problems. I don't want to go back to living in the 1800s but I do feel that we could learn from the way they lived. Maybe we could adopt some of their customs and bring some of the good old days into today's world.

PETERSON'S
getting you there

Analysis of Sample Essay 1B

1. There is an excellent four-paragraph organization. The introduction is fully developed with several pertinent illustrations. The body provides several additional points that support the writer's contention. The conclusion is a thought-provoking summary of the essay.

2. The use of contrast between past and present provides a fine frame for the essay. The theme of "gain and loss" is carried through with appropriate illustrations and a mature vocabulary.

3. There are no errors in sentence structure. The writer uses both simple and complex sentences effectively.

4. There is a consistent comma error, but no other mechanics errors.

Suggestions for Improvements

1. The second sentence of the opening paragraph seems ineffective in the context of so many mature comments. It could be rewritten: "This is especially true in comparing our world with the world of our grandparents."

2. There is a problem with pronouns and antecedents; this results in a lack of clarity. In the last sentence of the first paragraph, the singular pronoun "it" is incorrect since it does not agree with the plural "airplanes and automobiles." It would be better to write: "We gained airplanes and automobiles, but with modern means of travel we must suffer dirty air and pollution." So too, the second sentence of the concluding paragraph could be rewritten to clarify the pronoun, "they": ". . . but I do feel that we could learn from the way our grandparents lived." This change clarifies the use of the pronoun "their" in the subsequent sentence.

Essay 2A

Directions: Think carefully about the statement below and the assignment that follows it.

Topic: Our government is spending millions of dollars in the area of space exploration. This expenditure represents a misdirection of funds. It would be far better to use these funds to improve our own society and to upgrade our living conditions.

Assignment: What is your opinion of the idea that government funds should not be spent on space exploration but used for domestic purposes? Plan and write an essay that develops your ideas logically. Support your opinion with specific evidence taken from your personal experience, your observations of others, or your reading.

Take It to the Next Level

PETERSON'S

getting you there

Answers and Explanations

Sample Essay 2A

I can see the point of those who say that "this expenditure represents a misdirecting of funds." However, I feel it is necessary for humans to explore the stars and outer space in order to acquire more knowledge of the universe. Humans have always tried to learn more, even when it gets them in trouble. Wouldn't it be terrible if we bother some aliens and get destroyed by strange creatures who don't want us bothering them?

Anyhow, it is still important to send up rockets and space capsules to explore. The pictures we got to see and rock samples that come back are also fascinating. Someday maybe people will travel to far off countries and set up new civilizations. This would be a good chance to eliminate some of the overcrowded life on earth. We could also learn alot about what kind of gas or air, or surface other places have. This might help us back on earth too. The space program is also good for people's egos. It also may take their minds off of problems in our own world, which is not so bad.

We are spending far too much money on space travel and space exploration. As the question points out it would be far better to use these funds to help improve our own society and better our living conditions here on earth.

Analysis of Sample Essay 2A

1. There are several weaknesses in the essay. First, the writer does not take a clear stand. Does this student support or reject the thesis that space travel is of value and should be funded by the government? The first paragraph presents both views. The second paragraph basically supports the need for space exploration. The third paragraph, the concluding one, rejects this view, pointing out that too much money is needlessly spent on "space travel and space exploration." The essay tends to be confusing and disorganized.

2. The essay also contains many weaknesses in technical English. Problems in spelling and diction appear throughout (*humans* instead of *human beings* in the third sentence of the first paragraph; *alot* instead of *a lot* in the fifth sentence of the second paragraph; *off of* instead of *off* in the eighth sentence of the second paragraph). There are several awkward and ill-phrased sentences. In the second paragraph, the first sentence ends with the infinitive "to explore," but lacks an object of the infinitive. The second sentence of the second paragraph has a poorly ended verb clause. A better sentence would be, "The pictures and rock samples that came back to use . . . ." The word *good* is used three times in the second paragraph and should be replaced by more specific words, such as *valuable* or *important*.

3. The writer appears to understand the basic elements of essay organization, and the essay contains an introduction referring to the question, a development of supporting details, and a summarizing conclusion. Unfortunately, the lack of coherence strongly detracts from the value of the piece.

Sample Essay 2B

In our own country we have so many people who are unemployed and without jobs. Their families are without proper shelter and often don't have the money to buy the necessary food and clothing. If we took a portion of this money and provided employment for the jobless and homes for the homeless we would be doing our citizens a service. We could also use this money to develop research in medicine and find the cures for fatal diseases like cancer and HIV. Then we would be using our money correctly. What good is it to read about a flight to the moon when you are hungry or out of work.

I know that many people say that we have to be first in everything. That our national pride demands it. If we spend millions of dollars, we should be proud of the achievements of our scientists. Also we learn so many things about our vast universe and the world in which we live in.

Does this make good sense. I think that Charity begins at home. Lets not worry about what's happening on the moon. Let's be more concerned about what's happening here on the earth.

Analysis of Sample Essay 2B

1. The writer has a point of view that is clear and consistent.

2. Paragraph 1 provides excellent examples to support what is evidently the writer's position: that the money for space exploration should be used on earth to help society. (See under "Suggestions for Improvement" for the major flaw in this paragraph.)

3. The conclusion provides a summary and reinforces the writer's point of view.

Suggestions for Improvement

1. The author of this essay appears to have begun the essay in the middle. There is no introductory paragraph stating the issue or the writer's position. In the middle of the first paragraph the writer refers to "this money," but the reader doesn't know what "this money" is. While you don't need to restate the question word for word, you do need to include it in your introduction to provide the reader with a frame of reference.

2. Unfortunately, the many errors in punctuation, grammar, and usage seriously reduce the effectiveness of the essay and would doubtless lower the grade considerably. The writer should try to eliminate redundancies such as "unemployed and without jobs." End-stop punctuation is weak. The author uses periods instead of question marks to conclude the interrogative sentence in the last sentence of the first paragraph and the first sentence of the concluding paragraph. There is no reason to capitalize "Charity" (in the second sentence of the third paragraph), and although "Let's" is spelled correctly in the fourth sentence of the third paragraph, the necessary apostrophe is omitted in the same word in the preceding sentence. A careful proofreading of the essay might have helped the writer to locate and correct many of these errors.

More Practice Essays

For more practice, use the following quotations as writing prompts. Don't forget to:

- Set a timer for 25 minutes

- Read each prompt

- Decide whether you agree or disagree with it

- Then plan and write an essay within the 25 minutes

- Score it against the rubric on pages 248–251, use the free essay scorer on your CD, or use Peterson's satessayedge service (www.petersons. com/satessayedge). For more information, see the ad at the back of this book.

1. "Life is not a spectacle or a feast; it is a predicament."

2. "There is only one thing age can give you, and that is wisdom"

3. "Not to know is bad; not to wish to know is worse."

4. Public employees should not have the right to strike.

5. Every young American should serve the nation, either in the armed forces or in community service.

And now for a final congratulations! You're well prepared to tackle all sections of the Writing test! Put down your grammar book and pick up your calculator. Mathematics is next.

Chapter 7

Math Section— Enough Said

If *f*(*Chapter*) = A Bunch of Numbers, Then This Is the Math Section

The first thing we need to do is clear away a few misconceptions. Just as the SAT is not a measure of your intelligence, the SAT Math section is not an indication of your IQ, or even your math IQ. In fact, your performance on the SAT Math section is not even a precise indicator of your general math abilities. Some students who are not math whizzes in high school math classes ace the SAT Math section, and some students who have a 4.0 in high school math do not score as well as they would like on it. It's certainly true that being a good math student helps, but being a good math student and scoring well on the SAT Math section are not the same thing.

Scoring well on the SAT Math section means you are good at SAT Math, nothing more, nothing less. And being good at SAT Math is only important because many colleges like to use the SAT as part of their admissions criteria. Where you want to go to college plays a big part in determining how important the SAT Math section is for you. If you are planning on applying to engineering schools, for instance, a high math score may be more important than if you want to study English at a liberal arts college. In either case, colleges and universities do weigh the total score, so you should try your best on all three sections.

The New SAT

There are two basic changes to the Math section on the new SAT. The first is that one of the three question types is going the way of the dinosaurs. The old Math section included multiple choice, student-produced responses, and quantitative comparisons. The new Math section will only include multiple choice and student-produced responses. For many reasons, the

SAT test-makers decided to get rid of Quantitative Comparisons, so you don't have to worry about them. (Unless, of course, you love the SAT so much you want to know what it used to be like.)

> **Note**
>
> **Pacing**
>
> Spend about a minute on every question on the first pass. If you aren't getting anywhere in that time, move on and hit that problem again on your second pass.

The second change in the Math section is more important: more math concepts are being tested on the new test. On the old SAT you had to know a little algebra, a little geometry, and some basic number properties. On the new SAT you will need to know all the things from the old SAT plus some more advanced geometry, a little algebra II, and a new grab bag of math concepts just to keep things interesting.

On the whole, the new expanded topics are more complex and sophisticated than the old basic set of required knowledge. Don't run screaming into the hills yet, though. Just because the number of topics is expanding and the complexity of the topics is increasing does not mean that the Math section is actually going to be harder. Remember, the average score still has to be 500.

> **Note**
>
> The problems on the Math section get harder as the section progresses. Awareness of this order of difficulty is very important on the two multiple-choice Math sections. On the second problem in a section, answers that are easy to find are probably right, since that question appears early and, as such, is an easy question. Throughout this section, sample questions will be based on a hypothetical 21-question Math section.

Solving difficult problems on the old test involved knowledge of simple math concepts, multiple steps, and a good dash of cleverness. These convoluted, multi-step problems were no walk in the park. (Ask someone older about how easy the old Math section was.) The new Math section will still have some difficult questions that involve the simpler concepts, but it will also use the more sophisticated expanded topics to make questions harder.

The good news is that the problems involving knowledge of the harder topics won't demand clever techniques to solve as well. Basically, the old test made questions harder by expecting you to do ingenious things with simple concepts. The new test will make things harder by expecting you to do straightforward things with harder concepts. Therefore, if you grasp the more sophisticated topics, then you should be in good shape to do really well on the new SAT. If some of the more sophisticated topics elude you, you can still do well by mastering the basic materials. The bulk of this chapter is devoted to making sure you have a good grounding in both of these arenas, the old topics and the new.

Your Gear

There are two aids for test day: your calculator and the formula chart. You bring your calculator and the SAT provides the formula chart.

A Calculator Is Only as Accurate as the Fingers Punching the Buttons

The SAT would be a breeze if all the problems were just computation problems like $5235 \div 2.6$. You could just punch the numbers into your calculator and let it spit out the right answer. Of course, there won't be any problems that easy on the SAT. You will be expected to do a few steps of math reasoning before you get to the step where you pull out your calculator.

PEMDAS problems are the closest thing you will see to a straight computation problem. PEMDAS is an easy to way to remember a confusing math idea. It means:

(Parentheses Exponents) (Multiplication Division) (Addition Subtraction)

That is the order in which you do math operations when a problem requires you to perform multiple math operations. First, simplify what is inside parentheses. Next, simplify all the exponents. After that do the multiplication and division, then finally any addition and subtraction.

Here is an example of a problem where applying PEMDAS correctly is essential.

$$(3 + 4)^2[(2)(5 - 2)] =$$

Parentheses first:

$$(3 + 4)^2[(2)(5 - 2)] = (7)^2[(2)(3)]$$

Then exponents:

$$(7)^2[(2)(3)] = 49[(2)(3)]$$

265

Finally, multiplication:

$$49[(2)(3)] = (49)(6) = 294$$

If you didn't follow PEMDAS and did exponents before parentheses, you would have ended up with a different, wrong answer.

$$(3^2 + 4^2)[(2)(5 - 2)] = (9 + 16)[(2)(3)] = 25[(2)(3)] = 150$$

> **Note**
>
> For harder problems, the key will be to set up and manipulate equations properly. Once that's done, you can use your calculator.

In solving all problems, it is a good idea to write your work out. First, it makes things a lot less complicated because you don't have to do a bajillion steps in your head at once. And this, of course, will make it less likely that you will make a careless mistake. Second, if you write your work out, it is easier to catch a mistake. For instance, if the answer you came up with is not one of the answer choices, you can review your written work to catch any careless errors. But if you did all the work in your head, you won't have CAT scans to review your brain waves and catch your misstep.

There are three kinds of calculators you can use on the new SAT:

- A four-function calculator —adds, subtracts, multiplies, and divides.
- A scientific calculator—performs radicals, exponents, etc.
- A graphing calculator—displays graphs on screen.

You CANNOT use a calculator that prints out calculations, has a typewriter keypad, or makes any noises. As you might expect, you also can't bring a laptop or anything that needs to be plugged into the wall.

The best idea is to use a calculator you are comfortable working with. You don't want to eat up precious test-taking time by looking for the $\sqrt{}$ symbol. You might think that a snazzier graphing calculator will help you more than a simple four-function one, but the SAT just isn't designed to give an advantage to anyone with a fancy calculator. You can actually solve all the problems on the SAT without a calculator. Calculators just make getting the answer a little faster and easier.

What's the Volume of a Cylinder Again?

At the beginning of every Math section there is a set of formulas that show you how to determine the area of a circle or the volume of a cube. These formulas are the ones that the SAT tests the most, so it is nice to have them handy at the front of each section. This chapter will go over all these formulas. You will save time on the test if you commit them to memory. This way you'll avoid flipping back to the front of the section for every other problem. However, if on test day you're not entirely confident about the side relationships of a 30-60-90 triangle, it's nice to know that you can look this up.

You might take all three Math sections and never once use either the formulas at the front of the section or your calculator. That's fine. Realize, though, that you have these two tools at your disposal. Experiment with them, and when you take the sample Math sections in the back of this book, try to use them whenever possible. The more techniques, tools, and strategies you have, the better your chances are of finding a way to answer the math questions.

About Those Math Questions . . .

As stated earlier, the new Math section will contain two question types: multiple choice and student-produced response. You are probably very familiar with the multiple-choice format by now, so there is no need to go over it. Student-produced response, on the other hand, might sound a little vague and unclear.

The reality is very simple. Student-produced response just means you give the answer, instead of picking it from a list of multiple-choice answers. Undoubtedly, you have taken math tests in school where you had to produce the answer yourself. Most likely, you wrote your answer down on a sheet of paper.

The "sheet of paper" route won't work on the SAT. Instead, student-produced responses are placed on a grid-in answer sheet. If you've never done this before, some explanation of proper gridding-in is required. It's better to learn it now than on test day.

> **Note**
>
> The bulk of the problems on the Math section will be multiple choice, not student-produced response. This is good news, since guessing a right answer for a student-produced response is practically impossible, while your chances are much better on a multiple-choice problem. Review the "one question-one solution" discussion in chapter 2 to see why multiple-choice problems are preferable to student-produced responses.

PETERSON'S

getting you there

Here is what you will see on the answer sheet on the student-produced responses:

Here is how you would grid in $\frac{5}{11}$, 3.4, and 409.

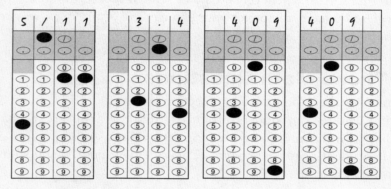

Points About Grid-Ins

1. Only mark one oval in each column.

2. The answer sheets are machine scored, so only answers with correctly marked ovals will receive credit.

3. It's a good idea to write your answer in the boxes above the grid to help you fill in the ovals accurately. This is not a requirement, but a helpful practice.

4. There might be more than one answer to a grid-in problem. If you notice this in solving a problem, don't fret about which one to put down. Just put down one of the correct answers because all correct answers are acceptable.

5. There's no way to record a negative number. Therefore, no correct answer will be negative. If you get a negative answer, go back to the drawing board.

6. Mixed numbers like $3\frac{1}{4}$ must be recorded as either an improper fraction, $\frac{13}{4}$, or as a decimal, 3.25. Either the fraction or the decimal is acceptable, but $3\frac{1}{4}$ is not. Since gridding in mixed numbers is a bit tricky, you can expect at least one mixed number answer.

7. If you get a decimal answer with a lot of digits, fill in the most accurate value the grid will allow. For example, if you get the answer 0.34567, record the answer as .345 or .346. If you don't fill in as many spaces as possible, for instance by answering .34 or .35, your answer will be wrong. (Notice on these examples that both the rounded and truncated responses are acceptable.)

8. Responses involving either fractions or decimals can be gridded in as either. For example, either of the following is an acceptable way to grid in 0.5.

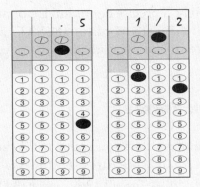

That is a lot to take in at one time. But once you work through the examples in the text and take the practice tests, you should be comfortable with student-produced response questions.

Numbers, Variables, Circles, and all that Other Math Stuff

The new SAT places all math questions into one of the following four categories:

1. Numbers and Operations

2. Algebra and Functions

3. Geometry and Measurement

4. Data Analysis, Statistics, and Probability

There are different ways to describe general math categories, but since these are the four categories the College Board uses, these are the four areas this book will use. The rest of this chapter will cover the basic and the *Take it to the Next Level* topics in each category to help you answer SAT math questions correctly.

Numbers and Operations

SAT arithmetic is all about how numbers work. The fancy phrase for this is, "number properties." There are a lot of detailed number properties that the SAT likes to test, finer points like, "Is 1 a prime number?" If you don't know this answer definitively, read on.

Math Speak

Math folks like math words because they have precise definitions. The SAT test writers like math words because they like to test if you understand those precise definitions. Fortunately, a precise definition is not necessarily a hard definition. In fact, almost all the math words on the SAT have pretty simple definitions. It is just a matter of knowing them well enough to be able to work problems with them.

Common Math Speak Terms

1. **Integer**
    Integers are like the numbers that you count with, such as 1, 14, and 28, but also include 0 and negatives of the counting numbers. **Consecutive integers** are integers that follow in sequence, like 19, 20, and 21 or −2, −1, 0, 1. If you want to get math fancy, and sometimes the SAT expects you to, you can represent consecutive integers like this, n, $n + 1$, $n + 2$, and so on. If you plug in any integer for n, you will generate a sequence of consecutive integers.

2. **Odd** and **Even**
    Odd numbers cannot be evenly divided by 2 while even numbers can be evenly divided by 2. −9, 5, and 13 are examples of odd numbers, and −18, 4, and 102 are examples of even numbers. Tuck it away in your brain that **zero is an even number**, since $0 \div 2 = 0$.

> ## Tip
>
> **Working with Evens and Odds**
>
> Addition
>
> even + even + even
>
> even + odd = odd
>
> odd + odd = even
>
> Multiplication
>
> even × even = even
>
> even × odd = even
>
> odd × odd = odd
>
> If you ever forget one of these rules you can always just plug in numbers to remind yourself.

3. **Prime Numbers**

   These are numbers divisible only by themselves and 1. Here's the list: 2, 3, 5, 7, 11, 13, 17, 19, and so on. Notice that **1 is not a prime number** and **2 is the only even prime number**.

4. **Digits**

   The numbers 0, 1, 2, 3, 4, 5, 6, 7, 8, 9, 0 are all the digits. **Distinct** digits are two digits that are not the same. 7 and 4 are distinct digits, but 6 and 6 are NOT.

5. **Quotient**

   This is the end result after you divide two numbers. 4 is the quotient of 12 ÷ 3. Not every two numbers divide evenly, which is why you might have a . . .

6. **Remainder**

   This is what is left over when a number is not divisible by another number. When you divide 5 by 2, you get: 5 ÷ 2 = 2 remainder 1.

7. **Product**

   The end result after you multiply two numbers together. 10 is the product of 2 × 5.

8. **Factor**

   Factors are whole numbers that multiply to give another whole number. Since 2 times 6 equals 12, 2 and 6 are factors of 12. (3 and 4 are also factors of 12.)

9. **Multiple**

    You start with a number, and then begin to multiply it by positive whole numbers. All these products (a previous term) are multiples of the original number. For example, 5, 10, 15, 20 are the first few multiples of 5.

Now that all these terms are swirling around in your skull, here's an SAT problem heavy on the Math Speak:

6. What is the difference between the number of positive integer factors of 12 and the number of positive integer factors of 8?

    (A) 0
    (B) 2
    (C) 4
    (D) 6
    (E) 8

In a problem like this, the difficulty is figuring out what is being asked. "Difference" means you are subtracting two things, but what exactly are you subtracting? To figure this out, you need to discover the number of positive integer factors of 12 and the number of positive integer factors of 8. Then you can subtract these two numbers.

How many positive integer factors of 12 are there? The factors are: 1×12, 2×6, 3×4, which adds up to 6. How about for 8? 1×8, 2×4. This adds up to 4. The difference between 6 and 4 is 2, choice (B).

Once you sort through the vocabulary, the problem becomes so simple you could ask a preschooler for the answer to 6 minus 4.

8.
$$
\begin{array}{r}
1\,D \\
+\ 2\,D \\
\hline
3\,E
\end{array}
$$

    If in the above addition problem D and E are distinct digits, how many possible values of D are there?

    (A) Zero
    (B) Two
    (C) Four
    (D) Five
    (E) Nine

Unpack the math terminology first. D and E are distinct digits, which means that they are 0 through 9 and do not equal each other. Now look at the addition problem. In the ones column, $D + D$ could equal E or $1E$. $D + D = E$, because there is not a one carried over to the tens column. You know this because the tens column equals three and not four.

From $D + D = E$ you can also see that E must be an even digit because two equal digits cannot add up to an odd number. This means E could be 8, 6, 4, 2, which means D could be 4, 3, 2, 1. D can't be zero because if it were D and E wouldn't be distinct. The answer is four, choice (C).

The last two problems were in the easy-medium range of difficulty. To see how math terms show up on harder problems, take a look at the following problem. This problem is typical of the way the old SAT used to make problems tough, and chances are good you will still encounter one or two hard math problems similar to this one.

21. $\dfrac{a}{b} + \dfrac{c}{d} + \dfrac{e}{f} \ldots$

If the above series is filled with positive consecutive increasing integers starting with a, such that $a > b > c > d > e > f$, then which of the following is less than $\dfrac{e}{f}$?

(A) $\dfrac{a+1}{a}$

(B) a

(C) $\dfrac{a+3}{a+4}$

(D) $\dfrac{a+4}{a+5}$

(E) None of the above.

The phrase *positive consecutive increasing integers* seems difficult, but unpacking it one term at a time takes the sting out of it. *Positive* means the numbers are greater than zero. *Consecutive* numbers are in order like 3, 4, and 5. *Increasing* means the numbers are going up, and you know what *integer* means. Putting that together, the series starts with an integer at a, and each succeeding letter increases by one integer. This means that $b = a + 1$, and $c = a + 2$. Seeing this, you can rewrite all the terms in the series in terms of a, including e divided by f, $\dfrac{e}{f} = \dfrac{a+4}{a+5}$. Doing this is helpful since the answer choices are all written in that manner.

PETERSON'S
getting you there

Now let's look at those answer choices. Choices (A) and (B) are too great because they are greater than 1, which $\frac{e}{f}$ isn't. Choice (D) equals $\frac{e}{f}$, so it's not what you're looking for. If you plug in numbers that fit the criteria, $a = 2$ for example, you will see that choice (C) is the answer.

Plugging in numbers from the get-go would have been another way to solve this problem. Once you unpacked the terminology, you could have made $a = 2$, or 3, or some other small integer since you don't want to make the computations too hard. Then you could have plugged in numbers for all the other variables. If you don't mess up the math, you would get to choice (C) again.

There might even be other ways to solve this problem. Never forget that there is usually more than one way to answer any SAT math problem. If you can't figure it out one way, try a different approach.

Fractions and Decimals

Fractions and decimals are two related, slightly different ways to talk about parts of a whole. For instance, if 5 of 10 pieces of a pizza have been eaten, then $\frac{5}{10}$ or $\frac{1}{2}$ of the pizza is gone. You could also say that 0.50 of the pizza is gone. You are saying the same thing because $\frac{1}{2} = 0.50$. The SAT will expect you to understand fractions and decimals and how they relate.

A fraction is a number made up of two integers and it looks like this $\frac{a}{b}$. The number on top, a, is called the numerator, and the number on the bottom, b, is called the denominator.

An important thing to remember about fractions is that they are actually division problems in disguise. A fraction means you are dividing, the numerator, by the denominator. The fraction $\frac{a}{b}$ really is the same thing as $a \div b$. Since $\frac{a}{b} = a \div b$, b cannot equal zero because dividing by zero is undefined. Keep this little nugget lodged in your brain because it might come up on a function problem. (We'll get to functions later.)

Note

The SAT will expect you to be able to perform math operations with fractions, like adding, subtracting, dividing, and multiplying. If you don't remember when you need a common denominator, or how to divide a fraction by a fraction, check out an Algebra I textbook for a refresher.

5. If $\dfrac{\dfrac{x}{4}}{\dfrac{2}{3}} = \dfrac{3}{8}$ then $x =$

   (A) 1
   (B) 2
   (C) 3
   (D) 4
   (E) 5

The standard, textbook approach to this problem is to solve for x. You do that by isolating x:

$$\frac{\dfrac{x}{4}}{\dfrac{2}{3}} = \frac{3}{8}$$

$$\frac{\dfrac{x}{4}}{\dfrac{2}{3}} \times \frac{2}{3} = \frac{3}{8} \times \frac{2}{3} \qquad \text{Here, both sides are multiplied by } \frac{2}{3} \text{ to eliminate the}$$

fraction in the denominator under x.

$$\frac{x}{4} = \frac{3}{8} \times \frac{2}{3}$$

$$\frac{x}{4} = \frac{6}{24}$$

$$4 \times \frac{x}{4} = \frac{6}{24} \times 4$$

$$x = \frac{6}{24} \times 4 = \frac{24}{24} = 1$$

A second way to solve this problem is to plug in the answer choices for x. Start with the middle value, 3, and see what you get.

$$\frac{\dfrac{3}{4}}{\dfrac{2}{3}} = \frac{3}{4} \div \frac{2}{3} = \frac{3}{4} \times \frac{3}{2} = \frac{9}{8}$$

As you can see, $\frac{9}{8} \neq \frac{3}{8}$. That value for x is too great. Since you know that choice (C) is too great, look at the remaining answer choices. Choices (D) and (E) are greater than (C), and since (C) is wrong, these will also be wrong. You can cross them out. All that remains are choices (B) and (A). You can plug in the value $x = 2$, and if choice (B) is wrong, then you know the answer must be (A).

Fractions also come in a hybrid form called mixed fractions. They look like this, $3\frac{2}{7}$. This number is mixed because it has an integer and a fraction. In longhand, $3\frac{2}{7}$ means $3 + \frac{2}{7}$.

What do you do if you need to rewrite this mixed fraction as an improper fraction? You could rewrite 3 as a fraction and add $\frac{3}{1} + \frac{2}{7}$. But there is a quicker way. Multiply the integer out front by the denominator ($7 \times 3 = 21$), then add that product to the numerator ($21 + 2 = 23$), and voila! You have it. In our example $3\frac{2}{7} = \frac{23}{7}$.

In the previous example, 3 was rewritten as a fraction. There is a simple way to rewrite integers as fractions. Make 3 the numerator of a fraction and 1 the denominator of a fraction. So $3 = \frac{3}{1}$. You can see that this is true if you recall that $\frac{a}{b} = a \div b$. You can rewrite any integer as a fraction by simply putting the integer into the numerator and 1 into the denominator.

As was said above, fractions and decimals express the same idea. To rewrite a fraction as a decimal, just divide the numerator by the denominator; remember $\frac{a}{b} = a \div b$. With a calculator this computation is very, very easy. Rewriting a decimal as a fraction is equally easy. Say you need to rewrite 0.19 as a fraction. First put 19 into the numerator. The denominator of a decimal equivalence is always going to be some multiple of 10. The question is, "What multiple of ten goes in the denominator?"

276

You figure that out by counting the places to the right of the decimal, and that number is the number of zeros in the denominator. In 0.19 there are two places to the right of the decimal, 1 and 9; so there are two zeros in the denominator, which means $0.19 = \dfrac{19}{100}$. If you aren't sure if you have correctly rewritten a decimal as a fraction you can always plug the fraction into a calculator to see if you get the correct decimal back.

All of the place values to the right of the decimal have funny names with "*ths*" at the end of them. Here is an example to refresh your memory about place values,

Take the number 934.167

9 is in the hundreds place, so the 9 means	900
3 is in the tens place, so the 3 means	30
4 is in the units place, so the 4 means	4
1 is in the tenths place, so the 1 means	$\dfrac{1}{10}$
6 is in the hundredths place, so the 6 means	$\dfrac{6}{100}$
7 is in the thousands place, so the 7 means	$\dfrac{7}{1000}$

3. Which of the following numbers has a value between 0.44 and $\dfrac{6}{11}$?

   (A) $\dfrac{1}{3}$

   (B) $\dfrac{9}{20}$

   (C) $\dfrac{6}{10}$

   (D) $\dfrac{2}{3}$

   (E) $\dfrac{5}{7}$

The easiest way to approach this problem is to rewrite $\frac{6}{11}$ as a decimal, and then rewrite the likely answer choices as decimals. Plugging into your calculator, $\frac{6}{11} \approx 0.55$, so you're looking for something with a value between 0.44 and 0.55. Considering the fact that 0.50 would be a value between these two values, and that $0.50 = \frac{1}{2}$, you want a fraction around one-half. If you eyeball the answer choices, (B) looks the closest to one-half. Try it first. $\frac{9}{20} = 0.45$. So (B) is the answer.

> **Note**
>
> Rewriting all the fractions in this problem as decimals using your calculator is one example of using your calculator to help you answer a problem. Note that it wouldn't matter what kind of calculator you use.

Percents, or Why Giving 110% Is Impossible

The concept of percent is related to decimals and fractions because it also deals with parts of a whole. Percent means "per hundred" or "divided by one hundred." If you want to rewrite a percentage as a fraction you simply put the number of the percentage in the numerator and 100 in the denominator. So 34% is equivalent to $\frac{34}{100}$, and simplifies to $\frac{17}{50}$.

You can also easily rewrite percentages as decimals. Recall that $0.10 = \frac{10}{100}$, and as we just saw $10\% = \frac{10}{100}$. So 0.10 is the same thing as 10%. If you want to rewrite a percentage as a decimal, simply move the decimal point two places to the left. For instance, 115% is equivalent to 1.15, or 0.5% is equivalent to 0.005.

An easy SAT problem with percentages might involve determining what percentage one number is of another. For example, the problem might read, "What percentage is 4 of 27?" The problem is asking how much of 27 is 4? In math, you write this as $\frac{4}{27}$. To find what percentage equals $\frac{4}{27}$, first use a calculator to divide 4 by 27. You get a decimal (0.148) which you can easily rewrite as a percentage (14.8% or 15%).

The answer to other percentage problems might not be so easy to see. However, you can always set up an equation like this, $\frac{4}{27} = \frac{x}{100}$. Since the right side of the equation is the fractional form of a percentage, if you find x, you know what percentage 4 is of 27. Solve for x by cross-multiplying,

$$\frac{4}{27} = \frac{x}{100}$$
$$(27)(x) = (4)(100)$$
$$27x = 400$$
$$x = \frac{400}{27}$$

At this point your calculator comes in handy, $\frac{400}{27} \approx 14.8$.

Percentage increase and decrease problems can be a little harder. You might see a problem where you are told that the price of bananas increased 10%, and then increased 15% percent, and you have to determine the percentage change of the price. In percent-change problems you must keep straight what is increasing or decreasing. In our banana problem, the original price increases 10%, and then the resulting second price increases 15%. If you guess that the total percent change is 25%, you will have missed that it is the second price that increased 15%. Because there are two prices involved, you can't just add up the two percentage increases.

This is why it is important to always keep track of what exactly is increasing or decreasing. Our banana problem might now seem like a real quandary, but a test trick simplifies it. Since the original price is not given, we can pick one. For ease's sake, pick 100 as the original price. This is a good number to use, because it is easy to see that 10% of 100 is 10. If the first increase is 10, then the price of the bananas is now:

$$\text{original price} + \text{increase} = \text{new price}$$
$$100 + 10 = 110$$

> **Note**
>
> This new price, 110, increased by 15%. You can see now why you can't simply add 10% and 15% together. The 10% increase was related to the original price of 100, while the 15% increase is connected to a different price, 110.

To determine the value of a 15% increase to 110, multiply 110 by 0.15, the decimal equivalent of 15%. This gives you $110 \times 0.15 = 16.5$. Adding 16.5 to 110 results in the final price of 126.5.

PETERSON'S
getting you there

What is the percentage change in going from 100 to 126.5? It is a 26.5% increase.

The ease of reading off this percentage increase is another reason why starting with the value of 100 works well.

In the example you just worked through, you were given the percentage increases and asked to find the percentage change. You might see a problem that asks the reverse; it will give you the percentage change and the final price of the item, and you will have to find the original price. There are similar formulas that are helpful for either kind of problem,

Decrease in value: Increase in value:

$$\frac{x - y}{x} = z \qquad\qquad \frac{y - x}{x} = z$$

where x is the original value, y is the second value, and z is the percentage change.

4. If the price of a computer is decreased by 25%, and after the decrease the price is $1237.50, what was the original price of the computer?

   (A) $412.50
   (B) $927.75
   (C) $1550.50
   (D) $1610.75
   (E) $1650

With the percentage change formula in hand, you don't have to get tangled up in which way the price went. Plugging in the values for this problem (it is a decrease in value),

$$\frac{x - y}{x} = z$$

$$\frac{x - \$1237.50}{x} = 0.25$$

$$x - \$1237.50 = 0.25x$$

$$x - 0.25x - \$1237.50 = 0.25x - 0.25x$$

$$0.75x - \$1237.50 = 0$$

$$0.75x - \$1237.50 + \$1237.50 = 0 + \$1237.50$$

$$0.75x = \$1237.50$$

Now calculate with your "electronic abacus," $x = \dfrac{\$1237.50}{0.75} = \$1650.$

Of course, if you already have too many equations to keep track of, you can reason your way through this problem. You could reason that since the price has decreased 25%, then $1237.50 equals 75% of the original price. Translating this into algebra, you get $0.75x = \$1237.50$. Either way, the answer is choice (E).

> Yet another way to approach the problem is to use common sense and look at the answer choices. You know that the price *decreased* to $1237.50, so the original price must be greater than $1237.50. This eliminates choices (A) and (B), giving you a one-in-three chance of guessing correctly.

Ratios and Their Relatives

A ratio is a way to compare two or more things and show how much of Thing 1 you have in comparison to Thing 2. For example, if you have 15 new-wave CDs and 10 hip-hop CDs, the ratio of new-wave CDs to hip-hop CDs is 15:10. Ratios, like fractions, can be simplified to simplist form, which means the ratio of new wave to hip-hop CDs can be simplified:

15:10 =
15 ÷ 5:10 ÷ 5 = (both sides are divided by 5 to simplify the ratio.)
3:2

Notice that with the ratio of your CDs it matters in which order you say the genres. The ratio of new wave to hip-hop is 3:2, but the ratio of hip-hop to new wave is 2:3.

Ratios can also be compared to other ratios. Suppose you had to determine which ratio was greater, 5:3 or 7:4 ? To accomplish this, first rewrite the ratios as fractional forms by putting the first number in the numerator and the second number in the denominator:

$$5:3 = \frac{5}{3} \text{ and } 7:4 = \frac{7}{4}$$

There are a couple of ways to determine which fraction, $\frac{5}{3}$ or $\frac{7}{4}$, is greater. You can rewrite both numbers as mixed numbers, or look for a common denominator:

$$\frac{5}{3} \; ? \; \frac{7}{4}$$

$$\frac{4}{4} \times \frac{5}{3} \; ? \; \frac{7}{4} \times \frac{3}{3}$$

$$\frac{20}{12} < \frac{21}{12}$$

Since 21 is greater than 20, the fraction $\frac{7}{4} > \frac{5}{3}$. This means 7:4 is greater than 5:3.

From a technical standpoint, ratios and fractions are not interchangeable, so your math teacher might quibble about rewriting a ratio as a fraction. For the SAT, though, you don't have to worry about such technicalities. If rewriting a ratio as a fraction helps you solve a problem, rewrite away.

There are 24 boys and 30 girls in the first grade class at Lakewood Elementary. What is the ratio of boys to first graders at Lakewood Elementary?

(A) 4:5
(B) 5:4
(C) 4:9
(D) 5:9
(E) 8:9

With ratios you always need to pay attention to what you are comparing. This problem asks you to compare boys and first graders. Now it's a matter of finding these two amounts and placing them in a ratio.

How many boys are there? 24.

How many first graders are there? 54, since it's the total number of boys (24) and girls (30).

The ratio of boys to first graders is 24:54. But you should suspect that this ratio can be simplified, especially since 24:54 is not an answer choice. 24 is divisible by 6 as is 54, 24:54 = 4 × 6:9 × 6 = 4:9. Choice (C) is the answer.

Algebra and Functions

You are probably either in an algebra class right now or recently finished one, so formal introductions are not in order. You already know that algebra means working with variables, solving equations, and so forth. SAT Algebra, though, is a little different from what you see in the classroom. You will have to do some basic algebra moves like factoring or simplifying, but you will not have to do any ten-step problems or work with really complicated algebraic expressions. Since all math problems on the SAT have to be workable in a reasonable amount of time, the algebra on the SAT cannot be too involved.

That's good news for you, but there is a catch: the test writers may tax your ingenuity with problems that require clever applications of a concept. Or, they may create problems that challenge your ability to identify the relevant concepts. To combat this, we'll make sure you are familiar with all the basic algebra concepts and also with the kinds of moves the SAT will expect you to make with that basic knowledge.

Here's a test-taking tip before we get to the meaty stuff: algebra questions that appear early on in a Math section will often just require solving for a variable. Pretty straightforward stuff. Later in a math section—as the problems become more difficult—you should expect that an algebra problem will require you to make a clever connection or see an "un-obvious" way to solve it. But in either situation, the problems should require about the same number of steps to solve.

Exponents and Roots, or the Rads and the Squares

Exponents are just shorthand for writing a number times itself. So instead of writing 4×4, you can write 4^2. The 4 is called the *base*, and 2 is the *power*, or *exponent*.

Here is a condensed version of how exponents function. Look it over, plug in some numbers (just for grins), and make sure you are comfortable with how exponents work.

PETERSON'S
getting you there

Working with Exponents

1. **Adding and Subtracting**

    You can add and subtract numbers with exponents if they have the same base and are raised to the same power.

    $$4r^2 + 7r^2 = 11r^2$$
    $$8t^3 - t^3 = 7t^3$$

    but $5k^2 + 8k \neq 13k^2$ or $13k^3$ since they are not raised to the same power.

2. **Multiplying and Dividing**

    You can also multiply and divide numbers if they have the same base.

    $$y^a y^b = y^{a+b}$$

    For instance, $s^2 \times s^3 = s^5$ makes sense if you see that

    $$s^2 \times s^3 = (s \times s)(s \times s \times s) = s^5$$

    You can count up the five s's

    $$\frac{x^a}{x^b} = x^{a-b}$$

    For example, $\dfrac{f^9}{f^4}. = f^{9-4} = f^5$.

3. **Raising Powers to Powers**

    You can also raise a number with an exponent to a power.

    $$(z^a)^b = z^{ab}$$

    So $(h^3)^5 = h^{15}$

    Let's try a problem.

9. $\left(\dfrac{x^2}{x^3}\right)^2 = 4$, then $x =$

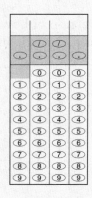

The good news about a problem like this is that there are no hidden tricks. You just have to solve for x. This should be simple after your review of how exponents work.

$$\left(\frac{x^2}{x^3}\right)^2 = 4$$

$$\left(\frac{1}{x}\right)^2 = 4$$

$$\frac{1}{x^2} = 4$$

But don't stop here. Since x is in the denominator, you need to move it to the other side of the equation.

$$\frac{1}{x^2} = 4$$

$$(x^2)\frac{1}{x^2} = 4x^2$$

$$1 = 4x^2$$

$$\frac{1}{4} = x^2$$

You might get stuck here if you don't know how to take the square root of a fraction. A little basic math can get things moving. What fraction times itself gives you $\frac{1}{4}$? $\frac{1}{2} \times \frac{1}{2} = \frac{1}{4}$. So $\frac{1}{2}$ is the answer.

Alert! Actually, there is another possible answer, $\left(-\frac{1}{2}\right)$, since it is also true that $\left(-\frac{1}{2}\right)\left(-\frac{1}{2}\right) = \frac{1}{4}$. But since you can't grid-in a negative answer, $\frac{1}{2}$ is the only answer for this problem.

The last problem illustrated something that you should always keep in mind when you are dealing with even exponents. When you see $x^2 = 16$, do not automatically assume that x has to equal 4, since it might also equal -4. This is the kind of trap that the SAT likes to lay for the inattentive student, so beware of it. When you are working with odd exponents, the story is different. If $x^3 = 27$, you know that 3 is the only true value for x because $(-3)(-3)(-3) = -27$.

PETERSON'S
getting you there

A relative of the exponent is the square root. It looks like this $\sqrt{}$, and it's the inverse of squaring a number. When you square 5, you multiply it by itself to get 5, but when take the square root of 25, you get the number that times itself gives 25.

$$5 \times 5 = 25, \text{ so } \sqrt{25} = 5.$$

Square roots can also be written as exponents like this:

$$\sqrt{y} = y^{\frac{1}{2}}.$$

Getting to the Roots

1. **Adding and Subtracting Roots**

   This is similar to exponents. You can only add or subtract expressions with roots if what is under the radical is the same. $4\sqrt{5} + 6\sqrt{5} = 10\sqrt{5}$, but there's not much you can do with $3\sqrt{3} + 2\sqrt{4}$. You probably won't see a problem like $3\sqrt{3} + 2\sqrt{4}$, but if you do, whip out your calculator and get busy with the $\sqrt{}$ key.

2. **Simplifying Square Roots**

   Like fractions, square roots can be simplified. To do so, factor the number under the radical, and factor any perfect squares out from underneath the radical.

   $$2\sqrt{12} = 2\sqrt{3 \times 4} = 2 \times 2\sqrt{3} = 4\sqrt{3}$$

3. **Multiplying Square Roots**

   You can multiply square roots together, and sometimes after you do this, you find a perfect square underneath the radical that you can then pull out.

   $$\sqrt{24} \times \sqrt{2} = \sqrt{24 \times 2} = \sqrt{48}$$
   $$\sqrt{48} = \sqrt{16 \times 3} = 4\sqrt{3}$$

   Since 16 is the square root of 4, you can factor it out from underneath the square root sign.

4. **Dividing Square Roots**

   Occasionally, you can find similar terms in both the denominator and numerator, which you can then divide out. Getting similar terms often requires factoring like in the example below, where $\sqrt{34}$ is restated as $(\sqrt{2})(\sqrt{17})$.

   $$\frac{\sqrt{34}}{\sqrt{17}} = \frac{(\sqrt{2})(\sqrt{17})}{\sqrt{17}} = \sqrt{2}$$

More Algebra and Functions

You already have been using algebra throughout this chapter. Look at the preceding pages and note how many times a **variable**—usually a letter like x—was used to denote an unknown numerical quantity. In a nutshell, that's algebra.

Algebra employs variables to represent unknown quantities. That's a simple definition, and some algebra problems are basic and straightforward:

$$65 = t - 40$$

Here, if you add 40 to both sides, you find a numerical value for t. You've solved an algebra problem, albeit an easy one. As you might expect, the algebra problems on the new SAT will typically be more difficult.

X-Ref

Before discussing functions, it helps to have a good understanding of basic algebra concepts such as variables, equations, and factoring. Functions are covered starting on page 298 after these fundamental algebraic ideas have been reviewed.

9. If $\left(\dfrac{x^2}{x^3}\right)^2 = 4$, then $x =$

287

Although you need a knowledge of fractions and exponents to answer this properly, there is an algebraic component as well. You have a variable, x, and you need to solve the equation to determine an actual numerical value for it. In this sense your goal is the same as it was for the equation $65 = t - 40$. Do the math necessary to determine the numerical value of the variable. Since SAT algebra questions can come in bewildering shapes, it's always helpful to keep this goal in mind. If you encounter a tough question with variables, and you're not sure where to start, ask yourself, "How can I determine the values of these variables?" Determining values for these unknown quantities is often the path to getting the right answer.

Equations

In the earlier part of an SAT section, you might see a problem where you are given an equation with one variable and have to solve for that variable. Since you have already done that a number of times in this chapter, you should be up to speed on that.

Things get a little more complicated if there are two equations and two variables, yet you can still solve for both variables because you have two equations. The general math rule is you can solve for as many different variables as you have equations. So if you have two equations and two variables, you're in business. If you have five variables and five equations, you're still alright. Luckily, you will most likely not see more than two equations and two unknowns.

With two variables, solve for one variable in one equation and then substitute that result into the second equation. For example, consider the following problem.

7. If $\dfrac{x + y}{11} = 1$ and $\dfrac{y}{x + 1} = 2$, then what is the value of $y - x =$

(A) -8
(B) -4
(C) 0
(D) 5
(E) 11

To find the answer to this problem you have to find x and y. Deciding which variable to start with is largely up to you. Solving for y in the second equation looks easiest:

$$\frac{y}{x+1} = 2$$

$$(x+1)\left(\frac{y}{x+1}\right) = (2)(x+1)$$

$$y = 2(x+1)$$

$$y = 2x+2$$

Now plug this value for y into the first equation, and you can solve for x, since that is the only variable in the equation.

$$\frac{x+y}{11} = 1$$

$$\frac{x+2x+2}{11} = 1$$

$$(11)\left(\frac{x+2x+2}{11}\right) = (1)(11)$$

$$3x+2 = 11$$

$$3x+2-2 = 11-2$$

$$3x = 9$$

$$\frac{3x}{3} = \frac{9}{3}$$

$$x = 3$$

You find y by plugging into either equation $\frac{y}{x+1} = 2$ (the original one) or $y = 2x+2$ (the equation you worked out first).

$$\frac{y}{x+1} = 2$$

$$\frac{y}{4} = 2$$

$$y = 8$$

In both cases, y equals 8, so $y - x = 8 - 3 = 5$.

PETERSON'S
getting you there

Inequalities, When Things Aren't Equal

An equation is when the stuff on the left side equals the stuff on the right side. An inequality is when the stuff on the left does *not* equal the stuff on the right side.

The same rules apply for solving an inequality as for solving an equation (if you do something to one side you have to do the same thing to the other side). But there is one important difference between the two. **If you multiply or divide by a negative number you have to switch the direction of the inequality.** There's a good reason for this, but it's not going to be covered here. The SAT doesn't test whether or not you understand why you switch it. It just tests if you know to switch it.

For example, if you need to solve for x in the following inequality, $-3x - 4 > 8$, use the normal techniques but remember to switch the sign.

$$-3x - 4 > 8$$
$$-3x - 4 + 4 > 8 + 4$$
$$-3x > 12$$
$$\frac{-3x}{-3} < \frac{12}{-3}$$
$$x < -4$$

If you forget to do the ole' switcheroo you get $x > -4$, and you can bet the farm that this incorrect answer will be lying in ambush somewhere in the answer choices.

6. If $9 > -3x - 3 > 6$, which of the following statements is true?

   (A) $-4 < x < -3$

   (B) $-\dfrac{5}{4} < x < -\dfrac{1}{4}$

   (C) $-3 < x < 1$

   (D) $2 < x < 4$

   (E) $\dfrac{5}{2} < x < \dfrac{9}{2}$

The rule for working with a double inequality is the same: if you do something to one side you have to do it to all three sides.

$$9 > -3x - 3 < 6$$
$$9 + 3 > -3x - 3 + 3 > 6 + 3$$
$$12 > -3x > 9$$
$$\frac{12}{-3} < \frac{-3x}{-3} < \frac{9}{-3}$$
$$-4 < x < -3$$

Choice (A) is the answer.

The Math section won't be riddled with inequalities, but there will be at least one or two. Remember to flip the sign when multiplying or dividing with negative numbers, and you should do well on these problems.

Absolute Value

Absolute value sounds imposing and extreme, but the explanation is simple. The absolute value of any number is how far it is from zero. The absolute value of 9 and -9 is the same (9) since both are 9 from zero. In math notation absolute value looks like two high straight fences surrounding a shy number.

$$|-9| = |9| = 9$$

The absolute value of something is always positive because distances, the distance from zero in this case, are always positive. There's no such thing as a negative mile, for instance. This means that whatever comes out of the absolute value symbols will always be positive.

Always do all the arithmetic inside the absolute value signs before taking the absolute value. For example, $|-6 -3| \neq |6 - 3|$ because $|-6 - 3| = |-9| = 9$ and $|6 - 3| = |3| = 3$.

6. If $|2(x - 3) + x| = 12$, then what is one possible value of x?

Note

This example might seem a bit strange since it asks for one "possible" value instead of a single value. However, there is usually at least one grid-in question on every test for which there is more than one correct answer. If you don't expect this, it can lead to uncertainty. Students are accustomed to a single correct math answer, and are suddenly faced with a question that yields more than one answer. They don't know which answer to grid-in, mistakenly thinking that only one answer will be counted correct.

Don't let this happen to you. When you encounter the more-than-one-correct-answer grid-in question, mentally say, "Oh, here's the more-than-one-correct-answer grid-in question." Then find an answer—any correct one will do—grid it in, and move on.

First simplify within the absolute value signs:

$$|2(x - 3) + x| = 12$$
$$|2x - 6 + x| = 12$$
$$|3x - 6| = 12$$

Without the absolute values, you would simply solve for x at this point.

$$3x - 6 = 12 \rightarrow 3x = 18 \rightarrow x = 6$$

Plug this value for x back into the equation with absolute values. It works, doesn't it? That's your answer. There is another possible answer, but there's no reason to waste time finding it. (It also turns out to be a negative number, so you couldn't grid it in even if you wanted to.)

When you encounter absolute value lines, think "positive."

Quadratic Equations

As you will see later in this chapter, equations can be graphed. Equations that look like $4x + 3y = 13$ are called linear equations because their graphs are lines. Linear equations only have variables that are not raised to a power other than one. In contrast, quadratic equations have variables that are squared, like x^2 or y^2. Equations with a squared variable are quadratic equations, and their graphs will not be a line.

Solving quadratic equations requires different techniques than the ones used when working with linear equations. Factoring is normally used. Check out the chart below to remind yourself how factoring works.

Factor Refresher

$$ab + ac = a(b + c)$$
$$(a + b)(c + d) = ac + ad + bc + bd$$
$$a^2 + 2ab + b^2 = (a + b)^2$$
$$a^2 - 2ab + b^2 = (a - b)^2$$
$$a^2 - b^2 = (a - b)(a + b)$$

If you encounter an equation that looks like the left side of one of the equations in the chart, "work it" until it resembles the corresponding equation on the right. This isn't always the key to solving the problem, but it often is, because it demonstrates your ability to factor and expand equations properly—a skill that the test-writers are interested in measuring.

> **Note**
>
> When you *expand* an expression, you take away the parentheses. When you *factor* an expression, you do the reverse by putting the parentheses back.

The second item in the chart involves FOIL, a method of expanding that is used when you are multiplying two groups of variables like $(a + b)(c + d)$. FOIL is a nice way to remember First, Outside, Inside, Last.

You multiply

the First terms, ac
the Outside terms, ad
the Inside terms, bc
the Last terms, bd

and then you add them all together:

$$(a + b)(c + d) = ac + ad + bc + bd$$

FOIL makes expanding simple, but factoring a quadratic expression like $x^2 - x - 12$ is not as straightforward. Putting the equation back into two sets of parentheses involves a little bit of guessing. To help guide your guess, think about FOIL and start with the first and last terms (the squared term and the number).

Beginning with the squared term, ask, "What would give x^2?" The variable x times itself is the answer, so the first terms in each parentheses is x. You now know:

$$(x \quad)(x \quad)$$

How about the 12? It is the Last term, and could be made with the factors 2 × 6, 3 × 4, or 12 × 1, since the product of all three is 12. The 12 also has a negative sign in front of it. This means one of the Last terms must be negative and the other positive because that is the only way to have −12 as the product. Our parentheses, then, must look like:

$$(x - \quad)(x + \quad)$$

For the final step, you must decide which set of factors to use. Since the middle term of the expression is $-x$, the Outside and the Inside terms must add up to negative one. Which of the three factor sets of 12 has a difference of one? Only 3 × 4. They must go in the Last places, and since adding up the Outside and the Inside results in a $-x$, the 4 must go with of the negative sign. Putting it all together:

$$x^2 - x - 12 = (x - 4)(x + 3)$$

You can always to check to see if you have factored correctly by using FOIL, $(x - 4)(x + 3) = x^2 + 3x - 4x - 12 = x^2 - x - 12$.

Being able to factor and expand quickly is important for the SAT. If you don't feel comfortable with both operations, spend some time making up your own expressions and working with them. Here are a few expressions to get you started.

Factoring and Expansion Practice

Expand the following:

$$(y + 4)(y + 6)$$
$$(x - 7)(x - 4)$$
$$(3x - 1)(2x - 9)$$

Factor the following:

$$x^2 + 10x + 16$$
$$y^2 - 7y + 10$$
$$10a^2 - 23a - 5$$

SAT problems will expect you to solve quadratic equations, but once you have factored a quadratic equation, solving it is pretty easy. Suppose you are given the quadratic equation $y^2 = 7 - 6y$ and asked to solve for y. The presence of a squared term, y^2, is the clue that tells you that you must factor to get the answer.

The first thing to do is to get all terms on one side of the equation. The other side will then equal zero. If possible, rearrange the terms so that the y^2 is positive.

$$y^2 = 7 - 6y$$
$$y^2 - 7 = 7 - 7 - 6y$$
$$y^2 - 7 = -6y$$
$$y^2 - 7 + 6y = -6y + 6y$$
$$y^2 + 6y - 7 = 0$$

Now you have to factor the quadratic equation so that you have two sets of parentheses.

$$y^2 + 6y - 7 = (y + 7)(y - 1)$$
$$y^2 + 6y - 7 = 0$$
$$(y + 7)(y - 1) = 0$$

How can you make this last equation true? Stated another way, for what values of y would the product of the parentheses be zero? A product is only zero if one of the factors is zero, so find values for y that would make each parenthesis zero. If $y = -7$ then the first parenthesis would be zero, and so the product would be zero. And, if $y = 1$, then the second parenthesis would be zero. Both $y = -7$ and $y = 1$ are correct answers.

> **Note**
>
> Quadratic equations usually have two solutions for one variable, so if a grid-in asks you for a solution to a quadratic equation, don't worry if you get two answers. As mentioned earlier, grid-ins sometimes will have more than one correct answer. Just pick one answer, grid it in, and move on.

PETERSON'S
getting you there

14.

x	1	2	3
y	$\frac{1}{3}$	0	-3

If the above table gives the relationship between x and y at certain values, which of the following equations could describe the table?

(A) $y = \dfrac{2x - 2}{x + 2}$

(B) $y = \dfrac{2x - 1}{x + 7}$

(C) $y = \dfrac{x^2}{2x - 1}$

(D) $y = \dfrac{2(x - 4)}{2x - 3}$

(E) $y = \dfrac{(x - 2)x}{x - 4}$

One way to solve this problem is to go through each answer choice and plug in the values from the table. If you can't identify another approach to the problem, go ahead and start plugging in values. However, you might want to wait until the second pass because this process can be time-consuming.

There is a shorter way, but it takes a bit of math cleverness to spot it. Notice that when $x = 2$, $y = 0$. *Scan the answer choices. You'll see that every one of them has y on the left and a fraction containing x on the right.* When $x = 2$, y is zero, so you're looking for a numerator on the right side of the equation that will be zero when $x = 2$. Answer choice (E) fits the bill, because the term would be zero when $x - 2 = 0$, which would make the entire numerator zero.

If you have some time, you could check the other answer values in the table to see if they also work. (They do.) Choice (E) is your answer.

Word Problems

In a word problem you are given a statement in regular old English. For example:

6. At Walt's Haberdashery, cowboy hats are three times as expensive as baseball caps. Tennis visors are half as expensive as baseball caps. If a single tennis visor costs $6.50, how much, in dollars, does a cowboy hat cost?

(A) 11.50
(B) 13.00
(C) 36.00
(D) 39.00
(E) 52.00

So far, the questions in this section have been littered with variables and equations. It was easy to see that algebra was involved. For word problems, the algebra is there, but you have to create the variables and formulas yourself. This may sound hard, but it's actually pretty simple once you do it a couple of times.

Start with the first sentence: "cowboy hats are three times as expensive as baseball caps." If you had to translate this into an equation, it would look like

$$1 \text{ cowboy hat} = 3 \text{ baseball caps (in price)}$$
$$1c = 3b$$
$$c = 3b$$

The variable c stands for "cowboy hats," and b stands for "baseball cap." Move on to the next sentence: "Tennis visors are half as expensive as baseball caps."

$$1 \text{ tennis visor} = \text{half a baseball cap}$$
$$1t = \frac{1}{2}b$$
$$2t = b$$

Note

Although you could use the variable x to stand for "tennis visor," it's much easier to use the first letter of the word, which is why we let $t =$ tennis visor.

297

Once you have translated the word problem into two algebraic equations, the rest falls into place. The question states that a tennis visor costs $6.50, so

$$2t = b$$
$$2(6.50) = b$$
$$13 = b$$
$$c = 3b$$
$$c = 3(13)$$
$$c = 39$$

Cowboy hats cost $39 dollars at Walt's Haberdashery, choice (D).

Sometimes it's hard to decide which strategy to use when faced with a particular problem. This is something best learned through practice, which is why there are three full-length practice SATs awaiting you after this chapter. However, spotting word problems is one of the easier tasks. Here are some clues:

- The problem has three to five text sentences.

- The sentences are filled with phrases like, "will be twice as old in three year's time," "is two-thirds as tall as the next building," or "weighs as much as three smaller machines."

- At one point, a numerical value is given.

The numerical value is the actual number that you plug in to your created equations. If you've set up your equations correctly, the answer will fall into your lap.

Functions, the Unappreciated Half of the "Algebra and Functions" Category

For the SAT, think of a function as a math machine. You will usually see the function as equal to some algebra expression like this:

$$f(x) = x^2 + x$$

When you feed the "function machine" values for x, it spits out values for $f(x)$. Put $x = 2$ into the function by replacing all the x's in the function with 2's:

$$f(2) = 2^2 + 2$$
$$f(2) = 4 + 2$$
$$f(2) = 6$$

You put a 2 into the function machine, and it spits out a 6. In Math Speak, when $x = 2$ then $f(x) = 6$, and this can also be written $f(2) = 6$.

Functions are typically described using the symbol $f(x)$. In some algebra classes, you may have talked about this symbol as "f of x."

You can change the guts of the function machine, but even if you do, it stills performs the same operation. It takes a value for x and gives you a value for $f(x)$. Suppose the function f is defined by $f(x) = \dfrac{x-2}{x-2^x}$. What is the value of $f(3)$?

Replace all the x's in the function with 3's:

$$f(3) = \frac{3-2}{3-2^3}$$

$$f(3) = \frac{1}{3-8}$$

$$f(3) = -\frac{1}{5}$$

A cardinal rule of functions is that for every x value that you put into the function machine, only **one** y value can come out. If there is more than one y value for one x value, then you are not dealing with a function. We'll talk about this more when we discuss the graphing of functions.

That's all you need to know about basic functions. If a question gives you a function and a value for x, then plug that value of x into the function machine and see what comes out.

Geometry: Euclid's Last Stand

Thankfully, you will see no geometrical proofs, so you can immediately stop worrying about *why* there are four interior right angles in a rectangle. Geometry on the new SAT focuses more on basic geometric figures and the formulae that accompany them. Like algebra, there is a limited amount of geometry that the SAT actually tests. This section will cover basic geometry information and ways in which it might appear on the SAT.

Lines and Angles

The line is the basic building block of most of the geometric figures. This makes it the best place to start.

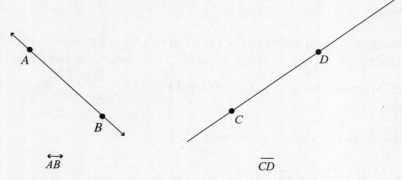

$\overleftrightarrow{AB}$ is, of course, a line. Those arrows at the end of the line mean that in Theoretical Geometry World, each end of the line goes on forever. $\overline{CD}$ is a

line segment because it is only a segment, or part, of the infinite line $\overleftrightarrow{CD}$. Note that the arrowheads are missing from the line segment symbol.

An **angle** is defined by two lines.

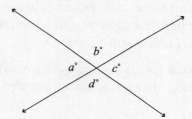

In the above figure, two lines intersect and form four angles. The sum of the measures of those four angles is 360 degrees. Since they are formed by two intersecting lines, the angles opposite each other are called **vertical angles**. Vertical angles are congruent to each other, so $a = c$ and $b = d$.

> **Note**
>
> If you think 360 is an unwieldy number, build a time machine and go back to ancient Babylon. You can blame this early civilization for deciding that one complete circular revolution equals 360 degrees.

Ninety-degree angles are a special angle in geometry. They have their own name, *right angles*, and their own symbol:

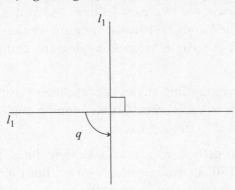

When two lines intersect to form a right angle, the two lines are said to be **perpendicular**. The symbol for perpendicular lines looks like this $l_1 \perp l_2$. In the figure above, you also know that the measure of angle q must be 90 degrees. Think about that for a moment if you don't see it right off.

Unlike perpendicular lines, **parallel** lines never cross, even if you follow them out forever. For a good mental image of parallel lines, think of railroad tracks. In "Math Write," parallel lines look like this $l_1 \parallel l_2$.

There is only a small chance you will see a math problem focused exclusively on perpendicular or parallel lines. However, both these concepts will appear throughout the Math section as part of larger geometric diagrams. For example, you might be given an intricate diagram and asked to find the measure of a specific angle. Nestled within the diagram will be two perpendicular lines ($l_1 \perp l_2$). Realizing that these lines form a right angle will be one important step toward finding the right answer.

If you cut across a pair of parallel lines with a third line, you create a juicy diagram with tons of congruent angles.

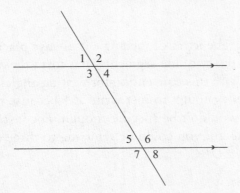

You know that ∠1 ≅ ∠4, ∠2 ≅ ∠3, ∠5 ≅ ∠8, and ∠6 ≅ ∠7 because they are all pairs of vertical angles. Angles 3 through 6 are called **interior** angles because they are on the insides of the two parallel lines. ∠3 and ∠6 are also called **alternate** angles, as are ∠4 and ∠5, because they are on alternate sides of the line cutting through. Alternate interior angles are congruent, so ∠3 ≅ ∠6 and ∠4 ≅ ∠5.

Angles 2 and 6 are called **corresponding** angles because their position at the two intersections corresponds to each other. Corresponding angles are also congruent, so ∠1 ≅ ∠5, ∠3 ≅ ∠7, and ∠4 ≅ ∠8.

If you put angles 3 and 4 together, you have a straight line. The angle measure of a straight line is 180, so m∠3 + m∠4 = 180. But there's more! Remember that ∠4 ≅ ∠5, so it must also be true that m∠3 + m∠5 = 180. This is actually a general rule: The measures of interior angles on the same side of the line cutting through always sum to 180.

> **Note**
>
> The reason a straight line is 180 degrees has to do with those Babylonians again. Cutting a line through the center of a circle makes two half-circles, and since a circle is 360 degrees, half a circle is $\frac{360}{2}$ = 180 degrees.

All these rules are important because some SAT questions will have you playing "Big Angle Hunter." You'll be given a diagram with intersecting lines or figures and asked to find the measure of a particular angle. You need to know all the different rules to help you track down and capture the necessary angle.

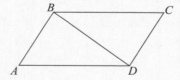

Angle *A* is written as ∠*BAD*. The letter of the angle is always placed in the middle, and the letters from the two line segments that form the angle are put on the sides. Notice that with this convention for writing angles, ∠*BAD* is the same as ∠*DAB*. It is not enough to just write ∠*A* because there are cases for which this method wouldn't be specific enough. For instance, for the figure above, if you wrote ∠*B* you could be referring to three different angles, ∠*ABC*, or ∠*ABD*, or ∠*DBC*.

14.

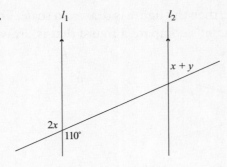

If $l_1 \parallel l_2$ then $y =$

(A) 15
(B) 20
(C) 25
(D) 30
(E) 35

This problem requires a little bit of algebra and a little bit of geometry, but the geometry comes first. Looking at the angles on the left, you can see that $2x = 110$ because they are vertical angles. Solving for x,

$$2x = 110$$
$$\frac{2x}{2} = \frac{110}{2}$$
$$x = 55$$

On the right side of l_2, you can see that $x + y$ and the mesure of the other angle sum to 180. The other angle measures 110 because it is an alternate interior angle to the known angle 110. This means $x + y + 110 = 180$, so you can solve for y,

$$55 + y + 110 = 180$$
$$165 + y = 180$$
$$165 - 165 + y = 180 - 165$$
$$y = 15$$

Way to go, Big Angle Hunter!

What You Can Figure from Figures

Whenever you encounter a figure, first see if there is a "Note: Figure not drawn to scale" disclaimer. If there is, then the figure will not be helpful to you in its present state, although you can sometimes redraw it to give you a better idea of what the question is asking.

If the disclaimer is not present, then the figure is drawn to scale. To cover all the details of what this means, let's compare a figure that is drawn to scale to one that isn't.

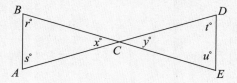

You can assume that:

1. *C* is a point along $\overline{BE}$ and $\overline{AD}$

2. $x = y$, since they are vertical angles

Even though this figure is drawn to scale, without further information, you should not assume anything else.

You shouldn't assume that:

1. $\overline{AC} = \overline{CD}$ because it looks that way.

2. $t = 60$ because it looks about that big.

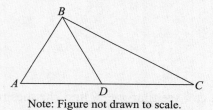
Note: Figure not drawn to scale.

You should assume that:

1. *ABD* and *DBC* are triangles.

2. *D* is on $\overline{AC}$.

3. $AD < AC$

4. m$\angle ABD$ is less than m$\angle ABC$

You shouldn't assume that:

1. $AD < AC$ because it looks that way.

2. m$\angle BAD$ = m$\angle BDA$

3. m$\angle ABD$ is greater than m$\angle DBC$

4. $\angle ABC$ is a right angle.

When a figure is drawn to scale, you can sometimes use it to eliminate answer choices that are definitely inaccurate. For instance, look back at the drawn-to-scale sketch. Suppose you were asked:

What is the measure, in degrees, of angle t?

(A) 20
(B) 50
(C) 60
(D) 70
(E) 120

Looking at it, you know that angle t is less than a right angle, so it must be less than 90 degrees. This means you can cross out choice (E), since there's no way this could be the correct answer. This incorrect choice is there to catch students who make a mistake in computation. There's no way that angle is 120 degrees, and there's also little chance that it's as small as 20 degrees, either. Choice (A) is highly, highly unlikely to be the right answer, so it can be eliminated as well. This gives you a one-in-three chance of answering the problem correctly simply by using your eyes.

With figures drawn to scale, you can often use your eyes to get a rough idea of the correct angle simply by comparing it to a known angle. If you're given a distance measurement in a figure, you also use that measurement to get a rough idea of the distances. Suppose that $\overline{AB} = 8$ in the drawn-to-scale diagram. $\overline{DE}$ looks about the same length, so you know that its length is somewhere around 8. Put another way, you know the length of $\overline{DE}$ isn't 24, because that would mean it's three times as long as $\overline{AB}$, and that's just not true.

Triangles and You

You probably aren't going to make a career out of triangles, though Pythagoras seems to have. It is still good to know a little about them because they are one of the SAT's favorite geometric figures. There are a few general triangle principles that the SAT tests, and there a few particular kinds of triangles that the SAT likes to test.

The triangle is tri-angled, meaning it has three angles. It also has three sides. There is one universal trait for triangles: the sum of the measure of the internal angles of all triangles is 180. That means if you know the measure

PETERSON'S
getting you there

of two angles of a triangle, you can always find the measure of the third. This is an important piece of knowledge when you are Big Angle Hunting for an angle like *x* below.

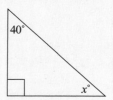

You know two angles measure, 40 and 90, and the measures sum to 130. Since the sum of the measures all three interior angles must equal 180, this means there are 50 degrees left (180 − 130) for ∠*x*.

The formula for the area of a triangle is a second general rule that holds for all triangles, $A = \frac{1}{2}(base) \times (height)$. The formula is simple enough, but it can be a little tricky to apply because problems usually won't just come out and tell you the "base is 30" and "the height is 12." The questions make you work to find one or both of these values. Further complicating things, the base and the height are not fixed values of a triangle. Only when you choose one is the other nailed down.

The base is always going to be one side of the triangle, but it can be any of the three. The height, on the other hand, will not necessarily be a side length. Once you pick the base, the height is the length of a line perpendicular to the base that runs to the angle opposite the base.

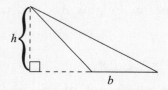 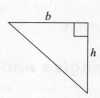

In the three different triangles above, the base and the height are picked differently. There is no set rule for how to pick which side to be the base. The only rule that should guide you is ease. Whichever base and height are easiest to find, pick them. Remember, that once you designate a base there is only one height that goes with it, or once you designate a height the base is locked in.

12.

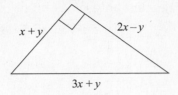

Which of the following is twice the area of the above figure?

(A) $x^2 + 2xy + y^2$
(B) $2x^2 + xy - y^2$
(C) $6x^2 + 2xy + y^2$
(D) $6x^2 + xy - y^2$
(E) $6x^2 + xy + y^2$

Don't let the combination of algebra and geometry throw you. Just deal with one at a time. Start with the geometry: pick the two sides that define the right angle as the base and the height. These two sides are $x + y$ and $2x - y$.

The question asks for double the area of the triangle, so we can drop off the one-half in the area formula, and just multiply the base times the height:

(base) (height) = double the area = the answer

$$(x + y)(2x - y) =$$
$$2x^2 - xy + 2xy - y^2 =$$
$$2x^2 + xy - y^2$$

This is choice (B). You had to use your old friend FOIL to find the right answer, illustrating once more how many SAT problems combine one or more concepts. If you're clear on the geometry and the algebra, this is one medium problem that you should have no trouble answering.

Well, Isn't That a Special Triangle?

There are many different triangles: acute ones, obtuse ones, big ones, little ones. On the SAT, though, a few different kinds of triangles show up again and again. These triangles are called "special triangles" because of their unique properties. The SAT likes to test you on these properties to see if you can identify and use them to solve problems.

Remember that crazy ancient Greek guy Pythagoras? He gets the credit for discovering one of the most important special triangles, the **right triangle**. A right triangle is a triangle with one angle that is 90 degrees. They are often easy to identify because they will have the box symbol for right angle (⌐) in them.

Since there are 180 degrees in a triangle, that only leaves 90 degrees for the two other angles; so the measures of the two other angles in a right triangle always sum to 90.

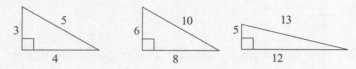

The sides of a right triangle have a definite relationship that Pythagoras summed up in his theorem $a^2 + b^2 = c^2$. a and b are the lengths of the two shorter sides of the right triangle, and c is the length of the side opposite the right angle. c is also called the **hypotenuse**. With the Pythagorean theorem, if you know two sides of a right triangle, you can find the third. This is a move that the SAT will expect you to be able to make (probably more than once).

Notice that the lengths of the three sides are given for each of the three right triangles above. These triangles are common right triangles, the 3-4-5, the 6-8-10, and the 5-12-13. All three adhere to the Pythagorean theorem: $3^2 + 4^2 = 5^2$, $6^2 + 8^2 = 10^2$, and $5^2 + 12^2 = 13^2$. Knowing these triangles can be helpful because you can quickly determine the value of their sides . For instance, if you see a right triangle with a hypotenuse of 10 and a second side of 8, you know that the third side must be 6.

10.

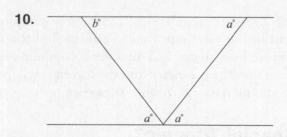

Note: Figure not drawn to scale.

If $a = 45$, then $b =$

(A) 30
(B) 40
(C) 45
(D) 60
(E) 90

The key to this problem is the angle between the two *a*'s on the bottom. You know that there are 180 degrees in a straight line. The two *a*'s take up 90 of those degrees, since . This leaves 90 for the angle in the triangle. Now you know two of the three angles of the triangle, so you can find the measure of the third, *b*.

$$b + 45 + 90 = 180$$
$$b + 135 = 180$$
$$b + 135 - 135 = 180 - 135$$
$$b = 45$$

The Mighty Isosceles

You probably won't see the words *isosceles triangle* on the SAT, but you will need to know how to work with one. An isosceles triangle has two sides that are congruent to each other. This is noted on a figure by putting little dashes through the sides that are equal, like this:

Here's the Big Angle Hunter fact about isosceles triangles: the angles opposite the two congruent sides are also congruent. In the above figure, this means $m\angle a = m\angle b$. There's a good reason for this, and you might have already slogged through the proof of it in your geometry class. For the SAT, the reason is secondary. Just remember that if the sides are congruent, then the opposite angles are congruent.

Isosceles triangles work the other way too. If you know two angles of a triangle are congruent, you can infer that the opposite sides are also congruent.

The right isosceles triangle is so special that the SAT includes the formulas for it at the beginning of every Math section. The measures of the three angles in an isosceles right triangle are always the same. The right angle is 90, so that leaves 90 degrees for the other two. Since the other two angles

PETERSON'S
getting you there

must equal each other, they must each be 45 degrees. Therefore, the three interior angles of an isosceles right triangle are always 45-45-90.

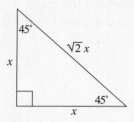

Consider how much you know about the 45-45-90 triangle. You know the angle measures and how the side lengths relate. Knowing how the sides relate is helpful since if you know one side, you can determine all three. For instance, you might know that one of the sides opposite a 45-degree angle is 10, then you can simply read off that the hypotenuse is $10\sqrt{2}$.

> **Note**
>
> If you want to know where the side relationships came from, use the Pythagorean theorem on the 45-45-90 triangle.

14.

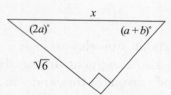

Note: Figure not drawn to scale.

If $a = b$, then $x =$

(A) $\sqrt{6}$
(B) $2\sqrt{2}$
(C) $2\sqrt{3}$
(D) $2\sqrt{6}$

(E) It cannot be determined.

Since it is a right triangle, you should be on the lookout for a special kind of right triangle. (And since you only know one kind of special right triangle at this point, you should have a good idea what to expect.) If you plug in what you know about a and b, you can see that both top angles equal $(2a)°$. A right angle plus two equal angles can only mean one thing: a 45-45-90 triangle.

You find the hypotenuse of a 45-45-90 triangle by multiplying the shorter side length by $\sqrt{2}$, so

$$\left(\sqrt{2}\right)\left(\sqrt{6}\right) = \sqrt{12} = \left(\sqrt{4}\right)\left(\sqrt{3}\right) = 2\sqrt{3}$$

Choice (C) is the answer.

The 30-60-90 triangle is the next super special kind of right triangle. It doesn't have a fancy name like "isosceles right triangle," but the SAT writers still like it enough to give it regular cameos on the test. Again, the drill is the same as with the 45-45-90 triangle. You will be expected to be able to identify a 30-60-90 triangle and then use its properties to solve problems.

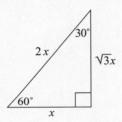

As you can see, the shortest side (the side opposite the 30-degree angle) is half the length of the hypotenuse. Stated the other way, the hypotenuse is twice the size of the smallest side. To find the length of the side opposite of the 60-degree angle, you take the length of the smallest side and multiply by $\sqrt{3}$. There are good reasons for these properties, but when preparing for the SAT concentrate on learning the properties, not the proofs that explain them.

The **equilateral triangle** is a triangle with three congruent sides. Since all three sides are congruent, all three interior angles are also congruent. In this sense, it's just like the isosceles corresponding side-angle love fest.

If three angles of an equilateral triangle are congruent, what must the measure of those angles be? You know they must sum to 180 degrees, so:

$$3s = 180$$
$$\frac{3s}{3} = \frac{180}{3}$$
$$s = 60$$

The interior angles of an equilateral triangle always measure 60 degrees. If you split an equilateral triangle down the middle, you end up with two 30-60-90 triangles.

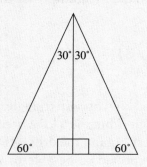

16.

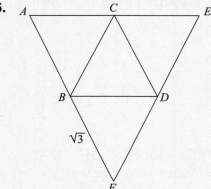

If each line segment in the figure above is congruent, what is the area of the entire figure?

A. $3\sqrt{3}$
B. $12\sqrt{6}$
C. $16\sqrt{3}$
D. $24\sqrt{3}$
E. $24\sqrt{6}$

This problem looks tough, but you know it must turn on the fact that each line segment is congruent. What can you infer from this fact? Each side of triangle *AEF* is two line segments, so *AEF* is an equilateral triangle with side lengths of $2\sqrt{3}$. To find the area, you need to pick a base and height. $\overline{AE}$ is as good a choice as any for the base, which means the height is the line from F to C,

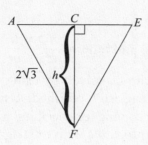

ACF is a 30-60-90 triangle, and you know two of the sides, $AC = \sqrt{3}$ and $AF = 2\sqrt{3}$. You only need one of these sides to find length CF, the height. If $AC = \sqrt{3}$, then the side opposite the 60-degree angle, CF, will be this length times $\sqrt{3}$.

$$CF = (AC)(\sqrt{3})$$
$$CF = (\sqrt{3})(\sqrt{3})$$
$$CF = 3$$

Once you have the height, plug in the values to the area formula for a triangle:

$$A = \frac{1}{2}(base)(height)$$

$$A = \frac{1}{2}(AE)(CF)$$

$$A = \frac{1}{2}(2\sqrt{3})(3)$$

$$A = 3\sqrt{3}$$

Note

This is not the only way to solve this problem. You also could have found the area of triangle ACF and then multiplied by 2 to find the area of the total triangle. Both methods lead to the same answer.

SOH-CAH-TOA

SOH-CAH-TOA is the acronym for the trigonometric functions for *sin*, *cos*, and *tan*. It stands for

$$\sin\theta = \frac{opposite}{hypotenuse}, \cos\theta = \frac{adjacent}{hypotenuse}, \text{ and } \tan\theta = \frac{opposite}{adjacent}$$

The new SAT will include problems that can be solved by using these trig functions. Don't worry, though, if your trig isn't polished. Using a trig function will always just be one method for solving (or checking) a problem. It won't be the only method. If you are comfortable with the trig functions and you see a problem that you can easily solve using them, go ahead. If you have never taken trig or have completely forgotten it, then don't give it a second thought. Just use the other methods outlined in this chapter to solve problems. There's no point in learning all about trig functions when there will always be an alternate method—involving a right triangle, typically—that you can use to answer the problem.

"Polygon" Isn't Slang for "Dead Parrot"

Any figure with three or more sides is a polygon. There are many polygons, but only a few actually make appearances on the SAT. Besides triangles, squares, and rectangles (all three are test favorites), there is the occasional parallelogram.

There is one rule that applies to all polygons. The measures of the interior angles of an *n*-sided polygon sum to $(n - 2)(180)$. Try this formula out on the one polygon we have worked with thus far, triangles:

$(3 - 2)(180) = 180$

You won't need this formula for triangles, but it could come in handy if you need to know the sum of the measures of the interior angles of an octagon.

Rectangles are polygons. They have four sides so the sum of the meaqsures of the interior angles is $(4 - 2)(180) = 360$. Rectangles have two important properties:

1. All interior angles are right angles.

2. Opposite sides are parallel and equal in length.

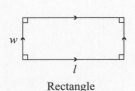

Rectangle

Square

All **squares** are rectangles. A square is a rectangle whose four sides are equal in length. With a rectangle, opposite sides are equal in length, and the length of a rectangle is traditionally longer than its width.

The **perimeter** of a polygon is the distance around its edges. Some polygons have perimeter formulae that make it easier for you to determine the perimeter. For a rectangle, the perimeter formula is $P = 2l + 2w$. This makes sense because if you add up the four sides you get

$$P = l + w + l + w = 2l + 2w.$$

This perimeter formula is true for squares too, but since $l = w$ for squares it simplifies to $P = 4l$. The area of a rectangle is $A = l \times w$. Again, for a square, replace the w with the l, and you get $A = l \times l = l^2$.

Since every side (s) of a square is the same, the area and perimeter formula for a square are usually written as $A = s^2$ and $P = 4s$, respectively.

9.

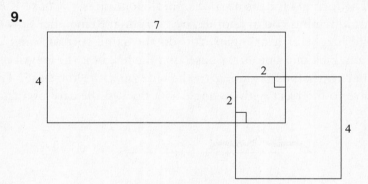

Note: Figure not drawn to scale.

The figure above is composed of a square and a rectangle. What is the measure of the outer perimeter of the figure?

(A) 18
(B) 22
(C) 26
(D) 28
(E) 30

Be sure you understand what the phrase "outer perimeter" implies. It means the parts of the figure's perimeter that are not contained within the figure, like the part of the square that is inside the rectangle and vice versa. Look at the part of the square that is inside the rectangle. Two of the angles are marked as right angles, and we know that the other two angles are right angles because they are angles from the square and rectangle respectively. This means all the sides opposite each other are parallel. If this is true, then the sides opposite each other must also be congruent. Therefore, the part of the square inside the rectangle is a square with side length 2. Once you know this, you can determine all the lengths of the outer perimeter.

Now add them up. Moving clockwise from the 7, you have

$$7 + 2 + 2 + 4 + 4 + 2 + 5 + 4 = 30$$

answer (E).

The **parallelogram** is like a parent of the rectangle. Both have opposite sides that are congruent and parallel, but the parallelogram's interior angles don't have to be right angles. A parallelogram's opposite interior angles are equal, and the measures of the angles adjacent to each other sum to 180 degrees. A rectangle is a special case of a parallelogram.

The formula for the perimeter of a parallelogram is the same as for a rectangle. The formula for the area of a parallelogram is $a = base \times height$, and this should remind you of another area formula. Remember how to find the base and height of a triangle? You do the same sort of thing with a parallelogram. Pick one side as the base, and the height is the length of a line perpendicular to the base running to the side opposite the base. The line does not have to intersect with an angle as it does in the case of a triangle.

15.

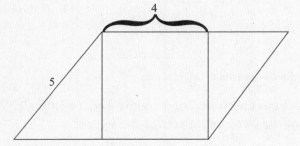

Note: Figure not drawn to scale.

The above figure is a square inside a parallelogram. What is the area of the parallelogram?

(A) 20
(B) 22
(C) 24
(D) 26
(E) 28

You need to pick a base and height that you can find. If you designate one of the vertical lines of the square as the height, then you at least know the height is 4. That makes the bottom (or the top) of the parallelogram the base. How can you find that length? Notice the two triangles. You can infer that they are right triangles because a square's interior angles are all right angles. Here comes a special triangle! You have a right triangle with sides 4, 5, and . . .

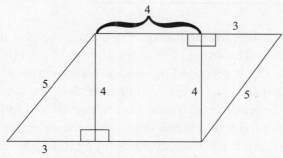

Note: Figure not drawn to scale.

Once you recognize the triangle as a 3-4-5 triangle, you know the shortest side is length 3. Add that to 4 and you get that the base of the parallelogram is length 7. The area is $A = base \times height = 7 \times 4 = 28$.

It is not a coincidence that a 3-4-5 right triangle just happened to be created by the square and parallelogram. Every section of the SAT is loaded with problems that contain critical keys to unlocking them. For SAT Geometry, the keys often come in the form of a special triangles. Once you learn all the keys to the SAT, you'll start recognizing them throughout the test. Use them properly and you'll get the right answer every time.

Similar and Congruent: When Things Look Alike

There are two conditions that must be met before a mathematician will say that two polygons are **similar**:

1. The measure of all the corresponding angles must be congruent.

2. The ratios of the corresponding sides must be equal.

It's the word *ratio* in the second half that really distinguishes similar from congruent. Here are two similar triangles.

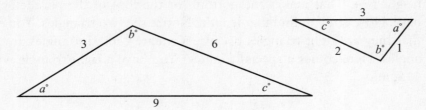

Look at the two conditions for similarity. The smallest angles in the two triangles are congruent. The same is true for the middle angles and the largest angles. Thus, the corresponding angles are congruent. The first condition has been satisfied. As for the second condition, the smallest sides have a ratio of 3:1. The same ratio is true for the middle and long sides. It doesn't matter that one triangle is much larger than the other one. As long as the ratio stays the same for each corresponding side, the figures are similar.

Congruent means congruent. Two geometric figures that are congruent are not just similar—they are exactly the same. All corresponding angles are congruent, and all corresponding lengths are equal. The symbol for congruent is like an equal sign with a wavy hairpiece on top of it ($\cong$). If line segments $\overline{PC}$ and $\overline{AD}$ are the same length, then $\overline{PC} \cong \overline{AD}$.

7.

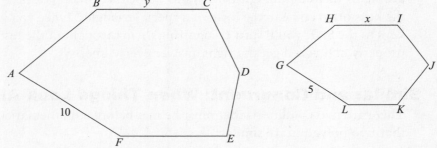

If polygons *ABCDEF* and *GHIJKL* are similar and $y + 2x = 32$, then $x =$

(A) 6
(B) 8
(C) 10
(D) 12
(E) 16

Since the polygons are similar, you know that corresponding sides have the same ratio. *AF* is twice the size of *GL* (10 and 5, respectively), so the corresponding lengths on *ABCDEF* are twice those on *GHIJKL*. This means $y = 2x$. Plug this into the equation given in the problem, and you can solve for x:

$$y + 2x = 32$$
$$(2x) + 2x = 32$$
$$4x = 32$$
$$\frac{4x}{4} = \frac{32}{4}$$
$$x = 8$$

The concept of congruency is more inflexible than the idea of similarity. With similarity, you have to remember the whole "ratio of corresponding sides" thing. If you have a problem dealing with similarity, expect the ratio aspect to play a crucial part in determining the right answer.

So far, every geometrical figure discussed has been very linear. It's time to get a bit "bendy."

Fun with Circles

For at least two and a half millennia, geometers have thought pretty highly of circles. Some have even gone so far as to worship them. The SAT test writers don't worship circles, but they do expect you to know a thing or two about them.

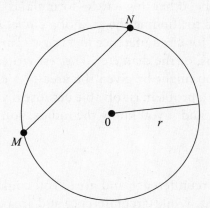

O is called the center of the circle. All the points along the edge of the circle are the same distance from O. That distance, *r*, is called the **radius**. The radius is any line that goes from the center to the edge of the circle. If a line starts at the edge of the circle, runs through O, and continues on to the opposite edge, it is called the **diameter**. By definition, every diameter is made up of two radii, so *diameter* = 2(*radius*). Any line segment whose endpoints are on the edge of the circle is called a **chord**, like $\overline{MN}$. The diameter is one particular chord, the longest one.

The **circumference** of a circle is the distance around the circle's edge. It's like the perimeter of a polygon. Since the circumference is not made up of straight lines, it's a little harder to calculate. Luckily for you, ancient mathematicians came up with a little tool to make calculating the circumference a lot easier. It's called **pi** (pronounced pie), and its symbol is π. Pi is the ratio of the circumference of a circle divided by its diameter.

$$\pi = \frac{circumference}{diameter}$$

The nice thing about π is that no matter how big or small the circle, the numerical value of π stays the same. At least since that wacky Pythagoras, mathematicians have been refining their calculations about the value of π. For the SAT, 3.14 is a good approximation of π (or just use the π button on your calculator).

Since $\pi = \frac{circumference}{diameter}$, when you multiply both sides of the equation by the diameter you get: *circumference* $= \pi \times$ *diameter*. This is one circumference formula for a circle, which is usually written $c = \pi d$. Recalling that the diameter is two times the length of the radius, you can see where another familiar formula for the circumference comes from, $2\pi r$.

In addition to circumference, the other big circle formula is the area formula. Pi comes in handy again for finding the area of a circle, $A = \pi r^2$. Notice that in both the equations for circumference ($c = \pi d = 2\pi r$) and for the area, all you need is the radius, or the diameter. The test writers like to exploit this fact. For instance, you might be given the area of a circle and asked for the circumference. Such a problem is solvable because if you know the area, you can find the radius, and if you know the radius, you can find the circumference.

Arcs and Sectors

Arcs and sectors are related to circumference and area. You could say the ideas are similar but not congruent. While circumference and area deal with the entire circle, arcs and sectors cover portions of a circle.

Any part of the circumference of a circle is called an **arc**. Consider the part, or arc, that goes from *A* through *B* to *C* in the figure below.

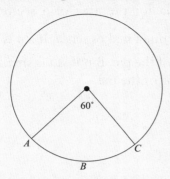

> **Note**
>
> This arc is called arc *ABC*, since it begins at *A*, goes through *B*, and ends at *C*.

There is a nice little formula for figuring out exactly what part of the circumference an arc is. Recall that there are 360 degrees in a circle. The angle of the arc is 60 degrees, which is $\frac{60}{360}$ or $\frac{1}{6}$ of the degrees of the circle. The arc angle and the length of the arc are directly related. Since the arc angle is $\frac{1}{6}$ of the circle's degrees, the arc length will be $\frac{1}{6}$ of the circle's circumference. So $arc ABC = \frac{1}{6}\ circumference$. The general formula is:

$$\text{arc length} = \frac{n}{360} \times c = \frac{n}{360} \times 2\pi r,$$

where *n* is the measure of the arc angle.

If you cut up a circle into pie pieces, the pieces of the pie are called **sectors**.

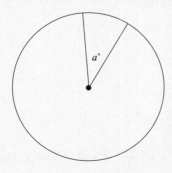

PETERSON'S
getting you there

You already know how to calculate the length of the arc of the sector; it depends on the measure of arc angle, $\angle a$. The area of the sector also depends on the arc angle. The formula for the area of a sector is $A = \left(\dfrac{a}{360}\right)\pi r^2$. If you think about it, this formula makes sense. If $\angle a$ is big, then the sector would take up a large chunk of the pie. But if $\angle a$ is small then the sector would only take up a small sector of the pie.

14.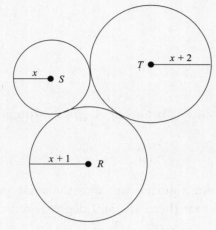

If the circumference of Circle T is 8π, what is the area of Circle S?

(A) 4π
(B) 9π
(C) 16π
(D) 25π
(E) 36π

There is a lot going on in the figure, but you need to focus on the information you have been given. Circle T has a circumference of 8π, which means

$$C = 2\pi r$$
$$8\pi = 2\pi(x + 2)$$
$$\frac{8\pi}{2\pi} = \frac{2\pi(x + 2)}{2\pi}$$
$$4 = x + 2$$
$$4 - 2 = x + 2 - 2$$
$$2 = x$$

Now you can find the area of Circle S, $A = \pi r^2 = \pi(2)^2 = 4\pi$, choice (A).

Tangency is the last major circle concept to know. A **tangent** to a circle is a line that touches the circle at one point. The figure below gives an example of a tangent line.

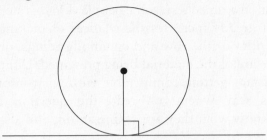

Notice that the tangent line is perpendicular to the radius that shares a point with it. Keep that fact in mind, because you might just need it on test day.

Data Analysis, Statistics, and Probability

Although many SAT-created categories have unwieldy and foreboding names, this one takes the cake. Yet the material covered under this heading is not as stiff as it sounds. When you look over a chart or graph in a newspaper, you are conducting *data analysis*. If you keep track of how many miles per gallon your car consumes (on average), that's *statistics*. As for *probability*, every student has pondered the question, "What is the probability that I could not study for this test and still get an excellent score?"

If that little pep speech didn't get you fired up about this section, here's something else that might cheer you. This is the last section of the level 1 math chapter. Stay diligent and soon you will have covered all the major topics that might appear on the SAT.

Interpreting Data

When you go into a sandwich shop for the first time, you have to look at the menu to see what they offer and how much everything costs. Often, the menu is a big board hung up somewhere behind the counter with all the items and prices. Glancing at it, you can quickly see that a small ham-and-Swiss is four bucks, and a chicken salad sandwich is four fifty.

You probably don't think about it when you are ordering, but in looking at the menu, finding what you want, seeing how much it costs, you have successfully read a table. The owners of the sandwich shop made the table (the menu up on the wall) to communicate their wares and prices, and you most likely had no problem correctly interpreting the table. That might not sound like much of a skill, but it is one that the SAT thinks is important.

There are a few basic rules to reading tables, graphs, and charts. First, always read the title. If you are going to understand and interpret a graph correctly, you need to know what the graph is about. This is something that people do regularly, but on a timed test, some people skip this step. It shaves off a few seconds, but greatly increases the chances of making an error. Second, read the axes titles or the row and column headings, or whatever other descriptions there are of the material being presented. Ultimately, you want to take a few seconds getting comfortable with what information is being presented. This way when you read the question about the information, you will know what they are asking about, and also where to find the answer.

The good news about these kinds of questions on the SAT is that all the information you need to find the answer will be right in front of you in the table, graph, or chart. Yes, you might have to do a little math to find the answer (you might have to do something like adding together the totals of two columns), but the answer will most likely only be a few steps away from what is right in front of you. Take a look at the graph and questions below:

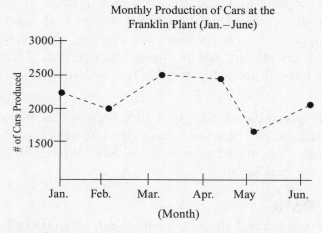

Monthly Production of Cars at the
Franklin Plant (Jan.–June)

The following two questions refer to the above graph.

5. What month had the greatest decrease in the number of cars produced compared to the previous month?

   (A) February
   (B) March
   (C) April
   (D) May
   (E) June

6. How many cars were produced at the Franklin Plant in February and March?

    (A) 2,500
    (B) 4,000
    (C) 4,500
    (D) 5,000
    (E) 6,000

The difficulty with the first question is untangling what it is asking. You are comparing each month with the previous month. Specifically, you are comparing the number of cars (not the percentage change). February and May were the only two months that were lower than the previous month. Just by eyeballing the graph, you can see that May is the greatest decrease. Choice (D) is the answer.

In the second question, look to see how many cars were produced in February and March (2,000 and 2,500 respectively). Adding these together, 4,500 is the sum, choice (C).

Every graph, table, and chart you see on the SAT will present numerical data in a visual form. Regardless of how ordinary or strange it looks, that's the fundamental purpose of this visual data. If you get a line graph like the one in the car-production problem, the goal is to make sure you understand what the question is asking, and then retrieve the necessary information from the graph. Harder problems might have stranger-looking graphs, or they might ask complicated questions about the information in the graphs, but the basic strategy remains exactly the same.

1. Determine what the question wants.

2. Look at the visual data to find the necessary information.

Chart reading is not rocket science. The more practice you get, the better you will be at handling these questions. If you currently feel uncomfortable with visual data, get some practice! Your local librarian can recommend reference books filled with various charts, tables, and graphs. Many newspapers have charts, tables, and graphs sprinkled throughout them. Start reviewing those newspapers (you can increase your vocabulary skills at the same time, if you recall.)

Charts, tables, and graphs are everywhere. The next time you come across one, make up an SAT-like question about it on the spot. When you can imitate the test and its questions, you will realize how knowledgeable about the SAT you have become.

Averages

There are four statistics words you will need to know for the SAT:

1. average (arithmetic mean)
2. median
3. mode
4. range

Once you know these four terms, you'll be good to go.

You'll never see the first word, *average*, by itself on the SAT. The test writers want to make sure you know exactly what kind of average they are talking about when they use the word, so it will appear as "average (arithmetic mean)." Don't let the stuff in the parentheses confuse you. What they mean by *average* is pretty simple, and it's probably what you mean when you use the word *average*.

The **average** (arithmetic mean) of a list of numbers is the sum of the numbers divided by the number of terms.

$$average = \frac{sum}{number\ of\ terms}$$

For instance, say you want to know the average (arithmetic mean) of your test scores in American history. Your scores in this class are 90, 80, 82, and 78. First add them up to get the sum:

$$90 + 80 + 82 + 78 = 330$$

There are four test scores, so divide the sum by four to get your average:

$$average = \frac{sum}{number\ of\ terms} = \frac{330}{4} = 82.5$$

Your average (arithmetic mean) score is 82.5. It doesn't matter that you never actually scored an 82.5. That's the number produced by summing up all the different tests and then dividing by the number of tests, so that's the average.

Median and mode are less commonly used, so you will not have as much experience working with them as you do with mean. Consider a set of numbers, {3, 8, 10, 4, 5, 9, 3}. You find the **median** of this number set by lining up the numbers from least to greatest {3, 3, 4, 5, 8, 9, 10}. The median is the number in the middle. Since there are seven numbers in the set, the fourth from the right, 5, is the middle number, and so it is the median.

Note On a big highway, the strip of ground between the opposing lanes of traffic is called the median. Thinking of this median strip of ground, directly in the middle with equal lanes of traffic on both sides, is a good way to remember the concept of a median.

What if there were one more number in the set, and the set was now {2, 3, 3, 4, 5, 8, 9, 10}? A set with an even number of numbers has no middle number. This is where the mathematicians step in and say that the median is the average (arithmetic mean) of the middle two numbers. In this case, the two middle numbers are 4 and 5, and their average is 4.5. Therefore, 4.5 is the median of the second number set.

The **mode** is simply the number that occurs most often in a set. In our first set of numbers, {3, 8, 10, 4, 5, 9, 3}, 3 is the only number that occurs more than once. That makes 3 the mode. If we modify the number set by taking away one of the 3's then we have {3, 8, 10, 4, 5, 9}. There is no mode to this set, since all the numbers occur just once. How about if we change the set again by adding an 8 and a 4 {3, 8, 10, 4, 5, 9, 8, 4}? Now we have two modes, 4 and 8, because both appear twice.

The **range** doesn't have any wrinkles like median and mode. It is always easy to calculate. The range is the difference between the greatest and least numbers of a set. The range of your American history test scores is 12, $90 - 78 = 12$. The range of the number set we worked with above is 7, $10 - 3 = 7$.

Statistics Recap

arithmetic mean, mean, or average	sum of numbers divided by the number of terms in set
median	middle number when set is lined up in numerical order
mode	number that appears most often in a set
range	difference between the greatest and least values in a set

PETERSON'S
getting you there

7. At the end of each day Tina turns in the number of projects she has completed. On the different days of one week, Tina turned in 4, 6, 9, 14, and 4 projects. For this particular week, what is the difference between the average (arithmetic mean) number of projects Tina completed and the median of projects Tina completed?

Cutting through all the words, {4, 6, 9, 14, 4} is the number set you are working with. The problem asks for the difference between the average and the median of this number set, so first you have to find the average and the median. The average is:

$$average = \frac{4 + 6 + 9 + 14 + 4}{5} = \frac{37}{5} = 7.4$$

For the median, arrange the set from least to greatest, {4, 4, 6, 9, 14}, and pick the middle number, which is 6. The difference between these two is $7.4 - 6 = 1.4$.

Probability

What are the chances? How likely is it? These questions are all questions about probability. There is a simple definition for the probability of an event occurring,

$$probability\text{-}of\text{-}an\text{-}event = \frac{number\text{-}of\text{-}was\text{-}event\text{-}can\text{-}occur}{number\text{-}of\text{-}possible\text{-}outcomes}$$

Flipping a coin is a straightforward example. What is the probability of flipping a quarter and it landing heads? When you flip a coin there are two possible outcomes, heads and tails. So the probability is $\frac{1}{2}$ or 0.5.

Let's try a little more complicated scenario. If there are 18 boys and 22 girls in a class, what is the probability that if one student is picked at random it will be a boy? Since there are 18 boys, there are 18 different ways that a boy could be picked at random. The total number of possible outcomes is the total number of students, $18 + 22 = 40$. So the probability of a boy being picked is $\frac{18}{40} = \frac{9}{20} = 0.45$.

That's your basic probability problem. If you are in the easy portion of the Math section and you come across a probability problem, "odds are" the question will be very straightforward. You'll have to determine the total number of ways an event could occur, and then place this number over the total number of possible outcomes. However, if the probability question is in the medium to hard portion of a section, finding the correct answer won't be as simple.

More Probability

Calculating the probability of multiple independent events is a little more involved. Say you have to flip the coin a second time, and you need to know the probability that it will land heads both times. The probability of the coin landing heads both times is the product of the two individual probabilities of the coin landing heads. The individual probabilities of the coin landing heads is $\frac{1}{2}$, so the product of these individual probabilities is $\frac{1}{2} \times \frac{1}{2} = \frac{1}{4}$.

The multiple coin tosses is an example of the general rule of multi-event probability: the probability of multiple events occurring is the product of the individual probabilities.

Probability problems can also involve geometry. For instance, take a look at the figure below,

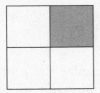

If a point is picked at random from the square, what is the probability that it will be in the shaded region? Since the shaded region makes up $\frac{1}{4}$ of the entire area, the probability the point would be in the shaded region is $\frac{1}{4}$. The same principles are involved in calculating the probability, but you are using geometry to determine the number of ways an event can occur and the number of possible outcomes. Since there are four quadrants of equal size, there are four possible outcomes, so the denominator of the probability is 4. The numerator is 1 because there is only one shaded quadrant.

12.

In the figure above the circular wheel is divided into 8 equal sectors. If the wheel is spun twice at random, what is the probability that the arrow will land on an even number and then a prime number?

(A) $\dfrac{1}{16}$

(B) $\dfrac{1}{12}$

(C) $\dfrac{1}{8}$

(D) $\dfrac{1}{6}$

(E) $\dfrac{1}{4}$

Since you have multiple events, you have to determine the probability of each event first. Then you can calculate the probability of both occurring.

What is the probability of landing on an even number? There are 4 even numbers out of 8 numbers total, so the probability is $\dfrac{4}{8} = \dfrac{1}{2}$.

What is the probability of landing on a prime number? To answer this, you need to go way back to the beginning of this chapter and remember that a prime number is a number divisible only by 1 and itself. 1 is not prime, but 2 is, so the number of prime numbers is 4 (2, 3, 5, and 7). This is the same as for an even spin, $\dfrac{4}{8} = \dfrac{1}{2}$. The probability of both occurring is the product of the two probabilities, $\dfrac{1}{2} \times \dfrac{1}{2} = \dfrac{1}{4}$.

There is a definite probability that you will encounter at least one probability question on the SAT, but the chances are very slight that there will be many of them. Probability questions on the SAT are like an important politician showing up at a public event: They always make an appearance, but they never stay around for long.

Take It to the Next Level

Fun with Symbols

One of the more difficult kinds of problems that shows up year after year on the SAT is the "Unfamiliar Symbol Problem." The problem begins by defining some new symbol and then expects you to work with that symbol. For instance, a problem might read:

For all integers, x, let $*x*$ be defined as follows:

$*x* = 2x$ if x is positive.

$*x* = x^2$ if x is negative.

Given this definition of $*x*$, $*-2* + *3* =$

Such symbol problems can be a little jarring, but remember, **everything you need to know about the symbol to solve the problem has been given to you.** This is always the case. Some students get freaked out because they think they're already supposed to have some experience working with $*x*$, but nothing could be further from the truth.

Relax, take a second to comprehend the definition of the new symbol, and then simply follow directions. The definition of the Unfamiliar Symbol will always tell you what you are supposed to do with the numbers given. In the example above, the definition says that if you see a positive integer between the stars, double it ($*x* = 2x$ if x is positive). If the integer between the stars is negative, square it ($*x* = x^2$ if x is negative).

For the actual computation, you have to add the two integers between the stars, -2 and 3. Since -2 is negative, square it, which is 4. Three is positive so double it, which is 6. Now add up the new values.

$*-2* + *3* = 4 + 6 = 10.$

331

When strange symbol problems appear on the test, there are usually two to four questions that pertain to them. That means understanding how a symbol works is important. When you see a weird symbol, take a little extra time to make sure you grasp it. You'll get that time back in the end because it will take you less time to deal with each related problem if you really understand how the symbol works.

10. Let it be defined that $< a , b >$ stands for the set of all integers between a and b, including a and b. For example,

$$< 2 , 5 > = \{ 2, 3, 4, 5 \}.$$

If x is in $< 3 , 7 >$ and y is in $< 7 , 10 >$, which of the following could be true?

  I. $x > y$
 II. $x = y$
III. $x < y$

  (A) III only
  (B) I and II only
  (C) I and III only
  (D) II and III only
  (E) I, II, and III

Tip

Questions with Roman numerals in them are very time-consuming, because you have to solve for I, II, and III. Since you only get credit for answering one question, always skip Roman numeral problems on the first pass. Do them on the second pass, and only after all regular problems have been attempted.

First, read the definition of the symbol and look at the example. Once you have it, look at the question. If x is in $< 3 , 7 >$, that means x must be 3, 4, 5, 6, or 7 because those are the numbers in that set. Likewise, y must be 7, 8, 9, or 10. Notice that x and y could both be 7, which means II *could be true*. You can take this fact and use it to eliminate any answer choices that do not contain II in them. This eliminate of choices (A) and (C), so if you're pressed for time, you could guess and have a one-in-three shot.

Since this section of the book is untimed, let's keep going. You know x could also be 3, 4, 5, or 6, less than the values in y, which means III *could be true*. However, the greatest possible value of x (7) is only equal to the least possible value of y (7), so Roman numeral I can't be true. Choice (D) is the answer.

Sequences

Math sequences put things in order according to some rule, like when a cheerleader shouts, " Two! Four! Six ! Eight!" This person is urging her team on with a sequence of numbers starting at 2, with each following number increasing by 2. "Starting at 2 and increasing by 2" is the rule that organizes that particular math sequence. Go team!

Other sequences have different rules that organize them. A sequence might start at 1, with each succeeding term being halved. That sequence would look like this: $1, \frac{1}{2}, \frac{1}{4}, \frac{1}{8}$, and so on.

Exponential series are a special kind of series. They are organized by a particular kind of rule. In exponential series there is a constant ratio between each consecutive term. That's a bit heavy with the Math Speak, so here's an example:

7, 21, 63, 189, 567, . . .

The constant ratio between each term is 3, as each term is three times greater than the one that precedes it. Because of the constant ratio you can write down an equation to describe this series as:

$7 \times 3^{n-1}$, where n is the number of the term in the sequence. For the equation, 7 is counted as the 1st term of the sequence, which means you plug in $n = 0$, and get $7 \times 3^{n-1} = 7 \times 3^0 = 7 \times 1 = 7$.

> **Note**
>
> Exponential series also go by the name **geometric series**. Both names refer to the same thing, sort of like how Venus and Aphrodite refer to the same mythical person.

You might wonder if the fractional series we looked at above:

$1, \frac{1}{2}, \frac{1}{4}, \frac{1}{8} \cdots$

is also an exponential series. It is. Each term is multiplied by $\frac{1}{2}$ to get the next term. So $\frac{1}{2}$ is the constant ratio. The equation for that exponential series is $1 \times (\frac{1}{2})^{n-1}$.

> **Note**
>
> Notice that the form of the equations for two the exponential series is the same: the first number in the series multiplied by a constant ratio raised to the $n - 1$ power.

PETERSON'S
getting you there

That is how exponential series work. On the new SAT you might be asked to do more than just identify an exponential series. You might be asked to apply one to a real-life situation.

13. A restaurant starts the lunch hour with 8 gallons of broccoli cheese soup. If by serving the soup to customers, the amount of broccoli soup is halved every 15 minutes, how much soup, in gallons, is left after an hour and a half?

    (A) 0.125
    (B) 0.150
    (C) 0.250
    (D) 0.50
    (E) 1.00

The first task is to identify that this situation can be described with an exponential series. The tip is the halving of the amount every 15 minutes. That is the constant ratio of decrease. Every fifteen minutes the amount of soup is divided by two, which you could also describe as "multiplied by one-half" since it means the same thing. The equation is:

$$8 \times \left(\frac{1}{2}\right)^{\frac{time}{15}}$$

Here the n-term is not just a simple number, but you find it by dividing the time elapsed by 15. Once you have the equation, the hard part is done. Just plug an hour and a half into the equation, which is 90 minutes. $90 \div 15 = 6$. Now all that is left is a little calculator work:

$$8 \times \left(\frac{1}{2}\right)^{6}$$

$$8 \times \frac{1}{64} = \frac{1}{8} = 0.125$$

Choice (A) is the answer.

21. The 2nd, 3rd, and 4th terms of a geometric sequence are $b\sqrt{3}$, $3b$, and $3b\sqrt{3}$ respectively. What is the 8th term of this sequence?

    (A) $9b$
    (B) $18b$
    (C) $27b\sqrt{3}$
    (D) $81b$
    (E) $243\sqrt{b}$

Since this is a geometric series, it is multiplied by a constant ratio. You can bet the farm that finding that ratio will help you solve this problem. To do this, look at the difference between the second and third term and ask yourself, "What times $b\sqrt{3}$ gives $3b$?" (These are the 2nd and the 3rd terms, respectively.) The b stays the same, but $\sqrt{3}$ becomes a 3. This can happen if $\sqrt{3}$ is multiplied by $\sqrt{3}$, since $(\sqrt{3})(\sqrt{3}) = 3$.

You now know the constant ratio is $\sqrt{3}$. Since the second term is $b\sqrt{3}$, the first term must be b. This means the form of the sequence is $b \times (\sqrt{3})^{n-1}$. To find the 8th term, plug in $n = 8$ into the form of the sequence,

$$b \times (\sqrt{3})^{8-1} = b \times (\sqrt{3})^7$$
$$= b \times 3^{\frac{1}{2} \times 7}$$
$$= b \times 3^{\frac{7}{2}} \times 3^{\frac{1}{2}}$$
$$= b \times 3^3 \sqrt{3}$$
$$= 27b\sqrt{3}$$

Choice (C) is correct.

Sets

A **set** is just a collection of things. A set of crayons is a collection of crayons. A set of dolls is a collection of dolls. Mathematicians like the notion of set. They like to organize and collect different math things together. And just as there are lots of different kinds of sets in real life, there are also lots of different kinds of sets in math. When you make a math set, you simply pick out the things that you want to collect together and call that your set. If you want to collect all the even numbers together, then call set M "the collection of all even numbers."

Mathematicians have names for the things that are within sets. They are called *members* or *elements*. If set T is defined as {1, 7, 10}, 1, 7, and 10 are the members or elements of set T.

PETERSON'S
getting you there

There are two basic concepts related to sets that the SAT will expect you to be familiar with:

1. **The union of sets**
   The union of two sets is just the combination of two sets (you're uniting them). For instance, if set G is the set of all positive even integers, and set F is the set of all positive odd integers, the union of F and G is all of the positive integers.

2. **The intersection of two sets**
   This is where two sets overlap, or share members. For example, if set M is {2, 3, 7, 9} and set N is {5, 7, 9}, the intersection of set M and set N is {7, 9} because they are the two members shared by both sets.

7. Set X is the integers 1 thru 5 inclusive, and set Y is the integers 6 thru 10 inclusive. Which of the following operations if performed on each member of set X would produce all the members of set Y?

   (A) Divide each member by 1.
   (B) Multiply each member by 2.
   (C) Multiply each member by 5.
   (D) Subtract 5 from each member.
   (E) Add 5 to each member.

You are performing an operation on each of the members of the set X, which will result in the members of set Y. What can you do to 1, 2, 3, 4, 5 to end up with 6, 7, 8, 9, 10? If you don't see it yet, look over the answer choices. If you add 5 to 1, you get 6, and if you add 5 to 2, you get 7. That looks promising, and if you keep going you will see the answer is choice (E).

Roots and Rational Exponents

The new SAT promises to have fractional exponents like $x^{\frac{3}{4}}$, and also negative exponents like z^{-3}. These look pretty bizarre, but fractional and negative exponents follow simple rules.

Let's start with fractional power. Expressed mathematically, a fractional exponent means:

$$d^{\frac{x}{y}} = \sqrt[y]{d^x}$$

Hopefully, many of you are math-savvy enough to understand what this means. If not, keep in mind that this is an advanced topic, so if looking at

$\frac{x}{dy} = \sqrt[y]{x}$ hurts your head, don't sweat it. Understanding basic radicals and exponents is all you need for the majority of the problems.

With a fractional exponent, the numerator gives you the power, while the denominator gives you the root. In the case of $7^{\frac{3}{4}}$, the 3 means that you would take 7 to the third power ($7 \times 7 \times 7 = 343$). The 343 would then be taken to the fourth root since the denominator is 4, so $7^{\frac{3}{4}} = \sqrt[4]{343}$. If you know the fourth root of 343 off the top of your head, good for you! You are a MATH GENIUS, or a computer masquerading as a human.

You probably won't have to actually solve a fractional exponent down to a single number, but you might be asked to simplify or do some computations with similar fractional exponents.

Working with Funky-Looking Fractional Exponents

Adding and Subtracting

Just as with integer exponents, you can add and subtract numbers with exponents if they have the same base and are raised to the same power.

$$2b^{\frac{2}{3}} + b^{\frac{2}{3}} = 3b^{\frac{2}{3}}$$

Multiplying and Dividing

As long as the numbers have the same base, multiply and divide away.

$$k^{\frac{2}{3}}k^{\frac{7}{2}} = k^{\frac{2}{3} + \frac{7}{2}} = k^{\frac{4}{10} + \frac{35}{10}} = k^{\frac{39}{10}}$$

$$\frac{c^{\frac{3}{4}}}{c^2} = c^{\frac{3}{4} - \frac{8}{4}} = c^{-\frac{5}{4}}$$

Negative exponents might seem like a strange idea, but they have a simple definition: $x^{-1} = \frac{1}{x}$. In the definition, you can see that when you take a negative power that is in the numerator, and you put it in the denominator, the power becomes positive. This is an illustration of a general rule with exponents: when you take a term raised to a power from the numerator and put it in the denominator, or vice versa, you switch the sign of the power.

For instance, recall that in dividing exponents $\frac{x^a}{x^b} = x^a x^{-b} = x^{a-b}$. When x^b is taken from the denominator and put in the numerator, it becomes x^{-b}.

16. If $z^{-4} = 81$, then $z^2 =$

A. $\dfrac{1}{9}$

B. $\dfrac{1}{3}$

C. 3

D. 6

E. 9

This is an excellent problem to plug in answer choices. To make sure you know how to solve for z, here is the textbook approach:

$$z^{-4} = 81$$

$$\frac{1}{z^4} = 81$$

$$z^4 \times \frac{1}{z^4} = 81 \times z^4$$

$$1 = 81z^4$$

$$\frac{1}{81} = \frac{81z^4}{81}$$

$$\frac{1}{81} = z^4$$

$$z^4 = \frac{1}{81} = \frac{1}{3} \times \frac{1}{3} \times \frac{1}{3} \times \frac{1}{3}$$

$$z = \frac{1}{3}$$

The second to last step is a bit intuitive. There's no easy, direct way to determine the fourth root of a number. Instead, you have to dabble with some small fractions, multiply them together four times, and see if you end up with what you need. In this case, $\frac{1}{3}$ turned out to be the fourth root of $\frac{1}{81}$.

The question asked for z^2, which you can find easily enough:

$$z^2 = \frac{1}{3} \times \frac{1}{3} = \frac{1}{9}$$

18. If $x^y = 25$ then $x^{\frac{y}{2}} =$

The key to this problem is the difference between x^y and $x^{\frac{y}{2}}$, which, of course, is that the second term is raised to the one-half power. But what does it mean for something to be raised to the one-half? Raising to the one-half is the same as taking the square root. So take the square root of x^y if you want to find out what $x^{\frac{y}{2}}$ is, $\sqrt{x^y} = \sqrt{25} = 5$.

Numbers and Operations is a big category, and we could take another 100 pages to define and delineate even more terms. Thankfully, we won't. What you have here are the basic terms and concepts that you will see throughout the new SAT. You might not see every advanced topic, but you can be 99.99% certain that you will encounter crucial topics like fractions, percents, exponents, and square roots.

So learn these terms! You'll see them on numbers and operations questions, as well as on other problems involving geometric figures, bar graphs, and algebraic equations. Speaking of algebra . . .

Radical Equations

A radical equation does not describe political revolution. It is just an equation that has a radical sign in it. You solve these equations the same way you would solve any equation, but you have to work with the radical.

6. If $3\sqrt{x} + 11 = 20$, what is x^2?

Take It to the Next Level

PETERSON'S
getting you there

The first order of business is figuring out what x is. Time once again to manipulate an equation to find a numerical value for a variable.

$$3\sqrt{x} + 11 = 20$$
$$3\sqrt{x} + 11 - 11 = 20 - 11$$
$$3\sqrt{x} = 9$$
$$\frac{3\sqrt{x}}{3} = \frac{9}{3}$$
$$\sqrt{x} = 3$$
$$x = 9$$

The second to last step, where both sides are squared, is a key idea to remember. With a radical equation, you want to isolate the segment under the radical on one side of the equation and have everything else on the other side. You can then square both sides to eliminate the radical.

> **Note**
>
> If $x = 9$ then $x^2 = 81$, so this is the value to grid in.

Radical equations look daunting to students who are uncomfortable with radicals and manipulating equations. Since you have just reviewed both radicals and equations, these problems should not make you anxious. It is yet another example of how understanding the basic set-up of the math problems goes a long way in helping you answer them correctly.

Direct and Inverse Proportion

Here's a statement most people would agree with: The more someone bugs you, the more annoyed you get. If they bother you a lot, you get really annoyed, and if they bother you only a little bit, you're only a little annoyed.

Anyone who has a brother or sister will probably agree with these facts. Mathematicians go one step further and use the term **direct proportion** to describe this. Mathematicians do this because they like to be precise, and it allows them to show off and use a formula:

$y = kx$

In this formula, y is your irritation, x is the amount you're being pestered, and k is a constant factor that makes sure that all the units and values work out right. The constant k stays the same, but as x increases, y increases. If x decreases, then y decreases. In other words, when one value decreases the other value decreases by a constant (k) amount. The equation $y = kx$ shows direct proportion between x and y.

Inverse proportion is the opposite of direct proportion. With inverse proportion, when one value increases, the other value decreases (and vice versa). For example, the amount of gasoline in a car's gas tank is inversely proportional to the number if miles driven on that tank of gas. If you fill up the gas tank completely, then you have a lot of gas but have not driven at all. As the amount of driving increases, the amount of gas in your tank decreases. This is shown mathematically as $y = \dfrac{k}{x}$.

Again k is a constant. As y increases, x must decrease for the equality to remain true, and as y decreases x must increase for the equality to remain true.

> **Note**
>
> You can plug in some numbers for x and y to help see this. Start with $k = 1$ and $x = 2$. You can see this makes $y = \dfrac{1}{2}$. Now increase x so that $x = 4$. What new fraction does this make y, and is the new fraction greater or smaller than one-half?

8.

x	y
2	6
3	9
4	12
5	15

Given the above table, which of the following could model the relationship between x and y?

(A) $y = \dfrac{3}{2x}$

(B) $y = \dfrac{5}{x}$

(C) $y = 2x$

(D) $y = 3x$

(E) $4 = yx$

First determine whether the relationship is direct or inverse. As x increases, y increases, so the relationship is directly proportional. This means you can cross out (A), (B), and (E), since these are all inverse relationships. You have only two choices remaining, (C) and (D), so take values from the table and plug them in to one of the answer choices. If they work, that's your answer. If not, there's only one choice left, so pick it.

Looking at the table, 2 times 3 is 6, 3 times 3 is 9, 4 times 3 is 12, and 5 times 3 is 15. Thus $k = 3$, which is (D).

Direct and inverse proportions can be shown using variables and formulas, which is why they fall under the category of algebra. A good first step on these questions is to ask, "Is this an inverse or a direct proportion?" Once you decide that, you can jot down the appropriate formula $\left(y = kx \text{ or } y = \dfrac{k}{x} \right)$ and start looking for numerical values to replace the variables.

Domain and Range

There are two concepts related to functions that need to be covered, **domain** and **range**. In Math Speak, the domain of a function is the set of values over which the function is defined. Translated into English, the domain of a function is all the values of x where the function makes sense.

The next million-dollar question is, "What does it take for a function to make sense?" An example might be more helpful than another Math Speak definition, so here is a situation in which a mathematician would say a function doesn't make much sense at all.

If f is defined by $f(x) = \dfrac{1}{x - 2}$, what is the value of $f(x)$ when $x = 2$?

If you replace all the x's with 2's, you get $f(2) = \dfrac{1}{2 - 2} = \dfrac{1}{0}$. As you might recall from algebra class, any fraction with a zero in the denominator is undefined. In other words, when you put the number 2 into this function, it doesn't make any sense. The answer you get back is not defined. This means that the domain of this function does not include 2. Are there any other values for x that this function is not defined for? Nope. So the domain of this function is, "All values for x except 2."

Lets take two more functions, $f(x) = x^2 + x$ and $f(x) = \dfrac{x - 2}{x - 2^x}$. What is the domain of these two functions? For the first one, you can input any value of x and the function will spit out a number. That means the domain is all values of x. How about the second function? You might suspect that there is a value of x where the denominator would equal zero, but can you find it? No, because there isn't one. Again the domain is all values of x.

The **range** of a function is all the values that the function can produce, or all the values that the function can spit out. Suppose f is defined by $f(x) = x^2$. No matter what value for x you put into the function, it will never spit out anything negative. The squared x means that the least value that the function will equal is zero (when $x = 0$). So the range of this function is from zero to as far as you want to go in the positive direction.

13. If f is defined by $f(x) = -x^4 + 4$, which of the following is not in the range of f?

    (A) -4
    (B) -1
    (C) 0
    (D) 5
    (E) None of the above.

The way to approach the problem without a graph is to think about the function term by term. The term $-x^4$ means that whatever positive or negative value you put into the equation, this part of the expression will be negative. So it is easy to see how the function could equal (A) or (B). How about (C), 0? Yes, when $x^4 = 4$ the function will equal zero. Choice (D), though, looks like it might be out of the range. The plus 4 is the only positive contribution to the value of the function. So the function's greatest value is 4 (when $-x^4 = 0$). Thus 5 is out of the range of the function, so the answer is (D).

Sketching the function on an xy-axis is another way to approach this problem. A rough sketch is all that is needed. The x^4 term means that the graph will have a parabola like x^2 would, only the parabola will be steeper in the x^4. Notice that there is a negative in front of the x^4 so the parabola will be upside down. The plus 4 part of the function means that when $x = 0$ the function equals 4, so the function must "crest" at four. Here is a **rough sketch** of this

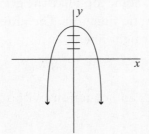

PETERSON'S
getting you there

Take It to the Next Level

From the sketch you can see that the function never gets higher than 4. Choice (D), 5, then is out of the range of the function.

When solving the problem using the graph method, the values of $f(x)$ corresponded to the values along the y-axis. If you graph a function, the values along the x-axis correspond to the x values in the function, and the values along the y-axis correspond to the values of $f(x)$. Since x corresponds to the x-axis and $f(x)$ to the y-axis, you can look at a graph of a function and read off the domain and the range. For instance, consider the two following graphs of functions.

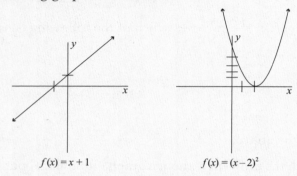

$$f(x) = x + 1 \qquad\qquad f(x) = (x-2)^2$$

Look at the graph on the left. The domain is all the possible values along the x-axis, and the range is all the possible values along the y-axis. Nothing's excluded here. The graph on the right tells a different story. Here, the domain is all the possible values along the x-axis, but the range is just the positive values of the y-axis.

Notice that the graphed function above on the left is written as $f(x) = x + 1$. It could also be written $y = x + 1$ because on a graph $f(x) = y$. This function is a linear function because it is a line, as you can see. Linear functions can always be put into the $y = mx + b$ form. If you see a function in that form, you know that its graph is a line. Viewed from the other direction, if you see a graph of a line, you know that the function it graphs can take the form $y = mx + b$.

All graphs on the SAT, though, aren't linear. Some look like the graph above on the right, which is the graph of a quadratic function. The graph of this quadratic will be a parabola instead of a straight line.

X-Ref

To refresh your memory about quadratics and equations with squared terms like x^2 in it, look back on page 284.

344

15. Which of the following is not the graph of a function?

(A)

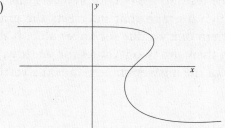

(B)

(C)

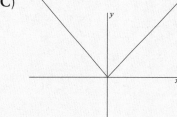

(D)

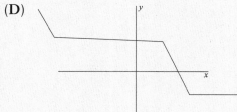

(E)

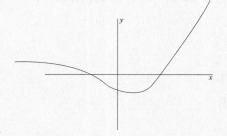

Remember the cardinal rule about functions: only one *y* value for every *x* value. Use the "vertical line test" to see if a graph meets this rule: If you can draw a vertical line through a graph that intersects the graph more than once, then there is more than one *y* value for an *x* value. If the vertical line intersects the graph twice, there are two *y* values for one *x* value, so it could not be a function. Which of the answer choices fails the vertical line test?

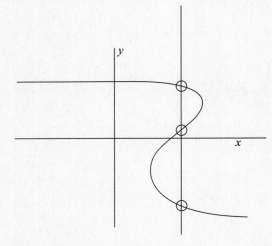

Choice (A) is the impostor function.

17.

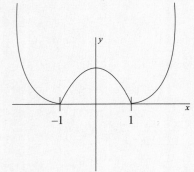

Which of the following functions is graphed above?

(A) $f(x) = |x - 1|$
(B) $f(x) = x^2 - 1$
(C) $f(x) = x^2 - 2$
(D) $f(x) = |x^2 - 1|$

(E) $f(x) = \dfrac{|x^2 - 2|}{x - 1}$

Take a second to examine the graph before getting to the functions. There are three important features to notice:

1. The graph is curved, so the function must be a quadratic.

2. The graph is always positive, which suggests that there are probably some absolute value signs involved, or everything is squared.

3. $f(x) = 0$ at -1 and 1.

Point 1 eliminates choice (A), since it is a linear function (x is not squared). Choices (B) and (C) can be negative (e.g. $x = 0$), which violates Point 2. Choice (E) does not meet Point 3. Choice (D) is all that's left, so (D) is the answer.

Multiple Figure Problems

One way that the SAT makes geometry problems harder is by piling on the figures. The usual story is that they will give you two or three figures, tell you something about one of the figures, and ask about a feature of one of the other figures. The key to such problems is that the figures have some kind of relationship, perhaps they share a side, or the diameter of one is the diagonal of another. Figuring out this relationship is critical, because it will unlock how to use the given information to find the answer. So when you see a multiple-figure problem, always ask, "What is the relationship between these two figures?"

17.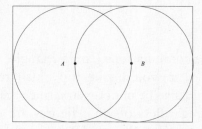

In the above figure, A and B are the centers of the two circles. If the area of each circle is 9π, what is the perimeter of the rectangle?

(A) 9π
(B) 30
(C) 36
(D) 45
(E) 18π

What is the relationship between the figures? Here's what you know.

1. First, the circles are congruent because they have the same area.

2. You can see that $\overline{AB}$ is a radii of both circles.

3. The diameter of the circles is the width of the rectangle, and the length of the circle is three radii. So length $= 3r$ and width $= 2r$.

That last point is the toughest to see, but if you take a pencil and start drawing radii, you will see that it is true. Now all you need to do is find the value of r, and you can determine the length and width of the rectangle. Since the area of the circles is 9π, the radius is

$$A = \pi r^2$$
$$9\pi = \pi r^2$$
$$\frac{9\pi}{\pi} = \frac{\pi r^2}{\pi}$$
$$9 = r^2$$
$$3 = r$$

That means the width of the rectangle is 6 ($2r$), and the length is 9 ($3r$). Placing these values into the perimeter formula for a rectangle gets you:

$$P = 2w + 2l$$
$$P = (2)(6) + (2)(9)$$
$$P = 12 + 18$$
$$P = 30$$

The answer is choice (B).

There are so many possible figure combinations (circle-triangle, rectangle-parallelogram, and so forth), that it would take too much time to go through every one of them. It would also be unnecessary, since the key to all combinations remains the same regardless of what figures are used. You need to figure out the relationship between the two figures—what common sides, angles, or points they share—and then use that knowledge to bridge the gap from what is given to you in the problem and what is being asked for.

Coordinate Geometry

Unless you slept all the way through algebra I, geometry, and algebra II, you are familiar with the coordinate plane.

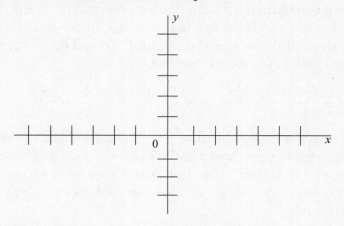

The coordinate plane is made up of two number lines. One runs up and down and is called the y-axis. The other runs right to left and is called the x-axis. The nice thing about the coordinate plane is that you can precisely locate everything on it. Every point on the plane has two coordinates, an x one and a y one. The x-coordinate tells you where along the x-axis the point is, and the y-coordinate tells you where along the y-axis the point is. The notation looks like this (x,y). So, $(4,-2)$, for example, means 4 along the x-axis and -2 along the y-axis. The coordinate plane below has that point graphed on it and also $(0,2)$.

Note

On a coordinate plane, all x values left of the y-axis are negative, while all x values to the right of the y-axis are positive. All y values below the x-axis are negative, while the y values above the x-axis are positive.

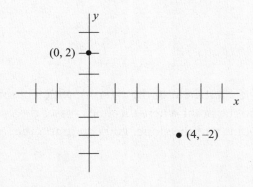

Take It to the Next Level

If a line were drawn between those two points, what would the slope of the line be like? It would lower moderately, going from left to right (and left to right is the direction you should always be going when using a coordinate plane). There is a mathematical definition for slope that is more precise than our eyeball description. The **slope** is the change in the y divided by the change in x, also called "the rise over the run." To find the slope, you need any two points along the line. For our line,

$$slope = \frac{change\text{-}in\text{-}y}{change\text{-}in\text{-}x} = \frac{y_2 - y_1}{x_2 - x_1} = \frac{2 - (-2)}{-4} = \frac{4}{-4} = -1$$

The slope is negative because the line goes down from left to right. Lines that go up from left to right have a positive slope. The 1 in the slope means that it changes one in the y-direction for every one it changes in the x-direction. Putting it another way, it rises one (or falls one in this case) for every one that it runs.

When you are calculating the change in x and y, it doesn't matter which point you make (x_1, y_1) or (x_2, y_2). Just be consistent with your choice in the numerator and denominator.

Slope is an important element when graphing linear equations. There is a basic form for all linear equations that looks like $y = mx + b$. In this format:

1. the slope is m,

2. b is the y-intercept, or the point where the line passes through the x-axis, and

3. the x and y values are for any point along that line.

If you start out with a linear equation like $-2x = y + 3$ and rewrite it in the above form, you can then read off the properties of that line much easier.

$$-2x = y + 3$$
$$-2x - 3 = y + 3 - 3$$
$$-2x - 3 = y$$
$$y = -2x - 3$$

The slope of the line is m (the coefficient of the x-term), which in this case is -2. The y-intercept is -3, so the point where this line crosses the y-axis is at $(0, -3)$. Since you have a point and the slope, you can graph the line.

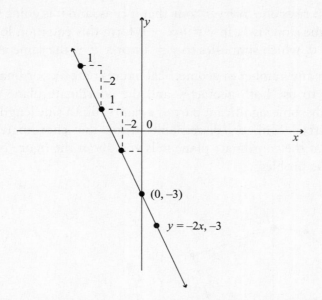

The line passes through the y-intercept at $(0, -3)$. The slope is -2, which translates to a "fall" of two for every "run" of one.

Let's try a problem.

11.

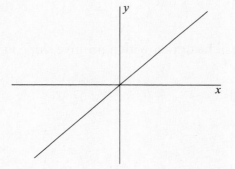

Which of the following is the equation for the line graphed above?

(A) $x = 2y$

(B) $2x = y$

(C) $x = y - 2$

(D) $x = y$

(E) None of the above.

You can place each of these equations into the form $y = mx + b$, but first look at the diagram and think about the line. What is the y-intercept? The line passes through the **origin**, the center of the coordinate grid at $(0,0)$. This makes the y-intercept zero.

Onto the slope. It rises one for every one that it runs, and it is going up from left to right, so the slope is 1. In $y = mx + b$ form this equation looks like this, $y = (1)x + 0$, which simplifies to $y = 1x$ or $x = y$, the same as (D).

The SAT will put any number of geometrical figures onto a coordinate plane and expect you to use both geometry and the coordinate plane to solve problems. Usually some significant part of a figure, like a side length, or the radius of a circle, will be discernable from the coordinate plane. Recognizing what the coordinate plane tells you about the figure is often a key to solving the problem.

16.

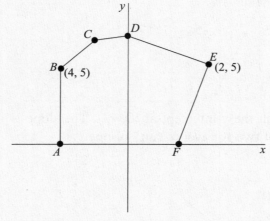

How many diagonals can be drawn with a positive slope in hexagon *ABCDEF*?

(A) None
(B) One
(C) Two
(D) Three
(E) Four

Diagonals are lines that originate and terminate at the points of the hexagon. Start with point *A* and picture all the diagonals that could be created. *AC*, *AD*, and *AE* all have a positive slope. (The slope of *AF* is zero, which is not positive.) That's three diagonals with a positive slope. For point *B*, *BD* is positive, but *BE* will have a slope of zero since the *y*-value for both points is 5. *BC* isn't a diagonal because it is one of the figure's sides. None of the other points can generate a new diagonal. The total is four, so the answer is (E).

Graphs

Remember functions? Well, the SAT has come to think that the graphs of functions are important, so you need to know something about them and how they work.

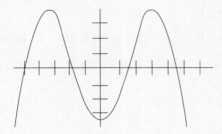

Inspect the graph of $f(x)$ above. How many times on the portion of the graph shown does $f(x) = 3$? Remember that on graphs $f(x)$ means y. The question is really asking, "How many different times does $y = 3$ on the graph?" The easiest way to see the answer is to draw the line $y = 3$,

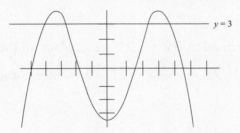

How many times does the $y = 3$ line intersect with the graph? 4 times. That is how many times $f(x) = 3$ on the graph shown.

In the previous problem you were given a graph of a function, and you had to answer a question about its behavior. The new SAT will expect you to be able to do this sort of reasoning with graphed functions.

The new SAT will also expect you to be able to work with simple transformations of functions and their graphs. That sounds intimidating, but don't run for cover yet. A transformation of a function is going from $f(x)$ to say $f(x + 3)$. This just means that instead of putting x into the

X-Ref

If you want a quick review of functions, turn back to page 298 in this chapter.

Take It to the Next Level

function, you are putting $x + 3$ into the equation. That is the transformation of the function. For example, if $f(x) = x + \dfrac{3}{x}$ then: .

$$f(x + 3) = (x + 3) + \frac{3}{(x + 3)}$$

Function transformations also involve the graph of a function. If $f(x) = -\dfrac{2}{3}x - 2$ then the graph of $f(x)$ is (notice that the function is in $y = mx + b$ form)

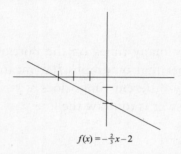

$f(x) = -\frac{2}{3}x - 2$

But what if $f(x)$ were transformed to $f(x + 2)$? First, replace all the x's with $x + 2$, and you get $f(x + 2) = -\dfrac{2}{3}(x + 2) - 2$, which simplifies to $f(x + 2) = -\dfrac{2}{3}x - \dfrac{10}{3}$.

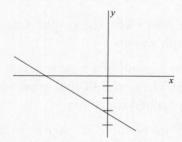

The transformed function is still a line with the same slope but with a different y-intercept, $b = -\dfrac{10}{3}$.

There are many steps to these transformation problems, and they involve healthy doses of geometry, algebra, and functions. If you can answer these questions with little problem, then it is a very good sign that you understand these basic math principles, and can apply them on easy, medium, or hard problems.

18.

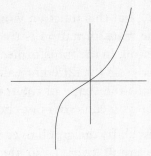

If the function graphed above is $f(x) = x^3$, which of the following is the graph of $f(x - 1)$?

(A)

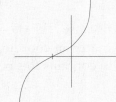

(B)

(C)

(D)

(E)

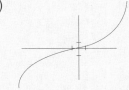

You might not be too comfortable with x^3, but this function works like all others. The first thing to notice about the transformation is that it won't change the basic shape of the original function. In the transformed function, $(x - 1)$ is being cubed instead of x, but $(x - 1)$ for different values of x is still just a number being cubed. That means the shape of the transformed function is the same. With this information you can cross out choice (E).

That leaves four answers. The -1 term just shifts the graph over 1. Answer choices (A), (B), (C), and (D) shift the graph over 1, so the question becomes, "Which shift is the right one?" To see which one is correct, when does $f(x - 1) = 0$? When $x = 1$,

$$f(x - 1) = (1 - 1)^3 = 0$$

So when $x = 1$, $f(x - 1). = 0$ That matters because $f(x - 1) = y$ in this case. For which graph does $y = 0$ when $x = 1$? Stated in coordinate grid terms, which graph has point (0,1)? Only choice (B) contains this point, so it is the answer.

If you do decide to answer a transformation function problem, save it for the second pass since these problems take time even when you know exactly what you're doing.

3-D Geometry

You won't get a pair of those cool glasses to see figures jump off the page, but harder geometry problems will involve the third dimension. Fortunately, there are only a few 3-D figures the SAT will expect you to work with.

The first is the **rectangular solid**. It is the three-dimensional version of the rectangle, which means that all of its sides are rectangles. Also, like the rectangle, faces of a rectangular solid opposite each other are identical.

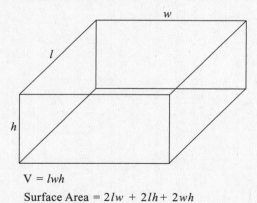

V = lwh

Surface Area = $2lw + 2lh + 2wh$

Recall how the rectangle and square are related. The rectangular solid and the cube are related in a similar fashion. The cube is a special kind of rectangular solid, namely the kind whose width, height, and length are all the same.

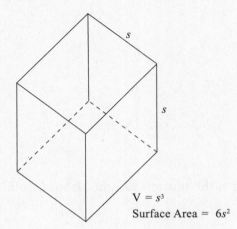

$V = s^3$
Surface Area $= 6s^2$

There is one more 3-D figure to inspect, the **cylinder**. Think of the cylinder as a bunch of circles stacked up on top of each other.

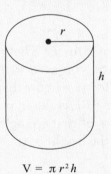

$V = \pi r^2 h$

Thinking of a cylinder as a bunch of stacked circles provides more than a good visual. It also gets your brain thinking of 3-D figures as multiple 2-D figures welded together in some way. The best approach to many 3-D figure problems is to treat them like multiple-figure problems. A rectangular solid is composed of six rectangular faces, but it also has triangles throughout its interior.

Take It to the Next Level

PETERSON'S
getting you there

Using these undrawn but present 2-D figures can be the key to answering a problem like the one below.

16.

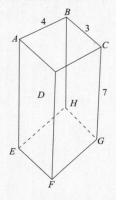

In the figure above, what is the shortest distance from *B* to *F*?

A. $\sqrt{14}$
B. $\sqrt{74}$
C.   10
D. $\sqrt{102}$
E.   14

The line *BF* is definitely the shortest route from *B* to *F*? The problem is figuring out how long *BF* is. To find this distance, you need to "uncover" the triangle *BFH*. This triangle is not drawn out for you in the diagram, but you can sketch it yourself or just imagine it. Line *BF* is the hypotenuse of right triangle *BFH*. If we find the two other sides of that triangle, then we can find *BF*. You know *BH* equals 7 since this is the height of the solid. You can find *HF* by looking at the bottom rectangle:

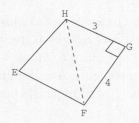

HF is the hypotenuse of the 3-4-5 triangle, so it is 5. Now you can try to find *BF*,

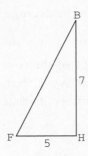

> **Note**
>
> You should not be surprised that a 3-4-5 right triangle just happens to appear in a place where you can use it. That sort of "coincidence" is what the SAT Math section is all about.

BF is the hypotenuse of this triangle. Using the Pythagorean theorem,

$$c^2 = a^2 + b^2$$
$$(BF)^2 = (HF)^2 + (BH)^2$$
$$(BF)^2 = 5^2 + 7^2$$
$$(BF)^2 = 25 + 49$$
$$(BF)^2 = 74$$
$$BF = \sqrt{74}$$

If you see a cube in a problem, don't see only the six squares that form its faces. Imagine all the other geometric forms that can be easily created. For example, drawing a diagonal on a face of the cube creates two 45-45-90 triangles. The key to answering a 3-D geometry problem often lies in finding these hidden figures.

Averages

There is another kind of average; it involves a conceptual wrinkle. It is called a **weighted average**. Consider the example below to see how a weighted average differs from a straightforward average.

In a group of 12 adults, 7 are 25 years old, and 5 are 32 years old. What is the average (arithmetic mean) of these 12 adults?

In the averages you worked previously, you were given a number set. You added up the numbers and then divided by the number of numbers in the set.

Here you are only given two numbers, 25 and 32, but the average is not just $\frac{32 + 25}{2}$ because there are more 25-year-olds than 32-year-olds. In this sense, 25 should have a greater weight in the average of the two numbers. You can give it the greater weight a few different ways, but the most straightforward is to multiply each age by the number at that age, and divide by the entire number of the group:

$$average = \frac{7(25) + 5(32)}{12} = \frac{175 + 160}{12} = \frac{335}{12} \approx 27.92$$

The age 25 was weighted more than the age 32 because there were more 25-year-olds than 32-year-olds.

You can still think of this weighted average as a regular average. You just took the average of the set {25, 25, 25, 25, 25, 25, 25, 32, 32, 32, 32, 32}.

Matrices

The word *matrix* probably conjures up images of a black-suited Keanu Reeves and a scowling Lawrence Fishburne. Put those images aside for the moment.

Matrices are queer little math entities that have some interesting applications if you are into quantum mechanics. But you don't need to worry about that for the SAT. You will need to be able to identify a matrix and then find its **determinant**. Sounds difficult, but it isn't. As for identifying a matrix, they look like this:

$$\begin{pmatrix} a & b \\ c & d \end{pmatrix}$$

The determinant of the above matrix looks like this:

$$\text{determinant} \begin{vmatrix} a & b \\ c & d \end{vmatrix} = ad - bc$$

Don't worry about what the determinant is, just make sure you understand how to calculate it. If the illustration is not clear, remember $ad - bc$ just means a times d minus b times c. So if you are asked to find the determinant just calculate $ad - bc$, the product of one diagonal minus the product of the other diagonal.

15. If $D = \begin{pmatrix} 2 & 5 \\ -6 & 7 \end{pmatrix}$, what is the determinant of D?

   (A) 16
   (B) 20
   (C) 30
   (D) 38
   (E) 44

The determinant is $ad - bc$, which in this case is $(2)(7) - (5)(-6) = 14 - (-30) = 44$. You see, all this talk of determinants and matrices sounds complicated, but actually calculating the determinant is pretty simple.

WHEW! Your brain should be full of numbers, rules, terms, and definitions. You could put the book down, go outside, and congratulate yourself for gaining a ton of knowledge or you could continue with some more word problems that will help you tackle the new SAT. If you want to tackle some more . . .

Speed (Rate of Motion)

SAT speed problems are a bit overrated in terms of their difficulty. They all involve the same familiar formula:

distance = rate $\times$ time

An easier speed problem will involve a *single* distance, rate, and time. A tougher speed problem might involve different rates, either:

- Two different times over the same distance, *or*

- Two different distances covered in the same time

In either type, apply the basic speed formula to each of the two events, then solve for the missing information by algebraic substitution. Use the same approach for any of the following:

- One object making two separate "legs" of a trip—either in the same direction or as a round trip

- Two objects moving in the same direction

- Two objects moving in opposite directions

PETERSON'S
getting you there

Here are two examples, each involving one of the first two scenarios:

10. Janice left her home at 11:00 a.m., traveling along Route 1 at 30 mph. At 1:00 p.m., her brother Richard left home and started after her on the same road at 45 mph. At what time did Richard catch up to Janice?

 (A) 2:45 p.m.
 (B) 3:00 p.m.
 (C) 3:30 p.m.
 (D) 4:15 p.m.
 (E) 5:00 p.m.

The correct answer is (E). Notice the distance Janice covered is equal to that of Richard—that is, distance is constant. Letting x equal Janice's time, you can express Richard's time as $x - 2$. Substitute these values for time and the values for rate given in the problem into the speed formula for Richard and Janice:

Formula: rate $\times$ time = distance
Janice: $(30)(x) = 30x$
Richard: $(45)(x - 2) = 45x - 90$

Because the distance is constant, you can equate Janice's distance to Richard's, then solve for x:

$$30x = 45x - 90$$
$$15x = 90$$
$$x = 6$$

Janice had traveled six hours when Richard caught up with her. Because Janice left at 11:00 a.m., Richard caught up with her at 5:00 p.m.

11. How far in kilometers can Scott drive into the country if he drives out at 40 kilometers per hour (kph), returns over the same road at 30 kph, and spends 8 hours away from home, including a 1-hour stop for lunch?

The correct answer is 120. Scott's actual driving time is 7 hours, which you must divide into two parts: his time spent driving into the country and his time spent returning. Letting the first part equal x, the return time is what remains of the 7 hours, or $7 - x$. Substitute these expressions into the motion formula for each of the two parts of Scott's journey:

Formula: rate $\times$ time = distance
Going: $(40)(x) = 40x$
Returning: $(30)(7 - x) = 210 - 30x$

Because the journey is round trip, the distance going equals the distance returning. Simply equate the two algebraic expressions, then solve for x:

$$40x = 210 - 30x$$
$$70x = 210$$
$$x = 3$$

Scott traveled 40 mph for 3 hours, so he traveled 120 miles.

Regardless of the type of motion problem you're solving you should always start with the same task: set up **two distinct equations patterned after the simple motion formula ($r \times t = d$).**

Rates of Work

Work problems involve one or more "workers" (people or machines) accomplishing a task. In work problems, there's an *inverse* relationship between the number of workers and the time that it takes to complete the job—in other words, the more workers, the quicker the job gets done. Here's the basic formula for solving a work problem:

$$\frac{A}{x} + \frac{A}{y} = 1$$

In this formula, x and y represent the time needed for each of two workers, x and y, to complete the job alone (individually), and A represents the time it takes for both x and y to complete the job working in the *aggregate* (together). So, each fraction represents the portion of the job completed by a worker. The sum of the two fractions must be 1, if the job is completed.

Regardless of which rate—individual or aggregate—you need to determine, a typical SAT work problem is a "no-brainer" if you know the formula. Just plug in what you know and solve for the unknown variable. The only curveball the SAT might throw at you is where one worker operates counter-productively to the other. You handle this scenario by *subtracting* one fraction from the other instead of adding them together—as in the following example:

12. A certain tank holds a maximum of 450 cubic meters of water. If a hose can fill the tank at a rate of 5 cubic meters per minute, but the tank has a hole through which a constant cubic meter of water escapes every two minutes, how long does it take to fill the tank to its maximum capacity?

   (A) 81 minutes
   (B) 90 minutes
   (C) 100 minutes
   (D) 112 minutes
   (E) 125 minutes

The correct answer is (C). In this problem, the hole (which is the second "worker") is acting counter-productively, so you must subtract its rate from the hose's rate to determine the aggregate rate of the hose and the hole. The hose alone takes 90 minutes to fill the tank. The hole alone empties a full tank in 900 minutes. Plug these values into our slightly modified formula, then solve for A:

$$\frac{A}{90} - \frac{A}{900} = 1$$

$$\frac{10A}{900} - \frac{A}{900} = 1$$

$$\frac{10A - A}{900} = 1$$

$$\frac{9A}{900} = 1$$

$$9A = 900$$

$$A = 100$$

It takes 100 minutes to fill the tank to its maximum capacity.

Mixtures

In SAT mixture problems, you combine substances with different characteristics, resulting in a particular mixture or proportion, usually expressed as percentages. Substances are measured and mixed by either volume or weight—but not by number (quantity).

13. How many quarts of pure alcohol must you add to 15 quarts of a solution that is 40% alcohol to strengthen it to a solution that is 50% alcohol?

   (A) 2.5
   (B) 3.0
   (C) 3.25
   (D) 3.5
   (E) 4.0

The correct answer is (B). The original amount of alcohol is 40% of 15. Letting x equal the number of quarts of alcohol that you must add to achieve a 50% alcohol solution, $.4(15) + x$ equals the amount of alcohol in the solution after adding more alcohol. You can express this amount as 50% of $(15 + x)$. Thus, you can express the mixture algebraically as follows:

$$(.4)(15) + x = (.5)(15 + x)$$
$$6 + x = 7.5 + .5x$$
$$.5x = 1.5$$
$$x = 3$$

You must add 3 quarts of alcohol to obtain a 50% alcohol solution.

Ages

Age problems ask you to compare ages of two or more people at different points in time. In solving age problems, you might have to represent a person's age at the present time, several years from now, or several years ago. Any age problem allows you to set up equations to relate the ages of two or more people, as in the following example:

14. Fred's age is twice what Geri's age was 8 years ago, and Holly's age is five years greater than Geri's age will be 1 year from now. If the total age of Fred, Geri, and Holly is 50, what is Fred's age in years?

PETERSON'S
getting you there

The correct answer is 14. Fred's age can be expressed in terms of Geri's, and Geri's age can be expressed in terms of Holly's:

$$F = 2(G - 8)$$
$$H = G + 6$$

Given that the total age of *F*, *G*, and *H* is 50, substitute these two expressions for *F* and *G* in the equation $F + G + H = 50$, then solve for *G*:

$$2(G - 8) + G + (G + 6) = 50$$
$$2G - 16 + G + G + 6 = 50$$
$$4G - 10 = 50$$
$$4G = 60$$
$$G = 15$$

To find *F*, substitute 15 for *G* in the equation $F = 2(G - 8)$:

$$F = 2(15 - 8)$$
$$F = 14$$

Interest on Investment

Tougher SAT investment problems usually involve interest and require more than simply calculating interest earned on a given principal amount at a given rate. They usually call for you to set up and solve an algebraic equation. When handling these problems, it's best to eliminate percent signs (or multiply by 100 to eliminate decimals).

15. Dr. Kramer plans to invest $20,000 in an account paying 6% interest annually. How much more must she invest at the same time at 3% so that her total annual income during the first year is 4% of her entire investment?

    (A) $32,000
    (B) $36,000
    (C) $40,000
    (D) $47,000
    (E) $49,000

The correct answer is (C). Letting x equal the amount invested at 3%, you can express Dr. Kramer's total investment as $20,000 + x$. The interest on $20,000 plus the interest on the additional investment equals the total interest from both investments. You can state this algebraically as follows:

$$.06(20,000) + .03x = .04(20,000 + x)$$

Multiply all terms by 100 to eliminate decimals, then solve for x:

$$6(20,000) + 3x = 4(20,000 + x)$$
$$120,000 + 3x = 80,000 + 4x$$
$$40,000 = x$$

She must invest $40,000 at 3% for her total annual income to be 4% of her total investment ($60,000).

In solving SAT investment problems, by all means size up the question to make sure your calculated answer appears to be in the right ballpark. But don't rely on your intuition to derive a *precise* solution. Interest problems can be misleading. For instance, you might have guessed that Dr. Kramer would need to invest more than *twice* as much at 3% than at 6% to lower the overall interest rate to 4%. Not true!

Now that you have the information you need to succeed, all that remains is to get some practice answering SAT-like questions in a timed format. That's what the next three chapters of this book are for.

Take It to the Next Level

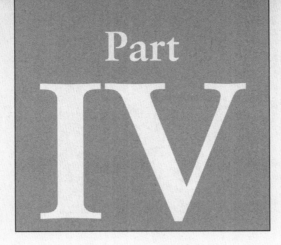

Part

IV

Taking
Three Practice Tests

PART IV

Chapter

8

Preface to the Practice Tests

The three practice tests in this book should be used to "test"-drive the new strategies and ideas you've learned. It's important that you don't just jump to these questions and start answering them before reading all that came before. To truly maximize your score, you should approach these tests with the attitude that you will use them to try out the various points and ideas covered in the earlier chapters of this book. Doing this will help you absorb the material discussed and make you a better SAT test-taker.

Make sure you take only one test at a time, and then look over the explanations to the answers. Everyone will want to read the explanations for the questions that they miss, but it's also a good idea to look at the answers for the other questions as well. The explanations can give you ideas about different ways to approach a problem.

Do your best, and remember that the goal is to learn something from every missed question, and even from some that you answered correctly.

Answer Sheets

SECTION 1

1	Ⓐ Ⓑ Ⓒ Ⓓ Ⓔ	6	Ⓐ Ⓑ Ⓒ Ⓓ Ⓔ	11	Ⓐ Ⓑ Ⓒ Ⓓ Ⓔ	16	Ⓐ Ⓑ Ⓒ Ⓓ Ⓔ
2	Ⓐ Ⓑ Ⓒ Ⓓ Ⓔ	7	Ⓐ Ⓑ Ⓒ Ⓓ Ⓔ	12	Ⓐ Ⓑ Ⓒ Ⓓ Ⓔ	17	Ⓐ Ⓑ Ⓒ Ⓓ Ⓔ
3	Ⓐ Ⓑ Ⓒ Ⓓ Ⓔ	8	Ⓐ Ⓑ Ⓒ Ⓓ Ⓔ	13	Ⓐ Ⓑ Ⓒ Ⓓ Ⓔ	18	Ⓐ Ⓑ Ⓒ Ⓓ Ⓔ
4	Ⓐ Ⓑ Ⓒ Ⓓ Ⓔ	9	Ⓐ Ⓑ Ⓒ Ⓓ Ⓔ	14	Ⓐ Ⓑ Ⓒ Ⓓ Ⓔ	19	Ⓐ Ⓑ Ⓒ Ⓓ Ⓔ
5	Ⓐ Ⓑ Ⓒ Ⓓ Ⓔ	10	Ⓐ Ⓑ Ⓒ Ⓓ Ⓔ	15	Ⓐ Ⓑ Ⓒ Ⓓ Ⓔ	20	Ⓐ Ⓑ Ⓒ Ⓓ Ⓔ

SECTION 2

1	Ⓐ Ⓑ Ⓒ Ⓓ Ⓔ	7	Ⓐ Ⓑ Ⓒ Ⓓ Ⓔ	12	Ⓐ Ⓑ Ⓒ Ⓓ Ⓔ	17	Ⓐ Ⓑ Ⓒ Ⓓ Ⓔ
2	Ⓐ Ⓑ Ⓒ Ⓓ Ⓔ	8	Ⓐ Ⓑ Ⓒ Ⓓ Ⓔ	13	Ⓐ Ⓑ Ⓒ Ⓓ Ⓔ	18	Ⓐ Ⓑ Ⓒ Ⓓ Ⓔ
3	Ⓐ Ⓑ Ⓒ Ⓓ Ⓔ	9	Ⓐ Ⓑ Ⓒ Ⓓ Ⓔ	14	Ⓐ Ⓑ Ⓒ Ⓓ Ⓔ	19	Ⓐ Ⓑ Ⓒ Ⓓ Ⓔ
4	Ⓐ Ⓑ Ⓒ Ⓓ Ⓔ	10	Ⓐ Ⓑ Ⓒ Ⓓ Ⓔ	15	Ⓐ Ⓑ Ⓒ Ⓓ Ⓔ	20	Ⓐ Ⓑ Ⓒ Ⓓ Ⓔ
5	Ⓐ Ⓑ Ⓒ Ⓓ Ⓔ	11	Ⓐ Ⓑ Ⓒ Ⓓ Ⓔ	16	Ⓐ Ⓑ Ⓒ Ⓓ Ⓔ	21	Ⓐ Ⓑ Ⓒ Ⓓ Ⓔ
6	Ⓐ Ⓑ Ⓒ Ⓓ Ⓔ						

SECTION 3

1	Ⓐ Ⓑ Ⓒ Ⓓ Ⓔ	9	Ⓐ Ⓑ Ⓒ Ⓓ Ⓔ	17	Ⓐ Ⓑ Ⓒ Ⓓ Ⓔ	24	Ⓐ Ⓑ Ⓒ Ⓓ Ⓔ
2	Ⓐ Ⓑ Ⓒ Ⓓ Ⓔ	10	Ⓐ Ⓑ Ⓒ Ⓓ Ⓔ	18	Ⓐ Ⓑ Ⓒ Ⓓ Ⓔ	25	Ⓐ Ⓑ Ⓒ Ⓓ Ⓔ
3	Ⓐ Ⓑ Ⓒ Ⓓ Ⓔ	11	Ⓐ Ⓑ Ⓒ Ⓓ Ⓔ	19	Ⓐ Ⓑ Ⓒ Ⓓ Ⓔ	26	Ⓐ Ⓑ Ⓒ Ⓓ Ⓔ
4	Ⓐ Ⓑ Ⓒ Ⓓ Ⓔ	12	Ⓐ Ⓑ Ⓒ Ⓓ Ⓔ	20	Ⓐ Ⓑ Ⓒ Ⓓ Ⓔ	27	Ⓐ Ⓑ Ⓒ Ⓓ Ⓔ
5	Ⓐ Ⓑ Ⓒ Ⓓ Ⓔ	13	Ⓐ Ⓑ Ⓒ Ⓓ Ⓔ	21	Ⓐ Ⓑ Ⓒ Ⓓ Ⓔ	28	Ⓐ Ⓑ Ⓒ Ⓓ Ⓔ
6	Ⓐ Ⓑ Ⓒ Ⓓ Ⓔ	14	Ⓐ Ⓑ Ⓒ Ⓓ Ⓔ	22	Ⓐ Ⓑ Ⓒ Ⓓ Ⓔ	29	Ⓐ Ⓑ Ⓒ Ⓓ Ⓔ
7	Ⓐ Ⓑ Ⓒ Ⓓ Ⓔ	15	Ⓐ Ⓑ Ⓒ Ⓓ Ⓔ	23	Ⓐ Ⓑ Ⓒ Ⓓ Ⓔ	30	Ⓐ Ⓑ Ⓒ Ⓓ Ⓔ
8	Ⓐ Ⓑ Ⓒ Ⓓ Ⓔ	16	Ⓐ Ⓑ Ⓒ Ⓓ Ⓔ				

SECTION 4

1	Ⓐ Ⓑ Ⓒ Ⓓ Ⓔ	8	Ⓐ Ⓑ Ⓒ Ⓓ Ⓔ	15	Ⓐ Ⓑ Ⓒ Ⓓ Ⓔ	22	Ⓐ Ⓑ Ⓒ Ⓓ Ⓔ
2	Ⓐ Ⓑ Ⓒ Ⓓ Ⓔ	9	Ⓐ Ⓑ Ⓒ Ⓓ Ⓔ	16	Ⓐ Ⓑ Ⓒ Ⓓ Ⓔ	23	Ⓐ Ⓑ Ⓒ Ⓓ Ⓔ
3	Ⓐ Ⓑ Ⓒ Ⓓ Ⓔ	10	Ⓐ Ⓑ Ⓒ Ⓓ Ⓔ	17	Ⓐ Ⓑ Ⓒ Ⓓ Ⓔ	24	Ⓐ Ⓑ Ⓒ Ⓓ Ⓔ
4	Ⓐ Ⓑ Ⓒ Ⓓ Ⓔ	11	Ⓐ Ⓑ Ⓒ Ⓓ Ⓔ	18	Ⓐ Ⓑ Ⓒ Ⓓ Ⓔ	25	Ⓐ Ⓑ Ⓒ Ⓓ Ⓔ
5	Ⓐ Ⓑ Ⓒ Ⓓ Ⓔ	12	Ⓐ Ⓑ Ⓒ Ⓓ Ⓔ	19	Ⓐ Ⓑ Ⓒ Ⓓ Ⓔ	26	Ⓐ Ⓑ Ⓒ Ⓓ Ⓔ
6	Ⓐ Ⓑ Ⓒ Ⓓ Ⓔ	13	Ⓐ Ⓑ Ⓒ Ⓓ Ⓔ	20	Ⓐ Ⓑ Ⓒ Ⓓ Ⓔ	27	Ⓐ Ⓑ Ⓒ Ⓓ Ⓔ
7	Ⓐ Ⓑ Ⓒ Ⓓ Ⓔ	14	Ⓐ Ⓑ Ⓒ Ⓓ Ⓔ	21	Ⓐ Ⓑ Ⓒ Ⓓ Ⓔ		

SECTION 5

1	Ⓐ Ⓑ Ⓒ Ⓓ Ⓔ	7	Ⓐ Ⓑ Ⓒ Ⓓ Ⓔ	12	Ⓐ Ⓑ Ⓒ Ⓓ Ⓔ	17	Ⓐ Ⓑ Ⓒ Ⓓ Ⓔ
2	Ⓐ Ⓑ Ⓒ Ⓓ Ⓔ	8	Ⓐ Ⓑ Ⓒ Ⓓ Ⓔ	13	Ⓐ Ⓑ Ⓒ Ⓓ Ⓔ	18	Ⓐ Ⓑ Ⓒ Ⓓ Ⓔ
3	Ⓐ Ⓑ Ⓒ Ⓓ Ⓔ	9	Ⓐ Ⓑ Ⓒ Ⓓ Ⓔ	14	Ⓐ Ⓑ Ⓒ Ⓓ Ⓔ	19	Ⓐ Ⓑ Ⓒ Ⓓ Ⓔ
4	Ⓐ Ⓑ Ⓒ Ⓓ Ⓔ	10	Ⓐ Ⓑ Ⓒ Ⓓ Ⓔ	15	Ⓐ Ⓑ Ⓒ Ⓓ Ⓔ	20	Ⓐ Ⓑ Ⓒ Ⓓ Ⓔ
5	Ⓐ Ⓑ Ⓒ Ⓓ Ⓔ	11	Ⓐ Ⓑ Ⓒ Ⓓ Ⓔ	16	Ⓐ Ⓑ Ⓒ Ⓓ Ⓔ	21	Ⓐ Ⓑ Ⓒ Ⓓ Ⓔ
6	Ⓐ Ⓑ Ⓒ Ⓓ Ⓔ						

Answer Sheets

SECTION 6

1 Ⓐ Ⓑ Ⓒ Ⓓ Ⓔ   5 Ⓐ Ⓑ Ⓒ Ⓓ Ⓔ   9 Ⓐ Ⓑ Ⓒ Ⓓ Ⓔ   13 Ⓐ Ⓑ Ⓒ Ⓓ Ⓔ

2 Ⓐ Ⓑ Ⓒ Ⓓ Ⓔ   6 Ⓐ Ⓑ Ⓒ Ⓓ Ⓔ   10 Ⓐ Ⓑ Ⓒ Ⓓ Ⓔ   14 Ⓐ Ⓑ Ⓒ Ⓓ Ⓔ

3 Ⓐ Ⓑ Ⓒ Ⓓ Ⓔ   7 Ⓐ Ⓑ Ⓒ Ⓓ Ⓔ   11 Ⓐ Ⓑ Ⓒ Ⓓ Ⓔ   15 Ⓐ Ⓑ Ⓒ Ⓓ Ⓔ

4 Ⓐ Ⓑ Ⓒ Ⓓ Ⓔ   8 Ⓐ Ⓑ Ⓒ Ⓓ Ⓔ   12 Ⓐ Ⓑ Ⓒ Ⓓ Ⓔ   16 Ⓐ Ⓑ Ⓒ Ⓓ Ⓔ

SECTION 7

For Questions 1–13:

Only answers entered in the ovals in each grid area will be scored.

You will not receive credit for anything written in the boxes above the ovals.

Section 1

20 Questions ■ Time—25 Minutes

Directions: Read each of the passages carefully, then answer the questions that come after them. The answer to each question may be stated overtly or only implied. You will not have to use outside knowledge to answer the questions—all the material you will need will be in the passage itself. In some cases, you will be asked to read two related passages and answer questions about their relationship to one another. Mark the letter of your choice on your answer sheet.

Musical notes, like all sounds, are a result of the sound waves created by movement, like the rush of air through a trumpet. Musical notes are very regular sound waves. The qualities of these waves—how much they displace molecules, and how often they do so—give the note its particular sound. How much a sound wave displaces molecules affects the volume of the note. How frequently a sound wave reaches your ear determines whether the note is high- or low-pitched. When scientists describe how high or low a sound is, they use a numerical measurement of its frequency, such as "440 vibrations per second," rather than the letters musicians use.

1. In this passage, musical notes are used primarily to

   (A) illustrate the difference between human-produced and nonhuman-produced sound.
   (B) demonstrate the difference between musical sound and all other sound.
   (C) provide an example of sound properties common to all sound.
   (D) convey the difference between musical pitch and frequency pitch.
   (E) explain the connection between number and letter names for sounds.

GO ON TO THE NEXT PAGE

2. All of the following are true statements about pitch, according to the passage, EXCEPT:

   (A) Nonmusical sounds cannot be referred to in terms of pitch.

   (B) Pitch is solely determined by the frequency of the sound wave.

   (C) Pitch is closely related to the vibration of molecules.

   (D) Pitch cannot be accurately described with letter names.

   (E) Humans' perception of pitch is not affected by the intensity of the sound wave.

Line   Margaret Walker, who would become one of the most important twentieth-century African-American poets, was born in Birmingham, Alabama, in 1915.
(5)   Her parents, a minister and a music teacher, encouraged her to read poetry and philosophy even as a child. Walker completed her high school education at Gilbert Academy in New Orleans and
(10)   went on to attend New Orleans University for two years. It was then that the important Harlem Renaissance poet Langston Hughes recognized her talent and persuaded her to continue her
(15)   education in the North. She transferred to Northwestern University in Illinois, where she received a degree in English in 1935. Her poem, "For My People," which would remain one of her most
(20)   important works, was also her first publication, appearing in *Poetry* magazine in 1937.

3. The passage cites Walker's interaction with Langston Hughes as

   (A) instrumental in her early work being published.

   (B) influential in her decision to study at Northwestern University.

   (C) not as important at the time it happened as it is now, due to Hughes' fame.

   (D) a great encouragement for Walker's confidence as a poet.

   (E) important to her choice to study at New Orleans University.

4. The passage suggests that Walker's decision to become a poet

   (A) occurred before she entered college.

   (B) was primarily a result of her interaction with Hughes.

   (C) was not surprising, given her upbringing.

   (D) occurred after her transfer to Northwestern University.

   (E) was sudden and immediately successful.

Questions 5–10 are based on the following passage.

Line   F. Scott Fitzgerald was a prominent American writer of the twentieth century. This passage comes from one of his short stories and tells the story of a young John
(5)   Unger leaving home for boarding school.
   John T. Unger came from a family that had been well known in Hades—a small town on the Mississippi River—for several generations. John's father had
(10)   held the amateur golf championship through many a heated contest; Mrs. Unger was known "from hot-box to hot-bed," as the local phrase went, for

her political addresses; and young John

(15) T. Unger, who had just turned sixteen, had danced all the latest dances from New York before he put on long trousers. And now, for a certain time, he was to be away from home.

(20)   That respect for a New England education which is the bane of all provincial places, which drains them yearly of their most promising young men, had seized upon his parents.

(25) Nothing would suit them but that he should go to St. Midas's School near Boston—Hades was too small to hold their darling and gifted son. Now in Hades—as you know if you ever have

(30) been there—the names of the more fashionable preparatory schools and colleges mean very little. The inhabitants have been so long out of the world that, though they make a show of keeping

(35) up-to-date in dress and manners and literature, they depend to a great extent on hearsay, and a function that in Hades would be considered elaborate would doubtless be hailed by a Chicago

(40) beef-princess as "perhaps a little tacky."

    John T. Unger was on the eve of departure. Mrs. Unger, with maternal fatuity, packed his trunks full of linen suits and electric fans, and Mr. Unger

(45) presented his son with an asbestos pocket-book stuffed with money. "Remember, you are always welcome here," he said. "You can be sure, boy, that we'll keep the home fires burning."

(50)   "I know," answered John huskily.

    "Don't forget who you are and where you come from," continued his father proudly, "and you can do nothing to harm you. You are an Unger—from

(55) Hades."

    So the old man and the young shook hands, and John walked away with tears streaming from his eyes. Ten minutes later he had passed outside the city limits

(60) and he stopped to glance back for the last time. Over the gates the old-fashioned Victorian motto seemed strangely attractive to him. His father had tried time and time again to have it changed to

(65) something with a little more push and verve about it, such as "Hades—Your Opportunity," or else a plain "Welcome" sign set over a hearty handshake pricked out in electric lights. The old motto was a

(70) little depressing, Mr. Unger had thought—but now ...

    So John took his look and then set his face resolutely toward his destination. And, as he turned away, the lights of

(75) Hades against the sky seemed full of a warm and passionate beauty.

5. The tone of line 28 can best be described as

(A) compassionate.
(B) sincere.
(C) sardonic.
(D) dismayed.
(E) understated.

6. The "Chicago beef-princess" (lines 39–40) can best be described as representing the Chicago upper class by way of which literary device?

(A) Anachronism
(B) Simile
(C) Apostrophe
(D) Metaphor
(E) Neologism

PETERSON'S
getting you there

7. The phrase "maternal fatuity" (line 42–43), suggests that

(A) John will not need linen suits and electric fans at St. Midas's.

(B) John's mother packed frantically and ineffectively.

(C) John's mother was excessively doting.

(D) John resented his mother packing for him.

(E) John never enjoyed linen suits or electric fans.

8. From the conversation between John and his father in paragraphs 3–6, it can be inferred that John feels

(A) rejected and angry.

(B) melancholic but composed.

(C) impassive and indifferent.

(D) resigned but filled with dread.

(E) relieved but apprehensive.

9. John's meditation on the town's sign in paragraph 6 serves in the passage primarily to suggest a contrast between

(A) John's love of Victorian things and his father's love of modern things.

(B) his father's commercialism and John's sentimentality.

(C) John's previous role as a part of the town and his new role as nostalgic outsider.

(D) his father's naivety and John's pragmatism.

(E) the old-fashioned atmosphere in the town before John's father influenced it and its current modernity.

10. The names Hades, St. Midas, and Unger suggest that the passage can be considered a(n)

(A) epic poem.

(B) euphemism.

(C) aphorism.

(D) satire.

(E) allegory.

Questions 11–20 are based on the following passage.

This passage discusses the work of Abe Kobo, a Japanese novelist of the twentieth century.

Line   Abe Kobo is one of the great writers of postwar Japan. His literature is richer, less predictable, and wider-ranging than that of his famed contemporaries,
(5)   Mishima Yukio and Nobel laureate Oe Kenzaburo. It is infused with the passion and strangeness of his experiences in Manchuria, which was a Japanese colony on mainland China before World War II.
(10)   Abe spent his childhood and much of his youth in Manchuria, and, as a result, the orbit of his work would be far less controlled by the oppressive gravitational pull of the themes of *furusato* (home-
(15)   town) and the emperor than his contemporaries'.

    Abe, like most of the sons of Japanese families living in Manchuria, did return to Japan for schooling. He entered
(20)   medical school in Tokyo in 1944—just in time to forge himself a medical certificate claiming ill health; this allowed him to avoid fighting in the war that Japan was already losing and return to Manchuria.
(25)   When Japan lost the war, however, it also lost its Manchurian colony. The Japanese living there were attacked by the Soviet Army and various guerrilla bands. They

(30) suddenly found themselves refugees, desperate for food. Many unfit men were abandoned in the Manchurian desert. At this apocalyptic time, Abe lost his father to cholera.

(35) He returned to mainland Japan once more, where the young were turning to Marxism as a rejection of the militarism of the war. After a brief, unsuccessful stint at medical school, he became part of a Marxist group of avant-garde artists.

(40) His work at this time was passionate and outspoken on political matters, adopting black humor as its mode of critique. During this time, Abe worked in the genres of theater, music, and photogra-

(45) phy. Eventually, he mimeographed fifty copies of his first "published" literary work, entitled *Anonymous Poems*, in 1947. It was a politically charged set of poems dedicated to the memory of his

(50) father and friends who had died in Manchuria. Shortly thereafter, he published his first novel, *For a Signpost at the End of a Road*, which imagined another life for his best friend who had

(55) died in the Manchurian desert. Abe was also active in the Communist Party, organizing literary groups for working-men.

Unfortunately, most of this radical

(60) early work is unknown outside Japan and underappreciated even in Japan. In early 1962, Abe was dismissed from the Japanese Liberalist Party. Four months later, he published the work that would

(65) blind us to his earlier oeuvre, *Woman in the Dunes*. It was director Teshigahara Hiroshi's film adaptation of *Woman in the Dunes* that brought Abe's work to the international stage. The movie's fame

(70) has wrongly led readers to view the novel as Abe's masterpiece. It would be more accurate to say that the novel simply marked a turning point in his career, when Abe turned away from the experi-

(75) mental and heavily political work of his earlier career. Fortunately, he did not then turn to *furusato* and the emperor after all, but rather began a somewhat more realistic exploration of his continu-

(80) ing obsession with homelessness and alienation. Not completely a stranger to his earlier commitment to Marxism, Abe turned his attention, beginning in the sixties, to the effects on the individual of

(85) Japan's rapidly urbanizing, growth-driven, increasingly corporate society.

11. The word "infused" in line 6 most closely means

(A) illuminated.
(B) saturated.
(C) influenced.
(D) bewildered.
(E) nuanced.

12. The author refers to "the orbit" of Abe's work (lines 12–13) to emphasize that

(A) his work covers a wide range of themes.
(B) the emperor is often compared to a sun.
C. Abe's travels were the primary themes in his work.
D. Abe's work is so different from his contemporaries' that it is like another solar system.
(E) conventional themes can limit an author's individuality.

377

13. From the sentence beginning "He entered medical school. . . " in lines 19–24, it can be inferred that

(A) Abe entered medical school because he was sick.

(B) sick people were sent to Manchuria during World War II.

(C) Abe wanted to help the ill and injured in World War II, rather than fight.

(D) illness would excuse one from military duty in World War II Japan.

(E) Abe never intended to practice medicine.

14. The author uses the word "apocalyptic" to emphasize that

(A) Manchuria suffered intensely as a result of the use of nuclear weapons in World War II.

(B) Abe was deeply affected by the loss of his father.

(C) there was massive famine in Manchuria at the end of World War II.

(D) postwar Manchuria experienced exhilarating change.

(E) conditions in Manchuria after World War II were generally horrific.

15. The word "avant-garde" (line 39) could best be replaced by

(A) experimental.

(B) dramatic.

(C) novel.

(D) profound.

(E) realistic.

16. Which of the following does the passage present as a fact?

(A) Abe was a better playwright than novelist.

(B) Abe's early work was of greater quality than his later work.

(C) The group of avant-garde artists of which Abe was a part were influenced by Marxism.

(D) The themes of *furusato* and the emperor have precluded Japanese literature from playing a major role in world literature.

(E) Abe's work is richer than his contemporaries' because he included autobiographical elements.

17. The phrase "blind us" in lines 65–66 refers to the

(A) absence of film adaptations for Abe's other novels.

(B) excessive critical attention to Abe's novel, *Woman in the Dunes*.

(C) difficulty in reconciling *Woman in the Dunes* and other later works with the form and content of his earlier works.

(D) challenge of interpreting Abe's more experimental works.

(E) overwhelming power of Abe's novel, *Woman in the Dunes*.

378

18. The author's main purpose in the passage is to

   (A) defend Abe's later works against the prevalent criticism of it.
   (B) advocate for Abe's work over that of his contemporaries.
   (C) explain the differences between Abe's earlier and later works.
   (D) argue that Abe is an even greater writer and artist than generally perceived.
   (E) demonstrate that Abe's work became less interesting after he left Manchuria.

19. The author of the passage is most likely a

   (A) film critic.
   (B) literary critic.
   (C) avant-garde artist.
   (D) translator.
   (E) novelist.

20. The author's attitude toward Marxism can best be described as

   (A) contemptuous derision.
   (B) reverent espousal.
   (C) skeptical tolerance.
   (D) respectful interest.
   (E) restrained impatience.

STOP Do not proceed to the next section until time is up.

Section 2

21 Questions ■ Time—25 Minutes

Directions: Solve the following problems using any available space on the page for scratchwork. Mark the letter of your choice on the answer sheet that best corresponds to the correct answer.

Notes:

1. You may use a calculator. All of the numbers used are real numbers.

2. You may use the figures that accompany the problems to help you find the solution. Unless the instructions say that a figure is not drawn to scale, assume that it has been drawn accurately. Each figure lies in a plane unless the instructions say otherwise.

Reference Information

$A = \pi r^2$
$C = 2\pi r$ $\quad A = \ell w \quad A = \frac{1}{2}bh \quad V = \ell wh \quad V = \pi r^2 h \quad c^2 = a^2 + b^2 \quad$ Special Right Triangles

The number of degrees of arc in a circle is 360.
The measure in degrees of a straight angle is 180.
The sum of the measures in degrees of the angles of a triangle is 180.

1. What percentage of 75 is 12?

   (A) 8%
   (B) 12%
   (C) 16%
   (D) 18%
   (E) 20%

2. If a circle is inscribed in a square of area 36, what is the area of the circle?

   (A) 36π
   (B) 24π
   (C) 12π
   (D) 9π
   (E) 6π

380

3. Which of the following could have a slope of one?

(A)

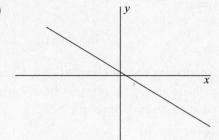

(B)

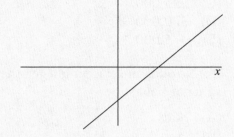

(C)

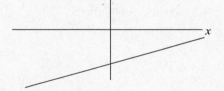

(D)

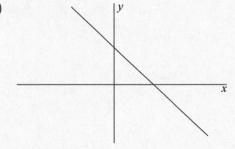

(E)

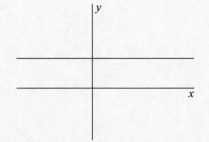

4. The first four terms of a series are 1, 4, 9, and 16. What is the eight term of this series?

(A) 49
(B) 56
(C) 64
(D) 72
(E) 81

5.

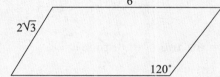

What is the area of the above parallelogram?

(A) 16
(B) 18
(C) 22
(D) 24
(E) 32

6. Which of the following fractions has the greatest reciprocal?

(A) $\dfrac{2}{9}$

(B) $\dfrac{4}{5}$

(C) $\dfrac{7}{3}$

(D) $\dfrac{2}{3}$

(E) $\dfrac{3}{13}$

GO ON TO THE NEXT PAGE

7.

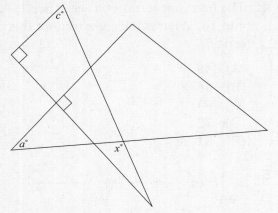

If $a = 60$ and $c = 50$ then $x =$

(A) 40
(B) 65
(C) 75
(D) 85
(E) 110

8. $\left[(2^2 + 2^2)^{-1} \right]^{-2} =$

(A) $\dfrac{1}{64}$

(B) $\dfrac{1}{16}$

(C) $\dfrac{1}{8}$

(D) 16

(E) 64

9.

Company A	☐	☐	☐		
Company B	☐	☐	☐	☐	☐

☐ = 150,000 widgets

According to the chart above, Company B produced approximately how many more widgets than Company A?

(A) 75,000
(B) 150,000
(C) 225,000
(D) 300,000
(E) 375,000

10. If x^x is odd, and x is an integer, then the value of x must be

(A) odd.
(B) even.
(C) less than one.
(D) an irrational number.
(E) None of the above.

The following description applies to questions 11–13.

The factorial of a number is the product of all the integers from one to the number. For example, 5 factorial is $5 \times 4 \times 3 \times 2 \times 1$. The notation for a factorial is the number followed by an exclamation point.

Thus $5! = 5 \times 4 \times 3 \times 2 \times 1$.

11. $\dfrac{6!}{3!} =$

    (A) 2
    (B) 16
    (C) 30
    (D) 88
    (E) 120

12. If $f(x) = (x!)^2$ then $f(3) =$

    (A) 16
    (B) 36
    (C) 172
    (D) 1080
    (E) 6282

13. If $y + 2 = x$, and y and x are integers, then $\dfrac{y!}{x!} =$

    (A) $\dfrac{1}{(y+2)(y+1)}$
    (B) y
    (C) $\dfrac{1}{y^2}$
    (D) $\dfrac{y}{x}$
    (E) $y(y-1)$

14. If the determinant of this matrix is -6, what is the value of n?

$$\begin{pmatrix} n & 4 \\ 5 & -7 \end{pmatrix}$$

    (A) -2
    (B) $-5\dfrac{3}{5}$
    (C) -7
    (D) -8
    (E) $-8\dfrac{3}{4}$

15. If $p + q = 2q + 6$, which of the following statements must be true?

    I. p is even
    II. q is even
    III. pq is even

    (A) I only
    (B) II only
    (C) II and III only
    (D) I, II, and III
    (E) None

16.

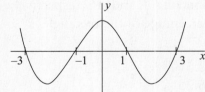

For the above graph, for which values of x is $y > 0$?

    (A) $-3 < -1$ and $1 < x < 3$
    (B) $x < -3$ and $-1 < x < 1$ and $x > 3$
    (C) $x < -3$ and $1 < x < 3$ and $x > 3$
    (D) $x > 3$ and $x > -1$
    (E) $-3 > x > 3$

PETERSON'S
getting you there

17.

A   B   C   D   E

The numbers from the number set {9, 11, 12, 15, 16} must be put in the above boxes according to these conditions:

Boxes A, C, and D contain numbers divisible by three.

Box B contains a prime number.

Which number must be in Box E?

(A) 9
(B) 11
(C) 12
(D) 15
(E) 16

18.

If, $\overline{AC} = 8$, $\overline{AB} = 4$, and D and H are midpoints on $\overline{CE}$ and $\overline{AG}$ respectively, what percentage of the rectangle is shaded?

(A) 12.5%
(B) 16.33%
(C) 20%
(D) 25%
(E) 30%

19. Raising $n^{\frac{-p}{n}}$ by which of the following will give the result n?

(A) $p^{\frac{-p}{n}}$

(B) $n^{\frac{n}{p}}$

(C) $\dfrac{p}{n}$

(D) $\dfrac{-n}{p}$

(E) $\dfrac{n + p}{p}$

20. If n is a positive integer and n, $n - 2$, and $n + 2$ are each prime numbers, then the set of those three numbers is called a prime triplet. How many different prime triplets are there where none of the set is greater than fifty?

(A) 1
(B) 2
(C) 3
(D) 4
(E) None.

21. If a circle has four tangents, each of which is perpendicular to two of the other tangents, then

(A) at most one pair of tangent lines is parallel.
(B) at most two pairs of tangent lines are parallel.
(C) all four tangent lines are parallel.
(D) a square is inscribed in the circle.
(E) one particular diameter could be perpendicular to all four tangent lines.

STOP Do not proceed to the next section until time is up.

Section 3

30 Questions ■ Time—25 Minutes

Identifying Sentence Errors

Directions: Mark the letter of your choice on the answer sheet that best corresponds to the correct answer.

Notes:

1. The following questions test your knowledge of the rules of English grammar, as well as word usage, word choice, and idioms.

2. Some sentences are correct, but others contain a single error. No sentence contains more than one error.

3. Any errors that occur will be found in the underlined portion of the sentence. Choose the letter underneath the error to indicate the part of the sentence that must be changed.

4. If there is no error, pick answer choice (E).

5. There will be no change in any parts of the sentence that are not underlined.

1. Despite the enormous voter drive, there
   A   B
   are still many city-dwellers who are not
                                C
   registered to vote. No error
   D   E

2. Debating the energy bill was the first
   A
   order of business for the Senate; to set the
   B   C
   calendar for the upcoming session

   was to follow. No error (E)
   D   E

3. The FDA did not conclude that the
            A
   negative side affects of the drug offset the
                 B   C
   drug's positive benefits. No error
                    D   E

4. Over the last decade, the information
                  A
   industry had grown into a multi-billion-
              B
   dollar industry that employs tens of
                    C   D
   thousands of workers. No error
                               E

385

5. Reading widely in her field, making herself
$\overline{\qquad}$ $\overline{\qquad}$
     A   B

available to students, and

her sophisticated research paid off for
$\overline{\qquad}$ $\overline{\qquad}$
        C   D
Professor Jackson: she was awarded

tenure last year. No error
            $\overline{\qquad}$
               E

6. One cannot perform multiple tasks

simultaneously if one is easily distracted
$\overline{\qquad}$ $\overline{\qquad}$ $\overline{\qquad}$
     A   B   C
by one's surroundings. No error
$\overline{\qquad}$ $\overline{\qquad}$
      D   E

7. In many ways emblematic of the sweeping
           $\overline{\qquad}$
               A
changes the state's agricultural industry
     $\overline{\qquad}$
        B
has undergone, strawberry farming
$\overline{\qquad}$
    C
had exploded in Central California.
$\overline{\qquad}$
     D
No error
$\overline{\qquad}$
  E

8. Of Armigo's two films, most critics agree
$\overline{\qquad}$ $\overline{\qquad}$
  A   B
that the second is best. No error
           $\overline{}$ $\overline{}$ $\overline{\qquad}$
             C   D   E

9. Most people in the neighborhood

agree that it is reasonable for the represen-
$\overline{\qquad}$ $\overline{\qquad}$
    A   B
tative to not acquiesce to the demands of
$\overline{\qquad}$ $\overline{\qquad}$
       C   D
the transit authority. No error
              $\overline{\qquad}$
               E

10. Although in many ways Canada is a
     $\overline{\qquad}$
       A
staunch ally of the United States,
$\overline{\qquad}$
      B
they have made their differences
$\overline{\qquad}$
    C
known on a number of important issues.
$\overline{\qquad}$
     D
No error
$\overline{\qquad}$
  E

Improving Sentences

11. Her first novel having been published, the author began to take notes for her second.

(A) Her first novel having been published
(B) Having been her most recent novel published
(C) Her first novel, having been published
(D) When having had her first novel published
(E) Having published her first novel

12. Van Gogh's early work has often been described as being in sharp contrast with his later work, despite there is a fundamental continuity between the two.

(A) with his later work, despite
(B) with his later work; despite the fact that
(C) with his later work, rather,
(D) with his later work, but
(E) with his later work, notwithstanding

13. After working on his serve for several days, rumors circulated that the challenger would win the rematch.

(A) After working on his serve for several days, rumors circulated that the challenger would win the rematch.
(B) After working on his serve for several days, the challenger circulated rumors that he would win the rematch.
(C) Rumors circulated that the challenger, after working on his serve for several days, would win the rematch.
(D) After having worked on his serve for several days, the rematch was rumored to be won by the challenger.
(E) After working on his serve for several days, rumors circulated, the challenger would win the rematch.

GO ON TO THE NEXT PAGE

14. The artist thought that it was important both to portray the subject truthfully, no matter the difficulty, <u>and revealing something new about the subject.</u>

(A) and revealing something new about the subject.

(B) and so he revealed something new about the subject.

(C) and to reveal something new about the subject.

(D) having thereby revealed something new about the subject.

(E) and revealing something about the subject that is new.

15. Max Planck was not only one of the founders of quantum <u>mechanics, but an accomplished pianist.</u>

(A) mechanics, but an accomplished pianist.

(B) mechanics; but he was also an accomplished pianist.

(C) mechanics; and he was also an accomplished pianist.

(D) mechanics, and an accomplished pianist.

(E) mechanics, but also an accomplished piano.

16. Coffee shops, <u>which were formerly found only in urban settings and near college campuses,</u> have been expanding in the last few years outside these circumspect domains.

(A) which were formerly found only in urban settings and near college campuses

(B) being formerly found only in urban settings and near college campuses

(C) which have been found formerly only in urban settings and near college campuses

(D) which were formerly found only in urban settings or near college campuses

(E) that were formerly found only in urban settings and near college campuses

17. Until the Chin dynasty changed this practice, most Chinese intellectuals did not travel to the imperial court <u>but remained in their native provincial centers.</u>

(A) but remained in their native provincial centers.

(B) and remained in their native provincial centers.

(C) but rather they remained in the native provinces.

(D) yet they remained in their native provincial centers.

(E) but remained in the provinces to which they were native.

18. The artwork of the late Renaissance was characterized by a deep sympathy for the human subject, <u>often portraying human frailties and failings.</u>

- **(A)** often portraying human frailties and failings.
- **(B)** and it often portrayed human frailties and failings.
- **(C)** human frailties and human failings being often portrayed.
- **(D)** although it often portrayed human frailties and failings.
- **(E)** though portraying human frailties and failings.

19. Pancho Villa's raid on Columbus, New Mexico, which was part of the tumult of the Mexican <u>revolution, therefore prompted a retaliatory expedition led by General Pershing.</u>

- **(A)** revolution, therefore prompted a retaliatory expedition led by General Pershing.
- **(B)** revolution, thereby prompting a retaliatory expedition led by General Pershing.
- **(C)** revolution, had prompted General Pershing to lead a retaliatory expedition.
- **(D)** revolution; a retaliatory expedition led by General Pershing thereby prompted.
- **(E)** revolution, prompted a retaliatory expedition led by General Pershing.

20. Philology, the study of words, no longer exists in academia as a distinct discipline because <u>it has been subsumed under the study of linguistics.</u>

- **(A)** it has been subsumed under the study of linguistics.
- **(B)** it was subsumed in the past under the study of linguistics.
- **(C)** it has been subsumed with the study of linguistics.
- **(D)** linguistics previously having subsumed it.
- **(E)** it had been subsumed under the study of linguistics.

Improving Paragraphs

Directions:

1. The following questions test your knowledge of paragraph and sentence construction.

2. The following passage is a rough draft of an essay. This rough draft contains various errors.

3. Read the rough draft and then answer the questions that follow. Some questions will focus on specific sentences and ask if there are any problems with that sentence's word choice, word usage, or overall structure. Other questions will ask about the paragraph itself. These questions will focus on paragraph organization and development.

4. Select the answer that best reflects the rules of English grammar and proper essay and paragraph writing.

Questions 21–25 are based on the following passage.

(1) An incredible hot-air balloon exhibition happened on September 5, 1862. (2) It was given by Glaisher and Coxwell, two Englishmen. (3) There was no compressed oxygen for them to breathe in those days. (4) They got so high that they couldn't use their limbs. (5) Coxwell had to open the descending valve with his teeth. (6) Before Glaisher passed out, he recorded an elevation of twenty-nine thousand feet. (7) Many believe they got eight thousand feet higher before they began to descend, making their ascent the highest in the nineteenth century.

(8) Now the largest balloon to go up in the nineteenth century was "The Giant." (9) The balloon held 215,000 cubic feet of air and was 74 feet wide. (10) It could carry four and a half tons of cargo. (11) Its flight began in Paris, in 1853, with fifteen passengers. (12) All of whom returned safely. (13) The successful trip received a great deal of national and international press because many thought the hot-air balloon would become a form of common transportation.

21. Which of the following offers the best combination of sentences 1 and 2 (reproduced below)?

An incredible hot-air balloon exhibition happened on September 5, 1862. It was given by Glaisher and Coxwell, two Englishmen.

(A) An incredible hot-air balloon exhibition was given September 5, 1862 by Glaisher and Coxwell, two Englishmen.

(B) An incredibly hot-air balloon exhibition happened on September 5, 1862, given by Glaisher and Coxwell, two Englishmen.

(C) Given by Glaisher and Coxwell, two Englishmen, an incredible hot-air balloon exhibition happened on September 5, 1862.

(D) Glaisher and Coxwell, two Englishmen, gave an incredible hot-air balloon exhibition, happening on September 5, 1862.

(E) Two Englishmen, Glaisher and Coxwell, gave an incredible hot-air balloon exhibition on September 5, 1862.

22. Which of the following sentences in the first paragraph appears to be out of order?

(A) There was no compressed oxygen for them to breathe in those days.

(B) They got so high that they couldn't use their limbs.

(C) Coxwell had to open the descending valve with his teeth.

(D) Before Glaisher passed out, he recorded an elevation of 29 thousand feet.

(E) Many believe they got 8 thousand feet higher before they began to descend.

23. Which of the following is the best revision for sentence 8 (reproduced below)?

Now the largest balloon to go up in the nineteenth century was "The Giant."

(A) Move "in the nineteenth century" to the beginning of the sentence and delete "Now"

(B) Add a comma after "Now."

(C) Begin the sentence with "Moreover,"

(D) Delete "now."

(E) Replace "to go up" with "exhibition."

24. Which of the following is the best way to combine sentences 9 and 10 (reproduced below)?

The balloon held 215,000 cubic feet of air and was 74 feet wide. It could handle four and a half tons of cargo.

(A) The balloon held 215,000 cubic feet of air and was 74 feet wide, which could handle four and a half tons of cargo.

(B) The balloon held 215,000 cubic feet of air and was 74 feet wide, handling four and a half tons of cargo.

(C) The balloon held 215,000 cubic feet of air and was 74 feet wide; it could handle four and a half tons of cargo.

(D) The balloon held 215,000 cubic feet of air and was 74 feet wide, and it could handle four and a half tons of cargo.

(E) The balloon held 215,000 cubic feet of air and was 74 feet wide, but it could carry four and a half tons of cargo.

25. Which of the following is the best way to revise sentences 11 and 12 (reproduced below)?

Its flight began in Paris, in 1853, with fifteen passengers. All of whom returned safely.

(A) Replace "whom" with "who."

(B) Make the second sentence read "Who all returned safely."

(C) Delete "of"

(D) Replace the period at the end of sentence 11 with a comma.

(E) Delete the period at the end of sentence 11 and change "returned" to "returning"

PETERSON'S
getting you there

Questions 26–30 are based on the following passage.

(1) On my nineteenth birthday, I began my trip to Mali, West Africa. (2) Some 24 hours later I arrived in Bamako, the capital of Mali. (3) The sun had set and the night was starless. (4) One of the officials from the literacy program I was working was there to meet me. (5) After the melee in the baggage claim, we proceeded to his car. (6) Actually, it was a truck. (7) I was soon to learn that most people in Mali that had automobiles actually had trucks or SUVs. (8) Apparently, there not just a convenience but a necessity when you live on the edge of the Sahara. (9) I threw my bags into the bed of the truck, and hopped in to the back of the cab. (10) Riding to my welcome dinner, I stared out the windows of the truck and took in the city. (11) It was truly a foreign land to me, and I knew that I was an alien there. (12) "What am I doing here?" I thought.

(13) It is hard to believe but seven months later I returned to the same airport along the same road that I had traveled on that first night in Bamako, and my perspective on the things that I saw had completely changed. (14) The landscape that had once seemed so desolate and lifeless now was the homeland of people that I had come to love. (15) When I looked back at the capital, Bamako, fast receding on the horizon, I did not see a city foreboding and wild in its foreignness. (16) I saw the city which held so many dear friends. (17) I saw tea-drinking sessions going late into the night. (18) I saw the hospitality and open-heartedness of the people of Mali. (19) The second time, everything looked completely different, and I knew that it was I who had changed and not it.

26. Which of the following is the revision of sentence 4 (reproduced below)?

One of the officials from the literacy program I was working was there to meet me.

(A) As it is now.
(B) One of the literacy program I was working's officials was there to meet me.
(C) There, was one of the officials from the literacy program I was working to meet me.
(D) One of the officials from the literacy program where I worked had been there to meet me.
(E) One of the officials from the literacy program where I would be working was there to meet me.

27. Which of the following is the best way to revise sentence 7 (reproduced below)?
I was soon to learn that most people in Mali that had automobiles actually had trucks or SUVs.

(A) Change "I was soon to learn" to "I was soon learning"
(B) Change "that had automobiles" to "who had automobiles"
(C) Replace "or" with "and"
(D) Add commas after "Mali" and "automobiles"
(E) Add an apostrophe to make "SUVs" read "SUV's"

28. Sentence 13 (reproduced below) would best be revised to which of the following choices?

It is hard to believe but seven months later I returned to the same airport along the same road that I had traveled on that first night in Bamako, and my perspective on the things that I saw had completely changed.

(A) As it is now.
(B) It is hard to believe, but seven months later I returned to the same airport along the same road that I had traveled on that first night in Bamako: my perspective on the things I saw had completely changed.
(C) It is hard to believe but seven months later I returned to the same airport along the same road that I had traveled on that first night in Bamako, and my perspective completely changed on the things I saw.
(D) It is hard to believe, but seven months later, when I returned to the same airport along the same road that I had traveled on that first night in Bamako, my perspective on the things I saw had completely changed.
(E) It is hard to believe, but seven months later I returned to the same airport along the same road that I had traveled on that first night in Bamako, and my perspective on the things that I saw having completely changed.

29. If you were to combine sentences 16–18 (reproduced below) into one sentence, which of the following would be the best choice?

I saw the city which held so many dear friends. I saw tea-drinking sessions going late into the night. I saw the hospitality and open-heartedness of the people of Mali.

(A) I saw the city which held so many dear friends; I saw tea-drinking sessions going late into the night; I saw the hospitality and open-heartedness of the people of Mali.
(B) I saw the city which held so many dear friends, drinking tea into late in the night, and the hospitality and open-heartedness of the people of Mali.
(C) I saw the city which held so many dear friends, I saw tea-drinking sessions going late into the night, I saw the hospitality and open-heartedness of the people of Mali.
(D) I saw the city which held so many dear friends, tea-drinking sessions going late into the night, the hospitality and open-heartedness of the people of Mali.
(E) I saw the city which held so many dear friends: tea-drinking sessions going late into the night, the hospitality and open-heartedness of the people of Mali.

30. Which of the following must be done to sentence 8 (reproduced below) to make it conform to the rules of written English?

Apparently, there not just a convenience but a necessity when you live on the edge of the Sahara.

- **(A)** Eliminate the comma after "Apparently"
- **(B)** Change "there" to "they are"
- **(C)** Add commas after "convenience" and "necessity"
- **(D)** Change "you live" to "one lives"
- **(E)** Add "Desert" after "Sahara"

STOP Do not proceed to the next section until time is up.

Section 4

Directions: Each sentence below has either one or two blanks in it and is followed by five choices, labeled (A) through (E). These choices represent words or phrases that have been left out. Choose the word or phrase that, if inserted into the sentence, would best fit the meaning of the sentence as a whole.

Example:

Canine massage is a veterinary technique
for calming dogs that are extremely _____.

(A) inept
(B) disciplined
(C) controlled
(D) stressed
(E) restrained

Ⓐ Ⓑ Ⓒ ● Ⓔ

1. The professor's oldest colleague was selected to give the _____ at the funeral.

    (A) eulogy
    (B) elegy
    (C) epigraph
    (D) eponymy
    (E) epitaph

2. The new team member's _____ was an encouragement to the rest of the team, who had become _____ by the string of defeats.

    (A) enthusiasm..elated
    (B) vigor..inundated
    (C) ebullience..dispirited
    (D) dourness..undone
    (E) excessiveness..downcast

3. By the end of the campaign both candidates had resorted to _____ the other.

    (A) commending
    (B) denigrating
    (C) mollifying
    (D) conceding
    (E) swindling

4. The cat _____ crept across the lawn, gracefully _____ the dog.

    (A) felicitously..enticing
    (B) swiftly..defeating
    (C) acrobatically..apprehending
    (D) maladroitly..undermining
    (E) deftly..eluding

5. The storyteller's _____ anecdotes earned her the _____ attention of the crowd.

    (A) compelling..rapt
    (B) pointed..spellbound
    (C) moribund..lucid
    (D) poignant..abrasive
    (E) meandering..distracted

6. The bill became bogged down in a(n) _____ of contentious issues in a Senate subcommittee.

    (A) marsh
    (B) sequence
    (C) iota
    (D) conundrum
    (E) quagmire

7. The outcome of the race seemed _____ before the leader's misstep on the final leg gave her competitors a(n) _____ of winning the title.

    (A) dubious..prospect
    (B) inevitable..hope
    (C) indubitable..air
    (D) assured..expectation
    (E) partial..endeavor

8. Though the new pharmaceutical regime was intended to be beneficial, its actual effect was _____, a result the medical community _____.

    (A) harmful..heralded
    (B) abundant..castigated
    (C) fortuitous..ignored
    (D) detrimental..lamented
    (E) negative..projected

9. The life of the lightening bug is _____ to human eyes: They live only twenty-four hours.

    (A) ludicrous
    (B) ephemeral
    (C) epic
    (D) ecstatic
    (E) incandescent

10. The kangaroo species _____ in the new environment where there was an abundant supply of food and a(n) _____ of predators.

    (A) stagnated..excess
    (B) bolstered..paucity
    (C) exploded..abundance
    (D) flagged..absence
    (E) flourished..dearth

396

11. With her speech, the politician attempted to _____ the fears of the _____ citizens.

- (A) intensify..disingenuous
- (B) ignore..alarmed
- (C) assuage..concerned
- (D) quell..disaffected
- (E) exploit..serene

12. The fencing champion was _____ with her rapier, but in most other sports she was rather _____.

- (A) adroit..awkward
- (B) adept..lithe
- (C) tenacious..passable
- (D) incompetent..clumsy
- (E) deft..skillful

13. Jane Goodall was at first a(n) _____ in her field, but since then she has received many accolades for her work.

- (A) acolyte
- (B) maverick
- (C) luminary
- (D) charlatan
- (E) miser

14. Alston was impressed by the philosopher's lecture, but Mario thought the lecture was better characterized as _____ than as erudite.

- (A) translucent
- (B) recondite
- (C) impeccable
- (D) specious
- (E) fictitious

15. The senior official _____ at the insinuation that his country's international trade policies were directly _____ the region's economic woes.

- (A) balked..responsible for
- (B) wrinkled..at fault for
- (C) staggered..inhibiting
- (D) blundered..implicated in
- (E) riled..accountable to

Questions 16–27 are based on the following passage.

The following passage was written by John Janovec, an ecologist who has worked in the Los Amigos watershed in Peru.

Line
The Amazonian wilderness harbors the greatest number of species on this planet and is an irreplaceable resource for present and future generations. Amazo-
(5) nia is crucial for maintaining global climate and genetic resources, and its forest and rivers provide vital sources of food, building materials, pharmaceuti-cals, and water needed by wildlife and
(10) humanity.

The Los Amigos watershed in the state of Madre de Dios, southeastern Peru, is representative of the pristine lowland moist forest once found
(15) throughout most of upper Amazonian South America. Threats to tropical forests occur in the form of fishing, hunting, gold mining, timber extraction, impending road construction, and
(20) slash-and-burn agriculture. The Los Amigos watershed, consisting of 1.6 million hectares (3.95 million acres), still offers the increasingly scarce opportunity to study rainforest as it was before the
(25) disruptive encroachment of modern human civilization. Because of its relatively pristine condition and the

GO ON TO THE NEXT PAGE

immediate need to justify it as a conservation zone, this area deserves intensive,
(30) long-term projects aimed at botanical
training, ecotourism, biological inven-
tory, and information synthesis.

On July 24, 2001, the government of
Peru and the Amazon Conservation
(35) Association signed a contractual agreement creating the first long-term permanently renewable conservation concession. To our knowledge this is the first
such agreement to be implemented in the
(40) world. The conservation concession
protects 340,000 acres of old-growth
Amazonian forest in the Los Amigos
watershed, which is located in southeastern Peru. This watershed protects the
(45) eastern flank of Manu National Park and
is part of the lowland forest corridor that
links it to Bahuaja-Sonene National Park.
The Los Amigos conservation concession
will serve as a mechanism for the
(50) development of a regional center of
excellence in natural forest management
and biodiversity science.

Several major projects are being
implemented at the Los Amigos Conser-
(55) vation Area. Louise Emmons is initiating
studies of mammal diversity and ecology
in the Los Amigos area. Other projects
involve studies of the diversity of
arthropods, amphibians, reptiles, and
(60) birds. Robin Foster has conducted
botanical studies at Los Amigos, resulting
in the labeling of hundreds of plant
species along two kilometers of trail in
upland and lowland forest. Michael
(65) Goulding is leading a fisheries and
aquatic ecology program, which aims to
document the diversity of fish, their
ecologies, and their habitats in the Los
Amigos area and the Madre de Dios
(70) watershed in general.

With support from the Amazon
Conservation Association, and in
collaboration with U.S. and Peruvian
colleagues, the Botany of the Los Amigos
(75) project has been initiated. At Los
Amigos, we are attempting to develop a
system of preservation, sustainability,
and scientific research; a marriage
between various disciplines, from human
(80) ecology to economic botany, product
marketing to forest management. The
complexity of the ecosystem will best be
understood through a multidisciplinary
approach, and improved understanding
(85) of the complexity will lead to better
management. The future of these forests
will depend on sustainable management
and development of alternative practices
and products that do not require
(90) irreversible destruction.

The botanical project will provide a
foundation of information that is
essential to other programs at Los
Amigos. By combining botanical studies
(95) with fisheries and mammology, we will
better understand plant/animal interactions. By providing names, the botanical
program will facilitate accurate communication about plants and the animals
(100) that use them. Included in this scenario
are humans, as we will dedicate time to
people-plant interactions in order to
learn what plants are used by people in
the Los Amigos area, and what plants
(105) could potentially be used by people.

To be informed, we must develop
knowledge. To develop knowledge, we
must collect, organize, and disseminate
information. In this sense, botanical
(110) information has conservation value.
Before we can use plant-based products
from the forest, we must know what
species are useful and we must know

398

their names. We must be able to identify
(115) them, to know where they occur in the
forest, how many of them exist, how they
are pollinated and when they produce
fruit (or other useful products). Aside
from understanding the species as they
(120) occur locally at Los Amigos, we must
have information about their overall
distribution in tropical America in order
to better understand and manage the
distribution, variation, and viability of
(125) their genetic diversity. This involves a
more complete understanding of the
species through studies in the field and
herbarium.

16. In line 6, "genetic resources" refers to

(A) plant seeds.
(B) different races of people.
(C) natural resources, such as oil.
(D) diverse species of plants and animals.
(E) cells that can be used in genetic cures
for diseases.

17. In paragraph 2, the author emphasizes
that the current environmental condition
of Amazonian South America is

(A) mostly unscathed.
(B) largely unknown.
(C) restorable through his project.
(D) irredeemable everywhere but in the
Los Amigos watershed.
(E) varying from destroyed to virtually
pristine.

18. In line 40, "concession" could be replaced, without changing the meaning,
with

(A) grant.
(B) acknowledgement.
(C) food supply.
(D) apology.
(E) compromise.

19. The author implies in paragraph 3 that the
agreement between Peru and the Amazon
Conservation Association is historic
primarily because it

(A) was the first time a South American
government had made an agreement
of any kind with the Amazon
Conservation Association.
(B) was the first long-term agreement
regarding land in the Amazon
Rainforest.
(C) represented the first time a South
American government had agreed to
renew a conservation agreement.
(D) is essentially a permanent conservation agreement.
(E) represents the first time such an
agreement had been made in the
form of a renewable contract.

20. The author's main purpose in the passage is to

(A) demonstrate that conservation efforts have been historically successful and so should be continued.

(B) garner support for opposition to destructive activities in the Los Amigos watershed.

(C) position the Los Amigos watershed agreement as a success towards the achievement of the vital goal of conserving the Amazonian rainforests.

(D) uphold the Peruvian government's progressive policies on management of the Los Amigos watershed as an example of government policy working toward conservation.

(E) argue that the study of pristine rainforests is essential for documenting and studying the myriad new species that the forests contain.

21. The author's tone in the passage can best be described as

(A) advocacy for his project over other competing projects.

(B) general praise for conservation projects in Amazonian South America.

(C) condemnation for the government of Peru for allowing destruction of the rainforest.

(D) passionate support for his and related projects.

(E) zealous advocacy for his point of view.

22. The work of Louise Emmons, Robin Foster, and Michael Goulding (in the fourth paragraph) are employed in the passage as

(A) colleagues of the author's in his botanical project.

(B) examples of the kinds of activities the author and his colleagues are trying to halt.

(C) examples of the influence of international scientists in Peru.

(D) scientists who represent new trends of study in Amazonian botany.

(E) scientists involved in projects related and amenable to the author's.

23. The author's botanical project involves all of the following EXCEPT

(A) studying plants in a laboratory.

(B) studying how plants are used by humans and animals.

(C) facilitating pharmaceutical use of plants.

(D) providing information on how to keep plant species flourishing.

(E) labeling plants in the Los Amigos area.

24. When the author says that the botanical project will "provide names," (line 97–100) he means that the project will

(A) help recognize new species.

(B) aid in the standardization of names for new species.

(C) participate in naming the region's different zones.

(D) publish information for corporations and researchers regarding the most appropriate names for specific plants.

(E) clarify the confusion surrounding the names of different organizations working in Amazonia.

25. When the author says that, "botanical information has conservation value," (lines 109–110) he means that

(A) a robust understanding of conservationism is aided by botanical information.

(B) conservationists should strive to preserve botanical information.

(C) speciation is important for conservation.

(D) political discussions about conservation should use botanical nomenclature.

(E) new drugs will be developed in the regions protected by conservationism.

26. Which of the following issues does the passage NOT address?

(A) Positive contributions of scientific research for conservation efforts

(B) Pollution of water sources in Amazonian Peru

(C) Economic importance of conserving the Amazon rainforests

(D) Specific efforts of the Peruvian government to maintain the integrity of Peruvian rainforests

(E) Examples of previous scientific research in Los Amigos

27. The author mentions areas outside the Los Amigos watershed primarily in order to

(A) imply that his future research will focus on these areas.

(B) draw a comparison between work in those areas and work in the Los Amigos area.

(C) underscore the interrelatedness of the ecosystems.

(D) emphasize that Los Amigos is the most pristine locale.

(E) praise the Peruvian government for its other conservationist undertakings.

STOP Do not proceed to the next section until time is up.

Section 5

21 Questions ■ Time—25 Minutes

Directions: Solve the following problems using any available space on the page for scratchwork. Mark the letter of your choice on the answer sheet that best corresponds to the correct answer.

Notes:

1. You may use a calculator. All of the numbers used are real numbers.

2. You may use the figures that accompany the problems to help you find the solution. Unless the instructions say that a figure is not drawn to scale, assume that it has been drawn accurately. Each figure lies in a plane unless the instructions say otherwise.

Reference Information

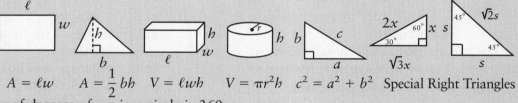

$A = \pi r^2$
$C = 2\pi r$ $\quad A = \ell w \quad A = \frac{1}{2}bh \quad V = \ell wh \quad V = \pi r^2 h \quad c^2 = a^2 + b^2$ Special Right Triangles

The number of degrees of arc in a circle is 360.
The measure in degrees of a straight angle is 180.
The sum of the measures in degrees of the angles of a triangle is 180.

---

1. Consider two sets of numbers: Set A includes all the positive integers and Set B includes all the negative integers. Which set has more members?

    (A) A
    (B) B
    (C) They contain an equal number.
    (D) Neither.
    (E) It cannot be determined.

2. If four sweaters cost p dollars, and the sweaters go on a half-off sale, how much would 12 sweaters cost in dollars?

    (A) $\dfrac{p}{2}$

    (B) $\dfrac{3p}{2}$

    (C) $2p$

    (D) $4p$

    (E) $6p$

3. $\dfrac{\frac{2}{3}}{\frac{4}{5}} =$

(A) $\dfrac{1}{3}$

(B) $\dfrac{8}{15}$

(C) $\dfrac{5}{6}$

(D) $\dfrac{15}{8}$

(E) $\dfrac{6}{5}$

4. If $3y = x$ and $y = \dfrac{10}{z}$, what is the value of z when $x = 3$?

(A) 1
(B) 3
(C) 5
(D) 7
(E) 10

5. If $y = mx + b$ where m is a negative constant and b is a positive constant, which of the following could be a possible graph of $y = mx + b$?

(A)

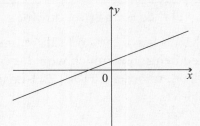

(B)

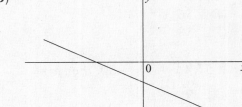

(C)

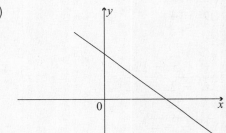

(D)

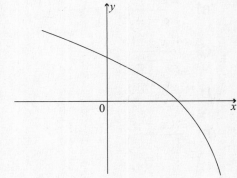

PETERSON'S
getting you there

6.

	Small (S)	Medium (M)	Large (L)
Hats (H)	$8	$12	$12
Shirts (SH)	$12	$12	$14

Hat & Shirt Prices at Moe's

If Moe's has a 25% off sale on medium-sized items, how much would it cost, in dollars, to order 2 H-M, 2 H-L, and 1SH-M?

(A) 51
(B) 53
(C) 55
(D) 56
(E) 58

7. If $5\sqrt{x} + 15 = 30$, then $x =$

(A) 9
(B) 10
(C) 12
(D) 14
(E) 15

8. $\dfrac{x^2 - x - 12}{2x^2 + 2x - 12} =$

(A) $\dfrac{x-2}{x-4}$

(B) $\dfrac{3(x-2)}{x-4}$

(C) $\dfrac{4(x-3)}{x-2}$

(D) $\dfrac{x-4}{2(x-2)}$

(E) $\dfrac{4(x-3)}{3(x-2)}$

9. If $f(x) = x^2$ is graphed on a standard xy-axis and then the graph is rotated 90° clockwise, which of the following graphs would result?

(A)

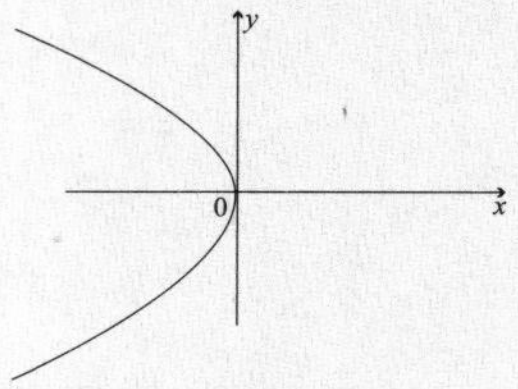

(B)

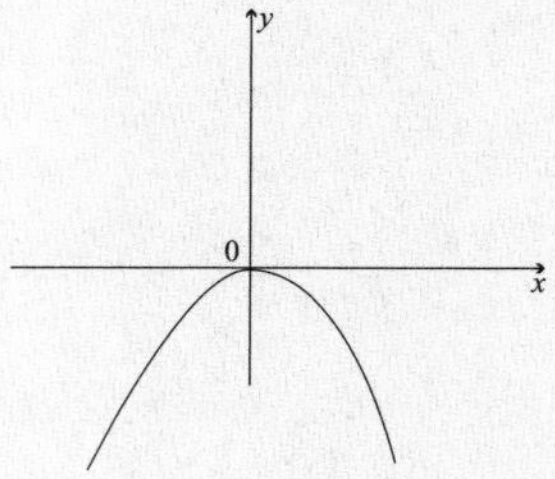

(C)

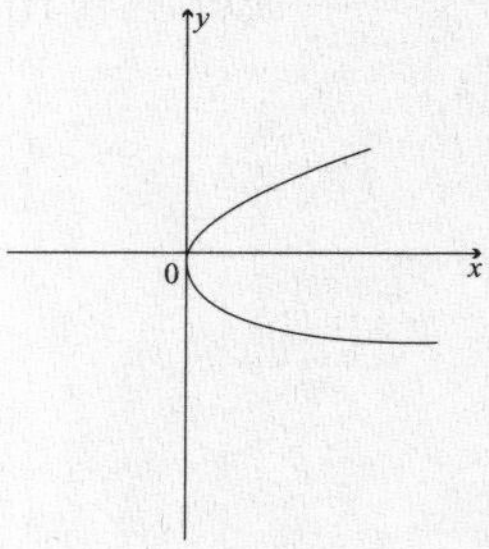

(D)

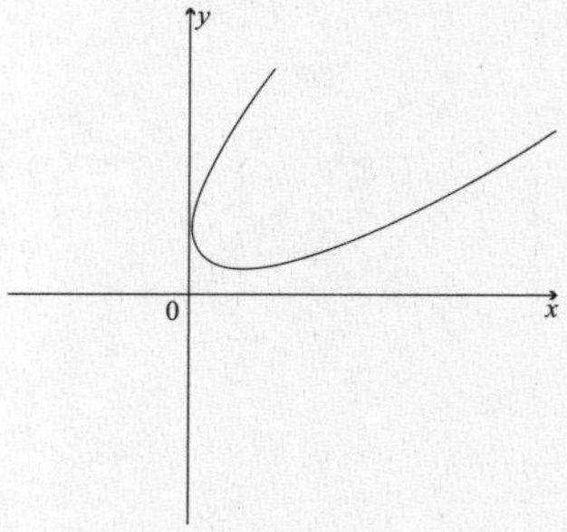

(E)

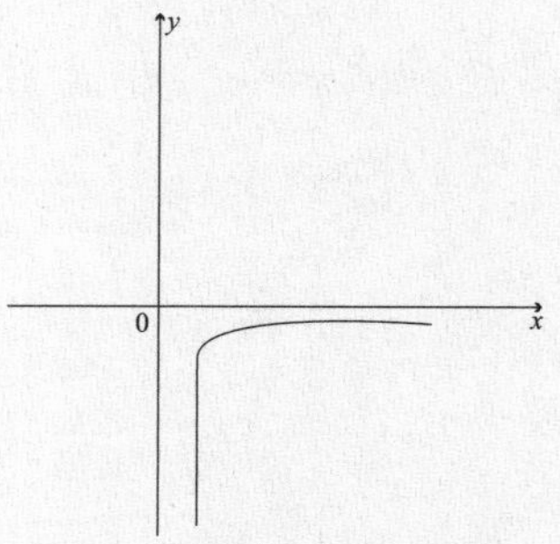

10. For which of the following ordered pairs (x,y) is $x - y > 2$ and $x + y > 4$?

(A) (1,3)
(B) (2,3)
(C) (4,0)
(D) (3,2)
(E) (4,1)

11. If x and y are positive integers and $\dfrac{x}{y} = \dfrac{1}{2}$, then $x + y =$

(A) $3x$
(B) $5x$
(C) y
(D) $2y$
(E) $3y$

12. Quentin buys three hot dogs with a ten-dollar bill and receives seven dollars and thirty-four cents in change. If the sales tax is seven cents per dollar (rounding to the nearest penny), which of the following choices, in cents, is closest to the actual price of a hot dog?

(A) 78
(B) 82
(C) 86
(D) 89
(E) 92

13.

If the two triangles above are congruent then $b =$

(A) 30
(B) 40
(C) 45
(D) 60
(E) It cannot be determined.

14.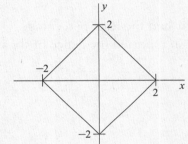

What is the area of the above figure?

(A) $2\sqrt{2}$
(B) 4
(C) 8
(D) 9
(E) 12

405

Questions 15–16 refer to the following chart.

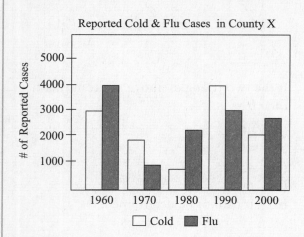

Reported Cold & Flu Cases in County X

15. Which year had the least percentage difference in reported incidence of flu and cold?

(A) 1960
(B) 1970
(C) 1980
(D) 1990
(E) 2000

16. In percentage terms, in what decade was the number of reported cold cases about 25% greater than the number of reported flu cases?

(A) 1960
(B) 1970
(C) 1980
(D) 1990
(E) 2000

17. If $l_1 \parallel l_2$, then which of the following pairs of angles must be congruent?

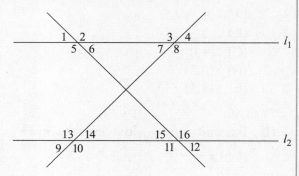

I. 6 and 12
II. 2 and 9
III. 4 and 10

(A) I only
(B) II only
(C) III only
(D) II and III only
(E) I and II only

18. If $-a^{-b^{-c}}$ is a positive integer, and a, b, and c are integers, then

(A) a must be negative.
(B) b must be negative.
(C) c must be negative.
(D) b must be an even positive integer.
(E) None of the above.

406

19.

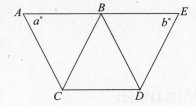

Note: Figure not Drawn to Scale

If all the line segments in the above figure are congruent, then

(A) $a > b$
(B) $a < b$
(C) $2a = b$
(D) $a = b$
(E) It cannot be determined.

20. Two boys and two girls are assigned to sit at a five-seat circular table, where the seats are numbered one through five. If neither boy can sit by the open seat, seat 3, how many different seating arrangements are possible?

(A) 2
(B) 3
(C) 4
(D) 5
(E) 6

21. There are 150 students in math courses at Dagmar High School. 73 are in geometry, 62 are in algebra, and 52 are in neither. How many students are in both geometry and algebra?

(A) 32
(B) 33
(C) 35
(D) 36
(E) 37

S T O P Do not proceed to the next section until time is up.

Section 6

16 Questions ■ Time—20 Minutes

Line

In 1953, Watson and Crick unlocked the structure of the DNA molecule and set into motion the modern study of genetics. This advance allowed our study of life to
(5) go beyond the so-called wet and dirty realm of biology, the complicated laboratory study of proteins, cells, organelles, ions, and lipids. The study of life could now be performed with more abstract
(10) methods of analysis. By discovering the basic structure of DNA, we had received our first glance into the information-based realm locked inside the genetic code.

1. Which of the following does the passage discuss as a change that the discovery of DNA brought to the study of life?
   (A) The study of lipids and proteins became irrelevant.
   (B) New and more abstract methods of study were possible.
   (C) Biology could then focus on molecules rather than cells.
   (D) Modern genetics matured past its Mendelian roots.
   (E) Information-based study of genes became obsolete.

2. The passage uses the phrase "wet and dirty" (line 5) to mean
   (A) haphazard guessing about the genetic code.
   (B) the work of Watson and Crick in discovering DNA.
   (C) information-based biological research.
   (D) the study of the genetic code.
   (E) involved laboratory practices in studying basic biological entities.

Although little-known today in the United States, Clark Saunders (1859–1941) cast a large shadow in the first several decades of the twentieth century, writing many widely read books on Native American, Spanish, and Anglo folklore. He also wrote extensively on the different cultures of California, the Sierras, and the Southwest. He was a major and influential contributor to *Sunset Magazine* in its early years. In his day, Saunders was important for introducing much of the American public to a person-sized understanding of the "Old West."

3. The passage presents Saunders as a(n)

(A) influential contemporary western writer.
(B) important historian of the West.
(C) a specialist of Native American studies.
(D) widely read author in his own day.
(E) the first editor of *Sunset Magazine*.

The history of rock and roll is inseparable from the development of blues and gospel music in the southeastern United States. Though the genre gained mass appeal through legendary figures such as Elvis Presley or the wildly popular Beatles, the musical roots of rock and roll extend far before such groups. In fact, many of the groups who popularized rock and roll were consciously attempting to emulate the work of blues greats such as B. B. King or Muddy Waters. The Rolling Stones are a good example of this trend, which developed in the late fifties and early sixties. The Rolling Stones, both then and now, have always explicitly stated their admiration and imitation of blues greats.

4. B. B. King is used in this passage as an example of a

(A) blues artist who was emulated by early rock bands.
(B) musical artist influenced by Elvis Presley.
(C) musician who incorporated aspects of rock and roll.
(D) musician who often played with Muddy Waters.
(E) gospel singer who influenced the Rolling Stones.

The following two passages deal with the political movements working for the woman's vote in America.

Passage 1

Line   The first organized assertion of woman's rights in the United States was made at the Seneca Falls convention in 1848. The convention, though, had little immediate
(5)   impact because of the national issues that would soon embroil the country. The contentious debates involving slavery and state's rights that preceded the Civil War soon took center stage in national debates.
(10)   Thus woman's rights issues would have to wait until the war and its antecedent problems had been addressed before they would be addressed.

In 1869, two organizations were
(15)   formed that would play important roles in securing the woman's right to vote. The first was the American Woman's Suffrage Association (AWSA). Leaving federal and constitutional issues aside, the AWSA
(20)   focused their attention on state-level politics. They also restricted their ambitions to securing the woman's vote and downplayed discussion of women's full equality. Taking a different track, the
(25)   National Woman's Suffrage Association (NWSA), led by Elizabeth Stanton and Susan B. Anthony, believed that the only way to assure the long-term security of the woman's vote was to ground it in the
(30)   constitution. The NWSA challenged the exclusion of woman from the Fifteenth Amendment, the amendment that extended the vote to African-American men. Furthermore, the NWSA linked the
(35)   fight for suffrage with other inequalities faced by woman, such as marriage laws, which greatly disadvantaged women.

By the late 1880s the differences that separated the two organizations had
(40) receded in importance as the women's movement had become a substantial and broad-based political force in the country. In 1890, the two organizations joined forces under the title of the National
(45) American Woman's Suffrage Association (NAWSA). The NAWSA would go on to play a vital role in the further fight to achieve the woman's vote.

Passage 2

In 1920, when Tennessee became the
(50) thirty-eighth state to approve the constitutional amendment securing the woman's right to vote, woman's suffrage became enshrined in the constitution. But woman's suffrage did not happen in one fell
(55) swoop. The success of the woman's suffrage movement was the story of a number of partial victories that led to the explicit endorsement of the woman's right to vote in the constitution.

(60)   As early as the 1870s and 1880s, women had begun to win the right to vote in local affairs such as municipal elections, school board elections, or prohibition measures. These "partial suffrages"
(65) demonstrated that women could in fact responsibly and reasonably participate in a representative democracy (at least as voters). Once such successes were achieved and maintained over a period of
(70) time, restricting the full voting rights of woman became more and more suspect. If women were helping decide who was on the local school board, why should they not also have a voice in deciding who was
(75) president of the country? Such questions became more difficult for non-suffragists to answer, and thus the logic of restricting the woman's vote began to crumble.

5. The word "antecedent" in line 11 can best be replaced by

   (A) antebellum.
   (B) referent.
   (C) causal.
   (D) subsequent.
   (E) abolitionist.

6. Which of the following does the first passage say was the first organized push for woman's suffrage?

   (A) formation of the National Woman's Suffrage Association
   (B) formation of the American Woman's Suffrage Association
   (C) convening of the Seneca Falls convention
   (D) Tennessee passing the Twenty-Second Amendment
   (E) "partial suffrages" of local woman's suffrage efforts

7. What national event does the first passage cite as pushing woman's voting rights to the background of the national consciousness?

   (A) Civil War
   (B) Suffrage movement
   (C) Prohibition
   (D) Passage of the Fifteenth Amendment
   (E) World War I

8. According to the first passage, the National Woman's Suffrage Association focused their efforts on

   (A) local elections.
   (B) constitutional issues.
   (C) prohibition efforts.
   (D) school board elections.
   (E) state elections.

9. The differences between the AWSA and the NWSA were ultimately resolved when

(A) the Twenty-Second Amendment passed.
(B) the two organizations were combined to form the NAWSA.
(C) the Civil War ended.
(D) prohibition passed.
(E) woman's suffragists won significant victories in the 1890 general election.

10. In Passage 1, the author's attitude toward the subject matter is

(A) intense scrutiny.
(B) distanced suspicion.
(C) mild censure.
(D) appreciative description.
(E) enthusiastic support.

11. Passage 2 locates the ultimate victory of the woman's suffrage movement with which of the following events?

(A) Tennessee approving the woman's voting rights amendment
(B) Congress passing the Twenty-Second Amendment
(C) The combination of AWSA and NWSA into NAWSA
(D) Woman earning the full vote in Wyoming
(E) Women's fruitful participation in local elections

12. When is the earliest success of the woman's suffrage movement that the second passage points to?

(A) 1848
(B) 1869
(C) 1870s
(D) 1880s
(E) 1920

13. Which of the following is NOT an example of a "partial suffrage" as described in the second passage?

(A) A mayoral election
(B) A school board measure
(C) Passage of the Fifteenth Amendment
(D) A state prohibition referendum
(E) Impeaching a city council member

14. The author of the second passage argues that the "partial suffrages" were most effective in bringing full voting rights for woman because

(A) through them woman were able to elect prosuffrage representatives.
(B) they showed women voting ably.
(C) they demonstrated that woman could participate in a full democracy.
(D) they demonstrated that woman could handle the intricacies of foreign policy.
(E) they established the power of the woman voter.

411

15. Which of the following questions is NOT addressed in either passage?

(A) When did the woman's right to vote become a constitutional amendment?

(B) What effect did the Civil War have on the woman's suffrage movement?

(C) What are the names of two leaders of the National Woman's Suffrage Association?

(D) What are "partial suffrages?"

(E) Which constitutional amendment gave women the vote?

16. The author of the second passage would most likely see the work of the

(A) AWSA as crucial for the ultimate success of the suffrage movement.

(B) NWSA as indispensable for "partial suffrages."

(C) NWSA as unimportant for the passage of the woman's voting rights amendment.

(D) Seneca Falls convention as the most important single event in the women's suffrage movement.

(E) the NAWSA as important for the unity of the woman's suffrage movement.

STOP Do not proceed to the next section until time is up.

Section 7

13 Questions ■ Time—20 Minutes

Directions for Student Produced Responses

Enter your responses to questions 1–13 in the special grids provided on your answer sheet. Input your answers as indicated in the directions below.

Answer: $\frac{4}{9}$ or 4/9

Answer: 1.4
Either position is correct.

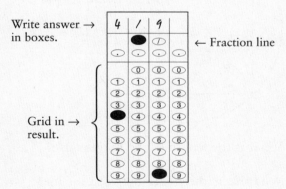

Write answer → in boxes.

← Fraction line

Grid in → result.

Decimal → point

Note: You may begin your answer in any column, space permitting. Leave blank any columns not needed.

- Writing your answer in the boxes at the top of the columns will help you accurately grid your answer, but it is not required. **You will only receive credit for an answer if the ovals are filled in properly.**

- Only fill in one oval in each column.

413

- If a problem has several correct answers, just grid in one of them.

- There are no negative answers.

- **Never grid in mixed numbers.** The answer $3\frac{1}{5}$ must be gridded as 16/5 or 3.2. If

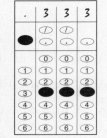 is gridded, it will be read as $\frac{31}{5}$, not $3\frac{1}{5}$.

Decimal Accuracy

Decimal answers must be gridded as accurately as possible. The answer 0.3333 . . . must be gridded as .333.

Less accurate values, such as .33 are not acceptable.

Acceptable ways to grid $\frac{1}{3} = .3333 . . .$

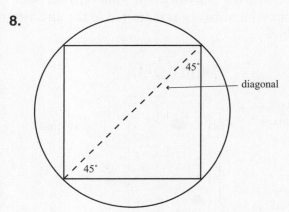

1. $[2(3^2)^2 + (4 - 3(4))^2] =$

2. Given that $22 - 3x > 13$, what is a positive integer that is less than x?

3. A phone company charges 40 cents for a completed long-distance phone call and 6 cents per minute on top of the initial fee. How much, in dollars, would a 30-minute long-distance phone call cost?

4. What is the least common multiple of 18 and 24?

5. If $|x - 3| > 2$, then what is one integer value that x cannot equal?

6. If the kth term in a series is generated by the equation $n = \dfrac{10(k + 1)}{k - 1}$, what is the eleventh term in the series?

7. Given $P(3, 2)$ and $Q(3, 6)$, what is the y-coordinate of the midpoint of the line segment defined by these two points?

8.

What is the length of the hypotenuse?

9. What is the difference between the mean and the median of the number set {7, 4, 3, 6, 2, 2}?

10. If line *a* and line *b* are perpendicular, line *b* and line *c* are perpendicular, and the slope of line *a* is $\frac{2}{5}$, what is the slope of line *c*?

11. If $f(x) = x^2 + 3$ and $x = y + 2$, when $y = 3$, $f(x) =$

12. If a square is inscribed in a circle and the area of the square is eight, what is the longest distance that a straight line could be that originated and terminated on the circumference of the circle?

13. What is the one integer that is between 999 and 1199 and satisfies these two conditions:
Its digits sum to seventeen.

Its tens and units digits are the same.

S T O P Do not proceed to the next section until time is up.

Section 8

Time—25 Minutes

Directions: Think carefully about the statement below and the assignment that follows it.

Consider the following statement.

Some people think that war is justified under certain circumstances.

Assignment: Write an essay in which you agree or disagree with the preceding statement. Develop your point of view on this statement and be sure to support your stance with sufficient details.

_____

_____

_____

_____

_____

_____

_____

_____

_____

_____

_____

_____

417

PETERSON'S
getting you there

S T O P When you are finished with your essay put your pencil down until the time allotted is over.

Answers
and Explanations

Section 1

1. **C**   The passage begins, "Musical notes, like all sounds, are a result of the sound waves created by movement." The author then goes on to talk about musical notes and how they illustrate properties of sound waves. Choice (C) captures this idea.

2. **A**   Pitch is determined by the frequency of the sound wave. This eliminates (B) and (E). Choice (C) seems to refer more to the intensity, so eliminate it too. The final sentence says that pitch can be described either in numbers or in letters, so eliminate (D). That leaves (A), the correct answer.

3. **B**   The passage states that Langston Hughes "persuaded her to continue her education in the North." And the passage uses this fact to explain her transfer to Northwestern. This is what (B), the correct answer, suggests.

4. **C**   The passage doesn't specifically say that Walker was writing poetry before she entered New Orleans University. Eliminate (A). Hughes recognized her talent, but he didn't create it, so eliminate (B). Hughes recognized her talent before she transferred to Northwestern, so eliminate (D). The passage, if anything, implies that Walker wrote poetry for some time before publishing anything, so eliminate (E). The passage makes reference to her parents' occupations and encouragement, implying that they had an influence on her decision to become a poet.

5. **C**   The author is poking a bit of fun at the Ungers, so eliminate (A), (B), and (E). His tone is more playful than downtrodden, so the answer is (C).

6. D The "Chicago beef-princess" suggests the wider high-class social world in Chicago. When one thing stands in for another, it is a metaphor. The answer is (D).

7. A Even if you do not know the definition of *fatuity* you can still get this question. John is going from Hades, which we can assume is hot, to Boston. He will probably not need the light suits and fans. The answer is (A).

8. B We know that John does not feel rejected, because he says he knows he will always be welcome at home. Eliminate (A). On the other hand, he does feel something negative, or he wouldn't cry. Eliminate (C) and (E). The handshake and the fact that John's tears are not mentioned until he has turned away from his father suggest that he is composed. The best answer is (B).

9. C If you were leaving home (and you were crying), why would you stop and look back? Most likely you would do so because you were sad to leave and wanted to get one last look before you went. Which of the answer choices matches this sentiment? Choice (C) does. The meditation on what the sign says serves to emphasize the quaintness of the town, of which John will no longer be a part. The other answers rely on your being distracted from the main emotions of the story.

10. E Hades is hell in Greco-Roman mythology. Midas represents wealth. Unger resonates with the hunger the family feels for the wealth and prestige of the North. In other words, the names suggest that the story uses the experiences of this one family to represent a larger situation. It is an allegory, choice (E).

11. C *Infused* is used to mean that his work was filled with the experiences he had in Manchuria. Eliminate all but (B) and (C). *Saturated* has something of a negative tone, and the author praises Abe's work, so eliminate (B). The answer is (C).

12. E The metaphorical use of orbit and gravitational pull is used in conjunction with the negative words "controlled" and "oppressive." Abe's work is not controlled by oppressive forces. Eliminate (B), (C), and (D). Choices (A) and (E) are similar answers, but (E) better captures the author's intent.

13. D Abe forged a medical certificate, so we know he was not actually sick. You can eliminate (A) and (B). The passage makes no reference to Abe helping the sick and injured, so eliminate (C). The sentence in the passage says that the forged medical certificate allowed him to avoid fighting. Choice (D) corresponds with that meaning. Choice (E) can be eliminated because you don't know what his intentions were for after the war.

14. **E** Even if you don't know the defintion of *apocalyptic*, you probably know that it is a negative word. Eliminate (D) (*exhilarating* is a positive word). There is no reference to nuclear weapons in the passage, so eliminate (A). There was *famine*, and Abe seems to have been *strongly affected by the loss of his father*, but neither of these answers is specific enough. Only (E) expressly answers the question.

15. **A** This question is a little bit more difficult than some vocabulary questions because you have to look in a few different places. The third paragraph, where the word appears, tells you that the avant-garde group was political and that Abe worked in various genres. The fourth paragraph refers to his earlier work, which was the work in the third paragraph, as "experimental and heavily political." Since one of these words is an answer choice (A), it is the best answer.

16. **C** This question basically asks you to distinguish between the author's opinion and the basic facts of Abe's career. Choices (A), (B), and (E) all contain evaluative opinions, so eliminate them. The author expresses strong opinions about the themes *furusato* and the emperor, but never presents any facts about their influence on Japanese literature in the world. The best answer is (C). The author presents it as a known fact that young Japanese artists after World War II were interested in Marxism.

17. **B** As always, go back to the passage to look for the context of the phrase. Shortly after the phrase appears, the author says that readers have wrongly decided that *Woman in the Dunes* was Abe's masterpiece. The author also refers to the lack of translations of Abe's earlier works. The answer that best summarizes these two things is (B).

18. **D** The author's purpose in paragraph 4 is to suggest that too much attention has been given to Abe's later work, as you just determined in question 17. So the answer cannot be (A). There is only a brief comparison to Abe's contemporaries, so (B) is too specific. (E) is not factually correct, since most of the work the passage discusses was produced in Japan. You are left with (C) and (D). (C) is too neutral; this author is opinionated. She/he does not suggest that Abe's later work is bad, but rather that his early work also deserves attention. Choice (D) is the best answer.

19. B The author is most interested in literary works. There is no reason to suspect that the author is an artist or writer. The tone is critical and scholarly. (B) is the best answer.

20. D The author of this passage does express many strong opinions, but not in regard to Marxism. You can therefore eliminate both (A) and (B). If anything, she/he is more positive than negative about the influence of Marxism on Abe's work. Eliminate (C) and (E), which imply a negative bias. The answer is (D).

Section 2

1. C With a calculator this problem is straightforward enough, but you do not need a calculator to solve this problem. The wording is a bit tricky, but to find the percentage of 75 that 12 represents, you would place 12 over 75. This can be simplified $\frac{12}{75} = \frac{12/3}{75/3} = \frac{4}{25}$. Percent means "of 100," so if you change the 25 in the denominator to 100, you'll have your percentage in the numerator. $\frac{4}{25} = \frac{4 \times 4}{25 \times 4} = \frac{16}{100}$. This is answer (C).

You could also have set up an algebraic equation, and then cross-multiplied to find the answer.

$$\frac{12}{75} = \frac{n}{100}$$
$$(12)(100) = (75)(n)$$
$$1200 = 75n$$
$$\frac{1200}{75} = \frac{75n}{75}$$
$$16 = n$$

2. D If a circle is inscribed in a square, then the circle is inside the square. You can find the length of the square's sides using the area formula for a square:

$$A = s^2$$
$$36 = s^2$$
$$6 = s$$

It might help if you draw a circle inside a square to visualize the next part. The side length of the square is the same as the diameter of the circle. Draw a diameter and you'll see that it's the same length as a side.

This is a key relationship that the two figures share. Once you know the circle's diameter is 6, its radius must be half that, 3. This radius can be placed into the area formula for a circle:

$$A = \pi r^2$$
$$A = \pi(3)^2$$
$$A = 9\pi$$

Choice (D) is correct.

3. B First, you are looking for a line with a positive slope, which means that it rises as you go from left to right. This eliminates choices (A), (D), and (E). Second, a slope of 1 means that it rises as much as it runs (it goes up at the same rate that it goes over). A line with a slope of 1 will be halfway between a line that is completely horizontal and a line that is completely vertical. Choice (B) is that line, since the rise in choice (C) is too gradual.

4. C To answer this question, you have to determine how the series is generated. The numbers are increasing, so it is very unlikely that either subtraction or division is involved. The numbers increase, and note how fast the increase is. Addition can be ruled out since the increase from one term to the next is too great; simple multiplication is also unlikely. Look at the four terms closely, and you'll notice that each number is the square of an ascending integer. The series is one squared, then two squared, then three squared, and so forth. This series then is generated by squaring the integers. Therefore, the eighth term is eight squared, 64. Choice (C) is correct.

5. B The area of a parallelogram is the height times the base. You do not know the height, but you can determine it by using the geometry of a triangle. If you drop a perpendicular from the top left corner to the opposite side (which you will call the base), then you have a triangle whose height is the height of the parallelogram. Measures of adjacent angles of parallelograms sum to 180, and so the bottom left-hand angle measures 60° (this is because the bottom right interior angle is 120°, and $180 - 120 = 60$). Surprise! This gives you a 30-60-90 triangle, and you can determine the height. Since the hypotenuse is $2\sqrt{3}$, the height is 3. The base is 6, and so the area is:

$$A = bh$$
$$A = (6)(3)$$
$$A = 18$$

That's choice (B).

6. A   To find the reciprocal, switch the numerator and the denominator. Once you've flipped the fractions over, look for a fraction where the numerator is greater than the denominator and where the difference between the two is greatest. Choices (A) and (E) look like the best candidates. The reciprocal of A is $4\frac{1}{2}\left(\frac{9}{2}=4\frac{1}{2}\right)$, and the reciprocal of (E) is $4\frac{1}{3}\left(\frac{13}{3}=4\frac{1}{3}\right)$. Choice (A) is the greatest.

7. E   Another sketch with more of the angles numbered is helpful here.

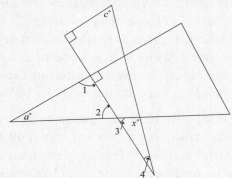

Angle 1 is 90° because its measure and the measure of the angle adjacent to it must sum to 180. Couple this fact with the given information $a = 60$, and it means that the measure of angle 2 is 30° since the measures of the angles in that triangle must sum to 180.

Angle 3 is also 30° since it is vertical with angle 2. If you can find angle 4, you could figure out angle x since you will have two of the three angles on that small triangle. To find the measure of angle 4, look at the big triangle with angles 4, c, and the right angle. Since a right angle is 90° and $c = 50$, the measure of angle 4 is 40° since the measures of the angles in the larger triangle must sum to 180. If the measure of angle $4 = 40$, and the measure of the angle $3 = 30$, then

$$180 = m\angle3 + m\angle4 + m\angle x$$
$$180 = 30 + 40 + x$$
$$180 = 70 + x$$
$$110 = x$$

Choice (E) is correct.

If you had no idea how to answer this question, you might have noticed that the figures were drawn to scale. Looking at x, it certainly looks greater than 90°. Choice (A) is highly unlikely as an answer, and (E) would be your best guess since it's the only choice greater than 90°.

8. E A problem like this takes a careful step-by-step execution, but fortunately nothing else is needed.

$$\left[\left(2^2 + 2^2\right)^{-1}\right]^{-2} = \left[\left(4 + 4\right)^{-1}\right]^{-2} = \left[\frac{1}{8}\right]^{-2} = \frac{1}{\frac{1}{64}} = 64, \text{ choice (E)}.$$

9. C Here you need to take care to read the chart correctly. Each complete box represents 150,000 widgets. Company B made one-and-a-half more boxes. That last box is not a full box, as you can see by its size and by the dashed lines on the right end. Choice (B) represents one box worth of difference (150,000 widgets), while choice (D) represents two complete boxes of widgets as the difference. Answer (C) is correct, since it shows a difference in production of one-and-a-half boxes (150,000 widgets + 75,000 widgets = 225,000).

10. A Since you are told that x is odd, you should suspect that the answer would have something to do with being odd or even or neither. That makes choices (A) or (B) the prime suspects. x cannot be even because an even number raised to an even power must be even. Try giving x an odd value, like 3. $x^x = 3^3 = 27$. This satisfies the facts given in the problem, since 27 is an odd number, so choice (A) is the answer.

11. E Do not be unnerved by the newness of this concept. All that you need to know about factorials is provided in the explanation. So be a good test-taking robot: Take the numbers they give you and feed them into the formula.

$$\frac{6!}{3!} = \frac{6 \times 5 \times 4 \times 3 \times 2 \times 1}{3 \times 2 \times 1} = 6 \times 5 \times 4 = 120, \text{ choice (E)}.$$

If you don't get flustered (and no self-respecting test-taking robot ever does), the problem is quite straightforward. You just apply the concept of factorial and then multiply to find the answer.

12. B Here replace x with three, and then solve:

$$f(3) = (3!)^2 = (3 \times 2 \times 1)^2 = (6)^2 = 36, \text{ answer (B)}.$$

13. A This one's the toughest factorial problem, but a clue is provided by the answer choices. Most of the answers are in terms of y. Therefore, you are probably going to have to manipulate $\dfrac{y!}{x!}$ so that only y's remain in the expression.

To do this, let's replace the x's with y's. Since, and y and x are integers, $x! = (y + 2)!$. Substituting this into the problem:

$$\frac{y!}{x!} = \frac{y!}{(y + 2)!} = \frac{y!}{(y + 2)(y + 1)y!} = \frac{1}{(y + 2)(y + 1)}$$

This is choice (A). You could also solve the problem by picking values for the two variables that are consistent with $y + 2 = x$, and then plugging the values into the factorial fraction and also into the answer choices. If only one answer choice matches the factorial fraction, then you have the right answer. If two answers match, then pick another set of values for the variables and repeat the process.

14. A You will probably recall that the determinant of a matrix is found by cross-multiplying. Since you know the end result is -6, all you need is the right set-up and the proper computation:

$$\begin{pmatrix} n & 4 \\ 5 & -7 \end{pmatrix} = -6$$

$$(-7)(n) - (4)(5) = -6$$

$$-7n - 20 = -6$$

$$-7n - 20 + 20 = -6 + 20$$

$$-7n = 14$$

$$\frac{-7n}{-7} = \frac{14}{-7}$$

$$n = -2$$

15. E First note that the question asks which statements *must* be true. Some statements could be true under the right conditions, but if they are not always true, they are not going to be the right answer for this problem.

Now, from $p + q = 2q + 6$, you can determine: $p = q + 6$ by subtracting a q from both sides. If p is odd then q is odd, and if p is even then q is even (since an odd plus an even is odd and an even plus an even is even). But neither of them has to be even or odd. Thus I and II are not necessarily true. The same is true for III, since p and q could both be odd, which would make their product odd. Choice (E) is the answer, since it's the only choice left standing.

One last point: this question should have been answered on the second pass. Once you saw the Roman numerals, you should have realized that it would take some time to answer, and that waiting until the second pass would allow you more time to get to questions that might take less time.

16. B Look at the graph and you'll see that there are three distinct regions in which x is greater than zero:

> (1) x to the left of negative three
> (2) x between negative one and one
> (3) x to the right of three

Once your eyes give you that information, it's up to your brain to decipher the wilderness of greater than/less than signs and find the answer that describes these three regions correctly. Choice (B) does this.

17. E Since the question asks which number must be in Box E, the conditions must only allow for one number to be in Box E. There is only one prime number, 11, and so it goes in Box B. 9, 12, and 15 are evenly divisible by three, and so they go in A, C, and D. You don't know what order, they are in, but it doesn't matter. That leaves 16 for Box E, which means choice (E) is the answer.

18. D Since B, D, E, and H are all midpoints on their respective lines, the rectangle is divided into four equal rectangles. The diagonal $\overline{CG}$ divides the two smaller rectangles it traverses into halves. One-half of each of these two rectangles is shaded, so a total of one of the smaller rectangles is shaded. Since the smaller rectangles are equal in size and there are four of them, one-fourth of the larger rectangle is shaded or 25%, choice (D).

19. D Since n is the same thing as n^1, you are looking to raise $n^{\frac{-p}{n}}$ so that the resulting exponent is 1. Remember that when you raise a number to an exponent, you multiply the exponents. What multiplied with $\frac{-p}{n}$ yields one? The answer is its reciprocal, $\frac{-n}{p}$.

$$\left(n^{\frac{-p}{n}}\right)^{\frac{-n}{p}} = n^{\left(\frac{-p}{n}\right)\left(\frac{-n}{p}\right)} = n^1. \text{ So (D) is the answer.}$$

427

20. A A straightforward way to start this problem is simply to start with the first prime number. 2 and 3 cannot be *n*, but 5 could since 3, 5, and 7 could form a prime triplet. Continuing on with the prime numbers to fifty, there is not another prime number whose closest primes are two more and two less than itself. Thus the answer is (A).

21. B If a geometry figure is described but not drawn, it's always a good idea to sketch the figure yourself. Draw a circle and then one tangent line. Next draw a second tangent line that is perpendicular to the first. Now draw a third tangent that also is perpendicular to the first. Your sketch can only look like this:

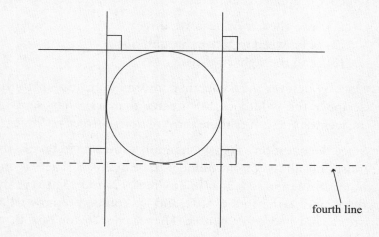

fourth line

Your lines could be rotated around, but the interrelationships of the tangents must be the same. The only place to draw a fourth tangent line that will be perpendicular to two other tangent lines is at the bottom of the circle.

Does this figure look familiar? It should, since it has the same appearance as the first geometry problem in this section, question 2. You have drawn a circle inscribed in a square. The fact that it is a square could clue you in to the fact that there are two sets of parallel lines. You might also recall from your geometry class that two lines that are perpendicular to the same line are parallel to each other. This means that both sets of tangent lines across the circle are parallel. Either way, the answer is (B).

Choice (D) is close, but the circle is inscribed in the square, not the other way around.

The fact that questions 2 and 21 employ the same figure shows you how two questions can use the same figure but vary greatly in terms of difficulty. A point to ponder is, "How did the test-takers make the last question harder?" First and foremost, no figure was included. This should spur you to draw any figure that is not given to you, and make a hard problem a lot easier to visualize and answer.

Section 3

1. **E** You should always take a close look at underlined pronouns in identifying sentence error questions. "Registered" in this sentence is an adjective, and "who" is a pronoun that represents "voters." Because it is the subject of the verb, "who," rather than "whom," is correct. In addition, there are no other errors in this sentence. So, the answer is (E).

2. **C** This sentence lacks parallel structure. "Debating" in the first part should be matched by "setting" in the second part. The answer is therefore (C).

3. **B** There's an error in diction here. "Affects" is a verb; "effects" is the noun form. "Side effects" is the desired phrase. Choice (B) is the answer.

4. **B** The error here is difficult to detect. The phrase *over the last decade* indicates that the growth is still continuing. This is also indicated in the present tense form of *employs* (D). Thus the first verb should be *has grown* instead of *had grown*. Choice (B) is the answer.

5. **C** Here is another case of missing parallel structure. This is a common mistake in this section. *Reading widely* and *making herself* need to be matched by another gerund in part C, such as *conducting sophisticated research*. The answer is (C).

6. **E** Using "one" might sound awkward to one, but it is not incorrect. Nor are there any other errors. The answer is (E).

7. **D** The tenses of the verbs in this sentence are not consistent; this is another favorite error in this type of question. *Has undergone* should be matched with *has exploded*. The answer is (D).

8. **D** In comparing two things (films in this case), one should use the comparative case of an adjective and not the superlative. *Best*, choice (D), is superlative and not comparative (*better* would be correct), and so it is incorrect.

9. **C** You *agree with* a noun, and *that* a phrase. (A) is idiomatically correct. There is no error in (B). You may use *reasonable for* with the construction here (subject + infinitive). No error there. *To not acquiesce* is acceptable for spoken speech, but in written language it should be *not to acquiesce*. There's the rub. The answer is (C).

10. **C** A country (Canada) requires the pronoun *it*, not *they*. The problem is therefore in choice (C).

11. **E** This sentence is unnecessarily wordy. *Having published her first novel, the author* is a lot snappier and more direct. The answer is (E).

12. **D** Here, *despite* is not used in a grammatically correct way. *Despite the fact that* is grammatically correct, but it is unnecessarily wordy and it is not appropriately joined with a semicolon. How about just *but*? That's the answer (D).

13. **C** This sentence might have sounded okay to you, but it has a misplaced modifier. These are very popular mistakes in the sentence correction questions. The phrase *after he had worked on his serve for a few days* modifies the noun *player*, so player must be right next to it. Only (B) and (C) accomplish this. Choice (B), however, changes the sense of the original sentence. The answer is (C).

14. **C** In sentence construction parallel parts of a sentence should have parallel forms. In this sentence the verbs *portray* and *reveal* are parallel, but in the original sentence construction they are not in parallel form. Choice (C) corrects this mistake.

15. **B** This is another favorite of the test writers: Any time you have "not only" you need to signal the contrasting phrase with "but also." The answer here is therefore (B).

16. **A** There is no error here. The answer is (A).

17. **A** There is not a grammatical error in the underlined portion, and none of the alternatives improve upon the original. Because you do not repeat the subject, there is no comma needed before the underlined portion. Were you to choose answer (C), you would need to add a comma. Choice (A) is the answer.

18. **D** Here the error is logical rather than grammatical per se. The first part of the sentence emphasizes sympathy, but the second part focuses on negative human qualities. You need a contrasting coordinator. That leaves (D) and (E). (D) is the better choice.

19. E It was not because Pancho Villa's raid was *part of the tumult of the Mexican revolution* that it *prompted a retaliatory expedition. Therefore* is misused. Simply delete it and you have a correct sentence. The answer is (E).

20. A There is nothing grammatically wrong with the underlined portion, and none of the other choices improve on the wording of the sentence. (A) is the best choice.

21. E Right away, you should notice two sentences in passive voice and think about making them active. Only (D) and (E) do that. (D) includes an imprecise −*ing* verb. The test writers love to throw these around. Sometimes they are the right answer, but you should always scrutinize them. Here (E) is a much sharper sentence.

22. A Doesn't sentence 2 seem too specific? It is really an explanation for why the men couldn't use their limbs. It should therefore follow sentence 4. The answer is (A).

23. D What is the logical connection between the two sentences? The first deals with the highest trip. The second deals with the largest balloon. *Now* has nothing to do with that. Neither does *in the nineteenth century*. You don't want to begin with either of these. *Moreover* represents paragraph 2 as an extension of the ideas in paragraph 1, which is also inaccurate. The easiest thing to do is simply get rid of now, (D).

24. C Sentence combination is huge in this section. This example is trickier than most. It already has an *and* in the first sentence, so if you use *and* again your sentence will start to sound like a run-on. Here, too, the −*ing* verb is imprecise. *Which* should really go very close to the noun it modifies, so eliminate (A). *But* implies a contrast, when all of these ideas are similar, so you can eliminate (E). Go with the semicolon (C).

25. D *All of whom returned safely* is not a complete sentence. It modifies "passengers" in the preceding sentence. Only (D) addresses that major problem!

26. E What's missing in this sentence is *where*. As it stands now, it implies that *literacy program* is the direct object of *working*. Choices (D) and (E) correct the error, but (D) makes undesirable changes to the verb tenses. (E) is the best answer.

27. B *That had automobiles* should not be separated by commas because it is an integral part of the category being described, not an added description. But it isn't correct in written English to write *people that*. It has to be *people who* (or *people whom* if what follows positions the people as the object of a verb). The answer is (B).

28. D The sentence as it stands is a bit of a disaster. It sounds like a run-on: it just goes on and on like the Energizer Bunny. So what you will want to do is make it more direct, showcasing the important parts and subordinating the descriptions that are really secondary. You also need a comma after *It is hard to believe*. Start with the easiest thing, and eliminate (A) and (C) off the bat. Which of (B), (D), and (E) makes the sentence more direct? Definitely not (E). Choice (B) gets rid of the second comma/and combination, which could be good. But is a colon really in order here? No. The best answer is (D).

29. A This is a little tricky because the repetition here does serve a purpose; it isn't just extra wordage that got in the author's way. Basically, the sentences are a list. When you have clauses that form a list (or other things requiring lots of words and/or punctuation), you separate them with semicolons rather than commas. (A) looks good. All of the other answers, except (D), change the sense of the original ever so slightly. (D) could be possible if it had *and* before the last clause, but (A) is still better.

30. B While it would be possible to add a comma after *convenience*, it doesn't make much sense to add one after *necessity*. Changing *you live* to *one lives* is possible, but not required. So is adding *Desert*. The comma after *apparently* isn't strictly required, but it is desirable. The only absolutely necessary change is to replace "there" with "they are" (choice B). "There are" might have been more difficult to rule against (though still incorrect), but the sentence doesn't even say *there are*; it just says *there*.

Section 4

1. A What is the name of the kind of talk that is delivered at a funeral? *Eulogy*. If you know this, the answer pops out at you. If you did not know it, consider each of the choices in their turn. *Epigraph* is a quote at the beginning of a piece of writing. *Eponymy* is something with the same name as something else. *Epitaph* is what is written on a gravestone. That leaves (A) and (B). *Elegy* is a poem written in memory. You don't "give" a poem. That leaves (A), the correct answer.

2. C On this dual-blank sentence, let's do the first blank first since we know that the blank was *an encouragement to the rest of the team*. Good spirits would be an encouragement to the rest of the team. You can eliminate (D) and (E). As for the second blank, what does a string of defeats do to a team? It discourages them. (A), *elated*, does not match this. Nor does (B), *inundated*. But (C), *dispirited*, fits well and you've already eliminated (D) and (E). Choice (C) is the best answer.

3. B You might not know what *resorted* means, but if you know it's a negative word, you can make an educated guess. Which of the answer choices is also a negative verb? (A), (C), and (D) are not. (E) is not a good answer because *swindling* has nothing to do with campaigning. Choice (B) is the best choice.

4. E The second half of the sentence gives more clues, so you ought to start there. What are cats most likely to do to dogs? Avoid them, probably—which will lead you to (E), the correct answer. But for good measure, let's eliminate the other possibilities. For a cat to *undermine* a dog isn't logical. Being undermined is something that happens to humans or projects, so you can definitely eliminate (D). One could say that a cat *enticed* a dog to do something, but it isn't good usage simply to say that the cat enticed the dog. Eliminate (A). Is it likely for a cat to gracefully *apprehend* a dog? No. Eliminate (C). The only possibilities left are (B) and (E). A cat might possibly defeat a dog in battle, but use the other clues. Defeat and "gracefully" don't go well together, and it doesn't make sense for a battle to happen while the cat is creeping across the lawn. Eliminate (B). The answer is (E).

5. A Attack the second blank first. The most likely adjective to describe attention will be something like *undivided* or *rapt*. (A), which includes *rapt*, is the answer. (B), which includes *spellbound*, is also possible. But *pointed* anecdotes doesn't make sense, so the answer is (A).

6. E You know the word is going to be negative: both *bogged* and *contentious* tell you so. Eliminate (B). Now think that the word is basically going to mean mess. You can eliminate (A) and (C). Conundrum is a confusing problem, not really a messy situation. (E) is the best answer.

7. B Here the first blank seems more approachable. The reference to a clear leader indicates that the outcome was known. Eliminate (A) and (E). For the second blank, the clue is that the leader *misstepped* and so rest of the competitors must have gotten a chance at the title, but they weren't assured a victory. Eliminate (D) and (C). The answer is (B).

8. D Consider the first blank. The word *though* indicates that the drug *was intended to be beneficial* but ultimately was not. Do any of the answer choices mean not beneficial? (A), (D), and (E) do. How would the medical community respond to a bad result? Ostensibly they would think that a bad result was bad. That eliminates (A) and (E). This leaves (D).

9. B A life that only lasts 24 hours is what in comparison to a normal human life? It is short. Which of the answer choices contains the notion of shortness in its meaning? (B), *ephemeral*, does.

10. E What is a species likely to do in an environment? It either grows in number or diminishes in number. Each of the first words, except in (B), could mean one of those things. Eliminate (B). When you discover that there is an abundance of food, you know that the first word will suggest that the kangaroos increased in numbers. Eliminate (A) and (D). Now you need the second part of the sentence. To grow in numbers, the kangaroos will need an absence or near absence of predators. Eliminate (C). You are left with (E).

11. C The best clue in this sentence is "fears." Citizens with fears can only be *concerned* or *alarmed*. That leaves (B) and (C). It's not particularly logical to say that a speech is designed to *ignore* something. On the other hand, it is common to use *assuage* with *fears*. The best answer is C.

12. A Let's attack the first blank. If the female is a fencing champion then she must be skillful with her *rapier* (her sword). Which of the first answer choices matches skillful? Choices (A), (B), and (E) do. (C) is possible but not likely. As for the second blank, the conjunction *but* indicates that her skillfulness in fencing is in contrast to her lack of skill in other sports. Which of the remaining second answer choices matches with this pre-guess? Only *awkward*, choice (A), does.

434

13. B There is a contrast drawn in the sentence between receiving accolades—praise, awards—and Jane Goodall's initial standing in her field. She must have met with a lack of support or outright disapproval. Eliminate (E) because it is illogical. Eliminate (C) because it goes with, rather than against, accolades. An *acolyte* is someone who assists a clergyman, so you can eliminate (A). You are left with (B) and (D). A *charlatan* is a fake, an incompetent. If the sentence said, "Some people thought she was a ——," *charlatan* might work, but it says she actually was "a —-." She couldn't have been a fake and later gotten awards. Eliminate (D). You are left with (B), a *maverick*, an independent thinker, a dissenter, a pioneer.

14. D This sentence is contrasting the views of Alston and Mario (the conjunction *but* clues you into this fact). Alston thinks that the lecture was *impressive*, which probably means smart, accurate, logical. Mario's view is in contrast to this. You can eliminate (A) and (C). *Recondite* is not likely to be a word to describe a lecture, so eliminate (B). You are left with *specious* or *fictitious*. *Specious* means logically false; *fictitious* comes from fiction, and presumably the philosopher didn't tell a story but rather made an argument. Choice (D) is the best answer.

15. A If you know that *insinuation* is a negative word, you can guess that the first blank will describe a logical response to a negative thing. *Balk* is a common word in this situation, but if you don't know that use the process of elimination. You can eliminate (B) and probably (D) because they are not negative words. Move to the next blank. If the official's response is negative, it's most logical that he is accused of having something to do with the *economic woes*. Eliminate (C). That leaves (A) and (E) as the most likely answers. But you don't "rile" *at* something; it's not good usage. Eliminate (E) and you are left with (A).

16. D The author is speaking generally in this first paragraph. Global warming and species extinction are two big, general problems; he refers to them in a positive light at "maintaining global climate and genetic resources." "Genetic resources" refers diverse species of plants and animals, choice (D).

17. E The author mentions that Los Amigos is relatively pristine, and that the rainforest is facing threats. Eliminate (A) and (B). He isn't talking in the passage about restoring the rainforest, but preventing future damage. Eliminate (C). He does not say that every other part of the rainforest is already destroyed beyond repair. Your logic should tell you that. Eliminate (D) and you are left with (E), the correct answer.

18. A First go back and get the context of the use of this phrase. It refers to land being set aside for conservation use. The only possibility is (A).

19. D This is a difficult question because it requires you to infer the answer. The best way to do that is to eliminate the least likely answers and then see what's left. The passage tells you that the agreement was "the first long-term permanently renewable conservation concession." There are two references to time in this sentence, so the answer must have to do with time—that leaves (B), (D), and (E). The author isn't really interested in the legal aspects, though, so eliminate (E). Because he includes both "long-term" and "renewable," the agreement probably wasn't the first contract that was simply one or the other. Eliminate (B). That leaves you with (D), the correct answer.

20. C This is a question that you should be asking yourself as you read through the passage. The passage begins by discussing the importance of conservation efforts in Amazonia and then links the work at the Los Amigos watershed with this goal. The correct answer will contain both of these things. (A) is too general. (B) isn't accurate—he doesn't focus on eliminating bad things but on continuing good things. (C) sounds good. (D) is incorrect because the passage is not primarily about the Peruvian government. (E) points to one issue that the passage discusses but lacks many of the other issues the passage discusses. (C) is the best answer.

21. D This question calls for a little nuance. He does advocate for his project, but does not position it against other projects. Eliminate (A). (B) is too general. (C) is not accurate—he does not condemn the government. (D) sounds good. (E) uses language that is too strong—he is not a zealot, but a scientist making his case in calm, rational language. (D) is correct.

22. E The author positions his project as complementary to other projects. These scientists are examples of the other amenable projects. The answer is (E).

23. E This is a tricky answer because the right choice is the one you'd least expect. The author focuses on working with plants in the watershed, but in the last word of the passage mentions an "herbarium," which through context clues and word study, you can guess means a laboratory where plants are grown. Eliminate (A). The author mentions studying "human-plant" interactions in paragraph 6. Eliminate (B). Somewhat surprisingly, the author is in favor of pharmaceutical use of Amazon plants, as he indicates in paragraphs 1 and 5 and implies in paragraph 6. Eliminate (C). (D) is obviously not the answer. You might think that because he focuses on naming, he means labeling, but in fact it is a scientist on another project, Robin Foster, who actually labeled plants. (E) is the answer.

24. B As always, first go back and read the section cited in the question. The sentence in which "providing names" occurs, mentions *communication about plants and the animals that use them.* You will recall that earlier in the passage, it was stated that one of the major projects in studying Amazonia was discovering new species. One hurdle for communication among scientists once a species is discovered is standardizing the name of the species. This is how "providing names" will *facilitate communication*. Choice (B) correctly points this out. (If you had difficulty with this question, notice that all the other choices mention issues not directly addressed in the passage. That is a strong indicator that an answer is incorrect.)

25. A The author's full argument goes, "To be informed, we must develop knowledge. To develop knowledge, we must collect, organize, and disseminate information. In this sense, botanical information has conservation value." The author is arguing that being informed is essential for conservationism, and so in this sense *botanical information has conservation value*. So even though (B), (C), (D), and (E) are all things the author might agree with, only (A) captures the meaning of the argument made here.

26. B You might confuse repeated use of the word watershed with an actual discussion of water pollution, but the author doesn't mention water pollution explicitly. The answer is (B). If you don't get this right away, you can arrive at it by eliminating the others. He does clearly mention all of the other choices.

27. C The author is talking about how his work at Los Amigos relates to other conservation projects, and how the Los Amigos area is related to other environmentally protected areas. Only (C) captures that meaning.

Section 5

1. C For every positive integer, there is a negative integer the same distance from zero. This means that there are an equal number of positive and negative integers. Therefore each set contains the same number of members, which is choice (C).

2. B Four sweaters cost p dollars, and so 12 sweaters at the regular price would cost $3p$ ($4 \times 3 = 12$). Since the sweaters are half-off, the 12 sweaters only cost half as much, $\frac{3p}{2}$, choice (B).

3. C This fraction looks complicated, but realize that the numerator and denominator are both fractions. You might then see that the numerator $\left(\frac{2}{3}\right)$ is less than the denominator $\left(\frac{4}{5}\right)$, and so this fraction is less than one. That eliminates (D) and (E) as possible answer choices. You have to simplify the fraction to find the answer, and since you're dividing fractions, remember to multiply by the reciprocal of the divisor:

$$\frac{\frac{2}{3}}{\frac{4}{5}} = \frac{2}{3} \div \frac{4}{5} = \frac{2}{3} \times \frac{5}{4} = \frac{10}{12} = \frac{5}{6}.$$ (C) is the answer.

4. E Here you just need to plug in and be careful. If $x = 3$ then $y = 1$ because

$$3y = x$$
$$3y = 3$$
$$\frac{3y}{3} = \frac{3}{3}$$
$$y = 1$$

If $y = 1$, then

$$y = \frac{10}{z}$$
$$1 = \frac{10}{z}$$
$$(z)1 = \left(\frac{10}{z}\right)(z)$$
$$z = 10$$

This is choice (E).

5. C $y = mx + b$ is the equation for a line, so the wiggly lines of choices (D) and (E) cannot be correct. A negative m means the slope is negative, so the line must slant down when viewed from left to right. That eliminates (A). The y-intercept b is positive, so the line must cross the y-axis above the x-axis. This is true of (C), so it's the answer.

6. A This problem requires a little careful decoding, but all the steps are straightforward. The first part of the order is 2 H-M, which are two medium hats. Usually the hats are $12 each, so two would cost $24, but since all medium-sized items are 25% off, the price is reduced. Twenty-five percent of 24 is 6, so together the two medium hats cost $18 ($24 minus $6). The next part is 2 H-L, which is two large hats, and together

438

they cost \$24. The last part of the order is 1 SH-M, one medium shirt, which costs \$9 since it is 25% off (\$3 is 25% of \$12, the normal cost of the medium shirt). Adding up $18 + 24 + 9 = 51$, answer (A).

7. A   The task here is to solve for x. The test makers are betting that the square root symbol will throw you off a bit.

$$5\sqrt{x} + 15 = 30$$
$$5\sqrt{x} + 15 - 15 = 30 - 15$$
$$5\sqrt{x} = 15$$
$$\frac{5\sqrt{x}}{5} = \frac{15}{5}$$
$$\sqrt{x} = 3$$
$$x = 9$$

Answer (A).

8. D   Here there is no shortcut. We have to factor and then simplify.

$$\frac{x^2 - x - 12}{2x^2 + 2x - 12} = \frac{(x - 4)(x + 3)}{2(x^2 + x - 6)} = \frac{(x - 4)(x + 3)}{2(x + 3)(x - 2)} = \frac{x - 4}{2(x - 2)}.$$ (D) is the answer.

9. C   The first thing to do is to have it clearly in mind what the graph of $f(x) = x^2$ looks like.

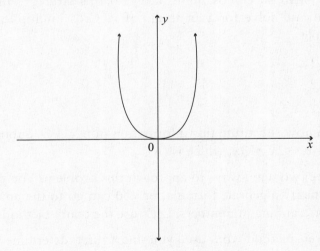

PETERSON'S

getting you there

This shape comes about as a result of the x^2 term. When $f(x) = x^2$, the fact that all x values are squared makes every y value positive (keep in mind that $f(x)$ acts as the y value). This graph has no negative y values, but to find the right answer, it must now be rotated clockwise. This means rotating to the right.

Here's a good way to visualize this. Hold up your left hand, and make a bowl-shape with your fingers on one side and your thumb on the other. The tips of your fingers and thumbs should all be point towards the ceiling. This is your graph before rotation. Now take your left hand and shift it 90° to the right; in essence, snap your wrist down. The tips of your fingers and thumb should now be pointing to the right. Find the answer choice that looks like the position of your left hand. (C) is the answer.

10. E The correct ordered pair has to satisfy two conditions, $x - y > 2$ and $x + y > 4$. Let's start with the first condition and take it from there. In order for $x - y > 2$, x must be greater than y by more than two. This eliminates choices (A), (B), and (D). Now you have only two choices left to check the second condition, $x + y > 4$. If you add the x and y values of choice (C) together you get 4, but the value must be greater than 4. Choice (E) has to be the correct answer.

11. A The best way to approach a problem like this is to use one of the equations and solve for one of the variables in terms of the other. Then you can place that answer into the second equation.

This problem succumbs quite nicely to this strategy. Take the first equation and solve for y in terms of x. Cross-multiplication makes this simple.

$$\frac{x}{y} = \frac{1}{2}$$
$$2x = y$$

You can now substitute this information into $x + y$. Subbing in for y: $x + y = x + 2x = 3x$, which is (A).

12. B There are two main ways to approach this problem. You can come up with a snazzy algebraic formula, or you can go to the answer choices and start cranking in numbers. Let's use the crank method.

Whichever method you use, you must first determine how much Quentin paid for the three hot dogs. This is done by subtracting $7.34 from $10, giving you $2.66. This is the price, including tax, of three hot dogs.

440

With the crank method, starting with the middle answer choice (C) often yields a clue, even if it's incorrect. Choice (C) has a hot dog at 86 cents. Add 6 or 7 cents sales tax to this, and then multiply by three. You get:

$$3(86 + 7) = 3(93) = 279$$

Tip

You can add the entire amount of sales tax per dollar, 7 cents, or you can take into account the fact that 86 cents is not quite an entire dollar, so Quentin might not owe the entire 7 cents sales tax. This might seem vague, but the question does allow for some wiggle room since it asks "which is closest to the price . . ." Whether you use 6 or 7 cents sales tax, the same answer works best both ways.

You know that Quentin spent $2.66, or 266 cents. Answer choice (C) comes out at 279 cents, which is 13 cents too many. This means that (C) is incorrect because it's too great. If (C) is too great, then (D) and (E) are even greater, so they must also be incorrect. This leaves (A) and (B). Try (B). If it also too great, then the answer must be (A). Here's (B).

$$3(82 + 7) = 3(89) = 267$$

This is only one penny off. If you use a 6-cent sales tax, it is only 2 cents off. (B) is closest to the price of the hot dog, so it's the correct answer.

13. D Since the triangles are congruent, you know that the bottom right angle on the left triangle is a right angle. You also know that the side opposite of b is $\dfrac{x\sqrt{3}}{2}$, and from this you can deduce that the side adjacent to b is $\dfrac{x}{2}$ by using the Pythagorean theorem. Here's what the computation would look like:

$$a^2 + b^2 = c^2$$

$$\left(\frac{\sqrt{3}x}{2}\right)^2 + b^2 = x^2$$

$$\frac{3}{4}x^2 + b^2 = x^2$$

$$\frac{3}{4}x^2 - \frac{3}{4}x^2 + b^2 = x^2 - \frac{3}{4}x^2$$

$$b^2 = \frac{x^2}{4}$$

$$b = \frac{x}{2}$$

The sides of this right triangle, then, are in the proportions of a 30-60-90 triangle. And since angle b is opposite the second largest side, its measure is 60°, choice (D).

14. C You can infer that the figure is a square since all the sides must be congruent because they are all formed by points equidistant from zero. To find the area of the square, you only need the length of one side. You can get this two ways: you can use the distance formula for two points or you can take a shortcut and realize that the square is cut into four 45-45-90 triangles by the y- and x-axes. The length of each non-hypotenuse side of these triangles is 2, so the hypotenuse must be $2\sqrt{2}$. This hypotenuse is also the length of the square's side, so place this value into the area of a square formula:

$$A = s^2$$
$$A = \left(2\sqrt{2}\right)^2$$
$$A = 4 \times 2 = 8$$

Choice (C) is the answer.

15. E The smallest percentage difference is going to be the year where the flu column and the cold column are closest. (The converse is not true for the greatest percentage difference.) Eyeing the chart is the fastest way to determine the answer. The values in the columns for 2000 look and are the closest, and so the percentage difference is the least. (E) is the answer.

16. D Cold cases (white bar) have to be greater than flu cases (shaded bar), so there are only two decades that could be the correct answer, 1970 and 1990, choices (B) and (D). In 1970, the number of cold cases is about twice as many as the flu (2,000 to 1,000), so the percentage difference would be 100%. This makes 1990, choice (D), the answer by default, but you can see that the percentage difference works out to about 25% since there were roughly 4,000 cold cases and 3,000 flu cases.

17. A You may want to save Roman numeral questions for the second pass! A judicious use of POE will help you out on this one, though. Looking at I, angles 6 and 12 are both formed by the same intersecting line, and they are congruent. Since I must be true, you can take this information and cross out any answer choices that do not have I in them. Surprisingly, this gets rid (B), (C), and (D). The answer is either (A) (I only) or (E) (I and II only). Since these are the only choices, you do not even have to worry about III. Check II, and if it must be true, then the answer is (E). If it isn't true, the answer must be (A). As it turns out, 2 and 9 are not congruent, so the answer is choice (A).

18. A This problem looks rather complicated, but the negative in front of the a simplifies it. If $-a^{-b^{-c}}$ is positive, then a must be negative and raised to an odd power. To get your head around this, consider that if a were positive, the entire expression could not be positive. So (A) *must be* true.

19. D The first thing to recognize here is that the figure is composed of three triangles, and since all the line segments are congruent, all the triangles are equilateral and congruent to each other. Equilateral triangles are all 60-60-60 triangles, and so both a and b are 60. Choice (D) is true.

20. C Since the boys cannot sit by seat 3, both girls always have to be sitting in seat 2 and 4. The boys have to be in seats 1 and 5.

If the first girl is in seat 2, then the second is in seat 4. If the first boy is in seat 1 the second boy is in seat 5. That is one arrangement. The boys could switch seats, and that is a second arrangement. The girls could also switch seats, and this would yield another two possible arrangements. That gives four total, (C).

21. E   There is a little formula that can be used, and you can draw up a Venn diagram if you like, but if you keep your head you can reason your way through this problem. If 52 students are in neither class, then 98 students are in algebra or geometry. The question states that "73 are in geometry and 62 are in algebra," so that would be a total of 73 + 62 = 135 students. Since this number is greater than the number (98) of students you found earlier, the difference between 135 and 98 must be the number of students enrolled in both algebra and geometry. This difference is 37 (135 − 98 = 37), choice (E).

Section 6

1. B   In reference to the discovery of DNA, the passage states, *the study of life could now be performed with more abstract methods of analysis.* (B) makes the same point, using the same key word, while all the other choices either go beyond what the passage actually states (e.g. (A), the passage does not say that the study of lipids and proteins became irrelevant; (C) basically says the same thing) or bring in topics not mentioned in the passage (e.g. (D), Mendelian genetics is not mentioned in the passage).

2. E   The passage contrasts "wet and dirty" study of lipids and proteins with the information-based study of DNA. In this sense "wet and dirty" involves intensive laboratory work with things like lipids and proteins. It is not *haphazard guessing* (A). Choice (E) states this correctly, also drawing on language in the passage (*information-based*).

3. D   The passage says that Saunders was a writer on Western topics who was widely read in the past. (D) fits with this. (A) does not. The passage does not say anything like (B), (C), or (E). Thus (D) is the best choice.

4. A   The passage reads, many of the groups who popularized rock and roll consciously were attempting to emulate the work of blues greats such as B. B. King. Choice (A) is an accurate paraphrase of the information given in the passage.

5. C   *Antecedent* means coming before. Even if you don't know the word, you can use word analysis to figure out that it has something to do with before. Don't confuse *ante-* with *anti-* (against). You can eliminate (D) and (E). *Referent* is a synonym for antecedent only in grammatical usage. Eliminate (B). You are left with *antebellum*, meaning before the war, or *causal*, meaning causing. *Causal* is more specific and more logical. (C) is the answer.

6. **C**   The passage begins by describing the Seneca Falls convention as the first organized attempt for woman's voting rights (read the first sentences of the passage to see this). AWSA and NWSA came after Seneca Falls. (D) and (E) refer to information provided in Passage 2. Choice (C) is the answer.

7. **A**   The passage states that the Seneca Falls conference did not have an *immediate effect* because the nation became *embroiled* in issues related to the coming Civil War. Knowledge of the dates of the Civil War will help you avoid confusing it with World War I. It was the Civil War, (A), that pushed the woman's voting rights movement to the background of the national consciousness.

8. **B**   Here it is best to go back to the passage and clarify in your own mind the distinctions drawn between the NWSA and the AWSA. The NWSA, which the question asks about, focused their efforts on federal and constitutional issues, whereas the AWSA focused on state-level issues. So (B) is the correct answer.

9. **B**   Don't be distracted by the wrong answers. Without even reading the passage, you could guess that the conflict between two organizations was resolved when they combined. The answer is (B).

10. **D**   The author of Passage 1 doesn't have a very strong opinion, so you can eliminate (A) and (E). Now you need to decide if the author's opinion, however subtle, is positive or negative. It seems positive. For example, the author describes the work of the NAWSA as *important*. Thus the correct answer will be positive. That eliminates (B) and (C). The answer is (D).

11. **A**   The first question is to determine what the "ultimate victory of the woman's suffrage movement" is. The first paragraph of the second passage makes it clear the author views the passing of the amendment to the constitution as the "ultimate victory," and this occurred with Tennessee approving the amendment. So (A) is the answer.

12. **C**   The *earliest* time that the second passage points to is the 1870s (the first passage refers to the Seneca Falls convention in 1848), and so (C) is the answer.

13. **C**   The second passage describes "partial suffrage" as the right to, "vote in local affairs such as municipal elections, school board elections, or prohibition measures." All of the examples but (C) refer to local affairs. Choice (C) refers to something mentioned only in Passage 1 (which was, moreover, before the 1848 Seneca Falls convention).

445

14. B The second passage argues that the "partial suffrages" showed that woman could "responsibly and reasonably participate in a representative democracy." These examples made the reasoning of nonsuffragists, that woman were not fit to vote, difficult to maintain. Choice (B) correctly points to this same idea.

15. E To answer a question like this you have to clearly have in mind which passage discusses what. Neither passage mentions the number of the amendment that gave women the right to vote. The second passage mentions when the amendment became law in the first paragraph, so you can eliminate (A). The first passage mentions the Civil War in the first paragraph. The first passage mentions the leaders of NWSA in the second paragraph. The second passage is all about "partial suffrages," and you've confirmed this in question 14. The only possible answer is (E).

16. A Recall that the author of the second passage saw the "partial suffrages," the local successes of the woman's movement in the 1870s and 1880s, as crucial to the ultimate success of the movement. The first passage says that AWSA focused on state-level issues. Choice (A) states as much and is the best choice. NWSA was specifically interested in federal and constitutional issues, so (B) is factually incorrect. The author of passage two agrees that the constitutional amendment was the ultimate success of the suffrage movement, so he or she would not agree with (C). (D) also contradicts that view. (E) is more difficult to eliminate, but the author of Passage 2 doesn't mention any differences within the suffrage movement. Choice (A) is the best answer.

Section 7

1. This one is all about PEMDAS.

$$[2(3^2)^2 + (4 - 3(4))^2] = 2(9)^2 + (4 - 12)^2$$
$$= [2(81) + (-8)^2] \, 162 + 64$$
$$= 162 + 64$$
$$= 226$$

2. Remember when you multiply or divide an inequality by a negative, you switch the direction of the inequality sign:

$$22 - 3x > 13$$
$$22 - 22 - 3x > 13 - 22$$
$$-3x > -9$$
$$\frac{-3x}{-3} < \frac{-9}{-3}$$
$$x < 3$$

The only two positive integers less than 3 are 2 or 1. Either one is an acceptable answer.

3. The cost will include the initial charge and the minute rate times thirty, $0.40 + 0.06(30) = 0.40 + 1.80 = 2.20$.

4. A good, no-nonsense way to find the least common multiple (LCM) is to multiply both numbers by increasing positive integers until both multiply to the same number.

$18 \times 2 = 36$	$24 \times 2 = 48$
$18 \times 3 = 54$	$24 \times 3 = 72$
$18 \times 4 = 72$	$24 \times 4 = 96$
$18 \times 5 = 90$	$24 \times 6 = 120$
$18 \times 6 = 108$	$24 \times 6 = 144$
$18 \times 7 = 126$	
$18 \times 8 = 144$	

Both numbers multiply out to 72, so this is the answer. Creating these two tables would take a lot of time if you didn't have a calculator, but since you do, make the most of it.

5. If x is any negative number, then the inequality will hold true because the absolute value bars will knock the value up well over 2. If you don't see this, plug in some negative numbers.

    Thinking positively, if $x > 5$ then the inequality is also true. The only remaining integers are 0–5. Plugging zero into the inequality, it still holds true. But if you plug 1–5 in, the inequality is not true. Thus any integer 1, 2, 3, 4, 5 is correct.

6. This problem works very much like a function machine. Take the number they give you and place it into the equation, then solve. For the eleventh term, k will be equal to 11, so

    $$\frac{10(k + 1)}{k - 1} = \frac{10(11 + 1)}{11 - 1} = \frac{10(12)}{10} = \frac{120}{10} = 12$$

7. If you do not see the answer by visualizing the points, you can always use the formula for the midpoint. It is just the average of the coordinates (in this case, the y coordinates)

    $$\frac{y_1 + y_2}{2} = \frac{2 + 6}{2} = \frac{8}{2} = 4.$$

8. You can use trigonometric functions to solve this problem, or you could use the Pythagorean theorem since this is a right triangle (the measure of the angles have to sum to 180 and you know the measures of two of the three angles, 40 and 50, sum to 90. This means the third angle must be 90.)

    $$a^2 + b^2 = c^2$$
    $$4^2 + \left(2\sqrt{5}\right)^2 = c^2$$
    $$16 + 20 = c^2$$
    $$36 = c^2$$
    $$6 = c$$

    The answer is 6.

9. The mean is the average, so we have to add up all the numbers and divide by the total:

    $$\frac{7 + 4 + 3 + 6 + 2 + 2}{6} = \frac{24}{6} = 4.$$

    The median is the number in the middle if you line up all the numbers from greatest to least. Since there is an even number of numbers, the median will be the average of the two middle numbers, {2, 2, 3, 4, 6, 7}. The median then is the average of 3 and 4, or 3.5. The difference between the two is 0.5 or $\frac{1}{2}$.

448

10. Draw this picture! Two lines that are perpendicular to the same line are parallel. To see this, draw one line perpendicular to another, and then draw a third line perpendicular to the second; it will be parallel to the first line).

That means a and c are parallel, which implies they have the same slope, $\frac{2}{5}$.

11. This might appear complicated, but a few careful substitutions and you will have the answer. When, $y = 3$, $x = 5$ because $x = y + 2$.

Now you need to plug this value of x into the function,

$$f(x) = x^2 + 3$$
$$f(5) = 5^2 + 3 = 25 + 3 = 28$$

12. The first step is to sketch the inscribed square.

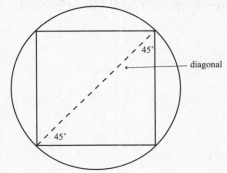

The sides of the square are $\sqrt{8}$ since the area is 8. You get this by working backward from the area of a square formula:

$$A = s^2$$
$$8 = s^2$$
$$\sqrt{8} = s$$
$$\sqrt{4 \times 2} = s$$
$$2\sqrt{2} = s$$

The longest straight line that originates and terminates on the circumference is the diagonal of the square. Now that you have the side of the square, you can find the length of its diagonal because two sides of the square and its hypotenuse make a 45-45-90 right triangle. The diagonal is the hypotenuse, so it will be $\sqrt{2}$ times greater than a side.

This means the diagonal of the square is:

$$\left(2\sqrt{2}\right)\left(\sqrt{2}\right) = 2\sqrt{4} = 2 \times 2 = 4.$$

449

13. Our range of numbers to meet the conditions is 1000 to 1198. The only way to meet the two conditions in the 1100's is to have the ones and units sum to 15 since with the two 1's (in the hundreds and thousands place) will make the sum 17. But this is impossible, since two numbers that are the same cannot sum to an odd number. Therefore, the answer must be in the 1000's. 1011 is far too less a sum of digits, and 1099 is too great, but not by much. Try 1088. It sums to 17.

Section 8

As you might expect, answers will vary. If possible, politely ask a teacher, fellow student, or some other person knowledgeable about formal essay writing to review your essay and provide feedback on ways in which the essay is commendable and on areas where it could be improved.

450

Scoring Worksheet

MATH				
	Number Correct	**Number Incorrect**	**=**	**Raw Score**
Section 2	_____	− (.25 × _____)	=	_____
Section 5	_____	− (.25 × _____)	=	_____
Section 7	_____	− (.25 × _____)	=	_____
CRITICAL READING				
Sections 1, 4, and 6	_____	− (.25 × _____)	=	_____
WRITING				
Section 3	_____	− (.25 × _____)	=	_____
Section 8	Go to www.petersons.com/satessayedge/ for instant online scoring and feedback.			

Score Charts

MATH				CRITICAL READING			
Raw Score	Math Scaled Score	Raw Score	Math Scaled Score	Raw Score	Verbal Scaled Score	Raw Score	Verbal Scaled Score
60	800	28	500	78	800	37	510
59	800	27	490	77	800	36	510
58	790	26	490	76	800	35	500
57	770	25	480	75	790	34	500
56	760	24	470	74	780	33	490
55	740	23	460	73	770	32	490
54	720	22	460	72	760	31	480
53	710	21	450	71	750	30	480
52	700	20	440	70	740	29	470
51	690	19	430	69	730	28	460
50	680	18	420	68	720	27	460
49	670	17	420	67	710	26	450
48	660	16	410	66	700	25	450
47	650	15	410	65	700	24	440
46	640	14	400	64	690	23	440
45	630	13	390	63	680	22	430
44	620	12	380	62	670	21	420
43	610	11	370	61	670	20	410
42	600	10	360	60	660	19	410
41	600	9	350	59	650	18	400
40	590	8	340	58	640	17	390
39	580	7	330	57	640	16	380
38	570	6	320	56	630	15	380
37	560	5	310	55	620	14	370
36	560	4	300	54	610	13	360
35	550	3	280	53	610	12	360
34	540	2	270	52	600	11	350
33	540	1	250	51	600	10	340
32	530	0	240	50	590	9	330
31	520	−1	220	49	590	8	320
30	510	−2	210	48	580	7	310
29	510	−3 and below	200	47	570	6	300
				46	570	5	290
				45	560	4	270
				44	550	3	260
				43	550	2	250
				42	540	1	240
				41	540	0	230
				40	530	−1	220
				39	520	−2	210
				38	520	−3 and below	200

Answer Sheets

SECTION 1

1 Ⓐ Ⓑ Ⓒ Ⓓ Ⓔ 6 Ⓐ Ⓑ Ⓒ Ⓓ Ⓔ 11 Ⓐ Ⓑ Ⓒ Ⓓ Ⓔ 16 Ⓐ Ⓑ Ⓒ Ⓓ Ⓔ
2 Ⓐ Ⓑ Ⓒ Ⓓ Ⓔ 7 Ⓐ Ⓑ Ⓒ Ⓓ Ⓔ 12 Ⓐ Ⓑ Ⓒ Ⓓ Ⓔ 17 Ⓐ Ⓑ Ⓒ Ⓓ Ⓔ
3 Ⓐ Ⓑ Ⓒ Ⓓ Ⓔ 8 Ⓐ Ⓑ Ⓒ Ⓓ Ⓔ 13 Ⓐ Ⓑ Ⓒ Ⓓ Ⓔ 18 Ⓐ Ⓑ Ⓒ Ⓓ Ⓔ
4 Ⓐ Ⓑ Ⓒ Ⓓ Ⓔ 9 Ⓐ Ⓑ Ⓒ Ⓓ Ⓔ 14 Ⓐ Ⓑ Ⓒ Ⓓ Ⓔ 19 Ⓐ Ⓑ Ⓒ Ⓓ Ⓔ
5 Ⓐ Ⓑ Ⓒ Ⓓ Ⓔ 10 Ⓐ Ⓑ Ⓒ Ⓓ Ⓔ 15 Ⓐ Ⓑ Ⓒ Ⓓ Ⓔ 20 Ⓐ Ⓑ Ⓒ Ⓓ Ⓔ

SECTION 2

1 Ⓐ Ⓑ Ⓒ Ⓓ Ⓔ 7 Ⓐ Ⓑ Ⓒ Ⓓ Ⓔ 12 Ⓐ Ⓑ Ⓒ Ⓓ Ⓔ 17 Ⓐ Ⓑ Ⓒ Ⓓ Ⓔ
2 Ⓐ Ⓑ Ⓒ Ⓓ Ⓔ 8 Ⓐ Ⓑ Ⓒ Ⓓ Ⓔ 13 Ⓐ Ⓑ Ⓒ Ⓓ Ⓔ 18 Ⓐ Ⓑ Ⓒ Ⓓ Ⓔ
3 Ⓐ Ⓑ Ⓒ Ⓓ Ⓔ 9 Ⓐ Ⓑ Ⓒ Ⓓ Ⓔ 14 Ⓐ Ⓑ Ⓒ Ⓓ Ⓔ 19 Ⓐ Ⓑ Ⓒ Ⓓ Ⓔ
4 Ⓐ Ⓑ Ⓒ Ⓓ Ⓔ 10 Ⓐ Ⓑ Ⓒ Ⓓ Ⓔ 15 Ⓐ Ⓑ Ⓒ Ⓓ Ⓔ 20 Ⓐ Ⓑ Ⓒ Ⓓ Ⓔ
5 Ⓐ Ⓑ Ⓒ Ⓓ Ⓔ 11 Ⓐ Ⓑ Ⓒ Ⓓ Ⓔ 16 Ⓐ Ⓑ Ⓒ Ⓓ Ⓔ 21 Ⓐ Ⓑ Ⓒ Ⓓ Ⓔ
6 Ⓐ Ⓑ Ⓒ Ⓓ Ⓔ

SECTION 3

1 Ⓐ Ⓑ Ⓒ Ⓓ Ⓔ 9 Ⓐ Ⓑ Ⓒ Ⓓ Ⓔ 17 Ⓐ Ⓑ Ⓒ Ⓓ Ⓔ 24 Ⓐ Ⓑ Ⓒ Ⓓ Ⓔ
2 Ⓐ Ⓑ Ⓒ Ⓓ Ⓔ 10 Ⓐ Ⓑ Ⓒ Ⓓ Ⓔ 18 Ⓐ Ⓑ Ⓒ Ⓓ Ⓔ 25 Ⓐ Ⓑ Ⓒ Ⓓ Ⓔ
3 Ⓐ Ⓑ Ⓒ Ⓓ Ⓔ 11 Ⓐ Ⓑ Ⓒ Ⓓ Ⓔ 19 Ⓐ Ⓑ Ⓒ Ⓓ Ⓔ 26 Ⓐ Ⓑ Ⓒ Ⓓ Ⓔ
4 Ⓐ Ⓑ Ⓒ Ⓓ Ⓔ 12 Ⓐ Ⓑ Ⓒ Ⓓ Ⓔ 20 Ⓐ Ⓑ Ⓒ Ⓓ Ⓔ 27 Ⓐ Ⓑ Ⓒ Ⓓ Ⓔ
5 Ⓐ Ⓑ Ⓒ Ⓓ Ⓔ 13 Ⓐ Ⓑ Ⓒ Ⓓ Ⓔ 21 Ⓐ Ⓑ Ⓒ Ⓓ Ⓔ 28 Ⓐ Ⓑ Ⓒ Ⓓ Ⓔ
6 Ⓐ Ⓑ Ⓒ Ⓓ Ⓔ 14 Ⓐ Ⓑ Ⓒ Ⓓ Ⓔ 22 Ⓐ Ⓑ Ⓒ Ⓓ Ⓔ 29 Ⓐ Ⓑ Ⓒ Ⓓ Ⓔ
7 Ⓐ Ⓑ Ⓒ Ⓓ Ⓔ 15 Ⓐ Ⓑ Ⓒ Ⓓ Ⓔ 23 Ⓐ Ⓑ Ⓒ Ⓓ Ⓔ 30 Ⓐ Ⓑ Ⓒ Ⓓ Ⓔ
8 Ⓐ Ⓑ Ⓒ Ⓓ Ⓔ 16 Ⓐ Ⓑ Ⓒ Ⓓ Ⓔ

SECTION 4

1 Ⓐ Ⓑ Ⓒ Ⓓ Ⓔ 8 Ⓐ Ⓑ Ⓒ Ⓓ Ⓔ 15 Ⓐ Ⓑ Ⓒ Ⓓ Ⓔ 22 Ⓐ Ⓑ Ⓒ Ⓓ Ⓔ
2 Ⓐ Ⓑ Ⓒ Ⓓ Ⓔ 9 Ⓐ Ⓑ Ⓒ Ⓓ Ⓔ 16 Ⓐ Ⓑ Ⓒ Ⓓ Ⓔ 23 Ⓐ Ⓑ Ⓒ Ⓓ Ⓔ
3 Ⓐ Ⓑ Ⓒ Ⓓ Ⓔ 10 Ⓐ Ⓑ Ⓒ Ⓓ Ⓔ 17 Ⓐ Ⓑ Ⓒ Ⓓ Ⓔ 24 Ⓐ Ⓑ Ⓒ Ⓓ Ⓔ
4 Ⓐ Ⓑ Ⓒ Ⓓ Ⓔ 11 Ⓐ Ⓑ Ⓒ Ⓓ Ⓔ 18 Ⓐ Ⓑ Ⓒ Ⓓ Ⓔ 25 Ⓐ Ⓑ Ⓒ Ⓓ Ⓔ
5 Ⓐ Ⓑ Ⓒ Ⓓ Ⓔ 12 Ⓐ Ⓑ Ⓒ Ⓓ Ⓔ 19 Ⓐ Ⓑ Ⓒ Ⓓ Ⓔ 26 Ⓐ Ⓑ Ⓒ Ⓓ Ⓔ
6 Ⓐ Ⓑ Ⓒ Ⓓ Ⓔ 13 Ⓐ Ⓑ Ⓒ Ⓓ Ⓔ 20 Ⓐ Ⓑ Ⓒ Ⓓ Ⓔ 27 Ⓐ Ⓑ Ⓒ Ⓓ Ⓔ
7 Ⓐ Ⓑ Ⓒ Ⓓ Ⓔ 14 Ⓐ Ⓑ Ⓒ Ⓓ Ⓔ 21 Ⓐ Ⓑ Ⓒ Ⓓ Ⓔ

SECTION 5

1 Ⓐ Ⓑ Ⓒ Ⓓ Ⓔ 7 Ⓐ Ⓑ Ⓒ Ⓓ Ⓔ 12 Ⓐ Ⓑ Ⓒ Ⓓ Ⓔ 17 Ⓐ Ⓑ Ⓒ Ⓓ Ⓔ
2 Ⓐ Ⓑ Ⓒ Ⓓ Ⓔ 8 Ⓐ Ⓑ Ⓒ Ⓓ Ⓔ 13 Ⓐ Ⓑ Ⓒ Ⓓ Ⓔ 18 Ⓐ Ⓑ Ⓒ Ⓓ Ⓔ
3 Ⓐ Ⓑ Ⓒ Ⓓ Ⓔ 9 Ⓐ Ⓑ Ⓒ Ⓓ Ⓔ 14 Ⓐ Ⓑ Ⓒ Ⓓ Ⓔ 19 Ⓐ Ⓑ Ⓒ Ⓓ Ⓔ
4 Ⓐ Ⓑ Ⓒ Ⓓ Ⓔ 10 Ⓐ Ⓑ Ⓒ Ⓓ Ⓔ 15 Ⓐ Ⓑ Ⓒ Ⓓ Ⓔ 20 Ⓐ Ⓑ Ⓒ Ⓓ Ⓔ
5 Ⓐ Ⓑ Ⓒ Ⓓ Ⓔ 11 Ⓐ Ⓑ Ⓒ Ⓓ Ⓔ 16 Ⓐ Ⓑ Ⓒ Ⓓ Ⓔ 21 Ⓐ Ⓑ Ⓒ Ⓓ Ⓔ
6 Ⓐ Ⓑ Ⓒ Ⓓ Ⓔ

Answer Sheets

SECTION 6

1 Ⓐ Ⓑ Ⓒ Ⓓ Ⓔ 5 Ⓐ Ⓑ Ⓒ Ⓓ Ⓔ 9 Ⓐ Ⓑ Ⓒ Ⓓ Ⓔ 13 Ⓐ Ⓑ Ⓒ Ⓓ Ⓔ
2 Ⓐ Ⓑ Ⓒ Ⓓ Ⓔ 6 Ⓐ Ⓑ Ⓒ Ⓓ Ⓔ 10 Ⓐ Ⓑ Ⓒ Ⓓ Ⓔ 14 Ⓐ Ⓑ Ⓒ Ⓓ Ⓔ
3 Ⓐ Ⓑ Ⓒ Ⓓ Ⓔ 7 Ⓐ Ⓑ Ⓒ Ⓓ Ⓔ 11 Ⓐ Ⓑ Ⓒ Ⓓ Ⓔ 15 Ⓐ Ⓑ Ⓒ Ⓓ Ⓔ
4 Ⓐ Ⓑ Ⓒ Ⓓ Ⓔ 8 Ⓐ Ⓑ Ⓒ Ⓓ Ⓔ 12 Ⓐ Ⓑ Ⓒ Ⓓ Ⓔ 16 Ⓐ Ⓑ Ⓒ Ⓓ Ⓔ

SECTION 7

For Questions 1–13:
Only answers entered in the ovals in each grid area will be scored.
You will not receive credit for anything written in the boxes above the ovals.

454

Practice Test 2

Section 1

20 Questions ■ Time—25 Minutes

Directions: Read each of the passages carefully, then answer the questions that come after them. The answer to each question may be stated overtly or only implied. You will not have to use outside knowledge to answer the questions—all the material you will need will be in the passage itself. In some cases, you will be asked to read two related passages and answer questions about their relationship to one another. Mark the letter of your choice on your answer sheet.

A bill is the form used for most legislation in the United State Congress. Only constitutional amendments and procedural issues affecting the House and Senate are adopted by a resolution, rather than a bill. Bills can be written to be permanent or temporary, general or special. A bill originating in the House of Representatives is designated by the letters "H.R.," signifying "House of Representatives," followed by a number that it retains throughout all its parliamentary stages. The number on the bill is determined by the order in which it was submitted during a particular session. Bills are presented to the President for action when approved in identical form by both the House of Representatives and the Senate.

1. From the passage, it can be inferred that a bill that is designated as H.R. 1 is the first bill

   (A) voted upon by the House of Representatives in a particular session of Congress.

   (B) submitted to the House of Representatives in a particular session of Congress.

   (C) sent to the Senate from the House of Representatives in a particular session of Congress.

   (D) originating in the House of Representatives signed by the President in a particular session of Congress.

   (E) debated on the floor of the House of Representatives in a particular session of Congress.

GO ON TO THE NEXT PAGE

2. It is implied in the passage that once a bill is passed in the House of Representatives that it might be sent to which of the following two places?

(A) Senate, conference committee
(B) Senate, House committee
(C) Senate, President
(D) President, Supreme Court
(E) President, Congress

Native American views of nature have important parallels in contemporary ecology. Through traditional customs and symbols like the medicine wheel, a circular arrangement of stones often interpreted as representing the relationship between Earth, air, water, and fire, Native Americans have long recognized and celebrated the connectedness among all natural things. Indeed, the Native American view of the world has always been consistent with that of Earth ecology—that Earth is a single system of interconnected parts.

3. The symbol of the medicine wheel is given as a(n)

(A) illustration of how Native Americans view the Earth as an interconnected system.
(B) example of the Native American understanding of the four elements.
(C) example of the interrelatedness of the four basic elements.
(D) critique of contemporary ecological understandings of the Earth.
(E) contrast to contemporary ecological understandings of the Earth.

4. Given what the passage states about Native American views of nature, which of the following scenarios most accords with a Native American view?

(A) Studying a microorganism removed from its habitat.
(B) Studying Earth through satellite images.
(C) Studying only animals and substances with spiritual symbolism.
(D) Studying a specific organism's interrelationships with its habitat.
(E) Studying a habitat as a whole.

Questions 5–12 are based on the following passage.

This passage is about Aaron Copland, one of the most celebrated American composers.

Line   Copland's music of the late 1920s culminates in two key works, both uncompromising in their modernism: the *Symphonic Ode* of 1929 and the *Piano*
(5)   *Variations* of 1930. The fate of these compositions contrasts sharply. While the *Piano Variations* is not often performed in concert, it is well known to pianists because, although it does contain
(10)   virtuoso passages, even those of very modest ability can "play at" the work in private. It represents the twentieth-century continuation of the great tradition of keyboard variations—the
(15)   tradition that produced such works as the Bach *Goldberg Variations*, and Beethoven's *Diabelli Variations*. Copland's *Symphonic Ode*, on the other hand, remains almost unknown: An
(20)   intense symphonic movement, it was considered unperformable by the conductor Serge Koussevitzky, otherwise the most potent American champion of

Copland's work during the first half of the century. Koussevitzky did perform a revised version in 1932; but even with a second, more extensive revision in 1955, the *Ode* is seldom played. It is Copland's single longest orchestral movement.

(25)

(30) Perhaps as a reaction to the performance problems of the *Symphonic Ode*, Copland's next two orchestral works deal in shorter units of time: the *Short Symphony* of 1933 requires fifteen

(35) minutes for three movements and the six *Statements* for orchestra of 1935 last only nineteen minutes. Yet, in fact, these works were more complex than the *Ode*; in particular, the wiry, agile rhythms of

(40) the opening movement of the *Short Symphony* proved too much for both the conductors Serge Koussevitzky and Leopold Stokowski. In the end it was Carlos Chávez and the Orquesta Sin-

(45) fónica de México who gave the *Short Symphony* its premiere.

It may have been partly Copland's friendship with Carlos Chávez that drew him to Mexico. Copland first visited

(50) Mexico in 1932 and returned frequently in later years. His initial delight in the country is related in his letter of January 13, 1933, to Mary Lescaze, in which he glowingly describes the Mexican people

(55) and the Mexican landscape. His interest in Mexico is also reflected in his music, including *El Salón México* (1936) and the *Three Latin American Sketches* (1972).

(60) Mexico was not Copland's only Latin American interest. A 1941 trip to Havana suggested his *Danzón Cubano*. By the early 1940s he was friends with South American composers such as

(65) Jacobo Ficher, and in 1947 he toured South America for the State Department.

(Some of the folk music he heard in Rio de Janeiro on this trip appears in his later works.) Copland in fact envisioned

(70) "American music" as being music of the Americas as a whole. His own use of Mexican material in the mid-1930s helped make his style more accessible to listeners not willing to accept the

(75) challenges of modern symphonic music.

5. What is the author's tone toward Copland's music?

(A) Strident skepticism
(B) Clinical objectivity
(C) Respectful description
(D) Qualified enthusiasm
(E) Unqualified praise

6. The word "virtuoso" in line 10 could best be replaced with

(A) ostentatious.
(B) intricate
(C) raucous.
(D) abstruse.
(E) publicized.

457

7. In the first paragraph the author states that *Symphonic Ode* and *Piano Variations* had different fates in that

(A) one was largely ignored while the other was almost universally praised.

(B) one, a simpler piece, won popular acclaim, while the other, a more complex piece, won critical acclaim.

(C) one, a simpler piece, became widely known by pianists, but the other, a more complex piece, remained largely unknown.

(D) one, featuring Mexican influences, was popular in Latin America, and the other, a modernist piece, was popular in the United States.

(E) both were initially acclaimed but only one became part of Copland's corpus of beloved works.

8. Koussevitzky is mentioned as an example of a(n)

(A) American conductor who admired Copland's work, but nonetheless found some pieces too difficult to perform.

(B) friend of Copland's who agreed to perform his less popular works.

(C) European composer who took issue with the difficulty of Copland's early work.

(D) musician who appreciated Copland's work but was unable to play it.

(E) European conductor who performed Copland's work.

9. The author of the passage believes that Copland's works immediately subsequent to the *Symphonic Ode* were possibly written

(A) for Copland's new relationship with Carlos Chávez and the Orquesta Sinfónica de México.

(B) to be simpler than the *Symphonic Ode*, on account of its difficulty in being performed.

(C) to be shorter than the *Symphonic Ode*, because the *Ode* was not being performed.

(D) to demand even more of conductors and musicians attempting to play Copland's music.

(E) to reflect Copland's new interest in Latin America.

10. In the sentence beginning "Yet, in fact, these works. . ." in lines 37–43 [second paragraph], the author suggests that

(A) parts of the *Short Symphony* simply weren't melodic enough to engage audiences.

(B) the *Statements* were too brief to warrant a formal performance.

(C) even those who admired Copland's work lost patience with the *Short Symphony* and *Statements*.

(D) the *Statements* and *Short Symphony* determined which performers were truly excellent and which were mediocre.

(E) the *Short Symphony* had melodies that were too quick to be played even by famous musicians.

458

11. The author suggests that Copland believed Latin American music

(A) was unfamiliar enough to a North American audience that he needed to introduce them to it.

(B) was different enough from North American music that incorporating aspects of it would make his music unique and exciting.

(C) influenced and was influenced by North American music.

(D) primarily originated in Mexico and Cuba.

(E) embodied the polar opposite of modernist aesthetics.

12. The sentence beginning "His own use of Mexican material. . . " in lines 71–75 suggests that the modernist music which also influenced Copland's compositions was

(A) superior in quality to his Latin American influences.

(B) dry and passionless.

(C) technically more challenging to perform.

(D) inaccessible but rewarding.

(E) outmoded by the 1930s.

Questions 13–20 are based on the following passage.

The following passage was written by Ed Lu, an astronaut, while a crew member of the International Space Station.

Line   Whenever I get a chance, I spend time just observing the planet below. It turns out you can see a lot more from up here than you might expect. First off, we
(5)   aren't as far away as some people think—our orbit is only about 240 miles above the surface of the Earth. While this is high enough to see that the Earth is round, we are still just barely skimming
(10)   the surface when you consider that the diameter of the Earth is over 8,000 miles.

So how much of the Earth can we see at one time? When you are standing on the ground, the horizon is a few miles
(15)   away. When in a tall building, the horizon can be as far as about 40 miles. From the International Space Station, the distance to the horizon is over 1,000 miles. So from horizon to horizon, the
(20)   section of the Earth you can see at any one time is a patch about 2,000 miles across, almost enough to see the entire United States at once. It isn't exactly seeing the Earth like a big blue marble,
(25)   it's more like having your face up against a big blue beach ball. When I look out a window that faces straight down, it is actually pretty hard to see the horizon— you need to get your face very close to
(30)   the window. So what you see out a window like that is a moving patch of ground (or water).

From the time a place on the ground comes into view until it disappears over
(35)   the horizon is only a few minutes, since we are traveling 300 miles per minute. When looking out a sideward facing window, you can see the horizon of the Earth against the black background of
(40)   space. The horizon is distinctly curved. The edge of the Earth isn't distinct but rather is smeared out due to the atmosphere. Here you can get a feel for how relatively thin the atmosphere is com-
(45)   pared to the Earth as a whole. I can see that the width of the atmosphere on the horizon is about 1 degree in angular size, which is about the width of your index finger held out at arms length. There
(50)   really isn't a sharp boundary to the atmosphere, but it gets rapidly thinner

459

PETERSON'S
getting you there

the higher you go. Not many airplanes can fly higher than about 10 miles, and the highest mountains are only about 6
(55) miles high. Above about 30 miles there is very little air to speak of, but at night you can see a faint glow from what little air there is at that height.

Since we orbit at an altitude about 40
(60) times higher than the tallest mountain, the surface of the Earth is pretty smooth from our perspective. A good way to imagine our view is to stand up and look down at your feet. Imagine that your eyes
(65) are where the International Space Station is orbiting, and the floor is the surface of the Earth. The atmosphere would be about 6 inches high, and the height of the tallest mountain is less than 2 inches, or
(70) about the height of the tops of your feet. Almost all of the people below you would live in the first one quarter of an inch from the floor. The horizon of the Earth is a little over 20 feet away from
(75) where you are standing. If you are standing on top of Denver, then about 15 feet to one side you can see San Francisco, and about 15 feet to the other side you can see Chicago.

13. The primary purpose of this passage is to

(A) provide a layperson's account of the Space Station's motion over the Earth.

(B) explain the relationship between the diameter of the Earth and the thickness of the Earth's atmosphere.

(C) answer the imagined question, "What do astronauts see from space?"

(D) give a glimpse of some of the daily activities of astronauts in space.

(E) discuss the thickness and composition of the atmosphere.

14. The second half of the second paragraph is primarily concerned with

(A) how one's location affects one's visual horizon.

(B) the thickness and density of the atmosphere.

(C) the speed of the International Space Station.

(D) the visual horizon from atop a tall building.

(E) being able to see all the Earth at once.

15. The author compares the view of the Earth from a downward-facing window in the International Space Station to

(A) holding a blue marble at arm's length.

(B) having your face up-close to a big blue beach ball.

(C) looking at the tips of your shoes when standing up.

(D) looking at an object that is on the ground fifteen feet away when you are standing up.

(E) the view from a high-flying plane.

16. In the passage, the author contrasts the view from a window looking "straight down" with the view from

(A) the observational deck.

(B) a sideward-facing window.

(C) a passenger airliner.

(D) a window looking "straight up."

(E) the circular windows on the space station.

17. The "faint glow" at night that the author speaks of in the passage comes from

(A) low-lying atmosphere.

(B) the outer edges of the atmosphere.

(C) the eastern horizon of the Earth just before sunrise.

(D) haze from foreign particulates in the atmosphere.

(E) the sun reflecting off aircraft in the high atmosphere.

18. In the last paragraph the author provides the thought exercise with the reader's height primarily to

(A) demonstrate the distance from Denver to San Francisco.

(B) give the reader a concrete sense of the proportions involved in looking down from the space station.

(C) point out that most humans live at a low altitude relative to the height of the atmosphere.

(D) illustrate the expansion of one's horizon at high altitudes.

(E) provide visual details of his activities in space.

19. The tone of the passage is best described as

(A) fairly technical.

B. highly professional.

(C) refreshingly irreverent.

(D) engagingly conversational.

(E) lyrically impassioned.

20. From the passage as a whole, it can be inferred that the astronauts' training

(A) did not prepare them for their free time in space.

(B) included a great deal of zero-gravity exercises.

(C) was more physical than technical.

(D) involved a strong background in math.

(E) focused on the astronauts' communication procedures and abilities.

S T O P Do not proceed to the next section until time is up.

Section 2

21 Questions ■ Time—25 Minutes

Directions: Solve the following problems using any available space on the page for scratchwork. Mark the letter of your choice on the answer sheet that best corresponds to the correct answer.

Notes:

1. You may use a calculator. All of the numbers used are real numbers.

2. You may use the figures that accompany the problems to help you find the solution. Unless the instructions say that a figure is not drawn to scale, assume that it has been drawn accurately. Each figure lies in a plane unless the instructions say otherwise.

1. If $x + 4y = 3$ and $x = -y$, then $y =$

    (A) -1
    (B) 0
    (C) 1
    (D) 2
    (E) 3

2. It takes Michael three hours to mow $2d$ acres. If Michael mows d acres at the same rate, how many minutes would it take?

    (A) 75
    (B) 90
    (C) 100
    (D) 120
    (E) 150

3. If $3f + 15 = 27$, then $3f - 6 =$

(A) 6
(B) 10
(C) 12
(D) 17
(E) 20

4.

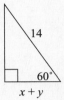

What is the value of $x + y$?

(A) 7
(B) $7\sqrt{2}$
(C) $7\sqrt{3}$
(D) 14
(E) It cannot be determined.

5. Steve bought a snack and a drink for $1.30. If the snack costs twenty cents less than the drink, how much does the drink cost?

(A) $0.50
(B) $0.55
(C) $0.65
(D) $0.75
(E) $0.80

6. If $f(x) = x + x^x$, when $x = 2$, $f(2x) =$

(A) 6
(B) 20
(C) 200
(D) 260
(E) 4096

7. If $\sqrt{x^2} = 2x + 3$, then $x =$

(A) $-x$
(B) -3
(C) x
(D) -1
(E) 4

8. If $|x + 1| > |y|$ then which of the following expresses the relationship between x and y?

(A) $x + 1 > y$
(B) $x + 1 > y$
(C) $x < y$
(D) $x > y$
(E) It cannot be determined.

9. 75% of 104 is the same value as 60% of what number?

(A) 130
(B) 133
(C) 136
(D) 140
(E) 144

10. If $3y - x = 12$ is the equation of a line, what is twice the value of this line's y-intercept?

(A) -2
(B) 2
(C) 4
(D) 8
(E) 24

463

PETERSON'S
getting you there

11.

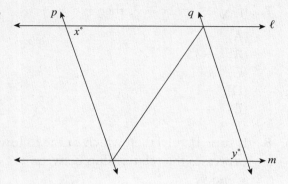

Given the figure above, which of the following must be a true statement?

(A) $x > y$
(B) $x < y$
(C) $x = y$
(D) $x + y = 90$
(E) $x - y = 90$

Questions 12–14 refer to the following definition.

Let $\in m$ be defined for any positive integer m as the number obtained when the first and last digit of m switch places.

For example $\in 4 = 4$, $\in 35 = 53$, and $\in 2003 = 3002$.

12. $\in 2323 - \in 2321 =$

(A) 2
(B) 20
(C) 200
(D) 2000
(E) 20,000

13. If A is a two-digit number between 10 and 20 and $(\in A)^2 = \in(A^2)$, then $A =$

(A) 11
(B) 13
(C) 14
(D) 16
(E) 18

14. If $A > B > C > D > E$, and each is a digit 1 through 9, then $ABCD - \in (ABCD)$ is

(A) less than zero.
(B) between zero and 100.
(C) between 100 and 500.
(D) between 500 and 1000.
(E) more than 1000.

15.

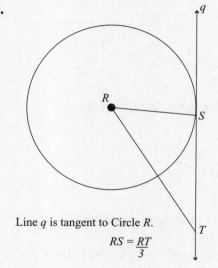

Line q is tangent to Circle R.

$$RS = \frac{RT}{3}$$

If $RT = 18$, what is the area of the above circle?

(A) 6π
(B) 12π
(C) 36π
(D) 81π
(E) 324π

464

16.

August and September Bassonet Sales

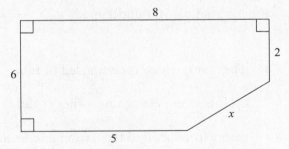

According to the above table, which of the following statements is true?

(A) September total sales are 3.5% greater than August total sales.

(B) September total sales are 2.5% less than August total sales.

(C) September total sales are 2.5% greater than August total sales.

(D) September total sales are 5.4% less than August total sales.

(E) September total sales are 5.4% greater than August total sales.

17.

What is the perimeter of the above figure?

(A) 24
(B) 25
(C) 26
(D) 27
(E) 28

18. Which of the following is the product of two prime numbers whose difference is twenty one?

(A) 46
(B) 51
(C) 55
(D) 57
(E) 58

19. What is the distance from the midpoint of $\overline{DE}$ to the origin, if $D(0,12)$ and $E(5,0)$?

(A) 5
(B) 6.5
(C) 8.2
(D) 12
(E) 13

20. If $-b^2 = (b - 7)(b + 3) - (2b + 2)(b + 5)$, then b equals

(A) $-1\frac{15}{16}$

(B) $1\frac{3}{8}$

(C) 2

(D) $2\frac{10}{11}$

(E) $5\frac{1}{3}$

21. Between 1950 and 2000, the population of Cree County tripled every ten years, except for the decade of the 1980s when the population of the country fell by one-half. If the population of Cree country was 1000 people in 1950, what is the population now?

(A) 40,500
(B) 72,900
(C) 121,500
(D) 218,700
(E) 243,000

STOP Do not proceed to the next section until time is up.

Section 3

30 Questions ■ Time—25 Minutes

Identifying Sentence Errors

1. The scientists found that there were less
    <u>   A   </u>
    <u>strands of</u> the mold they <u>were studying</u>
       B   C
    <u>than they needed</u> to conduct the experi-
         D
    ment. <u>No error</u>
         E

2. The painter <u>gave</u> a fantastic demonstration
         A
    for <u>Ada and I</u> and we <u>vowed to utilize</u> the
       B   C
    new technique in <u>our own work</u> . <u>No error</u>
              D   E

3. The team, which is <u>composed</u> of four
                 A
    cyclists, <u>compete</u> against other cycling
          B
    teams from <u>around the nation</u> and <u>around</u>
             C   D
    the world. <u>No error</u>
           E

4. <u>Depending on</u> which historian you <u>read</u>,
       A   B
    the *Pax Romana* was <u>either</u> as long as five
                     C
    centuries or as short as three. <u>No error</u>
               D   E

5. Because they <u>have extensively surveyed</u> the
  A
Lower Ohio Valley, <u>Louis and Clark</u>
  B
<u>were well prepared</u> to navigate uncharted
  C
<u>territory along</u> the Missouri River. <u>No error</u>
  DE

6. The administrator suggested that the staff

  <u>first focus</u> on contacting
  A
<u>prospective participants</u> for the upcoming
  B
seminar <u>and then</u> on <u>follow-up</u> with
  CD
previous speakers. <u>No error</u>
  E

7. The Ottoman Empire <u>initiated</u> <u>better</u> trade
  AB
relations with the Austrian Empire when

<u>its</u> border disputes with Russia
  C
<u>were resolved</u> (D). <u>No error</u>
  DE

8. The census statistics <u>was</u> a complex source
  A
of information, <u>in that</u> the demographers
  B
knew that certain groups of people <u>were</u>
  C
more likely to respond <u>than</u> others.
  D
<u>No error</u>
  E

9. <u>Because</u> of the large traffic jam, scarcely
  A
<u>no one</u> from the group <u>made</u> it to the
  BC
airport <u>in time</u> to catch the flight <u>to</u> the
  D
conference in San Antonio. <u>No error</u>
  E

10. <u>Even though</u> he had the title of
  A
<u>Vice-President</u> of Operations, his duties
  B
and responsibilities <u>were</u> not much greater
  C
than a <u>midlevel manager</u>. <u>No error</u>
  DE

Improving Sentences

Directions:

1. The following questions test your knowledge of English grammar, word usage, word choice, sentence construction, and punctuation.

2. Every sentence contains a portion that is underlined.

3. Any errors that occur will be found in the underlined portion of the sentence. If you believe there is an error, choose the answer choice that corrects the original mistake. Answer choices (B), (C), (D), and (E) contain alternative phrasings of the underlined portion. If the sentence contains an error, one of these alternate phrasings will correct it.

4. Choice (A) repeats the original underlined portion. If you believe the underlined portion does not contain any errors, select answer choice (A).

5. There will be no change in any parts of the sentence that are not underlined.

11. In an effort to make the Constitution <u>both more accessible and understandable to the public</u>, the House of Representatives has authorized the publication of a series of pamphlets about the Constitution.

    (A) both more accessible and understandable to the public

    (B) more both accessible and understandable to the public

    (C) more accessible to the public and more understandable for it

    (D) both more accessible and more understandable to the public

    (E) accessible to the public and understandable

12. Widely considered one of the most original poets of all time, <u>Gerard Manley Hopkins's poems display utterly nonconventional systems of rhyme.</u>

    (A) Gerard Manley Hopkins's poems display utterly nonconventional systems of rhyme.

    (B) Gerard Manley Hopkins's poems displayed utterly nonconventional systems of rhyme.

    (C) Gerard Manley Hopkins's poems have systems of rhyme that are utterly nonconventional.

    (D) Gerard Manley Hopkins wrote poems using utterly nonconventional systems of rhyme.

    (E) Gerard Manley Hopkins had written poems that were displaying utterly nonconventional systems of rhyme.

13. Eleanor Roosevelt, the wife of President Franklin D. Roosevelt, made an active contribution to many political <u>organizations, this included the Human Rights Commission.</u>

- **(A)** organizations, this included the Human Rights Commission.
- **(B)** organizations, being included the Human Rights Commission.
- **(C)** organizations, whose participation included the Human Rights Commission.
- **(D)** organizations; this including the Human Rights Commission.
- **(E)** organizations, including the Human Rights Commission.

14. <u>Sputnik was the first artificial satellite successfully propelled into orbit and began the space race between the United States and the Soviet Union, in 1957 it was launched by the Soviets.</u>

- **(A)** Sputnik was the first artificial satellite successfully propelled into orbit and began the space race between the United States and the Soviet Union, in 1957 it was launched by the Soviets.
- **(B)** In 1957, the first satellite and space race were beginning when Sputnik was launched.
- **(C)** Launched by the Soviets in 1957, Sputnik was the first artificial satellite successfully propelled into orbit, beginning the space race between the United States and the Soviet Union.
- **(D)** The launching of Sputnik was in 1957, the first artificial satellite was successfully propelled and the space race between the United States and the Soviet Union was begun.
- **(E)** The first artificial satellite successfully propelled into orbit was when Sputnik was launched in 1957, and the space race between the United States and the Soviet Union was begun as well.

15. The newly hired CEO stated clearly in her opening address to the company that her plans for reinvigorating the company were to cut back on discretionary spending, refinance the company's largest loans, and <u>her plans of keeping the company's holdings in the stock market.</u>

- **(A)** her plans of keeping the company's holdings in the stock market.
- **(B)** keep the company's holdings in the stock market.
- **(C)** to get the company to keep its holdings in the stock market.
- **(D)** her plans to keep the company's holdings in the stock market.
- **(E)** keeping the company's holdings in the stock market.

16. Typically, a restaurant's kitchen is divided into a number of sections, <u>each with a particular aspect of food preparation performed there.</u>

- **(A)** each with a particular aspect of food preparation performed there.
- **(B)** each corresponding to a particular aspect of food preparation.
- **(C)** where they each have their particular aspect of food preparation to perform.
- **(D)** which has a particular aspect of food preparation performed there.
- **(E)** they each correspond to a particular aspect of food preparation.

17. Domesticated over 5,000 years ago, the camel is a useful pack animal because <u>of its tolerance for hot sand, extreme temperatures, and it needs little drinking water.</u>

- **(A)** of its tolerance for hot sand, extreme temperatures, and it needs little drinking water.
- **(B)** of its tolerance for hot sand and extreme temperatures and its need for water is very small.
- **(C)** it can tolerate hot sand, extreme temperatures, and a lack of drinking water.
- **(D)** it can tolerate hot stand, withstanding extreme temperatures, and needs little water.
- **(E)** it can tolerate hot sand and extreme temperatures, and needs little water.

18. Legally, an agreement <u>among two people to commit a crime or concealing it</u> constitutes a criminal conspiracy.

- **(A)** among two people to commit a crime or concealing it
- **(B)** among two people to commit a crime or agreeing to conceal it
- **(C)** among two people committing a crime or concealing it
- **(D)** between two people to commit a crime or conceal it
- **(E)** between two people in the committing of a crime or the concealment of it

19. Not only was Sir Isaac Newton famous for his pioneering work in Physics, <u>he was also a talented and well-respected economic advisor to the king.</u>

(A) he was also a talented and well-respected economic advisor to the king.

(B) he had also been a talented and well-respected economic advisor to the king.

(C) but he was also a talented and well-respected economic advisor to the king.

(D) as he also was a talented and well-respected economic advisor to the king.

(E) but he had also been a talented and well-respected economic advisor to the king.

20. <u>If the high levels of stock market investment are to continue it will depend</u> upon both how long the stock market remains stable and its long-term durability.

(A) If the high levels of stock market investment are to continue it will depend

(B) If the high levels of stock market investment are to continue, depending upon

(C) If the high levels of stock market investment continue, it will depend

(D) Whether the high levels of stock market investment continue will depend

(E) Whether the high levels of stock market investment continue it will depend

Improving Paragraphs

Directions:

1. The following questions test your knowledge of paragraph and sentence construction.

2. The following passage is a rough draft of an essay. This rough draft contains various errors.

3. Read the rough draft and then answer the questions that follow. Some questions will focus on specific sentences and ask if there are any problems with that sentence's word choice, word usage, or overall structure. Other questions will ask about the paragraph itself. These questions will focus on paragraph organization and development.

4. Select the answer that best reflects the rules of English grammar and proper essay and paragraph writing.

Questions 21–25 are based on the following passage.

The following passage is part of an essay about the different meanings of the word "modern."

Line   (1) The word *modern* is a curious word (2) It is curious for all its different meanings. (3) If you take a freshman class in philosophy, for instance, your

(5)   professor might tell you about Rene Descartes. (4) Descartes was a French philosopher from the seventeenth century. (5) Many consider him as the first figure in modern philosophy. (6) So

(10)   if you are talking to a philosophy professor the word *modern* denotes anytime between about 1615 and now. (7) (Of course, some philosophers think that modern times ended a few decades

(15)   back and that we are already in to postmodern times.) (8) Other academics have a different timeline for the birth of modern times, or modernity. (9) And some historians point to the Industrial

(20)   Revolution in England as the beginning of modernity. (10) This dating technique puts the beginning of modernity at least a century after when the philosophers reckon the beginning of modern times.

(25)   (11) The philosophers and the historians have a bit of a discrepancy here.

     (12) Of course, you might think both the philosophers and the historians are a bit off on this whole modernity thing.

(30)   (13) Who thinks of the mud and cobblestone streets of Paris in the early decades of the seventeenth century as modern? (14) Then again, London a century later with the power of steam harnessed does

(35)   not strike most as the picture of modern times. (15) Most of us, when we think of what modern means, we are thinking about computers and cell phones and wireless networks. (16) We are not

(40)   thinking about some philosophical discourse that a Frenchman wrote four centuries back.

21. Which of the following is the best combination of sentences 1 and 2 (reproduced below)?

The word *modern* is a curious word. It is curious for all its different meanings.

(A) The word *modern* is a curious word. It is curious for all its different meanings.

(B) *Modern* is a curious word because it has all its different meanings.

(C) It is curious that the word *modern* has various different meanings.

(D) Curiously, the word *modern* has many different meanings.

(E) *Modernity* is a curious word for all its various different meanings.

22. Which of the following is the best way to revise sentences 4 and 5 (reproduced below) so that they are condensed into one sentence?

Descartes was a French philosopher from the seventeenth century. Many consider him as the first figure in modern philosophy.

(A) Descartes was a French philosopher from the seventeenth century, considering him the first figure in modern philosophy.

(B) Descartes was a French philosopher from the seventeenth century, whom many consider the first figure in modern philosophy.

(C) Descartes was a French philosopher from the seventeenth century, and many consider him the first figure in modern philosophy.

(D) Descartes was a French philosopher from the seventeenth century, so he was the first figure in modern philosophy.

(E) Descartes was a French philosopher from the seventeenth century and figuring him the first figure in modern philosophy.

23. Which of the following would be the best replacement for "And" at the beginning of sentence 9 (reproduced below)?

And some historians point to the Industrial Revolution in England as the beginning of modernity.

(A) However,
(B) Moreover,
(C) Even so,
(D) Considering this,
(E) For example,

24. Which of the following is the best revision of the underlined portions of sentence 10 (reproduced below)?

This dating technique puts the beginning of modernity at least a century after when the philosophers reckon the beginning of modern times.

(A) As it is now.

(B) at least a century after when the philosophers reckon it.

(C) at least a century after when the philosopher's date modernity's inception.

(D) at least one century after when the philosophers had reckoned the inception of modernity.

(E) at least a century after its having been reckoned by the philosophers.

473

25. Which of the following is the best revision of sentence 15 (reproduced below)?

Most of us, when we think of what modern means, we are thinking about computers and cell phones and wireless networks.

(A) As it is now.

(B) Most of us, when we think of what modern means, computers and cell phones and wireless networks coming to mind.

(C) When we think of what modern means, think about computers and cell phones and wireless networks.

(D) Most of us, when we think of what modern means, we are thinking about computers, cell phones, wireless networks.

(E) Most of us, when we think of what modern means, think about computers and cell phones and wireless networks.

Questions 26–30 are based on the following passage.

The following is a first draft of an essay about the growth of the department store industry in the 1920s.

Line   (1) Automobiles and radios became far more affordable in the 1920s. (2) By 1925 there was one automobile for every six people in the United States, by 1930
(5)   this had increased to one for every 4.6 people. (3) Also by 1930, about 4 in 10 American families owned radios. (4) The popularity of automobiles and radios led to the spread of chain stores of all kinds.
(10)   (5) Automobiles allowed consumers to travel further in search of the right item for the right price, while radios allowed businesses to advertise their products to a

larger group of people. (6) Those people
(15)   could be potential consumers.

(7) Many of our most famous department store chains first expanded during this time. (8) These include Sears, Roebuck; Woolworth's; the Great
(20)   Atlantic and Pacific Tea Company (the A&P); and Walgreen Drug. (9) Among the most successful department stores was Filene's in Boston and Macy's in New York. (10) Initially, department
(25)   stores were more like the malls of today. (11) Each department was leased to an individual owner. (12) Nowadays, virtually all departments are run by the larger company, including restaurants.

(30)   (13) Also, with their radio campaigns, the new department stores of the 1920s put on extravagant advertising spectacles. (14) Sometimes, they even hosted entertainment events to attract
(35)   consumers. (15) The Macy's Thanksgiving Day Parade, an attempt to capture the children's toy market, is one example of popular merchandising. (16) Bloomingdale's posted ads on all New York
(40)   public transit, pronouncing, "All Cars Transfer to Bloomingdale's."

474

26. Which of the following is the best revision of the underlined portions of sentences 5 and 6 (reproduced below)?

Automobiles allowed consumers to travel further in search of the right item for the right price, while radios allowed businesses to advertise their products to a larger group of people. Those people could be potential consumers.

(A) As it is now.

(B) a larger group of people, who could be potential consumers.

(C) a larger group of people, being potential consumers.

(D) a larger group of people, whom they made into potential consumers.

(E) a larger group of people, having the potential to become consumers.

27. "This time" in sentence 7 (reproduced below) is best made more specific. Which of the following phrases is the best revision?

Many of our most famous department store chains first expanded during this time.

(A) these years

(B) the twentieth century

(C) the same when automobile sales and radio sales were also on the rise

(D) the years described in the previous paragraph

(E) the 1920s

28. If you were to combine sentences 10 and 11 (reproduced below), which would be the most appropriate and precise punctuation mark to use?

Initially, department stores were more like the malls of today. Each department was leased to an individual owner.

(A) today 'each. . . owner.'

(B) today; each

(C) today: each

(D) today (each. . . owner).

(E) today, each

29. Which of the following is the best revision of the underlined portion of sentence 13 (reproduced below)?

Also, with their radio campaigns, the new department stores of the 1920s put on extravagant advertising spectacles.

(A) Moreover

(B) Too

(C) What's more to their radio campaigns

(D) In addition to their radio campaigns

(E) The radio campaigns being included

30. Which of the following sentences, if added at the end of paragraph 3, is the best concluding sentence for the passage?

(A) In the 20s, shopping and advertising started to look a lot like they do now.

(B) Other stores also had extravaganzas.

(C) So now get in your car and drive to a department store!

(D) Department Stores having become huge successes.

(E) Macy's Thanksgiving Day Parade was always a big hit.

STOP Do not proceed to the next section until time is up.

Section 4

27 Questions ■ Time—25 Minutes

Directions: Each sentence below has either one or two blanks in it and is followed by five choices, labeled (A) through (E). These choices represent words or phrases that have been left out. Choose the word or phrase that, if inserted into the sentence, would <u>best</u> fit the meaning of the sentence as a whole.

Example:

Canine massage is a veterinary technique for calming dogs that are extremely _____.

(A) inept
(B) disciplined
(C) controlled
(D) stressed
(E) restrained

Ⓐ Ⓑ Ⓒ ● Ⓔ

1. Jerome is a true _____ ; he rarely buys anything other than food, and even his food is plain and minimal.

   (A) hermit
   (B) teetotaler
   (C) gourmand
   (D) ascetic
   (E) fanatic

2. The property tax hike in Colson County was not just _____ by the county residents; a series of protests were even _____.

   (A) disliked..organized
   (B) espoused..planned
   (C) discouraged..theorized
   (D) bolstered..analyzed
   (E) detested..negotiated

476

3. There was criticism that the councilman was _____ when he seized the ceremony _____ by the girl's tragic death to speak out against his opponent.

   (A) militaristic.. negated
   (B) opportunistic..afforded
   (C) unreceptive..preempted
   (D) passive.. created
   (E) defeatist..overshadowed

4. The computer expert underscored that the new software would _____ the prior version; users could simply _____ the old one.

   (A) preclude..destroy
   (B) outdo..implement
   (C) infect..disregard
   (D) undermine..detach
   (E) supercede..discard

5. Romania has a long and _____ tradition of activist-poets, who through poetry have _____ the dignity and equality of humanity.

   (A) reputable..initiated
   (B) storied..articulated
   (C) tenuous..supported
   (D) tactile..decried
   (E) exemplary..countered

6. Dr. Patel expected the surgery to be _____ and laborious, but it turned out to be speedy and _____.

   (A) fragile..simple
   (B) compelling..forthcoming
   (C) intricate..straightforward
   (D) complicated..locatable
   (E) hard..mechanical

7. Despite the longstanding _____ between the clans, both clans _____ each other in the aftermath of the disaster.

   (A) feud..assisted
   (B) grudge..maligned
   (C) detente..withstood
   (D) skirmish.. ameliorated
   (E) alliance.. discounted

8. The oral tradition of the Bambara people of West Africa is rich with humor and _____, characteristics which are evident in the merriment of their every-day life.

   (A) irony
   (B) mirth
   (C) cynicism
   (D) history
   (E) mystery

9. Although *Astropithicus* has more subspe-cies than *Pthicalitius*, the latter populates the Earth with _____ numbers and in more _____ geographic regions.

   (A) greater..diverse
   (B) lesser..secluded
   (C) milder..remote
   (D) scanter..familiar
   (E) larger..ominous

10. It is generally _____ by medical practitioners that the last few weeks of a pregnancy are crucial in the _____ of the fetus.

    (A) acknowledged..progression
    (B) hedged..health
    (C) endorsed..birthing
    (D) accepted..development
    (E) negated..vitality

477

11. Though the organization espoused outward-focused ideals, in practice, it was quite _____.

    (A) gregarious
    (B) vigilant
    (C) insular
    (D) hermetic
    (E) idiosyncratic

12. The prosecuting attorney described the defendant's character as _____ and base, but the defense attorney rejoined that the prosecution was _____ the testimonials about the defendant.

    (A) dark..misunderstanding
    (B) nefarious..misconstruing
    (C) lackluster..misinterpreting
    (D) blustery..misapplying
    (E) motley..misrepresenting

13. Many believe that the new drug regime will be a _____ for helping cure diverse ailments related to spinal dysfunctions.

    (A) bane
    (B) panacea
    (C) module
    (D) fledgling
    (E) pariah

14. The executive charged that the whistle-blower's actions were so self-centered that they were not just _____ but even _____.

    (A) self-involved..altruistic
    (B) ill-tempered..narcissistic
    (C) egocentric..solipsistic
    (D) unduly..respectable
    (E) erratic..destructive

15. Technology, instead of alleviating the demands upon our time, has made the pace of modern-day life increase to a near _____ pace.

    (A) elicit
    (B) frenetic
    (C) lethargic
    (D) dilatory
    (E) cavalier

Questions 16–27 are based on the following passage.

The following passage tells the story of Juan Bautista Rael, an Hispanic-American scholar. It is adapted from a biography written by Enrique R. Lamadrid.

Line   Linguist and folklorist Juan Bautista Rael was a highly regarded academic pioneer. His major contribution to linguistics was collecting and documenting the *Hispano*
(5)   folk stories, plays, and religious traditions of northern New Mexico and southern Colorado.

        Rael was born on August 14, 1900, in Arroyo Hondo, New Mexico. Famous
(10)   for its spectacular setting north of Taos, the village lies in a deep, narrow valley between Taos mountain and the gorge of the Rio Grande to the west. His family prospered in sheep and cattle ranching
(15)   and owned a mercantile business that served surrounding *Hispano* communities as well as nearby Taos Pueblo.

        Juan's parents, José Ignacio Rael and Soledad Santistevan, raised a family of
(20)   four sons and a daughter. José Ignacio had the foresight to recognize the changes that were coming with the increasing Americanization of New Mexico and realized that a fluent
(25)   knowledge of English and a good education would be necessary for his

family to excel. Since local schools were rudimentary at best, the family relied upon its own resources to get the best (30) possible education for the children. Juan was a dedicated student from his earliest years, and his father's ambition was for him to become a lawyer and tend to the family lands and business. Juan's (35) elementary schooling was at Saint Michael's College in Santa Fe, and his high school studies were at the Christian Brothers' College in St. Louis, Missouri. The boy's semester-long absences from (40) his family led him to treasure the simple pleasures of village life. Summers are especially beautiful in Arroyo Hondo, and Christmas and Easter vacations were filled with colorful festivities and solemn (45) ceremony. Rael later reminisced about how much the *Pastores*, or Shepherds' plays, impressed him as a child. Un-doubtedly, the instincts and sympathies of Rael the folklorist can be traced to (50) these beginnings—watching rehearsals and performances depicting shepherds, hermits, and the rich ensemble of pastoral characters.

What became clear in his post- (55) secondary studies is that he was much more attracted to literature, philology, and the emerging disciplines of linguistics and folklore. His Bachelor's degree, from St. Mary's College in Oakland in 1923, (60) led to a Master's degree from the University of California at Berkeley in 1927. In the meantime, in 1923, he married Quirina Espinoza of Antonito, Colorado. Rael's first inclination was to (65) become an English teacher, but his bride helped convince him that his opportuni-ties and strengths would be as an Hispanist. After deciding on a university career of teaching and research, Rael

(70) relinquished his family inheritance in land, cattle, and sheep to his three brothers and his sister.

Rael realized that the wealth in northern New Mexico that interested (75) him was the vast repertory of folk narrative, song, and custom that had scarcely been documented. While teaching at the University of Oregon, he returned to Arroyo Hondo in the summer (80) of 1930 to begin compiling his famous collection of over five hundred *Nuevo Mexicano* folk tales.

By then his work had attracted the attention of pioneer *Hispano* folklorist (85) Aurelio Espinosa who invited Rael to Stanford in 1933. Rael completed his doctoral studies in 1937 there with a dissertation on the phonology and morphology of New Mexico Spanish that (90) amplified the work of Espinosa with the huge corpus of folk tales, later published as, *Cuentos Españoles de Colorado y Nuevo Mexico: Spanish Folk Tales of Colorado and New Mexico.*

(95) Well versed in the historic-geographic theory of transmission and diffusion of motifs, tale types, and genres, Dr. Rael set out on the formidable, almost quixotic task of gathering all the possible (100) versions and texts of the tales, hymns, and plays he was studying. The vast majority of tales are of European provenance, with only minimal local references. He meticulously traced the (105) shepherds' plays to several root sources in Mexico, and his study, *The Sources and Diffusion of the Mexican Shepherds' Plays*, is a standard reference on the subject. His ground-breaking study of the (110) *alabado* hymn, *The New Mexican Alabado*, is also a prime resource. But inevitably the historic-geographic

GO ON TO THE NEXT PAGE

approach led more to collection building than to analysis. Later generations of

(115) scholars would develop interests in performance-centered studies, but the collections of Rael continue to be an indispensable landmark in the field.

16. The author's attitude towards Dr. Rael's work can best be described as

   (A) laudatory.
   (B) engaged.
   (C) ambivalent.
   (D) disinterested.
   (E) condescending.

17. The passage primarily

   (A) analyzes the academic contributions of Dr. Rael.
   (B) contrasts Dr. Rael's work with the work of Dr. Espinosa.
   (C) tells the story of Dr. Rael's life and work.
   (D) discusses the basic assumptions of *Hispano* scholarship.
   (E) relates the story of the Rael family.

18. The passage implies that Rael decided that he would have more opportunity as a Hispanist than as an English teacher because

   (A) Hispanics weren't often hired to teach English.
   (B) Hispanic folklore would soon vanish.
   (C) he would have to live far from his family to teach English.
   (D) his English skills were mediocre.
   (E) becoming an Hispanist was a nearer match to his educational background.

19. The author probably uses the word "relinquished" in line 70 to emphasize that

   (A) Rael had had friction with his siblings.
   (B) Rael's family was very wealthy.
   (C) Rael had tried to be a rancher for some time.
   (D) Rael was relieved to be free of his family duties.
   (E) Rael's career path was difficult and not lucrative.

20. It can be inferred from the passage that northern New Mexico in the early decades of the twentieth century

   (A) had a ranch-driven economy.
   (B) was suffering severe economic depression.
   (C) was economically booming because of a newly opened southern railroad route to California.
   (D) had a strong public education system.
   (E) was not a primarily English-speaking region.

21. Which of the following best describes Dr. Espinosa's relationship to Dr. Rael?

   (A) Boss
   (B) Critic
   (C) Mentor
   (D) Pastor
   (E) Father

22. The word "corpus" in line 91 most closely means

   (A) religious text.
   (B) oeuvre.
   (C) published collection.
   (D) dissertation.
   (E) dialect.

480

23. According to the passage, which of the following of Dr. Rael's activities as a young man was most important for the development of his later academic interests?

- **(A)** Working on his family's ranch
- **(B)** Watching *Pastores* as a young man
- **(C)** Studying in a religious school
- **(D)** Reading books on the shepherds of northern New Mexico
- **(E)** Struggling to retain his Spanish when his schooling was in English

24. The phrase "diffusion of motifs" in lines 96–97 refers to

- **(A)** variations in the same stories that occur over time or by region.
- **(B)** adherence to standard literary structures.
- **(C)** variations in language use by region.
- **(D)** the surprising similarity of stories in different cultures.
- **(E)** the loss of folklore in more industrialized societies.

25. The word "provenance," line 103, could best be replaced with which of the following words?

- **(A)** Authority
- **(B)** Origin
- **(C)** Location
- **(D)** Destiny
- **(E)** Ethos

26. The main criticism the author offers of Dr. Rael's work is that it

- **(A)** focuses too much on the *Pastores*.
- **(B)** privileges Spanish-language stories over English-language stories.
- **(C)** focuses too much on European stories and not enough on Mexican stories.
- **(D)** doesn't offer enough analysis of the folklore.
- **(E)** includes too many materials, without differentiating between good and bad.

27. The passage suggests, in lines 97–101 that Dr. Rael

- **(A)** was mistaken about how much folklore was circulating.
- **(B)** traveled extensively as he gathered folklore.
- **(C)** was disorganized but intelligent in his methods.
- **(D)** had an historic insight about the source of New Mexican folklore.
- **(E)** developed an excessively technical model for the development of folklore.

STOP Do not proceed to the next section until time is up.

Section 5

21 Questions ■ Time—25 Minutes

Directions: Solve the following problems using any available space on the page for scratchwork. Mark the letter of your choice on the answer sheet that best corresponds to the correct answer.

Notes:

1. You may use a calculator. All of the numbers used are real numbers.

2. You may use the figures that accompany the problems to help you find the solution. Unless the instructions say that a figure is not drawn to scale, assume that it has been drawn accurately. Each figure lies in a plane unless the instructions say otherwise.

Reference Information

$A = \pi r^2$
$C = 2\pi r$ $A = \ell w$ $A = \frac{1}{2}bh$ $V = \ell wh$ $V = \pi r^2 h$ $c^2 = a^2 + b^2$ Special Right Triangles

The number of degrees of arc in a circle is 360.
The measure in degrees of a straight angle is 180.
The sum of the measures in degrees of the angles of a triangle is 180.

---

1. At full capacity, Thompson Paper Factory produces 200 sheets of paper per second. If the factory is operating at a quarter of its full capacity, how many sheets of paper will the factory produce in twelve seconds?

   (A) 600
   (B) 900
   (C) 1200
   (D) 2000
   (E) 2400

2. If $Z = \dfrac{2x}{5}$ and $Z = 3$, then $x =$

   (A) $\dfrac{5}{3}$

   (B) 2

   (C) 5

   (D) $\dfrac{19}{3}$

   (E) $\dfrac{15}{2}$

3. Which of the following is the greatest common factor of 32 and 42?

(A) 2
(B) 3
(C) 6
(D) 8
(E) 12

4.

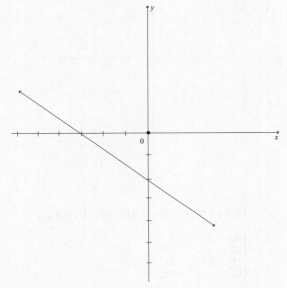

What is the slope of the above line?

A. $-\dfrac{3}{2}$

B. $-\dfrac{2}{3}$

C. $\dfrac{2}{3}$

D. 1

E. $\dfrac{3}{2}$

Questions 5–6 refer to the following table.

5.

3rd and 4th Graders at
Hyde Park Elementary

	Boys	Girls	Total
3rd	16	14	
4th			32
Total			

According to the table, how many students are there in 3rd and 4th grade at Hyde Park Elementary?

(A) 30
(B) 32
(C) 50
(D) 60
(E) 62

6. If there are 18 girls in 4th grade, how many boys are there in 3rd and 4th grade at Hyde Park Elementary?

(A) 18
(B) 22
(C) 26
(D) 30
(E) 32

483

PETERSON'S
getting you there

7. Which of the following is the value of the exponent when the expression $\dfrac{\left(m^{\frac{3}{4}}\right)^{-2}}{m^{\frac{5}{4}}}$ is simplified?

(A) $-\dfrac{11}{4}$

(B) $-\dfrac{29}{16}$

(C) $-\dfrac{3}{4}$

(D) $\dfrac{11}{4}$

(E) $\dfrac{29}{6}$

8.

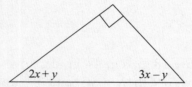

In the right triangle above, what is the value of x?

(A) 15
(B) 16
(C) 18
(D) 24
(E) 30

9. Taking the highway from Easton to Bethsaida is 7 miles longer than taking surface streets from Easton to Bethsaida. It is 31 miles total if you travel from Easton to Bethsaida via highway and return via surface streets. How many miles then, is the highway route?

(A) 12
(B) 13
(C) 15
(D) 17
(E) 19

10. If $f(x) = \dfrac{3x^2}{x^2 + 3x - 18}$, for what values of x is the function undefined?

(A) 0
(B) $-3,6$
(C) $-3,3$
(D) $2,5$
(E) $3,-6$

11.

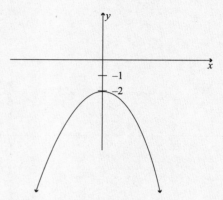

If $f(x)$ is graphed above, then $f(x) =$

(A) $x^2 + 2$
(B) $x^2 - 2$
(C) $-x^2 + 2$
(D) $-(x^2 + 2)$
(E) $-(x + 2)^2$

12.

If the above triangles are congruent, what is the value of y?

(A) 5
(B) $\sqrt{50}$
(C) 8
(D) $\sqrt{75}$
(E) 9

13. $(y + 2)^2 = (y - 4)^2$ is true when y equals

(A) 1 only
(B) 1 and −1
(C) 2 and −2
(D) 1 and 2
(E) 2 and 4

14. Z is the set of numbers 1 through 50 inclusive. How many members of Z are evenly divisible by 2 and 3?

(A) 6
(B) 8
(C) 14
(D) 16
(E) 25

15.

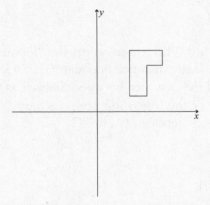

Which of the following figures is similar to the shape shown above?

(A)

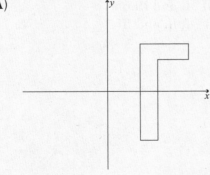

(B)

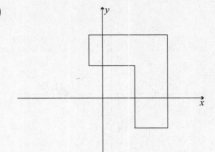

(C)

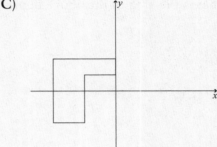

(D)

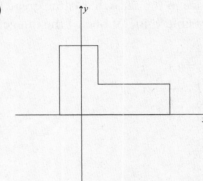

(E)

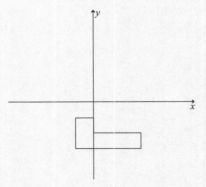

485

16.

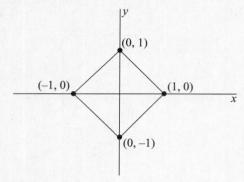

What is the area of the above figure?

(A) 1
(B) $\sqrt{2}$
(C) 2
(D) $1\sqrt{2}$
(E) 4

17. The sum of eight positive even integers is 50. If no integer can appear more than twice in the set, what is the greatest possible value of one of the integers.

(A) 8
(B) 18
(C) 22
(D) 24
(E) 32

18.

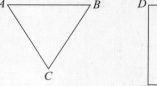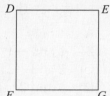

ABC is an equilateral triangle and *DEFG* is a square. If $\overline{AB} = \overline{DE}$, how many different ways can *ABC* be placed in *DEFG* such that two vertices of the triangle coincide with two corners of the square?

(A) 4
(B) 6
(C) 8
(D) 10
(E) 12

19. *G*, *S*, and *T* are three points that lie on a plane. If the distance between *G* and *S* is 9, and the distance between *S* and *T* is 5, which of the following are possible distances between *G* and *T*?

  I. 3
 II. 5
III. 14

(A) I only
(B) II only
(C) I and II only
(D) II and III only
(E) I, II, and III

20.

$B^{\bullet}$

$A^{\bullet}$ $D^{\bullet}$ $^{\bullet}C$

If $\overline{AB} = \overline{BC} = \overline{AC} = 6$, and D is the halfway between A and C, then $\overline{BD} =$

(A) $2\sqrt{3}$

(B) 3

(C) $3\sqrt{3}$

(D) $4\sqrt{2}$

(E) $4\sqrt{3}$

21.

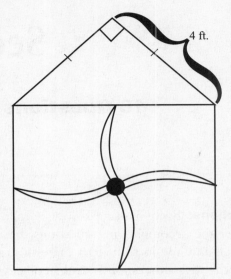

4 ft.

The figure above is the diagram of an industrial fan blade. If the fan's maximum blade speed is 100 revolutions per 10 seconds, what is the greatest distance (in feet) that any point on the blade could travel in 30 seconds?

(A) $100\sqrt{2}\pi$

(B) $200\sqrt{3}\pi$

(C) $600\sqrt{2}\pi$

(D) $600\sqrt{3}\pi$

(E) $1200\sqrt{2}\pi$

STOP Do not proceed to the next section until time is up.

Section 6

16 Questions ■ Time—20 Minutes

Directions: Each passage below is followed by a set of questions. Read each passage, then answer the accompanying questions, basing your answers on what is stated or implied in the passage and any introductory material provided. Mark the letter of your choice on the answer sheet that best corresponds to the correct answer.

Line Frederic Remington (1861–1909) has long been celebrated as one of the most gifted interpreters of the American West. Initially, his western images appeared as
(5) illustrations in popular journals. As he matured, however, Remington turned his attention away from illustration, concentrating instead on painting and sculpture. About 1900 he began a series
(10) of paintings that took as their subject the color of night. Before his premature death in 1909 at age 48, Remington completed more than seventy paintings in which he explored the technical and
(15) aesthetic difficulties of painting darkness.

1. The passage suggests Remington's major artistic accomplishments were

   (A) magazine illustrations.
   (B) sculptures.
   (C) paintings of nocturnal cityscapes.
   (D) paintings of nocturnal landscapes.
   (E) color studies.

Line The question of what counts as literature has been strongly debated over the last few decades both in and out of academia. Some argue that only the test of time
(5) ultimately vindicates a fictional work's claim to the status of literature. Their argument runs like this: if people still read, still reference, still care about a work of fiction decades or even centuries
(10) after its original publication, then that work clearly rises to the auspicious status of literature. Critics of this view, though, point out that this method of determining what is and is not literature by definition
(15) excludes contemporary works from consideration. We do not know, they rightfully contend, if a novel published in the last few years will be read in a hundred years or not. And so they ask,
(20) does this mean we cannot meaningfully discuss whether the work is important, or influential, or of great merit?

2. The author uses the word "vindicates" to emphasize that

(A) all works of fiction claim to be literature.

(B) all works of fiction are, in some sense, literature.

(C) literature is a much more prestigious category than fiction.

(D) the debate regarding what is literature is excessively erudite.

(E) for a work to establish itself as literature is an incredible feat.

3. The argument, given in the passage, against the "test of time" approach is that

(A) it excludes by definition all writing that is not fictional.

(B) it does not take trends in critical interest into account.

(C) it excludes contemporary fiction from the discussion.

(D) it allows contemporary works to be considered alongside the great works of centuries past.

(E) it gives too much weight to popular opinion.

Line   Since the sixteenth century, astronomers have recognized Mars for what it is—a relatively nearby planet not so unlike our own. The fourth planet from the sun and
(5)   Earth's closest neighbor, Mars has been the subject of modern scientists' careful scrutiny with powerful telescopes, deep space probes, and orbiting spacecraft. In 1976, Earth-bound scientists were
(10)   brought significantly closer to their subject of investigation when two Viking probes touched down on that red soil. The possibility of life on Mars, clues to the evolution of the solar system,
(15)   fascination with the chemistry, geology, and meteorology of another planet—

these were considerations that led the National Aeronautics and Space Administration to Mars. Project Viking's goal,
(20)   after making a soft landing on Mars, was to execute a set of scientific investigations that would not only provide data on the physical nature of the planet but also make a first attempt at determining if
(25)   detectable life forms were present.

4. Which of the following does the paragraph most emphasize as the motivation for the Viking trip to Mars?

(A) Fascination with chemistry on another planet.

(B) Four-century-old interest in the planet.

(C) The advancement of space exploration.

(D) Possibility of a space station on Mars.

(E) Possibility of life on Mars.

Questions 5–16 are based on the following two passages.

The following two passages discuss the English and Metric systems of measurement.

Passage 1

Line   It is an oft-repeated tale that the English measurement of the yard was standardized when an English royal stepped into disputes about the measurement's length
(5)   and declared the distance from his shoulder to the tip of his fingers as the standard yard. Unlike many colorful anecdotes from history, this one is true. Early in the twelfth century, the English
(10)   king Henry I established the length of the yard as the distance from the tip of his nose to the tip of his outstretched thumb.

In our scientific age such stories seem earthy at best and ridiculous at worst.

489

(15)   But not all ancient units of measure have such arbitrary origins. The mile is a good example of this. Though the mile is today counted as part of the English system of measurement, the unit dates back to
(20)   ancient Rome. The English word mile derives from the Latin term *mille*, which means one thousand. For the Romans, the *mille* was one thousand paces. A pace was two steps, or five feet roughly. This
(25)   meant the *mille* was 5,000 feet. In medieval Europe, however, the 220-yard furlong became the dominant measurement used. To reconcile the two measurements, the mile was lengthened to be
(30)   eight furlongs. This made the mile 5,280 feet. A sixteenth-century act of Parliament fixed this measurement for the mile.

It is true that the English system of measurement, the system that includes
(35)   the mile, the yard, the foot, and the inch, has a certain quirkiness to it because it has evolved through human history. This quirkiness might irritate scientists, but it is part and parcel of the tradition that
(40)   has been bequeathed, in its accumulated form, to the English-speaking world.

Passage 2

The metric system was conceived by twelve French scientists during the French Revolution. Like many innova-
(45)   tions during the French Revolution, the metric system was formulated as a scientific system that would replace traditional ways of ordering society. The revolutionaries did not see it as a
(50)   coincidence that length was meted in measures based on the size of a medieval king. Instead of these arbitrary standards, the metric system's basic unit of measure, the meter, was based upon the circumfer-
(55)   ence of the Earth. For the meter to be a

manageable size, it was defined as one one-forty-millionth of the Earth's circumference. They employed the word *meter* to harken back to the ancient
(60)   Greek word *metron*, meaning measure.

The rest of the metric system is even less arbitrary in origin. The other metric units of length were generated by either multiplying or dividing the meter by a
(65)   factor of ten. Thus a kilometer is 1000 meters, and a centimeter is one one-hundredths of a meter. It is the great asset of the metric system, at least for scientists, that units for measuring weight and
(70)   energy are also derived from the basic unit of the meter. For instance, weight is measured in grams, which are determined by the weight of one cubic centimeter of water.

(75)   France made use of the metric system compulsory in 1840. Other countries rapidly followed suit. The adoption of the metric system, also known as the international system, or S.I., coincided
(80)   with great advances in science. By 1900, over 35 countries had officially adopted its use. In the United States, the system has been dubbed "voluntary" and "preferred," but has never been made
(85)   compulsory.

The measure of the meter has been refined three times since its conception in 1791. The latest was in 1983 when the speed of light was employed to give the
(90)   greatest precision for the measurement to date. The distance that light travels in a vacuum in 1/299,792,458 of a second is the internationally accepted definition of a meter.

5. What is the author of Passage 1's attitude towards the English system of measurement?

   (A) Emphatic praise
   (B) Qualified acceptance
   (C) Neutrality
   (D) Strong criticism
   (E) Antipathy

6. In Passage 1, the story of Henry I is offered primarily to

   (A) demonstrate that the reader's preconceptions about the English system are wrong.
   (B) illustrate the role of the English monarchy in the development of the English system.
   (C) reveal how far back in time the English system goes.
   (D) provide a concrete example of how the arbitrariness of the English system developed.
   (E) suggest the practicality of the English system.

7. The word "earthy" in line 14 most closely means

   (A) unrefined.
   (B) musky.
   (C) impractical.
   (D) old-fashioned.
   (E) baffling.

8. By "reconcile the two measurements," (line 28–32) the author means

   (A) determine which one was accurate.
   (B) develop a new system of measurement without the inaccuracies of the old.
   (C) settle the public's disagreement over which was better.
   (D) find a metric equivalent.
   (E) cease using two different systems.

9. The author refers to the English system's "accumulated form" line 40–41 primarily to emphasize that the system

   (A) ceased to change once officially adopted.
   (B) derives from a variety of sources.
   (C) stretches back further than reliable written history.
   (D) continues to evolve.
   (E) was adopted wholesale.

10. The authors of the two passages would be most likely to agree that the metric system

   (A) has a shorter but equally interesting history as the English system.
   (B) has a history that reaches back as far as the English system's.
   (C) has a longer history than the history of the English system.
   (D) should not be thought of historically.
   (E) has a history that is equally long but less colorful than the English system's.

491

11. According to Passage 2, the invention of the metric system was

    (A) one of the greatest accomplishments of the French Revolution.
    (B) in contradiction to many of the other goals of the French Revolution.
    (C) a side-effect of the French Revolution's new calendar system.
    (D) one of many anti-traditionalist undertakings of the French Revolution.
    (E) left incomplete at the end of the French Revolution.

12. In the sentence beginning "In the United States. . ." (line 82) the writer suggests that the United States

    (A) has never seriously attempted to implement the metric system.
    (B) is likely to adopt the metric system fairly soon.
    (C) has created official policies regarding use of the metric system.
    (D) has attempted to require use of the metric system, but has been unable to enforce its policies.
    (E) reflects a clear bias for the superiority of the English system.

13. The word "refined" in line 87 most closely means

    (A) processed.
    (B) renegotiated.
    (C) made smaller.
    (D) challenged.
    (E) modified.

14. In Passage 2, the reason for the 1983 definition of the meter is probably that scientists

    (A) have determined that the new meter is a more manageable length.
    (B) have more sophisticated data on the circumference of the earth.
    (C) needed a way to bring the meter's length closer to the yard's.
    (D) have developed more accurate ways to calculate the original fraction.
    (E) wanted to disassociate the meter with the French Revolution.

15. In at least one of the passages all of the following are mentioned EXCEPT

    (A) the kings who ruled during the standardization of measurements.
    (B) the contemporary standing of the measuring system discussed.
    (C) terms from ancient languages.
    (D) the refinement of measurement standards in recent years.
    (E) the cultural heritage of each measuring system.

16. The author of Passage 2 conveys an implicit belief that the

    (A) metric system facilitates scientific endeavors.
    (B) United States has damaged its reputation in the international community by refusing to adopt the metric system.
    (C) metric system is best confined to scientific use.
    (D) French Revolution was a high point in the history of science.
    (E) metric system is a more fitting system for a democratic society.

S T O P Do not proceed to the next section until time is up.

Section 7

13 Questions ■ Time—20 Minutes

Notes:

1. All numbers used are real numbers.

2. All angle measurements can be assumed to be positive unless otherwise noted.

3. All figures lie in the same plane unless otherwise noted.

4. Drawings that accompany questions are intended to provide information useful in answering the question. The figures are drawn closely to scale unless otherwise noted.

Directions for Student Produced Responses

Enter your responses to questions 1–13 in the special grids provided on your answer sheet. Input your answers as indicated in the directions below.

Answer: $\frac{4}{9}$ or 4/9

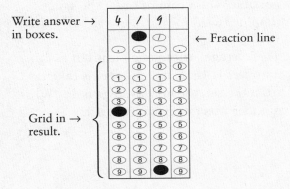

Write answer → in boxes.

← Fraction line

Grid in → result.

Answer: 1.4
Either position is correct.

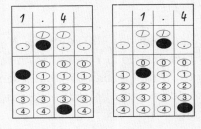

Decimal → point

Note: You may begin your answer in any column, space permitting. Leave blank any columns not needed.

- Writing your answer in the boxes at the top of the columns will help you accurately grid your answer, but it is not required. **You will only receive credit for an answer if the ovals are filled in properly.**

- Only fill in one oval in each column.

GO ON TO THE NEXT PAGE

- If a problem has several correct answers, just grid in one of them.

- There are no negative answers.

- **Never grid in mixed numbers.** The answer $3\frac{1}{5}$ must be gridded as 16/5 or 3.2. If

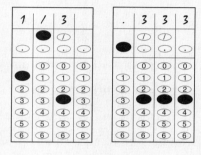

is gridded, it will be read as $\frac{31}{5}$, not $3\frac{1}{5}$.

Decimal Accuracy

Decimal answers must be gridded as accurately as possible. The answer 0.3333 . . . must be gridded as .333.

Less accurate values, such as .33 are not acceptable.

Acceptable ways to grid $\frac{1}{3}$ = .3333 . . .

1. If $2\sqrt{x} + \sqrt{x} = y$ and $2y = 12$, then what does x equal?

2. What is the product of the first five even integers?

3. Rider High has 400 students. A student will be picked at random from the student body. If the probability that a senior would be picked is three-eighths, how many seniors are there?

4.

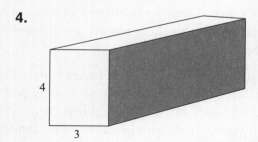

If the area of the striped side of the rectangular solid is 24, what is the volume of the box?

5. If the area of a circle is 16π, what is the diameter of the circle?

6. Lisa has three pizza toppings from which to choose: pepperoni, anchovies, and red peppers. If she can choose as many toppings as three and as few toppings as zero, how many different pizza orders are possible? (Lisa cannot order the same topping twice.)

7. The average (arithmetic mean) of five numbers is 16. If one number is taken from the set, the new average is 14. What number was taken from the set?

494

8.

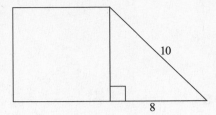

If the figure above is composed of a square and a triangle, what is the area of the square?

9. What is the slope a line that is defined by the following two points, $(-1, -2)$ and $(3,1)$?

10. Tom is twelve years older than Susan, and Susan is three times the age of Gina, and Gina is five years younger than Bo. If Bo is 15, how old is Tom?

11. For all positive integers, let $m*$ equal the greatest prime divisor of m. What does $(15*)(12*)$ equal?

12.

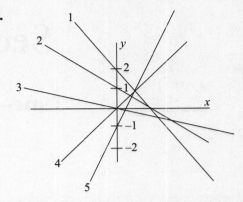

What is the sum of the y-intercepts in the above graph?

13. The sum of four positive distinct prime numbers is 21. What is the greatest possible value of one of those prime numbers?

S T O P   Do not proceed to the next section until time is up.

Section 8

Time—25 Minutes

Consider the following statement.

Innovation is primarily accomplished by an individual, though groups often do work out the details of an individual's innovations.

Assignment: Write an essay in which you argue for or against the preceding statement. Develop your point of view on this statement and be sure to support your stance with sufficient details.

GO ON TO THE NEXT PAGE

PETERSON'S
getting you there

STOP When you are finished with your essay put your pencil down until the time allotted is over.

Answers
and Explanations

Section 1

1. B The passage says that H.R. means House of Representatives and that the number is given according to, "the order it was submitted in a particular session." (lines 12–13) So the 1 means that it was submitted first in a particular session. Choice (B) is the correct answer.

2. C This is a tricky question. The major clue is that only three entities are mentioned in the passage: the House of Representatives, the Senate, and the President. You should suspect then that the answer will be the Senate and the President since those are the only other two entities mentioned in the passage. You can get confirmation for this hunch in the sentence that says "Bills are presented to the President for action when approved in identical form by both the House of Representatives and the Senate." Bills must pass both houses, so if the bills originate in the house, they have to go to the Senate before reaching the President. The answer is (C).

3. A The paragraph is about how Native Americans have "long recognized and celebrated the connectedness among all natural things." The medicine wheel illustrates this point because it emphasizes the connectedness of the four basic elements. So (A) is the best choice.

4. E Remember the Native American view stated in the passage is that all natural things are connected; so we should expect that the scenario will demonstrate this belief. (A) is specifically opposed to that. (C) is also, to a lesser degree. (B) is neutral toward the Native American idea—it neither contradicts it nor realizes it. (D) and (E) are in accord with the Native American view because they recognize the connectedness of an organism and its habitat. However, (D) mention studying a specific organism in its habitat, while (E) mentions studying a habitat as a whole. So, (E) is broader and, in this case, broader is better. The best answer is (E).

5. **C** Does the author portray Copland's music in a very negative or very positive light? Neither, so (A) and (E) are out. The author actually just describes the reactions of others to Copland's music and interjects little opinion of his or her own. That eliminates (D). Then again, the author is not *clinically objective* in tone (just think, the passage does not sound like a science passage). That makes (C) the best choice.

6. **C** The virtuoso passages are passages only a virtuoso could play—essentially, difficult. Eliminate (E). There is no negative judgment of that quality in the passage. That eliminates all but (C), which is the answer.

7. **C** The different fates were that the *Piano Variation* was known by many pianists, but played by few in concert, and the *Symphonic Ode* was largely unknown because it was too difficult. Choice (C) says as much, and so is the answer.

8. **A** In the passage, Koussevitzky is first mentioned in connection to the difficulty of playing the *Symphonic Ode*. The passage tells you that even he, a "champion" of Copland's music, did not conduct the piece until it had been simplified. Choice (A) correctly points this out. Don't be tricked by the difficult name into answering that he was European.

9. **C** The second paragraph begins, "Perhaps as a reaction to the performance problems of the *Symphonic Ode*, Copland's next two orchestral works deal in shorter units of time." So the author thinks that the pieces immediately subsequent to the *Symphonic Ode* were made shorter because the Ode was not being performed. Choice (C) says the same. (B) is tempting but the passage explicitly states that it was the length and not the complexity that Copland adjusted in the subsequent pieces.

10. **E** This sentence is essentially saying that, although brief, these works were also very difficult to perform. The answer is (E). This is essentially a vocabulary question, asking you to define "agile."

11. **C** First off, what does the passage state about Copland's views of the Americas and music? It says that Copland, "envisioned 'American music' as being music of the Americas." In other words, he thought they were related, or should be. (A), (B), and (E) run contrary to this meaning. (D) is irrelevant. The answer is (C).

12. **D** The Mexican material is more accessible to audiences. The opposite of accessible is inaccessible. (D) should look good to you right away. Don't get confused by (C). The emphasis in the sentence is on audiences, not musicians.

13. **C** You can eliminate (B) because it is too specific. You can eliminate (D) because the author never talks about eating or brushing teeth or other daily activities. (E) is also too specific. (A) is really off in emphasis; the author focuses on describing the Earth's appearance more than the trajectory of the Space Station. The answer is (C). It's also a good answer because it captures a little bit of the tone of the piece; the author seems to write the passage for an average person experiencing curiosity about seeing the Earth from space.

14. **E** The second half of the paragraph contrasts seeing the whole Earth to seeing just a limited part of it. But the emphasis is on seeing the whole Earth, because we've all seen limited parts of it. The answer is (E).

15. **B** Here you have to be careful because two different window views are discussed in the passage. The downward-facing window is discussed in the second half of the second paragraph. And there the author compares the view to looking at a big blue beach ball up-close, choice (B).

16. **B** This is where that second window view comes in. The author first discusses the downward-facing window and then contrasts it with looking through a sideward-facing window in the third paragraph. (B) is the answer.

17. **B** The passage discusses the "faint glow" in the last sentence of the third paragraph. There, he attributes it to the outer rim of the atmosphere. (B) says the same thing. (A) mentions the atmosphere, but it designates the wrong part of the atmosphere.

18. **B** Before the thought exercise is given the author states that, "a good way to imagine our view is to stand up and look down at your feet." In "imagining the view" through the thought exercise the reader gets a definite idea of the proportions of things within the space stations view (e.g. where San Francisco is in relation to Denver). Choice (B) says as much, and so is the best answer. Choice (C) is a tempting answer, because it is the idea with which the paragraph begins, but it ends up being too narrow a description of the thought exercise.

19. **D** You may be tempted to answer (A), because the passage can be confusing. But it's not dry or scientific, so "technical" just isn't a good word for it. Choice (B) doesn't capture it's informality. Choice (E) is too extreme—as far as poetic descriptions of the planet go, this one doesn't even rate. That leaves (C) and (D). Choice (C) isn't quite right, either, because it's not irreverent, it's just casual. Choice (D) best captures that sense.

20. **D** You don't know a lot about what the astronauts do from the passage, so you'll have to dig this answer up. Choice (A) seems silly, and would really be a disrespectful thing to say about the author. The SAT won't do that. So eliminate (A). There's no reference to gravity in the passage, so eliminate (B). There's no real reference to physical activity, so (C) seems wrong. You are left with (D) and (E). The astronaut uses a lot of numbers, and throws them around as though they were quite easy. (D) seems like a reasonable answer. There's no reference in the passage to *communication procedures*, which means you can eliminate (E) even though it's sort of a tempting answer.

Section 2

1. **C** This is the first question, so it should be one of the easiest, if not the easiest, questions in the section. For this reason, you don't have to expect anything too tricky about this problem. Substitute $x = -y$ into the first equation and solve for x:

$$x + 4y = 3$$
$$-y + 4y = 3$$
$$3y = 3$$
$$\frac{3y}{3} = \frac{3}{3}$$
$$y = 1$$

(C) is the answer.

2. **B** There are two main parts to this problem:

1. the use of the variable d, and

2. the change of units from hours to minutes.

Start with the variable since d is half as much as 2d, it should take him half the amount of time, or 1.5 hours. One hour is 60 minutes, and half an hour is 30 minutes, so 1.5 hours is 90 minutes. That's choice (B).

3. A There is more than one way to solve this problem, but all paths involve manipulating the equation. You can solve for f in the first equation, and then plug that value into the second equation. You could also just leave the $3f$ as is, and monkey with the formula this way:

$$3f + 15 = 27$$
$$3f + 15 - 15 = 27 - 15$$
$$3f = 12$$
$$3f - 6 = 12 - 6$$
$$3f - 6 = 6$$

Whichever path you take, if you manipulate the equation correctly you'll get choice (A) as your answer.

4. A The first thing to notice is that this triangle is a 30-60-90 triangle, one of the SAT's favorite triangles. Since you can read off the relationships between different sides of a 30-60-90 triangle, it can be readily seen that the $x + y$ side is half the length of the hypotenuse (which is 14). Half of 14 is 7, so (A) is the answer.

5. D Translating the English into algebra is the key to all word problems.

Since the snack costs twenty cents less than the drink, you can write down $d - 20 = s$. Since a snack and drink together costs \$1.30, you also know that $s + d = 130$. You have two equations and two variables. Substitute the first equation into the second and then solve:

$$s + d = 130$$
$$(d - 20) + d = 130$$
$$2d - 20 = 130$$
$$2d - 20 + 20 = 130 + 20$$
$$2d = 150$$
$$\frac{2d}{2} = \frac{150}{2}$$
$$d = 75$$

A drink costs 75 cents (\$0.75), so (D) is the answer.

Tip

For problems dealing with units of money, always decide whether you want to work in dollars or cents. If the amount of money is great, using dollars is typically the best way to go. On this problem, converting to cents might work better since you won't have to deal with any decimals.

6. D This problem looks really complicated, but don't let that ruffle your test feathers. With function problems, just plug in whatever the problem tells you to plug into the equation. Be a machine! Here, you are considering when $x = 2$, so $f(2x)$ is the same thing as $f(4)$. (Of course, the question could have just said $x = 4$, but that would have been too easy).

Now just replace every x in the problem with a 4:

$$f(x) = x + x^x$$
$$f(4) = 4 + 4^4$$
$$f(4) = 4 + 256$$
$$f(4) = 260$$

Your answer is (D).

7. D This one looks strange, and it is as straightforward to solve as it appears. If you only consider $\sqrt{x^2}$ to be x, then you only get the extraneous solution, and not the correct one. You start by squaring both sides and then factoring.

$$x^2 = 4x^2 + 12x + 9$$
$$0 = 3x^2 + 12x + 9$$
$$0 = 3(x^2 + 4x + 3)$$
$$0 = x^2 + 4x + 3$$
$$0 = (x + 3)(x + 1)$$
$$x = -3 \text{ or } x = -1$$

Checking both solutions in the original equation, you see that only $x = -1$ works. This is choice (D).

8. E If $|x + 1| > |y|$, what do you know about x and y? Not much actually. x could be -10 and y could be 5, and the inequality would be true. But x could also be 10,000 and y could be 9,998, and the inequality would still be true. This means you cannot nail down the relationship between x and y, so (E) is the answer.

9. A This question is almost all Math Speak, but hopefully you are getting better at this language. The whole thing sets up an equation. "Percent" means "divide by 100," and "is the same value" works the same as an equal sign. "What number" is Math Speak for "place a variable here." Here's the translation:

"75 percent of 104 is the same value as 60 percent of what number"

$$\left(\frac{75}{100}\right)(104) = \left(\frac{60}{100}\right)n$$
$$(0.75)(104) = 0.6n$$
$$78 = 0.6n$$
$$\frac{78}{0.6} = \frac{0.6n}{0.6}$$
$$130 = n$$

Choice (A) is the answer.

> **Note**
>
> The percentages were rewritten as decimals instead of fractions to make it easier to use your calculator. Dividing 78 by 0.6 is not something most people can do easily, but for a calculator, it's a cinch.

10. D Equations of lines can be put into the $y = mx + b$ form, and then the y-intercept, b, can be read off.

$$3y - x = 12$$
$$3y - x + x = 12 + x$$
$$3y = x + 12$$
$$\frac{3y}{3} = \frac{x}{3} + \frac{12}{3}$$
$$y = \frac{x}{3} + 4$$

If 4 is the y-intercept, and twice this number is 8, choice (D).

11. **C**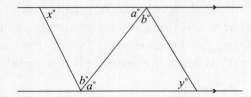

As you can see from this figure $a = a$, and $b = b$ because alternate interior angles are congruent. If two angles of a triangle are congruent to two angles of another triangle, what can you deduce about the relationship between the third angles? The third angles must also be congruent. If you don't see this, pick values for a and b and remember that the sum of the mesures of the interior angles of a triangle is 180. Choice (C) is the answer.

12. **D** These next three problems test your ability to deal with unfamiliar symbols. Recall that you will be told everything that you need to know about the new symbol. Carefully read the instructions and don't get rattled; everything you need to know about the new symbol will be handed to you on a platter.

In the subtraction problem, convert each term one at a time:

$\in 2323 = 3322$ and $\in 2321 = 1322$

(It's helpful if you write out the middle unchanging middle digits first, and then write the first and last digits.)

So $\in 2323 - \in 2321 = 3322 - 1322 = 2000$, choice (D).

13. **A** You know that A is a two-digit number between 10 and 20, which narrows the field of possible answers to 11, 12, 13, 14, 15, 16, 17, 18, and 19. This may seem like a lot, but the second part of the problem will narrow things down. The equation $(\in A)^2 = \in(A^2)$ looks confusing, but the key word is "equation." The two values are equal, even though you've flipped the first and last digits. Flipping 19 makes 91, which is quite a difference, and it's highly unlikely that $19^2 = 91^2$.

At this point, you might suspect that 11 was the answer because reversing the digits does not change the value of the number. That is a good suspicion, and if you see it, you can easily read off that (A) is the answer. If you did not have that suspicion, just dive into the problem trying different choices.

14. E Since each variable is a digit and the inequality is true, plug in some numbers to try to make the smallest difference possible:

$$A > B > C > D > E$$
$$5 > 4 > 3 > 2 > 1$$

Now look at the subtraction problem and plug in the numbers above:

$$ABCD - \in(ABCD) = 5432 - 2435 = 2977$$

The difference is greater than one thousand, so choice (E) is the answer.

> **Note**
>
> There is a theoretical path that leads to the same answer on this problem, but when dealing with weird symbols problems the theoretical path is usually not the best one to take. As you can see, generating some numbers and then placing them into the equation works well and didn't take too long.

15. C There's no answer choice that says, "It cannot be determined," so you have to realize that there is a way to determine the area of the circle. Since the area formula for a circle is $A = \pi r^2$ this means there has to be a way to find the radius of the circle, which in this case is line segment RS.

The two statements underneath the drawing give you the tools you need. If "line q is tangent to circle R," then angle RST is a right angle. And if $RS = \dfrac{RT}{3}$, then you can determine the value of RS since the problem gives you the length of $\overline{RT}$ as 18. For line segment RS, the radius will be 6, since $\dfrac{18}{3} = 6$. If you place this value of the radius into the area formula for a circle, you'll find answer (C) at the end.

$$A = \pi r^2$$
$$A = \pi 6^2$$
$$A = 36\pi$$

16. E All of the answer choices mention August and September total sales, so the first step in this problem is to figure out what these values are. In the table, August has two squares (1,000 each) and three triangles (50 returns each), so total August sales are:

$$2(1,000) - 3(50) = 2000 - 150 = 1,850$$

Doing the same box-and-triangle conversion, you should find that September total sales were 1950. Therefore, there were 100 more sales in September than in August. This lets you cross out (B) and (D), because they have September total sales as being *less* than August total sales.

The final three answers all have different percentages. The difference in monthly sales is 100 (1950 − 1850), so what percent of 1,850 is 100?

$$\left(\frac{n}{100}\right)1850 = 100$$

$$(100)\left(\frac{n}{100}\right)1850 = 100(100)$$

$$1850n = 10000$$

$$\frac{1850n}{1850} = \frac{10000}{1850}$$

$$n = 5.4$$

100 is 5.4 percent of 1850, which means that September total sales were 5.4 percent greater than August total sales. (E) says the same and is the correct answer.

17. C You cannot solve this problem unless you do some creative line drawing.

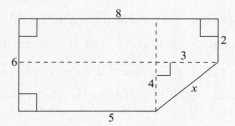

To find the unknown lengths, you have to subtract known values of opposites. Take the top and bottom sides, for instance. The larger top side is 8, and the lower part is 5, so the difference must be 3. A dashed line shows this value. Subtracting the right side (length 2) from the left side (length 6), you find another dashed line that has a value of 4.

From this sketch you can see that *x* is the hypotenuse of a 3-4-5 triangle, and so is equal to 5. This means the perimeter is 26, (C).

18. **A** Unpack the tangle of terms, and you'll find the answer. You are looking for two prime numbers that:

1. When you subtract them you get 21.

2. When you multiply them you get one of the answer choices.

It might not sound like enough information to find the answer, but it is. None of the answer choices are very great, so one or both of the prime numbers must be less than ten. If the two primes were greater, their product would not be as small as the answer choices. The difference between the two primes is 21, which means that one of the prime numbers must be small. Good candidates for the lesser prime are 2, 3, or 5.

Prime numbers starting in the 20s are 23, 29, 31, and 37. Use a little trial and error, and you'll realize that the difference between 23 and 2 is 21. Those are the two primes. What is 2 times 23? The answer is 46, choice (A).

19. **B** First, it always helps to draw a quick sketch of the scenario to get a better grasp on what is being asked.

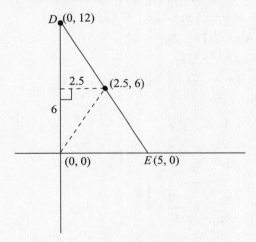

The first thing to determine is the midpoint of $\overline{DE}$, which you can do by using the midpoint formula:

$$\left(\frac{x_1 + x_2}{2}, \frac{y_1 + y_2}{2}\right) = \left(\frac{0 + 5}{2}, \frac{12 + 0}{2}\right) = \left(\frac{5}{2}, \frac{12}{2}\right) = (2.5, 6)$$

You can keep the x-value as a fraction if you like, but converting it to 2.5 will make it easier to punch into your calculator.

Looking at the dashed lines, you can see a right triangle with its hypotenuse from the origin to the midpoint of *DE*. It has sides of 2.5 and 6. Placing those values into the Pythagorean theorem yields:

$$a^2 + b^2 = c^2$$
$$2.5^2 + 6^2 = c^2$$
$$6.25 + 36 = c^2$$
$$42.25 = c^2$$
$$\sqrt{42.25} = \sqrt{c}$$
$$6.5 = c$$

It's choice (B).

20. A It's a big equation, but in the end it's just that: an equation. You have to pull out two different techniques—FOIL and PEMDAS—to solve it, but so long as you write out your work carefully, you will reach the right answer.

$$-b^2 = (b - 7)(b + 3) - (2b + 2)(b + 5)$$
$$-b^2 = (b^2 + 3b - 7b - 21) - (2b^2 + 10b + 2b + 10)$$
$$-b^2 = (b^2 - 4b - 21) - (2b^2 + 12b + 10)$$
$$-b^2 = b^2 - 4b - 21 - 2b^2 - 12b - 10$$
$$-b^2 = -b^2 - 16b - 31$$
$$-b^2 + b^2 = -b^2 + b^2 - 16b - 31$$
$$0 = -16b - 31$$
$$0 + 16b = -16b + 16b - 31$$
$$16b = -31$$
$$\frac{16b}{16} = \frac{-31}{16}$$
$$b = -\frac{31}{16} = -1\frac{15}{16}$$

Choice (A) is your answer.

21. A There's no table given for this question, so it's up to you to create one. In this respect it's like a diagram without a diagram given: You could conceivably answer it without the visual aids, but it's much easier with them.

For the table, start with the years:

1950 1960 1970 1980 1990 2000

Now place the number of people in Cree County in 1950 in the appropriate place, and then start multiplying by three.

1950 1960 1970 1980   1990 2000
1000 3000 9000 27000

In the 1980s, the population fell by one-half, so divide 27,000 by 2. Then go back to multiplying by 3.

1950 1960 1970 1980   1990   2000
1000 3000 9000 27000 13,500 40,500

Your answer is choice (A).

Section 3

1. A Something that can be counted requires "fewer" rather than "less." The answer is (A).

2. B In *for Ada and I*, *I* is used here as the object of a preposition (*for*). That should never be. *Me* is the object of a preposition, or a direct or indirect object. The answer is (B).

3. B Is the subject in this sentence singular or plural? *Team* is singular. Is the verb singular or plural? *Compete* is plural. The clause *which is comprised of four cyclists* obscures the subject-verb disagreement, but it is still there. (B) is the answer.

4. E Did you hear any mistakes in this sentence? Hopefully you didn't because there are not any. (E) is the answer.

5. A If you know that Louis and Clark were nineteenth-century explorers, the verb *have surveyed* might sound strange even before you read the rest of the sentence. If not, *were well prepared* suggests that the first exploration happened prior to an event which is, itself, in the past. The first verb should be *had surveyed*, and the answer is (A).

6. D There is a parallel structure problem here. *Focus*, a verb, should be paired with *follow up*, a verb, not *follow-up*, which is a noun. The answer is (D).

7. C Nothing in this sentence sounds wrong, but (E) is not the answer. Here's why, to whom does the *its* refer? It is not clear if it refers to the Ottoman or Austrian Empire. An ambiguous pronoun reference is an error, and so (C) is the answer.

8. A What is the subject, *census* (singular) or *statistics* (plural)? *Statistics*. *Census* is used as an adjective. The plural subject means you would need a plural verb, *were*. The answer is (A).

9. B *Scarcely no one* is a double negative. It should be *scarcely anyone*. (B) is the answer.

10. D This is a tricky question because the error arises with the implied part of the sentence. The full sentence with the implied part written out explicitly reads, "Even though he had the title of Vice-President of Operations, his duties and responsibilities were not much greater than a midlevel manager's duties and responsibilities." The short version should still say *manager's*. The answer is (D).

11. D After both, you especially need parallel structure. It should read *more accessible and more understandable*. The other answers only confuse the original. The answer is (D).

12. D The initial modifier should put you on the lookout for an incorrect noun, or reference to the "thing" that is being modified. You should examine the noun that directly follows the modifier carefully. Does the modifier modify the noun that follows it? Nope. The poet, Gerard Manley Hopkins, not his poems, is what is being modified here. The possessive form (*Hopkins's*) and the noun *poems* messes things up in the original and answer choices (A), (B), and (C). To make it work, you need to get rid of the possessive on the author's name. Only (D) and (E) do that. (E) makes an unnecessary change to the verb. The better answer is (D).

13. E The original underlined phrase is not glaringly obtuse or a grammatical disaster, but it is a little wordy. Also, *this includes the Human Rights Commission* is a complete sentence, so it would need to be attached with a semicolon. Only (E) addresses both problems without creating others.

14. C The most blatant mistake here is that, again, the clause that follows a comma is technically a complete sentence. The best way to approach this question is to read all the way through each of the answers to see if they contain problems. (B) has tense problems. (D) also has two complete sentences attached by a comma (this is called a comma splice). (E) just doesn't work. The answer is (C).

15. B The underlined portion of the sentence reads awkwardly for two reasons. First, it includes the phrase *her plans of*, which is redundant because the list is a list of her plans. Second, the preceding plans in the list are given in infinitive form (i.e. *to refinance*), but the last plan of action is not in infinitive form. Any answer choice that deals with these two issues will be the best choice. (B) is that answer choice.

16. B You know the correct answer won't be a complete sentence, because it is attached by a comma to the main clause. Eliminate (E). You will also want to cut down on wordiness, rather than add to it. Eliminate (A) and (C). *Which* suggests that the clause modifies a noun that comes just before it. That isn't the case. The answer is (B).

17. C Again, you want to move toward parallel structure as much as possible. You don't want nouns in one part of the list and verbs in another, as you have now. Change the noun *tolerance* to a verb, *tolerate*. You can narrow the field to (C) and (E). (E) is wrong because you don't use a comma in a two-items list.

18. D Guess what? Parallel structure again. *To commit a crime* needs to be followed by *(to) conceal it*. That leaves (D), without you even having to know that *among* suggests more than two people, whereas *between* suggests two.

19. C Here's the test writers' other favorite trick: "not only" with "but also." Only (C) and (E) use this construction. (E) makes the tenses unnecessarily complex. The answer is (C).

20. D The sentence as it stands is muddy and unnecessarily wordy. These are things to be avoided in good writing. "If" should be followed by a "then" clause. What follows here doesn't fit that logical pattern. So *if* is out. That leaves (D) and (E). (D) gets rid of the repetitive and vague *it* in the second part of the sentence. Good. The answer is (D).

21. D The original version should wave a red flag at you that it is repetitive and cumbersome and will need to be changed. (B) is even more vague and wordy than the original, despite being a single sentence. (C) is weak because it begins the essay with the word *it*, which is never a strong opener. (E) is suspect because the essay is about the word *modern* not *modernity*. (Yes, modernity is later introduced, but that does not change the point that the essay is about the word *modern*.) (E) is also unnecessarily wordy. That leaves (D).

22. B   Descartes is the thing that will link the two sentences. He is the subject of the first and the object of the second. This is a prime example of when to use *whom*. (B) is better than (C) and the others are longer than the original, not shorter. (B) is the answer.

23. E   What is the logical connection between the opinions of academics other than philosophers and the opinions of historians in particular? The latter is an example of the former. The answer is (E).

24. B   The original sentence is clunky because it has both *beginning of modernity* and *beginning of modern times*. You will want to replace the second with *it*. That leaves (B) and possibly (E). (E) adds unhelpful extra verbiage in other places, so (B) is the best answer.

25. E   Anything separated by commas should be detachable from the rest of the sentence. Remove the phrase between commas and you get *Most of us. . . we are thinking*. Bad. Most of us *think*. (E) is the only answer that addresses that problem correctly. (B) actually changes the sense by eliminating the subject of "think" so that it becomes a command.

26. B   Choices (C) and (E) have an imprecise and unclear −*ing* verb, so eliminate them. (D) is just a wordier alternative to (B), so eliminate it. (B) is so straightforward and clear that it is better than the original. The answer is (B).

27. E   The passage is talking about the 1920s. Be as specific as possible, without being wordy as in (C) and (D). The answer is (E).

28. C   The only punctuation marks that are possible here are parentheses, a semicolon or a colon. The second sentence gives more specific information to elaborate on the first sentence, so a colon is better than a semicolon or parentheses. The answer is (C).

29. D   What's wrong with the transition in the original? Is it a logical problem or a grammatical problem? It sounds weird and wordy, so it's a grammatical problem. The sense is logical, so keep it. Eliminate (A); it changes the sense. Which of the answers simplifies and clarifies the grammar? The answer is (D).

30. A   Eliminate (D) because it's grammatically incorrect. Eliminate (C) because it really doesn't go with the ideas in the passage. If you look back at the passage, you'll see that the last sentence is not about Macy's but Bloomingdales. (E) would be out of place, so eliminate it. You're left with (A) and (B). While (B) would be an adequate conclusion to the third paragraph, only (A) reflects back over the entire passage. The best answer is (A).

514

Section 4

1. D Jerome does not indulge much. He is an *ascetic*, (D). A *teetotaler*, (B), is someone who does not consume alcohol. A *gourmand*, (C), is someone who indulges a great deal in fine food. Neither (A) nor (E) have anything to do with indulgence.

2. A Begin with the first blank, since you know that it must be something negative since protests were planned. (B) and (D) are not negative, so eliminate them. Going to the second blank, *organized* fits well, while *negotiated* and *theorized* do not (you don't *theorize* about a protest event). This makes (A) the best answer.

3. B We know the first word will be negative, since it engendered criticism. All of the words are negative, so you can't eliminate anything yet. But what would a politician be if he "seized a ceremony" having to do with a "girl's tragic death to speak out against his opponent"? Not militaristic, or unreceptive, certainly not passive or defeatist. The answer is (B).

4. E All of the options in this question have a first word that could be something one software did to another. For the second word, all the choices, except (D), are things a user could likely do to software. *Preclude*, (A), means make something impossible, but the "prior version" clearly isn't impossible so eliminate (A). If the older version is *outdone*, you don't want to *implement*, or use, it. Eliminate (B). If something is *infected*, you don't want to *disregard* it, so eliminate (C). The answer is (E). *Supercede* means replace by being better, which would mean you could throw out, or *discard*, the now useless thing.

5. B Let's start with the first blank since it has to be paired with *long*. Which of the first answer choices pairs well with long? Only *storied*, *exemplary*, and *reputable* do (the others either are awkward or don't fit with the meaning of the sentence). Plug in the second answer choices of (A), (B), and (E) into the sentence. Can poetry initiate the dignity of humanity? No. Eliminate (A). Can it articulate, or express? Definitely. Choice (B) sounds too good to pass up.

6. C You should have a good sense of what kind of word goes in each blank because each blank has a pair. The second blank has a more obvious pair, so start with it. Which of the second answer choices goes with speedy? (A) and (C) are the best candidates. On the first blank, does *intricate* and *laborious* or *fragile* and *laborious* sound better? *Intricate* does because it provides a better contrast with the second half of the sentence. (Also, it is strange to speak of a surgery being *fragile*; someone in surgery might be in *fragile* health, but the surgery itself would not be *fragile*.) (C) is the answer.

7. A *Despite* at the beginning of the sentence is the main clue to unlocking the blank. You need one positive word and one negative word. Eliminate (B) and (C). Now what can clans do to each other? *Assist,* possibly *discount.* A problem is ameliorated, not a person or group of people. (A) is the better answer, especially since "feud" and "clan" are both words that seem to refer to the past.

8. B From the structure of the sentence, we can see that the word in the blank goes along with *humor* and *merriment.* Which of the answer choices fits with these two positive words? Only (B), *mirth,* does. (*Irony, history,* and *mystery,* are at best neutral terms in this context, not positive.)

9. A The Latin makes this sentence complicated. You can combat this by replacing the Latin words with the letters (A) and (B) in your head (i.e. although (A) has more subspecies than (B) . . .). The *although* is the key to the logic of the sentence structure. *Although* (A) has more subspecies than (B), (B) has greater numbers. (A) and (E) match this pre-guess for the first blank. (E) isn't really logical (how can a region be ominous?), so the answer is (A).

10. D Looking at the first blank, (B) and (E) can be eliminated because both are not conventional English. That leaves (A), (C), and (D). (A) is suspect, though, because *progression* is an odd word choice for the context. (C) is illogical. (D) is a best choice because it flows well in both blanks and because development is already a word you associate with "pregnancy" and "fetus."

11. C The word, *Though,* tells you that the ideals and the practices of the organization are at odds. So if the ideals are *outward-focused* then the practice must be inward-focused. Which of the answer choices matches this pre-guess? Only (C), *insular* (isolated, circumscribed), does. Hermetic means tightly sealed. It's not too far off in meaning, but it doesn't refer to group behavior.

12. B On the first blank we know that the word goes with *base,* and we know that the prosecuting attorney is probably not saying nice things about the defendant. (A) and (B) fit this (*motley* doesn't; even though it has a negative connotation, it means a random or ungainly assortment). This leaves *misunderstanding* the testimonials or *misconstruing* the testimonials, for the second blank. The latter is a better choice since the prosecuting attorney is more likely to be making the defendant sound bad on purpose than by mistake.

516

13. B This sentence is either really positive or really negative about the new drug regime. It is more likely positive since a new drug wouldn't come out if it was known to be really negative. So your inclination should be that the blank is very positive. Only (B) fits this, and it fits well. If you have extra time, you can check to see if there is a really negative response that might fit better. *Bane* could work in terms of meaning, but it doesn't work syntactically.

14. C The blanks in this sentence are a little more complicated because they must be considered together. The first blank is negative and the second blank is even more negative (in the same way, or to a greater degree). The second blank isn't negative in (A) and (D), so they are not it. That leaves (B), (C), and (E). Of the three, (C) is the best since *self-centered* and *egocentric* are synonyms and *solipsism* is a more negative form of both words. You might be tempted to go with (B) because you don't know what solipsistic means, but you can eliminate it because *ill-tempered* has little to do with *self-centered*.

15. B What is a good pre-guess for the blank? Really hectic (that is, opposite of *alleviating demands upon our time*). Only (B) matches this pre-guess, and it fits in the flow of the sentence.

16. A This is a global question since it cannot be answered by looking at one specific place in the text but has to be weighed considering the passage as a whole. Ask yourself, does the author present Dr. Rael positively or negatively, sympathetically or unsympathetically? The article describes Dr. Rael's career, generally in positive terms, and no criticisms of Dr. Rael's work is discussed. So the answer should be positive. That eliminates (C)—(E). (B) might seem appealing, but realize that an article can *engage* a person's work without being positive about that work. Also the passage more tells about Dr. Rael's work than *engages* it. So (A) is the best choice.

17. C Again this is a global question. To rephrase the question, what is the passage about? It tells the story of Dr. Rael's life with specific emphasis on his professional career. Choice (C) captures this. You might have been attracted by (E), but remember the passage only discusses the Rael family when it contributes to the story of Dr. Rael.

18. B You can answer this either as a detail question or as a global question; you will get the answer more quickly if you answer it as a detail question. You can find in paragraph 3 that "José Ignacio had the foresight to recognize the changes that were coming with the increasing Americanization of New Mexico and realized that a fluent knowledge of English. . . would be necessary." Choices (B) and (D) seem to echo this sentence. But the passage does not go on to say that Dr. Rael did not learn English. The answer is (B). If you answer it as a global question, use the process of elimination. The passage doesn't mention job discrimination. The passage refers to Rael studying far from his family, but doesn't mention that problem in regard to teaching. It strongly suggests that Rael was successful in American schools with English names, so eliminate (D). The passage doesn't specify what Rael studied before his Ph.D. Choices (C) and (E) are hard to eliminate, but an overall view of the passage should convey that the folklore was precious and disappearing.

19. E Relinquished means he gave something up, but the passage does not state that Rael was *relieved* to give up his family duties. Eliminate (D). There is no mention of sibling rivalry, so you can eliminate (A). The passage doesn't say if the family was wealthy or simply OK, so (B) is out. It certainly doesn't say Rael had tried to be a rancher, choice (C). That leaves (E).

20. E This question is similar to question 18, but it is definitely a global question. The basic gist of the passage is that Rael's work was important. He collected Spanish-language folklore and studied the particular Spanish used in the area. The answer is (E).

21. C Someone you study under is your mentor. This is a vocabulary question. The answer is (C).

22. B Corpus refers to a body of work. The only answer choice that reflects the idea of more than one book is (B).

23. B Looking over the choices, there is no reference to Dr. Rael enjoying working on the ranch (or using his scholarly pursuits to avoid it, which would already be using logic too strained for the SAT). The passage does mention his love of *Pastores*. Just after the mention of *Pastores*, the passage says this influenced his later work. Bingo. The answer is (B).

24. A This is a tough one. But "diffusion of motifs" seems to be related to the number of variants of a particular story. That eliminates (C) and (E). The passage goes on to emphasize how many variants there were, suggesting that the answer will emphasize difference more than sameness. Eliminate (B) and (D). The answer is (A).

25. B If you do not know the definition of *provenance* you are not lost on this one. Replace it with each of the answer choices and see which one makes the most sense. If you do know the definition of *provenance* (origin), then (B) pops out as the answer.

26. D The end of the seventh paragraph states, "But inevitably the historic-geographic approach led more to collection building than to analysis." This is the most critical sentence in the passage. The answer (D) includes the word "analysis" and is a fair paraphrase of this sentence. The answer is (D).

27. B This one is also hard. First of all, do you know what *formidable* and *quixotic* mean? Impressive, difficult, and errant—which is to say, traveling a lot. This comes from Don Quixote, who traveled a lot. He was also a little crazy, which is why the test writers try to trick you with (A) and (C). But these don't apply to Dr. Rael. Remember, the overall tone is "laudatory." (E) tries to trick you by getting you to admit that you were confused at this point in the passage. Admitting you don't know will never be the answer on the SAT. The answer is (B).

Section 5

1. A The wrinkle in this word problem is correctly translating what a "quarter" of the factory's capacity means. A quarter is one-fourth of something, so a quarter of full capacity—200 sheets of paper per second—is one-fourth of 200, or 50. If a quarter-capacity is 50 sheets per second, in 12 seconds the factory would produce 600 sheets since $50 \times 12 = 600$. Choice (A) is what's going on.

2. E This is a straightforward variable/equation substitution problem. If $Z = 3$ and $Z = \dfrac{2x}{5}$, then you substitute the value of 3 for Z in the second equation to get:

$$Z = \frac{2x}{5}$$

$$3 = \frac{2x}{5}$$

$$(5)3 = \frac{2x}{5}(5)$$

$$15 = 2x$$

$$\frac{15}{2} = \frac{2x}{2}$$

$$\frac{15}{2} = x$$

(E) is the answer.

3. A There are two prime ways to approach this problem. You can do a factor tree for both numbers, find the common factors, and then look down the answer list for the greatest one. If you don't know what a "factor tree" is, you could go through the answer choices one by one to see which is the greatest that divides 32 and 42. Start with choice (E), since it's the greatest number, and if it works, it's the answer. 12 doesn't work, so try the next greatest one, 8, choice (D). Eight doesn't work, and neither does 6 or 3. This leaves (A).

4. B If you understand the idea of slope, the answer will fall into your lap. If you have trouble with this problem, review pages 350–352 in the Math section to make sure you are perfectly comfortable with slope and linear equations in the form $y = mx + b$.

Viewed from left to right, the line descends, which means the slope is negative.
That eliminates choices (C), (D), and (E). A slope is "rise over run," meaning you look at the change in y-values as the numerator of the fraction, while the change in x-values is the denominator. The line drops two points along the y-axis for every three points it moves over on the x-axis, so the slope is $-\frac{2}{3}$, choice (B).

5. E You need to know the total number of students in each grade to answer this question. The table tells you there are 32 in the 4th grade, so you only need to determine the total in the 3rd grade. There are 16 boys and 14 girls in the 3rd grade, which makes 30 total. The overall total is 32 plus 30, which is 62, choice (E).

Note

The table is incomplete, but don't let this worry you. The SAT will always provide the information needed to answer the question, one way or another.

6. D If there are 18 girls in the 4th grade, then there are 14 boys in 4th grade ($32 - 18 = 14$). The table says there are 16 boys in 3rd grade, so there are a total of 30 ($16 + 14 = 30$) in the 3rd and 4th grade. Choice (D) is the answer.

520

7. A   Careful here. The problem asks for the value of the exponent, not the simplified expression. Simplifying this expression looks a little wiggy, but you need to be prepared to work with wacky-looking exponents problems like this:

$$\frac{\left(m^{\frac{3}{4}}\right)^{-2}}{m^{\frac{5}{4}}} = \frac{1}{m^{\frac{5}{4}}\left(m^{\frac{3}{4}}\right)^{2}} = \frac{1}{m^{\frac{5}{4}}m^{\frac{3}{4}}m^{\frac{3}{4}}} = \frac{1}{m^{\frac{5+3+3}{4}}} = \frac{1}{m^{\frac{11}{4}}} = m^{-\frac{11}{4}}$$

The exponent is $-\dfrac{11}{4}$, which is choice (A). If this makes no sense to you, you'll want to review the rules of multiplying and dividing exponents.

8. C   You can't solve this problem without a little help from the algebraic expressions. You know that the two expressions sum to 90 (because the measures of the interior angles of a triangle sum to 180), but there are two variables and only one equation: $2x + y + 3x - y = 90$ (They equal 90 since the right angle takes up the other 90°.)

If the y variables didn't subtract out when you added the two expressions, you could not solve for x. The whole point to this problem is to brain freeze students who look at it and say, "There are two variables and only one equation. It can't be solved!" If you just write out the equation, you can avoid this type of paralysis. Writing down your work saves the day!

$$2x + y + 3x - y = 90$$
$$5x = 90$$
$$\frac{5x}{5} = \frac{90}{5}$$
$$x = 18$$

(C) is the answer.

9. E For word problems, always translate the English into algebra. Call the distance from Easton to Bethsaida via highway x. Traveling this route is 7 miles longer than going on surface streets, so going via surface streets is $x - 7$. Traveling both routes is 31 miles, which translates to: $x + (x - 7) = 31$. Once you have an equation, you can solve for x:

$$x + x - 7 = 31$$
$$2x - 7 = 31$$
$$2x - 7 + 7 = 31 + 7$$
$$2x = 38$$
$$\frac{2x}{2} = \frac{38}{2}$$
$$x = 9$$

Here you might to double check that x is the highway route distance and not the surface street distance. Choice (E) is the answer.

10. E A function is undefined at a certain value, if at that value the function does not make any sense. For this function, the most probable way that it could be undefined is if the denominator is zero.

When is the denominator zero? Solve it like a quadratic to see:

$$x^2 + 3x - 18 = 0$$
$$(x + 6)(x - 3) = 0$$

The denominator is zero if x equals -6 or 3, which is choice (E).

11. D The graph is a parabola, so it will have an x^2 term in it. Sometimes that will help you cross out an answer choice or two, but on this question all answer choices have an x^2 in them. Even so, it was a good technique; it didn't work on this problem, but it will work on others.

The parabola is facing downwards, so the x^2 term must have a negative in front of it. If you don't see why, plug some numbers into $-x^2$. That eliminates (A) and (B).

Our last clue will come from where the figure crosses the y-axis. At this point, x must equal zero, which means that $-x^2$ will also be zero. When x equals zero on the graph, the value of $f(x$ is -2. So you are looking for an answer choice that has both $-x^2$ and -2. Although it's hiding a bit inside some parentheses, (D) is the answer since $-(x^2 + 2) = -x^2 - 2$.

12. D   With congruent triangles, corresponding angles and sides are congruent. Both are right triangles, so you should smell the Pythagorean theorem wafting about this problem as a method of solving for y.

$$a^2 + b^2 = c^2$$
$$y^2 + 5^2 = 10^2$$
$$y^2 + 25 = 100$$
$$y^2 + 25 - 25 = 100 - 25$$
$$y^2 = 75$$
$$y = \sqrt{75}$$

You might also have noticed that both figures are 30-60-90 triangles (you can infer this from the relationship between the hypotenuse and the smallest side of the triangle on the left). This means $y = 5\sqrt{3}$ which brings you once again to $\sqrt{75}$. Either method, choice (D) is correct.

13. A   Plug in the answer choices and see which ones make the equation true. Many of the numbers repeat and the equation isn't that involved, so this doesn't take as long as you might think. 1 works, but -1 doesn't. If you try all the answer choices, you will see that only 1 works, which makes (A) the answer.

14. B   There are multiple ways to approach this problem. Possibly the quickest is to count up the multiples of three that are even and 50 or less (if they are even, they will be divisible by 2). This list starts 6, 12, 18, 24 . . .

You might stop here and realize that the members of set Z are all multiples of 6. Even if you don't, you'll continue with: 30, 36, 42, and 48. 54 is the next item, but it's too great, so there are eight members of set Z. (B) is the answer.

15. D   With similar figures, the ratios of each pair of corresponding sides must be equal. The tricky part to this problem is the bent-leg formation of the given figure. The L-shape could roughly be described as, "three squares up, then one to the right." Choice (A) is too thin, i.e. there was no corresponding increase in width even though there is an increase in length. With (B), the small part of L seems to be too big, and with (C) the big part of the L is too large in proportion to the skinny part.
Now look at choice (D). The fact that the figure has been rotated makes no difference with similarity. If you draw the following dashed lines on choice (D), you'll see why it's the right answer.

523

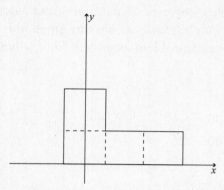

Here you have the same figure, "three squares, then one to the right." The squares are much larger, but they are in the same corresponding proportion. Choice (D) is correct.

16. C The figure is a square since the side lengths are all equal and all the angles are ninety degrees (if you don't see this, rotate the figure ninety degrees). To find the side length, it's Pythagoras time, but you get a shortcut since you have a special triangle. Each side length is the hypotenuse of a 45-45-90 triangle whose equal sides are of length one. So the hypotenuse/side length of the square is $\sqrt{2}$. Put this into the area of a square formula and you'll find answer (C):

$$A = s^2$$
$$A = \left(\sqrt{2}\right)^2$$
$$A = 2$$

17. B First, make sure you understand what all those words mean. You have eight numbers that are integers, and are also even, and when you add them up, they sum to 50. Furthermore, only two of the eight integers can be the same value. In other words, there are never three integers that are the same.

To find the greatest possible integer in the set, first make all the other integers as least as possible. The set could be 2, 2, 4, 4, 6, 6, 8, x. This would maximize x. Now solve:

$$2 + 2 + 4 + 4 + 6 + 6 + 8 + x = 50$$
$$32 + x = 50$$
$$32 - 32 + x = 50 - 32$$
$$x = 18$$

This is choice (B).

You can also start with the greatet numerical answer choice and then see if it works, but this will take more time than setting up a formula.

524

18. **E** Time to sketch! Here's one where two of the triangle's vertices coincide with two of the square's corners.

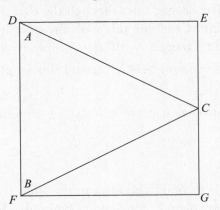

You could also have $\overline{AB}$ run along $\overline{DE}$. In fact, using $\overline{AB}$ you could put the triangle in the square four different ways (along $\overline{DF}$, $\overline{DE}$, $\overline{EG}$, $\overline{GF}$). Using $\overline{BC}$, you could put the triangle in the square four different ways also. The same is true for $\overline{AC}$. That is a total of 12 different ways that the triangle could be placed in the square such that two angles of the triangle coincided with two corners of the square. It means that (E) is the answer.

19. **D** You only know the distances between these points. You don't know their orientation in relation to each other. If T is on a line between G and S, then G and T are 4 away from each other ($9 - 5 = 4$). That is the closest that they could be to each other. But if T is on a line with S and G, and S is between G and T, then they are 14 away from each other ($9 + 5 = 14$). This is the farthest that they could be from each other. Therefore I is not possible, but II and III are. Choice (D) is the answer.

20. **C** If you connect A, B, and C, you have an equilateral triangle with a side length of six. $\overline{BD}$ cuts the triangle into two 30-60-90 triangles. This means that $\overline{AD} = 3$—because of the relationship between the sides of a 30-60-90 triangle—and so $\overline{BD} = 3\sqrt{3}$, choice (C).

21. **E** This problem has many steps, which is why it's number 21. First, ask yourself, "What point on the fan travels the greatest distance through one revolution?" The answer is the point on the corner tip of the fan blade, as it is the farthest from the axis of rotation. In going through one revolution, this point describes a circle because it rotates about a fixed point with a constant radius.

To find out how far this point travels, you need to determine the radius of this circle. This can be done with some help from the triangle shape at the top of the fan. The dashed lines through the two sides show that these sides are congruent. Combine this with the right angle, and you have a 45-45-90 right triangle with two sides of length 4. The hypotenuse of this triangle will be $4\sqrt{2}$, and this length will also be the diameter of the circle.

Therefore, in one rotation that point travels the circumference of the circle it describes:

$$C = \pi d = 4\sqrt{2}\pi$$

But there's more! In 30 seconds, the fan can do 300 revolutions. You know this because the problem states that maximum blade speed is 100 revolutions in 10 seconds, and you can multiply both of these numbers by 3 to get 300 revolutions in 30 seconds. This means that the farthest the point could travel would be:

$$300 \times 4\sqrt{2}\pi = 1200\sqrt{2}$$

Choice (E).

Section 6

1. **D** The passage reads, "As he matured, however, Remington turned his attention away from illustration, concentrating instead on painting and sculpture." (lines 5–9) So the passage links Remington's concentration upon painting and sculpture as key for his maturation. Eliminate (A). However, the rest of the passage focuses on his paintings, so the answer can't just be sculpture. Eliminate (B). We know he paints nocturnal scenes, so eliminate (E) (this answer isn't specific enough). He is a great artist of the American West, painting before there were any big cities in the West. The passage also implies that he paints natural scenes. The best answer is (D).

2. **C** Go back to the passage. In the same sentence with *vindicates* is *claim to the status of literature*. This phrase indicates that literature has more status than fiction. You can confirm this hunch in the next sentence, too. It says a *work clearly rises to the auspicious status of literature*. Again, the emphasis is on the loftiness of literature. Choice (C) best captures this sense.

526

3. **C** The passage states that the *test of time* method, *by definition excludes contemporary works from consideration.* Choice (C) is a reasonable paraphrase.

4. **E** There is only one topic that the paragraph mentions twice in relation to the exploration of Mars: detection of life. So this topic is the best candidate for what the paragraph most emphasizes as the motivation for the Mars exploration. The paragraph also concludes with this point. Choice (E) is the answer.

5. **B** Does the author of Passage 1 criticize the English system? He says it is quirky, but he does not outright criticize it. That eliminates (D) and (E). The author does not strongly praise the system either. That eliminates (A). The author is also not *neutral* toward it (he argues that it is part of the inheritance of the English-speaking world). That eliminates (C). Choice (B), *qualified acceptance,* sounds about right since the author does accept the system but still points out its *quirkiness.*

6. **D** What is Henry I's role in the passage? Not simply to demonstrate that the monarchy was involved in the development of the English system. Eliminate (B). The story of Henry I is definitely not included to *suggest the practicality of the English system,* since that is contrary to the basic thesis of the passage. Eliminate (E). The basic point of the passage is to argue that the English system developed arbitrarily over time. Choice (D) sounds like a good answer. (A) isn't right, since the author says the anecdote is surprisingly true. Answer (C) is off base, because the passage isn't simply interested in the length, but also the quality, of the English system's history. Choice (D) is correct.

7. **C** *Earthy* in context must mean something slightly better than ridiculous, because it is used in the discussion of the arbitrary nature of the English system. Choice (C) is the best answer.

8. **E** Go back to the phrase in the passage. It talks about one system developing in Rome and another in medieval Europe. They reconciled the two by making an estimate of one (the mile) that is an even number of the other (furlongs). Is that synonymous with *determining which one is accurate*? No. Eliminate choice (A). With developing a more accurate system? No. (B) is out. Settling the public's disagreement? Possibly. Hang on to (C). Finding a metric equivalent? Definitely not, so eliminate (D). Ceasing to use two different systems? Definitely. Between definitely (E) and possibly (C), pick definitely. The answer is (E).

9. B Again, use your knowledge of the main idea to help guide you. You can therefore eliminate (A) and (E). Does the English system continue to evolve? Use common sense—no. You are left with (B) and (C). The passage specifically mentions a variety of sources. (B) is the best answer. (C) is less good because it emphasizes the length of history instead of the quality of that history.

10. A You've established that the history of the English system is long and colorful. In the second passage, the author is also interested in history. So she/he would probably not happily agree that that history is less interesting. But there are dates in both passages. The English system goes back to the sixteenth century. Even if you forget that's actually the 1500s, you still know it's before 1840. So the history is factually shorter. That makes the answer (A).

11. D Go back to the reference to the French Revolution in the passage. The author specifically mentions its anti-traditionalist bent. So (D) looks good. She/he doesn't go so far as to indicate that the greatest accomplishment of the French Revolution was the metric system. Eliminate (A). The author indicates that the metric system was in keeping with the rest of the revolutionary thinking. So eliminate (B). There's no mention of the revolutionary calendar in the passage. Eliminate (C). (E) is the only tricky wrong answer. The passage says the metric system wasn't adopted in France until 1840, but it doesn't say it wasn't fully *invented* before then. The answer is (D).

12. C In the sentence in question, you find that it has been called, or *dubbed*, "voluntary" and "preferred." The implication is these are some sort of official designation, but they specifically are not required. Choice (C) sounds like a reasonable, noncommittal paraphrase. Eliminate (D). These words also don't suggest any pending official adoption. Eliminate (B). (A) overstates the case in the other direction: the view of the metric system reflected in the sentence in the passage is favorable. (E) overstates how favorable—the words in the passage are warm but don't suggest "superiority." The answer is (C).

13. E *Refined* in the passage is synonymous with recalculated. The passage doesn't say whether it's to make the meter smaller or bigger. That only leaves (E).

14. B There is no indication of any ideological shift motivating the 1983 move. That eliminates (A), (C), and (E). Which is more logical: new calculations of the Earth's circumference or new ways to calculate fractions? The former, especially where the speed of light is involved. The answer is (B).

15. A As soon as you find an answer that isn't addressed in one passage, you're done. Do both passages mention kings who were ruling at the time of their invention? No. Passage 2 talks about the French Revolution, which overthrew the king; it only mentions a king in regards to the English system. Choice (A) is the answer.

16. A Which of the answers is something that the author of Passage 2 would agree with but does not explicitly state? Which is most plausible? Choice (A) is the most reasonable answer on its face. You can find evidence for it when the author says *It is the great asset of the metric system, at least for scientists, that units for measuring weight and energy are also derived from the basic unit of the meter* and *The adoption of the metric system, also known as the international system, or S.I., coincided with great advances in science.*

Section 7

1. There is nothing fancy about this problem. Substitute and solve for x.

$$2y = 12$$
$$y = 6$$

$$2\sqrt{x} + \sqrt{x} = y$$
$$2\sqrt{x} + \sqrt{x} = 6$$
$$3\sqrt{x} = 6$$
$$\sqrt{x} = 2$$
$$x = 4$$

2. The first five even integers are 2, 4, 6, 8, and 10. Rev up that calculator start multiplying. The answer is 3,840.

3. If the probability that a senior would be picked is three-eighths, then seniors are three-eighths of the entire student body. Since Rider High has 400 students, the equation would be:

$$400 \times \frac{3}{8} = \frac{1200}{8} = 150$$

4. The volume of any rectangular solid is the length times the width times the height. The figure tells us the width and the height, and you can determine the length from what you know about the area of the shaded side. Start with the area of a rectangle formula and you can find the length:

$$A = l \times h$$
$$24 = 4 \times l$$
$$6 = l$$

Place this length of 6 into the volume formula for the box:

$$V = l \times h \times w = 3 \times 4 \times 6 = 72$$

5. First use the area of a circle formula to determine the radius.

$$A = \pi r^2$$
$$16\pi = \pi r^2$$
$$\frac{16\pi}{\pi} = \frac{\pi r^2}{\pi}$$
$$16 = r^2$$
$$4 = r$$

The diameter of a circle is twice the radius, so the diameter is 8.

6. There are some fancier ways to solve this problem, but the surest way is to count up the options. She could have:

1. No toppings.
2. Just a
3. Just p
4. Just r
5. a and p
6. a and r
7. p and r
8. All the toppings.

That is a total of 8. Sure, there's a fancier math way of handling this problem, but since you have the right answer, what does it matter? Is your SAT score in any way determined by whether you used the "fancy method" or not?

7. If x is the sum of the five numbers, you know:

$$\frac{sum}{number\ of\ items} = Average$$

$$\frac{x}{5} = 16$$

$$(5)\frac{x}{5} = 16(5)$$

$$x = 80$$

Make y the number taken away from the set y. You know that 80 minus y is the new sum, and that the new average is 14. With this information you can solve for y using the equation:

$$\frac{80 - y}{4} = 14$$

$$(4)\frac{80 - y}{4} = 14\ (4)$$

$$80 - y = 56$$

$$80 - 56 - y = 56 - 56$$

$$24 - y = 0$$

$$24 = y$$

8. Since the triangle is a right triangle, you can use the Pythagorean theorem to determine the third side of the triangle:

$$c^2 = a^2 + b^2$$

$$100 = 64 + b^2$$

$$36 = b^2$$

$$b = 6$$

If 6 is the length of one side of the square, the area of the square is the square of that, 36.

9. You need to remember the right formula for this one. At least you know that since you can't grid in negative numbers, the slope must be positive. Here's the rise over run calculation:

$$slope = \frac{rise}{run} = \frac{y_1 - y_2}{x_1 - x_2} = \frac{-2 - 1}{-1 - 3} = \frac{-3}{-4} = \frac{3}{4}$$

10. If you work backward from what you know, this problem contains no difficult steps. If Bo is 15 and Gina is five years younger than he, then Gina is 10. And if Gina is 10 and Susan is three times the age of Gina, then Susan is 30. And if Susan is 30 and Tom is twelve years older than Susan, then Tom is 42. There's your answer, 42.

11. This one tries to intimidate you with a new symbol and a complicated definition. By now, this sort of attempted distraction should not even faze you, as you are well aware that everything you need to know about the new symbol is right in front of you.

   The phrase *greatest prime divisor* means the greatest number that is prime and also divides the original number. So the greatest prime divisor of 15 is 5 since no prime numbers greater than 5 evenly divide into 15. As for 12, the greatest prime divisor is 3. This means $(15*)(12*) = (5)(3) = 15$.

12. The graph might look messy, but you only need to pick out the five y-intercepts and add them up.

   Line 1: at $(0, 2)$
   Line 2: at $(0, 1)$
   Lines 3 and 4: at $(0, 0)$
   Line 5: at $(0, -1)$

   Adding up these five y-values gives you: $2 + 1 + 0 + 0 - 1 = 2$

13. The problem says that the numbers are *distinct*, so none of the four numbers are the same. That's your first clue. Since the sum of the four numbers is 26, the numbers in the sum must be less than 21. Here's a Rogue's Gallery List of all the less prime numbers: 2, 3, 5, 7, 11, 13, 17, and 19. To find the greatest possible integer in the set, first make all the other integers as least as possible. The set could be 2, 3, 5, x. This would maximize x. Now solve:

   $$2 + 3 + 5 + x = 21$$
   $$10 + x = 21$$
   $$10 - 10 + x = 21 - 10$$
   $$x = 11, \text{ also prime.}$$

   11 must be the answer.

Section 8

As you might expect, answers will vary. If possible, politely ask a teacher, fellow student, or some other person knowledgeable about formal essay writing to review your essay and provide feedback on ways in which the essay is commendable and on areas where it could be improved.

Scoring Worksheet

MATH				
	Number Correct	Number Incorrect	=	Raw Score
Section 2	_____	− (.25 × _____)	=	_____
Section 5	_____	− (.25 × _____)	=	_____
Section 7	_____	− (.25 × _____)	=	_____
CRITICAL READING				
Sections 1, 4, and 6	_____	− (.25 × _____)	=	_____
WRITING				
Section 3	_____	− (.25 × _____)	=	_____
Section 8	Go to www.petersons.com/satessayedge/ for instant online scoring and feedback.			

Score Charts

MATH			
Raw Score	**Math Scaled Score**	**Raw Score**	**Math Scaled Score**
60	800	28	500
59	800	27	490
58	790	26	490
57	770	25	480
56	760	24	470
55	740	23	460
54	720	22	460
53	710	21	450
52	700	20	440
51	690	19	430
50	680	18	420
49	670	17	420
48	660	16	410
47	650	15	410
46	640	14	400
45	630	13	390
44	620	12	380
43	610	11	370
42	600	10	360
41	600	9	350
40	590	8	340
39	580	7	330
38	570	6	320
37	560	5	310
36	560	4	300
35	550	3	280
34	540	2	270
33	540	1	250
32	530	0	240
31	520	−1	220
30	510	−2	210
29	510	−3 and below	200

CRITICAL READING			
Raw Score	**Verbal Scaled Score**	**Raw Score**	**Verbal Scaled Score**
78	800	37	510
77	800	36	510
76	800	35	500
75	790	34	500
74	780	33	490
73	770	32	490
72	760	31	480
71	750	30	480
70	740	29	470
69	730	28	460
68	720	27	460
67	710	26	450
66	700	25	450
65	700	24	440
64	690	23	440
63	680	22	430
62	670	21	420
61	670	20	410
60	660	19	410
59	650	18	400
58	640	17	390
57	640	16	380
56	630	15	380
55	620	14	370
54	610	13	360
53	610	12	360
52	600	11	350
51	600	10	340
50	590	9	330
49	590	8	320
48	580	7	310
47	570	6	300
46	570	5	290
45	560	4	270
44	550	3	260
43	550	2	250
42	540	1	240
41	540	0	230
40	530	−1	220
39	520	−2	210
38	520	−3 and below	200

Answer Sheets

SECTION 1

1 Ⓐ Ⓑ Ⓒ Ⓓ Ⓔ
2 Ⓐ Ⓑ Ⓒ Ⓓ Ⓔ
3 Ⓐ Ⓑ Ⓒ Ⓓ Ⓔ
4 Ⓐ Ⓑ Ⓒ Ⓓ Ⓔ
5 Ⓐ Ⓑ Ⓒ Ⓓ Ⓔ

6 Ⓐ Ⓑ Ⓒ Ⓓ Ⓔ
7 Ⓐ Ⓑ Ⓒ Ⓓ Ⓔ
8 Ⓐ Ⓑ Ⓒ Ⓓ Ⓔ
9 Ⓐ Ⓑ Ⓒ Ⓓ Ⓔ
10 Ⓐ Ⓑ Ⓒ Ⓓ Ⓔ

11 Ⓐ Ⓑ Ⓒ Ⓓ Ⓔ
12 Ⓐ Ⓑ Ⓒ Ⓓ Ⓔ
13 Ⓐ Ⓑ Ⓒ Ⓓ Ⓔ
14 Ⓐ Ⓑ Ⓒ Ⓓ Ⓔ
15 Ⓐ Ⓑ Ⓒ Ⓓ Ⓔ

16 Ⓐ Ⓑ Ⓒ Ⓓ Ⓔ
17 Ⓐ Ⓑ Ⓒ Ⓓ Ⓔ
18 Ⓐ Ⓑ Ⓒ Ⓓ Ⓔ
19 Ⓐ Ⓑ Ⓒ Ⓓ Ⓔ
20 Ⓐ Ⓑ Ⓒ Ⓓ Ⓔ

SECTION 2

1 Ⓐ Ⓑ Ⓒ Ⓓ Ⓔ
2 Ⓐ Ⓑ Ⓒ Ⓓ Ⓔ
3 Ⓐ Ⓑ Ⓒ Ⓓ Ⓔ
4 Ⓐ Ⓑ Ⓒ Ⓓ Ⓔ
5 Ⓐ Ⓑ Ⓒ Ⓓ Ⓔ
6 Ⓐ Ⓑ Ⓒ Ⓓ Ⓔ

7 Ⓐ Ⓑ Ⓒ Ⓓ Ⓔ
8 Ⓐ Ⓑ Ⓒ Ⓓ Ⓔ
9 Ⓐ Ⓑ Ⓒ Ⓓ Ⓔ
10 Ⓐ Ⓑ Ⓒ Ⓓ Ⓔ
11 Ⓐ Ⓑ Ⓒ Ⓓ Ⓔ

12 Ⓐ Ⓑ Ⓒ Ⓓ Ⓔ
13 Ⓐ Ⓑ Ⓒ Ⓓ Ⓔ
14 Ⓐ Ⓑ Ⓒ Ⓓ Ⓔ
15 Ⓐ Ⓑ Ⓒ Ⓓ Ⓔ
16 Ⓐ Ⓑ Ⓒ Ⓓ Ⓔ

17 Ⓐ Ⓑ Ⓒ Ⓓ Ⓔ
18 Ⓐ Ⓑ Ⓒ Ⓓ Ⓔ
19 Ⓐ Ⓑ Ⓒ Ⓓ Ⓔ
20 Ⓐ Ⓑ Ⓒ Ⓓ Ⓔ
21 Ⓐ Ⓑ Ⓒ Ⓓ Ⓔ

SECTION 3

1 Ⓐ Ⓑ Ⓒ Ⓓ Ⓔ
2 Ⓐ Ⓑ Ⓒ Ⓓ Ⓔ
3 Ⓐ Ⓑ Ⓒ Ⓓ Ⓔ
4 Ⓐ Ⓑ Ⓒ Ⓓ Ⓔ
5 Ⓐ Ⓑ Ⓒ Ⓓ Ⓔ
6 Ⓐ Ⓑ Ⓒ Ⓓ Ⓔ
7 Ⓐ Ⓑ Ⓒ Ⓓ Ⓔ
8 Ⓐ Ⓑ Ⓒ Ⓓ Ⓔ

9 Ⓐ Ⓑ Ⓒ Ⓓ Ⓔ
10 Ⓐ Ⓑ Ⓒ Ⓓ Ⓔ
11 Ⓐ Ⓑ Ⓒ Ⓓ Ⓔ
12 Ⓐ Ⓑ Ⓒ Ⓓ Ⓔ
13 Ⓐ Ⓑ Ⓒ Ⓓ Ⓔ
14 Ⓐ Ⓑ Ⓒ Ⓓ Ⓔ
15 Ⓐ Ⓑ Ⓒ Ⓓ Ⓔ
16 Ⓐ Ⓑ Ⓒ Ⓓ Ⓔ

17 Ⓐ Ⓑ Ⓒ Ⓓ Ⓔ
18 Ⓐ Ⓑ Ⓒ Ⓓ Ⓔ
19 Ⓐ Ⓑ Ⓒ Ⓓ Ⓔ
20 Ⓐ Ⓑ Ⓒ Ⓓ Ⓔ
21 Ⓐ Ⓑ Ⓒ Ⓓ Ⓔ
22 Ⓐ Ⓑ Ⓒ Ⓓ Ⓔ
23 Ⓐ Ⓑ Ⓒ Ⓓ Ⓔ

24 Ⓐ Ⓑ Ⓒ Ⓓ Ⓔ
25 Ⓐ Ⓑ Ⓒ Ⓓ Ⓔ
26 Ⓐ Ⓑ Ⓒ Ⓓ Ⓔ
27 Ⓐ Ⓑ Ⓒ Ⓓ Ⓔ
28 Ⓐ Ⓑ Ⓒ Ⓓ Ⓔ
29 Ⓐ Ⓑ Ⓒ Ⓓ Ⓔ
30 Ⓐ Ⓑ Ⓒ Ⓓ Ⓔ

SECTION 4

1 Ⓐ Ⓑ Ⓒ Ⓓ Ⓔ
2 Ⓐ Ⓑ Ⓒ Ⓓ Ⓔ
3 Ⓐ Ⓑ Ⓒ Ⓓ Ⓔ
4 Ⓐ Ⓑ Ⓒ Ⓓ Ⓔ
5 Ⓐ Ⓑ Ⓒ Ⓓ Ⓔ
6 Ⓐ Ⓑ Ⓒ Ⓓ Ⓔ
7 Ⓐ Ⓑ Ⓒ Ⓓ Ⓔ

8 Ⓐ Ⓑ Ⓒ Ⓓ Ⓔ
9 Ⓐ Ⓑ Ⓒ Ⓓ Ⓔ
10 Ⓐ Ⓑ Ⓒ Ⓓ Ⓔ
11 Ⓐ Ⓑ Ⓒ Ⓓ Ⓔ
12 Ⓐ Ⓑ Ⓒ Ⓓ Ⓔ
13 Ⓐ Ⓑ Ⓒ Ⓓ Ⓔ
14 Ⓐ Ⓑ Ⓒ Ⓓ Ⓔ

15 Ⓐ Ⓑ Ⓒ Ⓓ Ⓔ
16 Ⓐ Ⓑ Ⓒ Ⓓ Ⓔ
17 Ⓐ Ⓑ Ⓒ Ⓓ Ⓔ
18 Ⓐ Ⓑ Ⓒ Ⓓ Ⓔ
19 Ⓐ Ⓑ Ⓒ Ⓓ Ⓔ
20 Ⓐ Ⓑ Ⓒ Ⓓ Ⓔ
21 Ⓐ Ⓑ Ⓒ Ⓓ Ⓔ

22 Ⓐ Ⓑ Ⓒ Ⓓ Ⓔ
23 Ⓐ Ⓑ Ⓒ Ⓓ Ⓔ
24 Ⓐ Ⓑ Ⓒ Ⓓ Ⓔ
25 Ⓐ Ⓑ Ⓒ Ⓓ Ⓔ
26 Ⓐ Ⓑ Ⓒ Ⓓ Ⓔ
27 Ⓐ Ⓑ Ⓒ Ⓓ Ⓔ

SECTION 5

1 Ⓐ Ⓑ Ⓒ Ⓓ Ⓔ
2 Ⓐ Ⓑ Ⓒ Ⓓ Ⓔ
3 Ⓐ Ⓑ Ⓒ Ⓓ Ⓔ
4 Ⓐ Ⓑ Ⓒ Ⓓ Ⓔ
5 Ⓐ Ⓑ Ⓒ Ⓓ Ⓔ
6 Ⓐ Ⓑ Ⓒ Ⓓ Ⓔ

7 Ⓐ Ⓑ Ⓒ Ⓓ Ⓔ
8 Ⓐ Ⓑ Ⓒ Ⓓ Ⓔ
9 Ⓐ Ⓑ Ⓒ Ⓓ Ⓔ
10 Ⓐ Ⓑ Ⓒ Ⓓ Ⓔ
11 Ⓐ Ⓑ Ⓒ Ⓓ Ⓔ

12 Ⓐ Ⓑ Ⓒ Ⓓ Ⓔ
13 Ⓐ Ⓑ Ⓒ Ⓓ Ⓔ
14 Ⓐ Ⓑ Ⓒ Ⓓ Ⓔ
15 Ⓐ Ⓑ Ⓒ Ⓓ Ⓔ
16 Ⓐ Ⓑ Ⓒ Ⓓ Ⓔ

17 Ⓐ Ⓑ Ⓒ Ⓓ Ⓔ
18 Ⓐ Ⓑ Ⓒ Ⓓ Ⓔ
19 Ⓐ Ⓑ Ⓒ Ⓓ Ⓔ
20 Ⓐ Ⓑ Ⓒ Ⓓ Ⓔ
21 Ⓐ Ⓑ Ⓒ Ⓓ Ⓔ

Answer Sheets

SECTION 6

1 Ⓐ Ⓑ Ⓒ Ⓓ Ⓔ	5 Ⓐ Ⓑ Ⓒ Ⓓ Ⓔ	9 Ⓐ Ⓑ Ⓒ Ⓓ Ⓔ	13 Ⓐ Ⓑ Ⓒ Ⓓ Ⓔ
2 Ⓐ Ⓑ Ⓒ Ⓓ Ⓔ	6 Ⓐ Ⓑ Ⓒ Ⓓ Ⓔ	10 Ⓐ Ⓑ Ⓒ Ⓓ Ⓔ	14 Ⓐ Ⓑ Ⓒ Ⓓ Ⓔ
3 Ⓐ Ⓑ Ⓒ Ⓓ Ⓔ	7 Ⓐ Ⓑ Ⓒ Ⓓ Ⓔ	11 Ⓐ Ⓑ Ⓒ Ⓓ Ⓔ	15 Ⓐ Ⓑ Ⓒ Ⓓ Ⓔ
4 Ⓐ Ⓑ Ⓒ Ⓓ Ⓔ	8 Ⓐ Ⓑ Ⓒ Ⓓ Ⓔ	12 Ⓐ Ⓑ Ⓒ Ⓓ Ⓔ	16 Ⓐ Ⓑ Ⓒ Ⓓ Ⓔ

SECTION 7

For Questions 1–13:
Only answers entered in the ovals in each grid area will be scored.
You will not receive credit for anything written in the boxes above the ovals.

Practice Test

3

Section 1

16 Questions ■ Time—20 Minutes

Directions: Read each of the passages carefully, then answer the questions that come after them. The answer to each question may be stated overtly or only implied. You will not have to use outside knowledge to answer the questions—all the material you will need will be in the passage itself. In some cases, you will be asked to read two related passages and answer questions about their relationship to one another. Mark the letter of your choice on the answer sheet that best corresponds to the correct answer.

Questions 1–4 are based on the following passages.

The following two passages represent two views of the value of hybrid cars, cars that are powered by gasoline and by electricity depending on whether they are in traffic or on the open road.

Passage 1

Line   Advocates of hybrids believe that they offer the best short-term solution to some long-term problems. By combining a regular gasoline-powered engine with an
(5)   electric engine, hybrids cut down on gas consumption and decrease the pollution caused by gasoline engines. These cars help auto makers meet government regulations for fuel efficiency and
(10)   emissions controls. Auto makers do not think that hybrids are the answer for the

future, but these small cars provide a way for conservation-conscious consumers to do something for the environment. Auto
(15)   makers see another benefit to the development process for hybrids. The technology that has gone into creating and refining the dual-powered hybrid will help with the longer term develop-
(20)   ment of cars powered by hydrogen fuel cells.

Passage 2

Opponents of hybrids believe that auto makers should be focusing on a longer term solution. They believe that either
(25)   hydrogen fuel cells or diesel fuel or both are better alternatives than hybrids. The cost of hybrids is higher than comparably sized gasoline-powered cars, forcing consumers who want "green" cars to pay

GO ON TO THE NEXT PAGE

(30) anywhere from $2,500 to $4,000 more. Opponents say that the higher sticker price means lower demand and less likelihood of automobile companies making their development dollars back.

(35) Naysayers point to Europe as an example of lack of demand. Gasoline prices are much higher there than in the United States, but no mass movement from gasoline-powered cars to hybrids has

(40) occurred.

1. According to Passage 1, hybrids are beneficial for all of the following reasons EXCEPT they

   (A) decrease gas consumption.
   (B) provide information for the development of hydrogen fuel cells.
   (C) decrease pollution.
   (D) provide an alternative for car buyers who want to protect the environment.
   (E) add to the profit margin for auto makers.

2. The lack of demand discussed in Passage 2 is said to result from

   (A) the lack of fuel efficiency of the hybrids.
   (B) the higher price of hybrids.
   (C) buyers' waiting for the alternatives to hybrids to come on the market.
   (D) the high price of gas.
   (E) a general lack of interest in conserving gasoline.

3. In Passage 2, *"green" cars (line 29) probably refers to the fact that the*

   (A) technology is new and relatively untested over a long period of time.
   (B) technology is experimental.
   (C) cars are environmentally friendly.
   (D) opponents are jealous because they did not come up with the technology first.
   (E) cars are expensive.

4. In contrast to Passage 1, the writer of Passage 2 uses

   (A) jargon.
   (B) a dismissive attitude toward the arguments of the other side.
   (C) a straightforward, direct style.
   (D) examples to support the argument.
   (E) complex sentence structures.

Questions 5–16 are based on the following passages

Achilles, the Greek hero, and Cuchulain, the Champion of Ireland, achieved mythical status because of their acts of courage. The following passages compare the two heroes and their heroic feats.

Passage 1—Achilles, Defender of Honor

Line   When Achilles heard that his friend Patroclus had been killed in battle, he became so despondent that his friends feared he might end his own life. When

(5) word of his complete and agonizing distress reached his mother, Thetis, in the depths of the ocean where she resided, she raced to his side. She found him in a highly distraught state, feeling guilty that

(10) he, in some way, might have been responsible for his friend's demise. His only consolation were thoughts of revenge for which he needed the help of

Hector. However, his mother reminded
(15) him that he was without armor, having
lost his recently in battle. His mother,
however, promised him that she would
procure for him a suit of armor from
Vulcan far superior to the one he had
(20) lost. Achilles agreed and Thetis immediately repaired to Vulcan's palace. Thetis
found Vulcan busy at his forge making
magical tripods that moved forward
when they were wanted, and retreated
(25) when dismissed. Vulcan immediately
honored Thetis's request for a set of
armor for her son, and ceasing his own
work, hastened to meet her demands.
Vulcan created a magnificent suit of
(30) armor for Achilles. The shield was
adorned with elaborate ornaments. The
helmet had a gold crest, and the body of
the armor was perfectly suited to his
body and of the very finest workman-
(35) ship. The armor was completed in one
night. When Thetis received it, she
descended to earth, and laid it down at
Achilles' feet at the first dawn of day.

Seeing the armor brought the first
(40) signs of life to Achilles that he had felt
since the death of his friend Patroclus.
The armor was so splendid that Achilles
was stunned at the sight of it. Achilles
went into battle with his new armor,
(45) consumed with rage and thirst for
vengeance that made him an unbeatable
foe. The bravest warriors fled from him
or were killed by his lance.

Passage 2—Cuchulain, Champion of Ireland

Line In days of yore, the men of Ulster sought
to choose a champion. They enlisted the
help of Curoi of Kerry, a wise man, to
help them reach their decision. Three
(5) brave men, Laegire, Connall Cearnach,
and Cuchulain indicated that they wished
to be considered. Each was told that he
would have to meet the challenge of a
terrible stranger. When the stranger
(10) arrived, all were in awe of him. "Behold
my axe," the stranger said. "My challenge is this. Whoever will take the axe
today may cut my head off with it,
provided that I may, in like manner, cut
(15) off his head tomorrow. If you have no
champions who dare face me, I will say
that the men of Ulster have lost their
courage and should be ashamed."

Laegire was the first to accept the
(20) challenge. The giant laid his head on a
block. With one blow the hero severed it
from the body. Thereupon the giant
arose, took the head and the axe, and
headless, walked slowly from the hall.
(25) The following night the giant returned,
sound as ever, to claim the fulfillment of
Laegires' promise. However, Laegire did
not come forward. The stranger scoffed
at the men of Ulster because their great
(30) champion showed no courage. He could
not face the blow he should receive in
return for the one he gave.

The men from Ulster were sorely
ashamed, but Conall Cearnach, the
(35) second aspiring champion, made another
pact with the stranger. He, too, gave a
blow which beheaded the giant. But
again, when the giant returned whole and
sound on the following evening, the
(40) champion was not there.

Now it was the turn of Cuchulain, who as the others had done, cut off the giant's head at one stroke. The next day everyone watched Cuchulain to see what (45) he would do. They would not have been surprised if he had not appeared. This champion, however, was there. He was not going to disgrace Ulster. Instead, he sat with great sadness in his place. "Do (50) not leave this place till all is over," he said to his king. "Death is coming to me soon, but I must honor my promise, for I would rather die than break my word."

At the end of the day the giant (55) appeared.

"Where is Cuchulain?" he cried.

"Here I am," answered Cuchulain.

"Cuchulain, your speech is morose, and the fear of death is obviously (60) foremost in your thoughts, but at least you have honored your promise."

Cuchulain went towards the giant, as he stood with his great axe ready, and knelt to receive the blow.

(65) The would-be champion of Ulster laid his head on the block.
When the giant did not immediately use his axe, Cuchulain said, "Slay me now with haste, for I did not keep you waiting (70) last night."

The stranger raised his axe so high that it crashed upwards through the rafters of the hall, like the crash of trees falling in a storm. When the axe came (75) down with a sound that shook the room, all men looked fearfully at Cuchulain. But to the surprise of all, the descending axe had not even touched him; it had come down with the blunt side on the (80) ground, and Cuchulain knelt there unharmed. Smiling at him and leaning on his axe, stood no terrible and hideous stranger, but Curoi of Kerry, who had

taken on the form of the giant to test the (85) champions. He was now there to give his decision.

"Rise up, Cuchulain," said Curoi. "There is none among all the heroes of Ulster to equal you in courage and (90) loyalty and truth. The Championship is yours." Thereupon Curoi vanished. The assembled warriors gathered around Cuchulain, and all with one voice acclaimed him the champion.

5. The word *despondent* in Passage 1 (line 3) means

(A) very depressed.
(B) in need of food.
(C) angry.
(D) embarrassed.
(E) belligerent.

6. Achilles' feelings of guilt were related to

(A) the loss of his armor.
(B) the loss of his last battle.
(C) his estrangement from his mother.
(D) the death of his friend.
(E) his relationship with Vulcan.

7. In line 21, the word *repaired* means

(A) glazed.
(B) retired.
(C) replenished.
(D) returned.
(E) untouched.

8. Although not stated directly in the passage, it is obvious that Vulcan

(A) blames Achilles for his friend's death.
(B) is a lower-level god.
(C) is extremely powerful.
(D) loves Thetis.
(E) does not wish to help Achilles.

9. Achilles' feeling as he went into battle can best be described as

(A) guilty.
(B) nervous.
(C) confident.
(D) depressed.
(E) arrogant.

10. According to Passage 2, when the men of Ulster wished to select a champion they enlisted the help of

(A) Curoi.
(B) the king.
(C) Laegire.
(D) Connall.
(E) Cearnach.

11. The challenge that the would-be champion had to meet involved

(A) fighting a giant with an axe.
(B) beheading a giant.
(C) competing against other men of Ulster.
(D) winning a match with the king.
(E) fighting Curoi of Kerry.

12. According to the passage, the giant was unusual because he

(A) was so tall.
(B) was so huge.
(C) defeated all his opponents.
(D) remained alive while headless.
(E) had three eyes.

13. The word *sorely (line 37) means*

(A) feverishly.
(B) utterly.
(C) angrily.
(D) bitterly.
(E) pitifully.

14. Cuchulain appeared as promised to meet the giant because he

(A) was afraid.
(B) knew the giant would not kill him.
(C) knew the giant was Curoi.
(D) did not wish to fail his king.
(E) gave his word.

15. In line 58, the word *morose* most nearly means

(A) serious and somber.
(B) riotous and humorous.
(C) indifferent and detached.
(D) informed and knowledgeable.
(E) satisfied.

16. Cuchulain is sometimes called the "Irish Achilles," probably because of his

(A) honesty.
(B) bravery.
(C) strength.
(D) wisdom.
(E) intelligence.

Questions 17–20 are based on the following passage.

This passage is adapted from The Myth of Culture *by Jo Lynn Southard, J.D., LL.M.*

Line Oppression of women is embedded in most, if not all, societies, its message usually couched in terms of the protection and promotion of traditional
(5) cultural practices. These practices are presented as natural and unremarkable, inherently beneficial to society by virtue simply of their connection with the past, with tradition. The call to preserve
(10) traditional cultural practices can wield enormous power, and it can be easily manipulated by those in power.

GO ON TO THE NEXT PAGE

In 1963, in the United States, Betty Friedan wrote of what she called the (15) "feminine mystique," which referred to the tradition (at that time pretty much unexamined—in fact, Friedan called it "the problem that has no name")—that being a wife and mother was a woman's (20) highest and only calling. It is a message still alive today, one that dies hard and severely limits women's life choices. In other cultures the message is much the same, sometimes going so far as to (25) harshly limit what a woman can wear in public, where she can travel, whether she can receive an education, whether she can work outside the home, and even whether she is to be allowed to learn to (30) read and write.

Time and again, in wars and revolutions, women are welcomed into the struggle for freedom from oppression, only to be forced back into the private (35) realm when freedom is attained. In the midst of a struggle or immediately after a change in power in a country, women are told that their particular issues must wait while the more pressing, "larger" issues (40) are addressed. Meanwhile, women are urged to return to the home to fulfill their traditional roles, one of which is to replenish a population decimated by the struggle itself. As a result, women's (45) issues—issues that affect half the population—never really become a priority.

International human rights law itself does far too little to respond to the needs (50) particular to women. Until very recently, virtually all precepts of international law ignored the concept of gender discrimination. Genocide, persecution, torture, and refugee status are still mostly defined by (55) race, religion, nationality, ethnicity, or membership in a particular social or political group. While all women fit into one or more of those groups, by definition these human rights abuses cannot be (60) said to be committed against women because of their gender, but rather are committed against all people. Human rights abuses against women *as women* (from denial of basic education or the (65) right to travel up to, until very recently, such heinous abuses as rape and mutilation) are pretty much ignored. In fact, even the Convention on the Elimination of All Forms of Discrimination Against (70) Women did not mandate the inclusion of women in the process of implementing the treaty. Decision-making, even when it comes to decisions about ending their own oppression, is simply not viewed as (75) a woman's "place." The decisions for ending discrimination under the treaty were and are made, in the main, by those who created and perpetuated the cultural traditions that enabled discrimination (80) and abuse to happen in the first place.

The traditions of the culture into which we are born have great influence over how we live our lives. Traditionally, most, if not all, cultures have defined (85) themselves from the point of view of the males in power. And it is natural for those who have power—even if they are kindly and well-meaning in other ways—to want to keep that power. (90) Patriarchy is the general rule in the public realm of government and religion, as well as in the private realm of the home. All of us receive messages about how we are to fit into our worlds—and, if we are (95) women, the traditional fit may be in serious need of alteration.

17. In the context of the passage, which of the following best explains Friedan's term, "the problem that has no name"?

(A) In Friedan's time, the problems specific to wives and mothers were kept secret.

(B) At the time Friedan wrote, problems specific to women were ridiculed, so women were embarrassed to speak of them.

(C) At the time the phrase was coined, the problem of the severe limitations placed on women's lives was not generally recognized.

(D) In Friedan's time, women's problems were not spoken of for fear that the men in power would retaliate.

(E) In Friedan's time, women were more satisfied with their lot than they are today and so did not speak out about their problems.

18. What is the meaning of the phrase "embedded in" as it is used in the first paragraph?

(A) An integral part of
(B) An acknowledged part of
(C) A shameful part of
(D) Written into the laws of
(E) Kept a secret from

19. In the context of the passage, the phrase "abuses against women *as women*" (line 63) most nearly means

(A) sexual abuse.
(B) abuse that can happen to both men and women.
(C) domestic abuse.
(D) abuse that, for the most part, happens only to women.
(E) abuse that is not taken seriously by men.

20. Reference to the Convention on the Elimination of All Forms of Discrimination Against Women (lines 68–70) primarily serves to

(A) make the writing style of the essay more appealing.
(B) achieve better overall organization of ideas in the essay.
(C) provide a concrete example to support the main point of the essay.
(D) cause the essay to seem more scholarly by appealing to authority.
(E) end the essay on a more optimistic note.

STOP Do not proceed to the next section until time is up.

Section 2

21 Questions ■ Time—25 Minutes

Directions: Solve the following problems using any available space on the page for scratchwork. Mark the letter of your choice on the answer sheet that best corresponds to the correct answer.

Notes:

1. You may use a calculator. All of the numbers used are real numbers.

2. You may use the figures that accompany the problems to help you find the solution. Unless the instructions say that a figure is not drawn to scale, assume that it has been drawn accurately. Each figure lies in a plane unless the instructions say otherwise.

Reference Information

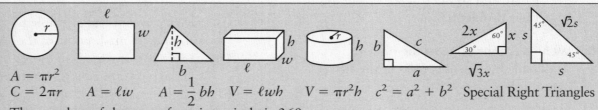

$A = \pi r^2$
$C = 2\pi r$ $\quad A = \ell w \quad A = \frac{1}{2}bh \quad V = \ell wh \quad V = \pi r^2 h \quad c^2 = a^2 + b^2$ Special Right Triangles

The number of degrees of arc in a circle is 360.
The measure in degrees of a straight angle is 180.
The sum of the measures in degrees of the angles of a triangle is 180.

---

1. $4 \times (7 + 1) - 6 =$

(A) 7
(B) 8
(C) 21
(D) 23
(E) 26

2. If angle α and obtuse angle β are supplementary angles, which of the following statements is true?

(A) $\alpha < \beta$
(B) $\alpha > \beta$
(C) $\alpha = \beta$
(D) $\alpha = 180°$
(E) $\beta = 90°$

3. If $x + 3y = z$, what is the value of y?

(A) $3(z + x)$

(B) $\dfrac{(xz)}{3}$

(C) $\dfrac{1}{3}(z - x)$

(D) $\dfrac{(x - z)}{3}$

(E) $-3(z - x)$

4. What is the volume, in cubic inches, of a rectangular solid of length 8 inches and width 6 inches if its height is one half its width?

(A) 120
(B) 144
(C) 168
(D) 192
(E) 576

5. What is the wall thickness, in inches, of a tube with an outer diameter of .750 and an inner diameter of .625?

(A) .0625
(B) .125
(C) .625
(D) .6875
(E) .750

6. A pair of pants sells for $6 more than 75% of its price. What is the price of the pants?

(A) $12
(B) $18
(C) $20
(D) $24
(E) $36

7. In the figure below, what is the value of α?

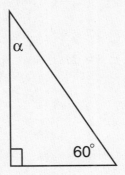

(A) 15°
(B) 20°
(C) 30°
(D) 45°
(E) 90°

8. What % of 5 is 90% of 50?

(A) 2.25
(B) 9
(C) 10
(D) 90
(E) 900

9. For what values of a and b is $(a \times b) < 0$?

(A) $a = 3, b = .0001$
(B) $a = -2, b = -.0001$
(C) $a = 7, b = 0$
(D) $a = -1, b = -19$
(E) $a = -2, b = 3$

10. How tall is a flag pole that casts a 60-foot shadow if a nearby fence post, four feet high, casts a 10-foot shadow?

(A) 40
(B) 36
(C) 30
(D) 24
(E) 15

11. What is the value of

$$\left(9x^3 - \frac{z^2}{2}\right)\left(\frac{y}{11}\right)$$

when $x = -1, y = 1, z = 2$?

(A) $\dfrac{25}{11}$

(B) $\dfrac{1}{11}$

(C) $\dfrac{-1}{11}$

(D) $\dfrac{-7}{11}$

(E) -1

12. In the figure below, if lines l_1 and l_2 are parallel, and l_3 transects l_1 and l_2 at an acute angle, which of the following statements is FALSE? (P, Q, R, S, T, and U are angles.)

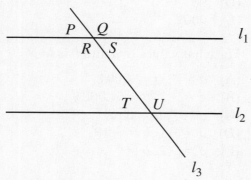

(A) $P = S$
(B) $P = Q$
(C) $T = S$
(D) $T = P$
(E) $R = Q$

13. A woman's coin purse contains 65 cents in 11 coins, all nickels and dimes. How many coins are dimes?

(A) 1
(B) 2
(C) 3
(D) 4
(E) 5

14. What percent of two gallons is a quart?

(A) 12.5%
(B) 25%
(C) 50%
(D) 67%
(E) 75%

15. In the figure below, $\overline{AC}$ and $\overline{BD}$ are chords of a circle that intersect at point E. $\overline{AD}$ is the diameter. If the measure of arc $AB = 40°$ and m$\angle CED = 60°$, what is the measure of $\angle CAD$?

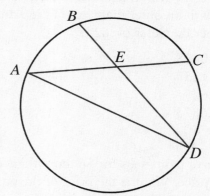

Note: Figure not drawn to scale.

(A) 60°
(B) 45°
(C) 30°
(D) 40°
(E) 15°

16. A shopper obtains a 30% discount on the price of a chair and pays \$420. How much was the original price of the chair?

(A) \$126
(B) \$450
(C) \$577
(D) \$600
(E) \$1,400

17. In triangle ABC, $m\angle C = 2m\angle B$, $m\angle A = 6m\angle B$. What is the measure of $\angle C$?

(A) 5°
(B) 15°
(C) 20°
(D) 30°
(E) 40°

18. If $\begin{matrix} a & b \\ c & d \end{matrix}$ is defined as $ad - cb$, then

$$\begin{matrix} a & b \\ c & d \end{matrix} + \begin{matrix} a & b \\ c & d \end{matrix} + 2cb =$$

(A) $ad - cb$
(B) $-2cb$
(C) 0
(D) $2ad$
(E) $-4cb$

19. If the base of a right triangle is $8\sqrt{2}$ and the hypotenuse is 18, what is the area of the triangle?

(A) 14
(B) $14\sqrt{2}$
(C) $56\sqrt{2}$
(D) 64
(E) $64\sqrt{2}$

20. If $a + b = 27$ and $3c - a = 0$, what does c equal?

(A) $3a$
(B) 27
(C) $27 - b$
(D) $9 - 3b$
(E) $9 - \dfrac{b}{3}$

21. If $0 \le a \le 3$ and $5 \le b \le 8$, what is the least possible value of $\dfrac{16}{b-a}$?

(A) 0
(B) 2
(C) 7
(D) 8
(E) 10

STOP Do not proceed to the next section until time is up.

547

Section 3

30 Questions ■ Time—35 Minutes

Identifying Sentence Errors

Directions: Mark the letter of your choice on the answer sheet that best corresponds to the correct answer.

Notes:

1. The following questions test your knowledge of the rules of English grammar, as well as word usage, word choice, and idioms.

2. Some sentences are correct, but others contain a single error. No sentence contains more than one error.

3. Any errors that occur will be found in the underlined portion of the sentence. Choose the letter underneath the error to indicate the part of the sentence that must be changed.

4. If there is no error, pick answer choice (E).

5. There will be no change in any parts of the sentence that are not underlined.

1. She poured over the travel brochure as if
   A   B
   she had never seen photographs of
          C
   snowcapped mountains before. No error
                         D   E

2. At the heart of the New England town
          A
   was the common, a public pasture for the
              B   C
   citizen's sheep and cattle. No error
   D   E

3. Being a real estate agent it requires passing
   A   B   C   D
   a licensing examination. No error
                            E

4. These oranges taste more sweetly than any
                        A   B
   others I've ever tried. No error
   C   D   E

5. In applying for the loan, one is required
      A   B
   to supply copies of your federal income
   C   D
   tax return. No error
               E

548

6. Coming from the rain forests, we
   <u>A</u>
   never dreamed that the desert could be
   <u>B</u>   <u>C</u>
   so beautiful. No error
   <u>D</u>   <u>E</u>

7. On the following day, the blizzard grew
   <u>A</u>   <u>B</u>
   even worst, surpassing all previous
   <u>C</u>   <u>D</u>
   records. No error
   <u>E</u>

8. All but seven passengers, three crewmen,
   <u>A</u>
   and a small dog was lost when the ship
   <u>B</u>   <u>C</u>
   sank. No error
   <u>D</u>   <u>E</u>

9. Everybody in the choir except for Meryl
   <u>A</u>   <u>B</u>
   and I had sung the hymn previously.
   <u>C</u>   <u>D</u>
   No error
   <u>E</u>

10. She wrote that they had visited Chartres
    <u>A</u>
    and saw the cathedral there. No error
    <u>B</u>   <u>C</u>   <u>D</u>   <u>E</u>

GO ON TO THE NEXT PAGE

Improving Sentences

Directions:

1. The following questions test your knowledge of English grammar, word usage, word choice, sentence construction, and punctuation.

2. Every sentence contains a portion that is underlined.

3. Any errors that occur will be found in the underlined portion of the sentence. If you believe there is an error, choose the answer choice that corrects the original mistake. Answer choices (B), (C), (D), and (E) contain alternative phrasings of the underlined portion. If the sentence contains an error, one of these alternate phrasings will correct it.

4. Choice (A) repeats the original underlined portion. If you believe the underlined portion does not contain any errors, select answer choice (A).

5. There will be no change in any parts of the sentence that are not underlined.

11. Noticing how close the other car was to him, his hands began to shake and he broke out in a sweat.

   (A) Noticing how close the other car was to him,
   (B) Noticing how closely the other car was following him,
   (C) When he noticed how close the other car was to him,
   (D) After noticing how close the other car was to him,
   (E) He noticed how close the other car was near to him,

12. The money had been split equally between the four gang members.

   (A) had been split equally between the four gang members
   (B) was split equally between the four gang members
   (C) had been split into equal shares between the four gang members
   (D) had been split equally among the four gang members
   (E) had been split equal by the four gang members

13. Hardcover books usually last longer than paperbacks; of course, paperbacks usually are less expensive to purchase.

   (A) than paperbacks; of course,
   (B) then paperbacks of course,
   (C) then paperbacks. Of course,
   (D) than paperbacks, of course,
   (E) than paperbacks, of course

14. In the six months since the truce was declared, several minor skirmishes occurring along the border.

 (A) several minor skirmishes occurring along the border
 (B) several minor skirmishes breaking out along the border
 (C) there have been several minor skirmishes along the border.
 (D) along the border there has been several minor skirmishes
 (E) the several skirmishes along the border have been minor

15. I have a fever of 101°, so I have lain in bed all day.

 (A) so I have lain
 (B) so I laid
 (C) but I lay
 (D) so I have laid
 (E) but I lied

16. The desire for public acclaim and recognition is universal, yet it is rarely achieved.

 (A) yet it is rarely achieved
 (B) yet its rarely achieved
 (C) yet it is rarely satisfied
 (D) however it is rarely achieved
 (E) yet it is achieved rarely

17. The computer has the capability for processing all the relevant data within a half hour.

 (A) has the capability for processing
 (B) has the capacity for processing
 (C) has the capability in processing
 (D) can process
 (E) processes

18. Neither one of the twins has been inoculated against polio.

 (A) Neither one of the twins has been
 (B) Neither one nor the other of the twins has been
 (C) Neither one or the other twin has been
 (D) Neither one of the twins have been
 (E) Neither one of the twins been

19. Not only reading in poor light but she warned that sitting too close to the television can strain the eyes.

 (A) Not only reading in poor light but she warned that sitting
 (B) Not only reading in poor light she warned, but sitting
 (C) She warned that not only reading in poor light but also sitting
 (D) In addition to reading in poor light, she warned that sitting
 (E) Not only reading in poor light, but she also warned that sitting

20. If I would have realized how much the music disturbed her, I would have turned the volume down.

 (A) If I would have realized how much
 (B) If I realize how much
 (C) Had I realized how much
 (D) When I realized how much
 (E) If I would have realized to what extent

Improving Paragraphs

Directions:

1. The following questions test your knowledge of paragraph and sentence construction.

2. The following passage is a rough draft of an essay. This rough draft contains various errors.

3. Read the rough draft and then answer the questions that follow. Some questions will focus on specific sentences and ask if there are any problems with that sentence's word choice, word usage, or overall structure. Other questions will ask about the paragraph itself. These questions will focus on paragraph organization and development.

4. Select the answer that best reflects the rules of English grammar and proper essay and paragraph writing.

(1) Advocates of a student dress code maintain that proper attire and proper behavior are interrelated. (2) If a student dresses correctly, they will also behave correctly. (3) At least, that's what is claimed.

(4) I do not believe that this is a valid assumption. (5) I know many young people who come to class in a very informal fashion. (6) They wear sweat suits or cut-off jeans. (7) Sometimes they dress so sloppily that teachers or their peers make remarks to them. (8) And yet their grades are quite acceptable, or often even more than acceptable. (9) I feel that as long as a person performs well academically, the way they dress should be of no concern to others.

(10) I suppose that one day psychologists will conduct studies to test whether or not attire affects behavior. (11) If these studies prove that poor attire results in poor behavior, then school administrators will be justified in trying to establish and enforce a dress code. (12) But until that day comes, dress the way you feel most comfortable.

21. Which of the following is the best way to combine sentences (2) and (3)?

   (A) If you dress well, you will behave well, at least so they say.
   (B) They claim that if a student dresses correctly, they will also behave correctly.
   (C) They claim that students who dress well also behave well.
   (D) As claimed by them, correct dress and correct behavior go hand-in-hand.
   (E) At least they claim that to dress correctly means you will behave correctly.

22. Which of the following best describes the chief purpose of sentence (4)?

   (A) To change the opinion of the reader
   (B) To prepare the reader for a second point of view
   (C) To offer an illustration or example
   (D) To provide a partial summary
   (E) To help the reader evaluate paragraph one

23. Which of the following is the best way to combine sentences (5) and (6)?

(A) I know many people who come to class dressed very informally in sweats or cut-off jeans.

(B) I know many students who dress informally, they even wear sweat suits or cut-off jeans.

(C) Many students I know come to class in sweats or jeans, this is informal dress.

(D) Students come to class dressed in sweats or other ways.

(E) If there are students who come to class dressed informally, wearing sweat suits or cut-off jeans.

24. Which of the following best describes the purpose of paragraph two?

(A) To provide a transition

(B) To continue the philosophy of the first paragraph

(C) To summarize the material previously offered

(D) To present material opposing that already presented

(E) To offer two diametrically opposing opinions

25. Which of the following is the best revision of the underlined portion of sentence (9) below?

I feel that as long as a person performs well academically, the way they dress should be of no concern to others.

(A) how they dress should be of no concern to others.

(B) the way they dress should not concern others.

(C) their dress should be of no concern to others.

(D) what they wear or how they dress should be their own concern.

(E) the way he dresses should be of no concern to others.

Questions 26–30 are based on the following passage.

(1) *Many early fans of jazz musician Miles Davis became aggravated and upset as they watched their hero change through the years.* (2) *The change involved not only the type of music he played but the way he behaved on-stage.*

(3) *Miles Dewey Davis was born May 25, 1926, in Alton, Illinois.* (4) *He grew up in East St. Louis.* (5) *He was given his first trumpet at the age of 13, and, in 1945, enrolled in the Juilliard School of Music.* (6) *Once in New York, Miles, in his own words, "followed [jazz great Charlie Parker] around down to 52nd Street," every night.* (7) *New York night life was interesting to the young jazz musician.* (8) *He'd write down Parker's chords and the next day play them in the practice rooms at Juilliard, instead of going to classes.*

(9) *Miles gradually, however, completely and finally broke away from the hard, aggressive temperament of the former bebop tradition.* (10) *He moved to a more subtle, cool, sometimes even gentle, kind of jazz, characterized by his* Birth of the Cool *album in 1949–50.* (11) *Later works, such as "Stella by Starlight," "Round About Midnight," his* Kind of Blue *album in 1959, and his* Sketches of Spain *album in 1960, continued to reveal a more gentle, open, and melodic musical style.*

(12) *In his early days, Miles's behavior was reserved.* (13) *He avoided interviews where he could and did not even respond to applause, remaining off stage unless he was playing.* (14) *By the late 1970s, however, when he had attained what some have termed a cult following of younger fans, he became more unguarded in manner, smiling and shaking hands with fans nearest the stage, waving to the audience, and giving generous, genial interviews.* (15) *Even the way he behaved in public changed over the years.*

553

26. Logically, the final sentence should be placed before

(A) sentence 8.
(B) sentence 9.
(C) sentence 10.
(D) sentence 11.
(E) sentence 12.

27. To improve unity, which of the following sentences would be the best one to delete from the second paragraph?

(A) Sentence 3
(B) Sentence 4
(C) Sentence 5
(D) Sentence 6
(E) Sentence 7

28. Which of the following is the best revision of Sentence 9?

(A) As it is now
(B) Gradually, however, Miles broke away from the hard, aggressive temperament of the bebop tradition.
(C) Miles gradually broke away and distanced himself from the hard, aggressive temperament of the bebop tradition.
(D) The hard, aggressive temperament of the bebop tradition, however, Miles gradually broke away from.
(E) The hard, aggressive temperament of the bebop tradition, however, was finally broken away from by Miles.

29. Which of the following sentences, if added, would most logically conclude the final paragraph?

(A) Even though Miles's music departed from its traditions, bebop continued to be a driving force in jazz and remains so to this day.
(B) Charlie Parker's influence on Miles Davis is emphasized in most of the biographies Miles's life has inspired.
(C) It was Miles's father who bought him his first trumpet and who enabled him to attend Juilliard.
(D) In spite of the changes that upset many of his early fans, Miles remained a formidable creative force in jazz throughout his career.
(E) Moving from East St. Louis to New York City must have been a shock to the young Miles.

30. In the context of the passage, which of the following is the best way to combine sentences 3 and 4?

(A) Miles Dewey Davis was born May 25, 1926 and, being born in Alton, Illinois, grew up in East St. Louis.
(B) Miles Dewey Davis grew up in East St. Louis and was born May 25, 1926 in Alton, Illinois.
(C) Growing up in East St. Louis, Miles Dewey Davis was born May 25, 1926 in Alton, Illinois.
(D) Born May 25, 1926 in Alton, Illinois, Miles Dewey Davis grew up in East St. Louis.
(E) Miles Dewey Davis: Born May 25, 1926 in Alton, Illinois; grew up in East St. Louis.

S T O P Do not proceed to the next section until time is up.

Section 4

27 Questions ■ Time—25 Minutes

Directions: Each sentence below has either one or two blanks in it and is followed by five choices, labeled (A) through (E). These choices represent words or phrases that have been left out. Choose the word or phrase that, if inserted into the sentence, would best fit the meaning of the sentence as a whole.

Example:

Canine massage is a veterinary technique for calming dogs that are extremely _____.

(A) inept
(B) disciplined
(C) controlled
(D) stressed
(E) restrained

Ⓐ Ⓑ Ⓒ ● Ⓔ

1. Her clear _____ of the situation kept the meeting from breaking up into _____.

   (A) grasp..chaos
   (B) vision..anarchy
   (C) knowledge..uproar
   (D) control..harmony
   (E) idea..laughter

2. The mayor remained _____ in her commitment to _____ the rise of unemployment among her constituents.

   (A) firm..uphold
   (B) wavering..identify
   (C) steadfast..stem
   (D) uncertain..staunch
   (E) alone..approach

GO ON TO THE NEXT PAGE

3. A _____ old stone farmhouse, it had been a landmark since before the Civil War.

    (A) corrupt
    (B) sturdy
    (C) rickety
    (D) ramshackle
    (E) vital

4. Because she thought her hateful cousin's behavior was _____, it _____ her to hear the adults praise him.

    (A) intangible..thrilled
    (B) putative..baffled
    (C) laconic..encouraged
    (D) insipid..demeaned
    (E) obnoxious..galled

5. A public official must be _____ in all his or her actions to avoid even the appearance of impropriety.

    (A) redolent
    (B) unctuous
    (C) baleful
    (D) circumspect
    (E) propitious

6. So many people turned out for the meeting that there were not enough seats to _____ them all.

    (A) count
    (B) ascertain
    (C) accommodate
    (D) delineate
    (E) delegate

7. The editorial accused the mayor of _____ for making promises he knew he could not _____.

    (A) hypocrisy..fulfill
    (B) revulsion..condone
    (C) impunity..reprise
    (D) liability..improve
    (E) petulance..verify

8. She was _____ as a child, accepting without question everything she was told.

    (A) obstreperous
    (B) recalcitrant
    (C) credulous
    (D) truculent
    (E) tearful

9. James Lovelock has posited the theory of *Gaia*, which says that the earth is a single living organism—independent and _____.

    (A) ambivalent
    (B) self-regulating
    (C) indolent
    (D) static
    (E) annihilative

10. With the computer program Windows, you can check for errors on your hard disk, as well as remove unnecessary files, thus _____ the performance of your computer.

    (A) embodying
    (B) adorning
    (C) impeding
    (D) optimizing
    (E) depreciating

11. My cousin Abebi is a/an _____ person—sociable, talkative, and a friend to all.

(A) obnoxious
(B) unpalatable
(C) gregarious
(D) parsimonious
(E) reticent

12. At the movies, I could forget myself and the way life really was, settle down in the plush theater seat with my popcorn, and _____ myself in the _____ on the screen.

(A) emerge..deception
(B) recuse..fantasy
(C) importune..emanation
(D) divulge..exudation
(E) immerse..illusion

13. In the fall, the chilly wind circles up under the eaves of the house, carrying the first _____ of winter.

(A) premonition
(B) spectacle
(C) meandering
(D) sighting
(E) sensation

14. When it became obvious that Ben had _____ money from the petty cash fund, he was fired.

(A) opportuned
(B) pilfered
(C) discounted
(D) required
(E) desired

15. Because Mandisa's job was so _____, she had a/an _____ of funds and was able to buy a boat and sail away to Greece.

(A) lucrative..superfluity
(B) arduous..penury
(C) remunerative..audacity
(D) powerful..mendicancy
(E) immodest..surfeit

Questions 16–27 are based on the following passage

Alexander Wilson was a poet and a naturalist. Born in Scotland in 1766, he emigrated to Pennsylvania in 1794 and soon became a full-time naturalist. This excerpt on hummingbird nests is from a nine-volume work titled American Ornithology, published in 1808–1814.

Line   About the twenty-fifth of April the Hummingbird usually arrives in Pennsylvania; and about the tenth of May begins to build its nest. This is generally fixed
(5) on the upper side of a horizontal branch, not among the twigs, but on the body of the branch itself. Yet I have known instances where it was attached by the side to an old moss-grown trunk; and
(10) others where it was fastened on a strong rank stalk, or weed, in the garden; but these cases are rare. In the woods it very often chooses a white oak sapling to build on; and in the orchard, or garden,
(15) selects a pear tree for that purpose. The branch is seldom more than ten feet from the ground. The nest is about an inch in diameter, and as much in depth. A very complete one is now lying before me, and
(20) the materials of which it is composed are as follows:—The outward coat is formed of small pieces of bluish grey lichen that vegetates on old trees and fences, thickly glued on with the saliva of the bird,

557

(25) giving firmness and consistency to the whole, as well as keeping out moisture. Within this are thick matted layers of the fine wings of certain flying seeds, closely laid together; and lastly, the downy
(30) substance from the great mullein, and from the stalks of the common fern, lines the whole. The base of the nest is continued round the stem of the branch, to which it closely adheres; and, when
(35) viewed from below, appears a mere mossy knot or accidental protuberance. The eggs are two, pure white, and of equal thickness at both ends. . . . On a person's approaching their nest, the little
(40) proprietors dart around with a humming sound, passing frequently within a few inches of one's head; and should the young be newly hatched, the female will resume her place on the nest even while
(45) you stand within a yard or two of the spot. The precise period of incubation I am unable to give; but the young are in the habit, a short time before they leave the nest, of thrusting their bills into the
(50) mouths of their parents, and sucking what they have brought them. I never could perceive that they carried them any animal food; tho, from circumstances that will presently be mentioned, I think
(55) it highly probable they do. As I have found their nest with eggs so late as the twelfth of July, I do not doubt but that they frequently, and perhaps usually, raise two broods in the same season.

16. In line 4, the word "fixed" most nearly means

(A) changed.
(B) improved.
(C) found.
(D) understood.
(E) undermined.

17. According to the author, all of the following are places where one could find a hummingbird EXCEPT

(A) on the upper side of a branch.
(B) on a moss grown trunk.
(C) on a white oak sapling.
(D) on a pear tree.
(E) in the meadow.

18. Why does Wilson mention the "old moss-grown trunk" and "strong rank stalk" (lines 9 and 11)?

(A) To compare relative sizes of birds
(B) To establish the birds' eating patterns
(C) To illustrate nontypical nesting behaviors
(D) To delineate plant life in Pennsylvania
(E) To complete a list of related flora

19. When Wilson remarks that the birds' nests resemble an "accidental protuberance" (line 36), he implies that

(A) the nests are messily constructed.
(B) nests may be destroyed accidently.
(C) the nests are usually invisible.
(D) the nests are designed to blend into their surroundings.
(E) most nests resemble the beak of the bird itself.

20. The phrase "little proprietors" (lines 39–40) refers to

(A) children in the orchard.
(B) eggs.
(C) naturalists.
(D) shopowners.
(E) nesting pairs of hummingbirds.

21. When Wilson remarks that he "never could perceive" hummingbirds feeding their nestlings animal food (lines 51–53), he is suggesting

- **(A)** that his eyesight is failing.
- **(B)** his limitations as an observer.
- **(C)** that animal food may, in fact, be eaten.
- **(D)** that no animal food is eaten.
- **(E)** that hummingbirds eat only at night.

22. The fact that Wilson has found nests with eggs "so late as the twelfth of July" indicates that

- **(A)** birds do not lay eggs before June.
- **(B)** most eggs are found earlier than July 12.
- **(C)** the eggs are not likely to hatch.
- **(D)** the birds began nesting late in the season.
- **(E)** some birds abandon their nests.

23. The hummingbirds' nest is composed of all of the following EXCEPT

- **(A)** moss.
- **(B)** lichen.
- **(C)** the wings of flying seeds.
- **(D)** a downy substance from fern stalks.
- **(E)** hummingbird saliva.

24. How does Wilson reconstruct the makeup of the nest?

- **(A)** By taking apart a nest that hangs in the orchard
- **(B)** By watching a hummingbird build a nest in the stable
- **(C)** By reading a report by John Audubon
- **(D)** By inspecting a nest that lies on his desk
- **(E)** By making a copy of a nest he has observed

25. Which of the following can be inferred about the hummingbirds' habits?

- **(A)** They flourish only in Pennsylvania.
- **(B)** Their broods each consist of a single egg.
- **(C)** They migrate in the spring.
- **(D)** They always raise two broods in a season.
- **(E)** They spend the winter in Pennsylvania.

26. The main purpose of this passage is to describe

- **(A)** the nesting behavior of the hummingbird.
- **(B)** the mating behavior of the hummingbird.
- **(C)** the relative size of the hummingbird.
- **(D)** hummingbirds in Pennsylvania.
- **(E)** young hummingbird fledglings.

27. If Wilson were to study crows, he would be likely to

- **(A)** stuff and mount them.
- **(B)** observe them in the wild.
- **(C)** read all about them.
- **(D)** mate them in a laboratory.
- **(E)** dissect them.

S T O P Do not proceed to the next section until time is up.

Section 5

21 Questions ▪ Time—25 Minutes

Directions: Solve the following problems using any available space on the page for scratchwork. Mark the letter of your choice on the answer sheet that best corresponds to the correct answer.

Notes:

1. You may use a calculator. All of the numbers used are real numbers.

2. You may use the figures that accompany the problems to help you find the solution. Unless the instructions say that a figure is not drawn to scale, assume that it has been drawn accurately. Each figure lies in a plane unless the instructions say otherwise.

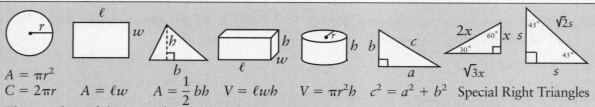

Reference Information

$A = \pi r^2$
$C = 2\pi r$ $A = \ell w$ $A = \frac{1}{2} bh$ $V = \ell wh$ $V = \pi r^2 h$ $c^2 = a^2 + b^2$ Special Right Triangles

The number of degrees of arc in a circle is 360.
The measure in degrees of a straight angle is 180.
The sum of the measures in degrees of the angles of a triangle is 180.

1. $\frac{1}{3} \times \frac{3}{5} \times \frac{5}{7} \times \frac{7}{9} =$

   (A) $\frac{1}{9}$

   (B) $\frac{3}{15}$

   (C) $\frac{35}{63}$

   (D) $\frac{3}{63}$

   (E) $\frac{35}{945}$

2. What is the value of $\left(\frac{1}{3}\right)c$ if $\left(\frac{5}{3}\right)c = 25$?

   (A) 2
   (B) 3
   (C) 4
   (D) 5
   (E) 6

560

3. What is 732,471 rounded to the nearest thousand?

- (A) 730,000
- (B) 732,000
- (C) 732,500
- (D) 733,000
- (E) 740,000

4. If Sally walks at an average speed of c miles per hour, how many miles does she walk in 4 hours?

- (A) $\dfrac{4}{c}$
- (B) $\dfrac{c}{4}$
- (C) $4c$
- (D) $4 - c$
- (E) $4 + c$

5. If a hiker can travel at a steady rate of 15 minutes per $\dfrac{3}{4}$ mile, how many hours would it take to walk 9 miles?

- (A) 1.8
- (B) 2
- (C) 3
- (D) 4
- (E) 6.75

6. When a positive number is added to the square of that number, the result is 42. What is the number?

- (A) 2
- (B) 3
- (C) 4
- (D) 5
- (E) 6

7. What is the least positive integer x, such that $|3 - x| \geq 4$?

- (A) 6
- (B) 7
- (C) 8
- (D) 9
- (E) 10

8. A rectangle is 3 inches wide and 4 inches long. Find the length of the diagonal of this rectangle.

- (A) 4.25
- (B) 5
- (C) 6
- (D) 7
- (E) 7.5

9. In the following figure, line c intersects the parallel lines a and b. What is the measure of angle β?

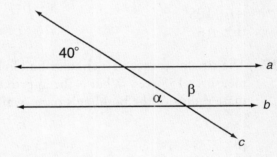

- (A) 110°
- (B) 120°
- (C) 130°
- (D) 140°
- (E) 150°

561

PETERSON'S
getting you there

10. Which of the following is a simplified form of $\dfrac{5x^2 + 12x + 4}{x^2 - 4}$?

(A) $\dfrac{5x + 2}{x - 2}$

(B) $\dfrac{5(x^2 + 2)}{x + 2}$

(C) $\dfrac{(5x + 2)(x + 6)}{x^2 - 2}$

(D) $5x + 2$

(E) $x + 2$

11. If one of the angles of an isosceles triangle measures 18°, which of the following could be the measure of another angle of the triangle?

(A) 72°
(B) 78°
(C) 81°
(D) 108°
(E) 162°

12. The circumference of a circular building measures 158 feet. What is the approximate radius of the building's outer wall?

(A) 7
(B) 25
(C) 50
(D) 76
(E) 101

13. The $\sqrt{x-7}$ is a real number if and only if

(A) $x \geq 7$
(B) $x = 0$
(C) $-7 < x < 7$
(D) $-7 < x < 0$
(E) $x \leq -7$

14. What is 7% of 60?

(A) .42
(B) 4.2
(C) 8.57
(D) 11.67
(E) 42

15. Which of the following are solutions to the equation $(x - a)(x - b) = 0$?

(A) $x = -a$ and $x = -b$
(B) $x = a$ and $x = b$
(C) $x = ab$
(D) $x = (-a)(-b)$
(E) $x = 2a + 2b$

16. If a circle has a diameter of 10 inches, how many square inches is the area of the circle?

(A) 5π
(B) 12π
(C) 25π
(D) 50π
(E) 100π

17. If $x + y = 4$, then $y^2 =$

(A) $16 - x^2$
(B) $x^2 - 16$
(C) $x^2 + 8x + 16$
(D) $16 - 8x + x^2$
(E) $16 + 8x - x^2$

18. If $-7 < x < -4$, which of the following could be a value of $5x$?

(A) -5.50
(B) -6.25
(C) -12.75
(D) -19
(E) -21.50

19. Which of the following numbers is greatest?

(A) .04
(B) .17
(C) .179
(D) .192
(E) .1912

20. If three different numbers are chosen, one from each of the following sets, what is the least sum these numbers could have?

C = {2,4,6}

D = {5,6,7}

E = {2,5,9}

(A) 9
(B) 11
(C) 13
(D) 15
(E) 16

21. If x and y are negative integers, and if $x - y = 1$, what is the least possible value of xy?

(A) -2
(B) -1
(C) 0
(D) 1
(E) 2

S T O P Do not proceed to the next section until time is up.

Section 6

16 Questions ■ Time—25 Minutes

Questions 1–2 are based on the following passage.

Line   In recent years the outsourcing of work to companies in India has grown exponentially. U.S. corporations interested in cutting costs in areas such as call
(5)   centers and data analysis have found a ready source of workers among India's huge and well-educated population. Some experts estimate that there are more technology engineers Bangalore
(10)   than in all of Silicon Valley, the hub of technology development in the United States. One reason that outsourcing is possible is the dramatic decrease in telecommunications costs. New types of
(15)   interactive software also encourage a long-distance workforce. Third, salaries for starting engineers in India are as much as 87 percent lower than those in the United States.

1. The word "exponentially" (line 3) means

    (A) an unknown variable.
    (B) the quality of a number.
    (C) relating to an exponent.
    (D) increasing in an extraordinarily large way.
    (E) symbolically.

2. The purpose of the passage is to

    (A) express indignation at the movement of jobs overseas.
    (B) explain why outsourcing is occurring.
    (C) suggest ways to combat outsourcing.
    (D) alert readers to the issue.
    (E) explain why there is no alternative to outsourcing overseas.

Questions 3–4 are based on the following passage.

Line President after president has appointed commission after commission to inquire into and report upon Indian affairs, and to make suggestions as to the best
(5) methods of managing them. The reports are filled with eloquent statements of wrongs done to the Indians, of perfidies on the part of the Government; they counsel, as earnestly as words can, a trial
(10) of the simple and unperplexing expedients of telling truth, keeping promises, making fair bargains, dealing justly in all ways and all things. . . . [A]ny one of [these reports], . . . read by the right-
(15) thinking, right-feeling men and women . . . would initiate a revolution, which would not subside until the Indians' wrongs were, so far as is now left possible, righted.
(20)   Helen Hunt Jackson,
                         A Century of Dishonor

3. What does Jackson mean by the phrase "a trial of the simple and unperplexing expedients" (lines 9–11)?

(A) the introduction of a lawsuit as quickly as possible
(B) a simple plea for justice
(C) a test of the court system as quickly as possible
(D) quick test of the government's actions
(E) a test of the use of straightforward action

4. The phrase "so far as is now left possible" implies that

(A) any interest in righting injustices to Indians is small.
(B) there are not enough "right-thinking, right-feeling men and women" to fight for the Indians' rights.
(C) there are some injustices that will no longer be able to be reversed.
(D) a revolution for Indian rights is unlikely.
(E) it is too late for a revolution for Indian rights.

Questions 5–12 are based on the following passage

The following speech was delivered at the height of the 1960s civil rights movement by Dr. Martin Luther King, head of the Southern Christian Leadership Conference and the movement's most eloquent spokesperson.

Line We have come to this hallowed spot to remind America of the fierce urgency of now. This is no time to engage in the luxury of cooling off or to take the
(5) tranquilizing drug of gradualism. Now is the time to make real the promises of democracy. Now is the time to rise from the dark and desolate valley of segregation to the sunlit path of racial justice.
(10) Now is the time to lift our nation from the quicksand of racial injustice to the solid rock of brotherhood. Now is the time to make justice a reality for all of God's children.
(15)   It would be fatal for the nation to overlook the urgency of the moment. This sweltering summer of the Negro's legitimate discontent will not pass until there is an invigorating autumn of
(20) freedom and equality. Those who hope

565

that the Negro needed to blow off steam and will now be content will have a rude awakening if the nation returns to business as usual. There will be neither
(25) rest nor tranquility in America until the Negro is granted his citizenship rights. The whirlwinds of revolt will continue to shake the foundations of our nation until the bright day of justice emerges.

(30)   But that is something that I must say to my people who stand on the warm threshold which leads into the palace of justice. In the process of gaining our rightful place we must not be guilty of
(35) wrongful deeds. Let us not seek to satisfy our thirst for freedom by drinking from the cup of bitterness and hatred.

We must forever conduct our struggle on the high plane of dignity and disci-
(40) pline. We must not allow our creative protest to degenerate into physical violence. Again and again we must rise to the majestic heights of meeting physical force with soul force. The marvelous new
(45) militancy which has engulfed the Negro community must not lead us to a distrust of all white people, for many of our white brothers, as evidenced by their presence here today, have come to realize
(50) that their destiny is tied up with our destiny. And they have come to realize that their freedom is inextricably bound to our freedom. We cannot walk alone.

As we walk, we must make the
(55) pledge that we shall always march ahead. We cannot turn back. There are those who are asking the devotees of civil rights, "When will you be satisfied?" We can never be satisfied as long as the
(60) Negro is the victim of the unspeakable horrors of police brutality. We can never be satisfied as long as the Negro's basic mobility is from a smaller ghetto to a

larger one. We can never be satisfied as
(65) long as our children are stripped of their selfhood and robbed of their dignity by signs stating "For Whites Only." We cannot be satisfied as long as a Negro in Mississippi cannot vote and a Negro in
(70) New York believes he has nothing for which to vote. No, no, we are not satisfied, and we will not be satisfied until justice rolls down like waters and righteousness like a mighty stream.

(75)   I am not unmindful that some of you have come out of great trials and tribulations. Some of you have come fresh from narrow jail cells. Some of you have come from areas where your quest
(80) for freedom left you battered by the storms of persecution and staggered by the winds of police brutality. You have been the veterans of creative suffering. Continue to work with the faith that
(85) unearned suffering is redemptive.

Go back to Mississippi, go back to Alabama, go back to South Carolina, go back to Louisiana, go back to the slums and ghettos of our Northern cities,
(90) knowing that somehow this situation can and will be changed. Let us not wallow in the valley of despair.

5. When King says in line 85 that "unearned suffering is redemptive," he means that it

(A) provokes police brutality.
(B) confers sanctity, or holiness, upon the sufferer.
(C) is bound to continue forever.
(D) strips children of their dignity or self-worth.
(E) will never be repaid.

6. In the passage, King's attitude is generally

(A) prejudiced.
(B) cynical.
(C) fearful.
(D) optimistic.
(E) neutral.

7. Which quotation best suggests the main idea of the speech?

(A) ". . . we must not be guilty of wrongful deeds."
(B) "We cannot walk alone."
(C) "We can never be satisfied as long as the Negro's basic mobility is from a smaller ghetto to a larger one."
(D) ". . . to remind America of the fierce urgency of now."
(E) ". . . this situation can and will be changed."

8. The tone of this speech can best be described as

(A) inspirational.
(B) boastful.
(C) defiant.
(D) sad.
(E) buoyant.

9. King's attitude toward white Americans appears to be based on

(A) noncommitment.
(B) contempt for authority.
(C) mutual distrust.
(D) mutual respect.
(E) negativism.

10. King's remarks indicate that he considers the racial problem a national problem because

(A) all white Americans are prejudiced.
(B) African Americans are moving to the suburbs.
(C) all areas of American life are affected.
(D) the United States Constitution supports segregation.
(E) laws will be broken if the problem is left unattended.

11. In the passage, King implies that the struggle for racial justice can be best won through

(A) marching on Washington.
(B) civil disorder.
(C) creative protest.
(D) challenging unjust laws.
(E) doing nothing.

12. In this speech, King specifically recommends

(A) nonviolent resistance.
(B) faith in God.
(C) Communist ideas.
(D) social turmoil.
(E) turbulent revolt.

GO ON TO THE NEXT PAGE

Questions 13–16 are based on the following passage

Line   Agustín Yáñez was the author of many short stories, most of them based in or around Guadalajara, Mexico, his hometown. "Alda," from which this

(5)   passage is excerpted, is from a collection entitled Archipiélago de Mujeres.
      I never met my first love. She must have been a sweet and sad child. Her photographs inspire my imagination to

(10) reconstruct the outlines of her soul, simple and austere as a primitive church, extensive as a castle, stately as a tower, deep as a well. Purity of brow, which, like the throat, the hands, the entire

(15) body, must have been carved in crystal or marble; the very soft lines of the face; the deep-set eyes with a look of surprise, sweet and sad, beneath the veil of the eyelashes; a brief mouth with fine lips,

(20) immune to sensuality; docile hair, harmonious and still; simply dressed in harmony with the obvious distinction and nobility of her bearing; all of her, aglow with innocence and a certain

(25) gravity in which are mixed the delights of childhood and the reverie of first youth. Her photographs invite one to try to imagine the timbre and rhythm of her voice, the ring of her laughter, the depth

(30) of her silences, the cadence of her movements, the direction and intensity of her glances. Her arms must have moved like the wings of a musical and tranquil bird; her figure must have yielded with

(35) the gentleness of a lily in an April garden. How many times her translucent hands must have trimmed the lamps of the vigilant virgins who know not the day or the hour; in what moments of rapture did

(40) her mouth and eyes accentuate their

sadness? When did they emphasize her sweet smile.
      No, I never met her. And yet, even her pictures were with me for a long time

(45) after she died. Long before then, my life was filled with her presence, fashioned of unreal images, devoid of all sensation; perhaps more faithful, certainly more vivid, than these almost faded photo-

(50) graphs. Hers was a presence without volume, line or color; an elusive phantom, which epitomized the beauty of all faces without limiting itself to any one, and embodied the delicacy of the best

(55) and loftiest spirits, indefinitely.
      I now believe that an obscure feeling, a fear of reality, was the cause of my refusal to exchange the formless images for a direct knowledge of her who

(60) inspired them. How many times, just when the senses might have put a limit to fancy did I avoid meeting her; and how many others did Fate intervene! On one of the many occasions that I watched the

(65) house in which my phantom lived, I decided to knock; but the family was out.

13. What does Yáñez mean when he says "I never met my first love" (line 7)?

(A) He loved unconditionally.
(B) His first love died young.
(C) He never fell in love.
(D) He fell in love with someone he never really knew.
(E) His first love was not a human being.

568

14. The description in the first paragraph moves from

(A) sound to sight.
(B) smell to sight to sound.
(C) sight to touch.
(D) sight to sound to movement.
(E) touch to sound to sight.

15. The word "docile" (line 20) is used to imply

(A) wildness.
(B) conformity.
(C) manageability.
(D) indifference.
(E) willingness.

16. Unlike the previous paragraphs, the third paragraph

(A) suggests an explanation for the author's behavior.
(B) describes the author's photographs of Alda.
(C) mentions the elusive qualities of Alda.
(D) compares Alda to someone else the author loved later.
(E) expresses regret for losing Alda's love.

STOP Do not proceed to the next section until time is up.

Section 7

13 Questions ■ Time—20 Minutes

Directions for Student Produced Responses

Notes:

1. All numbers used are real numbers.

2. All angle measurements can be assumed to be positive unless otherwise noted.

3. All figures lie in the same plane unless otherwise noted.

4. Drawings that accompany questions are intended to provide information useful in answering the question. The figures are drawn closely to scale unless otherwise noted.

Enter your responses to questions 1–13 in the special grids provided on your answer sheet. Input your answers as indicated in the directions below.

Answer: $\frac{4}{9}$ or 4/9

Write answer → in boxes.

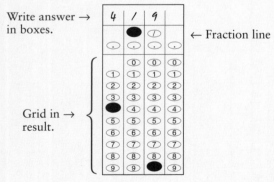

← Fraction line

Grid in → result.

Answer: 1.4
Either position is correct.

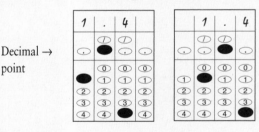

Decimal → point

Note: You may begin your answer in any column, space permitting. Leave blank any columns not needed.

- Writing your answer in the boxes at the top of the columns will help you accurately grid your answer, but it is not required. **You will only receive credit for an answer if the ovals are filled in properly.**

- Only fill in one oval in each column.

- If a problem has several correct answers, just grid in one of them.

- There are no negative answers.

- **Never grid in mixed numbers.** The answer $3\frac{1}{5}$ must be gridded as 16/5 or 3.2. If

| 3 | 1 | / | 5 |

is gridded, it will be read as $\frac{31}{5}$, not $3\frac{1}{5}$.

Decimal Accuracy

Decimal answers must be gridded as accurately as possible. The answer 0.3333 . . . must be gridded as .333.

Less accurate values, such as .33 are not acceptable.

Acceptable ways to grid $\frac{1}{3}$ = .3333 . . .

1. Let function f be defined by $f(x) = x^2 + 6$. If n is a positive number such that $f(3n) = 3f(n)$, what is the value of n^2?

2. What is the product of 5% of 7 and 7% of 5?

3. The sum of the length of three sides of a cube is 15 inches. What is the volume of the cube in cubic inches?

4. The average of 4 numbers is 8.5. Three of the numbers are 3, 7, and 9. What is the fourth number?

5. A container of apples sells for $6, which is $\frac{4}{5}$ of the original asking price. What was the original price?

6. Sixty-five percent of a group of students pass their driving test. If 260 people pass this test, how many took the test?

571

PETERSON'S
getting you there

7. What is one possible value for x if $\frac{1}{8} < x < \frac{1}{5}$?

8. If $3^x = 27$, what is the value of 2^{x+1}?

9. .003 is the same as the ratio of 3 to what number?

10. The area of square *ABCD* is equal to the area of rectangle *EFGH*. If *CD* = 4 feet and *EF* = 2 feet, what is the length of the rectangle's perimeter, in feet?

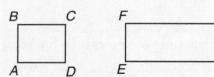

Note: Figures not drawn to scale.

11. What area remains when the area of a square with side 3 is subtracted from the area of a circle with radius 2?

12. In the following diagram, find the area of the triangle formed by dropping a perpendicular line from $\overline{AB}$ to Point *C*, given $x = 4$. Note that $\overline{AB}$ and $\overline{DC}$ are parallel.

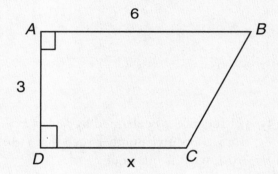

13. In the simple addition problem below, *A* and *B* are digits. What must *A* be?

$$\begin{array}{r} 0.AB \\ +\,0.BA \\ \hline 0.BB \end{array}$$

STOP Do not proceed to the next section until time is up.

572

Section 8

Time—25 Minutes

Topic

It has been said that "old age is not a defeat, but a victory." And yet it is extremely difficult for many people to meet the expenses brought on by long-term illnesses. The elderly, especially, are often at a loss when it comes to providing for health care for themselves or for family members. For this reason, the federal government should provide additional insurance to assist people during periods of long-term catastrophic illness.

Assignment

What is your opinion of the idea that the federal government should provide insurance for long-term catastrophic illness for the elderly? Plan and write an essay that develops your ideas logically. Support your opinion with specific evidence taken from your personal experience, your observations of others, or your reading.

Begin writing your essay.

If you would like your essay scored go on line at www.petersons.com/satessayedge

Assignment: Write an essay in which you argue for or against the preceding statement. Develop your point of view on this statement and be sure to support your stance with sufficient details.

574

STOP When you are finished with your essay put your pencil down until the time allotted is over.

Answers
and Explanations

12. D Although choices (A) and (B) might be appealing, the fact that the giant remained alive while headless was what made him so unusual.

13. B The context of the sentence supports definition (B), as the men of Ulster were completely or utterly ashamed.

14. E Cuchulain is a man to whom his word is his bond; he had to meet the giant because he gave his word.

15. A His speech is serious and sad because he is afraid of imminent death.

16. B The quality that Achilles and Cuchulain share is courage.

17. A Choice (A) addresses the three main points in the passage, having to do with culture, human rights law, and the exclusion of women from decision-making. Choice (B) is too narrow to be the main idea. Choice (C) is wrong because the passage does not discuss tradition overriding human rights law. Choice (D) might be deduced from the passage, but it is not really in the passage. Choice (E) is too narrow to be the main idea.

18. A This is the dictionary meaning of the word *embedded*.

19. D Choices (A) and (C) may seem attractive at first, but sexual abuse and domestic abuse can happen to both men and women. Choice (B) is illogical. Choice (E) is possible, but it is not the best answer.

20. C The example of the Convention supports the author's argument that women are excluded from important decision-making about their own treatment. The addition of the reference to the Convention does not make the essay more appealing, choice (A), or enhance organization of ideas, choice (B). The author is criticizing the Convention, not appealing to its authority, thus refuting choice (D), and her observations about the Convention are pessimistic, not optimistic, refuting choice (E).

Section 2

1. E If you remember to **Please Excuse My Dear Aunt Sally**, it will help you perform operations in the right order, which are: Parentheses, Exponents, Multiplication/Division, Addition/Subtraction. This means we must add the $7 + 1$ first, since they are enclosed within parentheses, then multiply by 4, and finally subtract 6, to get the answer 26.

2. A Supplementary angles are those that, when measured together, form a 180° angle. An obtuse angle has an angle measure greater than 90° but less than 180°. Because α and β are supplementary, we know that α + β = 180°, which means α = 180° − β. Since β > 90°, it follows that 180° − β < 90°, or α < 90°. Therefore, α < β.

3. C Since $3y = z - x$

$$y = \frac{(z - x)}{3}$$

or

$$y = \frac{1}{3}(z - x)$$

4. B The dimensions of the rectangular solid are: Length (l) = 8, Width (w) = 6, Height (h) = one half its width = $\frac{6}{2}$ = 3. Now plug these values into the formula for volume of a rectangular solid to find the answer:

$V = h \times w \times l = 3 \times 6 \times 8 = 144$ cubic inches

5. A As the cross-sectional diagram below shows, the wall thickness is one half of the difference in the two diameters.

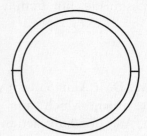

Subtract .625, the inner diameter, from the outer diameter .750, to get the difference in diameters, .125. Remember, .125 is the thickness of both walls. The question asks us to find the thickness of one wall, so you must divide .125 by 2 to get the right answer, .0625.

6. D To solve this problem, first, translate the words into algebraic form, then solve for the price, P.

The pants sells for $6 more than 75% of the price, which can be restated as:

$$P = 6 + .75P$$
$$P - .75P = 6$$
$$P(1 - .75) = 6$$
$$.25P = 6$$
$$P = \frac{6}{.25}$$
$$P = 24$$

7. C The sum of the measures of the angles of a triangle is 180°. Since we know the measures of two of the angles, we can compute the measure of the third:

$$180° - 60° - 90° = \alpha$$
$$120° - 90° = \alpha$$
$$30° = \alpha$$

8. E To figure this one out, translate the words into an equation, then solve for x. What % of 5 is 90% of 50 becomes

$$\frac{x}{100}(5) = \frac{90}{100}(50)?$$
$$\frac{5x}{100} = \frac{[(90)(50)]}{100}$$
$$5x = \frac{[(100)(4500)]}{100}$$
$$5x = 4500$$
$$x = 900$$

9. E For $(a \times b)$ to be less than zero, either a or b (but not both a and b) must be less than zero. All the other choices result in values that are either zero or greater than zero.

PETERSON'S
getting you there

10. D This problem can be solved easily using the method of similar triangles. Both the flag pole and the fence post form a right angle with the surface of the earth and the sun's rays strike both objects at the same angle, therefore we have two similar triangles. To solve a similar triangle problem, set up a proportion.

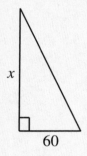

$$\frac{x}{60} = \frac{4}{10}$$

$$10x = 240$$

$$x = 24$$

11. E To solve this problem, plug in the values for x, y, and z, then simplify.

$$= \left(9x^3 - \frac{z^2}{2}\right)\left(\frac{y}{11}\right)$$

$$= \left((9)(-1)^3 - \frac{2^2}{2}\right)\left(\frac{1}{11}\right)$$

$$= (-9 - 2)\left(\frac{1}{11}\right)$$

$$= \frac{-11}{11}$$

$$= -1$$

12. B This is false because $\angle P$ and $\angle Q$ are supplementary angles and cannot be congruent because they cannot measure 90°. The other choices are all true because they are vertical angles, choices (A) and (E), alternate interior angles, choice (C), or corresponding angles, choice (D).

13. B Solve this one by translating the word into an algebraic relationship. We know the coins are only nickels or dimes. Of the 11 coins, we are asked to find x, the number of dimes. This means there are x dimes and $(11 - x)$ nickels. Now translate this information into algebraic form:

.65 = (value of a dime)(number of dimes) + (value of a nickel) (number of nickels)

$$.65 = (.10)x + (.05)(11 - x)$$
$$.65 = .10x + .55 - .05x$$
$$.65 = (.10 - .05)x + .55$$
$$.65 = .05x + .55$$
$$.05x = .65 - .55$$
$$x = \frac{.10}{.05}$$
$$x = 2$$

14. A To solve this one, translate the words into an equation, then solve for x.

What percent of two gallons is a quart or $(x\%)(2 \text{ gallons}) = 1$ quart

Next, convert gallons to quarts so the units match:

2 gallons = 8 quarts.

$$(x\%)(8 \text{ quarts}) = 1 \text{ quart}$$
$$\left(\frac{x}{100}\right)(8) = 1$$
$$8x = 100$$
$$x = 12.5$$

15. D To solve this problem quickly, recognize that m$\angle CAD$ = m$\angle EAD$, one angle of the triangle AED. If we can find the measure of $\angle ADE$ and $\angle AED$, we can subtract them from 180° to find m$\angle EAD$. We are given the measure of $\angle ADE$ in another form, as arc AB = 40°. This means m$\angle ADE$ = 20°. To find m$\angle AED$, notice that it is a supplementary angle to m$\angle CED$ = 60°. This means m$\angle AED$ = 180° − 60° = 120°. Now we can solve for m$\angle EAD$ = m$\angle CAD$.

$$m\angle CAD = 180° - 20° - 120°$$
$$m\angle CAD = 40°$$

16. D First, we must translate the words into an algebraic equation. Since the shopper pays 30% less than the original price (P), the equation is:

$$P - .30P = 420$$
$$(1 - .30)P = 420$$
$$.70P = 420$$
$$P = \frac{420}{.70}$$
$$P = 600$$

17. E Solve this problem by setting up an equation, solving for $\angle B$, then solving for $\angle C$.

$$m\angle A + m\angle B + m\angle C = 180°$$
$$6m\angle B + m\angle B + 2m\angle B = 180°$$
$$9m\angle B = 180°$$
$$m\angle B = 20°$$

Remember, the question asks us to find $\angle C$!

$$m\angle C = 2m\angle B = (2)(20°) = 40°$$

18. D $\dfrac{a}{c}\dfrac{b}{d} + \dfrac{a}{c}\dfrac{b}{d} + 2cb = (ad - cb) + (ad - cb) + 2cb$

$$= ad - cb + ad - cb + 2cb$$
$$= 2ad - 2cb + 2cb$$
$$= 2ad$$

19. C As the diagram below shows, before we can find the area, we must find the height of the triangle (x).

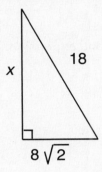

Solve for x using the Pythagorean Theorem:

$$x^2 + \left(8\sqrt{2}\right)^2 = \left(18\right)^2$$
$$x^2 = \left(18\right)^2 - \left(8\sqrt{2}\right)^2$$
$$x^2 = 324 - 128$$
$$x^2 = 196$$
$$x = 14$$

Now, find the area of the triangle using the formula for area of a triangle:

$$A = \frac{1}{2}\,\text{base} \times \text{height}$$
$$= \left(\frac{1}{2}\right)\left(8\sqrt{2}\right)\left(14\right)$$
$$= \left(7\right)\left(8\sqrt{2}\right)$$
$$= 56\sqrt{2}$$

583

20. E   Solve this problem in two steps. First, solve for *a* in the first equation:

$$a + b = 27$$
$$a = 27 - b$$

Second, plug this value for *a* into the second expression:

$$3c - a = 0$$
$$3c - (27 - b) = 0$$
$$3c = 27 - b$$
$$c = 9 - \frac{b}{3}$$

21. B   The least value for the expression is when the denominator is the greatest. This occurs when *b* is greatest, 8, and *a* is least, 0. This means that, within the constraints of the inequality, the least possible value for the given expression is $\frac{16}{8}$, or 2.

Section 3

1. A   The correct verb is *to pore over*, meaning "to study carefully."

2. E   The sentence is correct.

3. C   The subject is *being a real estate agent*. The pronoun it is superfluous.

4. A   Since taste is a verb referring to one of the senses, it should be modified by an adjective (*sweeter*), not an adverb (*more sweetly*).

5. B   *You are required is needed to agree with your tax return.*

6. E   The sentence is correct.

7. C   To compare weather conditions for two days, use the comparative *worse*.

8. B   When *all* refers to the total number of persons or things in a group, it takes a plural verb: *All . . . were lost.*

9. C   The preposition *except for* takes an objective pronoun: *except for Meryl and me.*

10. B   Since *wrote* is past tense, the events that preceded the writing must be described in the past perfect: *had visited* and *had seen*.

11. C   The sentence should be rephrased so that it does not seem as if *his hands* were *noticing*. Although (E) corrects the misplaced modifier, it creates a run-on sentence.

12. **D** The correct word is *among* (not *between*) the four gang members.

13. **A** The sentence is correct.

14. **C** The original sentence lacks a complete verb in the main clause. Both choices (C) and (E) provide a verb that agrees with the subject, but choice (E) changes the meaning of the original sentence.

15. **A** The sentence is correct. *So* establishes the cause-effect relationship; *have lain is the present perfect form of to lie.*

16. **C** The *it* does not refer to acclaim and recognition, which could be *achieved*. It refers to *desire*, which is either *satisfied* or *not satisfied.*

17. **D** The original uses five words where two will do.

18. **A** *Neither one* is singular and takes the singular verb form *has been.*

19. **C** The original idea poses two problems in parallel structure: (1) The two warnings must branch off grammatically from the subject that *warns*. (2) If the *not only* correlative form is used, it should be balanced by a phrase like *but also*. Only choice (C) meets both requirements.

20. **C** The sentence deals with a condition that is not a fact but a possibility. The verb used to express the condition contrary to fact should be in the subjunctive mood; the verb used to explain the possible conclusion should be in the conditional mood. The first clause should read: *Had I realized or If I had realized.*

21. **C** Choice (A) switches unnecessarily to the second person (*you*). Choice (B) has an agreement problem, using the plural pronoun *they* to refer to the singular noun *student*. Choices (D) and (E) are awkward. Choice (C) is best.

22. **B** Sentence (4) states that the material presented in the first paragraph, that a dress code is important, may not be valid. This paves the way for the presentation of another point of view.

23. **A** Choices (B) and (C) contain comma-splice errors. Choice (E) is a fragment. Choice (D) is awkward and omits details. Choice (A) is best.

24. **D** Paragraph one presents the opinion of those who favor a dress code. Paragraph two presents arguments against a dress code. Since paragraph two offers material opposing that already presented, choice (D) is best.

25. **E** The antecedent of *they* appears to be *a person*, but *they* is a plural pronoun and *person* is a singular noun. Choices (A), (B), (C), and (D) do not address this problem. Choice (E) does and is correct.

26. **E** Choice (E) is correct because sentence 15 introduces the topic of the way Miles's behavior changed over the years, which is described in sentence 12.

27. **E** It is not a particularly interesting thought, as it is too obvious; also it interrupts the flow of the sentences about Miles's admiration of Charlie Parker.

28. **B** It is clear and efficient. Examples of wordiness and redundancy in the other sentences are the phrase *completely and finally* in choice (A) and the phrase *and distanced himself* in choice (C). Choice (D) is convoluted and confusing. Choice (E) makes ineffective use of the passive voice.

29. **D** This is a logical conclusion to the discussion of the way Miles and his music changed over the years. The other sentences would be jarring, as they introduce new subjects.

30. **D** Choice (A) is unnecessarily complicated. Choices (B) and (C) sound strange because Miles's birth and his growing up are in reverse chronological order. Choice (E) does not fit the style of the rest of the passage, consisting of choppy phrases instead of full sentences.

Section 4

1. **A** Keeping a meeting from breaking up requires more than a clear *idea* or *vision*; it requires control, or a *grasp* of the situation.

2. **C** The word *commitment* signals the appropriate actions of the mayor; to be *steadfast* in her commitment, she must *stem*, or check, the increase of economic problems for the people who voted her into office.

3. **B** For the farmhouse to have been a landmark since before the Civil War, it must have been well built, or *sturdy*.

4. **E** If she thought her cousin was hateful, it is most likely that she found his behavior *obnoxious* (offensive) and that she was *galled*, or irritated, to hear him praised.

5. **D** *Circumspect*, meaning "watchful or wary," is the only choice that makes sense.

6. **C** *Accomodate*, meaning "to provide space for," is the only answer that makes sense.

7. **A** To make promises you know you cannot *fulfill* is *hypocrisy*. No other choice correctly fills both blanks.

8. **C** One who accepts without question is *credulous* (tending to believe readily).

9. **B** Living organisms are, by definition, *independent* and *self-regulating*. Choice (A) makes little sense, seeming to apply to a person who has the power of decision-making. Choices (C) and (D) run counter to the idea of life, since both indicate a lack of vitality. Choice (E) means "destructive."

10. **D** This is a definition sentence. Neither choice (A) nor choice (B) makes sense. Choices (C) and (E) are illogical, given the meaning of the rest of the sentence.

11. **C** To be *gregarious* is to be sociable. Except for choice (E), the other choices denote unpleasant traits. Choice (E) is wrong, because to be *reticent* is to be hesitant or reserved.

12. **E** To *immerse* oneself is to lose oneself, and a movie is an *illusion*. Look up the other words, and you'll find that one or the other of them makes no sense in the context of the sentence.

13. **A** *In the fall*, indicates that it is not yet winter, so the best answer is *premonition*, which means forewarning.

14. **B** Ask yourself, What kind of action, in regard to money, would get one fired? *Stealing* or *embezzling* will probably be the first words that spring to mind. Now look for a synonym of one of these words. Again, your vocabulary must be large enough to contain the word *pilfered*.

15. **A** Look up the other words and you'll find one or the other of them runs counter to the overall meaning of the sentence.

16. **C** In this context, the word *fixed* means situated or found, not its more common meaning—changed or altered.

17. **E** All of the other choices are explicitly mentioned by the author as the resting places of the hummingbird.

18. **C** Wilson states that nests are sometimes attached to such objects, but "these cases are rare" (line 12).

19. **D** The nest is not easily seen, but it is not invisible, as (C) suggests. Wilson describes seeing it from below (lines 35–36).

20. **E** Wilson refers to the proprietors darting around to protect the nest (lines 40–42).

21. C Wilson believes that hummingbirds *do* feed their young such food, saying, "I think it highly probable they do" (lines 54–56). However, he has not seen it.

22. B Since Wilson takes this to mean that hummingbirds may raise two broods (line 59), the only possible answer here is (B).

23. A According to the passage (lines 21–32), the nest is composed of bluish-grey lichen glued on with hummingbird saliva, the wings of flying seeds, and downy substances from fern stalks and from the great mullein (another kind of plant).

24. D Lines 19–20 show that Wilson is looking at something that "is now lying before me."

25. C It can be inferred from the sentence that the hummingbirds migrate into Pennsylvania (presumably from the south) "about the twenty-fifth of April." None of the other choices is supported by the passage.

26. A Although other details about the hummingbird are included, the passage focuses on hummingbirds' nesting.

27. B Most of Wilson's observations in this piece happen in the wild; it is safe to assume that he would study crows the same way.

Section 5

1. A The 3, 5, and 7 in both the numerator and denominator divide each other out, leaving a value of $\frac{1}{9}$.

2. D The quick method of solution is to divide both sides of the equation by 5. This leaves $\frac{1}{3}c = 5$. Another method is to solve for c first:

$$\frac{5}{3}c = 25$$

$$\left(\frac{3}{5}\right)\left(\frac{5}{3}\right)c = \left(\frac{3}{5}\right)(25)$$

$$c = \frac{75}{5} = 15$$

$$\frac{1}{3}c = 5$$

3. B Rounding to the nearest thousand means just dealing with the 2,471 part of the number. Since 471 is less than 500, round down to 2,000. This makes the rounded number equal to 732,000.

4. C The distance Sally walks is equal to the rate she walks multiplied by the time she walks, or $D = RT$. In this case, c = the rate she walks and 4 = the time she walks, which makes the answer $4c$.

5. C First, convert 15 minutes to hours to make the units of measurement match, 15 minutes = .25 hour. In this case, it is easier to work with decimals, so rewrite also $\frac{3}{4}$ mile = .75 mile. Now set up the following proportion and solve for x:

$$\frac{.25\text{hr}}{.75\text{mi}} = \frac{x\text{hr}}{9\text{mi}}$$
$$(.75)x = (.25)(9)$$
$$x = (.25)(9) \div (.75)$$
$$x = 3\text{hr}$$

6. E First, translate the words into an equation:

A positive number (x) is added $(+)$ to the square of that number (x^2) becomes: $x + x^2$. The "result is 42" becomes: = 42. So, the translation into an algebraic equation is:

$$x + x^2 = 42$$

In this case, it is fastest to just plug in the numbers until you find the correct answer, $6 + 6^2 = 6 + 36 = 42$.

An alternate solution is to solve the quadratic equation for x.

$$x^2 + x - 42 = 0$$
$$(x - 6)(x + 7) = 0$$
$$\Rightarrow x = 6 \text{ or } x = -7$$

Since x must be positive, $x = 6$.

7. B Solve this one by setting $|3-x| = 4$. The choice that fulfills this condition is $x = 7$. Thus, we have $|3-7| = |-4| = 4$.

8. B If you recognized the diagonal as the hypotenuse of a 3-4-5 triangle, you will know immediately that the length of the diagonal is 5. Otherwise, you can solve this problem by using the **Pythagorean Theorem**, which states: *the sum of the squares of each leg of a right triangle is equal to the square of the hypotenuse*, or $a^2 + b^2 = c^2$, where a and b are the sides of a right triangle and c is the hypotenuse. Using this formula, we have:

$$3^2 + 4^2 = c^2$$
$$9 + 16 = c^2$$

or

$$c^2 = 25$$
$$c = 5$$

9. D We know that, when a line intersects two parallel lines, both the measure of angle α and the 40° angle must be equal. We know that $\alpha + \beta = 180°$, and since $\alpha = 40°$, we have:

$$40° + \beta = 180°$$

or

$$\beta = 180° - 40°$$
$$\beta = 140°$$

10. A The expression can be factored to:

$$\frac{(5x + 2)(x + 2)}{(x + 2)(x - 2)}$$

The expression $(x + 2)$ can be divided in both the numerator and the denominator, leaving the answer:

$$\frac{5x + 2}{x - 2}$$

11. C We know the measure of one angle of the isosceles triangle and we know that the measures of two angles of the triangle must be equal to each other. Since the measures of all three angles added together must equal 180°, we have the following relations:

$$18° + 2\alpha = 180°$$
$$2\alpha = 162°$$
$$\alpha = 81°$$

or

$$18° + c + b = 180°$$
$$18° + 18° + b = 180°$$
$$36° + b = 180°$$
$$b = 144°$$

Thus, there are three possible answers (18°, 81°, or 144°). Only 81° is an answer choice.

12. B The circumference of a circle is $C = 2\pi r$. We are given $C = 158$, so we have:

$$158 = 2\pi r$$

or

$$r = 158 \div 2\pi$$
$$r \approx 25$$

13. A $\sqrt{x - 7}$ cannot be a negative number, so the only possible choice is the one for which $x \geq 7$.

14. B First translate the English into algebra:

What is 7% of 60

becomes $\quad x = \left(\dfrac{7}{100}\right)(60)$

$$x = 4.2$$

15. B To find the solutions to the equation, set $x - a = 0$ and $x - b = 0$. Solving for x yields the solutions, $x = a$ and $x = b$.

16. C The formula for the area of a circle is $A = \pi r^2$. Since the radius of a circle is $\dfrac{1}{2}$ the diameter, $r = 5$. By plugging 5 into the formula, the answer is obtained, $A = \pi 5^2 = 25\pi$.

17. D Solving for y:

$$y = 4 - x.$$

Squaring both sides:

$$y^2 = (4 - x)^2$$
$$= (4 - x)(4 - x)$$
$$= 16 - 8x + x^2$$

18. E   Solve this one by multiplying through by 5. This yields: $-35 < 5x < -20$. The only choice that satisfies this condition is -21.50.

19. D   It is easy to compare the numbers without getting mixed up if you make all the choices the same number of decimal places. Since .1912 has four decimal places, put zeroes in the other choices to make them all read four decimal places. It's faster to just do this mentally, but you are less likely to make a mistake if you can quickly write them in. Now it is easy to see that .1920 is the greatest number.

20. B   The combination with the least sum will have the three least different numbers. To satisfy this condition, choose:

$$C = \{4\}$$
$$D = \{5\}$$
$$E = \{2\}$$

This makes the sum $= 11$.

21. E   Solve this problem using the rules for signs and a bit of logical reasoning. Using negative integers approaching zero (0) will yield the least product. Start with -1, then decrease the values of x and y if necessary. The first two values that satisfy the equation are: $y = -2$, $x = -1$ $[-1 - (-2) = 1]$. Accordingly, $xy = 2$.

Section 6

1. D   *Exponentially* is related to the word *exponent*, but isn't used here in a math sense.

2. B   The tone of the passage should have told you that choices (A), indignation, and (E), resignation are incorrect. The content will tell you that choices (C) and (D) aren't correct. This is a straightforward explanation of why outsourcing is occurring.

3. E   If you read the question quickly and didn't go back to the passage, you might have chosen choices (A), (B), or (C) because each seems to work with the word *trial*. Always go back to the passage.

4. C   This is another example of why it's important to go back to the passage to check your answer. On a quick read of the question and the answers, you might have been distracted by the use of words from the passage and chosen any of one of the wrong answers.

5. B King urges his listeners to "continue to work with the faith that unearned suffering is redemptive." Even if you did not know the meaning of *redemptive*, you could infer that it promised something positive. Of the choices only (B) satisfies this condition.

6. D The last paragraph gives King's belief that ". . . this situation can and will be changed."

7. E This is stated in the last paragraph and sums up the point of the entire speech.

8. A King is attempting to inspire his listeners.

9. D Lines 46–51 state that this new attitude ". . . must not lead us to a distrust of all white people, for many of our white brothers . . . have come to realize that their destiny is tied up with our destiny."

10. C King states in lines 24–26: "There will be neither rest nor tranquility in America until the Negro is granted his citizenship rights."

11. C Paragraph four specifically mentions creative protest.

12. A The second paragraph discusses "the whirlwinds of revolt" that will continue until justice prevails; the third paragraph urges listeners to obey the law, as ". . . we must not be guilty of wrongful deeds." Thus "nonviolent resistance" is the best response.

13. D This is a completely literal statement. As the rest of the passage makes clear, the narrator never really knew Alda.

14. D To answer this synthesis/analysis question will require looking back at the paragraph and tracing its structure. The narrator describes what Alda looked like, speculates on what she sounded like, and guesses what she moved like, in that order.

15. C *Docile* has several connotations, but a look back at the citation in question will tell you that only two of the choices could easily be applied to hair, and (A) is exactly opposite to the meaning the narrator intends.

16. A In the first sentence of paragraph 3, the author suggests that his fear of reality was the reason he failed to meet Alda. This is the first time he has made such a suggestion. Paragraph 3 might also be said to support (C), but so do paragraphs 1 and 2. Choices (D) and (E) are not supported anywhere in the passages.

Section 7

1. The correct answer is n^2 = 2. Substituting $3n$ then n into $f(x) = x^2 + 6$ yields $f(3n) = (3n)^2 + 6 = 9n^2 + 6$ and $3f(n) = 3(n^2 + 6) = 3n^2 + 18$. Since we are given that $f(3n) = 3f(n)$, we know that $9n^2 + 6 = 3n^2 + 18$. Simplifying this expression gives us $9n^2 - 3n^2 = 18 - 6$ or $6n^2 = 12$, which is equivalent to $n^2 = \dfrac{12}{6}$ or $n^2 = 2$.

2. The correct answer is 0.1225. In order to get the relationships right in this problem, separate the problem into two components x and y. Let $x = 5\%$ of 7 and $y = 7\%$ of 5. Now you have simplified the problem to: what is xy. Just solve for x and y, then multiply them together to get the answer:

$$x = (0.05)(7) = 0.35$$
$$y = (0.07)(5) = 0.35$$
$$xy = (0.35)(0.35)$$
$$xy = 0.1225$$

3. The correct answer is 125 cubic inches. In a cube, all sides are of equal length. This means that each side has length $\dfrac{15}{3} = 5$. Now, just plug 5 into the formula for the volume of a cube (s^3) to get the answer:

$$V = s^3$$
$$= 5^3$$
$$= 125$$

4. **The correct answer is 15.** Solve this problem by setting up an equation, letting x be the unknown fourth number, then solving for x.

$$\frac{(3 + 7 + 9 + x)}{4} = 8.5$$
$$3 + 7 + 9 + x = (4)(8.5)$$
$$19 + x = 34$$
$$x = 34 - 19$$
$$x = 15$$

5. The correct answer is $7.50. To get this answer, translate the words into an equation, let x stand for the unknown original price, then solve for x.

$$6 = \left(\frac{4}{5}\right)x$$

$$6 = .80x$$

$$x = \frac{6}{.80}$$

$$x = 7.50$$

6. The correct answer is 400. Find this answer by putting the words into algebraic form, letting x be the unknown total number of people taking the test, and solving for x.

$$260 = 65\% \text{ of } x$$

$$260 = (.65)(x)$$

$$x = \frac{260}{.65}$$

$$x = 400$$

7. The correct answer may be any number in the range $.125 < x < .200$.

8. The correct answer is 16. Since $3^3 = 27$, $x = 3$. Substituting 3 into the expression yields the answer $2^{(3 + 1)} = 2^4 = 16$. Remember that the question asks what the value of the expression $2^{(x + 1)}$ is, **not** what the value of x is. (The value of x is 3.)

9. The correct answer is 1000. Remember, a decimal is an integer divided by some unit of 10. In this case, the ratio is 3 to 1000, or $\frac{3}{1000} = .003$.

10. The correct answer is 20 feet. First find the area of the square. We know its side has length $s = 4$ feet.

$$A = s^2$$

$$= 4^2$$

$$= 16 \text{ feet}$$

Now use the area just calculated to find the length of the long side of the rectangle. We are given that the two figures have equal area, which means the area of the rectangle is also 16 feet. Now solve for the rectangle's long side using the formula for area of a rectangle.

$$A = l \times w$$

Substituting $16 = l \times 2$

$$l = \frac{16}{2}$$

$$l = 8 \text{ feet}$$

You didn't forget the question, did you? It asks you to find the perimeter of the rectangle, **not** its length. The perimeter of the rectangle is

$$P = 2(l) + 2(w)$$
$$= 2(8) + 2(2)$$
$$= 16 + 4$$
$$= 20 \text{ feet}$$

11. **The correct answer is 3.57.** The area of a circle with radius 2 is:

$$A_1 = \pi r^2 = 4\pi = 12.57 \text{ to two decimal places.}$$

The area of a square with side 3 is:

$$A_2 = s^2 = 3^2 = 9$$

To find the answer, the area remaining, subtract the area of the square from the area of the circle:

$$A_1 - A_2 = 12.57 - 9 = 3.57$$

12. **The correct answer is 3.** Substituting the values given into the formula for the area of a triangle gives us:

$$\text{Area} = \frac{1}{2} \text{ Base} \bullet \text{Height} = \left(\frac{1}{2}\right) \bullet (6 - 4) \bullet 3 = \frac{1}{2} \bullet 6 = 3$$

13. **The correct answer is 0.** Any other digit could not produce this result.

Section 8

As you might expect, answers will vary. If possible, politely ask a teacher, fellow student, or some other person knowledgeable about formal essay writing to review your essay and provide feedback on ways in which the essay is commendable and on areas where it could be improved.

Scoring Worksheet

MATH				
	Number Correct	Number Incorrect	=	Raw Score
Section 2	_____	− (.25 × _____)	=	_____
Section 5	_____	− (.25 × _____)	=	_____
Section 7	_____	− (.25 × _____)	=	_____
CRITICAL READING				
Sections 1, 4, and 6	_____	− (.25 × _____)	=	_____
WRITING				
Section 3	_____	− (.25 × _____)	=	_____
Section 8	Go to www.petersons.com/satessayedge/ for instant online scoring and feedback.			

Score Charts

MATH			
Raw Score	Math Scaled Score	Raw Score	Math Scaled Score
60	800	28	500
59	800	27	490
58	790	26	490
57	770	25	480
56	760	24	470
55	740	23	460
54	720	22	460
53	710	21	450
52	700	20	440
51	690	19	430
50	680	18	420
49	670	17	420
48	660	16	410
47	650	15	410
46	640	14	400
45	630	13	390
44	620	12	380
43	610	11	370
42	600	10	360
41	600	9	350
40	590	8	340
39	580	7	330
38	570	6	320
37	560	5	310
36	560	4	300
35	550	3	280
34	540	2	270
33	540	1	250
32	530	0	240
31	520	−1	220
30	510	−2	210
29	510	−3 and below	200

CRITICAL READING			
Raw Score	Verbal Scaled Score	Raw Score	Verbal Scaled Score
78	800	37	510
77	800	36	510
76	800	35	500
75	790	34	500
74	780	33	490
73	770	32	490
72	760	31	480
71	750	30	480
70	740	29	470
69	730	28	460
68	720	27	460
67	710	26	450
66	700	25	450
65	700	24	440
64	690	23	440
63	680	22	430
62	670	21	420
61	670	20	410
60	660	19	410
59	650	18	400
58	640	17	390
57	640	16	380
56	630	15	380
55	620	14	370
54	610	13	360
53	610	12	360
52	600	11	350
51	600	10	340
50	590	9	330
49	590	8	320
48	580	7	310
47	570	6	300
46	570	5	290
45	560	4	270
44	550	3	260
43	550	2	250
42	540	1	240
41	540	0	230
40	530	−1	220
39	520	−2	210
38	520	−3 and below	200

Chapter 9

A Final Word—Whew!

Congratulations! You have just read through a mountain of SAT-related information!

If you have studied all the strategies and techniques, learned the formats for each section, and practiced on the sample questions, then you should feel pretty good about your chances on the real test. There's only so much preparation you can do, and if you've finished this book, you've done more than most people. Be confident about your chances on the real test, because at the very least, this book has shown you what to expect on the SAT, even in its "new" format. You would be surprised at how people's scores improve when they have an idea of what the test will be like. It makes a big difference when a test leaves the realm of "mysterious, unexpected exam" and becomes "just another standardized test."

That's all the SAT is, really; another standardized test. By now, you should realize that the SAT says nothing about your potential as a college student. If you do well on the test, then you're a good standardized test-taker, nothing more. But don't sell yourself short. You worked hard and it paid off. Your good score should help you get into the college of your choice, and that's no small thing!

We would wish you luck on the SAT, but if you've read this book, you won't need it. You will have made your own luck, and your SAT score will reflect it.